Corinth 1862

Corinth 1862

Siege, Battle, Occupation

TIMOTHY B. SMITH

University Press of Kansas

Published by the University Press of Kansas (Lawrence, Kansas 66045), which was
organized by the Kansas Board of Regents and is operated and funded by Emporia
State University, Fort Hays State University, Kansas State University, Pittsburg State
University, the University of Kansas, and Wichita State University

Library of Congress Cataloging-in-Publication Data

Smith, Timothy B., 1974–
Corinth 1862 : siege, battle, occupation / Timothy B. Smith.
p. cm. — (Modern war studies)
Includes bibliographical references and index.
ISBN 978-0-7006-1852-1 (cloth : alk. paper)
ISBN 978-0-7006-2345-7 (pbk. : alk. paper)
ISBN 978-0-7006-2346-4 (e-book)
1. Corinth (Miss.)—History—Siege, 1862. 2. Corinth, Battle of,
Corinth, Miss., 1862. I. Title.
E473.56.S65 2012
973.7'31—dc23
2012005829

British Library Cataloguing in Publication Data is available.

Printed in the United States of America

10 9 8 7 6 5 4 3 2 1

The paper used in this publication is recycled and contains 30 percent postconsumer waste.
It is acid free and meets the minimum requirements of the American National Standard
for Permanence of Paper for Printed Library Materials Z39.48-1992.

To
William J. Gully and Anel D. Crenshaw,
my great-great-grandfathers
Both of Company D, 36th Mississippi Infantry
Both in the siege of Corinth
Both wounded at the Battle of Corinth

CONTENTS

ILLUSTRATIONS

Maps

Photographs

PREFACE

Major General Henry W. Halleck, commander of the massive Union Department of the Mississippi, looked at the strategic situation in the spring of 1862 and immediately saw the keys to victory. Writing to Secretary of War Edwin M. Stanton on May 25, Halleck declared, "Richmond and Corinth are now the great strategical points of war, and our success at these points should be insured at all hazards." That was quite a statement, given the fact that major economic, industrial, and military centers such as Chattanooga and Atlanta were still in Confederate hands at the time. Nevertheless, Halleck named the Confederate capital and the almost unknown railroad crossroads at Corinth, Mississippi, as the two keys to Union success. The importance of Richmond was evident, but mention of the small town of Corinth seemed surprising, on the surface.[1]

Many others echoed Halleck's sentiments, however. One lower-level Federal described Corinth in Lincolnesque fashion as the "key that unlocks the cotton States, and gives us command of almost the entire system of Southern railroads." Certainly, Confederate officials agreed with Halleck's summation of Corinth's importance. No less an authority than Corinth's defender, P. G. T. Beauregard, argued to Richmond immediately after Shiloh, "If defeated here, we lose the Mississippi Valley and probably our cause." John Tyler Jr., son of the former president and now a Confederate officer, described Corinth as "the key to the Tennessee and Mississippi Valleys." A former Confederate secretary of war, Leroy Pope Walker, highlighted Corinth's significance when he referred to the two major railroads that crossed there as "the vertebrae of the Confederacy." Historians have long asserted that the Confederate cabinet in Richmond even deliberated whether to abandon the capital to defend Corinth.[2]

Corinth's obvious importance in the Civil War went through several phases. Initially, the town's strategic or tactical significance was less than its logistical importance. At first, Corinth served as one of Mississippi's, and then the broader Confederacy's, major logistical and mobilization hubs in the western Confederacy. The fact that it sat at the junction of two of the South's most important rail lines is enough evidence, but the mass of troops that came and went and finally concentrated at Corinth overwhelmingly confirms the town's initial importance as a military staging area.

Then, for a few months in early 1862, Corinth became a strategic and even tactical necessity. In fact, during the months of March, April, and May 1862, there was no more important place than Corinth in the western Confederacy and, arguably, in the South as a whole. Federal commanders concentrated almost all their power in the vast western theater on Corinth, forcing Confederate officials to do the same. The result was the iconic battle at Shiloh in April, fought over Corinth's railroads. Then came the month-long siege in May and the capture of the town and its railroads.

Corinth's significance to the war effort then morphed into another logistical realm, this time for the occupying Union forces. The town became the base from which Federal armies spread along the Memphis and Charleston Railroad eastward toward Chattanooga and westward to Memphis. The plan was to use this line, particularly from Corinth to Memphis, as the staging and support area for the Union advance down the Mississippi Valley, ultimately toward Vicksburg.

The role Corinth played in the Civil War changed yet again in the fall of 1862 as Confederate armies pushed forward in a massive offensive. Southern officers led their columns into Union-occupied areas of Maryland, Kentucky, and west Tennessee. Corinth became the focal point of the west Tennessee invasion, and the offensive resulted in a horrific battle in October. Although not as large as Antietam, and obviously overshadowed by it, Corinth was just as intense. The Federals repelled the offensive and retained Corinth, thus allowing the delayed Vicksburg campaign to move forward. From the Corinth–Memphis line, Ulysses S. Grant led his columns southward and eventually opened the Mississippi River, cutting the Confederacy in two.

The secured Federal bastion at Corinth had a more practical result as well. As the Union effort increasingly became a war to end slavery, the Federal government began to make provisions for contrabands, the official term for runaway slaves. Eventually, the government took over their care and began enlisting them into the Union army. Corinth, sitting on the brink of Confederate territory, was on the front lines of this racial war. Securing Corinth allowed the Federal army to care for and enlist thousands of former slaves in the most famous of all contraband camps in the western theater.

Despite its multifaceted significance, Corinth has received little attention from Civil War historians. Overshadowed by Shiloh, the highly significant May operations are often relegated to mere paragraphs, partly because the siege produced relatively little bloodshed. Yet much like the Tullahoma campaign in 1863, Corinth's capture by the Federals was extremely important. Taking place at the same time as the Antietam and Perryville campaigns, the October battle at Corinth has likewise been overshadowed. And beause historians have only recently begun to look at the social aspects of war, topics such as civilians, race, and politics at Corinth have rarely been discussed.

But Corinth's history has all the ingredients of a fascinating and important operation. Larger-than-life figures such as the still-learning Ulysses S. Grant, the carousing Earl Van Dorn, the dapper P. G. T. Beauregard, the portly and intriguing Sterling Price, the bookish Henry Halleck, and the rising William S. Rosecrans all took part in the campaigns. Natural phenomenon such as earthquakes and acoustic shadows baffled the soldiers, who were already confused by the fog of war. Brutal fighting that saw several brigades lose as much as 50 percent of their strength, and one lose 70 percent, attests to the vicious nature of the campaigns.

Before the late 1990s, however, only amateur and local historians gave Corinth and its surrounding operations any attention. Newspaper editor G. W. Dudley produced two short but important accounts of the local battles in the 1890s, *The Battle of Iuka* (1896) and *The Battle of Corinth and the Court Martial of Gen. Van Dorn* (1899). Monroe Cockrell located a lost copy of Dudley's latter account and reprinted it with a version of his own story in 1955. Major historians have only recently begun paying attention to Corinth. Peter Cozzens wrote *The Darkest Days of the War: The Battles of Iuka and Corinth* in 1997, and Earl Hess included the campaign in his study entitled *Banners to the Breeze: The Kentucky Campaign, Corinth, and Stones River* (2000). More recently, Steven Dossman added a short history entitled *Campaign for Corinth: Blood in Mississippi* to the much-lauded McWhiney series.[3]

As good as these works are, however, none gives Corinth its full due. Cozzens's well-received book covers only the fall campaign, primarily the battles themselves. The story is included with Perryville and Stones River in Hess's book. Inexplicably, little light has been cast on the siege; similarly, the occupation phases have produced few studies other than local investigations and journal articles. Fortunately, new approaches in Civil War historiography have opened the possibility for a more comprehensive examination of Corinth's history, including the civilians that both affected and were affected by the battles, the racial issues involved in the occupation, and the political overtones of military and social events. A comprehensive account of Corinth's important and significant role in the Civil War is impossible without this new approach, and the time has come, some 150 years after the fact, to produce such an analysis of the siege, the battle, and the occupation of Corinth. I hope this volume fills that need.[4]

Those numerous people who aided me in the research and writing of this book over the past twenty years are almost uncountable, but a few made extraordinary efforts. The staff members at the many archives and special collections I consulted were all helpful and supportive. Many academic friends and colleagues aided me in the process as well, including my colleagues at the University of Tennessee at Martin: David Coffey, Deidra Beene, Sandy King, and Sarah Conrad. Early on, several professors at Ole Miss encouraged the dreams of a young college student, and some read parts of my manuscript. Douglas Sullivan-Gonzalez, James J. Cooke, Harry P. Owens, and David G. Sansing were all great mentors. Harry Laver and Bill Robinson at Southeastern Louisiana University helped me locate a thesis on the siege. Patrick Hotard, the author of that thesis, was also helpful. John F. Marszalek and Michael B. Ballard at Mississippi State University, where I continued my graduate education, encouraged me greatly. Professor Marszalek went far beyond the call of duty, twice reading the initial version over a decade ago and then plowing through the revised version of some 900 pages. He is the epitome of a mentor and a friend.

Numerous staff members and volunteers at Shiloh National Military Park and the Corinth Civil War Interpretive Center also facilitated the process of finishing this book. My entire career in the National Park Service was encased within my work on this project, and I was fortunate to be around during the development of the Corinth center and even worked there occasionally. Jim Minor, Ashley Berry, Stacy Allen, Woody Harrell, and Tom Parson all aided me in one way or another. In addition to facilitating my research there, Tom Parson, the Park Service's chief authority on all things Corinth related, read the manuscript twice and made many helpful suggestions and corrections.

Other people in and around the Corinth community contributed to the process as well. Van Hedges graciously opened his massive collection of Corinth Civil War materials to me, as did Dr. William G. Jackson. Kristy White, Anne Thompson, and Gale Judkins helped me track down some elusive information on Corinth's citizens. Margaret Greene Rogers, now deceased, aided me in my initial research. Greg Williams allowed me to utilize his huge collection of Civil War regimental histories.

Working with the University Press of Kansas has been a wonderful experience. Mike Briggs supported the project from the first and ushered it through the publication process. Susan Schott and Larisa Martin made the marketing and editing aspects easy and enjoyable, and copyeditor Linda Lotz did a wonderful job on the text. The historians recruited by the press, Bill Shea and an anonymous reader, added many useful suggestions and comments. George Skoch created the wonderful maps.

Obviously, the group closest to me, and those who have probably had the most impact on me besides my God, is my family. My parents George and Miriam Smith apparently saw something worthwhile in my dream of research and writing. Early on, they funded several research trips to archives and special collections. Now that I look back on it and realize the cost of funding my own research trips, I see their sacrifice and love. I could not ask for better parents, and I love and cherish them dearly. My brother Danny Smith, a former newspaper editor, took the time to read the earliest draft nearly twenty years ago. Although the manuscript has changed drastically over time, his efforts are still visible in the finished product.

I began this project long before I knew there was a beautiful young lady named Kelly Castleman. As the focus of this book has changed over the years, so has my life, and only for the better. I am proud that Kelly is no longer a Castleman but a Smith, and together we have produced the two sweetest girls in the world, Mary Kate and Leah Grace. To them I give my unending love and thanks for their unending love and support.

Prologue

CROSSROADS

The spring of 1862 was a difficult one for Abraham Lincoln and his commanders. The year-old war had entered a vicious period, with large-scale battles producing tens of thousands of casualties. And those casualties were seemingly not garnering much fruit. A Federal attempt to capture Richmond, Virginia, the Confederate capital, was grinding to a halt amid massive bloodshed, while out West, several Union victories looked small compared with the bloody near-catastrophe at Shiloh. Not to be disrupted, however, Union commanders knew where the immediate, as well as the long-term, focal points were. John M. Schofield wrote in April that all Union troops were necessarily going to the Corinth front: "Something can be risked elsewhere, but nothing there," he wrote. As distinguished a Confederate figure as Robert E. Lee added his ideas on Corinth's importance. In forwarding orders for reinforcements to the critical crossroads, Lee wrote, "If [the] Mississippi Valley is lost [the] Atlantic States will be ruined." Because it was obviously so important, by the end of that year, Union generals would expend thousands of lives and tons of ammunition in first taking and then holding the small north Mississippi town. Indeed, the Federals would spend almost the entire bloody year wrestling for possession of Corinth.[1]

Despite it prominence in the spring of 1862, the town that became the South's vital staging area possessed a humble background. The hamlet itself dated back only to 1854, when word came that two major railroads would soon cross each other in central Tishomingo County. The Memphis and Charleston Railroad was to run from Memphis across northern Mississippi and Alabama and ultimately to Chattanooga, Tennessee, where other lines would connect it to the East. The Mobile and Ohio would run from Mobile, Alabama, northward to Columbus, Kentucky, on the Mississippi River. Surveyors staked out the routes of both railroads, and they crossed on a small parcel of land owned by William Lasley.[2]

Realizing the economic boom that would result, smart businessmen began to capitalize on the future crossing. Lasley sold his land at a profit. The two men who bought it, Houston Mitchell and Hamilton Mask, set to work building a town, and a hamlet quickly sprang up. These two entrepreneurs staked off their newly acquired land into streets and lots, sold their tracts, and began to gain their wealth. Fittingly, they named their little village Cross City in 1855. A petition for incorporation surfaced as the town grew, and the charter became official on March 12, 1856. The name was changed on the recommendation of the town's newspaper editor, W. E. Gibson, and Cross City became Corinth. Elections soon took place, with prominent local men becoming the selectmen, constables, judges, and justices of the peace.[3]

The small town continued to grow, especially with completion of the railroads. Corinth's first postmaster, Henry C. Hyneman, opened shop in 1856— interestingly, in a pink post office. The town's first brick building went up in 1857, and several churches of the Presbyterian, Baptist, and Methodist faiths soon opened their doors. Several saloons received licenses to operate, and numerous hotels began their functions.[4]

An educational institution also emerged in Corinth, the Corona Female College. It was housed in an impressive three-story domed structure that sat on five acres south of town donated by Houston Mitchell. St. Louis carpenter Martin Siegrist, a Swiss immigrant, moved to Corinth to build the structure, and it was completed by the summer of 1857. One student later remembered that the main hall had arches and pillars; the twenty-three rooms as well as the surrounding gardens were tastefully furnished and well kept. Officially opening in July 1857, the college soon boasted students from several surrounding states. The Reverend Leroy B. Gaston, a Presbyterian minister, served as president of the school, and his wife Susan was the principal. Despite the Unionism of the area, the Gastons were firmly Southern, declaring that no Northerners would teach in their school. By 1858, the college had ninety students and seven teachers, with a preparatory department consisting of a three-year program and a collegiate degree adding another year. "Oh, how hard we had to study," one student remembered, noting that "Mr. Gaston certainly had very little 'humbugery' about his examinations."[5]

By 1860, Corinth had grown to a population of around 1,200, prompting county officials to move the seat of government there for half of vast Tishomingo County; workers soon erected a brick courthouse in the center of town. Five churches, the college, three large hotels, and many smaller businesses had also emerged by the beginning of the new decade. The largest and most famous of these buildings was the brick Tishomingo Hotel, also built by Siegrist and operated by George Cox. It boasted two stories and stood adjacent to the railroad depot, facing the Memphis and Charleston Railroad. Another major hotel was Wiley Blount Pannell's Corinth House. An observer described in detail the small town as it looked in the early 1860s: "The houses are built after the Southern fashion," he noted, "with a front-door for every room looking toward the street. This is an odd feature to one used to Yankee architecture, but it is the universal style of the Southern states. The apartments of most of the houses are large and airy, and surrounded with immense porticos, where the high toned chivalry enjoy their siesta." He also noted that the people "consume almost unheard of quantities of Bourbon and rifle whiskey." "The yards of the rich are decorated with shrubbery," he continued, "and what is far more in accordance with good taste, forest-trees are left standing and neatly trimmed—a custom which has been too sadly neglected in the North." He also mentioned "several substantial brick and frame business-houses" and enumerated some of the shingles that advertised the shops.[6]

With all the churches springing up, a universal tug-of-war between good and evil emerged. There was lawlessness, of course. One judge described this scene in 1860: "They took a man up there to-day for running away with another man's wife, & gave him a pretty good whipping." He also described a wrestling match held in Corinth and noted, "I am fearful that the morals of Corinth are on the decrease." Yet the churches were active; they even held meetings for the black population, and some allowed blacks to join their membership. There were political events in Corinth as well, including speeches by luminaries such as Stephen A. Douglas and William Lowndes Yancey. Concerts and graduation exercises at the college added to the social activities.[7]

Although Corinth grew in educational, religious, social, and economic activity, everyone knew that the main lifeblood of the town was the locomotive. For years, the backwoods area of Tishomingo County had seen only river traffic from the nearby Tennessee River. Corinth itself obtained many of its supplies and did its trading at Pittsburg Landing, just across the border in Tennessee. Other landings in the eastern part of the county, such as Eastport, also provided an outlet for trade along the river. When the railroads extended passenger and mail service to Corinth, however, the town became tied to the larger regional and even national economy. The spike that completed the Memphis and Charleston Railroad was hammered in on April 1, 1857, just west of nearby Iuka; the ceremony brought a flurry of excitement as well as many new businesses and products.[8]

For a time, the Mobile and Ohio lagged behind its east-west counterpart, but it was soon completed as well. Service reached Corinth on January 10,

1861—ironically, one day after Mississippi seceded from the Union. There was great celebration, with the mayor and aldermen of Memphis coming out on the Memphis and Charleston to take part in the festivities. A local militia company, the Corinth Rifles, fired salutes, and one newspaper reported, "Corinth may now boast of being situated at the junction of the two longest railroads in the South, and we predict that in a few years she will occupy a position of prominence and independence, not even anticipated by her most sanguine projectors." Amid even greater celebration, railroad officials drove in the last spike for the Mobile and Ohio on April 21, 1861, at the Mississippi-Tennessee state line. Excursion trains brought dignitaries and tourists to the site, and a huge barbecue was held just north of Corinth.[9]

The presence of two major railroads in the southern portion of the United States brought new ideas to the formerly backwoods area. One visitor gave a good overview of the town's rise in prominence: "The place itself, although socially and politically insignificant, and not calculated ever to become of commercial consequence, yet, with the speculative greed strongly character-izing the age, had, upon the completion of the Rail-Roads, been laid off into streets, and lots sold at fabulous prices, on a plan as extensive as the City of Paris, with a plaza, or public square in the center."[10]

Despite the railroads and the potential to ship goods, agricultural endeav-ors around Corinth were actually smaller than in other parts of the state. There were some plantations, but the extreme northeastern portion of Mississippi was hilly and not well suited to large-scale farming. As a result, the society and culture around Corinth was very different from that on the big plantations along the Mississippi River. According to the 1860 census, only 4,981 of the roughly 437,000 slaves in Mississippi resided in Tishomingo County, which was one of the largest counties in the state. Along the Mississippi River, some counties had as many as 15,000 slaves each. Around the state capital of Jack-son, in Hinds and Madison Counties, there were 22,363 and 18,118 slaves, respectively.[11]

This lack of a major slave presence translated into a lack of zeal for seces-sion. One Corinthian, Walter A. Overton, noted in his diary during the seces-sion crisis of November 1860, "I hope the excitement will soon pop off and peace and quiet be restored." Governor John J. Pettus began talking of seces-sion in earnest after the election of Abraham Lincoln in November 1860, and the state legislature called for a secession convention. Tishomingo County was less than enthusiastic, much like its neighboring counties in northwest-ern Alabama and southwestern Tennessee. Overton later noted that he had voted for the "Union ticket" during the canvass for the secession convention delegates, and most of his neighbors had done likewise. The county voted nearly three to one for the cooperationist delegates, and it elected four anti-secession men to the convention, which assembled in Jackson in January 1861. Arthur E. Reynolds, Wright W. Bonds, Thomas P. Young, and John A. Blair all made their antisecession feelings known, including in the famous ballot cast on January 9, 1861, on the very ordinance of secession. The four men voted against the ordinance; all told, only fifteen delegates voted in the negative. Still, all four delegates from Tishomingo County signed the ordinance six days later in a show of support. Although the four men and the county as a whole did not support secession, they very much supported the war when it became inevitable. Unionist delegate Arthur Reynolds, in fact, was one of the first men to raise a unit for the Confederacy, ultimately becoming colonel of the 26th Mississippi. The large number of soldiers the county later sent to the Confederate war effort further attests to this support.[12]

The people of Corinth quickly began adjusting to war, just as they had earlier adapted to modernization. The earlier change had been welcomed, and the town's livelihood was staked to the boom the railroads brought. By the time the Mobile and Ohio Railroad was completed in April 1861, however, a mere nine days after the firing on Fort Sumter, the people of Corinth realized that the railroads would soon complicate if not destroy their lives. The railroads that had been the focus of so much economic and social celebration in the 1850s now made Corinth a valuable strategic point in the war, and both sides were determined to control it. An observer noted Corinth's placement: "Its importance is derived solely from its military association and strategic position, cutting as it does, the three great arteries of the South." A Corinthian noted the result in his diary on March 5, 1861: "Lincoln's inaugural address seems to purport war," he prophesied, "we shall have Squally times for awhile."[13]

1

The Great Rallying Point

With the coming of war, Corinth immediately found itself in a chaotic situation. In 1861, because of its railroads, the town became one of the chief centers of troop induction, organization, and supply in the entire western Confederacy. One Confederate described Corinth as "the great rallying point in the central south." The Memphis and Charleston Railroad was the Confederacy's only complete east-west rail link from the Mississippi Valley to Chattanooga, where it connected with other lines that led to the Eastern Seaboard. The only other such route was farther to the south, running from Vicksburg to Atlanta, but it lacked a link between Meridian, Mississippi, and Selma, Alabama, thus necessitating a detour down to Mobile and back up. The Mobile and Ohio Railroad was almost as important, being one of the only north-south lines in the western Confederacy. That the two railroads were of the same gauge made them even more helpful in logistical terms. Obviously, the crossing at Corinth was a primary strategic position.[1]

Although it was an important military locality, Corinth was not ideally situated for its coming role in the war. The town sat on low land in between two creeks bounded on their far sides by ridges. In short, the town sat in a depression where stagnant water gathered and sickness spread. "Corinth is built upon low lands and clay soil, so that in wet weather the place may very properly be denominated a swamp," one observer noted. Famous writer Ambrose Bierce labeled the town "the capitol of a swamp." Once war began and thousands upon thousands of troops concentrated there, there would be misery for all.[2]

Despite its Unionist leanings, Tishomingo County sent fifty-eight companies to the Confederacy; Corinth itself sent five. The prewar militia company known as the Corinth Rifles initially contained only thirty-four men, but they joined with another understrength company and formed a hundred-man unit that became part of the 9th Mississippi Infantry. Another company later went to the 26th Mississippi, and yet another to the 32nd Mississippi. The Corinth Minute Men joined the ill-fated 2nd Regiment of state troops, a part of the famed Army of Ten Thousand. A cavalry company soon became part of the 12th Mississippi Cavalry. Even Corinth's twenty-five-year-old mayor, James E. Stewart, left his post in 1861 to join the Confederate ranks.[3]

The recruitment and send-off to war at Corinth mirrored scenes throughout the nation. The women of the town sewed flags for the men as they marched off to war. One resident remembered, "The first Confederate flag that unfurled its silken folds to the breeze in our town was made by the ladies of Corinth, and [was] presented to this company [Corinth Rifles] by Miss Lydia Mitchell." The company captain accepted the flag and paid tribute to the patriotic women of Corinth. The cavalry company likewise received a flag. One day while troops were drilling "on the large lawn of the Corona Female College," one resident remembered, Mrs. Gaston and the students came out and surprised the men by presenting them with a hand-painted silk flag.[4]

Such ceremonial acts soon gave way to the realization that the men would be leaving their families. One Corinth woman described the departure of the Corinth Rifles to Pensacola, Florida: "We can never forget that sad morning in April, 1861, when good-bys were taken of our gallant soldier boys, looking so handsome in their new uniforms of Confederate gray, bugle and drum making sweet music." A large group of citizens gathered, and the Reverend J. W. Wells, the company's chaplain and the pastor of the Methodist Episcopal Church in Corinth, led them in prayer. "The troops were marched single file into the cars, bearing aloft the beautiful flag," the woman remembered. "As the cars moved off slowly, our very heartstrings were at their utmost tension," she added, and many tears were shed: "We lingered to catch a last glimpse."[5]

Most of Corinth's companies left the area and served elsewhere. Meanwhile, the Confederate and state governments soon sent many more Mississippians and other Southerners to town. In the early months of the war, Mississippi used Corinth as one of its troop staging areas. The small town's population mushroomed almost overnight as thousands of arriving troops camped in its vicinity and even occupied churches and other buildings in town. One of those raw recruits wrote home, "We are surrounded by excitement here all the time[.] From the breaking of the day to nine at night nothing greets your ears but the beating of the drums and the commands of the officers." Two of the initial eight Mississippi regiments were organized and equipped near Corinth—the 1st Mississippi at nearby Iuka, and the 2nd Mississippi at Corinth itself. As spring turned into summer, more companies rendezvoused at Corinth. Governor John J. Pettus ordered fifty companies to town in May 1861, and others arrived later that summer. These units eventually became the 11th through 17th Mississippi Regiments. Several other regiments were also formed at nearby Iuka. Most of the units organized in Tishomingo County eventually moved to Virginia because of the convenient railroad access to the East. Major General Reuben Davis's Mississippi militia brigade of the Army of Ten Thousand, however, made its way to Kentucky in the fall and winter of 1861. Many of these gathering troops suffered various shortages, such as one soldier who wrote to a friend from Corinth, "We have a full supply of guns but no ammunition except what we brought with us." Another related, "They yesterday marched us into town and took all our arms and equipment from us for to help equip a Regiment for Virginia." The soldier optimistically insisted that he "was glad of it for we shall get much better ones when we do get them."[6]

Eventually, the Confederacy also used Corinth as a concentration point. One Louisianan reported on arriving at the town, "Corinth is also a very pretty little town situated among hills but not high." Most of the early troops who encamped there faced a new military way of life that was wholly different from anything they had experienced at home. The excitement of the new soldiers' journey to Corinth quickly changed to the routine and harshness of army life. One soldier described his trip: "In every direction handkerchiefs were waving by ladies, men, boys, girls, children, and even negroes and you could not hear yourself think for the hollowing." Conditions became considerably worse when the troops arrived at Corinth itself. Army life disgusted many, especially the first recruits who had joined in eager anticipation of going off to war. "Our camp duties at first seemed very arduous," one recruit complained. "Rising so early for roll call, doing guard duty, etc." Then boredom set in as the soldiers realized they would not see any action for a while. The same recruit remembered how soldiers "put up arbors, made seats, tables, and cooking utensils." Another wrote home: "You can see men doing everything imaginable, some playing the fiddle, some dancing, playing cards, fighting chickens, doing everything." Then there were the unhealthy conditions. One Arkansan described Corinth "as a small country town, with the muddiest streets, the worst water and more fatal sickness than any place this army ever camped." Another wrote, "Water is scarce, inconvenient, and not very good." Another informed his wife, "I assure you I am tired of the place and the water is execrable." The result was mass sickness. A member of the 19th Louisiana in Corinth recorded that he had a "running off of the bowels." A future member of the 16th Mississippi wrote in his diary, "Measles and diarrhea were most annoying. The latter doubtless owing to bad water and unhealthy diet." Rough weather made matters even worse, with cold temperatures and occasional sleet and snow tormenting the men during that first winter of the war.[7]

Yet there were some exciting times. The soldiers took notice when famous units or people arrived. Governor Pettus came to camp in June 1861, and of course, the visits of Corinth's ladies made a major impression. Larger-than-life units also drew a crowd. One member of the Orleans Guard described that unit's reception in the spring of 1862: "Our arrival at the camp was hailed with a thousand hurrahs, and joy reigned throughout the camps when they learned that we were the Orleans Guard." Even P. G. T. Beauregard came out to the camp and reacquainted himself with the men he knew so well. "He appeared greatly moved at seeing us," one member wrote in his diary. He also noted proudly that this was the first time Beauregard had mingled with the troops since his arrival at Corinth.[8]

The soldiers gathering at Corinth felt the effects of war, even before they saw battle. One Louisianan noted: "Our little town of Corinth looks like it has been a flourishing little place once but now it is in quite a dilapidated condition." Spies were reported in town, which caused some concern. Some soldiers arrived with heavy hearts, such as future Confederate general Claudius W. Sears. When he left Holly Springs, he had just lost three small children to scarlet fever. His pregnant wife begged him not to go. Others felt the loss after they arrived in Corinth. "I feel very much depressed in spirits," Robert Moore wrote in June 1861, having "just lost one of my warmest and best friends, Cousin George L. Moore." He also noted the good-bye his unit had experienced: "The young ladies from our neighborhood left for home this morning. Tom's sweet-heart cried but he would not & I had to pinch him before he would cry." The lack of religious observances bothered many raw recruits. "It seemed very strange to see men out with guns on the Sabbath," Moore declared. "Pa does not allow us to handle a gun on Sunday," he explained.[9]

The citizens of Corinth were clearly affected by the influx of so many new people. Although passes were generally needed to go into town, there was quite a bit of interaction between the soldiers and the civilians. Some of it was not ideal. A Mississippi soldier wrote in his diary about the arrival of a new company: "a great many of them were a little tight," he wrote, and later told of several "boys marking time for bringing whiskey into the camp." One Corinth judge recorded in his diary that the soldiers had their own judicial system: "There was a great deal of excitement there. They drummed a fellow out of town. Tar[r]ed and cottoned an Irishman." He later described seeing "one ring fight, and several other minor fisticuffs[.] I expected to see some of them killed but there was not. . . . They had two women with them dressed in men's clothes, going Soldiering." The soldiers elaborated on the rough men congregating at Corinth and the danger they posed. One recruit wrote to a friend, "Three deaths occurred here yesterday, one being shot accidentally, second drowned and the other died of dysentery." Another wrote, almost proudly, to his mother: "Joe liked to of cut a man's throat." Despite the rough soldiers amidst them, most citizens were eager to help in any way they could. Susan Gaston of Corona College wrote, "They [soldiers] found the population ready to greet them with all the demonstrations of kindness which patriotism prompts."[10]

The removal of so many of Corinth's men led to hardship for the citizens who remained. One soldier's wife wrote in her diary, "My Husband left for Bowling Green Ky. this evening. . . . I did not go to see him off. I could not bear the Idea of parting with him under such dangerous Circumstances, he sent me his ambrotype which I prise above all things." To take care of the families left without a man at home during the war, the Tishomingo County Board of Police set up a commission in August 1861 "for the relief of families of absent soldiers." Each county district had a representative, and a special county tax was established to care for those families.[11]

Perhaps the greatest burden of all came later in the spring and summer, when dead soldiers began to be returned to the town, prompting one Corinth woman to describe "some of our soldiers' bodies [who] were brought home on their biers." The Corinth Rifles sent several bodies home from Pensacola, the victims of disease. Other Corinthians perished during early battles such as Manassas. These deaths stunned the citizens, who were not yet accustomed to such news. The townspeople also had to help care for the sick and dead from other communities who ended up in Corinth. One Louisiana soldier reported, "The people here are very kind to wait on our sick." Susan Gaston remembered that "every kindness [was] lavished upon the sick that was in the power of the kind hearted citizens."[12]

On a lighter note, the presence of soldiers provided entertainment for many of Corinth's citizens. Numerous reviews took place with "fifes and horns," one soldier remembered. A female resident of Corinth told of the festival atmosphere of military life: "Daily drilling was witnessed by citizens and visitors, and much interest was taken in the proficiency of the troops. As many as ten regiments were sometimes drilling on the field at one time. The social feature, the brighter side of life, had attention. Many entertainments were given the troops. There might have been some married men, but no tales were told." The soldiers also boosted the local economy. They employed local slaves to do such jobs as washing clothes. They also bought food from the locals. One soldier described how he and a friend often "went out in the country and got a good old family dinner" for only twenty-five cents. The locals apparently learned how to raise prices, however; one Louisianan complained that the cost of "every thing [is] very high and scarcely anything to sell." One

Confederate recruit organizing in Corinth even wrote of the local children's ingenuity: "The little boys and girls of the neighborhood brings in sweet cakes and lemonade every day and sell them to us."[13]

In addition to the influx of soldiers, the town became a major rail hub for the transfer of supplies, ammunition, and arms to the war front. "Cars are continually arriving and going off bringing and taking off troops," one soldier remembered. "There is a continual roaring of drums here," he added. Yet the supplies at Corinth were never sufficient for the number of troops, forcing a shortfall that many a soldier described.[14]

Corinth's logistical importance waned as the war entered its second year, however. As Federal forces came closer to northern Mississippi, state and Confederate officials began to use the convenient rail crossing less as an organization center and more as a military bastion. As the enemy came closer, military officials organized raw units farther south at more protected sites such as Grenada and Meridian. Corinth thus became more of a strategic locality of importance. Indeed, by the spring of 1862, the war had reached the doorsteps of Corinth, and Southern leaders were determined to hold on to it at all costs.[15]

The North seemed just as determined to take Corinth. Early in 1862, Federal commanders set out on what ultimately became an attempt to control the Mississippi Valley. Northern generals decided to bypass the impregnable Columbus, Kentucky, on the Mississippi River and instead use the Tennessee and Cumberland Rivers to invade what historian Thomas Connelly has called the Confederate heartland. This effort resulted in the capture of Forts Henry and Donelson and Nashville, Tennessee, in February 1862 and the occupation of Pittsburg Landing, only twenty-two miles northeast of Corinth, a month later. As early as February 1862, Union army commanders realized they had to neutralize the Confederate railroads that crossed at Corinth to weaken if not paralyze Confederate movement and transportation in the western Confederacy and provide a staging area for the campaign against Vicksburg and the rest of the Mississippi Valley. Henry Halleck wrote to Secretary of War Stanton in March 1862 that although the enemy's railroads had been cut in places, "we must take Corinth before we can seriously injure his communications."[16]

Two of the three major Federal armies operating in Tennessee were involved in the early operations against Corinth. The Army of the Ohio, under Major General Don Carlos Buell, who also commanded the department of the same name, made its way through the heart of Tennessee, occupying Nashville after the Confederate debacle at Fort Donelson. Major General Ulysses S. Grant commanded the other army—the Army of the Tennessee, which hailed from the department commanded by Halleck. This army, after its victories at Forts Henry and Donelson, continued up the Tennessee River to Pittsburg Landing. A third army, Major General John Pope's Army of the Mississippi, campaigned on that river and was also under Halleck's departmental command.[17]

Both Buell and Halleck tried to persuade Union army commander Major General George B. McClellan to give them the command of all forces in Tennessee. Halleck finally won on March 11 when he gained command of the new Department of the Mississippi. This department encompassed both former departments (Ohio and Missouri) as well as those west of the Mississippi River. In his new powerful position, Halleck ordered Buell, then at Nashville, to march overland to Pittsburg Landing and join the Army of the Tennessee for an attack on the railroads at Corinth. Halleck would lead the united armies himself. By April 5, Buell's advance force had arrived at Savannah, only a few miles downstream (north) of Pittsburg Landing.[18]

Confederate commanders had no choice but to concentrate their scattered forces south of the enemy. Corinth, because of the importance of the railroads, was chosen as the concentration point, and outlying areas, such as Eastport on the Tennessee River, were fortified and defended. This development brought in troops from almost every compass point, including the return of the Corinth Rifles from the coast. Generals also congregated. As one soldier told his wife, "All the Big Bugs are here Generals Johnson, Bouragard Brag." One Corinthian derisively wrote in his diary in March, "There are 5 Generals in town now and if we do not whip the Yankees this time it will not be for the want of [those?] articles." But Corinth's citizens wanted to do their part as well. During the spring, the local county government organized a commission to enroll men in the militia and contracted gunsmiths to repair private weapons.[19]

As more and more troops began to arrive at Corinth, entrenchments to defend the town began to go up. In March 1862, Braxton Bragg had his engineers find the best place to situate the earthworks and then had slave labor, augmented by soldiers, dig them. Soon, Bragg had a series of rifle pits dug around the east and north side of town, with several larger earthworks commanding the roadways. One staff officer described them as "enfilading redoubts for cannon, with continuous Earthworks or Rifle pits for infantry between." "Intrenchments are going up all along the line," another soldier wrote, "and we hold ourselves in hourly expectation of battle." When Albert Sidney Johnston and P. G. T. Beauregard arrived at Corinth, the two generals toured the works and pronounced them sound.[20]

The only thing missing was soldiers to fill those earthworks, and they came

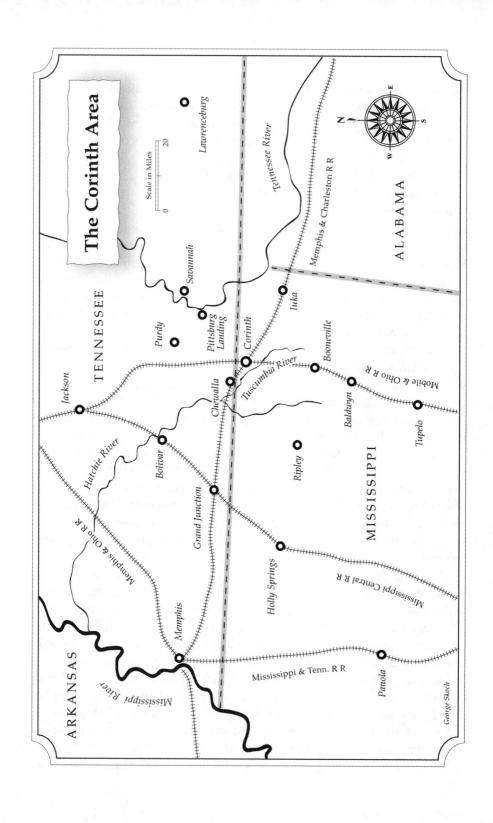

The Corinth Area

Scale in Miles
0   20

TENNESSEE

ALABAMA

MISSISSIPPI

ARKANSAS

Lawrenceburg

Savannah

Purdy

Pittsburg Landing

Corinth

Iuka

Chewalla

Booneville

Jackson

Bolivar

Ripley

Baldwyn

Tupelo

Grand Junction

Holly Springs

Memphis

Panola

Tennessee River

Tuscumbia River

Hatchie River

Mississippi River

Memphis & Charleston R R

Mobile & Ohio R R

Memphis & Ohio R R

Mississippi Central R R

Mississippi & Tenn. R R

N   E
W   S

George Skoch

from all over the Confederacy. One soldier described the scene: "Our main line of Briggades are now over 4 miles long making a citty of tents almost equal to Orleans." He went on to describe the sights and sounds of camp, including "Tatoo and I can here at one blast neare 100 bands playing." Another soldier, a new recruit, wrote, "The scenery is truly great here to one that never saw an army before. The hills for several miles around are covered with tents resembling hills of snow." Not everyone was optimistic about the results of the concentration, however. Upon viewing the unruly troops from other parts of the Confederacy, Bragg wrote to his wife, "I thought my Mobile Army was a *Mob*."[21]

Such a large concentration of soldiers—much larger than the initial organization of Mississippi troops in 1861—clearly had a greater effect on the town's population. One soldier cautioned his wife not to come to Corinth, as "all the women and children have left," and it would not be a very nice place for the next few weeks. The civilians that remained tried to maintain their normal lives amidst the growing Confederate army. Some civilians actively aided the army, such as one Corinthian who reported, "We went scouting and got as far as Burnsville." Others just wanted to protect their land and homes. "A regiment of soldiers have camped on my land," Judge Walter Overton wrote in his diary, "and there is no telling how much damage they are doing it. . . . They are cutting all the timber off of it and burning all the rails. If they stay long they will ruin it." Overton complained to Brigadier General Adley Gladden, who sent several of his aides and "the Provost Martial to see what damage they had done me," Overton wrote a few days later. "They came back and said they had done me no damage," Overton fumed. "If that is the way our friends treat us, Lord deliver me from our friends," he added. Later, he complained that "the soldiers have filled up my well . . . I would give a good deal to know who did it."[22]

While the soldiers camped in tents, the generals normally lodged with families in town. General Johnston quartered in the house of Major William M. Inge, who had attended West Point and was an officer on the staff of a Mississippi general in Virginia. Inge happened to be home on leave in March and April 1862 and met Johnston at the rail depot when he arrived. Inge tendered his home to the general and his staff to use as a headquarters. It was there that Johnston surveyed his declining strategic situation.[23]

Realizing the gravity of the state of affairs, Johnston and Beauregard determined to defend Corinth and its railroads by attacking Grant's isolated Union Army of the Tennessee at Pittsburg Landing before Buell and his Army of the Ohio could arrive. Johnston realized that his army would not be getting larger anytime soon, while the Union army would double. Johnston had to strike

immediately. All but the critically sick thus marched out of Corinth in early
April to attack the enemy. One common soldier reported, "The watchword
here is Victory or Death."[24]

Corinth's citizens watched the troops file out of town. Johnston himself
reviewed the units as they marched past his headquarters and provided stan-
dards to regiments who needed them. A witness described the "measured
tramp, tramp of moving troops, the bugle, fife, and drum." The bands played
various songs, their favorite being "The Girl I Left Behind Me." Johnston and
his staff then prepared to move to the front. Unbeknownst to the general, Mrs.
Augusta Inge had placed two sandwiches and a piece of cake in his coat
pocket before he left. Major Inge joined the marchers, serving as a volunteer
aide on another Mississippi general's staff.[25]

In what became known as the Battle of Shiloh, the Confederate Army of
the Mississippi surprised the enemy near Pittsburg Landing on the morning
of April 6, 1862, and, in a day of hard fighting, pushed the Federals back
toward the Tennessee River. By nightfall, a shaken Federal army hugged one
last, desperate line near Pittsburg Landing. General Johnston had been killed
during the day, but General Beauregard and the Southern commanders felt
sure they could finish the job the next morning.[26]

During the night, however, Buell arrived with the leading elements of his
army. With those three divisions of reinforcements plus others from his own
command, Grant ordered an attack at dawn. The stubborn Confederates gave
ground all day. By two o'clock in the afternoon, Beauregard knew he had no
choice but to retreat. The grand Confederate offensive, the success of which
directly hinged on the destruction of the Union Army of the Tennessee, had
fallen short of its goal. The mass of Confederates, now no more than 30,000
strong, made their painful way back to Corinth, struggling to comprehend
what had just happened. Bragg himself was speechless. He wrote to his wife
the day after the battle, "How to begin a letter confounds me. So much has
been crowded in a small space of time."[27]

The people left at Corinth spent several nervous days awaiting news from
the battlefield. A Confederate recruit, John Hooper Gates, had just arrived at
Corinth and described the ghost-town appearance of the place. "Our Reg.
[13th Tennessee] and nearly all the rest are gone out to the battlefield 12 or
15 miles from here," he wrote, "leaving only the sick at the tents." According
to Mrs. Inge, "Saturday, April 5, 1862, dragged its weary length along in much
expectancy. No engagement took place." The next morning, the residents
heard the thunder of artillery and knew Johnston had attacked. "It seemed that

the ground was vibrating with the shock," Mrs. Inge continued, "the agony of that day can never be written." As Susan Gaston remembered, "The sound of the guns first reached us on Sunday morning; we hurried from the breakfast table to the yard and listened to the continued roar. It was like far away sea waves when they strike the shore." A soldier in Corinth wrote home, "Heavy cannonading commenced in that direction this morning at 8 o'clock and kept up several hours." Then word began to trickle in that Johnston's army was winning a major victory, but many wounded were being sent back, prompting the yellow hospital flags to go up on nearly every building in Corinth. "The news is coming in from the field," John Gates wrote to his wife, and "it is said we are driving the enemy back down the river." At 6:00 P.M. he added more to his letter: "The news is coming in from the field very favorably but nothing authentic." That night, the wounded and stragglers began to appear, bringing the first real confirmation of the battle and its ferocity. Gates and the raw recruits of the 13th Tennessee, despite having no guns, were ordered to cook rations in preparation for going to the field.[28]

Worse news began to arrive the next morning. A shocked Mrs. Inge was sent word to have Johnston's room ready to receive his remains. His staff had temporarily taken his body to Shiloh Church and injected his veins with whiskey for preservation. Mrs. Inge watched as the staff brought Johnston's lifeless body into his room wrapped in army blankets. "It was lifted tenderly and carried to his room in Corinth and placed on an improvised bier amid silence and tears," she recalled. "Three days before he had left this room in all the vigor of mature manhood; now he was asleep in the same room, a martyr to his country's cause," she lamented. Mrs. Inge and several other ladies cleaned the body and uniform, wrapped Johnston in a Confederate flag, cut locks of his hair, and laid him in a simple white pine coffin, as no better one could be found. While cleaning the uniform, Mrs. Inge found one of the sandwiches and half the cake she had secretly deposited in Johnston's pocket. Before being taken south on a train, Johnston's body lay in state for several hours, and many residents of Corinth paid their respects.[29]

Soon a flood of soldiers would overwhelm the town. Hundreds of Federal prisoners, including Brigadier General Benjamin Prentiss, were brought to Corinth late on April 7. One of them, a member of the 14th Iowa, remembered, "We halted in the streets, threw ourselves down upon the ground to rest." They were then placed on railroad cars for shipment southward. An even larger number of wounded Confederate officers and men were brought back, including a mortally wounded Adley Gladden. Future U.S. senator William Bate was wounded so badly that surgeons wanted to amputate his leg, but he reportedly held them off with pistols. Major Inge returned to his wife, but he was badly bruised by a fall when his horse had been shot from under him. Thousands more trickled in over the next few days. One woman in Corinth remarked in her diary, "Nothing that I had ever heard or read had given me the faintest idea of the horrors witnessed here."[30]

For the most part, the citizens were eager to help. One soldier reported being allowed to spend the night in a "dwelling used to put cotton in and some lumber." He also said that the owner of the dwelling had set a comrade's broken arm. One civilian recorded in his diary on April 7, "I started to the battlefield this evening but could not get there. I stopped at Atkins' and helped to dress the wounded until 11 o'clock. The road is crowded with troops making their way back to Corinth. I fear we were badly worsted today."[31]

The Confederate wounded from Shiloh completely overwhelmed the medical facilities in Corinth. Southern surgeons converted almost every building, both private and public, into hospitals, where the Sisters of Charity, the Sisters of Mercy, and nurses from numerous cities across the South tended the wounded. The Sisters of Charity out of Mobile worked at Corona College; many other wounded were sent to the Tishomingo and Corinth House hotels downtown. Mrs. Ella King Newson, known as the "Florence Nightingale of the Confederacy," was in charge of the work at Corinth House. One Confederate soldier described the demise of so many of the wounded: "some pray to God to have mercy and others die cursing the 'Yankee sons of b_____s.'" A nurse at the Tishomingo Hotel also described some of the horror:

> The amputating table for this ward is at the end of the hall, near the landing of the stairs. When an operation is to be performed, I keep as far away from it as possible. To-day, just as they had got through with Mr. Fuquet, I was compelled to pass the place, and the sight I there beheld made me shudder and sick at heart. A stream of blood ran from the table into a tub in which was the arm. It had been taken off at the socket, and the hand, which but a short time before grasped the musket and battled for the right, was hanging over the edge of the tub, a lifeless thing. I often wish I could become as callous as many seem to be, for there is no end to these horrors. The passage to the kitchen leads directly past the amputating room below stairs, and many a time I have seen the blood running in streams from it.[32]

With such ghastly conditions, many healthy soldiers became sick in succeeding days. A nurse from Mobile who treated the sick in Corinth noted that she had seen "a whole Mississippi regiment sick," and "nearly all had a cough." A member of the 17th Louisiana wrote to his wife, "There is but six or seven men of the company well enough for duty and only one hundred and fifty eight of the Regiment fit for duty." Those not sick or wounded gagged at the gruesome sights. A pile of amputated arms and legs only grew larger outside the Tishomingo Hotel.[33]

The inhabitants and soldiers in Corinth expected to see fighting any day, and the Confederate authorities issued an order for all citizens to leave town. Susan Gaston remembered giving "advice to some who could leave, to hunt [for] a more desirable place of residence." One Louisianan wrote, "The women and children have been ordered out of Corinth a week ago and we are expecting an attack here." Fortunately, no battle came. Still, there was great unease about their situation. Many chose to leave, including the Inges, who removed to Aberdeen, Mississippi, and then on to Enterprise. Others chose to stay. Judge Overton did not leave town when the order was issued in mid-April, but by the end of the month, he was having second thoughts as a Federal advance on the town seemed more likely. Although unwilling to leave himself, he feared for his wife and children and took them southward to safety before returning to Corinth. "We started down the country and got as far as Holly Springs," he recorded in his diary in late April. He eventually deposited his family with kin at West Station in central Mississippi and then headed back home. "I found all things right at home," a relieved Overton wrote upon his return. "There is no indication of an engagement soon." Nevertheless, all eyes in the Confederacy turned toward Corinth in expectation of renewed fighting any day.[34]

Such a delay was fortunate for the Confederates defending Corinth because it gave them time to recover and stabilize their situation. One Southern soldier who arrived in Corinth from northwestern Tennessee after Shiloh noted in his diary that the soldiers in town "were worn out and presented a melancholy appearance." With the end of the rains and the beginning of warmer and drier spring days, however, the army began to recover its health. The weather alone did much to boost morale. Many soldiers were well enough to return to their commands, and the badly wounded were shipped south to towns that had the resources to take care of them—places such as Oxford, Okolona, West Point, Columbus, Brandon, Jackson, and Winona. Unfortunately, many of the wounded and sick soldiers sent southward never recovered from the deplorable conditions at Corinth. Small-town cemeteries along the rail lines to the south attest to the large numbers of Confederates who died along the way.[35]

After the debacle at Shiloh, the Confederate high command sent out urgent pleas for help. On April 10, President Jefferson Davis called on the governors of Georgia, Alabama, Mississippi, South Carolina, and Louisiana to "send forward to Corinth all the armed men you can furnish." Troops arrived from John C. Pemberton's department in South Carolina and Kirby Smith's command in east Tennessee, as well as newly organized units from the Deep South states. The major source of reinforcements, however, came from the trans-Mississippi. In the strategic concentration before Shiloh, General Johnston had called on Major General Earl Van Dorn, commander in that sector, to provide reinforcements. After his defeat at Pea Ridge on March 7–8, Van Dorn had made a quick trip to Corinth, where he met with Johnston and Beauregard to discuss future operations. The troops, in the meantime, made their way to Des Arc to board steamboats that would take them to Memphis and the railroad leading to Corinth.[36]

The Missouri troops that made up Major General Sterling Price's division of Van Dorn's command balked at the order to leave their homes west of the Mississippi River. The men argued that they had joined to defend Missouri and had no intention of going to Mississippi. They almost mutinied, but Price told "them that the road back to Missouri lay through Tennessee." Begrudgingly, the army finally moved eastward on April 8, but by that time, the Battle of Shiloh was already one day ended. Van Dorn continued nonetheless, and the first brigade left Des Arc that day on steamboats. "This was my first riding on [a] steam boat," one Confederate proudly noted.[37]

Even with such growing numbers, Beauregard was becoming more and more concerned about a Federal attack on Corinth. Amazingly, he wired Van Dorn on April 9, "Hurry your force as rapidly as possible. I believe we can whip them again." Van Dorn wired back the same day that his men were badly armed and needed the weapons taken in Beauregard's victory. Forced to explain his stretching of the truth about achieving victory at Shiloh, Beauregard replied, "I regret [I] have none; could not remove all I took, but we will take more. Come on." The theme of haste continued throughout the next few days. "Hurry up the movement" and "hurry forward" frequently appeared in messages between the commanders.[38]

By April 15, Price arrived in Memphis with the head of Van Dorn's army. "Reached Memphis and it is a large and handsome city full of flowers and beautiful women," noted one trans-Mississippian. As the men moved eastward, they continued to take in the new scenes. "Everything seemed to be on a grander and more magnificent scale than we had ever known it before," recalled an Arkansan. Over the next few days, the Memphis and Charleston Railroad demonstrated its value to Confederate troop movements by bringing one brigade per day into town, even amid the evacuation of so many wounded on trains moving in the other direction. "The cars are coming and going constantly," one woman in Corinth wrote, "and the noise is deafening." Not every ride on the railroad was ideal, however. The 6th Texas Cavalry, for example, had to ride flatcars the whole way, except for when the train stalled going up grades. Then the soldiers had to get off and hike up the long hills. An unfortunate few of Van Dorn's command, one soldier remembered, even "hoofed it to Corinth." Price's division of Missourians nevertheless made the trip and arrived in Corinth by April 24, causing a thrill among the people. Nurse Kate Cumming recalled, "I feel that we are now safe in Corinth," and she told Price so. She reported in her diary: "He gave me a very dignified bow, and, I thought, looked at me as if he *thought* that I was talking a great deal of nonsense." Later, more of Van Dorn's army arrived, and Van Dorn himself appeared on April 30. Others trickled in during the first few days of May.[39]

Many of Beauregard's soldiers did not know what to think of these westerners. One Missourian wrote, "The Missouri troops were the center of attraction, and a great many thronged our camp to look at us." One soldier even admitted to him, "They imagined that the Missourians had horns, but they saw we were 'just like any body else,' and seemed to be surprised." Of special note was Price. One soldier in Corinth remarked upon his arrival, "I believe him to be the greatest man of the day." The Shiloh veterans were not so impressed with the newly arrived Van Dorn. "He looked to me more like a dandy than the general of an army," one soldier wrote. Dandies or not, within a few weeks, more than 15,000 troops from the trans-Mississippi reached Corinth, and they expected to fight: "It is supposition that thare will be the largest battle that they ever has been," one trans-Mississippian wrote to his mother.[40]

While Van Dorn was making his way to Corinth and then setting up camp south of the town, units that were already there worked constantly on the system of earthworks and the abatis that lay in front of them. Work on the entrenchments had been restarted with a furious pitch after Shiloh. The fortifications began south of the Memphis and Charleston Railroad east of Corinth and continued around the town to the east and north before reaching the railroad again northwest of Corinth. These fortifications, some seven miles of them, in most cases lay along prominent ridgelines fronted by marshy, meandering creeks. Bragg's chief engineer, Captain Samuel Lockett, had originally laid out the fortifications, although Beauregard later corrected some of them on the north side of town. Five crescent-shaped works manned with siege guns guarded the roads from Pittsburg Landing and other river landings, which the Union army would obviously travel. This series of fortifications, which gained the sobriquet the "Beauregard line," was only two miles north of town and one mile from the center of town on the east. Confederate officials saw no need to construct works south and west of Corinth; few of the enemy would come from that direction, plus the Tuscumbia River ran in a crescent shape around the southern and western approaches to town. The combination of the river and the Beauregard line thus effectively shielded Corinth from any rapid advance by the enemy.[41]

Despite being their namesake, Beauregard was never completely satisfied with the earthworks' construction and kept his men busy strengthening them. Other generals were not that impressed either. When Price toured the fortifications, he thought little of them. His only remark, made "with a contemptuous smile," was, "Well, these things may be very fine; I never saw anything of the kind but once, and then I took them."[42]

Beauregard also knew that earthworks without soldiers were useless. By the end of April, the Confederate general had more than 70,000 men on his rolls, but lingering sickness kept some 18,000 of them in the hospital. There were others in the area, but he had no arms for them, prompting one of his generals, James Chalmers, to harshly assert that he had "no use for unarmed men at Corinth, and no arms to be put into our hands." Still, Beauregard did the best he could and shuffled his troops to cover all his fronts. "We are travling and moving ever two or three days wright around Corinth," a confounded soldier wrote to his wife. But there was method to the madness, and by May 1, Beauregard and company had gathered all available troops at the "great rallying point." Only time would tell if their efforts would be sufficient.[43]

2

"I LEAVE HERE TO-MORROW MORNING"

For the two Union armies at Shiloh, the days following the battle were filled with nauseous sights and smells and terrible camping facilities. The land that division commander William T. Sherman had described, only one month before, as "admirable camping ground for a hundred thousand men" had become incapable of sustaining an army half that size. The smell of dead and rotting human and horse flesh sickened the soldiers. Even worse, heavy downpours opened the shallow graves hastily dug after the battle. One soldier wrote to his wife, "It has rained and rained and rained until there was not one dry spot on which to set the sole of our foot in our tents or outside." These repulsive circumstances preyed on the troops both physically and emotionally. One surgeon told his wife, "I think the men will not suffer from it so much when all get away from the battlefield."[1]

The rain that opened the shallow graves had an even more devastating effect on the armies' infrastructure. The Tennessee River remained open, and vast amounts of supplies accumulated at Pittsburg Landing, but the rain made the roads almost useless. Units that camped several miles inland had to carry their provisions over seemingly bottomless paths of mud. One officer reported that road conditions had become "difficult even for horses."[2]

The Army of the Ohio had it even worse than the Army of the Tennessee. In the rush to get every available man to the battlefield on April 6, they had left their trains and baggage at Savannah. In the days after the battle, the men of Buell's army thus had to deal with the terrible conditions without much of their equipment, including cooking utensils and tents. One officer summarized that period as "two weeks . . . with every variety of discomfort that absence of its baggage and transportation in the most inclement weather could produce." Many reported diarrhea and other maladies, one blaming "the 'Stench' while encamped on the battle ground. It was horrible." There was also a lack of pure water. Buell reported "dysentery of a threatening type" rampant within the ranks of his army.[3]

Into this chaos came Henry Halleck to take personal command. He arrived on April 11 amid salutes but quickly went to work. In addition to the weather and sickness, Halleck faced political problems. The War Department had received word of Grant's alleged drunkenness during the battle at Shiloh. Many Northern governors also expressed great displeasure at the casualties their respective states had suffered. Halleck thus began the difficult process of smoothing these turbid waters even while he planned a campaign against the enemy at Corinth.[4]

Halleck immediately put his administrative strengths to work. He moved troops away from the horrible battlefield to locations where there was less mud and standing water. Buell's entire army moved to the bluffs overlooking Lick Creek, south of the battlefield. Along with the arrival of their baggage, the move "wrought a favorable change in the health of the army," one soldier reported. Halleck even went so far as to "camp out with them," setting up his headquarters near the landing. He also began disparaging his favorite target: Ulysses S. Grant. Halleck, who deemed the Illinoisan a sloppy administrator, even lambasted Grant for not requiring his command to properly fold their letters. As historian Steven Woodworth has surmised, "Halleck never understood Grant. How could this upstart from a Galena leather-goods store ever expect to win a war if he allowed his subordinates to fold letters improperly?"[5]

Halleck soon made several major changes in his jurisdiction. On April 15, he ordered the Army of the Mississippi to join the other two armies near Pittsburg Landing. This force, commanded by Major General John Pope, had recently captured Island Number 10 on the Mississippi River, in combination with the navy. In addition, these joint forces had opened the Mississippi River all the way to Fort Pillow, just above Memphis, as well as bagging the 7,000 Confederate troops defending the area.[6]

Pope, eager to continue his string of victories and the glory they amassed, wanted to march directly for Memphis. Halleck overruled him in favor of Corinth. At least one soldier agreed with Pope, writing that if Memphis fell, Corinth would prove "easy prey." Pope nevertheless obeyed. He moved his troops up the Mississippi River and into the Ohio at Cairo, which one soldier described as "almost submerged, the people being obliged to navigate the streets." Another reported that the water "threatened to wholly submerge the place." During the brief stop, the soldiers were allowed to disembark from the crammed transports and go into town. One soldier reported that "in 15 minutes not a particle of anything like bread, cake or cheese could be found in the town. It was literally cleaned out of everything eatable." Once they were under way again, the army's transports entered the Tennessee River, which one soldier described as "a lovely stream, and had it been at any other time than in a cold rain storm I should have enjoyed the trip exceedingly." Still, "the foliage on its banks is very thick and of a rich green and numerous high bluffs of solid rock, gray and moss-grown, frowned down upon us from either shore." On April 22, Pope's army disembarked at Hamburg Landing, four miles south of Pittsburg, and made its way inland to its assigned camps. Although a Confederate in Corinth noted in his diary that Halleck's numbers were "variously estimated at from one to 150,000," the addition of Pope's army and other units from Northern recruiting stations actually gave Halleck a little over 100,000 men for his forthcoming Corinth campaign.[7]

Such a huge gathering of soldiers was unprecedented and took time to organize, causing one Federal to remark, "[we] were a long time in getting the army in shape." To ensure control of this vast multitude, Halleck divided the armies into three wings, or "corps de armee," as many soldiers described it. On the left, in the vicinity of Hamburg, was the Army of the Mississippi under Pope. Buell's Army of the Ohio made up the center around Lick Creek. Grant's Army of the Tennessee on the old Shiloh battlefield became the right wing. So many troops meant the presence of many generals, and as one soldier wrote home, "It is nothing to see a general now."[8]

With all his men now concentrated, Halleck implemented a series of reorganizations that affected all three Union armies. The Armies of the Ohio and Mississippi underwent minor changes, but Halleck overhauled the Army of the Tennessee. Grant's original army had contained six divisions, but Halleck removed two of them to form a reserve. He also added one division from the Army of the Ohio, under Major General George Thomas. Command of the Army of the Tennessee then went to Thomas, and Halleck made Grant second in command of the entire force, "according to some French notion," as William T. Sherman recalled. Major General John A. McClernand commanded the reserve corps.[9]

This reorganization demonstrated Halleck's biases, which the general himself later explained: "It requires a *professional* man to conduct a law suit where a few thousand dollars are involved; but mere *politicians* can conduct armies where thousands of human lives, millions of money and the safety of the Govt itself are involved! I am tired and sick of military charlatans." After the reorganization, West Point graduates Thomas, Buell, and Pope commanded all three of the major armies. Furthermore, this maneuvering showed Halleck's lack of esteem for civilian officers such as McClernand and Lew

Wallace. Both these officers outranked Thomas and would have been entitled to command an army had they not been placed in the reserve corps. Wallace knew what the reorgainzation meant, informing his wife in early May that he and McClernand were considered "interlopers" and that "nobody but West Pointers have high commands in the front, and some of them are Brigadiers." Wallace termed the professional officers a "closed corporation" and realized that he and others were "undergoing the process of shelving."[10]

The reaction to Halleck's reorganization was varied. For those who had retained their commands, there was no problem. Those who were promoted, such as Thomas, could not have been more pleasantly surprised. But those who lost part or all of their commands were much less thrilled. Buell lost two of his divisions—one to the Army of the Tennessee and one to the reserve under McClernand—and he was not happy. Moreover, until recently, Thomas had served under Buell, but he now commanded an equal army. This problem ebbed somewhat with the subsequent return of Buell's division from McClernand's reserve corps.[11]

Those who had been "kicked upstairs" likewise showed their displeasure, but McClernand and Grant faced completely different circumstances. Both had influential supporters in Washington. President Lincoln backed McClernand, and Grant had a powerful congressional ally in Illinois representative Elihu Washburne. With removal thus out of the question, both men received promotions to seemingly less important appointments. The vain McClernand, who commanded the reserve, was particularly dismayed at receiving a position where he could achieve little glory.[12]

Grant emerged from the shake-up as the biggest loser. Because of his previous irritation, Halleck decided to put Grant in a position where he could effectively teach him proper military procedure. Halleck's April 30 order to Grant stated that it was "necessary that your headquarters should be near mine." To Grant, this proved almost more than he could bear. Although he retained his staff and escort, Grant had little to do. Sherman noted that Grant had ample free time and "frequently visited me." Grant became depressed and eventually determined to leave the army. It took his friend Sherman to talk him out of it. Grant stayed, but he remained unhappy.[13]

Meanwhile, Halleck continued to prepare for the campaign against Corinth. On April 27, he wired Washington that "as soon as the roads can be made passable we shall move." On April 29, he issued the necessary orders, and the troops marched out of their camps toward Corinth in what several Union soldiers described as a variation of the "First Epistle to the Corinthians." Halleck was sure that success awaited him. With fifteen divisions totaling more than 100,000 men broken into three wings and a reserve, he had no doubt that the major Confederate railroads at Corinth would soon be captured.[14]

Accompanied by War Department Assistant Secretary Thomas A. Scott, Halleck was in good spirits as his huge army lurched into motion in late April and early May. Soon, he moved his own headquarters toward Corinth, demonstrating that he aimed to make quick work of the enemy. On May 3, he was so bold as to inform Washington, "I leave here [Pittsburg Landing] to-morrow morning, and our army will be before Corinth to-morrow night." One of his soldiers wrote home that Halleck "says . . . we will be home to plow corn." Halleck obviously intended to make the twenty-five-mile march in only one or two days, and his soldiers were just as confident. "We have a mighty army here and they know it," wrote one Union soldier.[15]

Such confidence did not take into account the weather and Confederate resistance; the latter was rumored to number as many as 200,000. Bad water was also a major issue for both sides, and the closer to Corinth Halleck's army moved, the worse it became. But the terrain was the most troublesome issue. When the weather was mild, a Michigan soldier wrote home, "It is a most lovely country—far too lovely to be desecrated by such a scene of fratricidal slaughter as recently occurred here." In rainy or inclement weather, however, the terrain became nonnegotiable. "It is a very rough and uneven country hear," one soldier wrote to his sister, "more so than any part of Ohio." Halleck agreed with this soldier's assessment, writing to Secretary of War Stanton on April 29: "The heavy rains have caused another flood. Last night several of our bridges were carried away and roads rendered impassable." Three days later when he wrote again, he described how "the backwater of the Tennessee River from the flood has destroyed many of our bridges and overflowed the low lands and the creeks in our front." Apparently, Halleck was counting on better weather once his move began in earnest.[16]

The distance from Pittsburg Landing to Corinth was only twenty-two miles, but several major waterways swelled by the rain caused severe problems for the Federal armies advancing on the Confederate citadel. One Union cavalryman summarized the terrain well when he wrote, "Monstrous hilly country, this, and save a very few clearings, all heavily timbered." There were, to be sure, more easily traversed routes, such as the one the Confederates had used in April to make the trek to and from Shiloh in two days, but with more than 100,000 men, Halleck could not funnel all his divisions onto a single route. Some troops had to move over the poorer roads. The least obstructed route was on the Union right, where the Army of the Tennessee would basically follow the path of the Confederate advance and retreat to and from Shiloh. On what was known as the Ridge Road, Union forces could move in between Owl and Lick Creeks and face only smaller feeder branches of these major streams. In the center, where Buell's Army of the Ohio would move, the major impediment was Lick Creek. Buell already had his men working on bridging that stream and corduroying the roadways in the creek bottom. On the far left, where Pope's Army of the Mississippi was located, Lick Creek was not a factor. Still, the army would have to negotiate a route parallel to another major waterway, Chambers Creek, on its left flank. Many feeder branches stood in the way. Heavy duty thus fell on the engineers, one of whom jealously wrote, "But a slight conception of the amount of work performed can be entertained."[17]

Closer to Corinth, the armies would encounter other creeks. Chambers Creek took a huge turn to the northwest nearer to town, and both Pope and Buell would have to cross it, with Thomas marching through the headwaters region nearer Monterey. Then there was Seven Mile Creek, a major tributary of Chambers Creek that flowed southeastward, parallel to Chambers, a mile or so closer to Corinth. Finally, two creeks nearer to Corinth afforded the Confederates additional defensive locations. Phillips Creek flowed southward along the eastern section of Corinth's earthworks. Bridge Creek, into which Phillips Creek ran, was parallel to Phillips and about half a mile to the east. All three armies would have to negotiate these two creeks to get at Corinth's eastern and northeastern defenses.[18]

Halleck's bold plan also did not take into account the general's personality or his view of war. He was an old-school army officer, an 1839 graduate of West Point. He had written numerous works on military theory, including the influential *Elements of Military Art and Science* (1846); he had also translated Jomini's famous French work. Halleck's intellectual accomplishments eventually gained him the sobriquet "Old Brains." His writings reflected the belief that it was the commander's duty to mass overwhelming force at fractions of the enemy and thus capture strategic places, such as Corinth. Such operations normally utilized earthworks, like those Halleck had observed himself in France. Grant's surprise at Shiloh just a month earlier also influenced Halleck's thinking. As a result, a formula for a deliberate campaign emerged, with security being the commanding general's chief concern. Halleck thus drilled alertness into his officers and men. One soldier remarked, "We are in so imminent a danger of attack that it is impossible for even field officers to get a pass out of hearing of their commands." Another remembered thinking that Halleck obviously believed there was "a Beauregard or two lurking behind every bush." Another put it more succinctly in a letter to his wife: "we will not be

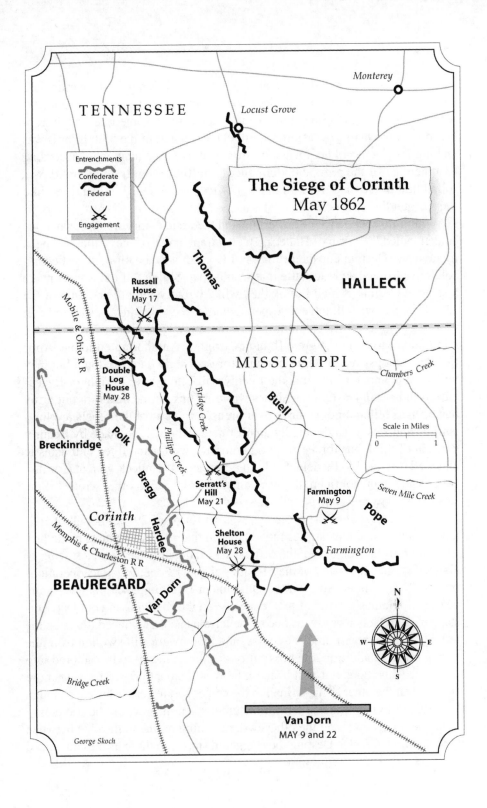

The Siege of Corinth
May 1862

TENNESSEE

Monterey

Locust Grove

Entrenchments
Confederate
Federal
Engagement

HALLECK

Russell
House
May 17

Mobile & Ohio R R

Thomas

MISSISSIPPI

Chambers Creek

Double
Log
House
May 28

Breckinridge

Polk

Bridge Creek

Buell

Scale in Miles
0   1

Bragg

Phillips Creek

Serratt's
Hill
May 21

Farmington
May 9

Seven Mile Creek

Corinth

Hardee

Pope

Memphis & Charleston R R

Shelton
House
May 28

Farmington

BEAUREGARD

Van Dorn

N
W   E
S

Bridge Creek

Van Dorn
MAY 9 and 22

George Skoch

caught with our britches down again." Federal soldiers reported wearing their equipment even at night, and Halleck had his officers wake up the men at 3:00 A.M. and have them in line at daybreak. Such caution sometimes led to trouble, however. On one occasion, Colonel David Stuart of the 55th Illinois was waking his sleepy soldiers when he stumbled over one man, who, according to a member of the regiment, "clinched him [the colonel], took him down, rolled him in the mud, hit him once or twice, and escaped unidentified into the surrounding darkness."[19]

With little knowledge of the terrain and theoretical impediments, what one soldier called the "firm of Halleck, Buell, Grant, and Co." nevertheless began to advance. Despite constant rumors of Corinth's evacuation, most Federal soldiers expected a great battle that would rival Shiloh. "If the Rebels make a stand at Corinth, which I think they will," wrote William Parkinson of the 11th Illinois, "we will have a desperate battle, & we are just as sure to be in it, as it comes off." He calculated his chances as "about one chance in five hundred not to be in the great fight at Corinth." Another noted in late April that "our troops are constantly moving forward and I have no doubt but they will soon be in a position that the Enemy will Either have to fight or Evacuate Corinth." Soldier Frank L. Jones wrote, "Thus far the health of our army has been excellent and we have every reason to believe the rebels are low-spirited and sickly. Undoubtedly an obstinate stand will be made by Beauregard, but I think our forces are too numerous, well disciplined enthusiastic and well disposed to be defeated by the Secesh." If Halleck won at Corinth, Jones said, "I am confident the war can not *last* long." Another wrote, "If the rebels lose they are gone up the Mississippi Valley."[20]

The official start of the campaign was set for April 29, but not all of Halleck's units or even his armies moved out on that day. A few units made preliminary moves even before the official start date, however. The left wing of Halleck's force, the Army of the Mississippi under Pope, began its operations on April 27, with the Army of the Ohio under Buell in the center advancing next, and Thomas's Army of the Tennessee on the right moving out last. This staggering of launch days was due to the terrain each army faced. Pope on the left had several major creeks to cross, and many were still swollen from the spring rains; in addition, the possibility of more rain had to be factored into the plan. Thus, Pope left first because he would have to move forward more slowly than the other armies. Buell in the center had fewer obstacles, although he still had to negotiate several large creeks. Thomas would be traversing much better ground than the other two, marching on the high ridge between Owl and Lick Creeks. Despite the staggered starts, all these armies advanced across a front of several miles, and all met some resistance and engaged in skirmishing with the enemy.[21]

The men themselves were impressed by the large number of troops and marveled that folks at home heard some news before they did. One Iowa soldier wrote home, "You know more that is going on in our army than we know." A Michigan soldier similarly wrote, "What would you think of there being a fight on our extreme right, 12 or 15 miles from here and we, hearing of it for the first time through the Chicago papers? Such a case has happened."[22]

In the advance toward Corinth, John Pope's Army of the Mississippi faced the most obstacles, and not all of them were terrain related. Having just arrived at Hamburg Landing a few days earlier, the army had rested and gathered wagons and supplies for its march. Pope had three divisions of infantry under Brigadier Generals Eleazer A. Paine, David S. Stanley, and Schuyler Hamilton (Halleck's brother-in-law) and one division of cavalry under Brigadier General Gordon Granger. Later in May, the army would be augmented by another division under the command of Brigadier General Jefferson C. Davis.[23]

Pope's initial moves began on April 27. With Paine and Stanley in front and Hamilton in reserve, the army moved forward about four miles toward Farmington in preparation to cross one of the major obstacles in its way, Chambers Creek. Pope later remembered that he and his army "saunter[ed] along slowly." The army camped around the Mt. Olivet Church area, which one soldier described as "a beautiful grove close by a primitive church." Because Buell's army to Pope's right had not yet advanced, on April 29, Stanley sent a large reconnaissance patrol—one brigade of infantry and two regiments of cavalry—westward from their camps to Monterey. They met a Confederate brigade commanded by Patton Anderson on the south side of the village, and there was some lively skirmishing with Anderson's Louisianans, including a company of the Washington Artillery. Nevertheless, the Federals returned to camp satisfied there was no major offensive threat at Monterey.[24]

Paine's division crossed Chambers Creek on April 30 and moved into what one artilleryman called "that hot bed of Rebeldom, Mississippi," but they returned to the division encampment the next day. Building roads took up the next few days, and one soldier described the "sapper and miner regiment" constructing them out of fences, bridges, and other items. Rough campsites also had to be cleared, the same soldier noting that "the place whare our regt camped was in a thicket whare a rabit could scarcly get through."[25]

On May 3, Paine again crossed Chambers Creek, while Stanley took up a position behind it near the Springer family's residence; Hamilton was still in reserve. One artilleryman described the creek as being "about 20 feet wide and 3 1/2 to 4 feet deep." He also noted that the undergrowth was so thick in the bottom that "our skirmishers were obliged to return to the road." Confederates under Brigadier General John S. Marmaduke did not contest the Chambers Creek crossing, but they did show some resistance when the army reached the next major obstacle, Seven Mile Creek. Pope labeled this a "bad creek," and it would indeed cause problems. Paine reported the enemy's presence at the crossing and sent a heavy force of skirmishers to drive them away. A sharp engagement occurred, during which the Federals captured some equipment and one Confederate captain who, "after he had thrown down his sword, offered to give . . . a fist fight." There was also some "very heavy cannonading." The retreating Confederates delayed long enough to burn the bridge over the creek, with Paine reporting, "We found the bridge destroyed and the road much obstructed by fallen timber." Union skirmishers went forward to secure the bridge site, and according to a member of the 10th Illinois, just as they were "climing and crouding through a lot of fallen trees . . . a volley of musketry was fiared at us but the brush being so thick that . . . prevented thare shooting from doing us any harm." The skirmishers moved on and, in Paine's words, "took up a strong position on the hill at the outlet of the swamp." Pope similarly reported that he had gained the "heights immediately north of the village," with an Illinoisan noting that they had formed a line at a large field "from which we could see Farmington." With the area secured, workers supervised by Paine himself soon cleared the road and rebuilt the bridge over Seven Mile Creek, which allowed the rest of the division to move forward. Again, the Confederates offered resistance as Paine slowly advanced, and more heavy skirmishing erupted around Farmington, some involving artillery. By the end of the day, elements of Paine's division, with Assistant Secretary of War Scott in tow, had made it all the way to Farmington, but Pope recalled them. He was worried that he had outstripped the other armies moving on his right. Paine withdrew to the high ground across (north of) Seven Mile Creek but made sure to keep two regiments in the swamp to guard the newly constructed bridge. One soldier noted that they were "left on picket in the slew by the bridge." Pope obviously did not want a repeat of that day's delay on May 4, when, as he wired Halleck, he would continue the advance.[26]

Pope did not advance his army again on May 4; only Stanley's division moved to Seven Mile Creek. Only the cavalry to the south made scouting rides toward the railroad, and one of Pope's soldiers was not impressed with the country. "We are now in the great state of Miss., about 6 miles from Corinth, near the line," he said. "The country through here looks very poor. About two thirds of it is woods. A few wheat fields, which is all headed out, and a few fields of cotton can be seen and also a few houses that are vacated. The water through here is very poor." Another had a similar view: "it is a broken worthless looking part of creation nothing to be seen but high hills and deep glens."[27]

Then it began to rain. Heavy downpours caused severe problems over the next few days, and Pope's divisions reported spending long hours in camp between May 4 and 7. Stanley wrote that "we had cold rains, lasting several days," and a lower-level soldier predicted, "it will stop our operations for several days." It did. "We attempted another advance," one soldier wrote, "but found the swamp entirely impassable." At least one whole company stationed on high ground in the swamp of Chambers Creek was isolated by the flooding and stranded for hours on an island. An Illinois soldier had a more comical take on the issue, recording in his diary that as he watched a cavalry unit trying to cross a creek, "many are tumbled off, and are ducked." A chagrined Halleck, having counted on good weather, wrote to Washington in understatement: "The heavy rains of the 4th and 5th have destroyed some of our bridges and greatly injured the roads. . . . This country is almost a wilderness and very difficult to operate in." One of his soldiers was just as chagrined: "We had every thing packed up and some of the troops commenced moving, but they had to be called back." Any Confederate who had taken part in the march to Shiloh just one month previously could have told Halleck of the difficulty he would face. His original timetable of reaching Corinth by the night of May 5 was completely unattainable.[28]

When the rains diminished on May 7, Pope went back on the offensive, ordering another reconnaissance toward Corinth the next day. This time, both Stanley and Paine were involved. Surprisingly, the bridge over Seven Mile Creek was still intact, and Paine recrossed it, taking a right-hand road between the creek and Farmington. Stanley followed and took the left fork through Farmington itself, while engineers strung a line of telegraph wire behind the advance. Both divisions skirmished with Wirt Adams's Mississippi cavalry, continually driving them back toward the main Confederate line of entrenchments. One Federal soldier from Illinois caught up in the pageantry of the advance wrote in his diary, "I thought it the pritiest sight I ever saw to see the two brigades and cavalry and artilry marching over that high open ground." He added that the men fixed their bayonets and, after a speech by General James D. Morgan, advanced "throu the woods and thick under brush over fences and through swamps and everything else that came in our way." Paine and Stanley, with Hamilton in reserve, went so far as to cross Bridge Creek, which was the easternmost creek fronting the Beauregard line of Confederate works. One colonel claimed to have reached within eighty rods of the Confederate earthworks. A newspaper correspondent noted that the Federals also "took a peep at the Memphis and Charleston Railroad." Paine and Stanley were surprised to get so close to Corinth with such little resistance, encountering only heavy skirmishing as they crossed Bridge Creek on an old bridge. Stanley noted that his men followed retreating skirmishers until they were "immediately under the guns of the enemy's battery in their principal intrenchment." A common soldier reported that Federal sharpshooters "went up near enough to shoot some of their gunners in their fort." Yet it was all for nothing. Paine reported, "a general engagement not being desired, orders were issued for the whole command to recross the creek." Surprisingly, Buell's left rested some three miles behind Pope's right. "There is entirely too much interval between us," Pope lectured Halleck. Stanley and Paine thus withdrew to camp, recrossing Seven Mile Creek. But Pope had knocked on Corinth's door.[29]

P ope's Army of the Mississippi had the toughest ground to traverse, thus leading to its early advance. Buell left his campsites next. Although he had to deal with the defiles of Chambers and Seven Mile Creeks, he was much better off than Pope, in that he could cross the streams farther up their courses, nearer the headwaters where they were much smaller. Since Buell was camped north of Lick Creek, however, he had to cross that major waterway first. The rains of early May only caused more problems. Encountering the numerous graves of Confederate dead did not help health or morale. One soldier wrote to his wife, "There must have been a great many of the wounded Rebels died on their retreat from the battle, as the road is strewn with Graves. I counted 120 new made graves on the sides of the road today, and one man was buried in the wagon track, and one of our wagon wheels went right through him — Such is war."[30]

Shiloh veterans all, Major Generals Alexander M. McCook, Thomas L. Crittenden, and William "Bull" Nelson and Brigadier General Thomas J. Wood commanded Buell's divisions, with a cavalry force under Colonel James S. Jackson. In the days prior to the campaign, Buell had his divisions working on the roads toward Corinth, especially around the two major fords he would use to get his men across Lick Creek. Buell planned to use the main road to Monterey, which crossed Lick Creek at Atkins Ford, and another more easterly path that crossed the creek at Greer's Ford. The two roads met each other south of Monterey, near the headwaters of Chambers Creek. To make the crossing of Lick Creek as easy as possible, Buell had his men bridge both ford sites, as well as corduroy the swampy bottoms through which the roads ran. "Woe to the man or beast that was unfortunate enough to step or fall off of the roads; that was the last of them, they sunk out of sight in a very short time in the quicksands," one soldier related. "Some of the mules that fell off of the corduroys were never found." Another told of a similar fate, as "horses become mired and sink down out of sight and are left to perish."[31]

Unfortunately, the terrain and the weather played havoc with Buell's preparations and his march. He did not seem to be impressed with the country to begin with, commenting, "All the roads are narrow, unimproved, dirt roads. Several small creeks, bordered by miry bottom-land, flow from the west and cross the direct road from Monterey. . . . The country is thickly wooded and has a dense undergrowth." One Federal went so far as to label the area the "forest primeval." One of Buell's soldiers echoed his thoughts: "The dense growth of vines and underbrush with the rains and stagnant pools of water was productive of miasmatic troubles. Fevers of all kinds as well as other diseases caused much sickness and many deaths." Many soldiers had to be sent from the front lines, one Indianan pointing out that "it is one continual convalescent camp from here to Pittsburg Landing." Those that could be evacuated went northward to various hospitals in the bigger river cities. A surgeon insisted, however, that he doubted the "proportion of deaths to the number of cases is much greater than in civil life," and according to at least one soldier, anyone could get a medical discharge from the surgeons for "5 to 25 dollars." Buell nevertheless finished his roadwork and started his move toward Corinth on May 2, when his cavalry and Nelson's division crossed Lick Creek at Greer's Ford and marched to Mt. Olivet Church, which Pope had already passed. The next day, Crittenden's and Wood's divisions likewise crossed at Greer's Ford, while McCook's men crossed at Atkins Ford.[32]

Then the rains began to pour again on May 4 and 5, halting Buell just as they had Pope. One poor soldier recorded in his diary, "This morning we got up pretty early for the water came in the tent like a river and run right over our blankets." The various divisions had made enough progress to encounter the enemy at the headwaters of Chambers Creek, where a little skirmishing took place, but the weather, not the enemy, stopped the advance. Buell reported, "Work was at once commenced on the roads in front, but heavy rains . . . prevented the advance of the troops and destroyed much of the work that had been done both in front and in rear." When the rains stopped, Buell put his men to work again and was soon advancing toward Chambers Creek with Wood on the right, McCook in the center, Nelson on the left, and Crittenden and the cavalry in reserve. Slight skirmishing took place, and future president James A. Garfield's brigade of Wood's division fought a small skirmish on May 6.[33]

The men soon had the Chambers Creek crossings in good condition, and Buell ordered an advance on May 8. Nelson crossed Chambers Creek in sup-

port of Pope's advance on Farmington, making his way to Nichol's Ford on
Seven Mile Creek amid slight skirmishing. McCook's men also encountered
only light resistance. But the situation still perturbed Buell, who reported to
Halleck that "Pope is reconnoitering with his whole force, 20,000 men." When
Pope withdrew that afternoon, Nelson returned to the east side of Chambers
Creek. Buell presumably breathed a sigh of relief.[34]

George Thomas's Army of the Tennessee, composed of divisions commanded
by Major General William T. Sherman and Brigadier Generals Thomas W.
Sherman, Stephen A. Hurlbut, Thomas J. McKean, and Thomas A. Davies, left
its encampments on the Shiloh battlefield later than the other armies. They had
many fewer terrain impediments and thus could outmarch the other armies.
The fact that two division commanders were named Sherman was a bit of a
problem, but the army managed to keep it straight. One soldier remembered
calling one of them "Port Royal Sherman," because of his prior service there,
and the more famous one "Steady-old-nerves," a dig at William T. Sherman's
notoriously nervous makeup. Some moves took place in April, when one soldier of the 7th Illinois noted, "This morning the whole army is in motion,
except the part sticking in the mud." "In a hurry we marched 4 miles," read
another soldier's diary on May 2. One surgeon wrote home on May 1, "We
struck our tents at Camp Shiloh day before yesterday and moved forward about
five miles." All of Thomas's divisions were on the move by May 4.[35]

    Thomas placed three of his divisions in the front line—William Sherman's
on the right, Hurlbut's in the center, and Thomas Sherman's on the left at Monterey. Davies and McKean were held in reserve. In this deployment, Thomas
moved forward through Monterey to the State Line Road, one soldier recording, "Our situation is now good—on the high hills that are about what is called
Pea Ridge." Thomas had fewer terrain problems due to the lack of major creeks
in his sector, but ironically, the lack of waterways led to a new problem. Halleck's far left flank, the left of Pope's army, was covered by Chambers Creek
and then Seven Mile Creek until he reached Farmington. Thus he had no worries about a flank attack from the south or east. Halleck did have to worry about
his far right flank, however, and that was probably why he placed his most
experienced division commander, William Sherman, on that flank. There was
no major waterway on which to anchor that flank; an additional concern was
that it rested not far from the Mobile and Ohio Railroad, meaning the Confederates could quickly concentrate troops there via the railroad. As a result, Sherman was given the task of holding the open flank. Thomas took special care to
see that Sherman's flank was re-fused and entrenched anytime it stopped. The

concern is evident in his words: "Major General Sherman's right flank being much exposed, [it] was intrenched immediately." McClernand's reserve corps watched the open right flank of the army as well, although he complained that, given the large space and the small numbers of his command, the task "is very great, indeed exhausting, if not oppressive." Despite its rearward position, the reserve did incur some casualties during skirmishing.[36]

Nothing came of Thomas's fears as the army held its position throughout the rainy days of May 4, 5, and 6. That time was hard on the rank-and-file soldier, however. The drinking water was awful, and one man complained that "it is full of tadpoles and wiggletales." The rain made it worse. One soldier of the 15th Illinois recorded in his diary that the men fashioned "booths to sleep in." Another noted years later that "this rain storm was memorable as being the hardest we encountered in our service." An Illinois soldier added detail: "We started early in the morning and it commenced raining soon after we started. We was all day coming. Sometimes stopping for one hour in mud knee deep. No place to rest. I can describe it in no better way than just [to] say it was *awful*." Even worse, the wagon train had been left far behind, and the men had no tents, cooking utensils, or equipment. "We just had to stand or sit in the rain," the soldier continued, until the wagons arrived late that night and "we hoisted our tents in the mud and water." "I know we will be put on short rations," he predicted. Once the rains stopped, however, Thomas moved his army forward like the others, making his way to Locust Grove. A portion of the line was again entrenched, particularly Sherman's re-fused right. There Thomas remained for several days while the action picked up on the other flank, which, ironically, was deemed more secure.[37]

By May 8, all of Halleck's armies were making solid and steady progress toward Corinth. Pope was already three-quarters of the way there, and the others were well over two-thirds of the way. And this was done despite all the weather concerns and the need to construct roadways. The armies had to continually repair roads as well as construct new linear ones to maintain good communication between the wings. Obviously, Halleck's original timetable had not been kept, but the armies were moving at good speed, considering the weather and the terrain.[38]

In fact, they may have been moving too easily. The lack of Confederate resistance calmed any nervousness that may have been present at the outset. The frequency and ease with which Pope, for example, was able to throw his units across Seven Mile Creek had lulled him, and perhaps others, into a false sense of security. But Pope was asking for trouble.

3

"THE BALL HAS COMMENCED"

As the huge Federal juggernaut continually lurched closer, Confederate commander P. G. T. Beauregard was not content to wait for the Federals to attack him. From his telegraph-equipped headquarters in Corinth, he made energetic preparations to defend the town, especially when activity began to pick up in late April. The Creole sent numerous scouts to his front, including brigade-sized units at major crossroads such as Farmington and Monterey. He thus knew when the Federals began their major move. As a result, he called his troops to the Corinth earthworks in late April, not knowing how soon Halleck might approach and give battle. He also urged forward the remainder of Van Dorn's men, but all these troops would not arrive until early May. One Louisianan, in fact, perfectly described the concern when he wrote in the early days of May that the "men were kept in a state of feverish excitement and anxious expectation."[1]

As would be expected of him, Beauregard's orders were a masterful set of minutiae that explained exactly how the Confederate army was to defend Corinth. Beauregard scattered the major corps of his army along the trenches fronting the eastern and northern parts of town. Within those lines, Leonidas Polk's command held the northern works along the Mobile and Ohio Railroad and Purdy road. To his right was Bragg's corps, which held the eastern trenches along the Pittsburg Landing and upper Farmington roads. William J. Hardee's men were placed on Bragg's right, holding the lower Farmington road and the Memphis and Charleston Railroad. John C. Breckinridge's small reserve corps was positioned on the extreme right flank to secure Hardee's right or to defend the extended area beyond the earthworks. It was also considered a "reserve to the right flank."[2]

In addition to Breckinridge, the Confederate commander wanted ample reserves for his line, and for that purpose he designated Van Dorn's command of three divisions. One division he centrally located, while the other two he placed behind the two wings of the army, north and east, respectively. In addition, Beauregard stipulated that one of the four brigades of each division of the other corps would be considered a division reserve to stand some 400 yards to the rear of the line of entrenchments. Cavalry was kept out front, and the artillery manned fortifications guarding major roads in and out of Corinth.[3]

The men themselves camped several hundred yards behind the lines and alternated their time in the trenches—by mid-May, a fourth of every brigade at a time. Regiments were to camp several hundred yards behind their place in line and were told to open good roads from their camps to the trenches to allow easy movement on foot and for the artillery. Obviously, battle was expected any day, and Beauregard was prepared.[4]

Despite the preparation, life in the Confederate camps was not very good, and morale plummeted, especially with the recent news of New Orleans' fall in late April and Norfolk's capture in early May. The recent action by the Confederate Congress to conscript soldiers also drove down morale, especially among men in twelve-month units, who were now required to serve two more years. "This law," one Confederate wrote in his diary, "caused a good deal of dissatisfaction among the troops and caused some desertions after the 12 month men times expired." Many of the units that mustered in at the beginning of the war were reorganized in April and May at Corinth, when their twelve months were up. "Many of the officers resigned and went home," remembered L. H. Graves, prompting the 20th Tennessee to elect a colonel who was twenty-two years old and a lieutenant colonel who was nineteen. Another soldier wrote that "some of the boys say they would enlist again but they don't like to be bossed." A Kentucky captain was livid that he was required to serve two more years and refused to be reelected by his company. He argued that "my company . . . is composed of more than two-thirds married men who went together with one condition, we could afford to give our country one year's service and could make arrangements to have our families cared for during that time." If the army had not accepted that condition at the time, he said, "we would not go in." Making it even worse for him, Kentucky was not even a Confederate state. In the bigger picture, the resentment of being conscripted for two more years as well as the shake-up in leadership on the company and even regimental level caused significant issues with Confederate unit effectiveness at Corinth.[5]

Conversely, the election of new officers gave some individuals an opportunity for advancement. A small few were even excited about their prospects, such as those who wished to be rid of their mediocre officers. One Confederate told of an artillery battery being broken up and added to another unit because of the "inefficiency of its officers." Another Confederate wrote home excitedly about the possibility of becoming his company's second lieutenant. The man originally appointed to the post had failed his qualifying exam, and C. H. George thought he had a good chance to get the spot. He wrote to his sister, asking her to "send me my sword and sash or the sword by its self as soon as possible." He also instructed her to have a local man make him a uniform "just like the last one only if he can get the lace put it on the sleeves." Obviously, he wanted to look the part of a second lieutenant.[6]

In addition to the chaos of reorganization, measles, mumps, and typhoid were prevalent in camp, continually driving down unit effectiveness as well as morale. Historian Bell Wiley has argued that as many Confederate soldiers died at Corinth as perished at Shiloh. Unit records bear this out; some companies were down to ten or twelve men. One Confederate remembered, "There were very few whose health was not affected by the pestiential air and unwholesome water of that swamp-surrounded village." William Kavanaugh recalled, "The rainy season had set in, the drinking water was of the worst, and the food supply not much better,—sickness prevailed throughout the camp, and many many deaths occurred here. I helped bury one of my neighbor boys." Another wrote to his sister, "I like this soldiering . . . and would like it a good deal better if I could get some good water to drink; the water here is cold but awful muddy and full of lime and very injurious to most of the men." One soldier lamented the lack of water, in that "we can't get to wash on account of scarcity of water and our clothes are getting very dirty as it is very dusty here at this time." Another Confederate agreed, writing home, "This is the filthiest place I ever saw in my life." At least one soldier noted all the sickness but admitted, "Many of them pretended to be sick, but they don't near all look so and this is true notwithstanding a fight is expected."[7]

The sickness and discontent were not confined to the lower ranks. Beauregard was not well, nor were Bragg and Breckinridge. A host of lower-level officers were ill as well, including Bushrod Johnson, Henry Little, Thomas Jordan, and Joseph Hogg. The sickness was bad enough for Beauregard to order a special train to depart at 9:00 every day from the Corinth depot to haul away sick soldiers. Some higher-level officers were not happy about other actions, such as when Beauregard's classmate James H. Trapier was placed in command of one of Polk's divisions instead of the ranking brigade commander, Alexander P. Stewart. Stewart filed a mild protest, but the situation was soon resolved when the regular division commander returned from sick leave. Whether the result of sickness or unhappiness, a weakened officer corps illustrated the weakened nature of the army itself.[8]

The commissary department was also having trouble keeping the men adequately fed, forcing Beauregard to cut the men's rations on April 30. That was followed by an order from the War Department to cut the rations even more, mainly in fresh meat. Beauregard protested, saying, "In the name of my men I must respectfully but urgently protest against such a reduction of the substantial part of the ration," and he later commented that "the greatest reduction has [already] been made that the meat ration will bear." By May 5, Beauregard was concerned that there was only three days' "subsistence for this army on the day of the enemy's demonstration in the front." He called on his chief of subsistence to keep at least ten days' worth of food. Fortunately, the ration situation became better as May passed, and the individual fare was boosted back to original levels by May 19. The food remained bad, however, as exemplified in an account by a member of the Orleans Guard. He related in his diary that he helped escort what he thought was a dead and badly decomposed body in a wagon, only to learn that it was not human but actually their meat ration. Many soldiers chose, one Confederate remembered, "to buy food that they like better than their rations," although they could not always get what they wanted. One Missouri Confederate bemoaned the lack of the finer things of life: "I crave buttermilk and butter all the time but I have not seen but two glasses full since I left home."[9]

In addition to the deplorable food situation, other items were scarce by late May. The army was having trouble procuring clothing and forage. The biggest problem was the water supply, however. One correspondent reported, "With every pint of fluid one has to drink a half ounce of dirt. You feel it scrape the throat as it goes down, and after it gets to the stomach it lays as heavy and indigestible as a bed of mortar." Beauregard ordered his engineers to "take immediate measures for the boring of artesian wells within the lines occupied by this army." Later, he had the men themselves digging wells, but they often dug too far down without adequate curbing for their own safety. Still, they found little water. Later, Beauregard hauled in water on railroad cars.[10]

The reduced rations and growing sickness caused sagging morale in the army. Desertion became a bigger problem the longer the campaign went on, with thirteen men leaving the 23rd Tennessee on one night alone. Commanders ordered pickets not to let anyone out of the lines without a pass from brigade or division headquarters and to shoot anyone who tried to go through without a pass. One Confederate remembered, "A detail of one-tenth of the army was placed in our rear to shoot us down if we ran." Those coming into the lines without a pass were immediately taken to headquarters for questioning. One Federal humorously noted that with so many Confederate deserters coming into their lines, "I think in ten days afterward there will not be enough Rebels left in Corinth to oppose our regiment." Another who noted a

Confederate lieutenant coming into their lines wrote to his wife, "I think that they are nearly played out when Commissioned officers begin to desert."[11]

As the Federals advanced, Beauregard issued a circular trying to bolster the army's morale, reminding the men of their "mingled banners" that allowed them to "meet our foe in strength that should give us victory." He called on the soldiers to "decide whether we are to be free-men or the vile slaves of those who are free only in name." He labeled the enemy "presumptuous mercenaries," "invaders of our soil," "despoilers of our homes," and "disturbers of our family ties." He called on each man to make sure his children could look back with pride and say, "Our fathers were at the battle of Corinth." Individual commanders issued their own similar rallying circulars at Beauregard's urging. He asked Breckinridge, for example, "Would it not be well to issue a short address to your troops? I think it would give a good effect."[12]

To boost the army's morale even more, Beauregard implemented a series of actions to punish cowardice and reward bravery. He ordered that one regiment's flag be taken away because it had left "its position in haste, without . . . orders, on the appearance of the enemy." On another occasion, he scolded units for retreating from "an imaginary enemy" and providing a lax picket guard. He also had a unit commander relieved. Conversely, he began a system of rewards for good actions, stipulating that the names of soldiers who "distinguished themselves" should be published by headquarters and that units should inscribe the names of their battles on their regimental colors. Later, Beauregard even devised a merit badge "to do full justice to the private soldier, who is seldom accorded his meed of praise and who rarely receives full credit for his gallant deeds."[13]

Throughout, Beauregard showed a confident tone: "Can the result be doubtful?" he asked his army. He ordered that all commanders "practice their commands in taking up the positions assigned for the defense of the lines," and he told them the strategy was a "defensive-offensive" one. They were to "await the approach of the enemy near our positions, then assume the offensive with great vigor and impetuosity before he can collect and deploy his forces." He also alerted unit commanders to take their troops to the sounds of the guns and stipulated that the army's motto should be "Forward and always Forward!"[14]

As part of his defensive-offensive plans, Beauregard had units positioned all across the spectrum of the Union advance, with elements as large as brigades manning forward outposts at Farmington and Monterey. These units had skirmished with the enemy on April 29. Other scouts watched the Federal advance as well, so Beauregard knew what was happening. When Pope advanced on May 3, Beauregard implemented his defensive-offensive strategy, calling his men to the lines again with three days' rations and 100 rounds of ammunition. "We were under arms all night momentarily, expecting an attack," one Mississippian wrote to his family, "as it seems to be our luck to fight on Sunday." Beauregard reasoned that if the Federals, with their huge numbers and siege artillery, ever made it to Corinth's doorstep, the campaign would be over. By early May, the Federals were getting extremely close; Pope's foray into Farmington was just four miles away, for example. Thus, Beauregard knew he had to strike Halleck's force or, better yet, one of his isolated armies before the enemy reached Corinth.[15]

Beauregard had his army positioned for a fight, with Hardee in command of the right wing that was supposed to hurl the enemy back. One sick captain recalled, "We had orders to march to our entrenchments around Corinth which were tolerable extensive. I was not able to march and therefore rode in a wagon but we had no fight but a rain and I got back to camp near midnight worn out with fatigue and salivated by physic I had taken." When no battle developed on May 3 and the rains of May 4 and 5 stopped everything, Confederate commanders allowed their men to remain in their camps but cautioned them to be ready to move "at a moment's notice." But the rains continued, ending all chance for a fight at that time. "It commenced raining yesterday evening," one soldier wrote on May 5, "and has rained very near all night pretty wetting and is still raining some this morning." And, he added, "there is mud a plenty here."[16]

By May 6, Beauregard was rethinking his entire deployment. He reasoned that the enemy would try to turn his right flank and cut his logistical lifeline to the south. Pope's advance on Farmington confirmed his thoughts. Thus, he began extending his line with new earthworks south of the Memphis and Charleston Railroad to cover the right flank. He ordered Van Dorn's reserve divisions to take a position on Hardee's right, with the ailing Breckinridge replacing Van Dorn as the reserve and positioning brigades strategically behind the line. Now on the right, Van Dorn and Price had taken advantage of the rainy lull to review their now concentrated troops. One civilian witness remarked, "The sight was quite imposing, as column after column marched along, with their flags flying in the breeze." Unfortunately, Beauregard then found that his left under Polk was also in danger from the wide sweep of the Federal advance. Beauregard ordered Breckinridge to man the trenches west of the Mobile and Ohio Railroad on Corinth's north face. The Confederate line thus ran from left to right: Breckinridge, Polk, Bragg, Hardee, and Van Dorn, with Bragg placed in tactical command of the original Army of the Mississippi units and Van Dorn in charge of the trans-Mississippi portion. Beauregard retained command of it all. What little army reserve there was had orders to respond to calls for assistance from the various corps commanders via a system of signals: one gun or rocket at night for a crisis on the left, two guns or rockets for the center, and three guns or rockets for the right. The result was predictable. One tired Confederate wrote on May 9, "Up to this date we have been having alarm after alarm and last night we were hurried to the breast works."[17]

Even during the reorganization, Beauregard kept his mind on the defensive-offensive strategy, and he soon had an opportunity to implement it. He knew that Pope was well out ahead of the other two armies, that there was a gap between Pope's right and Buell's left, and that once Pope crossed Seven Mile Creek and approached Farmington, he would no longer have the presence of major watersheds to cover his left flank. Substantial fighting had erupted on May 8 as Pope pushed several of his units across Seven Mile Creek into Farmington and Confederate units offered resistance. Beauregard sent other Confederate brigades in support, prompting one Georgian to write home: "As we passed out a sad spectacle met our eyes. The groans and cries of the wounded borne on litters from the scene of strife, their blood smeared garments and the dejected countenances of their comrades who had accompanied them from the battlefield, all these called vividly to mind the many once happy homes and firesides desolated by this unrighteous war."[18]

Beauregard was unmoved by the sights. In fact, he planned even more bloodshed. If he could hit an isolated part of Pope's army as it crossed Seven Mile Creek, he might be able to destroy a portion of Halleck's force. The rest of Pope's units would be back across the creek, and the other armies would be too far away to support him quickly. It was certainly a chance worth taking, and Beauregard scheduled an attack for the following day, May 9.

The plan was not complicated. Two divisions of Braxton Bragg's army corps, led by Brigadier Generals Daniel Ruggles and James H. Trapier, would move eastward out of the Corinth fortifications and engage the Federals who had crossed Seven Mile Creek at Farmington. While Bragg had the enemy's attention, Earl Van Dorn's three divisions of trans-Mississippians, led by Major Generals Samuel Jones, Sterling Price, and John P. McCown, would march southeast of Corinth to a point south of Farmington. Once Bragg had John Pope's attention focused on the Confederates coming from the west, Van Dorn would slam into his left flank and destroy the units south of Seven Mile Creek. Beauregard called his commanders together and told them of the plan.[19]

Pope played right into Beauregard's hands. On the night of May 8, while returning from that day's reconnaissance all the way to Bridge Creek, David Stanley left a brigade south of Seven Mile Creek while the other brigade and the whole of Paine's division crossed to the north side. The isolated brigade south of the creek was not ready for battle, illustrating the lack of major concern on the Federals' part. Brigadier General Joseph B. Plummer normally commanded the brigade of Stanley's division, but Plummer was sick that day, so the command fell to the senior colonel, John M. Loomis of the 26th Illinois. The serenity of the area may have lulled some of the Federals: one Union soldier described the area between Seven Mile Creek and Farmington as "a park-like plateau, with copses of wood here and there, and covered with blue-grass." Loomis positioned four companies of the 8th Wisconsin at Farmington, while the remainder of the brigade, consisting of the 11th Missouri and 47th Illinois, in addition to the Badgers and Loomis's own regiment, made camp at the edge of the Seven Mile Creek bottom just east of Dick Smith's cotton gin, which sat on the road. But Loomis was not happy. "The brigade was out of rations," he reported on the night of May 8, and expected to "be relieved next morning." The lone Federal brigade must have spent a fitful night.[20]

The next morning, May 9, no relieving brigade appeared, but the Confederates did. An 8th Wisconsin soldier recorded that "they came forward in line of battle, their flags fluttering over them and their bayonets glistening in the sunshine." Elements of Ruggles's division, spearheaded by Lucius M. Walker's brigade, were making their way toward Farmington, with Trapier's men on their left. Although one Confederate in Trapier's division remembered moving "slowly and cautiously . . . as we knew the enemy were near," Trapier's brigades did not see any major forces west of Seven Mile Creek; however, they did skirmish with a few infantry and cavalry regiments and some engineers corduroying the road near Nichol's Ford and farther up the watershed near the Lee and Shope homesteads. Not much happened, except that some Federal units ran. A court of inquiry was convened within a week because of it, as though Halleck and his commanders had nothing else to do. Nevertheless, the action picked up quickly nearer to Farmington. Ruggles ordered the majority of his brigades to follow behind Walker's deployed regiments before placing three of his brigades in line: Anderson's in the center, Major Daniel Gober's Louisianans on the left, and Walker's Louisiana and Mississippi regiments on the right. In reserve was Colonel James Fagan's Arkansas brigade. The majority of the fighting fell on Anderson's and Gober's men, as Walker was farther south.[21]

As Walker's men began to skirmish with the Wisconsin companies acting as pickets at Farmington, the Badgers' commander, Major John W. Jefferson, informed Loomis that he could not hold his position without help. Loomis notified division commander Stanley, who responded that a brigade from Paine's division was on the way. Loomis informed Jefferson that help was coming, but Jefferson responded that he would have to retire if he were not reinforced immediately. Reading the cards, the Federal telegraph operator in Farmington, along with Assistant Secretary Scott, "sent a hasty dispatch and cut his machine loose." This was fortunate, as bullets began peppering the house he was evacuating.[22]

Soon, Brigadier General John M. Palmer's brigade of Paine's division appeared from the Seven Mile Creek bottom, and a thankful Loomis began to make preparations to retire, "considering myself relieved," he noted. Unfortunately, Stanley also arrived and told Loomis to stay put, in case Palmer needed help. With that many Confederates on the attack, he would. It was a good thing that Loomis remained because, as Pope noted in his report, Stanley now had "eight regiments on the south side of the creek." Stanley also told Loomis to send one of his regiments to the left to occupy a bald knob the enemy could use to place artillery and outflank the line. Loomis sent the 11th Missouri. With the remainder of his brigade and one battery, he took a position to the rear of Palmer's men.[23]

Palmer's brigade, an all-Illinois unit composed of the 22nd, 27th, 42nd, and 51st Regiments, took position along a road leading into Farmington. The general himself, as division officer of the day, rode forward to check on the skirmishers. Suddenly, Palmer found himself under fire. He quickly wheeled around and headed back to his brigade, which he quickly formed. This being his first battle, Palmer later admitted that he used all the clichés he could think of, such as "stand firm," "fire low," and "don't fire until you see the whites of their eyes." The general later noted he did not need to repeat his words that day because "my eloquence may be found in almost any well-written military history." The words that would cause him the most embarrassment, however, came when a confident Palmer sent word back to Pope that he could "hold my position against the world, the flesh and the devil."[24]

Waiting in their hastily formed line, the Illinois regiments responded to the advancing Confederates with heavy fire and caused quite a few casualties. "The rebels gave one of their unearthly yells and started on the double quick," a Wisconsin soldier of Loomis's brigade wrote. "My heart was in my throat." Palmer had just ordered his artillery to fire down the road when the battery commander informed him that he only had time to get his guns away. "Get your guns off the field! What do you mean?" Palmer thundered. The artilleryman then pointed to the right at a line of Confederates that was about to take the brigade in the flank. Confederate artillery batteries were also firing rapidly, and the combined effect sent Palmer's men scurrying across a field to their rear into another belt of timber. The general himself rode among his retreating troops, grabbing the flag of the 27th Illinois before he was hit in the arm by a piece of shrapnel.[25]

And on came the Confederates. One Southerner remembered, "The roar of artillery, mingled with the rattle of musketry, and the swift tramp of horses inspired all with a desire to advance onward." Ruggles reported that "the contest of our infantry with the enemy was for the space of half an hour sharp and spirited, until we drove them before us." But then the second Union stand began to take a toll on the Confederates, as did an ill-advised Union cavalry charge that cost some forty-three casualties among the horse soldiers, despite one man's description of "sabers flashing and the horses running like mad." A member of the 2nd Iowa Cavalry later recalled Paine himself ordering the troopers forward: "You will charge that right hand battery with this cavalry; take and hold it at all hazards until I can get the infantry there to support you." The same trooper called the dash a "mad ride," made even more so by a dry ditch that stopped many of the cavalrymen, who probably were not that enthused about attacking a battery anyway. Still, one infantryman was impressed with the cavalrymen when they returned to camp: "they came in with their sabers almost covered with blood." But because of the odd cavalry assault, several Confederate miscommunications occurred, with one of Trapier's batteries firing into the Confederate advance and other batteries vacating their positions. Some entire regiments broke, such as the 36th Mississippi, which Anderson reported was brand new and "had enjoyed none of the privileges of drill and instruction." Parts of Gober's brigade likewise broke and had to be rallied. Nevertheless, the shaken but re-formed Confederate line soon continued forward, braced by the sight of Bragg himself, as well as the thought of Van Dorn coming in on the right. Eventually, they drove the Illinoisans from their second line.[26]

Meanwhile, Loomis waited while Palmer's men battled the enemy near Farmington, unable to fire either small arms or artillery for fear of hitting their own men to the front. Confederate artillery came raining down, however, with Loomis reporting, "We suffered considerably from the fire of the enemy." Soon, Palmer's men came racing back through Loomis's lines. The retreat of the ill-timed cavalry movement also broke Loomis's 26th Illinois, which fled, leaving only the 11th Wisconsin and 47th Illinois to fight the enemy. After several minutes of fighting across an open field, Loomis retired these units on Palmer's order, and a new line was formed nearer to the creek. The 26th Illinois quickly re-formed and added weight to the line, as did the recalled 11th

Missouri, which Stanley feared would be cut off. In this third major line, the fight raged again as Anderson's and Gober's Confederates continually moved forward, supported by artillery. Fagan's reserve brigade also entered the front line and fired several volleys at the Federals.[27]

Realizing he was outnumbered, Stanley decided that discretion was the better part of valor. Giving up the fight, he ordered Loomis to retire from the field, following Palmer across Seven Mile Creek but leaving the 11th Missouri to cover the withdrawal. The Missourians did so, finally crossing the creek about dark, ending the small engagement at Farmington. A member of that regiment recalled simply in his diary: "Fought the enemy and gave back to old camp." The Confederates had a different take: "The Yanks skeedaddled back to the main army towards the gunboats. We followed them about ½ miles through Tennessee Bottom wading mud up to our hips and gave up the chase." Even a Federal admitted the surprise of the Confederate advance. Beauregard, he said, drove "our advance back some two miles and almost scaring this wing of the Eagle." The enemy "drove Paine's division from the front like a drove of sheep," he concluded.[28]

The casualties were not confined to the Corinth side of Seven Mile Creek. Confederate artillery shelled the reserve Federal regiments deployed north of the creek. One Illinois soldier wrote, "A great many of them [shells] bursted close by us—they came a booming through the timber at an aful reat. Some of them going clear over our camp some times one would cut a large limb of the tops of the trees and made it a little dangerous in that way." Palmer's pride was also wounded. When he reported to Pope's headquarters later that night, he was met with laughter when he jokingly stated he had been able to "withstand the world and the flesh, but the devil was too much for me." Some of the staff officers reported his men would have run to the Tennessee River if not stopped. Palmer later noted that he "resented the imputation upon the courage of my troops" but added, "I am satisfied that a great many of them left the field very early."[29]

One member of a Northern regiment that came through the battle unscathed was "Old Abe," the eagle mascot of the 8th Wisconsin, who made his first appearance in battle at Farmington. The bird provided antics that the men quickly learned to love. When the small arms and particularly cannon fire began to increase, the Wisconsin soldiers hit the ground. Not to be outdone, Old Abe flew off his perch and prostrated himself on the dirt as well. The frightened bird, according to a member of the regiment, "flattened himself on the ground." As recorded in the regiment's official history, the bird's bearer "picked him up, with stern orders to keep his perch, but he refused to obey." The bearer tried to get the eagle up five or six times, but with no success, whereupon he threw the pole down and hit the ground himself. Old Abe, the story went, then "crept close to his side." When the bugle sounded and the regiment rose to move, however, the eagle "leaped voluntarily to his perch with the rising of the men." There he stayed until the close of the battle, making it safely through the ordeal. J. W. Greenman of the 8th Wisconsin proudly noted in his diary, "Our Eagle came safely through the fight."[30]

Pope, who watched the fight from a tall tree, could have made a major battle out of Farmington if Halleck had turned him loose. He later noted in understatement, "Both Palmer's brigade and my whole corps were greatly dissatisfied with this outcome." He could have easily sent the other brigades from Paine's and Stanley's divisions across the creek, but he was under strict orders not to bring on a major engagement. He did call for help on his suspended right flank, however, which was some three miles from Buell's left. Pope sent frantic messages to Buell and his commanders, one of which described the enemy "advancing fiercely" on his camps. Buell sent Crittenden's division southward as well as Nelson's before it was learned that his skirmishers were active around Nichol's Ford. Once matters calmed down, Pope informed Halleck of the fight. "I could not sustain them without passing the creek with my whole force, which was contrary to your orders, and would have drawn on a general engagement," he reported. Pope admitted that "our loss was considerable"; the small fight had cost Pope 16 killed and 157 wounded and missing. On the other side, Ruggles reported 119 casualties, the majority of them coming in Anderson's and Gober's brigades.[31]

Still, Farmington was a sharp little fight that certainly got the attention of the Federals. Hit by a massive array of Confederate units (with even more that were not engaged), it is no wonder that the two little Union brigades gave up their ground and retreated back across Seven Mile Creek. Several officers, including Pope, would later try to put a good spin on the retreat, but the fact remained that Beauregard had bloodied Pope's nose with a quick and surprising strike at Farmington.[32]

The battlefield said as much. In addition to the dead and wounded of both sides, who were removed to Corinth, the ground was thickly strewn with all sorts of weapons, blankets, overcoats, oilcloths, and knapsacks. A Louisianan remembered that Federal soldiers' letters "furnished some information and a great deal of amusement to the boys." One Confederate interestingly wrote that they also captured "a lot of coffins the Feds had made." A Confederate correspondent described the littered battlefield, saying, "They attempted to save nothing but themselves, and that they did most effectually." After the fight, Patton Anderson explained: "[The Federals'] surprise and hasty flight was evidenced by the manner in which these things were scattered through the woods and half-cooked breakfasts that lay around. Hogs and mutton, just butchered and not yet dressed, could be seen in many places." Lower-ranking Confederates told the same story. "No doubt they was completely surprised when we attacked the place," one wrote home, adding that the "boys got lots of love letters from Federals." There was so much loot, in fact, that Anderson detailed several men to police the battlefield and gather any supplies or equipment left by the retreating enemy. Confederates also gathered "spades, shovels, and pickaxes, &c.; also several hundred feet of telegraph wire." Before the Confederates left Farmington and returned to the Corinth trenches, they burned the bridge over Seven Mile Creek. Realizing there might be more action there in the future, since it was an important creek crossing, Anderson ordered Smith's gin burned as well (it had provided the enemy some cover during the battle), but not before taking a careful accounting of its worth so the owner could be reimbursed.[33]

Confederates also took Union soldiers' personal possessions left on the field. Albert T. Goodloe found a Bible owned by one of the "routed" Union soldiers. After using it throughout the conflict, he endeavored to find its owner after the war. The search took him twenty-two years, but Goodloe finally found the owner and returned it, at which time the Federal expressed his "great satisfaction at its return." Another Confederate wrote to his father that he was sending home "one or two relics of the Battle of Farmington brought from the enemy's camp." He also told of a friend who was "very lucky, having found in a knapsack a silver watch, and a valuable case of surgical instruments with other little articles of less value."[34]

Despite the loot, Braxton Bragg lamented the lack of real success: "Failing in my hopes of dining with general Pope to-day, as he seems to decline our company." But the biggest failure was Van Dorn's flank attack. The initial action of Ruggles's and Trapier's divisions to gain the enemy's attention worked to perfection, but the flank attack that would have rolled up and possibly bagged two entire Federal brigades south of Seven Mile Creek did not occur as planned. Bragg's far right brigade commander, Walker, kept his right flank on the Memphis and Charleston Railroad, and throughout the day he was ordered to contact and secure a hold on Van Dorn's left flank. But Van Dorn was nowhere to be seen for most of the day. Ruggles even delayed his advance for a time, but the trap did not shut.[35]

Van Dorn had left Corinth early enough the night before, with one woman proudly writing that she "saw them as they marched out. . . . They crossed a bridge opposite our bed-room window." He then formed his men southeast of Corinth, with, he said, his "left flank resting on the crest of the hill above the marshy bottom of the little creek in front of the intrenchments of Corinth."

Early on May 9, he moved to the right, but not soon enough to participate in the fight at Farmington. One of his soldiers, blinded to the larger context, remembered, "We had a good deal of marching afoot near this place . . . we thought we were going to get into a considerable battle . . . , but no battle worthy of note was fought." Sterling Price anticipated a battle as well; he wore his favorite battle shirt, which one soldier described as a "plaid hunting shirt of different colors." Van Dorn also itched for battle. One of his men remembered that the general "rode up to us and remarked, Boys lay down your blankets and when you get up to them just step right into them and give a yell. Says he lets reprieve ourselves for the Battle of Elk Horn." The troops responded with a yell, but one Missourian remembered, "[We] never caught up with them." An Arkansas soldier lamented, "Our battalion did not get to shoot any in the skirmish," although he noted that if the skirmish (as he called it) had been fought in Missouri or Arkansas, "it would have been called a battle." All Van Dorn related to Beauregard was that "natural obstructions—swamps, thickets, ravines, &c.—prevented my right flank from reaching the Hamburg road in time to cut off the enemy's retreat, although every effort was made to do so." One of his soldiers agreed, writing that the units "cross[ed] swamps, marching in line of battle through dense underbrush, over hill-tops, and across deep valleys." Van Dorn even blamed the Federals: "The enemy were too expeditious in getting out of the way to give us an opportunity to do anything more than skirmish with him." Illustrating Van Dorn's slight participation in the engagement, he lost only nine men in the entire operation. Beauregard, for his part, blamed the debacle on faulty guides.[36]

In actuality, Beauregard had simply not allowed enough time for Van Dorn to get into position, and therefore the trap had not shut. Still, Pope had taken a jolt. "At Farmington," remembered one Confederate veteran, "the invaders were utterly outdone and routed, throwing away knapsacks and other accouterments as they sought to escape from the yelling rebels." Another erroneously stated that they had driven the enemy nine miles. Yet another hyperbolically reported that the enemy had fled all the way to their gunboats. Despite these overstatements, the action at Farmington initiated major hostilities. One Federal remembered a "rumor [that] the ball has commenced."[37]

The engagement at Farmington, small though it was, had a tremendous impact on the campaign as a whole. The nonengaged Federals on the right, some of whom held reviews that day, heard the commotion and wondered whether the big battle everyone expected had come at last. Assistant Secretary of War Scott was quite shaken by his near capture that day; one Ohio sol-

dier described him as "thrown into a momentary panic." Scott reported to Secretary of War Stanton that night that he expected a major battle the next day,
observing, "It is now pretty clear that an overwhelming force will be massed
at Corinth to crush this army. In my judgement, which I respectfully offer for
your consideration, a heavy re-enforcement of infantry and artillery should be
sent here immediately, or we shall soon be the party besieged, and that, too,
in the heart of the enemy's country." Scott's dire forebodings made it all the
way to President Lincoln, who assumed the request for additional troops had
come from Halleck through Scott. Lincoln wrote to Halleck bluntly, "I beg
you to be assured we do the best we can. . . . Each of our commanders along
our line from Richmond to Corinth supposes himself to be confronted by numbers superior to his own." He ended: "I believe you and the brave officers and
men with you can and will get the victory at Corinth." In short, Halleck would
get no more troops. For his part, Halleck told Stanton he had never asked for
more troops.[38]

The skirmish also caused some hard feelings between Colonel Washington L. Elliott of the 2nd Iowa Cavalry and General Paine. Elliott was commanding a cavalry brigade elsewhere when he learned that Paine had ordered
his troopers to assault the Confederate battery. A soldier remembered that
Elliott was "very angry with Paine and cursed him vehemently." Paine retorted
that he had not expected the unit to go as far as it did and incur that many
casualties. A heated Elliott responded, "I want you to know that I have taught
that regiment to go to h__l if ordered there, but I didn't fetch them here to
have them ordered there."[39]

The main reason that Farmington loomed so large in the Corinth campaign,
however, was its impact on Union commanding general Henry Halleck. The
skirmish at Farmington upset his well-planned operation and showed him that
he was in for a bigger fight than he had expected. Deserters from the Confederate army told exaggerated tales of the proposed attack, inflating the numbers by some 35,000 men. It was almost as if Halleck suddenly became
intimidated by his nearness to Corinth and the possibility of battle. The result
was that he became extremely careful. He ordered the entire army to entrench,
and he gave the same order at every position the army took thereafter. If the
troops made any headway, they camped early and entrenched their positions.
Unit histories illustrate the point. The 57th Illinois recorded that on May 10,
"the 57th is introduced to the spade and shovel, and we commence throwing
up breastworks." Even a lowly Confederate noticed the change: "Fear seems
to have seized the invaders of our country," he wrote several days after Farmington.[40]

After the fight at Farmington on May 9, Halleck seemed to lose some of his nerve. Up to that point, his correspondence with officials in Washington had revealed a bold commander within his context of order, mass, and careful preparation; nevertheless, he had been intent on quick movements and a major battle for the possession of Corinth. On May 2, for instance, Halleck wrote to Stanton, "We expect a terrible battle, but our men will fight well, and all are determined to have a victory." The next day, he sent the message saying he intended to be at Corinth by nightfall the next day. On May 7, he reported to Stanton, "A severe battle will probably be fought." And during the entire time, his divisions were making steady progress toward Corinth. After Farmington, however, Halleck became much more cautious. On May 13, he wrote to Stanton, "We are gradually advancing on Corinth, but as the enemy is strongly intrenched, and his number equal if not superior to ours, it is necessary to move with great caution." On May 18, he sent a similar warning: "Country is so wooded and marshy that we are obliged to feel our way step by step." As late as May 28, he repeated his "feel our way" line. Obviously, the reports of Confederate reinforcements he received from deserters, many of whom had been sent into Union lines specifically to confuse Halleck, added to his worry. On May 6, he stated, "Deserters report that Beauregard has received large re-inforcements from New Orleans, South Carolina, and Georgia, and is very confident of being able to repulse any attack we may make." These reports convinced Halleck that he was outnumbered and that the abortive Confederate attack at Farmington on May 9 was merely an example of what could happen on a larger scale.[41]

Politics also had something to do with Halleck's anxiety. A transmission from President Lincoln hailing the victories in Virginia warned Halleck not to suffer a defeat that would dampen the outlook of the war. Perhaps looking for an excuse to throw up earthworks and catch his breath, Halleck took the message to heart and shifted the armies into a slow, creeping advance. For the rest of May, the Federal armies made only sporadic progress toward the town and its railroads. Units moved barely more than a mile before they stopped and sat for days. Then they would repeat the process, getting only a mile closer and becoming considerably more tired from all the digging. Halleck's movements up to May 9 had been sharp, forceful, and strong; then they became timid, cautious, deliberate, and slow. One Ohio soldier could only write, "Our army is proving the truth of the old saying that large bodies move slowly."[42]

This timidity is illustrated by the armies' moves over the next week. After Farmington, none of Halleck's divisions advanced for seven full days, although there was some minor skirmishing along the lines, such as a May 10 foray on Thomas's lines north of Corinth by Colonel Joseph Wheeler of the

19th Alabama. The only real movement was Halleck's effort to close the gaps between his armies. After Pope's frantic call on May 9, Halleck had sent word for Nelson's division to support Pope's right; Nelson marched at "quick-time" but arrived after the fighting had ended. Halleck soon made support of Pope a permanent part of his plan. On May 10, Buell moved his army southward some three miles, "the distance between my left and General Pope's right being too great for prompt support," Buell said. In order to connect with Pope's right, Buell kept Nelson at Nichol's Ford, moved Wood to the left to connect with Nelson, and sent Crittenden to Nelson's left. He kept McCook in reserve. All the divisions fronted Seven Mile Creek, which put them on line with Pope's forces.[43]

Over the course of the next two weeks, this cautious movement began to tax the nerves of Halleck's subordinates, one of whom wrote that he endured "slow, irregular, and inconvenient marches." Many soldiers wanted to move quickly and secure Corinth immediately, even if it meant a major battle. In particular, Halleck had to keep a tight rein on Pope, whom he considered rash. "Don't let Pope go too far ahead," he had prophetically warned Scott on May 9; "it is dangerous, and effects no good." Now Halleck correctly feared that Pope would get ahead of the rest of the army again and fall prey to the Confederates, resulting in a disaster of monumental proportions. Despite Halleck's efforts, Pope eventually moved ahead unsupported. Grant later wrote that Pope "got loose as it were at times." Incredibly, Halleck situated his headquarters in the center and on the right at various times. But if Halleck was so concerned about Pope, he should have positioned his headquarters with his most unreliable general, where he could keep a closer watch on him. Halleck did not, and it almost cost him a major defeat on May 9. He should have learned from that experience.[44]

4

"A Siege from the Start"

For the next two and a half weeks, Henry Halleck implemented his "feel our way step by step" mentality. Each of his armies moved forward on their respective fronts, but it would be a slow and methodical advance. He realized he had made some mistakes by letting Pope move ahead so quickly, by not watching his flanks carefully enough, and by allowing gaps to form between the armies. Halleck determined not to let such problems happen again. One of his soldiers thus described the two huge armies as "facing each other, both entrenched and each waiting for the other to advance, they seemed to be sparring for an opening, like two prize fighters in the ring." Another described it as "the two contending armies . . . arrayed at a distance of about four or five miles of each other and neither seems to wish to loose his advantage of ground by advancing on the other." Yet some soldiers were optimistic, describing the situation as "the Union coil . . . daily being placed around the rebels in Corinth. At every squirm they make[,] the coil become[s] tighter and the bones will soon begin to crack."[1]

Halleck had other matters on his mind, too. Assistant Secretary of War Scott was continually trying to tell Halleck how to run the operation, and various governors visited the army. These politicians liked to see the fighting firsthand, but as one officer told Indiana's Oliver P. Morton, "Too much danger for a governor here." "Not more for me than for you," the governor replied, but he was finally convinced to move to the rear. One of the politicians, Governor Louis P. Harvey of Wisconsin, perished at Savannah, Tennessee, in April when he fell into the Tennessee River and drowned. Then there were the newspaper correspondents, including soldiers, who wrote derogatory articles about the slow advance. Halleck soon banned all correspondents from his camps and stopped all soldier mail at Savannah. The correspondents would henceforth get only a summation of events posted on a bulletin board at Pittsburg Landing, a good distance to the rear.[2]

Even with all the care, heavy skirmishing erupted as the Union armies made their way across Seven Mile Creek, and fairly heavy fights broke out in front of each army as the weeks unfolded. Despite a scare and the resulting slowdown, Halleck was still intent on taking Corinth.

Reports and correspondence are full of soldiers' complaints about the elements, bad water, or mind-numbing tactics during the siege of Corinth. One soldier wrote with impatience in his diary, "Terrible cannon fire the whole day long. Why doesn't one arrive at the general question?" Another described the Union advance as "slowly coming ahead like snails." Yet another complained that "the further we go soldiering becomes harder and harder. The duty is very heavy for the men and the very hardest kind of duty." That duty, of course, was "intrenching ourselves at the end of every march," and it was particularly bothersome during the hot weather. One soldier remarked, "We are in the State of Mississippi where the sun comes down as hot as ever you saw in August." Another wrote to his sister that the heat had placed many soldiers "horse du combat," and "several men are constantly building boxes in which to inter the dead."[3]

Feeding such a gathering of men and animals was another problem. Even when the roads were good, it took an immense effort to provide enough food for such a large army. One officer reported "300 [wagons] waiting at Hamburg Landing to get their loads. After we started should think we passed 500 on the road." And he added, "You will recollect this was [just] on the road to Pope's army." An Ohio soldier in McClernand's reserve recounted that "mule teams by the thousand are passing here constantly going towards Corinth and returning, and 500 or 600 head of beef cattle passed towards Corinth to-day." A quartermaster in an Indiana regiment described the effort to bring up one regiment's food and forage: "From the great no[.] of teams that go there [Pittsburg Landing] to draw their supplies such as provisions and forage where we also get ours there has been an order that Quartermasters shall accompany their teams so as to Expedite business and prevent confusion. This causes me a trip to the Landing about three times a week and it takes 2 days to make it with a good deal of the night." Even worse, during rainy periods, transportation ground to a halt, depriving the soldiers. Sherman, in the midst of the heavy rains of May 4 and 5, reminded his troops, "Every ounce of food and forage must be regarded as precious as diamonds."[4]

The Confederates also sent rockets into the Union lines at intervals during the night, "with a view to harassing the enemy," Beauregard wrote. This apparently worked on some Federal soldiers, and one Ohioan described how the rockets went up "with a great roar." There was also the constant knowledge that a big battle would probably be fought soon against an extremely strong Confederate position. "We are now very near the great stronghold," wrote one Union soldier, obviously impressed with Corinth's might. Another described the Confederate fortifications as "reported to be very strong."[5]

The most common complaint was bad water, which, coupled with atrocious sanitation, caused horrible problems. One colonel reported that his men "have suffered considerably in the last two or three camps from the scarcity and quality of the water." A common soldier put it more bluntly: "Sometimes where we get water we have to skim off the green skum before we can get any so you need not wonder that we have the diarreah." A newspaper correspondent elaborated: "The water in and around Corinth . . . smells so offensively that the men have to hold their noses while drinking it. As our men advanced [toward Corinth] they found the water much deteriorated and very difficult to obtain." Units dug wells, but according to one Ohio soldier, "about the time we have it dug and fixed up nice and the ground policed then we leave."[6]

The constant skirmishing and the numerous false alarms that required units to sleep with their equipment on and to form even at night also bore heavily on the men's minds. One disgusted soldier wrote, "I ant particular whether I see any more of the Elephant or not." Another wrote to his wife, "If I am to be shot I want it to be in a regular battle not in a trifling skirmish." Numerous letters and diaries recorded the almost constant firing along the lines, as well as frequent cannonading. One Federal stopped his letter and wrote, "There went another cannon." Another elaborated that "'Secesh' balls flew thick all around us" and concluded, "The music of a shell bursting over our heads is not very charming to me." The skirmishers were more deadly. One soldier wrote of a particularly annoying Confederate sharpshooter hiding in the trees on Buell's front. He was finally killed by "three half breed Indians, . . . [who] crept silently through the grass and low shrubs that separated the lines." Another told of his experiences: "I have ben where the rifle balls fell like hail Stone on all sides of me then the grape and canister and Shell whised over my head a purfict storme. i felt Curious but i had to Stand the ground and fite a little. this was on picket guarde. i leveled my gun on one poor felow that had shot at me 3 or 4 times and he fell. i thought i had done rong for i hurd him say o dear and my hart farley jumped out of my side." One picket was scared just by an old hoot owl. "As there are some Red Skins among the Rebs I thought it might be one of them," he wrote to his wife. There were, not surprisingly, also cases of friendly fire. One soldier told his brother of a colonel who "went out to look after the pickets a few days ago, and one of the pickets drew up and shot him through the head and then challenged him." Another described an incident in which a soldier from the 6th Iowa shot someone who "was crossing over and beyond the guard line." Colonel John McDowell had ordered the sentinel to fire, but it turned out to be a soldier from a regiment down the line.[7]

Over time, soldiers became somewhat oblivious to the constant skirmishing. One Federal wrote to his wife that the men "will not stop a game of cards or the reading of a paper or the writing of a letter unless the Bull dogs (the cannons) commence barking." As concern about the dangers of skirmishing lessened, fraternization and trading with the enemy soon began to take place. "How far is it to Corinth?" one Union soldier shouted. His counterpart across the lines yelled back, "Its so d____d far, you'll never get thar!" Another Union soldier remarked, "It seems strange to me that enemys will stand inactive in sight—as we have for the past two days, and stranger still to see our men meet the 'Secesh' shake hands and converse with them. This has happened several times lately not over one hundred yards from me." An Ohio soldier recorded in his diary: "Today we are out on a reconnaissance and our men seen some of the rebels and they shook their handkerchiefs at our men and our men done the same." Some took fraternization to the extreme and made pacts with those on the opposite side that "they would not fire on each other." When orders came down the chain of command to secure a certain position, the Federals kept their bargain. A Union officer met with the corresponding Confederate officer and informed him that they had been ordered to take the position, and the Confederates willingly retired. An Illinois surgeon even recorded in his diary: "The Pickets got to friendly along the line, and would meet, and trade knives and play poker. Ross broke it up." Confederate officers also stopped the fraternization; one order revoking the action commented on soldiers "in the habit of meeting the sentinels of the enemy between the lines."[8]

Despite constant skirmishing, the boredom of trench duty soon set in. There was complaining, to be sure, especially about digging the fortifications. One colonel even noted how his men, "for pastime, have since sodded the works, splitting the sod with knives, and the rains have made them fresh and green." Still, commanders praised their men's performance. "The alacrity with which the men relinquished the rifle for the spade and then again grasped the rifle when the firing became heavy in front promises well for the future," one officer wrote. William T. Sherman even praised his volunteers, whom he did not think were up to the regulars' abilities. He once said that some state troops fought "like real soldiers" and later admitted, "I must also in justice to my men remark their great improvement on the march, the absence of that straggling which is too common in the volunteer service, and, still more, their improved character on picket and as skirmishers."[9]

The longer the siege lasted, however, the more the soldiers complained about Halleck's slowness and the lack of battle. Some began calling their commanding officer "Grandmother Halleck." "What under the sun our Halleck is waiting for we can't guess," one Illinoisan wrote. "One hour's march will commence the struggle now and you don't know how anxious we are for that little trip." Another told his wife, "I wrote you a few days ago that I thought the fight would come off in a few days. I have changed my opinion. It would not surprise me if it did not come off for a month." Newspaper correspondents picked up on the dissatisfaction and began to write derogatory columns about Halleck. Despite the delay, most soldiers on both sides continued to expect a major battle at any time, and many were prepared to die if it came. One Federal wrote to his father, "All of us are anxious for the fight so as to end our suspense." One member of Beauregard's army wrote to his sister, "I would not miss being in this fight for a heap, although I may get killed." An Illinois soldier was so concerned about the possibility of dying in the coming battle that he gave explicit instructions for his burial, telling his wife, "I will be home if I come in a box;" his captain had promised to send the soldiers home in the event of their death. He also told his wife, "I don't want my boy to have a step father for to beat and ruff him around."[10]

With so much potential for death, religion became an interest. One soldier told of hearing sermons and noted that there was no skirmishing on Sunday "for the first day for several days." One Federal abhorred the idea of fighting on Sunday: "I don't think our folks want to bring on the battle tomorrow as it is a Sunday, for there appears to be some dread of Sunday attacks." Another confided to his wife, "We trust in the Lord and ceap our Powder dry." Several Confederates fully believed that "God is on our side," and Jefferson Davis himself declared May 16 as a day of prayer. Not all were of a religious mind, however. One soldier wrote home early in the siege, "It did not look like the Sabbath at all, men were moving all day." Another wrote to his wife, "We know no Sabbath here." A soldier in the 11th Indiana agreed: "While there [at church] I cast my eyes round, I saw some men playing cards, others pitching horse shoes, and in the distance I heard the ringing of anvils." An Arkansas Confederate noted Jefferson Davis's order to "fast and pray" but observed that there was "no fasting in our reg't." He did mention that Hardee's entire corps was gathered to hear a sermon, however.[11]

Perhaps most exasperating of all were the problems caused by insects and other vermin. An Illinois trooper told of sleeping on the ground and how "the confounded lizards are working me into a fever. They are as thick as you ever saw grasshoppers. One of them ran into Allan Heald's shirt bosom yesterday and they say he moved rather sprightly for a few minutes. Lots of snakes here, cottonmouths, copperheads, rattlesnakes, and commoner varmint. There's also

a scorpion that looks like a lizard with a green head. They say it is poison-
ous." Another wrote of numerous bugs and "a few snakes and lizards in the
greatest abundance." One soldier wrote of "being in danger of having one of
the later [lizard] run up the britches leg." Another described the same thing
happening to a captain as he wrote a letter home: "It did not stop till it had
compassed the entire length of his body, emerging at his collar. Chaos ensued;
pen, ink and letter flew in different directions." The soldier went on to say that
the captain "had to draw another suit before he could appear in public again."
A member of the 15th Ohio told of a soldier who got a bug in his ear, whereupon General McCook, who was eating a meal nearby, ran over to the shouting man and poured whiskey in his ear, causing the bug to emerge. A member
of McCook's staff reprimanded the general for using whiskey when water
would have worked. Lice caused other problems. One Illinois soldier remembered, "Here is where I got the first graybacks on me, it made me homesick
and I wanted to see mama." After the war, an author devoted nearly an entire
chapter of his regimental history to lice or graybacks, gnats, mosquitoes, fleas,
ticks, jiggers, and the "black fly." This soldier told of one particularly humorous episode on the march: "I well remember seeing, one day, a celebrated,
robust brigadier general, who was afterward President of the United States,
engaged in chasing the *pediculus* along the seams of his nether garment, which
was spread out upon his knees in regulation style. The general had wondered
some distance back of his headquarters, and getting behind the largest tree he
could find he applied his energies to the work of 'skirmishing,' while the setting sun cast a mellow glow over the touching scene."[12]

Despite all the problems, the Federals also had some pleasant experiences.
One artilleryman wrote of listening to a "whip-poor-will for the first time,"
adding that he enjoyed "its song for more than an hour." Another noted that
his campsite was "a fine place to get flowers." Newspapers were a luxury in
camp, and as one Federal wrote, "We cannot get them for Love or Money."
When they did appear, however, they were consumed with great gusto and
sold for as much as fifteen cents each. They often brought news that heartened the troops, such as when the Federals learned of the Confederate evacuation of Yorktown in Virginia. The soldiers also welcomed the few breaks
from the hot temperatures, one Federal describing the nights as "deliciously
cool after sunset." He also remarked on the great abundance of apples,
peaches, chestnuts, and berries. "Saw peaches to-day larger than filberts," he
wrote. The soldiers also commented on the wildlife. An Ohio soldier wrote to
his wife, "Today some secesh hounds chased a deer into our picket line, and
the boys caught it, and have had it for their dinner. Sometimes there are wild
turkey, but they have not killed any that I know of, they generally are looking

out for larger game." During one skirmish, a member of the 55th Illinois described how "a magnificent buck came bounding along between the picket lines, and in full view of both armies. . . . He passed the entire front of the division unscathed, only to fall in front of the Fifty-third Illinois." Another soldier wrote, "The boys had a good deal of fun chasing squirrels and wild turkeys, but were not allowed to shoot them." Other soldiers reported that some members of the 15th Illinois and 56th Ohio were arrested for killing hogs and cattle. The guilty Ohians were made to cut a pole, string up the beef, and carry it around for hours before digging a hole and burying it, all on Lew Wallace's orders.[13]

There were also fun-loving times. One soldier in the 51st Indiana told of a quartermaster with the rank of major who kept "a barrel of fine old Kentucky whiskey" for "medical purposes." One night, a guard at regimental headquarters found the barrel and notified his friends. Soon, the whiskey was all but gone. The enterprising guard then called the major and told him that something in his wagon was leaking badly. "My whiskey," the major shouted, and ran to the wagon to save what was left. For his help in saving the whiskey, the major gave the guard a half pint for his "faithfulness." The soldier noted, "The day following was one of hilarity among the soldiers of the right of the regiment."[14]

On another occasion, a new sutler arrived near the camp of the 41st Ohio, whereupon one soldier dressed himself in an officer's uniform—"obtained no one knew how," one soldier remembered—and paraded himself around the sutler's wagon as General Nelson, the bombastic division commander in Buell's army. The private took several bottles of whiskey in a brusque manner and told the sutler he could get his money that night at the general's headquarters. One member of the regiment remembered, "If the bottles had been barrels they could not have held more merriment than came from the anticipated reception of the sutler when he should present his bill to Nelson."[15]

But despite the frolicking, many men grew impatient and could not understand why Halleck waited so long to attack. There was a great cry among soldiers that they were being wasted and that there were so many of them that the officers could not keep track of them all. One soldier in the 58th Indiana wrote that "the several Divisions seemed to be getting in each other['s] way. Sometimes we thought ourselves in the front and near the rebels. Pickets would be thrown out; strict orders would be given about making fires or noise of any kind, lest the enemy should discover our position. Later we would discover that a whole Division of our own troops were in front of us with blazing fires and stirring music." Another Indiana soldier wrote that his division was "marched and countermarched in almost every direction." Obviously, as

May wore on, the soldiers of the Federal army were beginning to get testy and hoped for a resolution.[16]

Halleck, Buell, Pope, Thomas, Sherman, Crittenden, McCook, Nelson, Stanley, Hurlbut: these Union leaders had led their men forward and were on the brink of taking what Halleck described as one of the two most important strategic locations in the Confederacy. The appearance of any of the major commanders thrilled the common soldiers. Conspicuously absent from the major affairs of the advancing armies, however, were several notable figures. McClernand, for example, chafed at his reserve role, and he played no major part until late in the campaign, when some of his units finally managed to get on the main line. Others of his command were chagrined as well, with one soldier telling another not to come back to the army: "We have enough of soldiers here that cannot do anything." Likewise, Lew Wallace was relegated to a reserve role and played no meaningful part in the advance, although the service he and McClernand performed behind the lines protected the logistical lifelines and covered the rear right flank of the armies as they advanced. Wallace, surprisingly, seemed to take his role in stride, writing in his memoirs decades later, "Somebody had to be in the reserve." The biggest shelving, however, was U. S. Grant. Halleck had promoted him into oblivion, and it almost cost the Union his services for the remainder of the war. Grant was right when he later wrote that Halleck's movement was "a siege from the start." And it was a siege in more ways than one. While Halleck implemented siege operations against Corinth, he basically had Grant under siege as well. Grant himself remembered, "For myself I was little more than an observer." In his memoirs he related that orders were issued without his knowledge, and advances were made without his input. One observer noted that Grant was "sort of 'fifth wheel to the coach,' upon which General Halleck expected to ride into prominence."[17]

Perhaps due to his muted role, Grant took the opportunity to scold one of the only persons he could during the siege: John A. McClernand. On a couple of occasions, Grant went through McClernand's pickets during the night, and they failed to examine passes. Grant brought the security failure to McClernand's attention, and McClernand passed the scolding down the chain of command. Ironically, Grant's tormentor Halleck was also involved in a security point mix-up, but this time, the contentious soldier yelled at the general himself that only "a pass signed by General Halleck" or some other officer would get him past the point. Halleck thundered that he *was* that man but had to appeal all the way up to the soldier's colonel.[18]

Grant mostly stayed behind the scenes, spending a lot of time moping around at the various headquarters. Pope remembered him lying around and talking about resigning. He also spent a lot of time with his friend Sherman. At times, however, Grant could not be quiet. On one occasion he produced a plan for Halleck's consideration: he thought Pope's army could withdraw from the line, march across the rear of the two other armies, and attack Corinth from the northwest, where the Confederate defenses appeared light. Halleck quickly put the general in his place, causing Grant to think he had proposed "an unmilitary movement."[19]

Making the situation worse, Halleck received word of Grant's unhappiness and scolded him even more, writing, "I am very much surprised, general, that you should find any cause of complaint in the recent assignment of commands." He noted that just because orders were not sent through Grant, he had "no more cause of complaint on that score than others have." Finally, Halleck lectured, "For the last three months I have done everything in my power to ward off the attacks which were made upon you. If you believe me your friend you will not require explanations; if not, explanations on my part would be of little avail."[20]

Grant became so agitated that he threatened to resign. In his memoirs he recorded, "My position was so embarrassing in fact that I made several applications during the siege to be relieved." Sherman, of course, talked his friend out of leaving the army after Grant confided to him, "I am in the way here." Sherman later told Grant, "You could not be quiet at home for a week when armies are moving." Fortunately for his career, and for the Union, Grant decided to stay.[21]

The Union advance on Corinth proved to be a disaster for those Tennesseans and Mississippians living in the area through which the armies marched. One soldier who was camped near Shiloh in early May recorded that "they are plowing corn here today," but that was the exception. A Union soldier wrote to his sister that the campaign was "destroying this Country fearfully and from here to hamburgh on the river will not get over it for at least ¼ of a sentory [century]." Another wrote, "We passed occasionally a farm, but they were generally destroyed by the desolating hand of war." Numerous examples of the citizens' plight can be found in contemporary records, and like the inhabitants of other battlefields, many lost their homes and other possessions. The inhabitants of the Shiloh battlefield just a few miles to the northeast, some of whom the Corinthians probably knew, could tell them a lot about the effects of war and the ravages produced by armies on the march. Now it was their turn to learn that awful truth.[22]

The Federal soldiers were not impressed with the locals or their region. One wrote to his daughter, "This country is not worth fighting for. I would not live in it for all that I have seen of it yet." Another described the inhabitants: "The principal part of the population consisted of negroes, alligators and mosquitoes." He went on to describe the locals: "I don't now remember that any of the Sixth boys got particularly stuck on the place. Nor did I ever hear of any of them deserting the regiment to remain there on account of being captivated by any of Corinth's tobacco-chewing, snuff-rubbing, fair-headed, sharp-nosed, hatchet-faced, yellow-eyed, sallow-skinned, cotton-dressed, flat-breasted, big-footed, bare-headed, long-waisted, hump-shouldered, stoop-necked, bare-footed, straddle-toed, sharp-shinned, thin-lipped, pale-faced, lantern-jarred, hollow-eyed, silly-looking, female damsels." Another described a family "of the class known as poor white, too proud to work, living from hand to mouth, and in fact it was very hard for one to see how they lived at all as there was nothing in the house and nothing outside except a small peach orchard." He added, "All, save the youngest, chewed tobacco." A Michigan soldier wrote home that he had a bad case of diarrhea, which he expected to keep "as long as I stay in the army or especially while we stay down in this God forsaken country. . . . Staying here will no doubt kill more men with sickness than will be killed by the bullet."[23]

Still, many of the farm boys from the Midwest were interested in the South's farming operations. Although farming was restricted in the area due to the fighting, some planters did have crops in the ground. The soldiers described fruit in abundance and took great pains to comment on the crops, especially noting the paucity of cotton. One soldier wrote to his parents, "We passed through several fields in which cotton grew last year but saw none planted this year." The farming operations made the soldiers miss their homes. "I expect you are busy planting up there," one Ohio soldier wrote to his brother. Many were amazed at the difference in seasons. "The seasons hear must be two months a head of central Ohio," one soldier wrote.[24]

There is no evidence of citizens being harmed, raped, or plundered, although with an army as large as Halleck's, there were bound to be some seedy soldiers who would not blink at committing some of the more benign depredations. One artilleryman reported capturing "6 or 8 prisoners mostly citizens nearly all of whom immediately became good Union men." But there are no accounts of more vicious acts such as murder or rape. In fact, one Illinois soldier described the reaction of some women to the Federals: "There were about a dozen real ladies at the springs yesterday, and they were quite sociable and so interesting that I could not help staying an hour after the column left[.] We were the first of our soldiers that the party had seen and they were much surprised that our boys behaved so well. None of them had ever been North, and they occupied about all the time I was with them in asking questions, principally though, about the conduct of our army." Most women stayed out of sight, however. Numerous Union soldiers recorded statements such as, "I hant seen a girl for two months" or "I have not seen a 'female' for over a month." One even admitted to his wife, "We have been isolated from female society for so long, that, we have become wild. We never see women here, no, my dear, only bide the time with patience."[25]

But there are numerous accounts of citizens losing personal possessions. One Union soldier lamented their loss, saying, "And these people were not secessionists originally." Another Federal wrote that the Union soldiers took freely: "The Union Army that is in this country have made use of all the rails enclosing the crops to build roads across the muddy bottoms." He described the agricultural efforts to grow corn and cotton but concluded, "They won't make much hereabouts this season." One soldier described some of the first artillery shots fired at Farmington, one of which hit a house "in which some Federal officers were enjoying a turkey dinner, and sent them scattering." A Union artilleryman described the effects of battle on another house on Sherman's front: "The fine house was set on fire by one of our shells and burned down," he wrote. "The apple and peach trees are many of them marked by our bullets, and the whole place is now abandoned to Ruin." The Confederates also told of the destruction of civilians' property. Bragg reported to Beauregard that one of his commanders "ordered the destruction of a log house on the lower Farmington road, now occupied by the enemy, and from which they seriously annoy and damage our pickets." And, Bragg told his commander, he would "probably hear some artillery for dislodging them." As noted earlier, Patton Anderson ordered the destruction of Dick Smith's cotton gin between Farmington and Seven Mile Creek because the enemy had used it for cover. He sent Captain G. P. Macmurdo and two of his men to take an account of the worth of the gin and then destroy it. Macmurdo reported that the gin house and machinery, the gin and a corn mill, three bales of cotton, and enough unginned cotton for five more bales were worth $960 in all. Then he set the entire complex afire. A Confederate captain similarly told of a family who had to leave their house "to get out of the way of our fortifications and entrenchments." Even worse, as the Federal army continually drew closer to Corinth, many began to worry about a bombardment. One Corinth nurse admitted, "We are beginning to feel a little nervous at the prospect of a shell waking us up some morning; certainly not a pleasant one to contemplate."[26]

Many citizens who realized they were caught in the middle of the fighting simply left home: "This is a doleful looking Country[. I] don't see eny body but soldiers," one Federal wrote home. Many reports mentioned troops moving directly through the small village of Farmington, which Major Daniel Gober described as "deserted." A remarkable number of locals remained, however, and they provided some intelligence to both sides. Given the strong Unionist bent of Tishomingo County prior to the war, it is not surprising that some citizens openly aided the Federals. Major John H. Foster of the 3rd Ohio Cavalry reported that during the May 9 skirmishing on Buell's front, he "went on to a Mr. Lee's, half a mile beyond there, and ascertained by Mr. and Mrs. Lee where the enemy's pickets had been, and that they had drawn them in that day." Similarly, Schuyler Hamilton reported that "the testimony of many citizens of the country" informed him of an aborted Confederate attack. Those reports convinced Hamilton that the enemy had turned around when they saw his division so strongly posted.[27]

Some citizens heartily aided the Confederates, however. The 5th Tennessee, like many regiments, had "washerwomen" attached to it. Other civilians aided military efforts. Anderson reported that right in the middle of the May 9 engagement at Farmington, a local citizen "approached me and said it was impossible for the brigade to get through a morass immediately in front." The citizen reported that he had talked earlier to Anderson's division commander, Ruggles, who had sent him to Anderson. Ruggles later confirmed the story. Others notified Confederate authorities of Union troop movements.[28]

Apparently, some Corinth citizens gave away too much information. On May 23, Beauregard issued orders forbidding anyone, soldier or citizen, from publishing any news of Confederate organization or troop movements. "We are not allowed to say any thing about the army in any way whatever," one soldier wrote to his sister. Beauregard's reason for doing this, he said, was based on "impending events and the proximity of the enemy." He stipulated that soldiers would be punished according to the army's regulations, but citizens would be "sent forthwith beyond the lines, and shall not be permitted to return within them again." The next day, May 24, Beauregard issued another order: "All newspaper and other correspondents are hereby ordered to leave this post by the first train, nor will they be permitted to return within 25 miles of the lines."[29]

The local citizens also had vast numbers of sick and wounded under their care. One ill Confederate captain, W. J. Stubblefield, wrote, "The people with whom we are staying are plain but very nice clever people . . . and they are careful to gratify each wish of ours in diet or otherwise but in turn we are careful not to be foolish nor more troublesome than we cannot help." The doctors and nurses who had borne the brunt of the Shiloh wounded had additional waves of wounded as skirmishes erupted every few days, Farmington on May 9 being the biggest. Wounded from both sides were brought into Corinth on May 9 and 10, and smaller numbers poured in continually.[30]

The nurses had to deal with freak accidents as well. As a group of women made bandages in the Tishomingo Hotel, using candlelight to see, the fire got too close to the cotton and, according to one nurse, was "communicated to some of the ladies' dresses." A man in the room put out the blaze, with little damage done. However, the nurse noted that she "was certain from the noise that the enemy had come to storm the hospital, for which I was laughed at considerably."[31]

Not all civilians were supportive of the soldiers, however. One Confederate wrote to his wife, "I took two men and started in the country to find something to eat." He went several miles "but could find nobody willing to sell me a chicken or any thing at all." He finally met a man with a wagon full of eggs, and he bought a whopping forty-three dozen for thirty-three and a half cents per dozen. "I have eaten nearly a dozen today," he wrote, and "if I could only have found some butter I would have lived like a lord for a few days."[32]

Then there were the pitiful individuals who had no other recourse but to beg for aid from the locals or the soldiers. One man described "helpless women pouring through our camp, with helpless babies in their arms and four or five little children following along behind, hurrying forward to seek charity."[33]

The plight of black civilians was even worse than that of the white, but fewer accounts of their actions have been documented. The Confederates used them as laborers, but they generally aided the Union forces. One slave gave away a masked Confederate artillery piece; another, described as a "Negro servant of an officer of the Forty-sixth Ohio," was captured by the Confederates and then escaped. He brought back intelligence, most of it wrong, about Confederate movements inside the town. A surgeon in the 72nd Ohio wrote to his wife, "Frequently runaway darkies come into our lines, but they seldom know much of importance." The Confederates' retribution for these actions could be cruel, as in the case of one Louisiana soldier who remembered a "black scoundrel" passing through their lines and giving away their position. Union artillery soon opened on them "with a precision of range conclusively showing that they were not shooting at random." The Confederate soldier went on to say, "Could the men have caught the dark hued rascal, there would have been a case of lynch-law, as their exasperation was very great."[34]

As bad as it was, the citizens of the Corinth area had no idea what was about to happen to them. If they thought picking up and moving away or living between two armies was bad, they were in for more trouble as May waned. If they thought the term *trapped* was wearisome, they would soon come to understand the mentality of another word that was even worse: *occupation*.

5

"A Constant Succession of Battles on a Small Scale"

By mid-May 1862, the Federal war effort seemed to be going nowhere. George McClellan's huge army on the peninsula of Virginia was stalled in front of Richmond, and Henry Halleck's comparable army was stalled in front of Corinth. Yet the lack of major movement did not translate into a lack of fighting. Skirmishing was rampant at Corinth as well as on the peninsula, and at times it reached fevered proportions. One Federal in front of Corinth wrote home that there was just skirmishing "enough to keep up the interest." As another described it, "The fight became verry warm the balls flying thick over our heads." This particular soldier went on to relate a poor decision he made and "how near I came to getting my napper taken (as the boys term it)." He wrote: "During the day I had thot there was a mullberry tree out on the road about a ¼ mile from wher we were laying so I shouldered my canteen as though I was going after water went out to the tree to get some berries. I had got up on the tree and was picking berries verry nice when bang went a gun & whiz came a bullet about a foot over my head cutting off the leaves and limbs." He added, "You may guess how soon I got down out of there. I soon had enough berries."[1]

Water was frequently a cause of conflict. One Illinois soldier, Joseph Skipworth, told of the lack of civility among the Confederates confronting them. "The rebels refused to let our men get water from a creek close to their quarters," he wrote with obvious resentment. "So our men brought up two pieces of artillery, musketry, and cavalry, and they was glad enough to give up the creek."[2]

Skirmishing all the while, the Federals continually crept forward, making a little progress day by day toward the Confederate bastion. But it was excruciatingly slow.

Within this general advance, George Thomas's Army of the Tennessee saw the first concerted action in mid-May. After several minor moves forward, always attended by throwing up a line of breastworks, Thomas's divisions took part in an across-the-board advance by all three armies on May 16 and 17, according to one soldier's diary, "in battle line under heavy cannon fire." On the first day, William T. Sherman advanced toward the Mississippi state line almost to the Russell house, where he entrenched his position. One of his artillerymen proudly wrote home, "I believe we are at last in ~~Missipissi~~ Messsppi. I can't spell it right it would seem." The other divisions of the army likewise moved forward on his left, with some units crossing the upper reaches of Seven Mile Creek and confronting Confederate skirmishers along Bridge Creek. Heavy pickets went forward from the Union lines, and skirmishing erupted across the front. Thomas reported, "There was considerable skirmishing between our pickets and those of the enemy, our pickets cautiously but steadily advancing from day to day and always holding the ground they had gained."[3]

Although one correspondent described the siege as "a constant succession of battles on a small scale," some of the skirmishing took on larger-than-normal proportions. Thomas W. Sherman, on the army's left, encountered a Confederate force at the Bridge Creek crossing on May 17 but easily drove them away and secured the crossing. The major fight on Thomas's front came that same day when William T. Sherman advanced a portion of his division to the Russell house, which sat on Phillips Creek, to dislodge Brigadier General James R. Chalmers's Confederate brigade. Sherman had met with Halleck and Thomas on the night of May 16 and planned the operation to deprive the enemy of the cover the house provided.[4]

Sherman prepared carefully. One member of the 72nd Ohio wrote to his wife, "Gen. Sherman frequently comes over here and looks about to see how things are being managed." On this day, he planned to use overwhelming force to take the house and the ridge on which it sat. Sherman asked Hurlbut, whose division was next in line, to provide troops to come in on the road south of the house, while two of Sherman's own brigades went directly from his lines. Brigadier General James W. Denver had just returned to the army and taken over command of the brigade formerly headed by Colonel Ralph Buckland at Shiloh. Denver and his brigade of all Ohio units, the 48th, 53rd, 70th, and 72nd, were tasked with moving around the enemy's left flank on a connecting road, while Brigadier General Morgan L. Smith's brigade, consisting of the 8th Missouri, 55th Illinois, and 54th and 57th Ohio, were to make the main attack down the road toward Russell's. Hurlbut's troops soon moved out, as did Denver with the 70th and 72nd Ohio. The main body moved forward behind skirmishers "jumping from tree to tree in admirable style," according to one soldier. Smith placed the 8th Missouri in the lead once they were past a small branch of Phillips Creek and headed for the Confederate lines. It was around 3:00 P.M. when the action began in earnest.[5]

Sherman described the Confederate resistance as "obstinate." Chalmers held his position, causing Smith to report that the enemy brigade was "very well commanded." Many of the Mississippians fired from the Russell house itself and its outbuildings, and the Union soldiers could hear "some of the officers entreating and ordering their men to hold their ground and not run from the damned Yankees." Chalmers came close to flanking the Missourians on the right, but Smith sent the 54th Ohio to secure that position. A similar threat came on the left, and companies of the 55th Illinois deployed to secure that flank. The main problem the Union forces encountered, however, was a lack of suitable terrain to deploy the artillery that accompanied each wing of the attack. But as soon as Smith's men moved forward far enough, a good place opened up and the cannoneers of Captain Edward Bouton's Battery I, 1st Illinois Artillery were deployed. They soon drove the Confederates back. A charge by the Missourians and Illinoisans of Smith's brigade sent Chalmers farther back, across Phillips Creek toward Corinth. One Ohioan noted, "After all their bragging they don't like to see the point of the bayonet coming at them any better than other people."[6]

In the midst of the attack, a Confederate officer still in the Russell house called for his men to return, telling them loudly that the "damned cowardly Yankees were running." Lieutenant Colonel James Peckham, commanding the 8th Missouri, described the result: "A ball from the well-aimed rifle of private R. M. Snyder, Company G, who was within 50 yards, sped its way to the head of the rebel, and deprived him forever of his command." After driving the Confederates away, Smith pursued them for several hundred yards across the creek but then halted and left a strong force to hold the position while he recalled his brigade. One surgeon wrote to his wife, "We followed the rebels a mile, and slept on the ground they had abandoned." The men left at Russell's spent a frightful night, worrying that they would be overrun before securing the position with entrenchments. They held on, though, and over the next few days, Sherman's men erected "a very excellent parapet," the ground around the Russell house being "one of great natural strength."[7]

Sherman was justly proud of his men's accomplishments, calling it "the prettiest little fight of the war." Smith alone had carried the position with eight companies of the Missouri regiment and two of the Illinois unit. But even then, there was a disagreement over who had actually taken the house. An Illinois captain turned up a canteen of whiskey he had obtained from the house, using it as evidence that the Illinois soldiers had won it. Smith "quietly sampled the contents of the canteen," one soldier wrote, and then settled the issue. He told the Missourians that the Illinois men had undoubtedly captured the house because, "if that [Missouri] regiment had got into the house first, nobody else would ever have found a canteen of whiskey there."[8]

For their part, the remainder of the brigade showed obvious disappointment, one soldier lamenting that "they could not become hotly engaged." A similar thought ran through Denver's command. He arrived on the flank just as the affair was ending and had to struggle to keep his men from firing on Smith's troops, thinking they were the enemy. Hurlbut's troops likewise played no major role. If the resistance had been greater, however, the two flanking columns certainly would have come in handy, as Sherman had prepared to close in on the house from three directions. Still, casualties were fairly high for a skirmish lasting less than two hours. Smith's brigade lost ten killed and thirty-one wounded, mostly from the 8th Missouri and 55th Illinois. Chalmers made no report, but Federal officers counted as many as twelve bodies left on the field, among them a captain and two lieutenants. Smith took only one prisoner. One Federal officer summed up the result, stating that the Confederates had "left some guns and some blood behind them at different places."[9]

The Army of the Tennessee continued skirmishing with the Confederates over the next few days, one artilleryman noting that a "beautiful afternoon began with Cannon shells by the rebels, but soon we returned the fire with the same stuff which they sent us." With the Phillips Creek crossing secured near the Russell house, Sherman and the rest of the army made another advance on May 21, this time crossing Phillips Creek. The army took a position running southward from the Russell house (which they destroyed on May 24) along a dominant ridge overlooking a branch of Phillips Creek. Sherman, whose right was continually re-fused to guard against a flank attack, held the right; Hurlbut, Davies, McKean, and T. W. Sherman continued the line southward until it reached Buell's forces, which had moved southward to close up the gap between himself and Pope. Skirmishing occurred as the divisions moved forward, with Davies uncovering an entire Confederate brigade across Phillips Creek. A few shots from the division's artillery sent the enemy back toward the town's entrenchments.[10]

While Thomas drew ever closer to Corinth, posting his May 21 line overlooking the Phillips Creek branches, Buell likewise moved forward after several days of intermittent skirmishing. So little movement took place prior to May 17, however, that division commander Wood even took the opportunity to drill his men: "During the occupation of this camp several lessons were given in the division drill, more especially in those tactical movements most likely, in all probability, to be made in actual conflict." The men were obviously not as enthused about the project as General Wood was. Other commanders did the same, with numerous soldiers' accounts relating various incidents. One drill in the Army of the Tennessee's Second Division even brought out General Davies, who, one soldier wrote, wore "a chapeau, epaulets and gorgeous uniform in full regulation style, making the volunteer officers in their fatigue, service suits look cheap." He added, "That was the first and last time we saw such finery." The 57th Illinois drilled so much during the siege that its regimental historian recorded, "We will not soon forget the cotton fields of Mississippi." On another occasion, Bull Nelson took the opportunity to draw his division up in a hollow square and present the 24th Ohio with a new flag labeled "Shiloh."[11]

When the time came to advance, Buell and Pope personally reconnoitered the ground across Seven Mile Creek together. Buell then moved his army forward methodically on May 17, skirmishing as he went. Wood's division took up a new line at the Driver house, with Nelson on his left and Crittenden on Nelson's left near a log church, connecting with Pope to the south. McCook remained in reserve. All the frontline divisions erected a line of earthworks. One of McCook's reserve soldiers knew a good thing when he saw it, writing home, "We are laying about in the woods and in the tents doing nothing. This is what I like about the Reserve. For I don't think it is the best of fun in throwing up intrenchments especially on such hot days as we are having down here." The next day, Buell moved forward again, this time to the widow Serratt's house overlooking Bridge Creek. A new line of entrenchments, or "ditches," as the soldiers referred to them, was dug. General Wood reported that his men dug "a continuous line of intrenchments, consisting of an epaulement, with the ditch inside." The men also placed a line of abatis to the front. Despite the breastworks, Confederate skirmishers still harassed the troops. Wood described how "the slightest exposure of the person was sure to be followed by the sharp crack of the rifle." One sharpshooter in particular caused damage on Crittenden's front. A brigade commander, Colonel Samuel Beatty, reported, "One of the enemy having climbed a tree, caused much annoyance for some time, but was finally shot and seen to fall heavily to the ground." A similar incident took place elsewhere, with the killer remarking to his son, "Old Butternut come down a dead man and we had a good jollification over it." Cannonading was also common, with one Federal describing an artillery duel as "very exciting and amusing. Viewed the affair with as much . . . interest as we are accustomed to look upon a horse-race." He also mentioned that Scott, the assistant secretary of war, "amused us all while he witnessed the encounter."[12]

Other soldiers had personal issues at the time. One pitiful Confederate told of being on the main line when he received a letter informing him of his daughter's death. "We were expecting an attack from the Yankees every moment," he wrote, but "I am glad they did not come — I was no longer a man — Completely unnerved, I was a child, yes almost an infant in feeling and there I fear I could not have done my duty." A Union counterpart similarly wrote of receiving the sad news that his mother had died: "The news came with stunning effect on me for I did not know that Mother was sick." On a lighter note, members of the 50th Illinois got caught by a Confederate advance while they were out cleaning in front of their camps. In the hurry to get back to their weapons, one lieutenant's belt got caught in a shrub bush, and the entangeld officer yelled at his company, "Halt and hold this hill at all hazards." On another occasion, famed Confederate cavalryman Nathan Bedford Forrest participated in a patrol during which he scouted the front and somehow managed to get behind some forward Federals. When he made his appearance, the obviously frightened Union soldiers hastily made their way back toward their lines. Forrest remembered, "I Suceded in gaining thir rear . . . they wair not looking for me I taken them by surprise they run like Suns of Biches."[13]

The major skirmish on Buell's front occurred on May 21 when a brigade of Nelson's division, commanded by Colonel Thomas D. Sedgewick, made a reconnaissance toward Bridge Creek and a large, round hill that stood between the creek and the widow Serratt's house. The impatient Nelson wanted to move forward, but he could not do so unless Wood's division on his right cleared the hill. "General Nelson bet him a barrel of whiskey," one soldier remembered, that he could clear the hill and then sent Sedgewick to do so. Sedgewick led his brigade of mostly Kentuckians in the 1st, 2nd, and 20th Regiments, along with the 31st Indiana, an artillery battery, and a cavalry detachment, past the Driver house and toward the hill. Just past the widow's house, Sedgewick's skirmishers became so heavily engaged that he had to deploy additional men just to maintain his line. When the Confederates threatened to turn his left flank, Sedgewick had to send more men into line, and he eventually deployed his entire brigade. Despite opening up with artillery on the Confederates, Sedgewick reported that the enemy's "fire seemed to increase instead of diminishing," and he later stated that after nearly an hour's firefight, "the result of the contest seemed doubtful."[14]

Fortunately for Sedgewick, another artillery battery was able to enfilade the Confederate line, and he moved his men forward under that cover. The fighting raged all the way to Bridge Creek, where Sedgewick crossed carefully, being concerned that the enemy was "endeavoring to draw us farther into the woods." With his orders fulfilled, Sedgewick wisely stopped the advance west of the creek and positioned the 31st Indiana to hold the ground until dark. The brigade had lost twenty-six men wounded, three of them mortally. A later examination of the area found thirty-five "newly-made graves," leading Sedgewick to believe he had bested the enemy in the two-hour fight. A soldier remembered that the skirmish "was really none of our fight"; it had been precipitated by Nelson. To make up for his haste, Nelson sent the brigade the whiskey he had promised Wood in the bet.[15]

The fighting during mid-May was not limited to engagements with the enemy; a breach also developed between Buell and his commander. Halleck was not satisfied with the pace of Buell's May 17 advance and wrote, "I do not understand the reason for the delay." Buell thought it was up to him and Pope to mutually work out the best time to move, but Halleck insisted he was "entirely mistaken." The delay, Halleck scolded, "deranges my plans." He later criticized Buell again, stating, "Your not moving this morning, as agreed upon, has caused great embarrassment," and he added that he might have to recall Sherman from the Russell house because Thomas's wing was isolated due to the lack of movement on Buell's part. According to one of Buell's staff officers, the two generals also had words face-to-face over the matter, Buell griping to Halleck, "I do not think there is any man who can rebuke me." Halleck did not contain his scalding complaints about Buell to the man himself; he voiced his disfavor with Buell throughout the army. To Sherman, Halleck wrote, "General Buell, without reasonable excuse, has failed to occupy the position assigned to him yesterday. You will therefore use your own discretion about holding Russell's." To Pope, he wrote, "Are you in position? General Buell's delay is very embarrassing." Pope responded, "I regret the delay in this movement, but desire to be acquitted of the fault of any part of it."[16]

Halleck continued the scolding the next day, writing to Buell: "I have observed to-day that my instructions have not been carried out in two respects. First. Your army corps does not occupy the position assigned to it. Your right was directed to occupy Driver's and hold the road at that place. As you did not take that position yesterday, General Thomas was obliged to secure it. He will be directed to move to the right at 10 A.M. to-morrow, and it is expected that you will occupy this place at that hour. Second. In making the advance all the army corps were directed to intrench themselves. . . . I find intrenchments on the right and left wings, but none on the center." Buell responded that he was under the impression he could use his own judgment and that he was unaware of any orders to entrench. Halleck let it rest, but his faith in Buell had been shaken. The skittish commander later made it plain to Buell: "I therefore wish the line from Farmington to Russell's made as secure as possible, so that we can proceed to press the enemy in front."[17]

With the tempest going on to his right, Pope's Army of the Mississippi likewise moved forward after the lull at Farmington, but only "by degrees every day," as one soldier declared. Pope sent frequent cavalry scouts southward toward the Memphis and Charleston Railroad, "mak[ing] all the fuss and demonstration you can to make the enemy believe you are about to attack him." The ruse generally worked. One Confederate even declared that the enemy was operating west of Corinth early in the siege, and several Federals wrote that they nearly had Corinth surrounded. The cavalry raids normally netted little real action, although at least one trooper found the terrain more difficult than the enemy. "My confounded horse fell down with me in a creek the other day," he wrote, "threw me out on the bank in a bunch of blackberry bushes and then crawled out over me, stepped on my foot in the melee by way of showing sympathy, I suppose. It don't hurt my appetite any and hasn't put me off duty." Others had horse trouble as well, such as Colonel George Boomer of the 26th Missouri in Hamilton's division. Generally regarded as having the best horse in the army, Boomer lost the animal when he loaned it to his chaplain to visit the sick in the rear. Apparently, a Confederate general had been eyeing the horse for a while and sent a man to capture it. The Confederate officer later sent Boomer a note of thanks for the horse.[18]

After Pope's personal reconnaissance with Buell, all three of his divisions moved forward on May 17 to Farmington itself. Paine was on the right, connecting with Buell; Stanley was in the center at Farmington itself; and Hamilton was on the left, with his flank re-fused to guard against another flank attack like that which was supposed to take place on May 9. Obviously cautious after their May 9 surprise, the divisions threw up substantial earthworks and utilized a system of signals: one shot to warn of approaching danger, and two shots to notify regiments to sound the long roll. To add to the security, one officer reported that Paine's division "encamped in double lines, and threw up strong earthworks in front of both lines." Stanley reported, "These trenches were made to conform with the nature of the ground, following the crest of the ridges and provided with such flanking arrangements as could be improvised by the eye. They consisted of a single ditch and parapet in the form of a parallel, though constructed with less work, and only designed to cover our infantry against the projectiles of the enemy." One lieutenant gave more detail, writing home that "our Earth Works are made of *Sand bags*." One private recalled a different issue: "Our regiment's line ran through a grave yard; we did not like the ghastly idea of digging among the graves, but an invading army has no respect for the rights of property or person, alive or dead. The ditch however was dug broader than usual, and shallow enough to not disturb the denisons of the silent city."[19]

From this position at Farmington taken on May 17, the men could hear Sherman's action at the Russell house. Several forays went forward, reconnoitering Pope's front toward Bridge Creek. On the night of May 20, Colonel William H. Worthington of Hamilton's division was killed by friendly fire. "His fate throws a gloom not only on the Third Division, but the whole Army of the Mississippi," Hamilton reported. In another reconnaissance, Paine received the wrath of Pope, who scolded, "The movement of the First Division of this army this morning was entirely unauthorized. Such movements tend to dispirit and harass the troops, and must result in the demoralization of the command." Pope reminded his commanders that no moves were to take place without written orders or oral authorization from one of Pope's staff officers. On yet another occasion, according to a 10th Illinois soldier, both sides' skirmishers got mixed up in the dark, resulting in a small body of Confederates moving between the Union skirmishers and the main army. They were quickly surrounded and captured.[20]

The constant skirmishing kept Halleck moving toward Corinth, however. But he obviously still had concerns. He had to feed and control his huge armies, and every step toward Corinth lengthened his already taxed supply lines back to Pittsburg and Hamburg Landings. Eventually, he would come to the Confederate fortifications, and who knew what that might bring. Additionally, he continually worried about his flanks—Sherman on the right, and Pope on the left. As it turned out, Sherman had his situation well in hand. Pope no longer had Chambers and Seven Mile Creeks to shield him on his left, however, and Beauregard had plans to test him once again.

While the Confederates battled Thomas's and Buell's advances, they saved their biggest effort for Pope. On May 20, Beauregard saw another opportunity to destroy part of the Federal army, and he set into motion a plan similar to the one he had used on May 9. This time, however, Beauregard involved the entire army. He could only hope the results would be better this time around.

By the third full week of May, P. G. T. Beauregard knew something had to be done to stop the juggernaut of advancing Federal forces. Their slow pace did little to alleviate his concern; in fact, the more careful Halleck was in advancing, the less opportunity Beauregard had to exploit another mistake, as he had tried to do on May 9 at Farmington. The Confederates in the ranks were tiring, having been in full force in the trenches for days in response to the May 17 general advance by Halleck's armies. By May 20, Beauregard began formulating firm plans to attack Halleck and try to even the odds.[21]

Beauregard had to do something, because life in the Confederate trenches had become nearly unbearable. Illness kept almost half the army on the sick list. Beauregard later blamed the massive sickness on a lack of good water, labeling the area around Corinth "badly supplied with water for a large force." Earlier in May, rains had provided at least some fresh water, but now everything was scorchingly hot. One soldier remembered, "Almost the whole army attended the sick call every morning. All the water courses went dry, and we used water out of filthy pools." Another observer recalled that "the soil is as easily affected by the drought as by rains, and the result is that at the present time the clay is baked perfectly solid, and the ground filled with fissures." Another noted that it was so hot that "a man can hardly get enough of the rarified stuff they call air here to fill his lungs." What chagrined Beauregard most, however, was the lack of good food. He described the fare as "not fit to eat" and laid the blame at the door of the Confederate commissary in Richmond. A captured Confederate officer confirmed that there was nothing but "rye coffee and horsebeef" in Corinth. The lack of vegetables and fruit caused problems, and Beauregard even noted scurvy among his troops. A detailed study of the sickness at Corinth by staff officers concluded that "bad food, neglect of police duty, inaction, and labor, and especially the water insufficient, and charged with magnesia and rotten limestone, had produced obstinate types of diarrhea and typhoid fever." No wonder half the army was on the sick list and morale was low.[22]

Late in May, Beauregard tried to boost the morale of his soldiers. He received word of Benjamin Butler's famous declaration that any New Orleans woman who insulted Federal soldiers would be treated as "a woman of the town plying her avocation." He distributed it to the men, calling Butler the "Haynau of the North." One soldier remembered, "The infamous New Orleans Order of Gen. Butler was read at all dress Parades to the whole Army." A Mississippian wrote home, "I think few prisoners will be taken here as, if that is their game, . . . termination will be the best way of working on their feelings." Though not going that far, Beauregard called on his soldiers to rise to the occasion and "drive back from our soil these infamous invaders."[23]

But the minor skirmishing and sharpshooting were doing the Confederates little good, and Beauregard knew he had to think bigger. He soon envisioned an attack strikingly similar to that of May 9, with Van Dorn again marching around the Union left flank. This time, however, the attack was to unfold into a general engagement, with the various Confederate corps attacking in echelon. Beauregard planned for Van Dorn to make the flank march, with support from Hardee. The attack would then proceed northward as Bragg, Polk, and Breckinridge took up the advance and rolled up the divisions of

Buell and Thomas. It would not be simple, however; Polk and Breckinridge would have to move their commands from the north and northwestern sides of Corinth, which would leave those areas unguarded. Van Dorn and Hardee also had a long route to cover, and success would depend on them moving into their assigned positions on time—something that had not occurred on May 9. It would take finesse and clockwork, but if all went according to plan, Beauregard envisioned a great victory.[24]

The Creole set the day of the attack as May 21. Obviously, Van Dorn had the farthest to travel, and having learned from the debacle on May 9, he set out to clear his path and get into position early. In particular, this new plan involved Van Dorn's divisions negotiating Clear Creek, which was not as large or as daunting as Seven Mile Creek but still posed problems. Van Dorn, wary of starting so soon, informed Beauregard that he would like to delay the attack, at least until May 22. "It is dark and rainy," Van Dorn wrote on May 20, "but the movement is within possibility." He informed Beauregard of his work to "reopen the crossing of Clear Creek" but then stated, "If it is not of the greatest importance, . . . I must say that the promises are not so bright as they would probably be by starting to-morrow evening. It is extremely dark and will rain heavily, I think. Men will not be cheerful, and many will remain, under plea of sickness, who would otherwise go." Hardee likewise counseled caution, telling Beauregard, "Much of the route has not been examined." Because of such hesitation, Beauregard wisely rescheduled the attack for the next day, "on account of the weather." Hardee wrote to Beauregard, "I am pleased the movement was deferred."[25]

Beauregard then sent out detailed instructions for his corps to move into position on the evening of May 21 and be ready to attack early the next day. He placed Colonel Daniel W. Adams in charge of the "invalids," who were to man Corinth's earthworks once all the units had marched out of the lines. Beauregard specifically admonished Van Dorn, after the failure on May 9, to "make ample allowance for delays before getting into position." The troops were issued three days' rations, with two more uncooked. The medical department issued instructions that all nonseriously wounded soldiers should be sent back to their original camps for treatment, while all seriously wounded men should be treated on the field and sent to the medical headquarters. A Kentuckian in Breckinridge's corps remembered the preparation: "It seemed a fight to the finish was at hand & from the preparation made by the surgeons for the care of the wounded we felt that ere the sun went down many a scene of carnage would be witnessed." Another remembered that Breckinridge addressed his old Kentucky brigade, telling them, "Boys I shall try to be with you men to-day."[26]

On the late afternoon of May 21, Confederate units began to file out of the Corinth earthworks to deploy in their attack positions. Van Dorn and Hardee marched out of Corinth toward the Clear Creek area to the southeast. Bragg moved his men forward out of the eastern trenches and deployed his two divisions just west of Bridge Creek. It was the vanguard of this movement that led to the lively skirmish with Sedgewick's brigade at the widow Serratt's that afternoon. Polk advanced from his position north of Corinth to a point in between the Mobile and Ohio Railroad and the Purdy road, and Breckinridge advanced on his left with a re-fused line to cover the northern approaches to Corinth and the army's left flank. Officers issued directives to their commands; Bragg, for instance, told his men not to fire randomly, not to stop and plunder, to leave prisoners for later capture, and not to place too much importance on enemy artillery. "We lose more men by retreating from it," the old Mexican War artillery officer surprisingly admonished, "than it would cost to charge and capture it, and we rely too much on our batteries to drive off imaginary foes from concealed places. Let our infantry press on and carry destruction before it and we shall suffer less and achieve more."[27]

Unfortunately, problems quickly developed for the Confederates during the long night of May 21, mainly due to the muddy roads caused by the recent storms that moved through the area. An exhausted Hardee was up by 2:00 A.M. on May 22, and things were clearly not going according to plan. He informed Beauregard at 2:30 A.M., "The road is blocked up with troops, wagons, and artillery." He added that many generals were missing due to sickness, and that the 3:00 A.M. start time for the march would not be possible. Hardee was convinced he would not be in position to attack until six hours later, around 9:00 A.M. One common soldier summed it up in a letter to his father: "We were marched out to attack the enemy but as the roads were almost impassable our troops were delayed several hours." Beauregard thus had to make some quick adjustments. He notified Bragg, Polk, and Breckinridge of the delay and advised them to try to cover their fronts with pickets and skirmishers so the enemy would not detect their presence. Polk and Breckinridge were having difficulties of their own, however. Breckinridge found that the area between the railroad and Purdy road was too small for his command, and Polk notified Beauregard that they were adjusting.[28]

Meanwhile, Van Dorn was trudging along. He stopped at 8:00 A.M. on May 22 and informed Beauregard: "I am now on the cross-roads leading to Dickey's Mill and about the intersection of the Burnsville road. I have been delayed by bad management and stupidity of officers, unexpected defiles, &c., and I am sick with disappointment and chagrin, but will push the enemy when I do reach our position. I feel like a wolf and will fight Pope like one. Have patience with me; you will hear my guns soon." Beauregard's reaction to Van Dorn's note is not known, but he was probably sicker with disappointment and chagrin than Van Dorn was. Nevertheless, he penned a hurried reply to the general, telling him, "We are all ready here." He also asked Van Dorn to notify Bragg when he started his attack: "My fear is we may not hear your guns well enough." He also admonished him not to fire on Bragg's troops, which would be coming in from the west.[29]

For the next several hours, Beauregard and Bragg waited, hoping to hear the report of Van Dorn's guns or, better yet, to receive a message from him saying that he had started his attack. Polk and Breckinridge waited north of town. Noon came, and no attack. Then, in the early afternoon, Beauregard received a short note that said simply: "General Beauregard: I have written. Cannot attack, and am retiring. E. Van D." A shaken Beauregard had to gather his wits quickly and get his now vulnerable army back to its entrenchments. He hastily composed a note to his corps commanders. To Polk he addressed a sharp note at 2:00 P.M. that read in its entirety: "Get your troops and those of General Breckinridge back into their former positions in camp."[30]

Beauregard later received a communication from Van Dorn dated noon on May 22. The contents probably made Beauregard seethe with anger. "It pains me to say," Van Dorn reported, "that I have, after consultation with Generals Hardee and Price, determined to return to my intrenchments. I have found unexpected difficulties, topographical and otherwise, and I have been delayed until this hour, and yet not in position. It is too late to begin a general engagement, and I cannot wait to hear from you to get orders. I have therefore determined to act myself and return. I will explain more fully when I see you." Van Dorn wrote again later, saying, "General, don't be too much disappointed with me, you can't imagine what I have had to contend with." Once again, Beauregard's carefully laid plans had fallen through on Van Dorn's watch. And once again, Van Dorn blamed everyone but himself. One Confederate colonel, S. M. Meek, summed up the feeling in a letter to his wife: "Better luck next time."[31]

The rank and file of the Union armies were probably ignorant of the May 22 movement. Higher-level commanders soon realized the magnitude of the aborted attack, however. One division commander described deserters who told him that 70,000 Confederates had marched out of the earthworks, on the attack. Many higher-echelon Federals reported odd happenings on May 21 and 22 and quickly surmised what was going on. Thomas, on the right flank, reported on May 21 that the Confederates seemed to be up to some kind of deployment outside the Confederate works—obviously, deployment for the attack that was to commence the next day. "Our pickets reported that there appeared to be great commotion in Corinth," Thomas stated, "and there was every indication that the enemy would attack the right wing in force." Thomas later erroneously heard from Confederate deserters that "Bragg and Van Dorn were to have attacked . . . , but found on sending their scouts forward that we already held the position they intended to have taken up; consequently they withdrew."[32]

Hamilton, who would have borne the brunt of the attack on the extreme left, also reported increased activity. "The troops were thrown into the intrenchments on the report of Capt. Thomas H. Botham, Third Michigan Cavalry, that the enemy was advancing in strong force," he reported. Hamilton also said his extended pickets had been driven in for some distance, obviously by Confederate skirmishers shielding the main Confederate attack force from the Union pickets. Hamilton later claimed to have been told by citizens that as many as 40,000 Confederates had been poised to attack, "but finding it [Hamilton's division] so strongly posted and the troops so vigilant, they marched down the hill and then marched up again, without attempting to make any attack." Although the sight of a re-fused Federal flank could have entered into Confederate planning, it is highly unlikely that Hamilton scared off the entire Confederate army.[33]

Yet the realization of the aborted attack led to another slowdown in the Federal advance. Over the greater part of the next week, the Federals held their positions in the forward entrenchments, waiting to see if another attack was coming. They even began to solidify their positions, bringing up reserve units and placing them on the front lines despite rain on May 23. They were getting close to Corinth and a caged enemy, but the Union commanders did not know how the Confederates might respond, so they prepared for every eventuality.[34]

Although small-scale skirmishing took place along the lines, only a few minor engagements erupted over the next week, prompting one Corinth citizen, Walter Overton, to write in his diary on May 24: "I have heard nothing from the army. I don't know whether they are doing anything or not. All seems as quiet as if there were not an enemy in 100 miles of here." Union diaries and letters mention numerous noncombat activities such as drill, pay, and "whiskey rations." Nevertheless, on May 24—ironically, the same day Overton reported no activity—Stanley made a foray forward of his lines. Stanley reported to Pope that the Confederate skirmishers on his front had become "exceedingly annoying and insolent." The division commander thus sent Colonel Joseph Mower with five companies of his regiment (the 11th Missouri) and five companies of the 39th Ohio, along with an artillery battery, to clean out the nest in front of the Union lines. Stanley accompanied Mower and even encountered the enemy in an open field. "Coming out of the woods with the members of my staff," Stanley wrote, "I found myself within a few hundred yards of their front, but, I suppose thinking us their officers, they made no attempt to molest us." Stanley returned and sent Mower forward with his Missourians and a section of artillery, and the combined effort "started them scampering in all directions." For good measure, Stanley had the artillery throw a dozen shells into Corinth. He described the affair as "a very pretty little exploit."[35]

There was minor skirmishing on Buell's front as well. On May 27, McCook's reserve division of Buell's army moved forward toward widow Serratt's house and skirmished with the enemy near Bridge Creek. McCook deployed two brigades in his front line, but the Confederate resistance on his right was so strong that he had to bring up his reserve brigade to support that flank. With so much firepower, McCook succeeded in driving the Confederates across the creek, and his skirmishers followed the enemy all the way to within a few hundred yards of their entrenchments. McCook ordered them to halt but to hold their position.[36]

Given the aborted Confederate attacks of May 9 and 22 on Pope's left flank, Hamilton, with his line re-fused to the east, took no chances. He continually sent out patrols and reconnoitering parties into the area to his south. On May 24, for example, he sent out the 5th Iowa and a portion of the 4th Minnesota, along with artillery, to the Memphis and Charleston Railroad to the south. Hamilton happily noted that the patrol returned "without seeing any large body of the enemy." On May 26, another patrol consisting of the 10th Iowa and two companies of the 26th Missouri made their way to the Danville road and on toward Corinth. They encountered the Confederates in force at the entrenchments and had to retire, but the march eased Hamilton's fears about his flank.[37]

While these few patrols came and went, the Federals strengthened their lines for the possibility of a renewed attack. Thomas's Army of the Tennessee made preparations for part of McClernand's reserve corps to take a position in the front lines; the reserve of Buell's Army of the Ohio, McCook's division, took a position in front as well, on Serratt's Hill with other forward units. There was also an effort to take nearby McGee's Hill. The biggest reorganization took place on Pope's front, however. Another division of the Army of the Mississippi—the Fourth, commanded by Brigadier General Jefferson C. Davis—arrived at Hamburg Landing from Arkansas on May 25 and 26 and marched forward to take its position in the lines on May 27. With four divisions, Pope decided to divide his army into two wings. Major General William

S. Rosecrans, who had arrived at Pittsburg Landing on May 23, took command of Paine's and Stanley's divisions as the right wing, while Hamilton took over his division, now under Jacob Plummer, and Davis's division as the left wing. No sooner had Rosecrans taken command than his horse was shot out from under him on May 28.[38]

With almost every available man in the front lines, and certain that Beauregard had no more surprise attacks up his sleeve, Halleck regained his nerve and ordered another general advance on May 28. Major skirmishing erupted. One Federal wrote to his brother, "We advanced on double quick driving the rebel pickets in, in great haste and the rascals never made a stand until they run clear in to there entrenchments." An artilleryman noted in his diary, "The Rebels will either evacuate Corinth, or get ingloriously whipped."[39]

Pope's four divisions moved forward, with Rosecrans on the right and Hamilton on the left, again keeping a wary eye to the south for a flank attack. Given his fondness for climbing trees to look at the enemy, Pope scouted the area, causing Halleck to send an uncharacteristically jesting message: "General Pope up a tree / The Rebels for to see." Others did the same, one soldier writing in his diary, "The soldiers are climbing high trees and looking with spy glasses." Nevertheless, Stanley and Paine took position on the ridge east of Bridge Creek, throwing up heavy double lines of earthworks that ran diagonally away from the Corinth entrenchments. The lines fronted a large Confederate work south of the railroad, outside the main line of entrenchments. Stanley ordered his artillery to shell the area, whereupon the Confederates responded with their guns. "Engaged the enemy near Farmington, Miss., and one of the most terrific artillery duels that has been fought during the war ensued," remembered a member of the 11th Missouri in overstatement. Another noted that the bombardment "dun us little harm as they went two high and far over us without exploding." The Union infantry under Stanley was also involved in a small fight at the crossing of Bridge Creek, mainly battling Patrick Cleburne's Tennessee and Arkansas brigade. Hearing that the skirmishers had been driven in, Hardee sent Cleburne out the lower Farmington road, where he met Stanley around the Shelton house. "Suffice to say that the result was satisfactory to the Second Division," Stanley reported. Cleburne, who admitted some eighty to ninety casualties, blamed his problems on Colonel Robert D. Allison of the 24th Tennessee. Cleburne said that Allison had not moved forward as ordered, thus throwing off the rest of the advance. When Cleburne "upbraided Colonel Allison with his shameful dilatoriness," the colonel only muttered something about thick underbrush. Cleburne went on to say that he had found Allison "dismounted and with his uniform off." Because of the Confederates' problems, Stanley noted, "the lesson they received permitted our pickets to remain in peace." Illustrating the lopsidedness of the affair, one Confederate officer inquired of his Federal foes what kind of weapons they were using; he intimated that the Northerners had killed some of the Confederates at a range of 500 yards. Despite the theatrics, not all Federal units enjoyed the day. The 5th Minnesota broke during the fight.[40]

Buell also advanced on May 28, with the southern divisions of his army swinging from east to west on Wood's northern division, which moved very little. McCook moved back to Serratt's Hill and took firm control of it, providing, as Buell reported, "a commanding and very important position less than a thousand yards from the enemy's works." The Confederates contested McCook's position in heavy skirmishing but were unable to drive him off the hill. Nelson moved forward and took the upper Farmington road crossing of Bridge Creek from Alabama and Louisiana troops, with Sedgewick's brigade doing most of the fighting as the Confederates tried three times in vain to dislodge the Federals. Driving the enemy back, Sedgewick's men followed them with "a yell and a cheer" and cut off a company of the 21st Louisiana, capturing officers and privates. Despite three killed and twenty wounded, this encounter made the Federals "masters of the hard-earned bridge," one Federal recalled. Crittenden also moved forward, supporting Nelson in his advance. All divisions heavily entrenched their new positions. By the end of the day, Buell reported that his line extended "in a direct line two miles and two-thirds." A correspondent noted that the army had "worked itself up into the very teeth of the rebel works."[41]

Thomas's Army of the Tennessee also moved forward on May 28, at some points driving over Confederate picket lines with ease. The advance was so rapid in one area that a Confederate colonel who had been asleep when the ruckus started "came out of his tent rubbing his eyes and giving orders to our men, who were now rushing past him." Federal Colonel William Camm humorously said of his Confederate counterpart: "Seeing his mistake, he politely lifted his hat and exclaimed, 'Beg your pardon, gentlemen, I have made a mistake.'" Of course, he was taken into custody. William T. Sherman led the way on his part of the line. As Sherman moved south, the area north of Corinth became more of a concern, and part of McClernand's reserve moved forward on Sherman's right—specifically, John A. Logan's brigade of Brigadier General Henry M. Judah's division (formerly McClernand's). The reserve troops, generally occupying the works vacated in each forward movement, provided a vital service, securing the right flank of the armies as they moved forward; they also performed reconnaissance and made raids on the

Mobile and Ohio Railroad, much as Pope had done to the south. Now they were finally getting into the real action.[42]

The Confederates skirmished mainly with Thomas around a "double log building, standing on a high ridge." The Southerners had removed the chinking between the logs, leaving spaces to fire through. Sherman secretly deployed Denver's and Morgan L. Smith's brigades, supported by Logan's brigade of Judah's division and James C. Veatch's brigade of Hurlbut's division. He ordered his artillery to "demolish the house or render it decidedly uncomfortable to its occupants." The infantry then rushed the line so quickly that the Confederates could hardly get off a volley. Generals Grant and Thomas were on the scene watching, and Thomas recalled that the resistance to this move was "more determined . . . on the part of the enemy than any we had previously made." The Confederates later made a surprising advance, prompting Sherman's artillery commander, Ezra Taylor, to ask the general, "Hadn't I better give them some shells left oblique?" Sherman nervously replied, "Yes, yes—quick, quick." The Confederate assault did not amount to much, and by the end of the day, Thomas's lines were within a few hundred yards of Corinth's northern works, particularly a large salient that sat on the Mobile and Ohio Railroad. Thomas's divisions entrenched their position and, as one soldier noted, listened to "the sounds of his [the enemy's] drums and sometimes of voices in command and the railroad cars arriving and departing at Corinth." One soldier remembered that they could even see the Confederate entrenchments "at some places."[43]

In contrast to the general advance of May 28, Thomas noted that there was "comparative quiet all along the front" the next day. One Federal colonel even reported the strange capture of enemy prisoners: "Soon after my pickets were posted, . . . two of the enemy walked leisurely across the bridge into our lines." The only minor skirmishing took place on Pope's front, including some artillery fire from the detached Confederate work on the railroad. One soldier described how a Federal shot cut the Confederate flagpole, "and thare flag bowed to the dust great cheering from our side." He also noted that the infantry had orders to storm the fort, but when the Confederates stopped firing at about the time the assault was to begin, it was canceled, Pope thinking the artillery had done away with the enemy guns. Later in the day, the Confederates opened up again, but it was too late to assault at that point.[44]

Thus, by May 28, Halleck had at last arrived in front of Corinth, his three armies stretching from the Memphis and Charleston Railroad east of Corinth to the Mobile and Ohio Railroad north of town. Most of the lines lay within a mile of the enemy earthworks. The lines were so close, in fact, that Union soldiers reported hearing "the rebel drums in their camps." Others could hear "the cars . . . in motion all night on the roads going south and west of Corinth, and we could hear the whistle." It had been a long time since Halleck's boast to the War Department that he would be at Corinth's doorstep on May 5. Still, he was there now.[45]

But the cautious Halleck was not yet ready to hurl his armies at Corinth's defenses. He had options. He could attack; he could maneuver around the south and west side of town and break Beauregard's supply lines; or, better yet, he could bombard Corinth into submission with his siege guns, which were gathering even then.

The effort needed to position the big weapons was astounding. One Illi- noisan reported that the guns needed "10 horses hitched to each one." One soldier told of the guns in Sherman's division being hauled by oxen, thus lead- ing to the nickname the "ox battery." Another soldier marveled at the sight of the big guns going into position: "they were the heaviest ordnance we had at that time, taking ten or fifteen yoke of oxen or twenty horses to pull them." One artilleryman wrote home that the army had "quite a number of heavy Siege Guns," but they were not necessarily needed at this close range—or what one soldier called within "bomb shot" of Corinth. A Union officer wrote to his wife that the lines were "so close that we could shell their encampments far beyond their entrenchments, over which our smallest guns could throw their missiles." Still, the big guns were there and were ready for use, along with what one soldier described as "eight mortars." Once in position and fir- ing, the guns were even more impressive. A Minnesota soldier described the result of the action: "They fired them all at once[;] they made a tremendous nois." Another commented that "one of the siege guns was let loose, which fairly shook the earth, farther than that no damage was done." Interestingly, several of the cannon emplaced amid the Union battle lines had helped repel the last Confederate attacks at Shiloh on April 6.[46]

With all that firepower, Halleck wisely decided not to attack. Instead, he prepared to wait out the Confederates in a siege. But Beauregard was a sly general himself and had different ideas.

6

"To the Last Extremity"

By late May 1862, P. G. T. Beauregard and his Confederates manning the Corinth entrenchments could not hold out much longer. They already suffered from bad water, and Halleck would soon be cutting their supply routes. Even then, Halleck's cavalry was making a raid into the Confederate rear, with Colonel Washington L. Elliott leading a small cavalry brigade in an effort to break the Mobile and Ohio Railroad at Booneville, twenty-two miles south of Corinth. Accompanied by the 2nd Iowa Cavalry and the 2nd Michigan Cavalry, commanded by Colonel Phil Sheridan, Elliott reached the town early on May 30 and at dawn destroyed the track, switches, and depot as well as a well-stocked train of twenty-six cars. Sheridan reported the damage was done with "alacrity," perhaps foreshadowing his later work in the Shenandoah Valley in 1864. He also noted that he captured the "personal baggage of General Leonidas Polk." Elliott's raid threw the Confederates into some confusion. One lowly soldier reported to his wife, "It is said the Yankee Cavalry are all over the Country behind us."[1]

Beauregard had a lot to think about in the latter part of May, even before Elliott's raid. Although the situation at Corinth was reaching crisis stage, he still commanded a vast department and carried on correspondence across his realm. He utilized the department's resources in instituting cavalry raids in Halleck's rear, hoping to force the Federals to withdraw some of their troops advancing against Corinth. He also had to deal with the loss of some of his officers. At the request of Arkansas officials, for example, Beauregard dispatched Thomas C. Hindman to take command in that state on May 26. That same day, he lost his inspector general of the army, Brigadier General Daniel M. Frost. During the siege, Samuel B. Maxey was under arrest, and Brigadier General Joseph L. Hogg died of dysentery on May 16; he passed away in a private residence and was buried near Corinth. Beauregard's main problem was Halleck, however, and not just on the battlefield. He and his Federal foe carried on a correspondence over paroled prisoners, whom Beauregard did not want to feed with his meager supplies. Occasionally, each side delivered paroled prisoners to the other. Former secretary of the interior Jacob Thompson delivered one mass of Union prisoners to the Federals at Farmington. The main concern was Halleck's effective soldiers, however, not prisoners. Beauregard knew full well that when Halleck opened with his siege guns, Corinth would be untenable. But to leave the earthworks and attack the Federals now would be suicidal. Evacuation was the only other option.[2]

Beauregard had been thinking about evacuation as early as May 9, when he instructed his commanders on what to do "in case we have to retire from this position." That retreat was contingent on a disaster at Farmington on May 9, however; it was not a general withdrawal by choice. A week and a half later, he began to think more of an evacuation and started to delicately mention the possibility of a future withdrawal to the War Department in Richmond. Beauregard knew he was not in favor with the commander in chief, Jefferson Davis, given his run-ins with the president during the first year of the war in Virginia. In fact, that was one of the many reasons Beauregard had been sent west to be second in command to Albert Sidney Johnston. The Creole knew that if he gave up Corinth now—without a major fight, no less—Davis would be unhappy; after all, Corinth was in Davis's native Mississippi. Thus Beauregard began to put out potential fires in his rear even before they flared up.[3]

In a subtle query sent to Richmond on May 19, Beauregard seemed to be supporting the idea of maintaining his position at all costs. "I deem it advisable to lay before the Department, in as few words as practicable, my reasons for still holding this position against a much stronger force of the enemy in my front, even at the risk of a defeat, instead of retiring into the interior of the country," he wrote. Then he couched possible evacuation by emphasizing a supposed controversy over which way to retreat—along the Mobile and Ohio Railroad south, or along the Memphis and Charleston Railroad westward. That way, Beauregard was not advocating evacuation so much as introducing the topic to Richmond officials. He ended with talk of holding Corinth "to the last extremity."[4]

Beauregard got what he wanted from the War Department in the form of a note from Robert E. Lee, no less. He assured Beauregard that the Confederacy had faith in him and then gave the Creole the sentence he needed for political cover: "Should, however, the superior numbers of the enemy force you back, the line of retreat indicated by you is considered the best." Beauregard had at least planted the thought of retreat in the minds of his superiors.[5]

By the time Lee's note arrived in Corinth, however, Beauregard and his commanders were already working on an evacuation. Although there is evidence that Beauregard was drawing up plans for the withdrawal even earlier, he first met with his generals to discuss the subject on May 25. The commanders of the four corps of the Army of the Mississippi (Polk, Bragg, Hardee, and Breckinridge) were all there, as well as Van Dorn and Price. After the meeting, Hardee went so far as to "reduce my views to writing." In a note written that night, he explored Beauregard's various options, quickly dismissing an attack on the enemy. "I am clearly of opinion that no attack should be made," Hardee wrote. "To attack him in his intrenchments now would probably inflict on us and the Confederacy a fatal blow. Neither the number nor instruction of our troops renders them equal to the task." He likewise dismissed the idea of waiting for Halleck to attack. In fact, the slow Halleck would bombard the city into submission before he attacked outright. The only other option was to evacuate, and Hardee advocated doing so as soon as possible. Once Halleck opened up with his siege guns, Hardee wrote, "it will be difficult to evacuate the place in good order." Beauregard agreed.[6]

Verbal orders went out to the commanders the next day, May 26, and were quickly followed by written orders. Beauregard called another meeting of the commanders, at which time he required each one to provide details of the movement from memory, for his own corps as well as everyone else's. Beauregard also issued instructions to his outlying garrisons at places such as Pocahontas and Chewalla west of Corinth and Bear Creek and the Eastport area east of town to fall back with the army when it evacuated.[7]

Beauregard's orders called for the evacuation to begin on the night of May 28 and to be completed by dawn on May 29. The baggage and provision trains were to be loaded and ready to depart by noon on May 28, and they were not to stop until they had crossed south of the Tuscumbia River. The ammunition and ambulance trains were to remain with their parent brigades longer, but they too would eventually move to the rear of the baggage trains south of the river. Once all the trains were safely across the Tuscumbia, the officers in charge were to open sealed orders telling them where to go.[8]

Once the trains were out of Corinth, the troops would begin to file out of the entrenchments. They were to deposit their baggage into the wagons by noon on May 28 and return quickly to the trenches, "as it may become necessary to take the offensive." One brigade of each corps was to move in front of the trenches in line of battle in case Halleck attacked. This movement caused the various skirmishes all along the line encountered by Cleburne and others on May 28. If Halleck demonstrated no resistance, the troops were to file out of the trenches at 3:00 on the morning of May 29. Hardee's corps would move along the main Danville road east of the Mobile and Ohio Railroad, across the Tuscumbia River, through Rienzi, and on to Baldwyn. Bragg's troops would depart Corinth to the southwest, moving to Kossuth and a crossing of the Tuscumbia River; from there, the corps would make its way to Baldwyn. Breckinridge and Polk would take the same route as Bragg to Kossuth but would follow different roads southward to Baldwyn.[9]

To keep the Federals from suspecting anything, the corps commanders were to keep "a sufficient number of drums from each brigade . . . to beat reveille at the usual hour, after which they can rejoin their commands." Once the infantry left, only cavalry pickets would remain in the trenches, where they would stay until all major bodies of the army had crossed the Tuscumbia. At that point, the chief of cavalry was to recall his troopers for the retreat. As the cavalrymen fell back, they were to destroy all bridges and roads. The army was then to concentrate at Baldwyn, where "the best defensive position will be taken . . . , due regard being had to a proper and sufficient supply of wood and water for the troops and horses."[10]

Van Dorn's army received much the same instructions, except his baggage trains were to leave by dawn on May 28 and his men were to march southward across Clear Creek, east of the Mobile and Ohio Railroad. The trans-Mississippians were not to stop at Baldwyn, like the rest, but were to make their way to Guntown. Otherwise, all other orders regarding trains and infantry, cavalry, and drummers were the same.[11]

It was a complex set of orders that the inexperienced Confederate army had to implement like clockwork, and there were doubters, given the problems just a portion of the army had experienced in keeping schedules on May 9 and 22. And the entire operation depended on getting the large amounts of stores, ammunition, and supplies out of Corinth prior to the evacuation. That would take time. The efficient organizer Braxton Bragg was in charge of removing all supplies from Corinth, and he had men loading trains and wagons throughout the day on May 28 in preparation for a dawn departure the next morning. But things were not going well. By early afternoon on May 28, Bragg informed Beauregard: "The prospect at the railroad is not encouraging. Things move very slowly—a want of management with the cars, as well as sick." He stated that the medical department was getting along better since a regular train had been augmented with a mail train for the sick and the nurses, but he could not see evacuating according to plan by dawn on May 29 "without abandoning arms, ammunition, baggage, &c., which we cannot afford to lose." Bragg told his commander that the operation should be delayed, even at his own personal expense: "My baggage is gone, but I am prepared to bivouac for one day in order to save what we can"—a noble offering from Bragg.[12]

Later that afternoon, Bragg had better news, stating that all the sick had departed and that the supplies were being taken south as fast as possible. "If we had cars all could be off by 12 to-night," he said. But the cars were not available. Therefore, Beauregard decided to delay the operation by one day, "considering," as he said, "that we have still so much yet to be removed." All the times and routes would remain the same, but the army would depart by dawn on May 30 instead of May 29. The wagon trains had already left, however, so Beauregard sent word to stop them wherever they were and start again the next day.[13]

Meanwhile, Bragg had many men working at the tracks: "A sufficient and permanent force of negro laborers was employed by the quartermaster's department for loading and unloading the cars at the railroad depot," one report noted. And work they did, through the night, loading trains and sending them off while waiting for more to arrive. But by the next morning, May 29, Bragg was becoming exasperated. The longer the evacuation was delayed, the better the chance the Federals would learn of it and do something to stop it. Bragg had to work hard and fast. The plan could not be delayed another day. With the Federals advancing to within a mile or less of the outer works on May 28, the situation seemed that much more critical.[14]

The stress was evident in Bragg's correspondence with Beauregard. "I have found it necessary to take charge here personally," Bragg wrote to his commander from the railroad depot at 11:30 A.M. on May 29. He said he could save the ammunition and the sick and possibly the hospital supplies, but much of the baggage would have to be destroyed. "I find [personal] trunks enough here to load all trains for a day," Bragg informed Beauregard; "they are being piled for burning, and great is the consternation." Bragg even had to form his guard to keep looters and presumably the owners of the trunks away. Apparently, more than just personal baggage was destroyed. Colonel J. B. G. Kennedy of the 21st Louisiana later reported that he lost "all my books and papers at the evacuation of Corinth." Several tents were also set on fire, but unfortunately, it was later learned they contained small arms. Still, Bragg reported that the main cause of the delay was a lack of trains: "there is great want of cars," he wrote, yet ended, "all is going on well . . . , nothing in our power will be left undone. It is the first time I have played chief quartermaster, but it is no difficult task." By that afternoon, however, Bragg was in a worse mood. "We are moving subsistence and quartermaster's stores as fast as trains can be had," he informed Beauregard, but fumed: "The chiefs of these departments have never been to the depot, and know not and seem to care not what goes on. I am working in the dark, but doing much." By later that afternoon, matters had gotten somewhat better again, and Bragg was working on getting Polk's subsistence on the trains, as well as the heavy guns from the defenses.[15]

Individual soldiers commented on Bragg's ill humor during the loading process. Eugene Falconnet described the chaos in his diary: "the whole town was crowded with men." On one occasion, several soldiers were ravaging the surplus officers' trunks piled in the mud near the depot. "Bragg happened to go to the Depot at that time," Falconnet wrote, and he wore "that terrible smile on his lips, which he has when he is mad." Soldiers described the smile as a "Tiger grin." Falconnet "saw a soldier pick up something from a trunk which was to be burnt up and he [Bragg] ordered immediately the sentinels to fire on the man." According to the shocked soldier, the balls missed the looter but "may have hit some innocent person somewhere else." He added that Bragg "caused the sentinels to fire several times in my presence."[16]

But Bragg's ill humor was well earned, as the situation around the railroad crossing and the depot was indeed a mess as afternoon turned into evening. The two railroads had been told to send all available trains and cars to Corinth, and they arrived to a stalled effort, especially around the depot and the crossing. Some trains went out north and east to the entrenchments, where they were loaded with army stores, but most arrived amidst the chaos at the depot platforms. Charles S. Williams, assistant superintendent of the Memphis and Charleston Railroad, was still irritated by the situation in mid-June, when he recorded his actions on that night: "empty trains were arriving constantly on the main track behind trains that were loaded or loading, and the side tracks, as well as the main track, so crowded that it was impossible to make up trains without stopping the process of loading, which was, under the circumstances, the most important of all other matters; hence the last train that came in must be loaded and be the first to go out. This will account, I hope satisfactorily, for so many trains being together and the trains not leaving as they were loaded." In addition, there was no time to argue about which cars belonged to which railroad, and several trains went "around the Y" to the other road. According to Williams, goods were sometimes loaded onto cars with no directions concerning where they were supposed to go—out westward toward Memphis, or southward toward Tupelo. Thus, many of the cars had to be switched. His railroad, in fact, was "frequently blocked up at the Mobile crossing by trains standing across." Once the track was cleared, the Memphis and Charleston workers began making up their trains, but it was well after midnight on May 30 before the heavy ordnance was loaded.[17]

Nerves grew raw. Bragg issued orders for sentinels to keep anyone without a pass away from the depot. When one lieutenant without a pass made his way there, Bragg's chief quartermaster, Colonel L. W. O'Bannon, "with loud curses ordered him to go to work loading the cars." The lieutenant refused, whereupon O'Bannon, one soldier wrote, "struck him, knocked him down and stamped and kicked him, and then had him put under guard." The stunned soldier reported, "Next morning that officer was shot by order of Genl. Bragg, without having a hearing."[18]

As Bragg fought the pile of trunks at the depot, Beauregard oversaw the evacuation throughout the day and into the night of May 29. He continually kept trains running out to the entrenchments north and east of town, and the soldiers cheered as each train appeared, hoping to trick the enemy into thinking reinforcements were arriving. Beauregard also had to tinker with his orders in the fluid situation. He approved Van Dorn's request to leave his position an hour early on the night of May 29 and admonished him to be sure to obstruct the roads as he went. He also changed the place of rendezvous from Baldwyn to Guntown, as scouts had reported that the latter was more defensible.[19]

Beauregard gave specific directions on when light batteries, heavy artillery, and other units should depart, and he moved up the timetable of the infantry's departure, telling his commanders to keep each corps' best brigade as a rear guard. He made sure campfires were maintained in the original lines to deceive the enemy, and he reminded the troops to continue cheering each time an empty train arrived in Corinth.[20]

Several other odd orders went out, such as an effort to render all wells in the vicinity useless. Obviously, Beauregard wanted to make conditions as difficult as possible when the enemy took over. He even ordered that the "artesian-well machinery" be removed. With regard to signal rockets, which one Federal reported "all eyes were directed to," the general also gave orders concerning when the rockets were to be used. One bit of odd war-fighting machinery concerned Beauregard most during the evacuation, however. The Confederates believed the enemy had some type of observation balloon. One of Beauregard's commanders decided it was a hoax, but the Creole expressed his concern that such a balloon could uncover all his plans for the surprise evacuation. "I am glad to hear of the sham balloon," he wrote. "I hope it is so, for I fear that more than their artillery at this moment." Later, he admonished his commanders to keep regular fires going during the night "on account of [the] balloon."[21]

There was indeed an odd object rising above the trees, but it was most likely one of the scouting towers Pope's men had constructed on his lines. Pope had graduated from climbing trees to building towers. On May 20, he informed Halleck, "I am building a lookout in front of my camp about 90 feet high, from which I can see into Corinth and note every movement of consequence. I can see the town now from the top of the trees." An engineer gave a better description: "a remarkable observatory [was] erected in a tall oak tree near Farmington, from the top of which a full view of the enemy at Corinth could be obtained; the height of the tree was increased by a framework of tall poles on which was built a platform." A colonel described a similar effort that included attaching a spar to a tall pine tree. He noted that it was built by "ship-builders and sailors" and that men on a "truck" were hauled up with a rope that ran through a pulley at the top. But it was awkward. "The tapering top mast bent with weight," the colonel noted.[22]

For once, a major Confederate evacuation went off like clockwork, once it began. Beauregard, who frequently produced complex and flamboyant plans, seemed at his best on May 29 and 30. The last trains left Corinth at around 4:30 A.M., with Williams, the Memphis and Charleston official, on the last train going west. The Confederate military superintendent of railroads, Colonel R. B. Hurt, was on the last train going south on the Mobile and Ohio, and he notified those guarding bridges south of town to fire their spans as he passed. It was a miraculous job of withdrawal, but the Confederates still left a large amount of items. One soldier who marched through commented on the "blankets, quilts, all kinds of bed fixings, tin plates, tin pans, cups, knives, forks, all kinds of clothing piled up for burning." Susan Gaston reported the next morning, "Across a vacant lot in front of an encampment could be seen a thousand articles cast off by the retreating party. Coats, haversacks, camp utensils, boxes of provisions and every description of camp equipage save ammunition. Whatever would lighten the soldier on a hasty march was here cast away. The sight was painful, the silence oppressive."[23]

The ingenuity of the Confederate soldier was not thwarted by the withdrawal. Before leaving the trenches, the men constructed "Quaker guns"—logs painted to resemble cannon—and put them in normal gun emplacements. One Federal approaching the works later remembered "a log painted black and set on a wagon . . . I suppose they thought they would scare us with it." Another described how his regiment was "confronted by a mammoth gun, that threatened to blow the Union clear over the north pole." Later, the Federals discovered it was a log painted to look like a columbiad. Yet another mentioned a "masked battery of logs." Straw dummies fitted with uniforms and bearing broad smiles manned the works, and one Federal wrote in his diary that the troops "examined their wooden guns and miniature men."[24]

The various Confederate commands left the trenches when ordered. One Confederate complained that "after being in line of battle for 48 hours and having some very brisk cannonading we took up our line of march." Colonel

Joseph Wheeler, commanding a brigade, remembered, "I silently marched the brigade to Corinth, and slowly marched toward the Tuscumbia River." Yet another wrote to his wife, "We marched all night—we have bin ever since then." Susan Gaston reported the passing of a column at Corona College: "A noise of passing crowds but not a word, in silence, in darkness, marching as with muffled feet our regiments went by. More than one time I rose from my sleepless couch pushed back the lattice and listened to the continued movement, so quiet, so strange. On on for hours, not a word of command heard, but on thousands went." But not all was quiet, especially as dawn neared. One soldier remembered, "The town was in a blaze of fire and the arsenal was roaring and popping and bellowing like pandemonium turned loose as we marched through Corinth." By that time, nothing but drummer boys and cavalry pickets remained to add wood to the fires that were supposedly cooking Confederate breakfasts. One Confederate in the 50th Alabama recorded in his diary that they left "2 of our company deployed as skirmishers." The musicians made their way up and down the lines sounding different orders on their drums. The Confederates spared nothing; Beauregard even used rockets as guides and ordered all direction boards on roads south of Corinth removed.[25]

As dawn approached on May 30, the Confederate army was quietly slipping away from Corinth, marching to the south and southwest. "We bade farewell to Corinth," one Confederate wrote. "Its history was black and dark and damning. No little speck of green oasis ever enlivened the dark recesses of our memory while at this place. It's a desert that lives only in bitter memories. It was but one vast graveyard that entombed the life and spirit of once brave and chivalrous men. We left it to the tender mercies of the Yankees without one tear of sorrow or regret, and bade it farewell forever." Once it reached the Tuscumbia River, some six miles south of Corinth, Beauregard's army was in relative safety. Yet the Confederates had to be on guard for a pursuit and for the Union cavalry raid that was even then going on south of Corinth.[26]

John Pope watched the signs with concern throughout the night of May 29 and convinced himself that the Confederates were mustering another attack on his position. This was certainly not the first time he and Scott had jumped to conclusions; he had often reported in previous weeks that the enemy was either attacking him or evacuating Corinth. Throughout the month of May, many common soldiers' letters and diaries also mentioned the frequent rumors that Corinth had been evacuated. "We are in just such a state of suspense at this time," one Federal wrote as early as May 8, "as to whether Corinth is evacuated or not that I scarsely know what, or how to write." Federal commanders reported hearing many trains coming and going in Corinth for several days, and the combined effect convinced Halleck as well. The Confederates had also started rumors of a grand offensive, and some of these leaked into Union lines, where they were reinforced by fake deserters Beauregard had sent out. And then there were the empty trains that, after evacuating the vast stores from Corinth, came back into town blowing their whistles while the troops cheered, giving any listening Federal the idea that reinforcements had arrived. Taking in all this evidence, Pope sent word to Halleck before dawn that he was surely about to be attacked in force.[27]

But Beauregard had pulled off a complete hoax. One common Federal soldier summed up the reaction when he wrote home the next day: "I reily believe that all our leaders are just as much taken aback as we are." Indeed, while the Confederates marched south, the Federals were bracing for the attack they had convinced themselves was coming at dawn. William Rosecrans reported "remarkable activity in the rebel camp," with trains "running from the north and west and passing down toward our left." David Stanley said that "the continued running of cars from Corinth to our left and the beating of drums and moving of troops in the same direction induced me to report to the general that he must expect the whole weight of their attack to fall early upon our left." Pope reported the massive buildup on his front up the chain to Halleck. "I have no doubt, from all appearances, that I shall be attacked in heavy force at daylight," Pope warned Halleck at 1:20 A.M. on May 30. By dawn, however, he reported that twenty-six trains had left during the night, and dense smoke billowed from Corinth. "Everything indicates evacuation and retreat . . . I am pushing forward," he notified Halleck. By then, the Confederates had disappeared, and the only battle left to fight was for the honor of getting into Corinth first.[28]

For his part, Ulysses S. Grant claimed he had never expected a major Confederate attack. In his memoirs, he alleged that he had men, former railroad workers, who could tell if a train was carrying a load by putting their ear to the rail and listening. They had supposedly informed Grant that loaded trains departed Corinth and empty trains came back in. Whether Grant disregarded the information or felt reluctant to tell Halleck, fearing another rebuke, the Federals did not use it. As it turned out, the railroaders had judged correctly.[29]

While the top Federal brass was scurrying for cover on the left, lower-level division commanders of the Army of the Mississippi were sending out reconnoitering parties and responding to threats of their own. When a horse managed to get loose behind one of Pope's divisions, the sleeping soldiers were ordered to fall in. "The frightened horse frightened the men," one member of the 6th Indiana remembered, and several men were killed and wounded in the melee. Despite the chaos, Rosecrans reported "a series of explosions" around dawn and "dense columns of smoke . . . along the line of these explosions." He realized what had happened then. Several regiments from Stanley's and Paine's divisions moved forward and found the Corinth defenses empty.[30]

Despite the scrambling in the Army of the Mississippi to his south, Don Carlos Buell was not so sure an attack was coming. The day before, he had recommended a major advance toward Corinth, consisting of several divisions. He had asked Halleck for cooperation from Pope, who declined, saying he could not advance without starting a major battle. Buell was prepared to move on his own, but when word arrived that Pope was about to be attacked, Buell determined that his divisions could just as well support Pope as take the offensive, and he decided to wait.[31]

All the while, Buell's own commanders were gathering intelligence about what was happening in the Confederate lines. "An escaped rebel" informed Nelson of the evacuation, and Nelson sent word to Buell at about 4:30 A.M. that the Confederates were evacuating and he was pressing forward. Later, according to a Buell staff officer, Nelson himself arrived with confirmation of an evacuation, "his horse foaming." On one section of the lines, what one soldier described as a "jubilant old darkey . . . in a high state of excitement" came forward waving a large white flag. "Dey's all gone, boss, shuah," he told the Union officers. "Ole Burygard and his army done lef' las' night. If dey hand't I couldn't neber hab come heah. You-uns can jess walk right into de town ef yer wants to." But having just heard from Pope and then Halleck a couple of hours earlier that the Confederates were on the attack, Buell hesitated. Eventually, his men found the Confederate entrenchments empty and continued into Corinth. One Federal wrote home that his unit "went on right up to the works & lo & behold there was no enemy then we then pushed forward & was the first regt on the works. . . . we gave 6 harty cheers & away we went our company in advance on quick time & was the first regt in Corinth."[32]

Over on the Union right, the men of the Army of the Tennessee also heard the commotion and were not sure what to make of it. "Various were the conjectures as to what it meant," one officer remembered. Sherman's "suspicions were aroused" with the arrival and departure of so many trains. Then came the "curious explosions" around 5:00 A.M. and the thick smoke rising from the town. Sherman telegraphed Halleck, looking for information and reporting that Corinth was "enveloped in dense smoke, yet the rebels are in my front." In a breach of the chain of command (the order should have gone through Thomas), Halleck telegraphed back directly and told Sherman to move forward and see what was happening. Sherman had already anticipated such an order and had his men ready. They moved forward toward the Confederate lines and found, as one astonished soldier related, "the enemy's chief redoubt . . . within 1,300 yards of our lines of intrenchments, but completely masked from us by the dense forest and undergrowth." Wondering whether the enemy works were empty, and having no artillery to draw fire, Sherman's troops stopped for a while until Captain C. F. Clarke of General Denver's staff bravely (or stupidly) rode forward by himself and found the entrenchments deserted. Sherman's men then moved forward. The 72nd Ohio stopped at the entrenchment and, as one soldier proudly remembered, gave "three hearty cheers for the Stars and the Stripes." Sherman's men found Corinth "completely evacuated." M. L. Smith's brigade made the initial pursuit of the Confederates through town and to the college, then pressed on toward the Tuscumbia.[33]

The cheering was universal as each army's lead elements occupied the vaunted Confederate earthworks. One Army of the Tennessee soldier noted to his wife, "We advanced in line of battle to their breastworks early yesterday morning, and found no one to defend them against us. With loud cheering our boys leaped over them, and advanced two miles further through and beyond the town." The same cheering was heard over in the Army of the Ohio, one soldier admitting, "We did our full share of yelling and prancing around." Another commented that the soldiers' gladness "resounded with the pent-up cheers of men who were wearied with long waiting and patient watching." As the 8th Wisconsin moved into Corinth amid shouts of victory, one member recorded that "Old Abe" was "whirling and dancing on his perch."[34]

Most Federals were not at all impressed with the Confederate works, once they saw them, and several wished they had stormed these defenses much earlier. The Confederate trenches, one Federal wrote, "were worse constructed than those we had erected." Pope recalled that the earthworks "were of no formidable character. They were built of earth and heavy logs, and whilst they afforded excellent shelter for troops they were not of themselves a formidable obstacle." A newspaper correspondent wrote, "I had been led to suppose that the fortifications were really formidable. But such was not the case. I admire the engineering which dictated the position of the intrenchments, but that is all that deserves the slightest commendation." Still, he admitted that "the zigzag course of the line gave the defenders the command of all the feasible approaches, and hundreds could have been mowed down at every step made by an assailing army, even from the imperfect earth-banks which had been thrown up." Colonel William Camm chose to differ, describing the section he went over as "extensive, well engineered and executed. It would have been a bloody job to have stormed them had the Johnnies fought as well as they usually do." One Federal was more critical of the entrenchments' defenders: "the rebels bilds vary good brest works but never stay to try hit[.] thay don't know wheter hit will stand a conion ball or not."[35]

Some of the Federals entering Corinth met Mr. Harrington, the mayor's clerk, "who asked protection for private property, and for such of the citizens as had determined to remain." They also found good artesian wells that, surprisingly, the Confederates had not destroyed. One Union surgeon wrote to his wife that he "had the first good drink of water I have had since I left Ohio." The various units also rounded up any lingering Confederates, mostly, according to one 7th Iowa soldier, "pickets who were sacrificed to make a show of resistance." Most got away, however, with one Federal noting, "I could but laugh to see the Rebel Cavalry put spurs to their horses and gallop off." Mrs. Gaston hid one soldier in civilian clothes at Corona College; he had "been placed upon guard, and did not understand the last order given when the pickets were ordered in."[36]

Some Federals were no more impressed with Corinth than they were with its defenses. "It is a miserable looking place surrounded by swamps and frogponds," one Ohio soldier wrote. An occasional dead body lying around "render[ed] the scene more ghastly," another Federal remembered. One soldier stated, "We spent a good deal of the time looking around this late rebel stronghold," and a disappointed Federal noted that the enemy "left us the empty camp grounds." Another recalled that the "Tishomingo Hotel had been badly splintered by our artillery shots, and many other buildings showed marks of the siege." Halleck himself reported to Washington that Corinth was "in flames," and the various division commanders supported his claim. Nelson, who was probably the first division commander in Corinth, reported that he "found the town on fire, but . . . [was] deterred from any serious attempt to extinguish the flames by the frequent explosion of shell; found artillery and musket ammunition in close proximity to the fire, which I ordered to be moved." General Davies remembered that "everything was in flames around the depot except the two hotels and the private buildings. I ordered the two telegraph lines passing through the town to be cut, which was done. The depot platform was on fire, which as far as possible was arrested, saving the depot and the houses adjoining." Buell reported that his divisions found about 100 Confederates who were apparently too ill to be evacuated. One of his soldiers discovered a pile of skillets that had not been removed, "but no stores of any importance," Buell stated. "The little that the enemy did not carry away he destroyed."[37]

Most of the buildings in Corinth "displayed hospital or white flags," General Davies remembered, but the Stars and Stripes soon made its appearance.

The 39th Ohio went directly to the courthouse and raised its flag over that building. Davies went through the town to the college, which he referred to as the "Gaston Institute." He described it as "a large one [building], upon an eminence southwest of the depot, where a rebel flag was flying from the dome. I ascended to the roof, my staff following, and ordered it to be hauled down and the Stars and Stripes raised in its place. This was done, after some difficult climbing, by two of my staff." Mrs. Gaston found the general to be "a courteous gentleman," but she got into a verbal debate with a "young colonel," causing "an ill suppressed smile on the General's face [and] . . . smiling among my companions," she remembered. As the spat continued, the argument "made the Gen' turn away to hide his merriment." Mrs. Gaston objected to the Union flag being raised on a private residence; "my Southern blood bubbled up to the surface," she recalled. She told the officers, "My husband is a Southern man, he sympathizes with the Confederate cause. This flag is a misrepresentation of his sentiments." According to Mrs. Gaston, "Before sunset it was taken down and carried to 'Safe Quarters' and never again was the owner insulted by its shadow upon his roof." Given the independence of its citizens, many of the Federals were surprised to find that Confederate generals had maintained their headquarters in private homes, "generally occupying the finest residences in the place," one observant correspondent wrote. "Our commanders are all quartered in tents," he noted, although at least one soldier reported differently during the siege. One Federal soldier even sent his wife roses "plucked from the garden at his [Beauregard's] Quarters."[38]

The Federal commanding general entered Corinth quietly, dressed in plain clothes. Fittingly, Halleck's horse stumbled when it tripped on a downed telegraph wire. Chiding him was a nearby sign asking, "Halleck outwitted—what will Old Abe say?" Another posted on a building read, "These premises to let; inquire of G. T. Beauregard." When the bombastic generals under Halleck began to arrive, however, there was a debate about who should be given the honor of arriving first. A major in Buell's army got into a scuffle with a major in Pope's army over who should raise the flag over the Corinth courthouse. Nelson arrived and arrested Pope's major, accompanied by a long string of curses. Then Pope arrived and began arguing with Nelson; the two got into a "cursing match," according to Stanley. A member of the 39th Ohio who witnessed the exchange was amazed at Pope's "universal knowledge . . . of cuss words and with what artistic ease grace and vihme could use them." And, the soldier recalled, "he seemed to enjoy it too. I know the boys did." Because Pope was senior to Nelson, the latter had to endure his wrath. He sat on his horse "immovable as a statue and never replied, apparently did not hear one word of the whole tirade," an onlooker marveled.[39]

Despite the theatrics, the truth slowly dawned on the victorious but unsuspecting Federals: "The rebs made their last appearance at Corinth, Miss," was how one rank-and-file soldier put it. Another noted, "The agony and tension is over." Halleck soon caught his breath from the surprising developments and organized his command. He ordered all units out of Corinth except for one division of Buell's army, McCook's, as garrison troops. Halleck ordered his nearest army, Pope's, to pursue the Confederates southward toward Booneville. Some of Buell's cavalry and artillery followed the Confederate retreat route toward Kossuth, but according to one observer, they found the way so "obstructed by fallen trees and burned bridges" that they could not get through. Sherman's men later scouted and patrolled that area.[40]

By the afternoon of May 30, the Confederate army was some fifteen miles south of Corinth, and it seemed that Beauregard had made his getaway. The only units left near Corinth were rearguard brigades holding the crossings at the Tuscumbia River. There, the pursuing Federals, led by abducted guides, made contact, but there was little fighting that night and over the next few days. For at least one Confederate company, however, another enemy created more of a fuss in camp than did Halleck's pursuit. Johnny Green told the humorous story of finding "a great big rattlesnake" coiled on top of his blanket one morning during the retreat. He rolled out of bed quickly, and another member of the company caught the snake live. Then, "with this pet in his hands he was running nearly everybody out of camp until the Capt made him kill the creature." Despite such natural enemies, the rear guard left their posts on June 2 while the rest of the army filed southward. Beauregard soon designated Tupelo as the army's new base, as "Baldwyn was found to offer no advantages of a defensive character, and being badly provided with water." The main body of the Confederate army left the Baldwyn area on June 7 and was in camp at Tupelo by June 9, although Breckinridge's corps was soon transferred west to Oxford. Only cavalry pickets were in place several miles to the north, watching for any pursuit or advance by the enemy.[41]

By all accounts, Beauregard had stolen a march on Halleck and everybody else, his Confederate soldiers included. One Southern infantryman wrote home that "no body here was dreaming of such a thing." The operation went very well, and the Confederates managed to bring off the vast majority of their guns, supplies, ammunition, and stores. The only major miscue was the burning of railroad bridges at Cypress Creek, west of Corinth, before the last seven trains out of town had passed that point. The men in charge of the train contemplated returning to Corinth but correctly surmised that, by that time, the bridges south of town would be burning as well. The Confederates were thus forced to damage the locomotives and burn the sixty-plus cars filled with supplies. But many of the local people appropriated the goods first. One Confederate officer complained that the conductors who were supposed to destroy the cars "and the country people all got drunk, or most of them, from liquor on the trains." Still, the cars were mostly burned, and the locomotives were damaged by fire and the removal of parts, which were buried in nearby swamps or thrown into creeks. (The always industrious Sherman soon had the 52nd Indiana, known as the "railroad regiment," searching for the missing parts and repairing the trains. They soon had an engine working on one side, and when the "one-legged" engine appeared in Corinth, thousands of Federals let loose a shout of joy.) Despite the minor problems on the Memphis and Charleston Railroad, the overall retreat was a truly magnificent affair; Shelby Foote has described the evacuation as "the greatest hoax of the war."[42]

Pope's Army of the Mississippi followed Beauregard toward Tupelo and found the Tuscumbia River a "considerable stream, with extensive swamps on both sides, and the only bridge over it having been destroyed." There was some fairly heavy skirmishing, and Rosecrans reported that at one point it seemed the Federals were "in some danger of losing part of a battery" while another unit "came near being entangled." Pope soon got across the river, however, and continued on to Booneville. Halleck later ordered Buell to support the Army of the Mississippi, which he did with Nelson's and Crittenden's troops, moving out on June 4. Pope on the left and Buell on the right confronted the Confederates at Twenty Mile Creek, with Rosecrans reporting, "We touched the rebel front at five points."[43]

One Union soldier lamented to his sister, "We did not come up with any of them but a few cavalry in the rear." Still, Pope captured a substantial number of stragglers and some equipment, including one Confederate who protested that his weapon was private property, given to him personally by Sterling Price "not more than fifteen minutes before." Also captured, according to one Federal, was "a regimental band of rebels, consisting of 16 men, who were discovered secreted in the brush." They also gained numerous slaves who saw their chance at freedom and took it. One Illinois soldier remembered, "The Negroes flocked into camp, hailing the Union army as deliverers and believing that the 'Year ob Jubilee had shorely come.'" Pope grossly inflated the numbers he captured, however, allegedly reporting 10,000 prisoners and 15,000 stands of arms. This capture did not occur, of course, but such rumors made their way into the newspapers, both Union and Confederate. Pope and Halleck argued over who actually issued the report, and Davis and Beauregard ultimately had words over the matter as well. Even Beauregard and Halleck bickered about the report. Pope was not the only one who exaggerated the results. One Federal soldier inflated the success of the pursuit, stating, "We drove them out of the state . . . , and then [they] came back this far." In actuality, the Confederates lost only a modest number of troops and supplies on the retreat south, and Halleck recalled his hot and thirsty men on June 10. The Federals received little more from the chase than a prominent new officer—Phil Sheridan, although Buell referred to the little-known colonel (at the time) as only "the officer in command of the cavalry advance." The Union armies thus returned to the vicinity of Corinth to await the next phase of the war. Some of the officers reinstituted drill as early as June 1, no doubt to the chagrin of the soldiers.[44]

The town of Corinth was now occupied, and the anxiety could be heard in the residents' voices. Susan Gaston wrote, "The night previous [to the evacuation] had been one of painful excitement to some of us who had watched the unusual demonstrations with much anxiety." The next morning, however, "brought to us the realization of Beauregard's evacuation and the rapid advance of the Federal army." As the Confederates left and the Federals took over, massive fires ravaged the town, destroying public property as well as some private homes. Fortunately, most of the citizens of Corinth had evacuated prior to the army's departure. Several Federals commented on the deserted nature of the town, although there were probably quite a few citizens left; they were just hiding. One Union correspondent, for instance, reported, "Much more damage would have been done but for our timely arrival. The place is entirely deserted, except by one or two families." An Illinois soldier added that those who remained "were as shy of the yankees as a wild deer would be of his pursuers." Another reported that the Union army "found but two or three men and a few women and children." Another wrote that the poor citizens "walked curiously around, observing the movements of the soldiers, astonished at the comparatively handsome uniforms they wore, and gratified that the fears they had felt had not been realized." One soldier summed it up by saying, "Corinth seemed truly a deserted place."[45]

The Union soldiers could see that Corinth had once been a nice town. One wrote, "Corinth is a fine looking little place, and contains a thousand or fifteen hundred inhabitants. The dwellings are generally neat, and the places of business numerous and respectable looking." Another wrote to his sister, "Corinth is a beautiful place. . . . 500 Yankees in two years would make it a town of 40,000." There was, of course, some damage to private dwellings. One Union battery commander reported that "several shells went through the house and the roof was nearly torn off." A colonel reported, "The house near which their artillery was posted was several times struck by our shells, and the torn appearance of the trees and buildings around evidenced the fearful accuracy of our shots." The worst part for civilians, obviously, was death. The Federals periodically shelled the town later in the siege, doing unknown damage, but at least one shell hit near the depot in town, killing an engineer and wounding four others.[46]

Although Susan Gaston remarked that no one was willing to guide the Federals in their pursuit, the few citizens who remained in Corinth were smart enough to give the Federals all the information they needed. Some showed the soldiers where the Confederate generals had stayed. Others reported rumors they had heard, such as the Federals having a steam trench-digging machine. One Federal wrote, "They got some queer notions into their heads in regard to us." Numerous Federal reports mentioned gaining intelligence from the citizens. Sherman remembered, "From the best information picked up from the few citizens who remained at Corinth it appeared the enemy had for some days been removing their sick and valuable stores." Another Federal reported that "a citizen informed us that the main body of troops had left about 2 o'clock in the morning and the rear guard at daybreak." He later related that "a negro" had told him of a cannon not far ahead, and "an old man captured by the Iowans" had informed him of enemy pickets not far up the road. Mrs. Gaston confirmed that the old man, Mr. Kincaid, had been forced against his will to direct the Federal pursuit. He "resisted all he could," she wrote, but "they told him to either go peaceably or he should be tied upon his horse."[47]

Little is known of the functions of the town government during and after the chaotic evacuation. No town records exist, or at least none have been found, which indicates some destruction of the town's public buildings. It is clear, however, that the board of selectmen and the mayor, Edward C. Gillenwaters (who was elected to complete Mayor Stewart's unexpired term), were ousted when the Federals took over Corinth. Gillenwaters and his government were dismissed, and martial law was instituted for the remainder of the Union occupation. Various regiments and officers served as provost guard and provost marshal, including the 15th Iowa and future Grant cabinet member Major William W. Belknap. One soldier described the duty: "Our regiment is camped just in the edge of town," he wrote. "We have therefore nothing to do but to go into the streets and guard the different army store houses in the town and patrol the streets. We have no drill or any other duty, outside of this, to do." They also guarded a few Confederate prisoners who were brought in, but most of them took the oath of allegiance. "A few are spunky to the backbone," a soldier wrote, "and declare they will join the Secesh army and fight again if released." The Confederate post office at Corinth also ceased to exist with Beauregard's evacuation.[48]

The government of Tishomingo County, led by the board of police and Sheriff John G. Barton, continued to function as best it could. The board of police and the probate courts operated through the evacuation and Corinth's capture. Records indicate that the board met regularly, the registrar continued to record deeds, and the courts continued to hold sessions through the end of May. Other functions of county government attest to its continuance as well, such as recording bonds for administrators and appraisals. But after the Federal capture of Corinth, the county government lost part of its area of authority and operated in exile from Corinth; most actions were taken in the infrequently occupied old courthouse at Jacinto. Decades later, one county historian remarked that the primary work of the board of police during the Union occupation was "caring for the families of absent soldiers, raising the number of volunteers called for and dodging the Federal troops quartered in the county." Many county functions understandably took a drastic downturn when the change took place in June (for example, the probate court had very little on its docket), but they soon resumed and, for the most part, continued throughout the war with little interruption.[49]

No evidence of foul play is found anywhere in the records or sources, and one Ohio soldier wrote to his wife, "But few families remain in the town. These were of course in no way molested." A Union correspondent noted, "The wealthy females looked from the windows of their mansions upon the Union troops, affecting the greatest scorn and disdain for the Yankees, who viewed them in return rather in a spirit of pity than revenge." In fact, one soldier reported that a young boy came up to him and said, "I thought from what our soldiers told us that you-all were great beasts that would eat us up, but you look just like we-uns!" The lack of harm was appreciated, but the fact remained that the citizens of Corinth now lived amid a vast battleground— and an occupied one at that.[50]

7

"Most Anxious Period of the War"

Thus ended what one Confederate general termed "those tedious days of Halleck's approach to Corinth." It had been a significant month of tedious days, however. The loss of Corinth was a major blow to the Confederacy. Not only did the South lose its strategic crossroads, but it also lost a continuous route to the east. From now on, trains heading east would have to move along an indirect pathway through Mobile and Atlanta. Moreover, before the loss of Corinth, the interior of the Confederacy had lived in total safety. Now, Corinth's capture brought Federal troops into Mississippi very near Vicksburg, and it allowed other places in the Deep South, such as Memphis, to fall. Most important, Confederate offensive operations were significantly curtailed due to the town's loss. Corinth had served as a major hub for Mississippi's early war organization and then for the Shiloh offensive, and its loss deprived the South of flexibility in launching strategic counterattacks. Needing a major transportation and logistical center from which to support offensive operations on the scale of Shiloh, the South would have to depend on the next tier of railroad cities to the south, Jackson and Meridian. But both of them proved to be too far south to aid any advance into Tennessee.[1]

The Confederacy's desperate position after the loss of Corinth was clear to all. One Union correspondent detailed the dwindling hope. "All the citizens of Corinth, and I believe of the rebel States, believed the place would be held at all hazards," he wrote, "and the chagrin and disappointment at its evacuation, without a blow, were deep and bitter. I talked with several who, up to that hour, had never faltered in their faith, but who now look upon their cause as past the remotest chance of a resurrection, and are adapting themselves to their new and changed circumstances. They say that if the South could not defend Corinth, they cannot hold their ground at any other point, and it is idle to prolong a war which is desolating twelve States." Writing home, one Confederate soldier similarly told his wife, "I feel that all is at stake there [Corinth] and that unless we whip the Yankees there and whip them thoroughly the whole valley of the Miss. is lost and Richmond itself as that city can only be saved by a victory at Corinth or thereabouts." Perhaps he took his view to the extreme, but this soldier was correct in his assessment of Corinth's importance to the Confederacy. A Union soldier likewise wrote to his mother, "It will give us all the valley of the Missippi." Perhaps Henry Halleck said it best to Abraham Lincoln himself: Corinth's value "in a military point of view is worth more than Richmond." And now, with Corinth's fall, Confederate fears of losing the Mississippi Valley suddenly seemed more real. The inner heartland of the Deep South was in grave danger, and the South had no transportation and logistical hub from which to launch a counteroffensive to regain its lost territory. The Mississippi Valley's logistical back had been broken.[2]

The events around Corinth in May 1862 certainly did not occur in a vacuum, although many soldiers had a feeling of being secluded in some great wilderness with no connection to the real world. The nation was watching, with many national as well as small-town newspapers running stories about the action near Corinth. The *New York Times* and *New York Herald*, for example, ran front-page stories titled "Retreat of the Rebel Army from Corinth" and "The Evacuation of Corinth." One newspaper correspondent told his readers that "Corinth was indeed a stronghold, and its importance could not have been over-rated. It is the key that unlocks the Cotton States, and gives us command of almost the entire system of Southern railroads, and nothing but despair could have prompted its abandonment. While there was a shadow of hope for the Confederacy, policy would have compelled the insurgents to hold the town." Others followed the progress of the Union armies, or the lack thereof, through the many letters sent home by the men in the ranks. Most disturbed, of course, were the families who received the terrible news from north Mississippi that their loved ones had been killed or had died from disease. Political and military officials were also watching, knowing that Corinth was the key to unlocking the Confederate inner sanctum in the west. With Corinth's fall, congratulatory messages ran furiously between Secretary of War Edwin Stanton and George B. McClellan and other commanders. Even President Lincoln knew about Corinth's fall as early as May 30. "Corinth was evacuated last night and is occupied by our troops today—the enemy gone South to Okolona on the Railroad to Mobile," he informed one of his generals.[3]

The commanding generals, of course, garnered most of the public's attention in the actions around Corinth. Henry Halleck had his backers, one of whom was William T. Sherman, who described the Confederate evacuation of Corinth as "a clear back-down from the high and arrogant tone heretofore assumed by the rebels." However, the conqueror of Corinth was more usually criticized in the Northern papers. The *Chicago Tribune* reported, "Halleck has thus achieved one of the most barren triumphs of the war. In fact, it is tantamount to a defeat." The general was viewed as too cautious, and the Northern press thoroughly chastised him for letting Beauregard steal a march on him. Detractors also existed inside the army. One Iowa colonel wrote, "If he had his own way he would shovel the Southern Confederacy into the Gulf of Mexico in a few years." Lew Wallace later wrote, "Corinth was not captured; it was abandoned to us. At dawn of May 30th we marched into its deserted works, getting nothing—nothing—not a sick prisoner, not a rusty bayonet, not a bite of bacon—nothing but an empty town and some Quaker guns. The strategic advantages remained to us, because, with all his leisure, it was not possible for General Beauregard to destroy or take them away." Lower-level Federals felt the same way. One soldier wrote to his wife, "They have put us to a good deal of trouble *for nothing*." Another wrote in his diary, "The great battle of Corinth has proved to be a humbug." Yet another surmised, "I don't know a man in the whole army that ain't sorry we did not give them a try at least two weeks ago." Perhaps the campaign answered the question of Halleck's competency as an organizer and a strategic commander, but it gave no indication of his competence as a tactical general. He organized the three armies beautifully, but he led them to what many described as an empty victory, and it took him a month to do it. But he did accomplish his goal, and he did so in the way he had determined to do it—with order and sense.[4]

The petty dispute among the armies as to which one entered Corinth first made matters worse for Halleck. Buell reported that Nelson had been the first to sound the alarm that the Confederates were retreating and stated, "I have no doubt myself that the honor is due to Major-General Nelson." When he was not credited with the honor in public statements, Nelson complained to Halleck that "the official telegraph has been made the medium of the wrong." Conversely, Pope claimed that his regiments had entered the town first, and numerous newspapers reported that their states' regiments had been the first to fly their flags in Corinth. Perhaps Sherman summed up the dispute best, saying, "But in fact there was no honor in the event."[5]

Despite the fact that he lost Corinth, Beauregard received mostly praise for his generalship. The same *Chicago Tribune* that insulted the victorious Halleck called the evacuation "a victory for Beauregard, or at least . . . one of the most masterly pieces of strategy that has been displayed during this war." The *Cincinnati Commercial* reported, "Beauregard had achieved another triumph." News of his cunning spread all over the North. His generals likewise praised the campaign. Leonidas Polk related the story to his daughter in some overstatement: "We have deemed it advisable, after having kept the enemy employed six weeks in digging and embanking all the way from the Tennessee River to Corinth, and just when he had spent millions of dollars, and lost thousands of men by the climate and water, and when he had just got ready to open his heavy batteries,—to bid him good morning and to invite him down a little farther South. How he likes it we have not heard." The common soldiers also thought as much. One wrote, "Gen. Beauregard by completely deceiving his own Army, deceived the enemy."[6]

In truth, however, Beauregard had lost Corinth, and his army and political leaders knew it. James Phelan, one of Mississippi's senators in Richmond, wrote to Jefferson Davis describing the retreat: "You can scarcely magnify the deplorable condition of the Army of Corinth—both morally and physically—at the time of the retreat from that place." Senator Phelan went on in more detail: "Deaths numerous; Desertions, by no means, rare; whilst a general spirit of despondency seemed to pervade the entire march." A soldier noted in his diary, "Beauregard has allowed Halleck to dig him out of Corinth," and he wondered where the army would go next: "I do not know. Down into Mexico I expect before we stop." Even one of the Federal soldiers could not fathom Beauregard's strategy: "This is to me a strange move I am not able to comprehend it. Perhaps this is because I am not a military man but it does seem to me that if I had been a commanding General fortified as they were I would rather have taken my chances of successfully resisting our forces than to have Evacuated. What Effect this will have apon the rebellion I cant tell but it seems to me it will be very damaging. It seems to me that an Evacuation under the circumstances was about Equal to a defeat." Another Federal crowed, "I think it was better for us for them to evacuate, and worse for them than tho we had had a hard battle and whiped them. It demoralises their army and causes the people of the South to loose confidence in their leaders." The terrible loss of supplies also weighed on the Confederates' minds, and several mentioned the loss of personal effects. One soldier wrote home asking for clothes. "We lost everything at Corinth except what we had on and we are the dirtiest men you ever saw," he wrote. Despite the grand way in which the Confederates left Corinth, the evacuation was still a severe loss for the South.[7]

In Richmond, the disappointment was overwhelming. Concerned that his pre-evacuation hinting might have been insufficient to thoroughly prepare the government for such a loss, Beauregard tried to put the campaign in the best light in his report dated June 13 from Tupelo. He blamed his strategic defeat on several factors, including the enemy's larger numbers, his own dwindling force of only 45,000 effectives due to sickness, and, incomprehensibly, the accomplishment of "the purposes and ends for which I had occupied and held Corinth." He reminded Jefferson Davis that Robert E. Lee himself had approved the evacuation, although in actuality, Lee had approved only a possible evacuation route. He also accused the Federals, whom, he noted, had "declined my offer of battle twice," of having the gall to avoid separating their units, to entrench their lines, and to move cautiously. Beauregard went to great lengths to dispute the victory claims of the enemy, calling them "inaccurate, reckless, and unworthy." He concluded that Halleck's report of the affair, based on Pope's exaggerated numbers, "may be characterized as disgracefully untrue," although he conceded that Halleck may have been "duped by his subordinate."[8]

It is not known what President Davis's reaction was when he read these excuses. The president had clearly not heard enough, however, because he sent his aide, William Preston Johnston (son of his late friend Albert Sidney Johnston) to inspect the army and interview Beauregard. The Creole was not completely comfortable with the process, asking Johnston "to what end [his] mission . . . tended." Beauregard believed it showed Davis's lack of trust in him, and he threatened to request a court of inquiry. Although that never came about, it would not be Beauregard's last run-in with Davis.[9]

But what was done was done, and the war was certainly not over; new campaigns loomed in the future. Thus, as Beauregard's tired force reached safety near Tupelo and Halleck called off his chase, both armies took stock of where they were and what had been gained and lost. Both also entered a period of complete reorganization. This change would be evident both in the landscape around Corinth, as the Federals threw up new fortifications, and in the armies that would defend or attack those fortifications in the coming campaigns. This two-month-long interlude saw not only the overhaul of the structure of the various armies but also a complete turnover in command. Each army replaced commanders, and each made many adjustments at lower levels as well. New leaders with new ideas would soon be leading both armies around the same old battlegrounds of Corinth, Mississippi.[10]

Despite their fears and the rumors of a strongly fortified town, Federal commanders saw firsthand just how weak Corinth actually was once they arrived on site. One soldier of the 53rd Ohio wrote to his sister, "Their breastworks not near as formidable as I expected. Not as good as those we put up in 24 hours." And those weak fortifications existed only on the east and north sides of town. Now that the Union occupied Corinth, any Confederate counterattack would probably come from the south or west, which was totally open and had no defending earthworks. Therefore, one of the first Federal acts of reorganization was the establishment of a new line of fortifications. This was a priority, because there were many reports of enemy movements. One Federal wrote home, "We have been moving through Tishomingo County, Mississippi, generally following either sounds or sights or anything else that would indicate to us the nearness of the Enemy."[11]

The old Beauregard line ran only north and east of Corinth, defending the sector from which the Union armies had approached. Only the Tuscumbia River stood in the way of a Confederate attack from the south or west. Halleck thus ordered the construction of a new line to remedy this lack of security. A series of earthen forts that ran from the tips of the old Confederate fortifications went up south and west of the town and was dubbed the "Halleck line." In all, Halleck erected six forts, each designated by a letter of the alphabet. Battery A lay within the old Confederate works southeast of Corinth. From that point, Batteries B and C continued the line to the west. At Battery C, the line turned northward, with Batteries D through F extending north toward the Memphis and Charleston Railroad. Each battery commanded a major avenue of approach, whether a road or a railroad, and Halleck planned for rifle pits and trenches to connect the six forts. One officer described the fortifications as "isolated earthworks for cannon supported by flanking rifle pits" that "continued and perfected [the defenses], forming an entire circle following the brow of an elevated range of hills surrounding the place, with an abatis of heavy oak timber . . . six hundred yards in breadth felled down the slope in front throughout their whole length." The 81st Ohio got the dubious duty of felling the timber for the abatis, clearing a 4-mile-long, 300-yard-wide strip over the summer. They complained a lot, one soldier arguing that it would take an army of 100,000 men to man such a line. But the duty was mitigated to some extent, according to one Ohioan, by "the adjoining fields [that] furnished an ample supply of green corn, and the orchards [that] yielded peaches and apples." The forts and abatis went up over the summer of 1862, but progress on the trenches lagged behind. When completed, however, the Beauregard and Halleck lines would encircle the town and provide defense from any direction.[12]

While the security issues were worked out, the turnover in command began as well. With time to think after the stunning victory, and suffering from a bout of diarrhea (which he called "the evacuation of Corinth"), Halleck first wrote his official report of the Battle of Shiloh. There were also bigger issues. On June 10, the day the pursuit ended, Halleck revoked the organization he had employed during the siege. Special Field Order No. 90 returned the three

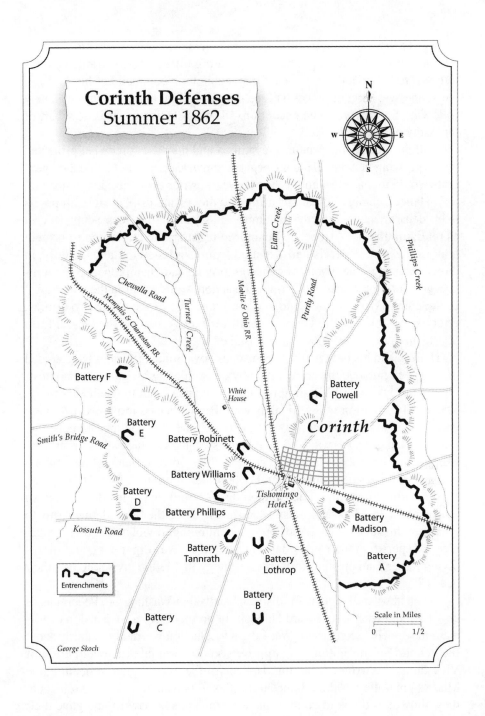

Corinth Defenses
Summer 1862

N
W   E
S

Chewalla Road

Elam Creek

Phillips Creek

Memphis & Charleston RR

Turner Creek

Mobile & Ohio RR

Purdy Road

Battery F

White House

Battery Powell

Corinth

Battery E

Smith's Bridge Road

Battery Robinett

Battery Williams

Battery D

Tishomingo Hotel

Battery Phillips

Kossuth Road

Battery Madison

Battery Tannrath

Battery Lothrop

Battery A

Entrenchments

Battery B

Battery C

Scale in Miles
0   1/2

George Skoch

respective armies to their former commanders. This reorganization had no bearing on Buell and Pope, but it made a big difference to Grant. Thomas returned to his own division, and Grant again took command of his Army of the Tennessee. Circumstances had seemingly reverted to the days immediately following Shiloh, with one exception—Thomas's division was now part of the Army of the Tennessee.[13]

With his command structure revamped and his base somewhat protected by the growing new line, Halleck began an unwise operation that Federal generals would repeat throughout the war years. After achieving his major victory, Halleck began to break his army into pieces and disperse it to all points in his department. Fearing the oncoming hot season in the Deep South, as well as realizing the need to occupy captured territory, he attempted to protect major cities the Federals had wrestled from Confederate hands. Oddly, in direct contrast to the theory of concentration he had championed in his writings and during the siege of Corinth, the action would result in the withdrawal of the entire Army of the Ohio and the scattering of the other two armies, effectively stopping the Union's southward movement in the west. Philip Sheridan, in fact, called it a "fatal mistake."[14]

Halleck had his backers then, as he does now. Some historians have argued that Halleck pursued the correct path by consolidating his gains and not testing the furious central Mississippi summer in an attempt to reach Vicksburg. The supply situation was critical as well. But Halleck's move has routinely been treated as a momentum crusher, allowing the Confederates to retake the initiative and carry the war back into Tennessee and Kentucky. Historian Kenneth W. Noe describes Halleck's choice as "the worst decision of his career." Perhaps Halleck's biographer John F. Marszalek summed it up best, however. "Halleck did something that violated the very military rules that he had so long espoused," Marszalek writes. "He had allowed the Confederate Army to escape by his delays. . . . [And] he was continuing to violate his own principles—dispersing rather than massing troops. He was organizing and resupplying rather than pushing forward, a strategy that left many scratching their heads."[15]

When news of the plans for dispersal arrived in Washington, Federal leaders glanced a wary eye toward Halleck. In no mood for a suspension of forward movement, Secretary of War Edwin M. Stanton worriedly inquired about the general's future plans. "I suppose you contemplate the occupation of Vicksburg," he wrote, reminding Halleck of the overall plan of opening the Mississippi Valley. Although the authorities in Washington seemed reluctant, they allowed Halleck to control his department as he saw fit and gave their approval for the scattering of the armies.[16]

Halleck began by dispatching Buell and the four-division Army of the Ohio eastward toward Chattanooga, another important Confederate city that had become a major Union objective. Buell already had one division under Major General Ormsby M. Mitchel in the area, and throughout the summer, he repaired the Memphis and Charleston Railroad as he went, making slow progress. One Ohio soldier described the efforts in his diary: "We had to build a railroad bridge and then we went on again." Another reported, "We are guarding a water tank and bridge. The water tank was burned down by the rebels, but it is now almost rebuilt. They have formed themselves into guerilla parties and are continually scouring the country, tearing up the railroad track and burning cotton where ever they can have a chance." Obviously, the progress was slow.[17]

In addition to sending divisions east, Halleck sent forces westward toward Memphis, which had been outflanked by Corinth's fall and occupied on June 6. William T. Sherman became an acting corps commander when he took his own and two other divisions westward. The Federals repaired the railroad as they moved along, leaving small garrisons in important places as they passed. One Union soldier wrote to his wife, "We have got soldiers all along the railroad a guarding it," although, he continued, "we havent mutch hard work to do now the most we have to do is to stand guard and picket." At Memphis itself, one soldier described the defenses that went up over the summer: "We are a putting up good stout breast works close by the river and a round part of the town. We don't have to work on the breast works, for we have a bout six hundred negroes a working on them." He also noted the presence of five gunboats in the river.[18]

Other troops under McClernand held the delicate supply lines to Corinth and Memphis, while the rest of the Army of the Tennessee remained in Corinth under the command of a newcomer from the eastern theater, Major General E. O. C. Ord. One artilleryman wrote home, "The old fellow looks just like a Russian Marshal with his fierce Mustachios and beard." Also at Corinth was the Army of the Mississippi under Pope and later Rosecrans, when the former moved to the Virginia theater.[19]

The top spot in the Mississippi Valley changed as well when Lincoln called Halleck to Washington, leaving Grant in command. Lincoln had been seeking someone to serve as general in chief ever since he and the secretary of war had fired McClellan, and he decided on Halleck. Obviously, Halleck's performance in the march to and siege of Corinth had convinced Lincoln and his advisers of the general's organizational and operational expertise. Before leaving, Halleck praised the men he had led for the past three months. "The major-general commanding the department in giving up the immediate command of the troops now in the field . . . desires to express to them his appreciation of the endurance, bravery, and soldierly conduct which they have exhibited on all occasions during the present campaign." The next day, Grant officially took command, and Halleck left for the domes and spires of Washington.[20]

In his new position as commander of two armies, three departments, and some 80,000 troops, Grant seemed almost overwhelmed. And he became increasingly nervous in the days following his elevation, now that he had the entire department resting on his shoulders. He later referred to those days as the "most anxious period of the war." His men had confidence in him, however. "The more we see of him as commander," wrote one Northerner stationed in Corinth, "the more we are satisfied with Gen. Halleck for making him his successor."[21]

Now on the defensive, Grant had to be ready to take whatever the Confederates hurled at him. But by August, he still had some 78,869 "aggregate present" with which to confront the myriad problems facing him. One Ohio soldier perhaps overthought the situation when he wrote that Grant had plenty of "Chaplains behind the breastworks to proclaim the terms of salvation to the sinful tribes of secessia." Whether his numbers would prove enough, only time would tell.[22]

If Grant thought he had it bad, it was worse in the Confederate army fifty miles to the south. Sickness, low morale, and a number of other issues confronted Confederate commanders that summer. One of the most common reasons for poor morale was the institution of strict discipline and harsh punishment for the most trivial of crimes. One soldier reported that "to prevent complete disorganization, the men were restricted to their regimental boundaries. . . . We really suffered from the stagnation of prison life without books or papers or even strangers to talk with." Braxton Bragg, already known as a harsh disciplinarian, received the brunt of the criticism. "Great complaint is made of Genl. Bragg in consequence of alleged tyranny amounting to brutality and murder," Senator Phelan informed Jefferson Davis. "It is alleged," Phelan continued, "and, at present, I do not doubt the charge—that he has had several soldiers shot upon his mere order, without the shadow of a trial, and that too, for comparatively trifling offenses." One popular tale boasted that Bragg executed a soldier for shooting a chicken. Actually, the ball aimed at the chicken glanced and hit a small black child. There were also reports that both Beauregard and Bragg illegally dismissed officers for failing examinations given by a "military board" set up by the generals. Lower-level officers bore this out, and one captain of the 10th Mississippi wrote to his wife that, even during the siege, "there has been an examining board of three officers here to examine all commissioned officers as to their competency. The Board is sitting in our regiment now, and they are cutting off heads pretty fast." He added, "I expect mine will come off during the day, as little time has been afforded me to qualify myself for the multifarious duties devolving upon a Captain." Another soldier summed up the hatred of Bragg: "I should not be surprised if Genl. Bragg should receive a ball in his back from one of his own men some day as many have sworn to shoot him."[23]

The food allotment was also insufficient, forcing the soldiers to get eatables any way they could. One Confederate reported having "a big mess of roasting ears today. How we got them is nobodys business." Fortunately for the common soldier, the water situation at Tupelo was much better than at Corinth, although it was not perfect. One soldier wrote, "If we get anything like good water we haf to go from one mile two two miles from our camp." The almost never-ending drill was also hard on the men. Many officers instituted a "rigid course of drill," causing one Louisianan to complain to his wife: "They form us in line of battle early in the day, they march us around three miles from camp, and they make us do exercises until 9:00 on an empty stomach. I believe there is neither justice nor humanity in this." A Confederate general explained that the army was "waiting . . . for the tide to rise, . . . but diligently at work . . . drilling and disciplining our army and getting it ready for work."[24]

Another problem that confronted the Confederates in the summer months was the turnover in command. By August, the Army of the Mississippi had changed hands three times, and Van Dorn's Army of the West four. Beauregard himself was the chief casualty, having affronted Jefferson Davis one too many times. When he left without authorization on sick leave, Davis replaced him with Bragg. Presumably, the tales of executions skyrocketed. In his new position, Bragg seemed almost overwhelmed. "Please define the limits of my command," he pleaded in a wire to Richmond on June 23. Davis's reply extended the department to include all of Mississippi, Alabama, Louisiana east of the Mississippi River, and small portions of Georgia and Florida.[25]

With this clarification, Bragg began to make changes, mostly to corps commands in the Army of the Mississippi. The Army of the West also went through a series of changes, which the trans-Mississippi soldiers welcomed. "Van Dorn is not only unpopular with his division," Senator Phelan wrote to Davis, "but is the butt of their jeering and ridicule." Phelan gave the example of a jingle often heard in camp: "Who lost the Battle of Elkhorn / Van Dorn— Van Dorn / Who do we wish had never been born / Van Dorn—Van Dorn." Many of the soldiers also blamed him for the debacles of May 9 and 22 at

Farmington. Some declared that Van Dorn had been "too drunk to attend to business."[26]

Van Dorn ultimately went south to Vicksburg, while Sterling Price made the long journey to Richmond for a consultation with the president in the hope that he could convince Davis to send him and his trans-Mississippians back to Arkansas. There they could actively campaign instead of milling around camp for months at a time. In contrast to their feelings for Van Dorn, the trans-Mississippians loved their old "Pap" Price. He was one of them, and they knew he wanted to lead them back home. Such an astute observer as Senator Phelan wrote, "Price's men do idolize him and he can hurl them against obstacles at which other men would quail." Phelan went on to put Price's status in context: "I do not hesitate to assert that there does not exist, in this army, one particle of [similar] enthusiasm towards any other General—unless it may be in a limited degree—Genl. Breckinridge."[27]

Davis refused Price's request, and harsh words were spoken. Price even hit the table with his fist, which, as one onlooker remembered, "set the inkstands and everything upon it a-dancing." With Van Dorn transferred and Price in Richmond, Major General John P. McCown, the senior officer present, had command of the Army of the West. He took charge on June 20, but Price returned by July 2. The Confederate high command seemed to be playing musical chairs.[28]

Then the entire dynamic of the war in the west changed dramatically. With seemingly competent leaders at the helm of every major district by mid-July, Braxton Bragg and company, including deported Tennessee governor Isham G. Harris, who was pushing for the recapture of his state, began to envision a bold plan to regain the losses incurred in recent campaigns. The scheme would not only defend east Tennessee, which had come under increasing pressure from Buell, but also take the war through Kentucky and into Northern territory. At present, Major General Kirby Smith's force was all the Confederacy had to defend east Tennessee, and he had too few troops to do so. Although Buell had started almost two months earlier, he had to repair the Memphis and Charleston Railroad as he traveled. Consequently, Bragg conceived a plan that would send the Army of the Mississippi from its base at Tupelo across Alabama to Chattanooga. There, he would outflank the Army of the Ohio and be as close to Kentucky as Buell was. From this position, Bragg could move into Buell's rear, cut him off from reinforcements and supplies, and destroy him. If that attempt failed, he could simply hold a line defending Georgia and the interior of the South.[29]

With approval from Richmond, Bragg began to implement his plan on July 22. He began the move to Chattanooga by sending the troops at Mobile ahead;

the tail end of Bragg's column would replace the garrison. More than a few Mississippians lamented the fact that they had to leave their state. One wrote home to express his distress at "bid[ding] farewell to old Mississippi, the dear old state that gave me birth." No doubt the Missourians were not sympathetic. By July 24, Bragg had moved his headquarters to Chattanooga, and only Price remained in north Mississippi to keep Grant busy, trying to make it impossible for him to reinforce Buell.[30]

By late August, the Confederates had regained some parity in numbers because Grant had indeed sent several divisions east. He had retained the entire Army of the Tennessee but only two divisions of the Army of the Mississippi. To make matters worse, Grant commanded divisions that were scattered from Corinth to Memphis. But Price still had only two divisions, or 15,000 men, at his disposal. The future was uncertain for both generals.

Ulysses S. Grant's major concern at the time was the defense of Corinth, the main garrison on his line. But because so many general officers were taking sick leave and going home for a few weeks, his army grew weaker. The officers no doubt enjoyed their leave, but the soldiers were not so sure of their superiors. "I have not so much confidence in some of our Cols who are acting Brigs," one soldier wrote, "as they come verry near getting us into several bad scrapes." Grant nevertheless kept troops stationed in several outlying areas, such as Kossuth and Rienzi, to watch for approaching Confederates. The major encampment was Camp Montgomery, a few miles south of Corinth, where the soldiers dug wells, built hospitals, and fashioned ovens for baking bread. The men relished the calmer days of summer compared with those in May. One soldier reported to his brother, "We are now stationed ten miles from Corinth in a little place named Kossuth and have very good times here and also good quarters in a large store from which everything has been taken when we came there." In Corinth itself, engineer James B. McPherson was revamping the destruction left by the Confederates. "All around town are the foot-prints of Gen. McPherson," one newspaper reported. "New Railroad buildings are going up as if by magic." Around the town, Union soldiers manned the line of breastworks, including on the north and east sides at the old Confederate entrenchments.[31]

Yet both Grant and Rosecrans were still dissatisfied with the defenses of Corinth itself. Workers continually labored on the Halleck line, but by August, both generals saw they had too few men to work on the lengthy line, much less man it in the event of an attack. Rosecrans, in fact, labeled the Halleck line "utterly useless to our small command," and he lobbied hard for a new line. After discussing the idea of a shorter line closer to Corinth, the two generals made an on-the-spot survey, accompanied by Captain Frederick Prime, an engineer. Grant and Rosecrans identified a favorable position for the line in the vicinity of Corona College. Orders immediately went out for the construction of five batteries, much like A through F on the Halleck line. These batteries, later named for the artillery commanders who manned them—Robinett, Williams, Phillips, Tannrath, and Lothrop—ran in a semicircle extending in a southwesterly fashion from Battery Robinett, north of the Memphis and Charleston Railroad northwest of Corinth, to Battery Lothrop, close to the Mobile and Ohio Railroad and almost directly south of the town. Contraband blacks under their superintendent, Captain William B. Gaw, worked tirelessly on the line. Prime supervised, and soon the majority of the forts were erected. These new defensive works made Corinth even more formidable, especially against an attack from the south or west, and they provided more peace of mind to the Union high command.[32]

The lackadaisical attitude of some of the rank-and-file soldiers around Corinth also worried the generals. Security became lax as the men settled into their camps and nothing happened for weeks on end. One sick soldier who left Corinth in mid-May returned in July and was amazed at the quietness of the area. "When I got back here I found our army in possession of Corinth and everything quiet," he wrote to his mother, "where at the time I left nothing but fighting was talked of or looked for by everybody." The only major event was a Fourth of July celebration in town. "We have had a celebration here today that has convinced the citizens at least that we have not forgotten the Birthday of our Nation. The Batteries of our Division fired a National Salute of 34 guns at noon amid the cheers of the assembled Infantry," one soldier wrote home. Despite the patriotic celebration, the soldiers continued to be more interested in creature comforts than in watching the enemy. One soldier related an incident in which fifteen men and an officer were supposed to be on picket duty on a road in front of their camp when they were suddenly attacked by Confederate cavalry. "Not one was on guard—some were away picking berries, some back in the shade reading, and some even had their guns apart cleaning them. Even their look-out in advance of their outpost was in a thicket picking berries," he remembered.[33]

Clearly, the life of the common soldier at Corinth during these summer months was mostly comfortable. "The weather is perfectly delightful, excruciatingly so, our tents are all sheltered by large unbragious trees, under which the men lie and bask in holy ease, eating peaches, figs and apples, reading amorous novels, or lazily puffing a cigeratt," one Iowan wrote. Another described his camp as having "a good well and . . . a bake oven[.] Our company has got a splendid brick oven we have all the soft bread now that we want which is quite a rarity to us after living on hard bread and crackers long as we have." Members of the 8th Wisconsin particularly enjoyed playing with their eagle, "Old Abe." The soldiers marveled as the bird caught "crazy bugs with his claws in puddles of water" and played with minié balls rolled on the ground by the men. Visits by luminaries, such as state governors, also brought excitement into the camps, and rumors and news from other theaters traveled widely. One soldier described such a rumor to his brother: "One of our boys says the blacksmith told him that he heard the doctor say that we were actually going east." News of the implementation of a draft also heartened the soldiers. And, of course, payday always lifted morale.[34]

Although newspapers from all over the North were sometimes available, the soldiers gained most of their news from a local paper. Editor Elbridge D. Fenn began publishing a weekly multipage paper, the *Corinth War Eagle*, on July 31, offering a three-month subscription for two dollars. The paper contained a blend of news from around the nation and the world, as well as poetry, entertaining stories, and other features. Several Corinth businesses, such as the Tishomingo and Corinth hotels, purchased advertisements, as did sutlers. The paper also provided other services, such as a listing of arrivals at the hotels and notices of unclaimed letters in the post office.[35]

Whenever there was a death or bad news arrived from home, however, the soldiers found camp to be a lonely and inhospitable place. One soldier described a pitiful sight: "R. F. Woods of this Co. was buried . . . it was the hardest looking funeral I ever saw in peaceable times; it was raining when they buried him, they took him off to the grave, through the rain." One soldier even reported "some deaths caused by homesickness." The most notable death was that of Union General Joseph B. Plummer, who died suddenly in August. Bad news also caused problems in camp. When the members of a Minnesota artillery battery learned about a massacre of white men by Sioux Indians in August 1862, they were infuriated. They relished every bit of news they could glean from letters or papers: "We read in the papers about the Indian Massacre and resulted in upsetting everyone in camp," wrote one soldier. He later reported that several men tried to get furloughs to return home, but only five who had families were allowed to go. "Since I was not married," he wrote, "I had to remain."[36]

Several small skirmishes erupted over the summer, despite one wag's declaration that the troops mostly "fight flies, fleas, and lizards." Federal commanders thus had to remind their men to follow army regulations. On one occasion, Ord sent complaints of an "offensive smell" in the camps, particularly that of the 12th Illinois, to the brigade commander, Richard J. Oglesby.

The future Illinois governor inspected his camps and reported to Ord that "the inspector must have carried the smell with him when he rode through the camp." One soldier remembered that Oglesby's comments "ruffled the feathers at headquarters," and he had to apologize. A lower-level incident likewise illustrated the growing discipline problem. One soldier told of men being captured while on patrol, and others deserting to the enemy. "Thare has been sum 2 or 3 men shott for deserting in Corinth," he wrote home.[37]

The Federals closely observed the local people during the summer of 1862. "We have seen some of the inhabitants and they present contrast enough to our northern people," one soldier wrote. "Where they dare be they are impudent enough and when provoked it is astonishing how they will sputter. They most emphatically know how to be abusive and how to brag—two things Southern people know especially such as are blessed with secession proclivities at least." He went on to say that "one of these women threatened to put a bullet through my head last night." In contrast, another reported to his brother, "I have seen many very good looking girls down here."[38]

Usually, the soldiers found certain aspects of Southern society to be comical. One Federal wrote: "They are a hard looking set of people. It takes about two to make a shadow. They must certainly starve unless they get help." Artilleryman William Christie told his brother that the locals repeatedly used the term "right smart." For instance, one farmer told him the ground "gives a right smart yield of cotton." Christie concluded that it was "a strange mixture of bad grammar and poor English." The area's farms were especially interesting to midwestern farm boys. "Hog and Negro are the principle kinds of stock raised here in this country," one of them wrote.[39]

The Federal soldiers also got their first look at slaves, as Corinth quickly became a haven for those fleeing bondage in northern Mississippi. The recent changes in Union policy toward slaves stated that they would not be returned to bondage, and one Union soldier at Corinth remarked that the army brought in "nigars by the hole sale. Thay ar leving thar masters every day and coming in our lines." Many others were sent north. One colonel wrote to his aunt, "They flocked into my camp in great crowds, and I shipped them as fast as I could get transportation. They are all in a free state by this time." Some of the Union soldiers displayed racist attitudes, such as the one who confessed, "Most of them seem to me to be almost another family of the human race something distinct and separate physically and mentally."[40]

Since the Corinth area had been reluctant to secede, not all the locals were loyal to the Confederacy or its troops. There was much smuggling of goods to the Union forces, as well as selling to and buying from the Federals in Corinth. There were also frequent claims about being a Unionist. One Federal soldier wrote home: "It looks a little rough some times to go and take all such stuff a man has got and him pleading up Unionism all the while for you can't find a man down here but what is all right, if he sees a foraging train coming, all I have to say is that if they are Union men that some of them has to sacrifice a great deal and if they aint it's a good joke on them."[41]

The most frequent occasions for destruction came when the Union troops went foraging for food. Many Federals left accounts of their expeditions and the results they had on the population. One soldier described an effort west of Corinth: "Our regiment went out with a foraging train yesterday; . . . there were about 150 six mule teams in the train; we went out about seven miles to a rich old planter's and opened a hole in his fence, went in and loaded all the teams with corn and fodder out of one man's field and the worst of it was that they did not even take the trouble to ask for it." He told his sister, "I thought then, if the scale was turned and the rebels were in the North making so free with everything they wanted, that you folks up there living in peace and quietude, would begin to see the magnitude of this war." The Federals occasionally gave farmers receipts for all they took. One soldier wrote to his sister, "On emerging from this swamp we came to a cornfield and immediately entered it with about fifty teams. In 20 minutes the field of 10 acres were swept clean and the fodder piled on the wagons. We then turned and came back, leaving the Division quartermaster to pay the owner five dollars per acre as he was a Union man." Another soldier told of befriending a local farmer: "The old man from whose well we get our drinking water is becoming softened a great deal by our good treatment of him. . . . We get along first rate with him now and, seeing that we have almost worn out his Bucket and rope by continual hauling, we took up a subscription yesterday and raised money enough to buy a new rig for him."[42]

In addition to the local Southerners, the newly occupied town of Corinth attracted all sorts of Northern civilians in the summer of 1862. Some were notorious for their desire to make a quick buck. Ord later commented to the secretary of war, "The place was being overrun with cotton-buyers, speculators, whiskey-sellers, and refugees from draft at the North." Ord had a simple solution: he instituted his own draft and inducted as many of the shady characters as he could catch into the army. There was "a stampede of them by every outlet," Ord noted, but he was able to "put some of these vagabonds in the ranks."[43]

Local people were sometimes willing to aid the Federals. The students at Corona College offered well water to Union troops who had marched several miles through the hot and dusty terrain. Others sold meals to the soldiers for moderate sums. On other occasions, the locals provided Federal officers with intelligence about Confederate movements or intentions. At the same time, some citizens worked against the Union. One soldier wrote home, "Our Pick-etts is pestered. Some boys are prowling round both day and night for a chance to nab us. We ammong our selves think the tormentors is citizens."[44]

Of course, the same citizens could have been the source of both support-ing and opposing actions. Such was the paradox of wartime Mississippi.

8

"A Deeper Design"

By September 1862, the grand Confederate offensive had begun as armies all across the South marched and prepared to invade the United States. The defensive war waged by the South up to this point was put on hold, and Southern leaders bet on one massive movement. If successful, the war could end in a matter of months. If it failed, the war might end as well, but with the destruction of the Confederate armies. Southern leaders took this risk in an attempt to equalize the advantage the Federals held in almost every category: larger armies, better equipment, and more capable generals. Corinth and its surrounding outposts would play a major role in this crisis of the war.

Far to the east and north of Corinth, Robert E. Lee's Army of Northern Virginia slowly made its way northward. By the middle of September, the army had moved into Maryland, only to meet the larger and better-equipped Union force under George B. McClellan. Although Lee and his army had repeatedly defeated stronger Union masses on Southern ground, this time, they fought on enemy soil. Could Lee achieve a victory in Northern territory and thus gain foreign support for his cause?[1]

Braxton Bragg had similar ideas. He too planned a Northern invasion, arousing pro-Confederate sentiment in Kentucky and destroying Federal installations on the way. Like Lee, Bragg had moved out of Confederate territory by mid-September and made his way northward. He established contact with Kirby Smith and formulated plans to capture Federal cities on the northern bank of the Ohio River. He faced far fewer Federals than Lee did, and they suffered badly from disorganization. Could Bragg pull a victory out of the campaign?[2]

Van Dorn and Price sat on the western flank, and their task was to hold the west Tennessee Federals in place to prevent Grant from sending reinforcements to stop the invasions by Bragg and Lee. If the Federals broke loose, though, Price was to follow and constitute another invasion force that would meet Bragg "on the Ohio and there open the way to Missouri." Bragg obviously threw in the line about further action in Missouri to persuade Price to go along with the plan. Price was already disappointed that the Confederacy had not sent him and his troops back to the trans-Mississippi, and the inactivity of June, July, and August had done little to improve Price's feelings while his native state lay unprotected.[3]

It would take big planning and risk-taking if the Confederacy hoped to capitalize on the momentum it now had. But the gains, if successful, would be well worth the risk.

The task of holding north Mississippi and the Federal troops stationed there fell mainly to Sterling Price. Born to wealthy Virginia aristocrats in 1809, Price had settled in Missouri, where he eventually became speaker of the Missouri house, a representative in Washington, and governor of the state. As one of the principal secessionists in Missouri, Price had failed in that endeavor, but he soon entered the Confederate army as a general officer and fought at Wilson's Creek and then in Van Dorn's debacle at Pea Ridge before crossing the Mississippi River. By September 1862, Price and his small army of around 15,000 men were the sole Confederate forces in northern Mississippi. But their job was clear: ensure that no more Federals left the area.[4]

And reports indicated that Federals were leaving Mississippi by the division, prompting Price to move as well. Although Van Dorn in Jackson dreamed of his own offensive, Price felt that he could not wait and set out toward Nashville on September 7. Before leaving, he notified Van Dorn that he had moved "immediately against Iuka in accordance with orders just received from General Bragg, who again instructs . . . to follow Rosecrans." Price thus advanced his two divisions under Brigadier General Dabney H. Maury, a West Pointer from Virginia, and Brigadier General Lewis Henry Little, a native of Maryland, a Mexican War veteran, and widely known as Price's "right hand man." The seven brigades contained some of the famous Missouri regiments, as well as the 3rd Louisiana and the 2nd Texas, both of which were well known for their skill on the parade field. The Texans were veterans of Shiloh. A cavalry brigade of about 3,000 men under Frank C. Armstrong and a light artillery battery attached to each brigade completed the small army's organization.[5]

The Confederates trudged northward through mid-September. The march toward Iuka included a rarity in America: a camel served as a beast of burden for officers of the 43rd Mississippi. Horses were afraid of the camel, and many interesting experiences took place along the way. The army, camel and all, marched through northern Mississippi in sweltering heat that turned every road into what one soldier described as "fearfully dusty" trails. Before the soldiers reached Iuka, however, the weather changed, and rain peppered the troops. The dusty trails then became ribbons of mud. One soldier described the effect: "every wagon stalled ascending one big hill."[6]

There was a small confrontation when Price arrived at Iuka, and the Federal commander, Colonel Robert C. Murphy of the 8th Wisconsin (the "Eagle Regiment") panicked. After the Federal decision to abandon the railroad east to Alabama because of a lack of troops, Grant had left Murphy at Iuka to guard and remove the many military goods in the town. Unfortunately, Murphy left without destroying the supplies. One Confederate noted, "We came upon them so unawares that 'twant much to whip them—they did not even have time to burn their stores." Price was ecstatic about his capture, notifying Bragg that Rosecrans had left "several Hundred thousand dollars' worth of army stores." One Confederate foot soldier put it more bluntly: "We captured a good many commissionary stores—the Yanks live like fighting cocks," he mused. He also noted that the morale and health of the men were good: "With the exception of fatigue and a blister on one foot I feel better than I have for a month."[7]

Price soon found himself in a quandary, however. He received conflicting reports that Rosecrans was both at Nashville and at Corinth. It turned out that three of Rosecrans's divisions had moved north, but Rosecrans himself and two divisions were still at Corinth. Meanwhile, Bragg was writing, "I have anxiously expected your advance, and trust it will not longer be delayed." Price knew Rosecrans was at Corinth, but he could not disregard Bragg's order to move to Nashville. The Missourian forwarded Bragg's note to Van Dorn, stating, "I cannot remain inactive any longer, and must move either with you against Rosecrans or toward Kentucky." Price seemed to need someone to give him a little nudge and tell him exactly what to do.[8]

That nudge came early on September 19. A courier from Van Dorn arrived in Iuka with the news that Jefferson Davis had placed Van Dorn in command of both armies in Mississippi on September 11. Van Dorn immediately ordered Price to evacuate Iuka and march to Baldwyn, where the two armies could combine. With the decision made for him, Price issued the necessary orders to get his command ready and to load the captured stores. He planned to march at daylight the next day, September 20.[9]

Ulysses S. Grant intended to have his say, however. He knew that as long as the two Confederate forces in Mississippi remained separated, they were less of a threat. If they united, the two armies would constitute a dangerous enemy. The best course of action for the Federals was to eliminate Price and thus make a Confederate concentration impossible. Unfortunately, the Northerners were as confused about Price's position as Price was about Rosecrans's. On September 7, reports had come in that the two Confederate forces had united and planned an attack. But where? To cover his entire line, Grant moved the two remaining divisions of Rosecrans's army to Corinth. These two, along with the one division of the Army of the Tennessee that remained there, constituted the town's garrison. Rosecrans, whose task it was to see that outposts such as Rienzi and Jacinto had sufficient guards, commanded the entire force. Similarly, E. O. C. Ord, with two divisions of the Army of the Tennessee, moved from Corinth toward Memphis. He took over the position previously held by McClernand, who had already left for Washington. Ord was to guard the stretch of track between Corinth and Memphis. Grant now had three capable subordinates to command his "three grand divisions": Sherman at Memphis, Rosecrans at Corinth, and Ord in the center.[10]

Then the Federals captured a Confederate deserter who told them that Price and Van Dorn had united and intended to move into Kentucky. This news caused a flurry of activity throughout the Federal command. Grant did not know which way the Confederates intended to go, but he reasoned that Corinth was the most likely spot. He responded by moving Hurlbut's division out of Memphis, which was not mentioned as an objective in any of the rumors, to Bolivar, which was much closer to Corinth. That allowed the troops under Ord, who had not yet settled in their new area, to move back to Corinth and help repel an attack there. With the help of the railroads, Ord brought nearly 8,000 men into Corinth within twenty-four hours. This quick movement was amazing, especially considering that the lead train jumped the track, causing a delay of approximately four hours. Not everyone rode the rails, however, and the oppressive heat took its toll on the swiftly marching column. "We marched fifteen miles without stopping to get a drink," one soldier reported, but when they reached Corinth, they were heartened by the reaction of the students at Corona College. "On passing through the town, by the college grounds, the young lady students worked hard at drawing water from the well and giving it to the men to quench their thirst," one thankful Federal remembered. Despite the delay of marching troops and derailing trains, Grant soon had a respectable force with which to defend the crossroads town.[11]

But the situation changed rapidly as more details became known. By the evening of September 11, Grant had enough information to wire Halleck that he thought an attack on Corinth, from the southwest, would come within forty-eight hours. Grant called in all his outposts and braced for the attack from Price's estimated "36,000 to 40,000" men. At that time, Price was actually southeast of Corinth with 15,000 men, but his mere presence seemed enough reason for Grant to call his divisions into Corinth.[12]

Instead of an assault on Corinth, the attack came at Iuka. Seeing an opportunity, Grant determined to do all he could to trap Price. He made up his mind to gamble that Van Dorn could not reach Corinth in less than four days. If Price tarried at Iuka for an extended time and did not make his getaway across the swamps of Bear Creek—the only obstacle that could keep him in the area long enough for Grant to catch him—Grant thought he could get to Iuka, destroy or capture Price and his army, and move back to Corinth within four days to do battle with Van Dorn. He wired Halleck to that effect on September 19. In the message sent from Burnsville, Grant informed Washington that he thought "it will be impossible for Price to get into Tennessee."[13]

Grant had indeed done everything in his power to prevent Price from crossing the Tennessee River. He thus put into motion his plan to strip Corinth of its defenses and attack Price. In the unlikely event of an attack on Corinth while its garrison was away, Grant left a small guard under Brigadier General Thomas J. McKean in the town and in outlying areas. These troops, the 7th, 50th, and 57th Illinois, took up positions where they could warn of an attack from the west early enough for reinforcements to get back to Corinth. All these preparations left Grant feeling confident about the safety of his rear. Now he could concentrate on destroying Price.[14]

With Corinth protected, Grant put all his energy into tracking down the elusive Price. Because Rosecrans was familiar with the area where the operations would take place, he was the logical person to develop the plan. Unfortunately, he created a complicated proposal that would require precision and coordination. Surprisingly, Grant gave his wholehearted approval to Rosecrans's complex scheme, which called for two separate columns to converge on Iuka and the Confederate army there. Rosecrans, leading one wing, would position his two divisions at Jacinto, about ten miles southeast of Corinth. The other wing, led by Ord, would position three divisions at Burnsville, about the same distance down the Memphis and Charleston Railroad toward Iuka. Rosecrans would march into Iuka from the south, while Ord marched on the roads north of the railroad. After Ord had captured the Confederates' attention to the north, the plan called for Rosecrans to sweep into the Southerners' rear and take them by surprise. When Ord heard Rosecrans's guns, he was to launch his attack, and the two wings would catch Price between them like a pecan in a nutcracker.[15]

But Rosecrans's wing became increasingly late as it marched toward Iuka. Its divisions were commanded by Charles Hamilton, a West Point classmate of

Grant's and a Mexican War veteran, and David Stanley, a West Point graduate and regular army officer who had turned down the rank of colonel in the
Confederate army. Seven miles to the northeast, Ord was busy preparing for
his much shorter march. His three divisions, commanded by Brigadier Generals John McArthur, Leonard F. Ross, and Thomas A. Davies, had moved out
of Corinth and massed at Burnsville by noon on September 18. They then
moved to their positions northwest of Iuka, where they skirmished with
Maury's Confederates.[16]

To the south, Rosecrans's infantry marched forward. A member of Hamilton's division, Samuel Byers of the 5th Iowa, remembered that he and his regiment marched "as light-footed and as light-hearted . . . as if we were going
to a wedding." By noon, the column had reached Barnett's Mill, but Rosecrans made a terrible error in judgment there. Two roads meandered southward out of Iuka. The easternmost road, known as the Fulton road, paralleled
the western road, known as the Jacinto road. The two roads were only a couple of miles apart, although the distance between them grew the farther south
they ran. In the master plan, which Rosecrans himself had drawn up, the Federals were supposed to block both the Fulton and Jacinto roads. Price would
then be trapped as the Federals cut off all avenues of escape. Surrender or a
difficult crossing of the Bear Creek swamps would be his only choice. But
Rosecrans marched from Barnett's Mill with his entire force on the Jacinto
road. He had decided that the deep woods in that area of Mississippi would
nullify any chance for the two separated divisions to support each other.
Besides, nearer to Iuka, the Bay Springs road meandered between the two
main byways. Rosecrans reasoned that he could keep his infantry together
until he reached that road and then cross one division over. He furnished
Hamilton with a guide and, "without further instructions," told him to march
on the Jacinto road. Although Rosecrans used sound military logic, he made a
critical blunder. At noon on September 19, the Fulton road remained open,
and it would remain unguarded throughout that night and into the next day.[17]

By 4:00 P.M., Rosecrans was nearing Iuka, but he was two hours behind
his revised schedule, which constituted a delay of almost seven hours from
his original timetable. Because of this, Grant and Ord concluded there was no
way Rosecrans could fight that day. It would be a momentous conclusion.[18]

Watching Ord's Federals advance slowly northwest of Iuka, it came as a
great surprise to Price that the enemy also threatened his rear. At about 2:30
on the afternoon of September 19, an excited courier arrived to report that the

enemy, in heavy force, was making its way toward Iuka on the Jacinto road. Price suddenly had a major problem, but he acted decisively. He pulled Louis Hébert's brigade out of Little's division and sent it southward down the Jacinto road. The Missourian simply told Little to "prevent their further advance." He hoped to stall the Federal divisions on the Jacinto road until he could decide how to get out of Iuka. Thinking better of the idea, Price also sent John D. Martin's brigade after Hébert.[19]

It was a good thing he did, because Rosecrans was getting nearer to the town with every passing minute. By 4:00 P.M., the Federal skirmishers leading Rosecrans's march had pushed the Confederate cavalry back nearly to Iuka. The Union troops filed past the Dick Rick house, some stopping to have a drink from the well in the yard; a sign above the gate leading to the house read "Iuka 2 miles." The Federal brigades continued on, passing a small log church on the left and ascending a long slope to the top of the next hill. But as the Federal skirmishers drove forward, they stumbled into what one soldier of the 5th Iowa described as "a hornets nest" deployed on the reverse slope. The Battle of Iuka had begun.[20]

Hébert's Confederate brigade hit Hamilton's division centered on the 11th Ohio Battery atop the commanding ridge. As the Union cannoneers wheeled their pieces into line, Lieutenant Cyrus Sears and his officers readied the men for the test that would come. Their six guns—two rifled six-pounders, two smoothbore six-pounders, and two twelve-pound howitzers—stood defiant, ready to meet the enemy. The Confederate line had by this time advanced into the hollow below and fired into the Union line, but the Ohioans held their fire. An anxious sergeant could see no reason for the delay, but a corporal informed him that no order had been given to open fire. Sears, commanding the battery, sided with the sergeant and later stated, "It was the last straw." He ordered the battery to open up on the advancing Confederates.[21]

Hamilton later recalled that "the battle at this time had become terrific," and officers continued to bring reinforcements to the front. But the initial line had to deal with the Confederate assault, which, after three attempts, drove the Union infantry away from the Ohio guns. One grizzled participant remembered, "Sword and bayonet were crossed. Muskets, revolvers, knives, ramrods, gun swabs—all mingled in the death-dealing fray." Lieutenant Henry Neil, now in command in place of the wounded Sears, soon had little to lead. The battery ceased to exist except for six lone cannon and their accessories standing atop the wooded hill. All but four horses had fallen, along with a like percentage of the men, several of whom had been bayoneted at their posts. The survivors of the battery succeeded in spiking three of the cannon before they fled, but the Confederates could rightly claim victory amid the devastation. One Confederate later remembered the pitiful sounds of "the rattling of chains and harnesses on wounded artillery horses, only a few yards away."[22]

By this time, Price himself was on the field and took action to drive the Federals farther back. He sent in Martin's brigade, two regiments on each flank. He also called for the other two brigades of Little's division. But tragedy soon struck the command. While Little was moving regiments around the field, he encountered Price. The two sat on their horses in the hollow that faced the Union battle line, perhaps 100 yards east of the road. While Price sat with his back to the battle and Little faced the conflict, a minié ball narrowly missed Price as it passed under his arm and hit "square in the forehead" of General Little. The bullet entered on the "line of the scalp over the left eye," according to an eyewitness, and made its way through the general's brain, stopping just under the skin at the back of his head. Little flung his arms upward and fell from his horse, "Trumps," into the arms of an aide standing nearby. A crowd gathered to offer assistance, but Little was dead.[23]

Price was devastated by the loss of his friend and trusted subordinate — right before his eyes, no less. But the battle continued as the Confederates fought for survival. And the fight only grew more heated. Despite the Union retreat, the Federals soon re-formed their line and managed to counterattack, retaking the battery. The Confederates returned, continuing the seesawing that would see the battery change hands three more times. Union fire from the rear did not help the defense, and the Federals ultimately gave up the fight at sundown. The Confederates held the field.[24]

Casualties were high, given the small number of men engaged. The Federals reported 790 losses, while the Confederates reported 525, although that number is almost certainly too low. Obviously, the battle would have been even bloodier if Ord's Union force had attacked from the north, but fortunately for the Confederates, he did not. After he and Grant had decided that no battle would take place that day, Ord returned to his camp and stayed there all night, never even hearing the sound of the guns. Grant later wrote that the wind had been blowing in "the wrong direction to transmit sound towards either Ord or me."[25]

In Iuka, a relieved but grieving Sterling Price, after entertaining thoughts of continuing the battle, wisely decided to retreat. Fortunately, Rosecrans's faulty decision and Price's hard fight had kept the Fulton road open. The next morning, Price's tired and bloodied army retreated out of Iuka and eventually toward Baldwyn and safety. One Confederate officer was unable to see the benefit of the entire operation, though. "I am totally at a loss, as well as everybody else, to know what we accomplished by it," he noted in his diary.[26]

Rosecrans's dazed column wasted little time in following the retreating Confederates toward Iuka the next morning, even firing a few artillery rounds at the tail end of the Confederate column. Just outside the town, the Federals met a delegation of Iuka citizens led by Sam Dewoody, who carried a bed sheet on a broom handle. Ord's forces also arrived and learned, to their dismay, that Rosecrans had fought the afternoon before. Once they entered Iuka, the Federals found that they had captured only an empty town full of dead and dying Confederates.[27]

Grant also traveled to Iuka for a firsthand view. There, he discovered that the Fulton road had been left open and that Price, at that very moment, was making good his escape. Grant was quite upset with Rosecrans, which would cause problems in the future. He immediately ordered Rosecrans's two infantry divisions, as well as the cavalry, to pursue, but Grant did not stop there. His major concern was for Corinth itself, and he began sending his men back to the crossroads town. Realizing that more than half the time Van Dorn needed to arrive had passed and that Corinth remained very lightly defended, Grant immediately ordered Ord back to the town. In fact, rumors that the Confederates had taken Corinth began swirling as early as September 21. "Various reports were passing that Price is already in Corinth," August Schilling wrote in his diary, "and is being pressed by Rosecrans. We surely would appreciate to know the truth." Later, when he reached the town, Schilling found that the fortifications had been strengthened with "embankments and hurdles encircled in order that an inner line of defense could hold because of the small number of soldiers. The siege guns were already in position." Meanwhile, Rosecrans's two divisions moved back to Jacinto, ending the small but deadly campaign.[28]

The troops that were expected to defend Corinth against the Confederate attack were in poor shape, however. One soldier reported on the march back to Corinth: "We are very short of rations, to-day, and I have had no breakfast. I don't expect anything to eat until we get to Corinth." When they finally returned and had a meal, they found that all their baggage and tents had been "drawn to the breast-works for fear of a raid on the camp." The soldiers were displeased, to say the least, to find their carefully crafted bunks and camps "destroyed." Another soldier reported that the men had placed their wet blankets in wagons before the march, and they "must have got into a wagon-train bound for other parts, for that was the last we ever saw of them." It was not a perfect situation, but they were back at Corinth and ready to defend it.[29]

Despite the recent disturbance, the area around Corinth was quiet for the first time in several days—at least for now. Whether and when a battle over the town developed depended on the new Confederate commander in north Mississippi. That commander was Earl Van Dorn, a native of Mississippi and a West Point classmate of Rosecrans. He had a reputation for action, and he had already made his decision. Even before the campaign that culminated in the battle at Iuka, the Mississippian had focused his attention on a grander scheme. At the center of his plan was an advance into west Tennessee and then a push into Kentucky and the southern reaches of the United States. Bragg, who was still making his way northward in Kentucky, had ordered the two Confederate generals in Mississippi to do all they could to help his invasion. A parallel advance to the west would certainly do that, and it could accomplish much more. It might even bring the vain Van Dorn the glory he had always wanted. But the Union garrisons left in Mississippi had to be attacked before any advance northward could be made.[30]

Van Dorn was many things, but inexperienced was not one of them. He was, however, impulsive. According to historian Charles Elliott's novel thesis, while fighting the dashing but ill-prepared Comanche, Van Dorn had learned the slashing attack he would implement for good and bad in the Civil War. He used it at battles such as Pea Ridge, and he would use that style of fighting in a campaign against Corinth. Situated at Jackson, Mississippi, in the late summer of 1862, and in command of the district around Vicksburg, Van Dorn had planned how he might work with Price to contain Federal units in Mississippi, liberate west Tennessee, and form a junction with Bragg in Kentucky. After securing the area around Vicksburg, he had ordered his own headquarters and as many troops as possible to go north to Holly Springs. After being "marched and counter-marched about the state," as one soldier put it, they arrived in the early days of September. Van Dorn informed Price that he would be ready to work with him by the middle of the month, but by the time he reached Holly Springs, Price had already moved toward Iuka.[31]

At Holly Springs, three brigades were led by Brigadier Generals Albert Rust, John B. Villepigue, and John S. Bowen, all constituting a division under Major General Mansfield Lovell. Once he arrived, Van Dorn immediately began searching for Price. He led an expedition toward Bolivar in which he almost captured a Federal brigade, but he learned nothing of Price's whereabouts. On September 23, Van Dorn sent out more scouts with a letter for Price. The searching finally paid off, and Van Dorn and Price worked out the details of a merger at Ripley on September 28.[32]

Despite a thunderstorm that hit the area on the evening of September 27, the two forces met as planned the next day. But then a potentially serious dispute occurred within the army's command. It was common knowledge that the two generals did not like each other, but their relationship had remained professionally friendly. It was Price's chief of staff, Thomas Snead, who caused the near rupture. Having seen all of Price's correspondence with Van Dorn, Snead announced that he would not serve under the Mississippian and submitted his letter of resignation to Price. In the letter, he called Van Dorn incompetent and rash and surmised that Van Dorn would, little by little, take over Price's army. In his blistering attack, Snead reminded Price that this was the second time he had resigned rather than serve under Van Dorn. Had the issue remained buried among headquarters gossip in northern Mississippi, little chaos would have ensued, but the story was leaked to the press, and correspondents broadcast it throughout the South. The *Charleston Mercury*, for example, stated that Snead's charge "most certainly does seem unjust." Price, a little older and perhaps a little wiser, dealt with the matter more calmly. He wrote back to his young officer and noted that although he and many other Missourians felt the same way as Snead, this was certainly the wrong time and place for such comments. Price showed enormous patience, and he encouraged Snead to support Van Dorn's command. Snead eventually withdrew his resignation, and the potentially crippling disruption soon quieted.[33]

With this situation shrugged off, the generals began to reorganize their troops for the coming campaign. Very little in Maury's division, unengaged at Iuka, changed. In Little's division, however, Hébert officially took Little's position, and Colonel Bruce Colbert of the 40th Mississippi assumed command of the brigade. These two divisions then combined with the lone division Van Dorn had brought to Ripley to constitute the Mississippian's army. Price retained command of his two divisions, which were still officially known as the Army of the West but were referred to as Price's Corps. Hébert and Maury still answered to Price; Lovell, who had the same command, answered only to Van Dorn, who commanded the whole.[34]

Van Dorn named his force the Army of West Tennessee, even though none of the soldiers had spent any appreciable time in western Tennessee and the army did not occupy a single inch of ground in that area. Van Dorn so named his army because that was where he planned to take it and reclaim that territory for the Confederacy. But the first stop was Corinth.[35]

While contemplating attacks on Memphis or Bolivar, both of which had numerous drawbacks, Van Dorn surmised that a victorious assault on Corinth would not only bring that important post back into Confederate hands but also serve as an excellent jumping-off point for the invasion of west Tennessee, the purpose for his action in the first place. Van Dorn realized that "the taking of Corinth was a condition precedent to the accomplishment of anything of importance in West Tennessee." Terming the town the "strongest but the most salient point," he simply could not leave such a large Union garrison in his rear as he moved north.[36]

Van Dorn also reasoned that, since Shiloh, he had become personally knowledgeable about the area in question; he also had a detailed map, captured from the Federals at Iuka, and he knew the Federal commander, a fellow West Point graduate. In addition, the Mississippian had about 22,000 men, a much greater number than the estimated 15,000 Rosecrans had inside Corinth at the moment. The trick would be to attack and win before Rosecrans's other divisions, thought to be at Jacinto, could arrive. Speed would thus determine the success of the operation. The longer the Confederates delayed, the more formidable the Corinth defenses would become and the more men Rosecrans would have to man them.[37]

Despite the advantages, the attack on Corinth also involved major dangers, including a larger defending garrison than at Memphis or Bolivar and rail connections to the north. In addition to a lightning attack, carried out before the enemy could call in troops from the surrounding countryside, Van Dorn envisioned an attack from the northwest that would cut the railroads coming from Federal-held garrisons. The plan was risky, to say the least, but Van Dorn considered the attack "a military necessity, requiring prompt and vigorous action."[38]

Price agreed with the advance northward and even the attack on Corinth, but he disagreed with Van Dorn's timing. One of Price's staff officers later recalled that the Missourian "strenuously advised against it." Price believed the army should postpone the attack until after the arrival of the exchanged Fort Donelson prisoners, due at Holly Springs shortly. Van Dorn, supported by Lovell, countered that waiting would only give the enemy time to strengthen Corinth's fortifications. As the decision was announced, Van Dorn noted that Price "seem[ed] despondent." "No! You quite mistake me," Price thundered. "I have only given you the facts within my knowledge and the counselings of my judgment. When you reach Corinth you shall find that no portion of the army shall excel mine either in courage, in conduct, or in achievement."[39]

With the decision made, Price and Lovell readied their commands. Van Dorn told the two commanders to provide three days' rations for their men. To feed them past those three days, army wagons and others found along the way should be sent to Holly Springs, where they would be loaded with foodstuffs. For this trip, the wagons would be guarded by what one soldier called "convalescents or weakly men," thus taking no able-bodied man from the ranks. Van Dorn also presented the timetable. On September 29, Lovell would lead the way with his division; Price's two divisions would follow the next day. The three divisions would march from Ripley toward Bolivar, keeping the Federals confused as to their real intentions. At the last moment, Van Dorn would turn southeast and, after a rapid march, attack the unsuspecting enemy at Corinth from the northwest.[40]

Van Dorn, whom Maury later insisted was "one of the ablest and most audacious and aggressive soldiers which our side produced during the war," felt confident that his latest scheme would result in a great victory. He even wired Richmond of his plans. "No army ever marched to battle with prouder steps, more hopeful countenances, or with more courage," Van Dorn later wrote, "than marched the Army of West Tennessee out of Ripley on the morning of September 29 on its way to Corinth."[41]

Federal commanders kept a close watch on the confusing enemy movements to the south. With the help of good scouts and plenty of cavalry, which Grant "kept well to the front," he and his subordinates knew almost every move the Confederates made. And by September 23, Grant and his subordinates had stabilized the situation around Corinth itself. Although a lack of troops forced him ultimately to abandon the Memphis and Charleston Railroad between Corinth and Memphis, some troops—Ross's and Hurlbut's divisions at Bolivar—still covered the middle segment of Grant's line. That left two divisions of the Army of the Tennessee to defend Corinth alongside the two divisions of the Army of the Mississippi under Stanley and Hamilton. The Second and Sixth Divisions of the Army of the Tennessee were no longer controlled by their original commanding officers, however. John McArthur had obtained permission for a leave of absence, and Thomas Davies, a New Yorker who had graduated from West Point the same year as Robert E. Lee and Joseph E. Johnston, had transferred from the Sixth Division to take over W. H. L. Wallace's old Shiloh command, veterans of the Hornet's Nest. Thomas J. McKean, at the time commanding the Corinth garrison, took Davies's Sixth Division. Only a year younger than Davies, McKean had also graduated from West Point, but two years after Davies. A native of Pennsylvania, McKean had fought in the Mexican War as an enlisted soldier.[42]

Then, in a surprising move on September 26, Grant moved his headquarters to Jackson, Tennessee, in order "to superintend the movement of troops to whatever point the attack might be made upon." There was apparently more to it than that, however. Rosecrans later stated that Grant's movement added to the "embarrassments in preparing the place [Corinth] to resist a sudden attack." John Fuller, a brigade commander in Stanley's division, stated after the war that there existed a "positive dislike between Grant and Rosecrans—a breach which was never healed." Stanley, one of the division commanders at Corinth, agreed. He wrote, "A general quarrel arose between Generals Grant and Rosecrans." This quarrel, resulting from the mix-up at Iuka that left the Fulton road open and allowed Price to escape, no doubt became quite heated and could have contributed to Grant's decision to move his headquarters away from Rosecrans.[43]

Despite the temporary calm and normality, tension still filled the Federal commanders as several small skirmishes broke out. Rumors also spread about larger Confederate activities, one of which claimed the two major Confederate forces had begun moving toward Ripley. Keeping an eye on Van Dorn at Bolivar, Hurlbut reported on September 27 that the Confederates had apparently gone eastward. He confirmed the report on September 30. The next day, confirmation of Price's arrival at Ripley came from Rosecrans. All this activity, as well as the numerous rumors, sent alarm throughout the Union high command.[44]

One of those rumors mentioned an attack on Memphis. Very soon, Grant learned that the supposed movement on Memphis was just a ruse to cover "a deeper design; one much more important to his [Van Dorn's] cause." Grant did not yet know what that design was, but another report mentioned Corinth. "It has been rumored for some time that Price was meditating an attack upon this place or somewhere upon the forces in this vicinity," one Union soldier wrote from Corinth in late September. Rosecrans thus stepped up his efforts to make the town's defenses more formidable. During his absence in Iuka, workers had completed the five new inner batteries but not the connecting earthworks, so Rosecrans had his work cut out for him. "Colored engineer troops organized into squads of twenty-five each" began to labor in earnest. Soldiers of the quartermaster department led these squads, and Captain William B. Gaw commanded the entire operation. The batteries received extra attention, and the line of batteries was extended on both ends. A new earthwork north of town, Battery Powell, was started to the right of Robinett; another, Battery Madison, lay south of town, in the southeast quadrant of the railroads' crossing. But there was not enough time to connect them with rifle pits.[45]

As the fortification continued throughout the latter days of September, Corinth became more formidable. In addition, Rosecrans ordered an abatis laid on the northern and western side of Corinth, constructed from the trees that still stood in front of the works. Rosecrans also called in the outposts, essentially Hamilton's and Stanley's divisions at Jacinto, bringing them "within short call." Subsequently, however, Rosecrans sent Stanley back out westward to Kossuth to "cover all the Hatchie crossings."[46]

By the first of October, some holes remained in the Corinth works, but they were becoming stronger by the hour, with most of the work being done on the western and southern approaches to the inner line. Little work had been done on the sections between Battery Robinett and Battery Powell, which was itself incomplete. A thin line of abatis lay between Robinett and the Mobile and Ohio Railroad, but nothing stood in the way of an attacking force sweeping through the area from the railroad eastward to Powell. But surely, Rosecrans believed, any major attack on Corinth would come from the south or west, and it was there that he put the majority of his effort. Van Dorn, however, was not a predictable commander.[47]

9

"My Position Is Precarious"

By the early days of October, the nationwide Confederate offensive was in shambles. Robert E. Lee had suffered enormous losses at Antietam in Maryland, and with that, the Confederate invasion in the east failed. The hope of Lee and others that Marylanders would rise up and join the Confederacy was dashed, as most opted not to do so. Then Abraham Lincoln used the strategic victory in Maryland as a justification for issuing his preliminary Emancipation Proclamation. Many people at the time, as well as countless historians since, argued that the proclamation ended any chance the South had for foreign recognition and thus doomed the Confederacy.[1]

In Kentucky, Bragg's invasion remained ostensibly on schedule, but numerous problems were emerging there as well. As in Maryland, the throngs of Kentuckians who were supposed to flock to the Confederate army were nowhere to be found. Instead, frightened masses in Indiana and Ohio were rising up and forming units for the defense of their states. Bragg was having leadership problems as well. He was unable to get Kirby Smith to work with him, and lower-level commanders were refusing to follow orders and losing precious men in needless battles. On top of it all, the enemy was reorganizing and moving out to confront Bragg.[2]

Mississippi was a problem area too. When Price became hemmed in at Iuka, the entire plan seemed doomed. After he miraculously extricated himself and united with Van Dorn, however, the two once again seemed ready to lead the third prong of the fall invasion. But the Confederates had to take Corinth first, and that required stealth, quickness, and surprise.

Despite the failure elsewhere, Van Dorn still had high hopes for success in his part of the Confederate advance. Thus, his army, motivated by its motto "Conquer or die," confidently moved northward toward the center of the Federal line in northern Mississippi and western Tennessee. On September 29,

Lovell and his division left Ripley and marched toward Pocahontas, Tennessee. The next morning, Price and his two divisions moved out. The plan called for Van Dorn to march toward Bolivar, threatening that place until the last moment; then he would suddenly change course and move on Corinth from the northwest.[3]

By nightfall on September 29, Lovell had moved about six miles to the north, camping for the night close to the Lucker house. Meanwhile, Price's men had marched to the west of Ripley and set up camp. The next morning portended a heat wave as Lovell marched on into Tennessee, stopping at Metamora, a small village just south of Pocahontas. Price's troops, in the meantime, marched back through Ripley and turned north, following the general direction of Lovell's troops and camping close to the little village of Jonesborough that night. A "fair assembly" of women, as one soldier recalled, urged the soldiers on and gave them food along the way. On October 1, both commands, particularly the Missouri troops, were overjoyed to leave Mississippi. One veteran remembered, "It seemed to put joy & mirth in all the Missourians' hearts to get out of the State of Miss, not that we disliked the state but we wanted to go north." Another noted that despite "dew [that] is almost like a shower of rain," he was confident and happy and hoped to send "a Yankee home with a 'bug in his ear.'"[4]

Up to this point, Van Dorn had succeeded in fooling the enemy, but he also managed to confuse his own officers in the process. Almost no one except for Price and Lovell knew Van Dorn's intentions. He had dropped hints about drawing the enemy out of Corinth, but the other officers knew nothing more. To further confuse the Federals, Van Dorn sent out cavalry detachments toward Bolivar and Corinth. Colonel William Falkner moved with his regiment toward Corinth for the sole purpose of breaking the Mobile and Ohio Railroad north of town. This would not only hide Van Dorn's true intentions but also keep reinforcements from reaching Corinth by rail. Another regiment moved toward Bolivar. By the time the Confederates reached Pocahontas, however, the time had come to stop the game and make a run toward Corinth.[5]

Van Dorn notified his commanders that they were to turn their divisions eastward toward Chewalla, Tennessee, only ten miles northwest of Corinth. On October 2, Lovell was to march toward Chewalla and use cavalry to feel out the enemy's position. Price was to have his divisions ready to march "at short notice," the time of departure depending on what came of Lovell's probe. One obstacle stood in the way, however. A portion of the 3rd Michigan Cavalry had earlier destroyed Davis Bridge across the Hatchie River. Lovell's men repaired the bridge while Van Dorn and some of his generals gathered at the Davis house, which stood on the left of the road about 100 yards west of the river. Once the bridge was rebuilt, the army began to move. Lovell's division left its camps with Armstrong's cavalry in the vanguard. Price soon received orders to follow. One Confederate colonel who was still in the dark reacted with bewilderment. "Took the Corinth road," he wrote in his diary, "a very puzzling move for me."[6]

Higher-ranking officers were equally unaware. When John Bowen went with Lovell to the Davis house that morning, he was shocked. They found Van Dorn working on a map of Corinth with a local citizen, the map merely "a crude sketch on a sheet of letter paper." After Bowen and Lovell left, an alarmed Bowen voiced his concern about the need for better maps and reconnaissance.[7]

Despite the growing alarm, the march continued, with Van Dorn using only minor detachments to secure the rear of his marching column. Wirt Adams and his Mississippi cavalry regiment, along with the attached 2nd Arkansas Cavalry, remained on the west bank of the Hatchie River to guard the recently rebuilt bridge. In the event of a setback, Van Dorn would need the bridge as an avenue of escape. After crossing the Hatchie, Van Dorn left his wagon train behind as well, along with Edwin R. Hawkins's 1st Texas Legion and the St. Louis Battery to defend it. These units halted where the Bone Yard road left the main road running south; it later crossed the Hatchie at Crum's Mill before finally connecting with the Ripley road west of the river. The remainder of the army moved in an easterly direction toward Chewalla, tiring rapidly in the increasing heat and growing hungrier by the hour. One soldier wrote that many of the men were "broak down and left by the roadside marched to death and suffering with hunger."[8]

Before they reached Chewalla, the Confederates discovered that Young's Bridge across the Tuscumbia River was partially damaged as well. Van Dorn sent Bowen, who had been an engineer before the war, to repair it. As the soldiers began to work on the bridge, Federal skirmishers opened a brisk fire on them, forcing a temporary stoppage. The Confederates finally pushed the Federals back, and handpicked members of the 1st Missouri repaired the bridge. But Van Dorn chafed at the lost time, waiting impatiently as the men rebuilt the structure.[9]

While he waited, Van Dorn called his generals together and, for the first time, told them of his plan. The news openly devastated many of them; they could hardly believe that Van Dorn was going to assault the Corinth works. Bowen and Rust were especially distraught at the thought of assaulting enemy breastworks, and they were upset that Van Dorn had not confided in them sooner. Van Dorn was in a testy mood, earlier complaining of "the worthlessness of engineer officers." He now responded harshly that their "duty was to obey orders," and he did not have to tell his plans to those of lower rank. Rust recalled, "I expressed myself strongly against it" and even went so far as to declare that "it was impossible to succeed in the attack." But Lovell silenced the complainers. "If we could not succeed we had better lay down our arms and go home," he argued. His mind unchanged, Rust later confided to one of Price's staff officers that the attempt was "madness." Van Dorn remained firm, however, and the Confederates soon passed over the repaired bridge, continuing their long journey toward Corinth. There was nothing Rust or anyone else could have said to change Van Dorn's mind.[10]

Nearer to Chewalla, the Southern column met more Union pickets. After Armstrong finished "skirmishing lightly with the enemy for several hours," one soldier recorded, the Confederates finally drove them away. Apparently, the Federals were elements of Grant's old bodyguard, Ford's Independent Illinois Cavalry Company, and Rosecrans enjoyed telling the general that they were "reported to have run in the most disgraceful manner." Nevertheless, Van Dorn quickly occupied Chewalla's abandoned camps and earthworks, which one surprised Confederate described as "quite extensive being I think fully 200 yards in diameter." After taking a small amount of supplies, Van Dorn's army bivouacked there on the night of October 2.[11]

Unfortunately for the Confederacy, Van Dorn's elaborate plan had already begun to unravel, and he did not seem to know it. The plan depended on speed and surprise, but the skirmishing at Young's Bridge and Chewalla had provided the Federals with ample knowledge of Van Dorn's whereabouts, and it also gave them time to prepare. Confederate commanders hoped the enemy had not penetrated behind the cavalry screen and seen that the entire army was moving toward Corinth, but they could not be sure. In fact, Federal infantry at Chewalla had observed infantry and artillery units in line of battle behind the cavalry screen on October 2. They knew Corinth was the target.[12]

Reports quickly arrived at Grant's headquarters about an enemy movement. Both Hurlbut at Bolivar and Rosecrans at Corinth kept cavalry out to watch, and those scouts provided vital information concerning the whereabouts of the Confederate army. After the Confederate concentration at Ripley, Grant had already felt confident that the attack would come at Corinth; accordingly, he had ordered Rosecrans to bring in his outposts. Rosecrans promptly obeyed. This caused at least one soldier who had been expecting a battle and the possibility of dying to write home that he planned to "use up my money at the sutlers or on some better food than the rations." When the Confederates marched toward Pocahontas, however, Grant hesitated. He had garrisons at both Corinth and Bolivar, so all he could do was wait until Van Dorn tipped his hand. He ordered Rosecrans to send all trains to Jackson, and he told Hurlbut to fortify all bridges north of Bolivar. Fortunately, the cavalry guard, posted in a ring around Corinth at such places as Burnsville, Jacinto, Kossuth, and Bone Yard, soon gave Grant more information. Two units even patrolled the road in the rear of Van Dorn's marching army. Colonel Albert L. Lee's cavalry brigade marched across the Hatchie River at Crum's Mill, some six miles south of Davis Bridge; the 7th Kansas Cavalry similarly marched from its camps at Rienzi to Ripley and were positioned behind Van Dorn. Brief skirmishes pinpointed the Confederate position. But even then, Grant could not determine the exact direction of the Confederate attack—Corinth or Bolivar. In Corinth, quartermasters received orders to forward only necessary articles to the brigades. At Bolivar, orders went out for the troops to keep their cartridge boxes on.[13]

By October 2, however, Grant had the information he needed. Hurlbut at Bolivar reported that there was "evidently a movement eastward going on in front of me." Then the skirmishing at Chewalla verified reports that the Confederates were on their way to Corinth. Grant informed Halleck, "It is now clear that Corinth is to be the point." "My position is precarious," he added, "but [I] hope to get out of it all right."[14]

Although Grant was convinced that Van Dorn would attack Corinth, Rosecrans "doubted if they would venture to bring their force against our command behind defensive works." He later testified that he could not help but think "it was in their interest" to move on Bolivar and Jackson. But if Corinth was indeed the target, Rosecrans was sure that Van Dorn would first cut the Federal communication and supply lines and force him to come out of those defenses and fight in the open. Further perplexing Rosecrans was the fact that Stanley, near Kossuth, reported there were no Confederates in sight at the Hatchie, and he doubted there were any for three miles across the river. By that time, of course, the Confederates had already passed that position and were indeed on the Hatchie, just farther downstream (north). Rosecrans thus stayed on guard, "prepared for whatever they might do."[15]

Part of Rosecrans's preparations consisted of strengthening the garrison at Corinth. He had numerous divisions in and around the town that he could call in quickly if needed. One surgeon in the 12th Iowa wrote home, "We can get reinforcements if we can have 2 or three hours time. I can not say that our position looks all together safe, but I presume that our men feel safe." Most notably, Rosecrans posted Hamilton and Davies just south of the town, across Bridge Creek. He also decided to call in other outlying units. The 11th Ohio Battery, the unit so badly mauled at Iuka just thirteen days earlier, returned to

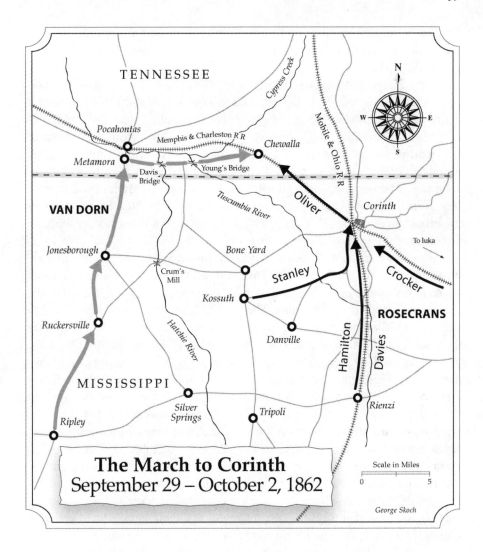

The March to Corinth
September 29 – October 2, 1862

George Skoch

active duty on October 2. Completely refitted by Captain Henry Neil at Iuka, the battery had remained there until the latter part of September. When the refurbishing was complete, its orders were to secure a guard from Marcellus M. Crocker, who commanded a brigade at Iuka, and proceed to Corinth. By the evening of October 1, the battery was ready to leave, but Crocker would not supply the guard to accompany them. Neil grappled with the question of whether to gamble on an unguarded trip to Corinth. He ultimately decided to take the risk, although he was afraid that guerrillas would capture the battery

and that he would be "shot up first and court-martialed afterward." To provide some protection, Neil mounted cannoneers and had them ride in the
advance.[16]

The battery made the trip safely, and when the men entered the Union
lines, they did so "amid the hurrahs and tears of the infantry that had seen it
destroyed under the terrible fire of the 19th of September," one soldier remembered. As one Federal put it, the battery "had come back from the regions of
the dead to aid in the terrible struggle now going on between the same
armies." Glad to be back in Napoleon Buford's brigade, Neil told Colonel
John B. Sanborn, commanding the 4th Minnesota, to stay right beside his battery. If he did so, no Confederate would get to the guns. Neil later stated that
the brigade "looked much smaller than before Iuka but that made us think all
the more of it."[17]

As time passed and Rosecrans gathered his army, it became increasingly
clear that Corinth was the Confederate target. One Union surgeon in town
wrote to his wife, "The first positive indication we had of the approach of the
enemy in force was on Thursday. The regular train from Columbus failed to
come in on Thursday night and we soon learned that the rebels had torn up
the track." Taking no chances, Rosecrans sent out additional scouts. One large
group was the Union Brigade, a battalion of companies made up of the remnants of the regiments that had surrendered at Shiloh's Hornet's Nest. Rosecrans ordered them south of Corinth to the Tuscumbia River to look for any
Confederate movements in that direction. The unit was camped at Danville,
"enjoying our fruit and pursuing our usual avocations of guard mounting,
reposting and jay-hawing," one of the soldiers remembered. But the unit's
commanding officer was sick when the order to move arrived, leaving command to Captain John G. Fowler. Unfortunately, Fowler immediately "commenced drinking catawba wine," one soldier remembered, and was soon "so
gloriously drunk that the whole Brigade noticed it and laughed and yelled at
him as if he were put there for their special amusement." Fowler gave all sorts
of strange commands and would then "give a yell like an Indian war-whoop
and be answered by loud shouts from the men." Tiring of the nonsense, Captain David B. Henderson ordered several men to remove the captain from his
horse and arrest him. The silly affair cost the brigade precious time, and the
men were late in arriving at their destination. Henderson confided to a friend,
"My great regret is that I did not put a ball through Fowler's rotten carcass."[18]

Rosecrans also sent part of John Oliver's brigade of McKean's division
northwestward toward Chewalla: "You had better send enough to make a
brigade with axes &c to obstruct the roads," Rosecrans ordered McKean. One
regiment, the 15th Michigan, had earlier taken a position at Chewalla, along

with a company of Illinois cavalry, and had erected some crude breastworks. It was these men that skirmished with the advance guard of the Confederate army. Oliver and the 14th and 18th Wisconsin Regiments, along with a section of the 1st Minnesota Battery, joined them near sundown on October 1. One member of the 14th Wisconsin, initially thinking it was only "a straggling band of bush whackers" to the front, recorded that they found the 15th Michigan "badly broken up and with their camp equipage making for a more friendly country." The Michiganders "insisted" there were more Confederates out there than bushwhackers, as Oliver soon found out for himself. When he "reached the heights above Chewalla," he reported that the enemy was advancing toward the town. Though he encountered only enemy scouts, Oliver ordered his men to deploy in line of battle on a ridge south of town covering the roads that led southwest to the Tuscumbia bottom, the supposed route of the Confederates; he did not know that the main Confederate body was situated near Pocahontas. He and others of his command erroneously believed the Confederates were near Kossuth, south of their position. To make sure, Oliver sent scouts out on several occasions to "feel vigorously for the enemy." He also sent scouts out on the Bolivar road toward Young's Bridge. Each time, to Oliver's dismay, the scouts on the Bolivar road found the enemy, and those sent toward Kossuth did not, although they did hear drums in that direction. He therefore decided to change his front, covering both the Tuscumbia River roads as well as the Bolivar road. Eventually, he withdrew to cover both.[19]

Not wanting to "bring on more trouble than we could care for," Oliver welcomed a message from McKean ordering him to move even farther back than the junction his men currently held. He notified his regiments to fall back on the crossroads at Alexander's, while the rear guard continued to skirmish with the enemy. Oliver soon arrived at Alexander's and formed his men in a strong position, one that would "thoroughly command the road," he said. While the regiments formed the new line, the skirmishers continued to fall back in front of the advancing enemy.[20]

Oliver continued to worry, even during his withdrawal. He realized that the railroad to the north provided an easy means of travel for the Confederates, so he sent a patrol to scout it. Still not convinced that the main Confederate body was near Chewalla, he also sent the 18th Wisconsin to guard Smith's Bridge over the Tuscumbia, just to the west. Although the Badgers saw nothing, the small patrol on the railroad found what Oliver had feared. Oliver quickly reported the news to McKean and waited for developments, but by this time, the sun had set. During the night of October 2, one of Oliver's men surprisingly recorded in his diary, "Laid in line of battle all night [but] there was no alarm"; Oliver would have disagreed. He notified McKean that the enemy was "advancing apparently on all roads" and cautioned that his cavalry "now here are completely worn out and *discouraged*." That was a pretty good description of the jumpy Oliver himself.[21]

Growing more confident by the hour that Corinth was the Confederate target, Rosecrans and his commanders had men on the march throughout the evening and nighttime hours of October 2, concentrating at Corinth. There was little sleep at Oliver's headquarters near Alexander's, for instance. He wanted to withdraw closer to Corinth but could not move until he received orders; he was somewhat comforted, however, by the arrival of reinforcements. The 16th Wisconsin of Colonel Benjamin Allen's brigade had come to the front and taken a position beside Oliver's troops. McArthur also arrived from his court-martial duty and toured the defenses with the nervous Federal commander. Oliver had reason to be anxious. By the night of October 2, when Oliver and McArthur were at Alexander's, the entire Confederate army was camped at Chewalla, closer to Alexander's than Alexander's was to Corinth.[22]

While one part of McKean's division fought the Confederates on the Chewalla road, the remainder camped inside the outer ring of earthworks, just south of that road. Allen's brigade camped there, as did Crocker's, which had just completed the long march from Iuka. Crocker had still been at Iuka on October 1 when he received orders to make a forced march, "posthaste," to Corinth. A train arrived to haul the equipment and the sick, but the men themselves marched. One member of the 15th Iowa remembered, "Our men set fire to all the houses along the line of march to-day." When the brigade reentered Corinth, the deplorable water situation did not help their fatigue. One soldier reported: "Water is very scarce. I took six canteens and started to find water, but to get it I must have traveled in all four miles." Nevertheless, Mc-Kean's division was soon present and ready to fend off any attack the Confederates might hurl at them.[23]

Meanwhile, Rosecrans also called the other Union divisions toward Corinth, which was exactly what Van Dorn had hoped to avoid; his advantage of surprise was gone. Stanley's division, after a roundabout march from Jac-into to Corinth via Kossuth, arrived in time to help thwart the Confederate general's plans. He had moved his division closer to Corinth by October 1 and then marched to Kossuth and back to the Tuscumbia River. Thus, it was most likely Stanley's drums that Oliver heard from Chewalla. While at Kossuth, Stanley sent a patrol that scouted all the way to the Hatchie, finding nothing; he also sent a few regiments to act in conjunction with Lee and his cavalry reconnaissance. On October 2, Stanley's division, minus three regiments left at Kossuth, went into camp nearer Corinth, although at least one soldier recorded that they got lost a couple of times: "We wandered around like lost sheep all day." The division was exhausted, having marched more than thirty-five miles in the last twenty-four hours in a heat wave and with little water to drink. And nerves were frayed. At one point, Stanley cursed a teamster for driving too fast on such a hot day, whereupon the driver took out a pistol and forced Stanley to sheath his sword. "They eyed each other closely for a moment," one eyewitness recorded, "and then Stanley deliberately put up his sword and told the driver to go on." Stanley later remarked to a colonel: "He is a good one."[24]

Rosecrans also called in his units south of town. Camped at Clear Creek, Hamilton was near Corinth by October 2. Davies had also moved closer, to Camp Montgomery, two and a half miles south of Corinth. But there they stayed until the Federal high command figured out exactly what was going on. "We were under marching orders all day but did not march," one Iowa soldier recorded in his diary. As if oblivious to the growing storm, on October 2 a portion of Davies's division participated in a dress parade.[25]

By October 2, Rosecrans was convinced that Van Dorn would attack Corinth, but he was still unsure whether Van Dorn would attack directly or force him out of his defenses to fight on open ground. Earlier, Van Dorn had sent a regiment of cavalry, Falkner's Mississippi troopers, to cut the Mobile and Ohio Railroad and the adjacent telegraph line north of Corinth. The regiment reached its objective at Ramer's Crossing on October 2 and quickly went to work cutting the railroad. After succeeding in their mission, the Confederates had to flee when members of the 17th Wisconsin arrived to support a portion of the18th Missouri. Nevertheless, the Confederates succeeded in breaking both the telegraph line and the railroad, ending direct communication between Rosecrans and Grant. Thereafter, the Federal commanders could communicate only by couriers traveling a circuitous route from Corinth through Farmington to Bethel, where the telegraph was still operational. It took seven or eight hours.[26]

During these hours of uncertainty, Rosecrans even entertained thoughts of marching out of Corinth before a battle began. On October 2, perhaps still doubting that the town was the Confederate target, he ordered Stanley, located near Kossuth, to look into the best "possible means . . . of marching . . . across the Hatchie." His plan envisioned leaving only a small force at Corinth while the rest marched westward across the river. Once across, the Federals would enter the Ripley road, get behind the advancing Confederates, and, Rosecrans said, "push those fellows to the wall." He even mentioned this plan to Grant, but no answer was recorded. Whether Rosecrans realized the move was impossible because the Confederates were already near Chewalla and would be too far out of reach if they gained the Ripley road, or whether he simply decided to drop the matter, he said no more about it. By that time, Rosecrans had plenty of other worries. The Confederates had pushed Oliver back, and their main body was evidently at Chewalla. Ironically, the Confederates had pushed Rosecrans, it seemed, to the wall.[27]

Events progressed during the night of October 2, indicating that the Confederates were going to attack the Corinth defenses directly. Nearly convinced, Rosecrans once again called in his divisions, this time all the way into Corinth's fortifications. He planned to place them around the old Confederate works and thus force Van Dorn to deploy his army far outside of town. Rosecrans could then fall back grudgingly, skirmishing all the while, into the inner works on the College Hill line. There, he would dispute the Confederate advance with everything he had. To this end, during the nervous night of October 2, Rosecrans sent messages to all four division commanders, ordering each to have his division up and ready to move or fight by 3:00 A.M. Each division also received orders to carry three days' rations and 100 rounds of ammunition. In the understatement of the war, Rosecrans began his orders: "There being indications of a possible attack on Corinth. . . ." Rosecrans still rated the attack as only a possibility, but he acted more emphatically than this opening sentence implied. He did not make plans for a "possible" attack; he planned for an all-out battle that would involve all his divisions.[28]

Rosecrans ordered McKean's division to stay where it was: south of the Memphis and Charleston Railroad. McKean's right would rest on the railroad near Battery F, the northernmost fortification on the Halleck line. But Rosecrans was having a hard time gaining information from the division commander, and staff officers lectured McKean: "The General commanding desires to hear from you" and "The Genl. Com'dg has been awaiting report from you all night." Nevertheless, by daylight, McKean had his division, consisting of Allen's and Crocker's brigades, up and deployed in the position ordered by Rosecrans. At least one Federal, Cyrus Boyd of the 15th Iowa, thought they had merely been turned out to drill: "thinking that the weather was hot we were going out to drill before breakfast as had been our habit in hot weather." The division actually deployed in two lines, both perpendicular to the Memphis and Charleston Railroad.[29]

Camped at Clear Creek, Hamilton also received orders to move his division by 3:00 A.M. on October 3. He was to march to a point north of Corinth and east of the Mobile and Ohio Railroad, covering the Purdy and Pittsburg Landing roads as well as the space between the two. The two brigades marched through the dark: "As the grey of morning appears we come in sight of the noted place," one soldier remembered. The division marched through Corinth, some of the men unaware of what was coming until they reached a hollow. There, as Joseph Risedorph described it, they saw "the ambulances corralled and the attendants engaged in tearing yellow strings on their arms and otherwise preparing for to take care of the wounded." Risedorph said, "This was the first premonition that any of us had that a battle was imminent." Still, Jeremiah Sullivan, commanding one of Hamilton's brigades, reported that the "prospect of again meeting General Price aroused the enthusiasm of the troops." When the division reached its proper position, a portion of the 10th Missouri went forward under Major Leonidas Horney to scout the area. Additional orders soon arrived instructing Hamilton to move farther out the Purdy and Pittsburg Landing roads to the old Confederate works. By 10:00 A.M. on October 3, both Sullivan's and Buford's brigades had moved into position guarding the works less than three miles from Corinth. Only the 5th Iowa was farther south, where the Pittsburg road came into the old Confederate works east of Corinth. "It was a post of honor for us," recalled one member of the regiment. Portions of that regiment were further dispersed to guard other avenues of entry, such as the Farmington roads, where sections of artillery also stood guard. One soldier of the 5th Iowa, John Quincy Adams Campbell, wrote in his diary, "We ensconced ourselves behind the old earthworks of the enemy."[30]

Davies's division, though ordered to move at the same time as the others, experienced a delay due to "some mistake in the telegraph," he believed. After realizing that Hamilton's division had marched away, Davies telegraphed Rosecrans to receive instructions. Although some of the men of the 12th Illinois stationed at Burnsville moved by rail into Corinth, the majority of the division did not leave Camp Montgomery until after daylight on October 3. The already weak division thus grew weaker as the men marched from camp in the rising temperatures, but they made it to Corinth. One member of the 7th Illinois of Silas Baldwin's brigade remembered that the troops seemed "to be ignorant of anything hostile any where in Northern Mississippi." When they were ordered to march at the double-quick, however, it led them "to think that there is something coming this way." As they moved out the Chewalla road, past Battery Robinett and a white house to the north, artillery fire from Oliver's skirmishing to the northwest made them think for sure that a battle was coming. Marching through Corinth, Davies reported to Rosecrans, and the commanding general told him to march northwestward out the Memphis and Charleston Railroad for one and a half miles and deploy his division between that railroad and the Mobile and Ohio. Davies formed his division where the Columbus and Chewalla roads crossed. On the way out, the division met incoming cavalrymen, and the common jabs took place: "Yes, boys, the rebels are out there, the cavalry are runnin'." A cavalryman replied, "There are more rebels out there than you will want to see." Davies put two brigades, commanded by Brigadier Generals Pleasant Hackleman and Richard Oglesby, in line and held the third, Baldwin's, in reserve. His artillery deployed to cover both the railroad and the Chewalla road. By 10:00 A.M., the units had taken position and opened communication with Hamilton on their right.[31]

Like Hamilton to the east, Davies did some late rearranging of his own. He received permission to move his division farther north, to a field at the junction of the Columbus road and a small trail called the "bridle path," 800 yards in front of the inner works. There, he sent out the 7th Illinois of Oglesby's brigade, along with the 7th Iowa and artillery of Hackleman's brigade, to reconnoiter. Davies moved farther north when word came from Rosecrans to guard the old Confederate works and also to look to the bridle path, which, Rosecrans declared, "will need your attention." Davies moved his two brigades into the Confederate trenches 1,000 yards to the north, sending out skirmishers to the front and two companies to the railroad on the right to meet Hamilton's line. Baldwin remained in reserve at the junction of the Chewalla and Columbus roads. This deployment allowed a continuation of the line that Hamilton's command had begun, but a gap remained between Davies's division and McKean's units around the Turner Creek headwaters.[32]

Rosecrans also ordered Stanley's division of two brigades, still commanded by John Fuller and Joseph Mower, to march to a point "near General Grant's old headquarters" south of Corinth and await further orders. Stanley had his men, some still at Kossuth, up and marching early. One surgeon in Fuller's brigade told his wife, "While we were at Kossuth we were ordered to march forthwith to Corinth. . . . We left Kossoth at 12 o'clock at night." By midmorning, Stanley had reached the point assigned him, just south of Corinth near the Whitfield residence. A soldier of the 39th Ohio reported to his wife, "To our surprise we found a battle raging." Stanley quickly formed his division into "parallel lines of battle" facing west. All regiments, including those lately at Kossuth, were present except for the 5th Minnesota, which was still guarding a bridge over the Tuscumbia River. Rosecrans was much relieved to see the whole division in Corinth, and one soldier of the 39th Ohio remarked, "He jerked off his hat and jumped down off his horse and fairly danced for joy."[33]

Rosecrans's medical director, surgeon Archibald B. Campbell, also prepared for battle, taking over a commissary depot recently erected in Corinth for a makeshift hospital. He had his men prepare the place, getting medicines, surgical instruments, cots, bedding, and even buckets of water ready for the influx of wounded they knew would come shortly. All was done, Campbell reported, "some time before the first wounded man was brought in."[34]

Thus, by 10:00 A.M. on Friday, October 3, Rosecrans was ready for a fight. His army had taken position, with almost every man in line. Rosecrans's main line extended along the old Beauregard line with Hamilton on the right, Davies in the center, and McKean on the left. To strengthen the defense further, Stanley's full division remained in reserve just south of town. The available cavalry took advantageous positions at points south of Corinth and also on the flanks of the army. Their orders were simply to guard the approaches to Corinth that the infantry could not cover. Moreover, Oliver remained out in front of the line, slowing the Confederate advance.[35]

Obviously, Rosecrans had an overall plan. With everything set, he called his division commanders together and explained his wishes to each commander, ordering them "to hold the enemy at arm's-length by opposing him strongly in our assumed positions." To McKean on the forward outpost, he gave specific instructions: McKean and his men were to "hold their ground as long as possible. If they should be forced by the enemy in force, let them rally . . . and allow the enemy to *cover* very close." He added, "The great object is to ascertain the strength of the enemy without exposing our own." He also gave detailed instructions to the men in the ranks: "Tell the field officers not to stand behind trees but pass along the line and instruct the men how to act—Let the Brigadiers see to this." Should the Confederate pressure become too strong, Rosecrans wanted his divisions to fall back slowly, but only after the Confederates had been forced to deploy. The units were then to fall back to a spot "determined by events and the movements of the enemy," but the eventual goal was to draw the Confederates toward the inner defenses of Corinth, where "the use of our batteries and the open ground in the immediate vicinity of Corinth" could be utilized. The idea was to tire and bloody the enemy by the time they reached the inner defenses so that Rosecrans could easily repel any assaults against the fortifications.[36]

For any observant Federal veteran of Shiloh, it was a plan not unlike the one Grant had used to win the battle there. Rosecrans would trade space for time, slowly falling back to a stout last line, where the enemy would be stopped. In the meantime, reinforcements could arrive from Jackson and Bolivar. If all went according to plan, the enemy would be destroyed.

By the evening of October 2, the Confederate army was drawing closer to the entrenchments that ringed Corinth. At Young's Bridge, the troops enjoyed themselves by picking and eating the plenteous muscadines from nearby swamps. The main army then crossed the bridge and proceeded to Chewalla, where it spent the night. The next morning "before sunrise," according to one soldier, the army ate a hurried breakfast brought forward from the wagons in the rear. Then, even before some had finished, the long column began its march. Once again, Lovell moved in the lead; Price, dressed in his multicolored battle shirt, led his two divisions right behind. As the Confederates marched out of their encampments at daylight on October 3, they soon came into contact with Oliver's skirmishers and then his entire force. This encounter made the Confederates anxious, and at daylight, three distinct earthquake tremors shook the area, adding to the concern. One Confederate remembered that many of his comrades thought it was an "ominous report." A comet also appeared, another alleged omen.[37]

Men of both sides quickly gathered their wits and prepared for the day. One officer eloquently wrote, "The first rays of an unclouded sun glimmered from the bayonets of our army already hastening to the Feast of Death prepared by the weird sisters of Destiny." Oliver was not quite so poetic. By the morning of October 3, he no longer had just cavalry and advance skirmishers before him; he had the entire Confederate army. Moreover, he had lost some of his troops. The 16th Wisconsin of Allen's brigade had returned to its own command earlier that morning. Still, Oliver seemed up to the task. As the Confederates drew nearer to Corinth, he gave them stiff opposition. But the sound of fighting off to the northwest was not comforting for the rest of the army. One cannoneer stationed near Battery F remembered, "The thundering became louder and closer and we knew Price was advancing."[38]

Spirited skirmishing took place as Villepigue's brigade marched toward Oliver's command at Alexander's. Villepigue's artillery immediately fired on the Federals, but Oliver held his ground through the fighting, all the while realizing the building strength of his opposition. He recognized the danger and hoped to receive permission to withdraw and form a line in the old Confederate works on the east side of Cane Creek. McKean gave him that order, and a relieved Oliver quickly sent his command to the rear. The regiment at Smith's Bridge likewise received orders to retire. The Confederates, elated at gaining the position so easily, closely followed the retiring Federals.[39]

While the Federals were crossing Cane Creek, one of Oliver's Minnesota guns was disabled and lost. The axle of the gun had been broken at Shiloh and now came completely apart. One of the cannoneers described what happened: the gun "broke its axle by recoil, was dragged by the prolonge rope until it broke, and was then spiked and thrown into a creek." Chief of artillery for the Sixth Division, Captain Andrew Hickenlooper, reported, "Being hotly pressed we were obliged to abandon it." Another gun from the 1st Minnesota Battery stationed at Battery F replaced the broken gun in line. As Oliver withdrew, he ordered the bridge across Cane Creek destroyed. A party of axmen did the work, and the bridge lay in shambles by the time Oliver fell back, some of his skirmishers barely making it across. The Federals also cut a tree to block the road to further delay the Confederate advance.[40]

Oliver continued withdrawing his brigade southward until he crossed the railroad. He took a position on "Cane Creek Bluff," just to the left of and in line with the old Confederate works. McArthur, authorized by Rosecrans to take command of the area to the front, ordered Oliver to hold that position, "which was a strong one and easy to hold against anything but an overwhelming force." He also promised to return with reinforcements. The position was indeed crucial. It commanded both the Chewalla road and the railroad.[41]

Oliver immediately sent out skirmishers to cover his front and flanks. Then he noted movements in his rear, but these turned out to be reinforcements coming to strengthen his position. True to his word, McArthur had returned with Allen's brigade, which moved into line, extending it to the left. A brigade from Davies also arrived. Davies had sent two regiments of Baldwin's reserve to Oliver at the double-quick to fill the gap to his left. McArthur, the only general in the area except for McKean in the rear at Battery F, took command of all three brigades.[42]

As the skirmishing increased around Cane Creek, the Confederates finally drove Oliver's skirmishers back. Still three miles from Corinth, Lovell saw that the time had come to deploy; the Federal resistance had become more than simple skirmishers could handle. Scouts returned to report that the Federals were in "considerable force" on the hills looming east of Cane Creek. To attack, however, the Confederates had to cross the creek. Arriving at the dismembered bridge, Lovell and his brigades discovered not only the disabled cannon but also the fact that the Federals had them and the bridge in the sights of their remaining guns. Lovell saw that he had to cross the unbridged creek, which was dry; only then could he form his division for the attack. The Confederates repaired the bridge under the heavy fire of the Union guns and began the crossing process. Soon, Van Dorn's entire army was deploying east of Cane Creek.[43]

It was now 10:00 A.M. Van Dorn arrived at the front and ordered the deployment of his force in one long line curving around the Federal defenses. Unfortunately, he thought only of the present operation. He kept no general reserve to exploit a breakthrough or to plug a gap. Each division had reserves of its own, but no general reserve existed. Van Dorn obviously intended to sweep right over the Union position and win the victory quickly. He seemingly knew nothing of the inner fortifications, the Federals having built them after his departure in the spring. He had done a poor job of reconnaissance, so he had no plan to follow the fight at the outer works.[44]

Moreover, the present attack was not going well. As the Confederates deployed, the Federal artillery was wreaking havoc on them. Amazingly, General Price's band had marched the entire way at the head of the column, right behind the skirmishers. As the band began to play "Listen to the Mocking Bird," a Federal shell hit squarely at the forks of a large oak tree directly above them, showering the band with fragments and splinters of tree limbs. One officer remembered, "The Mockingbird hushed its dulcet strain and the boys shouted with glee as the band and negro camp followers 'skedaddled' to the rear."[45]

The deployment nevertheless continued. As soon as Lovell's division crossed the creek, he ordered it to march south and form on the right of the Chewalla road. The brigades took their position in one line. Rust, taking the place of Villepigue in the vanguard, marched to the end of the line and established his position at the extreme right. Bowen's brigade followed and took position on Rust's left, while Villepigue's brigade went into line on the left, his left resting on the Memphis and Charleston Railroad. To secure the flank, Colonel William H. Jackson's cavalry brigade moved onto Rust's right.[46]

Price led his corps to the left of Lovell's division on a military road cut by Van Dorn himself the previous spring, crossing Cane Creek farther to the north behind a tall ridge. He placed Maury on the right, near the Walker house, touching the railroad and Lovell's left. Two of Maury's brigades, John Moore's and Charles Phifer's, were on the front line, and William Cabell's brigade was put in reserve. Hébert placed his division to Maury's left; Elijah Gate's, Martin Green's, and John Martin's brigades were up front, while Colbert's brigade remained in reserve. Hébert's troops, except for the skirmishers, were somewhat shielded from the Union line by a tall, wooded ridge, behind which they deployed. Frank Armstrong's brigade of cavalry watched for any flanking maneuvers on the left.[47]

The entire line faced a "belt of fallen timber," as one soldier described it, perhaps 400 yards wide. Skirmishers moved out from each unit, and minor fighting took place while the units readied for the advance. The Union artillery all along the line opened up on the formed Confederates, whose artillery responded in kind. The heavy volume of fire coming from the Union guns did little damage in the ranks of the Confederate army, however, although one officer on Price's staff was killed.[48]

Despite the growing carnage, some comical incidents occurred. James Newton, a member of the 14th Wisconsin posted with the skirmishers, remembered how nervous he and his friends were as they watched the Confederate skirmishers come closer, prodded by their officers. They "did not seem to obey them very willingly," he noted. The Confederates finally moved forward, but very slowly. Newton and his friends fired on the obviously frightened Southerners and then ran a short distance away, only to see that the Confederates were running too. Newton and his friends determined among themselves never to run again, and with clear consciences they moved forward to their original line. A moment later, the Confederates reappeared. Then they "saw something to run for," Newton remembered. The whole Confederate army was moving forward.[49]

Confederate skirmishers had similar problems. Those of Bowen's brigade swept away the Federal skirmish line, quite possibly Newton and his comrades. They made their way up the hill toward the enemy line, some of which lay behind the old earthworks of the Confederate line. One soldier quipped that these had been "too well constructed by Beauregard." Union artillery knocked huge limbs down from the trees above them, but the skirmishers continued toward the Federal line. Then they realized their folly and found, to their dismay, that they had advanced alone. One Confederate remembered, "We went down the hill much faster than we ran up it."[50]

Despite such episodes, serious work lay ahead. With his army deployed in an arc northwest of Corinth, Van Dorn made his headquarters at the Murphy house and began preparing for the attack. He planned to begin the attack on his right with Lovell's division, where he knew the Confederate earthworks did not extend. Van Dorn hoped the Federals would take troops off their right to reinforce their assailed left, which in fact was already happening. That would weaken the Union right, thereby giving Hébert and the Confederate left an excellent opportunity for a stunning victory.[51]

The day that Van Dorn longed for had finally arrived. Yet all was not well. He surely realized that his greatest allies, speed and surprise, had both fallen by the wayside, but he was determined to attack anyway. Dressed in his colorful hunting shirt, Price was also set for battle, riding up and down his line, already under fire from the enemy. The troops were ready. The lines had formed. The time seemed right—right for the meeting of two old West Point classmates, and right for the taking of Corinth.[52]

10

"WE WERE OBLIGED TO FALL BACK GRADUALLY"

By midmorning on October 3, Earl Van Dorn's Confederate army was poised and ready for the attack. Amid the growing heat, Confederate commanders rode up and down the lines steadying their troops. They could see the strong Federal works on the hills to the front, and they knew these entrenchments well, having constructed and manned them earlier in the year. Now, instead of being behind their protection, they were attacking them. Van Dorn nevertheless ordered the assaults to begin, with Lovell on the right opening the attack; it would then gradually progress down the line toward Hébert on the far left. When the Federals removed some their troops from that area to withstand Lovell's attack, Van Dorn believed Hébert would be able to walk into Corinth.[1]

But Rosecrans's Federals were just as determined. The blue-clad infantry and artillery stood at their posts atop the range of hills overlooking Cane Creek, watching every move the enemy made. The undeniable sight of the Confederate army fanning out in attack formation in front of them finally convinced everyone that they were about to engage in battle. Rosecrans himself later testified that "by 11 o'clock it became apparent that, instead of a feint, the enemy was in full force." The battle had come.[2]

Mansfield Lovell's line faced a formidable series of hills crowned with guns and men, but the Confederates were confident they could take them. Lovell thus ordered his entire line forward, which brought the division directly in front of McKean's men. Oliver, McArthur, and Baldwin formed a solid line in front of the Confederates, with six regiments and a number of guns. Baldwin's two regiments, the 7th and 57th Illinois, had deployed in the earthworks on the right, leaving only one regiment of his brigade out of the action. That unit, the 50th Illinois, was back with Davies at the junction of the Chewalla and Columbus roads to act as the division's reserve. Similarly, only two of the three regiments that made up McArthur's brigade were in this line. The 16th Wisconsin and the 21st Missouri—the latter newly arrived from Kossuth and, more recently, from Battery E, where it "had just got settled in its tents"— deployed alongside the other brigades. McArthur's third regiment, the 17th Wisconsin, remained in reserve. Oliver's command finished out the line. The 15th Michigan and the 14th Wisconsin, along with a battalion from the 18th Missouri, took their positions in line. Oliver's only other regiment, the 18th Wisconsin, had moved to Smith's Bridge earlier and thus did not take part in the early action near Cane Creek. McArthur added six guns to these infantry-men. William Z. Clayton's two guns of the 1st Minnesota Battery were still fighting hard. A section of Captain Henry Richardson's Battery D, 1st Missouri Light Artillery, and a section of Lieutenant Charles H. Thurber's Battery I, 1st Missouri Light Artillery, added firepower to the infantry regiments. With this assortment of men, McArthur, who was in immediate command of all the troops, waited for the inevitable Confederate attack.[3]

McArthur had some advantages going into battle. The entire Union line, studded with artillery, sat on the brow of a hill that commanded the open area to the front. Also, a portion of troops on the right were behind fortifications. Moreover, McKean's position contained at least some water, which was des-perately needed on this hot October day. There were three artesian wells at Battery F and one at Battery D. Many units went thirsty throughout the day, but a fortunate few in McKean's division did not.[4]

It was the open nature of the ground to the front, however, that proved most beneficial to the Federals. A Minnesota artilleryman, Thomas Christie, was clearly pleased with his unit's effectiveness. "We had some splendid long range practice," he wrote to his sister nearly a month later. It was "the first time . . . we have had a chance to use our guns as they should be used, to play on heavy columns instead of scattered skirmishes. At the very first shot from our rifle we had the range and plumped a Hotchkiss percussion Shell right into the midst of the Greybacks, whom we could see plainly marching along at a 'Right Shoulder shift.' The way they scattered was a caution to snakes, and wherever a bunch of them could be seen we would plant a shell or spher-ical case, till you could not see their backs for the dust. Some reckless scamps among them returned our fire with their muskets although they were a half mile distant, but I noticed that they sent no more men up that road." Christie was a veteran of Shiloh, but he found Corinth to be a much different battle. "I should like to get my revenge out of them in this way to compensate for the way we had to fight them at Shiloh—at short pistol range—and compelled to use nothing but canister and short-timed shells. We may be in many a fight yet and see death and wounds enough, but I doubt if we ever see another such time as we had there."[5]

Despite the artillery's success, problems were developing in the Union line. One issue involved unity of command. Silas Baldwin tried to take command of the forces when he arrived at Oliver's position, evidently not knowing that McArthur was present. He issued orders at the same time McArthur did, often requiring regimental commanders to decide which order to obey. Lieutenant Colonel Frederick J. Hurlbut of the 57th Illinois reported forming his line on McArthur's orders but then getting a command from Baldwin to move to the earthworks. "Having reported to General McArthur I did not obey the order, but reported the order to General McArthur," Hurlbut said a few days later.[6]

The main problem was the pending Confederate attack, however. General Rust, on the right of Lovell's division, led the way for the Confederates. He had split his brigade in order to give the right a head start, with the 3rd Kentucky moving to the right and beginning the assault. After the Kentuckians became engaged, the remainder of the brigade moved forward, but the Federals on the rise in front responded with devastating fire. A thick forest had thus far sheltered the Confederates, but they came in full view as they pressed forward. The Union guns bellowed repeatedly, and Rust reported later, "It appeared that the entire line would be swept away." Another observer wrote, "Terrific volleys of shell, grape, and canister" took their toll on the advancing Confederates. "They were equal to the occasion," Rust later explained, as the Confederates closed ranks and kept moving.[7]

While Rust's brigade struggled toward the Federal works, so did Bowen and Villepigue, who advanced only a few moments behind Rust. "Villepigue threw one leg over the pommel of the saddle, and stroking his beard, with his horse's nose right against [a Mississippi regiment]," one soldier remembered. A member of Bowen's brigade described their advance in detail: the brigade "moved forward from the open field in which it had been deployed, into a strip of woodland thickly covered with undergrowth, under a desultory fire from the enemy's skirmishers, and a battery in front." As these two brigades marched to the front, they came to the same clearing Rust encountered and took casualties from the Federal artillery. Like their comrades on the right, they too closed up and continued on.[8]

The Federals were outnumbered but gave a good account of themselves, one officer noting to his wife, "Our men stood the shock nobly, delivering the most steady and effective fire that I have seen during the war. It told fearfully on the enemy, . . . but it had no effect in checking their march. They advanced on the double quick in the utmost disregard of human life." In Oliver's brigade,

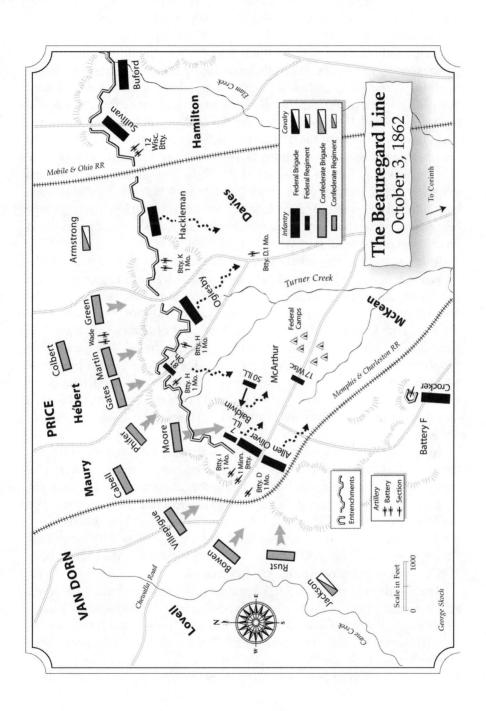

The Beauregard Line
October 3, 1862

Infantry
Federal Brigade
Federal Regiment
Confederate Brigade
Confederate Regiment

Cavalry

To Corinth

VAN DORN
Lovell
PRICE
Hébert
Maury

Jackson
Rust
Bowen
Villepigue
Cabell
Phifer
Moore
Gates
Martin Wade
Green
Colbert
Armstrong

Buford
Sullivan
Hamilton
12 Wisc. Btty.
Mobile & Ohio RR

Hackleman
Davies
Btty. K 1 Mo.
Oglesby
Btty. D 1 Mo.
Btty. H 1 Mo.
Btty. H 1 Mo.

Turner Creek

McKean
Federal Camps
McArthur
17 Wisc.
50 Ill.
Baldwin
7 Ill.
Allen Oliver
Memphis & Charleston RR
Crocker
Battery F

Btty. I 1 Mo.
1 Minn. Btty.
Btty. D 1 Mo.

Elam Creek

Corinth
Chewalla Road
Cane Creek

Entrenchments
Artillery
Battery
Section

Scale in Feet
0   1000

George Skoch

the 15th Michigan's chaplain, Thomas M. Brady, was in the thick of the fight, encouraging and ministering to his men. Oliver reported, "Father Brady, respected and beloved by all his flock, both Catholic and Protestant, for his kindness and good offices, was with me under the hottest fire, and volunteered to go for ammunition, and, when brought up, I think helped to give it out." William Lowndes of the same Michigan regiment retrieved a set of Union colors that had been left on the ground—the flag of the 14th Wisconsin. Similarly, when the color-bearer of the 21st Missouri, Sergeant Gus Stevens, ran to the rear, another member of the regiment, Jesse Roberts, chased him down, brought the flag back, and carried it throughout the fight. Stevens ultimately lost his stripes, which Roberts soon acquired. Despite such bravery, McArthur soon began to feel the pressure of the Confederate advance, and some of his men began to flee from the line. Moreover, McArthur worried about the gap that loomed to his immediate right, between his right flank and Davies's left.[9]

That gap had been somewhat plugged by the arrival of Baldwin's brigade. However, when the Confederate attacks began, it was still large enough for the Confederates to exploit, and the opportunistic Southerners did so. By the time Lovell attacked, Maury's division had taken a position to his left. Since the gap in the Union line fronted Moore's brigade of Maury's division, Van Dorn ordered Maury to aid Lovell's assault. Maury quickly sent the inactive Moore to support Lovell. Crossing a cornfield, Moore sent out skirmishers, who quickly found the enemy's advance guard, which the Confederates drove back into their works. With the exact location of the line pinpointed, Moore's men threw off their blankets and knapsacks and began their assault on the Federal line.[10]

Moore turned his brigade to the right and flanked the troops in his front—the right of McArthur's line. When the brigade reached the fallen timber, the men charged and made quick work of the Federal defenders. In fact, the brigade completed the entire operation, one Confederate remembered, "with but little opposition." The only problem the Confederates encountered came on the far left, where the 42nd Alabama had a small scrap with a regiment from Davies's division. Still, Moore succeeded in flanking McArthur's position, causing the Federal line to begin to crumble.[11]

The 7th Illinois, on McArthur's extreme right, took the brunt of Moore's attack. One member of the regiment remembered the Confederates "emerging from the timber in solid column, about forty rods to our right, moving directly across the unprotected works." When Moore first threatened the exposed right flank, the 7th Illinois received orders to change its front and face the oncoming Confederates. After doing so, the regiment poured volleys into the enemy, temporarily slowing the Confederates. McArthur then ordered them to charge, which, he reported, "they attempted to do." The charge accomplished little against the overwhelming number of Southerners, however, and Moore continued to crumble the right flank of McArthur's line while others penetrated elsewhere. One 7th Illinois soldier remembered the helpless feeling: "Rebels in our front, rebels on our right and rear; rebels on our left and rear; soon the right and left columns will meet." Colonel Andrew J. Babcock and his Illinoisans had no choice but to withdraw.[12]

While McKean's right caved in, Lovell's division made other penetrations. By this time, Rust's brigade had almost reached the railroad. In fact, the 9th Arkansas had to detour to the east of the road in order to miss a deep cut. While doing so, it also drew closer to the Union troops on the hill and took corresponding casualties. The 3rd Kentucky, on the far right, likewise felt the fierceness of the battle. It had moved forward alone until it became obvious that a great gap had opened between it and the remainder of the brigade. Fearing that his right was in jeopardy, Colonel A. P. Thompson called for reinforcements. Rust immediately sent the 7th Kentucky, his only reserve.[13]

The main body of Rust's brigade pressed up the hill to the left. "In a few seconds," Rust reported, "I here lost over 100 men and officers." Yet Rust could not halt his command; doing so would make them stationary targets for the already destructive Union artillery. He ordered bayonets fixed and commanded his men to charge to the top. The order brought a cheer, and the Confederates quickly carried the hill. The 9th Arkansas, which had detoured to the left of the railroad cut, was the first to reach the Union line. Right behind them came the remainder of the brigade, although the right wing, consisting of the 3rd and 7th Kentucky, arrived too late to make a difference in the assault. Although they had "rushed impetuously forward," as one soldier noted, the flanking Kentuckians arrived just in time "to witness the flight of the enemy."[14]

Villepigue, on the far left of the division, also had to contend with the Federals on the hill and took devastating fire from the Union guns. The "deadly fire of the enemy and the nature of the obstructions in front of us" stopped the brigade, Villepigue reported, but he soon had his men up and going again. By the time the 9th Arkansas of Rust's brigade had taken the Union lines in their front, the 33rd Mississippi had secured the section of works confronting it. The Mississippians, led by Colonel David W. Hurst (who had voted against secession at the state convention), arrived on the hill not long after the Arkansans swept over the top. In fact, it was probably in this charge that Hurst himself went down, thrown from his horse and disabled so badly that he had to leave the service. By this time, Villepigue's brigade was so disjointed that the general could locate only the lone Mississippi regiment. The other regiments had vanished from sight.[15]

In the center of Lovell's line, Bowen's brigade saw the least action of all. The success of the brigades on his right and left "rendered the work comparatively easy for my brigade," Bowen remarked. Although the men did not take part in the fiercest fighting, the 22nd Mississippi was one of the first units to reach the top, breaking the Federal line where the 14th Wisconsin stood at essentially the same time as the 9th Arkansas and 33rd Mississippi entered the enemy position. One of the Mississippians remembered finding a Wisconsin boy in the trenches, holding a dead man. "Are you hurt?" the Confederate asked. "No," replied the Federal, "but this is my poor dead brother, and I could not leave him. I would not mind it for myself so much, but for his poor wife and little baby." Another Confederate in Bowen's brigade described wounding a Union "Superior Officer, whose fine horse with elegant saddle &c, dashed up to the 22nd [Mississippi] just as it halted after pursuing the enemy two hundred yards, but wheeled and dashed wildly away through the woods." Nevertheless, Bowen reported taking a "salient near the railroad and driving the entire infantry force from the trenches."[16]

McArthur quickly recognized the helplessness of the situation. Moore's brigade had begun to move around the Federals' right flank and into the rear of the line, and other portions of his line were similarly falling apart. He thus ordered a withdrawal, one artilleryman noting, "We never limbered to the rear without the General's orders." The Federals made several stands, and Colonel David Moore's 21st Missouri even counterattacked for a moment, but nothing could stop the Confederate onslaught until they called off the chase a few hundred yards inside the Federal line.[17]

The Federals lost dearly in the assault. Several officers went down, including Colonel Moore of the 21st Missouri. Moore had lost a leg at Shiloh, and when his horse was shot from under him, the colonel fell to the ground, "bruising severely my amputated leg," he later wrote. The Federals also lost the use of several caissons and two guns, one of them the "Lady Richardson" of Richardson's Battery D, 1st Missouri Light Artillery. Major George H. Stone, commanding Davies's artillery, reported that one of the drivers panicked and ran, leaving the frightened horses to bolt, which broke the limber pole. Without a limber, the gun could not be hauled away. One Confederate claimed they also captured "six sleek, beautiful, coal-black horses, who were immediately enlisted into the rebel service." The other piece, a gun of the 1st Minnesota Battery, literally fell apart, and the soldiers sent it to Corinth for repair. The remaining gun of the battery soon replaced it in a new line.[18]

As the Confederates drove the Federals out of their works, they left a path of destruction. "Our division was ordered to fall back," one Union surgeon reported, "which they accomplished in pretty good order leaving our dead and badly wounded upon the field." Indeed, the dead and wounded of both sides lay all around. The heat of the day also caused many soldiers to fall out of ranks and roam the rear, looking for water. Cavalrymen sent to the rear for water provided some relief, but the scene was still awful. One Confederate coming upon the wounded color-bearer of the 14th Wisconsin, to whom he gave morphine, thought it ironic that after trying to kill each other, they tried to "repair the damage done." Union soldier James Newton could attest to the chaos. After he and his comrades rejoined their regiment east of Cane Creek, they fell back with the rest of McArthur's line. Newton, however, got caught "between two fires" and laid down in a ditch, hoping to survive uncaptured, but the Confederates soon discovered him. As he wrote to his parents days later, the enemy was "on both sides of the ditch and when they came up—why I surrendered." He later went to the rear to help with the dead and wounded of both armies.[19]

The Federals used the lull to retire to a new line closer to Battery F. McArthur patched together another line but soon had to change the front slightly as the Confederates approached again. Two fresh regiments—the 50th Illinois, sent personally by Davies, and the 17th Wisconsin—joined the tired veterans on this second line of defense. McArthur placed the regiments that had fallen back from the original line beside these two fresh units and again waited for the Confederates to attack. This line contained, from right to left, the 17th Wisconsin, 57th Illinois, 7th Illinois, and 50th Illinois, with the 16th Wisconsin and 21st Missouri on the left flank. While they waited, the guns of the forward 1st Minnesota Battery moved to the rear and took a position at Battery F. In their place, a section of Battery F, 2nd Illinois Artillery, commanded by Lieutenant J. M. Mitchell, came forward and deployed. This line was formed on the north side of the Memphis and Charleston Railroad and almost parallel with it.[20]

The new line, which faced northward, forced the remainder of McKean's division to change its front, but that consisted solely of Crocker's brigade. The men had stood in line of battle all morning directly south of Battery F, facing west, logically thinking the attack would come from that direction. Two regiments, the 11th and 13th Iowa, formed the line of battle. The other two regiments, the 15th and 16th Iowa, formed in column directly in the rear. When McArthur fell back to his second position, Crocker changed his front to face northward. He put the 15th and 16th Iowa in line of battle on the right of Bat-

tery F—on "a naked high ridge," recalled one member of the 15th Iowa—and
deployed the 11th and 13th Iowa in column behind the front line. With this
deployment, McKean had a hastily formed line that ran from McArthur's position north of the railroad to Crocker's brigade, and then to the artillery at Battery F. To make it stronger, this line contained six guns. McArthur had a
section of Mitchell's 2nd Illinois Artillery, Battery F, and the remaining two
guns of the 1st Minnesota Battery on the right of the fort, while one section
of the 3rd Ohio Battery, commanded by Captain Emil Munch, took position
inside Battery F.[21]

Subsequently, Oliver's tired brigade, having borne the brunt of the action
for two days, was allowed to withdraw out of the line, and it deployed in
reserve. There, a battalion of the 18th Missouri reinforced it. This action left
only three brigades—McArthur's, Baldwin's, and Crocker's—in the front line.
Rosecrans might have had something to do with Oliver's retirement; he
seemed very displeased with Oliver's conduct throughout the day. Although
Rosecrans's general plan was to fall back steadily, Oliver's actions on that
morning must have been too fast for his superior's liking. Rosecrans even
wrote to Grant that Oliver "acted feebly and fell back." Throughout the day,
Rosecrans continually sent messages to his division commanders urging them
to battle for the area in front of the inner works. "I wish it distinctly understood that the extreme position is not to be taken until driven to it," he wrote.
Later, he added, "The enemy will doubtless feel your position, but do not
allow this to hasten your movements." Obviously, Rosecrans wanted his divisions to fall back only after forcing the enemy to fight. In this context, Rosecrans ordered McKean to support Oliver and watch him closely. "He has no
brains," Rosecrans said. He told McKean that he could replace Oliver if necessary and "put the 2 little brigades in the Hands of Genl. McArthur."[22]

While the Federals took advantage of the respite, the Confederates also
welcomed the calm, even taking the time to bury some of their dead. Officers
gathered the scattered remnants of commands, and Lovell reported his
progress and inquired about future operations, indicating, of course, that Van
Dorn had thought only about the initial assault, not what to do afterward. But
the opening actions of the Battle of Corinth no doubt pleased the Confederates. "The conflict was short and bloody," Lovell remembered, and the Union
troops had taken their toll on the Confederates before retreating in front of the
massive pressure. Still, in only a matter of minutes, Lovell's and Moore's
sweeping attacks had not only driven the Federal troops back but also secured
all the outer works confronting these brigades. The two guns they captured
added to these gains. The Confederates found the splendid twenty-pounder
Parrott gun named "Lady Richardson" smashed against a tree, and Rust and

Bowen apparently had words over whose brigade actually captured the piece. More humorously, W. G. Whitfield of the 35th Alabama told a story about his comrades who were the first to reach the gun. One soldier, he remembered, "jumped a stride" the gun but "immediately dismounted to cool off as it was a very hot gun."[23]

Despite the success, the fog of battle took over. When Lovell's men carried the Union line, they did not know what Van Dorn wanted them to do next. Moore had received orders to make a junction with the left of Lovell's division, but in the confusion, he had not done so. Lovell concentrated his gains by ordering Rust and Villepigue to form in line of battle ahead of the hill just carried, with Bowen forming on the hill itself. Rust, who had inadvertently ended up north of the railroad, marched his brigade to the south side of the tracks and took position there. The other two brigades also formed in their ordered positions. So did Moore. Then the brigades waited until Lovell could contact Van Dorn.[24]

When the action picked up again, however, it was not the Confederates who initiated it. Skirmishers on both sides were still in contact as the Confederates merely followed up the Union withdrawal, moving through the 17th Wisconsin and 21st Missouri camps and locating the re-formed Federal line north of the railroad. The two skirmish lines were in contact for perhaps forty-five minutes as Lovell reorganized his scattered command. During the spirited skirmishing, McArthur decided to put some distance between his line and the enemy by driving the enemy skirmishers back. Portions of McArthur's and Baldwin's commands thus charged the shadowing Confederates and drove them rearward, "making a fearful inroad among the rebels," according to one excited Union soldier. An equally excited captain in the 50th Illinois told his men, "Boys if we cannot break their line, they can have my life." An Illinois surgeon was also caught up in the spirit of the attack, writing to his wife, "During the fight on this line our brigade consisting of the 57th, 7th, and 50th Illinois made a charge on the run at their extreme right and drove them back a half mile capturing some prisoners." Despite the overblown rhetoric, it was the first major Union counterattack of the day. The Federal defense was stiffening.[25]

The counterattack took the lead members of Moore's brigade by surprise and caused some confusion in the Southern ranks. The 42nd Alabama mistook Confederate skirmishers as the enemy and fired into them. One member of the Alabama regiment wrote of the mix-up in his diary: "Advancing some two hundred yards I was suddenly almost stunned by a tremendous fire seemingly in our face[.] Our regiment replied in a deafening roar falling on its face. . . . It proved to be the 2d Texas Regiment we were firing into and Col. Lanier ordered us to retreat to avoid any more danger." Although the mix-up soon

ended, McArthur's men surprised the Confederates and drove Moore's skirmishers back some three-quarters of a mile, through the camps of the 21st
Missouri and 17th Wisconsin and onto the main line of Moore's brigade.[26]

McArthur even tested Moore's brigade before more Confederates—the 1st
Missouri of Bowen's brigade, which had ranged far ahead of its parent unit—
arrived on the left of the Union line. The two sides exchanged volleys at no
more than fifty paces, according to Major Edwin Moore of the 21st Missouri.
But then everything went wrong for the Federals. Two other regiments in the
rear of the charging Union soldiers, the 15th Michigan and 14th Wisconsin of
Oliver's brigade, fired into the back of the line, causing considerable confusion among McArthur's charging soldiers. McKean had sent the two regiments at McArthur's request, but "they failed, however, to comprehend the
situation of affairs, and after firing an unnecessary volley retired precipi-
tously." Colonel Babcock of the 7th Illinois reported, "From some unknown
reason [they] fired into us, fortunately doing little damage, but causing the
men to break." McArthur's men fell back, and the fighting finally ended when
the Confederates, almost out of ammunition, stopped their pursuit. McArthur,
who had a horse shot out from under him, formed yet another line in the rear.
Coming across the colors of a disorganized regiment, McArthur, according to
one member of the 50th Illinois, "lifted his Scotch cap and shouted, 'What
regiment is this?'" Told it was the 50th Illinois, he planted the colors there and
re-formed the line. The Confederates did not respond. Obviously, both sides
were tiring in the extreme heat of the day. One Union soldier of the 7th Illinois reported, "There is a lull now; the rebels seem hesitating. The heat is
intense; no water; the men are famishing; some of the Seventh fall in their
tracks, fainting and exhausted under the scorching sun." But it was only the
beginning.[27]

While Lovell and Moore were making quick work of the Federals in the
vicinity of the railroad, Price similarly assaulted the works to the east and
northeast. Van Dorn, who had watched the initial movements of Lovell's
brigades, soon rode to Price's sector, where the battle was also heated. Price
himself rode up and down the lines of Maury's and Hébert's commands, one
staffer reporting that he did so "in the presence of every danger, with calm
and thoughtful form and with a countenance that indicated profound concern."
Phifer's brigade of Maury's division and Gates's, Green's, and Martin's
brigades of Hébert's division formed the front line of Price's wing, with Cabell
and Colbert in reserve. The officers positioned the various units and addressed
the men in stirring tones. John Martin spoke to each of his regiments indi-

vidually, telling the 38th Mississippi, for instance, "Attention! Men of the 38th! You are about to enter a severe engagement. I count largely to-day on you. Be cool, take aim, and fire low. What if you are killed! You will die in a glorious cause." Meanwhile, Price ordered his field batteries to deploy on the tall ridge in front of the massed infantry, but his chief of artillery informed him that the horses could not bring the guns to position, so only a few batteries unlimbered.[28]

The Confederate brigades prepared to assault the Union works occupied by Davies's division. Having already lost the services of Baldwin's brigade, this division was far below strength, and Davies realized he could do no more than slow the Confederate advance unless reinforcements came quickly. Indeed, Davies had only two small brigades supported by two batteries. Oglesby's brigade, alongside Captain Frederick Welker's Battery H, 1st Missouri Light Artillery, held the left. Hackleman was on the right, supported by Lieutenant Charles Green's Battery K, 1st Missouri Light Artillery. But soon Davies had even fewer men at his disposal. Baldwin, now over to the left with McArthur, called for reinforcements, and Davies sent the 50th Illinois, the last reserve he had except for a section of Battery D, 1st Missouri Light Artillery.[29]

Everyone knew what was coming next. While awaiting the inevitable attack, one member of Hackleman's brigade betrayed the nervousness felt by many: "In front of our position, running down to the edge of the woods one-half mile, was a gentle slope which had been cleared, or rather the timber had been fallen. Looking down and beyond through the opening vistas we discovered a large body of infantry on the move towards our left. Every once in a while we would catch a glimpse of their colors. Our pulses beat quick for we apprehended and anticipated their intention." An Ohioan in Oglesby's brigade similarly wrote, "Every now and then a rebel officer would ride out of the woods to take a view of our defenses, and it was evident that they were marshaling for a charge upon our works."[30]

By this time, Davies realized that the gap separating his left from Baldwin and the rest of McArthur's command was going to cause him problems. Rosecrans had alerted him to the issue, and Davies had sent what little force he could spare to cover the small "bridle path" that ran between the two divisions. He sent the 81st Ohio, totaling 218 men, and a section of Welker's Battery H, 1st Missouri Light Artillery. The regiment, commanded by Colonel Thomas Morton, took position with nothing on either flank and behind entrenchments that one soldier called "a slight affair . . . [that] would only serve as protection against musketry." Even worse, the regiment guarded a section of the works that looked northwestward, allowing the Confederates to plant an enfilading battery to rake their line. One corporal remarked, in understatement, "There was not an enlisted man in all that line, nor a commissioned officer, that was in love with this state of affairs."[31]

By the time Davies sent out reinforcements for other commands and covered the bridle path, he had only two depleted brigades to cover his weak front. A soldier of the 81st Ohio recalled, "The regiments were stretched to their utmost capacity in a thin line, but yet there were immense gaps which could not be filled." And worse, the Confederates were starting to move forward. The Union skirmishers scampered back into the earthworks ahead of the Southern surge. As the Confederates slowly came into sight, one of Hackleman's men remembered, "On they move[d], our eyes following them in their march." An Ohioan watched through a small opening in the woods: "A great number passed this opening; tramp, tramps, tramp, they kept coming." As they finally began the assault, the Confederates encountered the vast strip of felled timber but were not stopped. One Ohioan explained that the abatis, felled back in the spring when the Confederates had held those works, "had lost much of its strength by that time." Once they were clear of the abatis, the Confederates "charged the enemy's position with the most determined courage," an onlooker observed. By then, the Federals behind the works had begun pouring a devastating fire into the faces of the oncoming Confederates.[32]

The initial contact came at the 81st Ohio's position (guarding the bridle path). While Moore's charge to the west assaulted the empty works and hit McArthur's command on the flank, causing those units to retreat, the 42nd Alabama of Moore's brigade engaged the 81st Ohio in a long-distance affair. But the main attack on the Ohioans came from Phifer's men. Portions of the 7th Illinois, far to the left, fired obliquely into Phifer's charging brigade. This fire "staggered the enemy but did not prevent their onward march," Davies recalled. That fire soon ceased because Moore's brigade quickly engaged the 7th Illinois and caused it to retreat. To the right, the 81st Ohio also had to fall back, but not before wounding many of the attacking Confederates. The Confederates' return fire fell short of the Union line, causing one Ohioan to yell, "Shoot higher, you d____d rebels, you're doin' no good!" Soon, however, the Confederates' power became obvious as they quickly entered the Ohioans' lines. Artillery horses fell, and some members of the 81st Ohio, making a last stand, were bayoneted in the trenches. Seeing that the Confederates vastly outnumbered them, Morton's Ohioans retreated to the rear, leaving behind the two guns of Battery H.[33]

Part of Phifer's brigade, supported by Cabell in the rear, also hit the left of Oglesby's brigade. On the left, Gates's brigade supported the attack. Martin's and Green's brigades also charged the Union works, striking them farther down the line in the direction of Hackleman's men. A staff officer marveled as he watched the men move "up a steep ascent, over the heavy interlaced trunks and entangled branches of an original forest skillfully felled in accordance with the rules of military art, and in the face of a solid array of cannon and musketry securely sheltered, pouring upon their ranks a fire so rapid and continuous as to lose all distinctiveness of sound and beneath which the earth trembled and sun appeared to reel." Confederate officers were "riding around trees, jumping their horses over them or dismounting to lift aside heavy branches." The men were having similar trouble, their line broken to the point that they advanced "in two and threes," one soldier remembered.[34]

As the Confederates came nearer the Union line, they were led by able officers such as John Martin, who escorted his brigade forward, waving his hat. Bruce Colbert (former member of the Mississippi secession convention) and Martin Green both had horses shot from under them. With the Confederate flood nearing, Oglesby soon found his weak brigade "hotly engaged with the enemy," but he had trouble maintaining the line. The brigade had placed only three regiments on the line; the fourth, the 22nd Ohio, had been left behind to guard the town. When the 81st Ohio moved away to cover the bridle path, Oglesby was left with only two regiments. The 12th Illinois held the left of the brigade, while the 9th Illinois held the right and joined with Hackleman's men. When Phifer hit Oglesby's left flank, he therefore fell on the left flank of the 12th Illinois. That regiment, in the process of trying to move to the left to connect with the 81st Ohio, fell back to save itself. Its retreat uncovered the flank of the 9th Illinois, and it too gave way, uncovering Hackleman's left in the process. Chaplain Marion Morrison of the 9th Illinois remembered, "Soon the enemy came through the large gap thus made, and attacked us simultaneously in the front and rear." These flanking movements, along with the frontal assaults carried out by Hébert's brigades, immediately uprooted Oglesby's command and sent the troops running to the rear. One Confederate described the scene as "the yanks taking to their heels and getting out of danger."[35]

With Oglesby's men falling back on his left and his own flank uncovered and wide open to attack, Hackleman saw that he could not hold his position. But his men continued to fire even after Oglesby fell back. One officer reported that the artillery "continued pouring grape and canister into the ranks of the enemy, apparently without effect, though they must have suffered severely." Knowing his position was untenable, Hackleman quickly sent word to Davies about the disaster on his left and asked for orders. Davies replied that the brigade should pull back, and Hackleman began "retiring in perfect order," one officer later claimed.[36]

One Federal soldier of the 7th Iowa wrote in his diary that the Confederates "came up on us with overwhelming forces and compelled us to leave the

Breastworks." Another left a more graphic description of the fight on Hackleman's front. "We see them emerge from the forest and commence ascending the hill," he noted. "Our men on top, behind the earthworks, are pouring volley after volley down into their ranks. But there is a whole division of Rebels and they are massed together. Good Heavens! What a sight! I can see the red flash of our men's guns as they fire into the moving mass. For a moment or two they are checked. . . . On they move—they have reached the breastworks—one climbing over—our men are falling back."[37]

As the surging Confederates made their way up the incline toward the Federal lines, they saw what one Southerner described as the Federals running "like a drove of Sheep." Another Confederate remembered, "They ran like hens running from a hawk." At least one Federal saw it differently. James Thurston of the 52nd Illinois recorded in his diary a much calmer scene: "We were obliged to fall back gradually as the enemy were too much for us." Regardless of the differences in interpretation, Price had taken the old Confederate works. The Federal line had dissolved, and several cannon had been captured. One of the rounds the cannoneers managed to get off, however, landed in Green's brigade, killing twelve Mississippi soldiers.[38]

According to staff officer John Tyler, a "wild shout of triumph" went up as the Confederates realized they had taken the works. Tyler went on, "Our soldiers stood once more within the works their own hands had erected." And the men of Price's command could hear the shouts of Lovell's troops farther to the right, indicating success in that quarter as well. One excited Missourian, sitting atop a captured gun, remarked to his colonel, "Well, Colonel, you mounted fellows are tolerably useful in camp, and serve a good purpose on the drill ground but we don't need you much in a fight." Since not a single officer on horseback had made it up the hill, Colonel James McCown could only agree.[39]

Yet the Confederates suffered numerous losses in this victorious assault on the Federal line. Captain Absalom Dantzler of the 37th Mississippi, a member of the state legislature, was hit above the shoulder blade, the bullet clipping a major artery. One of his soldiers took him rearward and remained with him until he died. "He talked as long as he had breath," the soldier wrote to Dantzler's wife. "He was as calm as if in common conversation perfectly satisfied to die." Colonel John D. Martin, commanding Hébert's fourth brigade of Mississippi and Alabama troops, was also mortally wounded in the action. He took a shot within twenty yards of the Federal works while leading his brigade against an angle in the Union line. It is quite possible that a Union soldier of Hackleman's brigade described Martin's wounding: "I can see a rebel Gen'l ride in front and wave his sword—his men move on—I see him roll off his horse and the steed prancing down the hill." Removed to the rear, Martin died at 5:00 that afternoon, his last words being "God Bless Rosa and my children" and "Oh, God! Forgive my sins." Martin, only thirty-two at the time, had become a prominent citizen in Memphis, working as a surgeon at the city's hospital. He also proved to be a real leader, as his exploits at Shiloh and Iuka demonstrated. Price reported that Martin's actions "won for him a place in the heart of every Mississippian and the admiration and confidence of his superior officers." Command of the brigade fell to Colonel Robert McLain of the 37th Mississippi.[40]

Despite the death blows delivered to the enemy, the Federal commanders were not confident that they could form a new line. In the retiring Union mass, General Davies did not know what to do, even asking his aides, "Do you think we can form another line?" He must have received a positive answer, because he soon positioned the division in a new makeshift line. The new deployment was situated about 1,000 yards behind the unit's former position at the old Confederate trenches—the same place they had formed earlier that morning. There, the two brigades fronted an open field and waited for the Confederates. Knowing that he desperately needed more men, Davies sent a message to Baldwin, ordering him to rejoin the division. The messenger was shot, but he kept going until he came to a large Confederate force, Moore's brigade. He then returned and reported that the Confederates had moved between Davies and McKean. This news disturbed Davies even more, but he still formed his line, hoping his two nervous brigades were ready to meet the next Confederate assault.[41]

The victorious Confederates of Price's command halted just inside the captured works, letting out a victory cheer all along the line. The cheer and the lull were entirely deserved. In only a matter of minutes, the troops of Price's Corps had swept up the slopes and carried the Union lines, capturing several prisoners and guns. They had also driven a wedge of troops between two Federal divisions. Moreover, contrary to the report of Hackleman's artillery doing great damage, this had been accomplished with very few casualties, Martin's mortal wounding being the most notable one. Price attributed this success to the "impetuosity with which the charge was made." A rumor throughout the Confederate army further boosted Price's confidence. L. H. Graves of the 6th Texas Cavalry remembered, "Gen. Price came galloping up & said that we had killed the commander in chief of the enemy Tom Rosecrans—he (Gen Price) was much enthused." No doubt Van Dorn was also happy. Thinking the outer fortifications were all he would face, he must have believed the hardest fighting was over. Price and Van Dorn met on the main road behind the lines, feeling good about their men's work.[42]

No cheers went up on the Union side. McKean had been driven from his line around Cane Creek, and Davies had lost the works to the east. The commands were also in a state of disarray. Baldwin's entire brigade, for example, was fighting with McArthur. In addition, the gulf between McKean's and Davies's divisions was greater than ever, and Confederates completely filled that gap. And the opening was no longer just an unmanned line. The farther south the Union line withdrew, the larger the Turner Creek watershed became, forming a barrier between the Union divisions. A corresponding gap, though not as large, between Moore and Phifer on the Confederate side was the only respite.

Thus far, too, Stanley and Hamilton had not been engaged. What the Federals once perceived as a blessing, however, soon became an area of concern. When Davies had fallen back and the Confederates had followed a short way, Hamilton to his right had done very little, to the point that his soldiers even found time to write letters home. He still held his position at the old Confederate works with Buford's brigade, although Sullivan on the left had fallen back a short distance and changed his front to face the Confederates. Now the Southerners were nearing Hamilton's rear and seemed ready to cut him off and capture or destroy him.[43]

To do so, Price's men finally began the pursuit that brought them near Davies's second line of defense, passing Union encampments along the way. One soldier remembered, "The tents were standing, and all the appurtenances of a camp were left, including a well-constructed bakery." The Confederates soon formed up and placed two batteries, Landis's and Guibor's, in position to fire on the Federal line. The Federals met the artillery fire, and the two lines "had a brisk artillery fight" for about forty-five minutes, one soldier recalled. The Confederate artillery finally drove its Federal counterparts away, and the infantry prepared to assault.[44]

Before Price's troops could attack, however, Davies ordered his two remaining brigades to withdraw a second time, this time down the ridge between Turner and Elam Creeks. Davies only intended the second line to slow the Confederates, he reported, causing "them to form line of battle in my front, which they did." Before any musket shots were fired, Davies again had his two brigades march to the rear, some 800 yards back, where they formed another line. This third line of defense lay at the junction of the Chewalla and Columbus roads, only about 1,500 yards in front of Battery Robinett and the main line of defense for the town of Corinth. This was the location of Davies's original position earlier that morning. As the lines formed, Davies sent another urgent plea for reinforcements.[45]

While Hackleman and Oglesby formed their lines, Davies directed yet another withdrawal. This time, the troops withdrew another 950 yards to a point less than 750 yards in front of Robinett. Davies pointed out that this was the only position "from the Confederate breastworks where the small force under my command had any hope of meeting the enemy with success." Meanwhile, Davies received an order from Rosecrans that he was not to take the "extreme position," the inner line of defense, until forced to do so. Davies ignored the order and formed his line near a dwelling called the "White House." Fortunately, Batteries Robinett and Williams were close enough to cover the line's left flank with their big guns; also, the Elam Creek swamp covered the right flank, and Turner Creek covered the left. The center contained a large open field that the Federals could also use to their advantage. Davies formed his brigades on this line on the northern edge of the field. Hackleman formed the 52nd Illinois, 2nd Iowa, and 7th Iowa from right to left, with the Illinoisans resting on the Elam Creek swamp. To their left, Oglesby formed the 12th Illinois, 81st Ohio, and 9th Illinois, with the artillery on the high ground on the left near the house in the southern portion of the field. These guns covered both the field and the roads that led behind the line. With his brigades formed, Davies waited, he said, for "the whole army of Price and Van Dorn [which] would soon make its appearance and give us battle."[46]

The Confederates did not disappoint. Price soon had his men moving forward toward this new line. The first day's battle at Corinth was about to get vicious.

Major General Henry W. Halleck commanded the massive Federal army bearing down on Corinth in May 1862. Known as "Old Brains," he employed methodical, careful, and orderly thinking in the campaign and eventually won Corinth with little bloodshed. He transferred to Washington, D.C., in the summer of 1862 to command all the Federal armies. (Courtesy of Library of Congress)

Major General Ulysses S. Grant, the castigated victor of Shiloh, was promoted to Halleck's meaningless second in command during the advance on Corinth. When Halleck transferred east, Grant took control of the department, overseeing the military operations as well as the developing contraband situation. (Courtesy of Library of Congress)

Major General William S. Rosecrans arrived at Corinth in late May 1862 and eventually took control of the Army of the Mississippi upon John Pope's transfer east. Rosecrans commanded the Corinth region, where he battled Sterling Price at Iuka and then Earl Van Dorn and Price at Corinth. To reward his victory, Lincoln promoted Rosecrans to command the Army of the Cumberland. (Courtesy of Library of Congress)

Brigadier General Grenville M. Dodge took command of the troops and post of Corinth in late October 1862. Although better known for his postwar work on the transcontinental railroad, Dodge was an important factor in the Union's contraband policy. At Corinth, he oversaw the establishment of the contraband camp and the enlistment of former slaves into the Union army. (Courtesy of Library of Congress)

General P. G. T. Beauregard took
command of the Confederate Army of the
Mississippi upon Albert Sidney Johnston's
death at Shiloh. It fell to him to defend
Corinth and its railroads against Halleck's
larger armies, but Beauregard wisely
evacuated the town, keeping his army
intact. He did not survive another run-in
with Jefferson Davis, however, and turned
control of his army over to Braxton
Bragg. (Courtesy of Library of Congress)

General Braxton Bragg served as a corps
commander at Shiloh and then under
Beauregard during the siege of Corinth,
personally overseeing the loading of a vast
assortment of supplies before the
evacuation. When Jefferson Davis relieved
Beauregard of command, Bragg was his
successor. He would be the longest-serving
commander of the Army of Tennessee.
(Courtesy of Library of Congress)

Major General Earl Van Dorn was a hard-luck commander who wished for glory and sought it at every opportunity. Defeated in Arkansas at Pea Ridge, Van Dorn transferred his command to Corinth for the siege. He eventually took command in Mississippi when Bragg moved east and then northward into Kentucky in the fall of 1862. It was Van Dorn's idea to attack Corinth, but his inadequate leadership resulted in a serious defeat for the Confederacy. He would later have more success commanding the cavalry, until a jealous husband ended his life. (Courtesy of Van Hedges)

One of the most revered commanders in the Confederate army, Major General Sterling Price moved east with Van Dorn after the debacle at Pea Ridge, fighting in the siege as well as at Iuka later that fall. He effected a concentration with Van Dorn, but his trans-Mississippians were devastated at Corinth. He eventually got his wish to return to the trans-Mississippi, although his troops remained east of the river. (Courtesy of Library of Congress)

Corinth's main importance revolved around the railroads that crossed there. Looking westward from town along the Memphis and Charleston Railroad toward Batteries Robinett and Williams, this typical scene shows the dynamic railroad presence in Corinth. (Courtesy of Dr. William G. Jackson)

The celebrated Tishomingo Hotel sat at the junction of the railroads in Corinth. After Shiloh, it was used as a hospital, and it saw action during the October battle, even sustaining some damage. The Confederate surge reached the porch of the hotel. Although it survived the battle, the hotel did not survive the war, succumbing to flames set by retreating Confederates in January 1865. (Courtesy of Van Hedges)

Corona College was a major landmark just south of Corinth. Female students from all over the South attended the school before the war, but the fighting eventually ended all classes. The Federals built a large fort surrounding the college after the October battle but burned the building upon their evacuation in January 1864. (Courtesy of Dr. William G. Jackson)

Long thought to be a photograph of Battery Robinett, recently discovered evidence indicates that this is the only known photograph of Battery Powell, which saw heavy action during the second day of the October battle. The Confederates momentarily took possession of the redoubt but had to give it up when the Federals counterattacked. (Courtesy of Dr. William G. Jackson)

This view of Battery Robinett shows the horror of war. The dead Confederate in the foreground fell on the second day of the attack. (Courtesy of Library of Congress)

Once the Federals won the October battle, it fell to them to bury the dead. For days, Confederate wounded and dead alike were located across the battlefield. This view, looking toward Corinth from the front of Battery Robinett, shows the recently gathered dead Confederates, including Colonel William P. Rogers at left. (Courtesy of Library of Congress)

Although occupation life was much easier than fighting battles, the Union army still kept firm control of its troops, often dispensing punishment. Some offenses carried the death penalty. This view shows the offender immediately before his sentence was carried out. Note the garrison assembled to watch in the background. (Courtesy of Dr. William G. Jackson)

Programme of the
Grand Military Ball
given by the
Commissioned Officers of the Garison of Corinth
on
(New Year's Eve (Dec. 31st 1862)

Order of Dances.

1. Quadrille
2. do. —
3. Waltz. —
4. Quadrille. — Lieut Fish
5. Sicillian Circle. —
6. Cotillion. —
7. Polka. —
8. Cotillion — [illegible]
9. Shottische. —
10. Quadrille. [illegible]
11. Spanish Dance. —
12. Cotillion, Capt [illegible]
13. [illegible]

Once the fighting ended and the much more peaceful Union occupation began, life in Corinth returned to a kind of normal. Newspapers operated, church congregations gathered, and social events took place, including the famous New Year's Eve ball at the Tishomingo Hotel. This dance card shows the partners of an anonymous woman for several dances during the evening. (Courtesy of Van Hedges)

Corinth thrived during the occupation. This view shows a typical street scene and one of the buildings being used as the Federal commissary. The buildings are facing south on Front Street. (Courtesy of Van Hedges)

Knowing that they would be stationed at Corinth for quite a while, soldiers built commodious quarters all over the landscape. This portion of a lithograph shows the wooden barracks of the 52nd Illinois Infantry. (Courtesy of Van Hedges)

Another portion of the same lithograph shows the only known rendering of the contraband camp and the enlistment of former slaves in Federal regiments. (Courtesy of Van Hedges)

After the war, the Federal government disinterred the Union dead on the nearby battlefields and buried them in Corinth National Cemetery. This view shows the gates to the cemetery around the turn of the twentieth century. (Courtesy of Shiloh National Military Park)

This 1890s-era view shows the original site of Battery Robinett and the view from the ridge into Corinth. Colonel William P. Rogers was buried at the fort, on Rosecrans's orders. His grave was not yet permanently marked, but a large memorial would eventually go up. (Courtesy of Shiloh National Military Park)

By the turn of the twentieth century, most of the earthworks nearest to Corinth, including all the forts of the inner line, were obliterated. Only small portions of the works are discernible in this 1890s-era view of one of the covered passageways connecting the Federal forts. (Courtesy of Shiloh National Military Park)

11

"VICTORIOUS SO FAR"

Thomas McKean was determined to hold his position around Battery F despite the retreat of Davies's division to his right, across Turner Creek. Rosecrans had already expressed his displeasure at what he considered Oliver's hasty withdrawal, and McKean was determined to be pushed when he fell back again. Moreover, Rosecrans had notified him that Hamilton on the far right would begin a flank attack any minute. "The object will be as far as possible to keep your troops fresh and constrict our line of defense until we can develop a flank movement with Hamilton's Division," Rosecrans informed McKean that afternoon. McKean thus reported, "I considered it best to retain my present position for the purpose of engaging the attention of the enemy until such movement could be effected." As a result, action picked up again along the Memphis and Charleston Railroad. But the Union counterattacks north of the railroad could delay the Confederates pushing toward Battery F for only so long, and by 3:00 P.M., a mass of Southern soldiers was putting pressure on the Federal line once more.[1]

By this time, McArthur and Baldwin had fallen back across the railroad to Battery F, where Crocker's brigade held the line. Skirmishing quickly erupted as the idle guns of the 1st Minnesota Battery moved forward and fired on the approaching Confederate lines. One of its cannoneers reported that the officers required them to hold their fire because the tree line reduced visibility to only thirty yards; they also wanted to try to fool the Confederates into thinking there were no guns at Battery F. Union skirmishers were also on the front. "We begged for permission to shoot our cannon," August Schilling remembered. "We grumbled that we had to watch and wait." Just then, "all of a sudden a cannon ball whizzed just above our heads from the enemy front. . . . We saw the smoke of the second cannon shot and then heard the next ball whiz passed, much closer than the first one." They got their answer, Schilling remembered, and the Minnesotans opened up. Two guns of the 3rd Ohio Battery inside Battery F also erupted, and they soon drove the Confederate gunners away. "Our artillery which had chose good positions, poured grape and canister into their ranks with terrible effect," one Federal recalled.[2]

One Minnesotan gave a detailed description of the artillery duel:

> When our gun was heated it was mighty hard work to ram down the charge, which was my duty as I was No. 1. Nothing is so exciting as working a gun in real action. The sound of the discharge almost raises us off our feet with delight. Before the smoke lifts from the muzzle I dash in, dip the brush in the sponge bucket and brush out the bore using plenty of water, then seize the sponge staff and sponge it out dry. No. 2 then inserts the cartridge which I ram home, then the shot, shell or canister, whichever it may be and it is sent home, then I spring out beside the wheel and fall flat. "Ready" shouts the Gunner. No. 3 (who has been serving vent while I loaded) now pricks the cartridge, No. 4 jumps in and inserts a friction primer, to which his lanyard is attached, in the vent, springs outside the wheel and straightens his lanyard. The Gunner gives a turn or two to the elevating screw, taps on the trail and has it carried round a little, and then, "Fire" "Take that,—you" says No. 4 as the gun rushes back with the recoil. The other numbers run her forward at the command "By hand to the front" while I load.

The artilleryman added, "While you have been reading this description we would fire 3 or 4 shots, so rapidly do we work."[3]

But right in the middle of the artillery action, new orders for McKean arrived from Rosecrans, changing the plan. Davies's successive withdrawals in the center prompted Rosecrans to order McKean to fall back to a position in touch with Davies's newest line. McKean's third line, according to Rosecrans, was to have its right on Davies's left across Turner Creek and its left on Battery E: "swing your left back as fast as possible it is too much exposed," Rosecrans ordered. Old Rosy also ordered McKean to fill the three artesian wells at Battery F and the one at Battery D to ruin them for enemy use.[4]

Baldwin's and McArthur's brigades moved to the rear as ordered, which left only Crocker's brigade at Battery F. The two front regiments, the 15th and 16th Iowa, remained in line as a rear guard on the east side of Battery F, along with two companies of skirmishers from the 13th Iowa; the 11th Iowa and the remainder of the 13th Iowa withdrew and formed a line to the rear, covering the road on which the other units moved. Those two units would not participate in the forthcoming action, prompting one member of the 11th Iowa to tell his family back home that the regiment was not engaged during the battle. McKean planned to have the two front regiments withdraw before a fight, but the Confederates struck first. A member of the 15th Iowa was ill about his comrades' retreat: "The regiments held as a Reserve fell back toward our Camp without helping us any." A disappointed member of the 13th Iowa similarly recorded, "As soon as they charged the reserve was ordered back. We fell back about half a mile and formed again. The 15th and 16th fought them."[5]

It would be known as the fight for Battery F.

Mansfield Lovell's division swung into action a second time. In their new position, Rust and Villepigue could see in the distance a strong Federal redoubt "well flanked with infantry," Lovell reported. A formidable expanse of fallen timber around one side added to its strength. He noticed it, but since the timber stretched only to the left of the work, Lovell surmised that there were "no obstructions to the north, in the direction of Price's right," or, essentially, Moore's brigade. Lovell reported this to Van Dorn, who immediately told Moore to attack. Bowen's brigade also received orders to move on the fort on the right.[6]

In addition, William Cabell was ordered to send two regiments to support Moore. Still in reserve behind Phifer, Cabell quickly sent the 19th and 20th Arkansas across the upper reaches of the Turner Creek watershed. When the two regiments arrived, Moore led his men forward toward the Federal fort. Along the way, he had his troops change their front, moving the left wing up so that the brigade now faced southwest. Then the troops came to the railroad, which lay parallel to their line. The brigade quickly crossed the road and made ready for the assault, but they suddenly took point-blank fire from the fort and from the infantry on its flanks. "On crossing," Moore related, "the enemy opened on us a most terrific fire from the brow of a hill not more than 75 yards distant." Moore had stumbled into a den of angry Federals.[7]

Moore's men were equal to the test, however, as were some of Bowen's troops. The 1st Missouri moved on the battery from the Confederate right. The two wings acted in unison and forced the Federals to fight viciously for their ground. One Union soldier observed that the Confederates moved toward their line and got off the first volley, which, he said, "laid out many a man for us." A member of the 15th Iowa, Phillip Hippert, also remembered the opening Confederate attack. He and the other Iowans could see the Confederates coming but were told to hold their fire. "Three or four times I raised my gun to fire," he recalled, "when a voice we were accustomed to obey said: 'Hold on, Hippert; hold on.' Turning my head and looking back," the Iowan continued, "I saw right by the colors that good old gray horse, with Colonel Belknap in the saddle, as cool as a cucumber, while the rebel bullets were flying like hail." But when the Confederates raised the rebel yell, the Union infantrymen could not hold back any longer. "Somebody commenced firing and we shot away in the smoke not knowing exactly where to aim as the enemy were in lower ground than we," remembered Cyrus Boyd of the 15th Iowa.[8]

When finally let loose, the Federal fire was heavy. Moore took casualties from the artillery fire as well as the rifles of the 15th and 16th Iowa, which Belknap reported was done "in full volleys." Crocker's infantry fire checked Moore's progress for a moment, but Moore soon had his men re-formed and charging again. This time, Moore's men were more successful, although the Iowans gave almost as good as they got. One member of the 15th Iowa wrote home, "Our regiment engaged the enemy in close conflict about forty minutes but they outnumbered us and we had to fall back. I had a good place behind a tree, I shot nine times at a good mark but I can't say that they had any affect but I felt cool and done it deliberately." Just as heroic a spectacle was the 15th Iowa's commander, Lieutenant Colonel William Belknap (in charge of the regiment because the colonel was sick). Belknap, according to Crocker, "was everywhere along the line, mounted, with sword in hand, encouraging by voice and gesture his men to stand their ground." Not to be outdone was the 16th Iowa's commander, Lieutenant Colonel Addison Sanders. Although Sanders was severely wounded in the thigh, and his horse had been hit in several places, he would not leave the regiment. Yet despite the sound leadership, the Confederates drove the Federals from around the fort. The 1st Missouri of Bowen's brigade had moved ahead of the rest of the regiments and suddenly appeared on the opposite side of the fort. They drove the Federals away and took the redoubt while "commenc[ing] a murderous fire upon the unprotected left and rear of the 15th Iowa," one of the members of that regiment recalled. The Union infantry fell back, but they succeeded in removing the guns before the Confederates arrived. Soon, the Union infantry received notification that all the artillery had safely moved to the rear and they could now retreat. Battery F, which the Confederates found "to be a strong work, in a fine position, and well constructed," thus fell to the Confederates. The Southerners had taken a giant leap in their move toward Corinth. After taking the Beauregard line, they had also cracked the Halleck line.[9]

The victorious Southerners found the nearby Federal camps to their liking. The perceptive Federals, some of them veterans of Shiloh, had taken the precaution of dropping the Sibley tents so that they lay flat on the ground and would not be shot up. One retreating Federal remembered, "I could see the Rebs tearing the Sutlers tents away and going for the goods." The troops had little time for sacking, however, because the brigades soon formed in line of battle once again. No one seemed to know what to do next, though. Moore, separated from his division, sent a courier to Maury asking for instructions. Before he received a reply, Lovell and his staff arrived. In consultation with Moore, they decided to form a line perpendicular to the railroad facing southeast, and Moore moved his troops into line with his left resting on the railroad. For the better part of the next hour, Lovell's brigades kept busy receiving ammunition and forming on Moore's right. Villepigue and Bowen deployed in the front line, while the bloodied soldiers of Rust's brigade continued to form the reserve.[10]

When the two frontline Iowa regiments fell back before the determined Confederate attacks, they withdrew to a position next to the other two regiments of the brigade. There, they formed on the right of the main line and waited for the Confederates, who were "declining to follow," Crocker remembered. Another Iowan recalled, "The rebels did not follow as we supposed they would." Crocker had done his job by halting the Confederates for forty-five minutes, giving the rest of the troops time to move to the rear. Even the hard-fighting Crocker was moved by the experience. Sitting beside Belknap of the 15th Iowa during the fight, Crocker asked, "Do you know, old fellow, what I am thinking about?" Belknap responded, "What, colonel." "I wish I was back in Des Moines," Crocker muttered. Nevertheless, the three battle-weary brigades—McArthur's, Oliver's, and Baldwin's—now moved to the third line, an extension of Davies's position, while Crocker covered the movement with his brigade.[11]

The hands of Price's watch neared 3:00. The original Federal line at the entrenchments had fallen around noon, and the Confederates had spent the next three hours reorganizing and following Davies's various retreats. Each stop, as Rosecrans and Davies had hoped, had caused the Confederates to deploy, only to find nothing to attack. But by 3:00 P.M., Price finally had the Federals in a no-retreat situation, and he made plans to assault their formidable position. The Confederates realized the sturdiness of the Union line, however, with one commander remarking, "Here we saw danger ahead." Another wrote, "We had been double quicked about three miles, and drawn up in line of battle on one side of a narrow field, with the enemy's guns just on the other side, in plain view." He admitted, "I freely confess I had but little courage and less confidence left."[12]

But while the Southerners prepared for their charge, events took place to their left that would have a marked effect on the result of the battle. Directing the slow retrograde movement, Rosecrans suddenly became more offense minded. He realized this was the main Confederate attack and that Van Dorn did not intend to draw him out of his fortifications. For Davies's part, he had been trying to tell Rosecrans that all day, sending urgent pleas for reinforcements throughout the early afternoon. Rosecrans finally saw that the Confederates indeed "meant mischief." Now they presented him with a golden opportunity. He thus ordered Hamilton into action.[13]

Hamilton's division had not fought at all that day; Buford reported that the division was "engaged all the day in watching the enemy." Only a few cavalrymen had appeared before their lines, and they quickly galloped away. The soldiers of Hamilton's division had heard the commotion to their left and realized the Confederates had moved behind the original positions assigned them by Rosecrans. Obeying his last orders to cover the Purdy road, Hamilton had gradually turned his division to the left, pivoting on its center and establishing itself on the Confederate's left flank, eventually facing due west; only the extreme right regiment, the 26th Missouri, was re-fused to face northward and watch the flank. The division stood on the ridge containing the Purdy road, facing the valley of Elam Creek and the Mobile and Ohio Railroad. One soldier in the 4th Minnesota told of the lack of action: "We change[d] front and marched to the South West, where we lay on our arms to get a few minutes rest and escape the burning sun, whose rays have become almost unbearable." The regiment's colonel, John Sanborn, commented that "more men were carried off the field on litters from the effects of sun-stroke than from wounds." Like other commanders, he even resorted to hauling water in wagons out from Corinth, some of which inadvertently became lost between the contending sides. One artillery officer yelled at a lost wagon team to "get out of this," and, as an Illinoisan recalled, "they got." But without orders, Hamilton did not dare move any farther. He merely placed Captain Henry Dillon's 6th Wisconsin Battery between the brigades and held the remainder of his artillery in reserve on the right, ready to cover that open flank and move to any threatened point.[14]

Around 2:00 P.M., Hamilton finally received word from Rosecrans, but it only made the confusing and bewildering situation more chaotic. First of all, like Davies and McKean, Hamilton was told not to take up the "extreme position" until forced to do so. That was plain enough. But then Rosecrans informed Hamilton of Davies's retreat and ordered him to move his division to the *left* of Davies's division and attack the Confederate flank. Hamilton knew that had to be a mistake: if he moved into position on Davies's *left*, he would have to move across Davies's rear, which would totally remove any chance of an attack against the Confederates' exposed left flank. Hamilton returned the order to Rosecrans with that explanation written on the back; he was already anxious due to his tenuous position as well as recent bouts of nervousness and a palpitating heart. Rosecrans sent Colonel Arthur Ducat, his chief of staff, back to Hamilton with revised orders. Ducat was reluctant to go, protesting that the ride was terribly dangerous and that he had four children, but Rosecrans sent his subordinate anyway. When the new order arrived, Hamilton read that he should march his division south until the head of the column arrived near Davies's *right* flank. At that point, Hamilton should turn his brigades to the west and attack the Confederates on that flank. Rosecrans had gotten his left and right mixed up in the heat of battle.[15]

While Hamilton and Rosecrans had trouble over orders, Davies endured a different kind of trouble from the Confederate infantry. Like McKean, he had received news of Hamilton's intended flank attack, but as of yet, he had heard nothing from Hamilton himself. Nor had he received any of the reinforcements he had been pestering Rosecrans about all day. It seemed he would face the Confederates alone.[16]

Until help arrived, Davies had only two brigades with which to form his line and try to hold the position across the narrow ridge between Turner and Elam Creeks. Richard Oglesby realized the situation and lectured his troops: "Men, we are going to fight them on this ground. If there's dying to be done, men, I pledge to you my word I'll stay with you and take my share of it." Fortunately, this line contained eleven guns, all that remained in the division. But the infantry still lay in open timber on the north side of an open field on either side of the Chewalla road. As the men lay down in line, one soldier of the 81st Ohio positioned his head right behind his standing captain's foot. Pointing at the captain's foot, he told his comrade next to him, "Its got to go through *that* before it hits me."[17]

The Confederate attacking force had a huge numerical superiority, containing Phifer's, McLain's, Gates's, and Green's brigades, while Colbert's and Cabell's brigades continued to form the reserve. Van Dorn himself rode among the troops, encouraging the weary. Unfortunately for them, ineptitude and a lack of leadership squandered the massive Confederate numbers. As the units formed, a mix-up occurred when the left of Hébert's division obliqued too far to the right, thus moving behind Green. As a result, Green moved forward to fight the Federals alone. Members of other brigades related that only "skirmishing continued during the balance of the day."[18]

Green's Missouri brigade nevertheless moved forward and made its way toward the Union line situated on the north side of the field near the White House, which was already being used as a hospital. Realizing it would be better to have the enemy cross the open field rather than to retreat across it under fire, Davies quickly retired his brigades to force the enemy to move through the open. Thus, the line formed south of the White House, in the rear of the artillery and the open field. Those Federals not facing the field fronted a "thick underbrush," one soldier recalled. Due to the terrain and the fact that the infantry was prone on the ground, it was hard to see exactly where the Union line was. One Federal reported, "The rebels came up within 100 yards of us before we seen them, or they seen us, but we let into them first." Davies reported sending the enemy "a welcome in one of our 20-pounder guns, to which politeness they returned the compliment." Landis's battery, attached to Green's brigade, responded and deployed in the rear of the Confederate line on "a little ridge," one Missouri Confederate remembered, and poured over the Union line with fire. Guibor's battery also took up the fight, despite the presence of civilians running out of a small cabin nearby. Federal soldiers on the opposite side of the field related the result of the barrage. One described "shells bursting over us and limbs falling on them which cannonballs would cut off when they passed over us." Another of the 2nd Iowa described "shells and every other missile of death sweeping over our heads."[19]

Soon the infantry took up the fight. As the Confederate soldiers burst out of the woods at the double-quick, covered by Landis's and Guibor's guns, they immediately met the fire of Davies's artillery. The division's guns, despite their small number, played havoc on the charging Confederate line as it tried to cross the open field. These eleven guns—three guns of Battery D, four of Battery K, two of Battery H, and two of Battery I, 1st Missouri Light Artillery—had recently concentrated on the left of the line. The artillery deployed at a "pleasant range" and "poured a steady stream, staggering their advancing column," one Federal remembered. The Confederates endured the artillery fire, but they had little with which to respond. Price reported that he could find no place, except for Landis's and Guibor's positions, from which the guns could fire and produce favorable results. The ground was hilly and knobby. The eleven Union guns, along with some infantry support, thus broke the Confederate charge.[20]

The Confederates were not willing to let eleven guns stop their progress, however. They had driven the Federals to within a shot of Corinth, and this was no time to stop. They re-formed and charged again. Once more, their line broke, and Green's brigade had to fall back under the immense pressure of the Union artillery. "The [Confederate] infantry essayed time and again to advance," Davies reported, but the artillery drove them back each time.[21]

Despite the success of blunting the frontal attacks across the field, Davies was growing more and more concerned as the afternoon wore on. He had still heard nothing from Hamilton, his artillery was running out of ammunition,

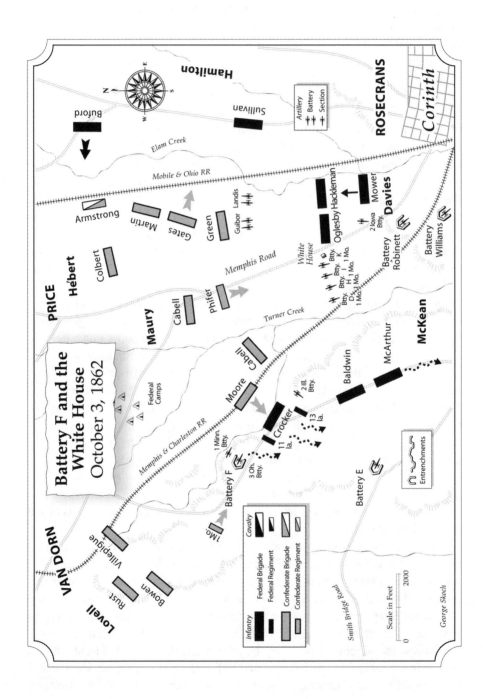

Battery F and the White House
October 3, 1862

Hamilton

ROSECRANS

Corinth

Buford

Elam Creek

Mobile & Ohio RR

Sullivan

Artillery
Battery
Section

Armstrong

Martin

Gates

Green

Guibor
Landis

Colbert

PRICE

Hébert

Memphis Road

White House

Oglesby Hackleman

2 Iowa
Btty.

Mower

Davies

Btty. K
Btty. I, 1 Mo.
Btty. H, 1 Mo.

Battery
Robinett

Battery
Williams

Cabell

Phifer

Maury

Turner Creek

Btty.
D, 1 Mo.
1 Mo.

McKean

Cabell

McArthur

Federal
Camps

Moore

Crocker

Baldwin

2 Ill.
Btty.

13
Ia.

Memphis & Charleston RR

1 Minn.
Btty.

11
Ia.

Battery F

3 Oh.
Btty.

Battery E

Entrenchments

VAN DORN

Villepigue

1 Mo.

LOVELL

Rust

Bowen

Cavalry

Infantry

Federal Brigade
Federal Regiment

Confederate Brigade
Confederate Regiment

Scale in Feet

0   2000

Smith Bridge Road

George Skoch

and the Confederates were attacking again. Davies's position was desperate, and he sent yet another urgent plea for help. Making matters even worse, the Confederates were moving to his right. If this movement succeeded, the enemy would be between his division and Corinth. That threat soon subsided, however, when Hackleman sent a regiment to deal with the flankers. The 52nd Illinois on the division's right flank moved eastward, across the Mobile and Ohio Railroad. The Illinois regiment, with Colonel Thomas W. Sweeny commanding, succeeded in driving the small number of Confederates away and secured that sector. To make sure, Lieutenant Colonel John S. Wilcox moved farther to the right with two companies and, after a small skirmish, drove a few other Confederates back. In the fight, Wilcox reported to his wife, "I saw one of the rebel skirmishers step upon the track some 60 rods distant." The Confederate took a shot at Wilcox, but he ducked, and the bullet passed harmlessly overhead. With the flank secured and no sign of more Confederates, the regiment moved back over the railroad and rejoined the fighting there.[22]

Davies still needed reinforcements, however, and a few came in the form of the small Union Brigade composed of remnants from different units that had surrendered in the Hornet's Nest at Shiloh: the 8th, 12th, and 14th Iowa and the 58th Illinois. This unit had just arrived from a march south of Corinth, which one member described as "very hot and dusty . . . [a] good many of the boys were sunstruck." On the way into Corinth, one of Davies's staff officers met the unit and ordered it to move at the double-quick, to which one captain responded that it was "impossible for our boys were falling sunstruck every moment, some of them whom died." Nevertheless, they did the best they could but soon found more trouble the closer they got to the battle. One soldier described their feelings as they approached the White House lines: "The loaded ambulances that came pouring in from the field satisfied us." When they finally arrived, the Union Brigade moved to the extreme left of the line, where it deployed to cover the artillery's position at the edge of the field. Beyond these small numbers, however, Davies had no new troops to deal with the charging Confederates. He ordered his infantry to lie down until the Confederates came within very short range; then they were to rise and fire.[23]

The Confederates were indeed charging again. Green's brigade, one soldier remembered, came "forward in a steady line, firing as they advanced." But this time, some of the Confederate high command's ineptitude had subsided, and Phifer's brigade was in support on the right. Having finally received orders to attack, the brigade moved on Green's right and hit the Federal line near the Union Brigade. As the Confederates emerged again, the Union line rose "as one man . . . from its concealment," one onlooker observed, and fired directly into the faces of the Confederates. The Southerners "fell like the leaves of autumn," one Federal remembered. But then they closed up and came again. A Confederate in the 6th Texas Cavalry of Phifer's brigade agreed: "The trees were tumbling in every direction and the limbs fly through the air. The ground bursting into holes and ditches by the mighty force of the cannon balls, but once we went through it all up to the very mouth of the battery." The two Federal brigades, situated "upon a gentle rise of ground and in full view of the field," then poured another volley into the Confederate line, which broke again and fled to the rear. One member of the Union Brigade described the action: "The boys being of the best metal they poured the grape and canister into them until they came right up to the mouth of the pieces." He added, "The last shot killed five men within three feet." Another Iowan wrote home, "They come and we open upon them with a hearty cheer—we go at it cheering." The Federals also took casualties, however. One Iowan described how the Confederate "hard shot and shell cropt the trees, [and] hissed over our heads."[24]

One member of the 81st Ohio, Charles Wright, had an almost surreal, slow-motion experience in the middle of the carnage. He later remembered looking about him at all the beauty of the fight: "The afternoon sun shone on the powder-stained faces of the men, the polished rammers glint and glisten amid the wreaths of battle smoke." Looking up, he saw "floating proudly and defiantly above the flaming guns—is the Starry Flag, bullet riven but 'a thing of beauty and joy forever!'" His calm was shattered, however, when he touched elbows with his friend next to him and saw that he had been wounded, the bullet having "torn its way along the side of his head." Wright told him to go to the rear, to which his friend responded, "I am not hurt bad enough yet!"[25]

During the assault, the main Federal line remained intact, but portions of the Union Brigade on the far left fled from Phifer's repeated attacks, which momentarily took a couple of the guns. One member of the Union Brigade, E. B. Soper, recalled, "We poured volley after volley into the advancing lines with seemingly little effect, as they continued to advance." "The guns boys left their pieces," another soldier reported. A captain in the Union Brigade laid the blame on the unit's few numbers: "Our second fire convinced them that our numbers were few, when they came rushing upon us, pouring in the most deadly fire as they came." When portions of the Union Brigade bolted, some soldiers hid until nightfall; others were captured, and one member of the 12th Iowa, Silas Crossman, outran his pursuers. Shot in the musket by a chasing Confederate who constantly called on him to halt, Crossman sped toward the Union lines in the rear. "The boys say that he so stretched his legs in running that his cartridge box struck the ground at every jump," remembered the 12th

Iowa's historian. According to the regimental history, Crossman "reached a rail fence, turned a somersault over it, and lay exhausted so near our lines that his pursuer dared not follow."[26]

Their partial success on the Union Brigade's front encouraged the determined Southerners not to quit. They re-formed and attacked the Federal line once more, drawing near to the artillery but again falling short. Casualties were mounting. Many had been killed and wounded by this time, and officers were not immune. Lieutenant Colonel James C. Parrott of the 7th Iowa reported to his wife the several close calls he had that day: "A ball went through my holster and buried in the horn of my saddle, . . . and my horse was badly wounded." Parrott was also hit: "It was merely a glancing shot [and] it scarcely raised the skin, but left quite a severe bruise." He later reflected to his wife, "One half inch closer and your hubby would have been numbered among the dead."[27]

The rapid firing of the Union guns soon expended all the ammunition, but Davies had made provisions to get more from Corinth. Twice, a six-mule team brought ammunition to the front, which the cannoneers soon fired. The team traveled back a third time, but before it could return, Green charged again. Knowing that empty guns could provide no support and would only be prizes ready for capture, Davies ordered Major George H. Stone, commanding the division's artillery, to limber up and proceed to Corinth. There, Davies told him to refill the limbers and "take the most favorable position he could get in line with Fort Robinett." The artillery crews did so, as one Federal remembered, "looking more like coal-heavers than soldiers, with perspiration streaming down their faces blackened with gunpowder." As the artillery filed to the rear, only the infantry remained to hold the position. Thanks to the artillery's work, however, there were far fewer attacking Confederates and much less daylight. The artillery had gained almost an hour and a half for the Northern army by its obstinate defense of the White House line.[28]

Without artillery support, Davies's brigades now had to stop the Confederate assaults on their own. But their options were limited. They could not hold without artillery support, and they could not fall back. The only other alternative was to attack. To drive the Confederates away this time, the two Federal brigades charged. They surprised the Confederates with such pluck and pushed the enemy at bayonet point across the field and back into the woods on the other side. Davies described it: "After a well-directed volley the order was given to charge, when the enemy was forced back at the point of the bayonet with great slaughter across the open field." One Confederate of the 3rd Missouri Cavalry later wrote that the effect was to isolate his regiment and the 4th Missouri. The Missourians simply "turned and cut our way back," he recalled. It was during this Union attack that Colonel James Baker of the 2nd Iowa fell mortally wounded.[29]

The Federal advance fell solidly on Green's Missourians, who by this time were entirely used up. Thus far, Green's brigade had done most of the fighting on the Confederate side. Granted, the narrow ridge did not provide a lot of room for maneuver, but inexplicably, Hébert and Price had not ordered Gates's brigade, formed right behind Green's, to help. One member of the idle brigade remembered that his unit lay in a large field with weeds over four feet high. As the men waited, bullets clipped the top of the weeds. Another wrote that the brigade "was not hotly engaged at no time during the day—we were used principally this day for flanking purposes, while other commands were engaging the enemy in front, we would form our line and advance making a detour to the left and north, thereby slowly but surely oppressing them back." Up ahead, Green's brigade had indeed run into stiff resistance, but Gates had no orders to move forward and therefore formed to the left and rear of Green. Many of the Missourians of Gates's brigade wished to help their friends, but no orders came. Gates thus remained in position, as did McLain and Colbert. Only Phifer launched any supporting attack.[30]

It is unclear why the Confederate commanders in the area insisted on piecemeal attacks at the White House when a concerted effort might have gained an open road into Corinth. Davies's men were tired and outnumbered, and the Confederates had ample firepower in the area to dislodge them—six brigades in all. Perhaps Van Dorn cannot be totally faulted, however, because he had the entire operation to oversee, and his whereabouts at any particular time are not known. But Van Dorn had been in the area earlier, and he had seemingly competent commanders in that sector who should have ordered more men into the fight. Hébert, the division commander, certainly should have employed more of his brigades, but Hébert was already acting strangely, perhaps due to sickness. Price, the corps commander, could have taken up the slack left by Hébert, but he had his own problems that could have attributed to his less than formidable attack. One Missourian noted that Price had been wounded: "Early in the day Genl. Price was wounded by a piece of a shell from the enemies Batteries though not sufficient to disable him from duty—he received an ugly wound in the left arm, but he remained astride of his Old Sorrel Horse and directed his men as though nothing unusual had happened." Although Price seemed to be continuing unfazed, his wound, weariness, and loss of blood could have affected his judgment later in the day.[31]

Just as Davies's division was at the breaking point, relief came. Rosecrans had finally ordered Stanley, still formed south of town, to send one of his brigades to Davies's support "through the woods by [the] shortest cut." Stanley's men might have provided support all through the day, especially in the gap between McArthur and Davies; however, Rosecrans, like Price, did not order his reserves into battle when they were most needed. Throughout the battle, Stanley's division had only changed its front from a westerly position to one facing north, with his left resting near Battery D and some elements as far north as Battery E. Now, with orders from Rosecrans, Stanley detailed Mower's brigade to help Davies, and they soon marched northward "with loud cheers, although sadly distressed for the want of water," Stanley reported. The general accompanied them a portion of the way, urging them to hurry, to which Colonel William A. Thrush of the 47th Illinois retorted, "The men are already almost utterly exhausted; to move them faster will render them unfit for action." Perhaps because of Thrush's boldness, Stanley returned to his other brigade. Mower thus led his men toward town, where the quartermaster of the 8th Wisconsin had a barrel of whiskey open, allowing the men to fill a cup as they marched by. The brigade moved northward past Battery Robinett and out the Chewalla road several hundred yards, to a point behind Davies's line. There, they stopped to await orders, which Mower soon received. He moved the brigade forward, and by 5:00 P.M., his troops were in position, with their right on the Mobile and Ohio Railroad and their left on the Chewalla road.[32]

The confusion of battle soon got the best of Mower's brigade, however. He formed the line with the 26th Illinois on the far right near the railroad and the 11th Missouri, 8th Wisconsin, and 47th Illinois continuing the line to the left; the Illinoisans took a position to the right rear of the shaky Union Brigade's line. Soon, Davies's battle-hardened veterans withdrew through Mower's line, leaving his men to face the oncoming Confederates across the bloody field near the White House. One Wisconsin soldier described the Confederate attack: "They made a charge, yelling like so many screech owls or devils. . . . They came right on, like a great wave, overwhelming everything in its progress." Right in the midst of this attack, Mower realized he had gone in too far to the right, so he immediately sent the 47th Illinois to the left and tried to move each regiment in that direction as well. But in the process of moving, the Illinoisans were caught in a "galling fire," as Mower described it, during which their commander, Colonel Thrush, went down with a bullet through his heart. That threw the regiment into confusion. Officers in other units, realizing that the fresh but shaken brigade was the only brace that could strengthen the Federal position enough to hold it, worked to steady the unit. Even Oglesby and Hackleman came forward, trying to re-form Mower's men to provide some relief for their own brigades.[33]

Almost surreally, an event occurred right in the middle of Mower's fight that almost caused both sides to pause. The 8th Wisconsin had brought along its famous eagle mascot, "Old Abe," and he got loose when his tether either became untied or was shot in two. It was well known in the regiment that Confederate officers had told their men to capture or kill the bird. Price was rumored to have said that he would "rather capture him than the whole brigade." As Old Abe flew upward, many heard shouts from the Confederate lines: "There he is—the Eagle—capture him, boys!" A Wisconsin soldier remembered, "Catching sight of our Eagle those in front of our regiment gave forth an unearthly yell and started to capture it." One member of the 47th Illinois wrote, "Suddenly he was seen to spring aloft and soar away over the heads of the combatants; a halt of the lines as they paused upon both sides to watch the eagle's flight." Then, the Illinoisan continued, "the sharp-shooters in gray began to fire at the circling bird as he rose higher and higher with exultant cries." The Wisconsin troops watched in horror as the bird circled the area and the Confederates shot at him. At one point, "there was a wavering of a wing—was he hit?" Just as quickly, Old Abe flew back down. "The smoke suddenly cleared and the eagle saw the gleam of the colors below and with magnificent swoop returned to his perch beside the Union flag," one soldier remembered. The bird then jumped to the ground, one soldier reminisced, ducking "his head between his carrier's legs." Unable to get him to resume his perch, his bearer received permission to take him rearward to camp, where he remained for the rest of the battle. Upon examination, it was found that the eagle had been hit in the feathers, but not close enough to the body to wound him seriously.[34]

Despite these marvelous theatrics, the battle continued to rage. The offense-minded Mower ordered his shaky command to charge, and portions of it did, driving back the Confederates who had ranged toward the Federal line. Numerous soldiers fell during Mower's advance and subsequent retreat. One was Edward Cronon of the 8th Wisconsin. He left a vivid description of his wound, later writing: "At first . . . , I felt a jolt or shock at my shoulder and turned partly around to see who or what hit me, and saw nothing and then faced the enemy again." He continued, "I was wounded but did not discover the fact until I was so informed by my Lieut . . . [who] said, 'Ed, you are shot.'" Cronon protested that he was not, but then his lieutenant showed him "the blood pouring from the sleeve of my blouse." "Then I began to say cuss words," Cronon remembered, "and was never so mad in all my life."[35]

More significantly, both Oglesby and Hackleman also fell wounded while trying to rally Mower's brigade. While near the 81st Ohio's position, Hackleman was hit in the neck, the ball cutting his esophagus and damaging his trachea before exiting near the spine. One Ohioan remembered, "I saw him quivering in his saddle and slowly falling from his horse." A member of the regiment laid down his gun and caught Hackleman, but everyone considered his wound mortal, including Hackleman himself. Able to speak but not to swallow, he garbled, "I am dying, but I die for my country. If we are victorious, send my remains home; if not, bury me on the field." Stretcher bearers soon found an ambulance and carried him to the Tishomingo Hotel (which, like many other buildings, had become a hospital) for treatment. Similarly, while discussing the situation with Colonel Augustus Chetlain, Oglesby took a shot that entered his chest near the left armpit and lodged against the spine. He fell from his horse, which ran into the Confederate lines. One Missourian recorded in his diary that they had Oglesby's "horse, saddle and bridle and also glasses." This wound, like Hackleman's, appeared to be a fatal one. After Oglesby fell, bleeding freely, Federal soldiers likewise saw to his care. But he refused their attention, pointing to his brigade and stating, "Never mind me; look yonder (pointing to the enemy); I have seen my troops victorious." Oglesby was also taken to the rear, in the same ambulance as Hackleman, to the Tishomingo Hotel. Command of Hackleman's brigade fell to Colonel Thomas W. Sweeny of the 52nd Illinois, who had commanded a brigade of W. H. L. Wallace's division in the Hornet's Nest at Shiloh. Oglesby turned over his command to Colonel August Mersy, commanding the 9th Illinois.[36]

Unfortunately, at least one soldier, Charles Cowell, reported that Mersy was "so drunk he could hardly sit on his horse." And that was not the only report of drunkenness among officers at Corinth. A surgeon in the 12th Iowa wrote to his wife that some were "found not able for duty because of the amount of liquor they had taken." He added, "It [is] a fact that can not be denied that almost all of the officers indulge in the dram of liquor."[37]

Despite the loss of two key Federal commanders, nothing seemed to work for the Confederates; the Union line even had the audacity to advance. The Confederates lost officers as well, including Colonel Eugene Erwin of the 6th Missouri and Colonel Archibald MacFarlane of the 4th Missouri, who were wounded. An event that took place in Sweeny's brigade showed just how intense the Union defense was. Officers reported to Sweeny that the barrels of their guns had become so heated that the men could hardly hold them and the charges exploded inside the barrels. Sweeny, seeing that the fight must continue, ordered his men to fight until the guns burst.[38]

The arrival of fresh Federal troops, no matter how unstable, certainly affected the Confederates. General Green reported that "as we would break the lines of the enemy, they would bring fresh troops." Green also noted that his left flank was open to Hamilton to the east. Fortunately, he had Gates's idle brigade, which had already moved to the left of the line, on his flank; Francis M. Cockrell's 2nd Missouri did most of the maneuvering. Federal skirmishers were hurriedly moving forward, nearing the Confederate artillery in the gap that had formed between Gates and Green. The guns opened on the Federals "with shell & grape," as one Confederate recalled, and "they 'skedaddled' in double quick time."[39]

Finally, after numerous attacks had netted the Confederates almost nothing, a lull came over the battlefield. The Confederate charges ended, and they began to build up strength on the right flank for another charge on Davies's weak left. This attack would, they hoped, break the line and allow the Confederates to chase the Federals into Corinth. One Federal reported the larger Confederate numbers: "They came up in three lines deep and we only had one, so we had to retreat back about 80 rods so as to give the guns at the fort a chance." Aware of the enemy buildup on his left, Davies wisely called his troops back. He knew the state of his division and the state of Mower's brigade. He also knew of Hackleman's and Oglesby's woundings. Davies put all this information together and saw that there was no way he could withstand another attack, especially one on the flank, where the remnants of the shaken Union Brigade stood. He ordered his men to withdraw and form a fifth line at Battery Robinett.[40]

Fortunately, some portions of Mower's men had settled down by this time and were providing relief to Davies's hard-pressed line as it fell back. At least a portion of Hackleman's men, led by the 7th Iowa's Colonel Elliott Rice, also made a stand between the White House and Battery Robinett. But most continued to go rearward. As they fell back, the 47th Illinois passed the body of their dead colonel, William Thrush. One private seemed to think the colonel was still calling to them from the dead to hold their positions: "My brave men, let not my mangled corpse fall prey to these vile traitors." Captain Nelson T. Spoor's 2nd Iowa Battery made the most significant stand, however, unlimbering on a hill within 300 yards of the White House and effectively providing rearguard cover for Davies's and Mower's men as they retired. One particular Confederate column moved toward the battery on the Chewalla road, but Spoor reported, "This column advanced to within 60 yards of the battery, exposed to a most destructive fire of canister before it broke and retired in confusion."[41]

The Confederates offered little opposition to the withdrawal other than skirmishers, thanks in part to Spoor's fire as well as Robinett's twenty-pound

VICTORIOUS SO FAR 199

Parrotts, which shelled the woods to the front. David Stanley later wrote that a Confederate prisoner had told him that Sterling Price himself was on the scene, and one of the fort's shells "just missed his head." Nevertheless, after holding the White House line for more than two hours, the tired and thirsty Union soldiers filed "at common time" back through the abatis and into line on the east side of Robinett, where they met the division's artillery. The resupplied guns stood in a line, ready to confront the Confederates once more. There, the soldiers also met wagons loaded with barrels of water. One Ohioan remembered that the boys did not even wait to fill their canteens; many simply "climbed into the wagons by dozens, and sank their hot faces down into the barrels and drank."[42]

Earl Van Dorn intended to order an assault on Davies's new line, but Price talked him out of it. The Missourian pointed out that the Confederates were out of ammunition, extremely worn out by the fighting and the heat, and too disorganized to attack. Glazed with blood now from two slight wounds, Price concluded by stating, "I think we have done enough for to-day, General, and the men should rest." In addition, darkness had begun to fall over the land, and the Confederate high command had learned of the presence of a major Union body on their left flank. They could waste no time charging Davies because they now had to look toward the left flank's security. Van Dorn thus ordered an end to hostilities on that front, concentrating instead on securing the open flanks of Hébert's division.[43]

To remedy Phifer's open right flank, Cabell's brigade, minus the 19th and 20th Arkansas, which had earlier helped Moore and were thus on the west side of Turner Creek, moved to plug the gap in the Turner Creek bottom. The brigade was fresh; it had seen no action thus far. Because of its small numbers, however, its effectiveness was questionable. Indeed, it could play little part in an attack on the inner lines, if one took place. Cabell admitted that he contented himself "with holding the position I had and watching the movements of the enemy." Despite the brigade's lack of action, its commander managed to be slightly wounded in the foot by a spent ball. Cabell reported that the wound "gave me a good deal of pain at the time, but did not disable me."[44]

The critical flank was on the Confederate left, however. While Davies made a determined stand in front of the White House, by nightfall, Hamilton was almost in position to launch the attack that would roll up the Confederate line from the east. By the time Hamilton received the correct orders, though, many valuable hours had been lost, and Davies could not hold out much longer. Despite the late hour, Hamilton continued his march. Soon, Sul-

livan's brigade arrived in position near Davies's right, but perpendicular to
that line, moving up to and parallel with the Mobile and Ohio Railroad. Sullivan was ready to attack, but Hamilton had lost sight of Buford's brigade in
the rear, and he dared not send just one brigade to the attack. Waiting for
Buford to come up was the only option, and the men of Sullivan's brigade par-
ried several threats to their line, including a Confederate attempt to place a
battery on the railroad itself to enfilade Sullivan's right.[45]

At the time, Buford was more than half a mile north of Sullivan's position.
When he began his march behind Sullivan's column, he became aware of a
Confederate force to the west that looked strong and apparently contained
artillery. Several of his regiments had even begun to fire, but Buford, according to one Minnesotan, rode up rapidly and ordered the men "to stop firing,
remarking that there was no one in front to fire at." He then went on to
describe the surreal situation: "But the words are scarcely out of his mouth
before a ball strikes his horse, which convinces the old man that there is something in front." A similar incident occurred as the 4th Minnesota's colonel,
John B. Sanborn, was talking with a staff officer from headquarters. The ball
hit the aide in the chest, knocking him off his horse. Miraculously, the round
had hit a book in his pocket and caused no major damage. Nevertheless, with
all the lead flying around, Buford perceived a major enemy force and
promptly deployed his brigade to meet it. While Sullivan continued the march
southward and deployed in the intended position half a mile to the south,
Buford moved his brigade westward toward the supposed enemy, which, in
reality, consisted of only a small force with artillery. The men of the 4th Minnesota did most of the skirmishing, with the 59th Indiana aiding them. One
Indianan wrote to his wife that the enemy "were trying to plant a battery. . . .
This was the first opportunity I ever got for a shot at the Rebels. I cannot say
that I hurt anybody but I can only say I tried." Learning of the mistake, Hamilton ordered Buford to disengage and follow Sullivan. Buford responded by
telling Hamilton, "The enemy is in my front and I am going to fight him."
Hamilton knew better and again ordered Buford to withdraw. Finally, Hamilton sent Buford a "peremptory order" to fall back. This time, Buford obeyed,
but he left one regiment, the 4th Minnesota, to fight the Confederates. One of
that regiment's soldiers later claimed to have captured six Confederate cannon but for some unknown reason left them, writing that it was "a great big
mystery too big for the private to unravel." By this time, however, night was
approaching, and any chance of a flank attack by Hamilton's division had vanished. Whether through another mistake or direct dereliction of duty, Buford
had led his brigade to a point half a mile north of Sullivan. In doing so, he

squandered a golden opportunity to win the day. Several simple mix-ups that day had cost the Union army a badly needed flank attack.[46]

Some good did result from Hamilton's movements, however. While Buford moved into position, Sullivan, though not attacking outright, engaged the left flank of the Confederate line, Gates's brigade, and captured around 100 prisoners. This development, Hamilton remembered, "immediately checked the enemy's advance on the town and caused him to change front." Had the Confederates not detected the presence of Union infantry on their flank, Davies might have faced another attack, and it seems doubtful that he could have withstood it. Hamilton gave the Confederates a "terrific scare," according to Rosecrans, and with it, the Confederate assault ended on October 3.[47]

Hamilton's presence also contributed to a major shuffling of Confederate brigades to meet the threat. Price was so concerned about Hamilton that he ordered the recently deployed Cabell to march across the Confederate rear to the left flank. Cabell reported to Hébert, who put him into position on his open flank, along with Gates and others who had moved to the area. Cabell's brigade deployed, facing Hamilton, to repel the attack that all thought would come. Several batteries also took the Federals under fire. The Federal action, as beneficial as it was, was not without loss, however. The movement cost the services of General Sullivan. In the latter part of the action, he received "a severe contusion" and turned his brigade over to Colonel Samuel A. Holmes of the 10th Missouri. Holmes reported that he found Sullivan "very much exhausted and barely able to keep his saddle."[48]

Whereas there was major action on Davies's line late in the day, McKean and Stanley on the far left saw very little. First scolded for withdrawing too quickly and then reprimanded by Rosecrans for counterattacking when his orders called for him to slowly give ground, McKean had begun to move toward the new line after the loss of Battery F, but he was not quite sure what to do. Fortunately, he received further orders to withdraw all the way into the defenses of Corinth. Davies had withdrawn into those defenses, the orders stated, and McKean had nothing on which to anchor his right. McKean thus kept his columns moving down the ridge west of Turner Creek until they reached the inner works. But the Confederates still did not appear in large numbers on McKean's front. Crocker's brigade, aided by the 10th Ohio Battery and a section of the 2nd Illinois Artillery, constituted the rear guard and kept the enemy at bay, although Captain H. B. White, commanding the Ohio battery, had a horse shot out from under him during minor skirmishing. The only major confusion came when all four brigades—including Oliver's, who reported that his brigade joined the others in line "fuller than could hardly have been expected from us"—came to the relatively few openings in the abatis that fronted the inner Federal line. It was fortunate that a weak Confederate pursuit gave them enough time to make it through fairly easily.[49]

Lovell was indeed slow in moving forward after the fight at Battery F, but his caution was warranted. Although Bowen labeled him "very undecided" and noted that he "seemed to be awaiting orders," Lovell's hesitation was not totally due to incompetence. He was aware of the continuation of the Halleck line to the south. Concerned that there might be more Federals manning those field fortifications, Lovell obviously did not want to plunge ahead and find a major force on his right flank and rear. The affair at Battery F had been serious, and a large enemy force at Battery E or D, on his right, could prove disastrous. And that possibility was not out of the question; Battery F had been manned, after all, and Stanley's division had earlier rested its left on Battery D, with portions of Fuller's brigade moving all the way up to Battery E. Thus, Lovell wisely moved forward cautiously, detouring somewhat to the right to determine what, if any, resistance was at those forts. Bowen reported that the division "made a circuitous detour to the right (this was about 4 o'clock) and waited in line of battle." Eventually, according to Bowen, Lovell "was convinced that three redoubts and a line of encampments in their rear had been abandoned by the enemy several hours before."[50]

No fighting came of this maneuver because darkness was imminent and the Federals had already withdrawn. Accordingly, the Confederates did not pursue vigorously, although they did partially overtake a wagon train and captured a few mules, which Bowen used to haul off the captured "Lady Richardson" gun. McKean led his men into the defenses while Lovell's troops stopped for the night along a tall ridge west of Corinth, overlooking the Federal line. But Lovell can hardly be blamed for moving slowly. On the left, Price himself gave his men an hour's break after taking the initial earthworks at noon, and his advance the rest of the afternoon had been anything but quick and overwhelming.[51]

At last, darkness crept over the field, bringing an end to the slaughter. Price rode among his bloodied command, "sympathizing with the suffering," staff officer Tyler noted. He added, "Wherever he went cheers followed him. The wounded threw up their caps and even the dying waved to him their hands." Yet many welcomed the growing darkness, especially because it relieved the heat of the day. Many wagons carrying water rolled through the Confederate dead and wounded to the troops in the field, but there was not nearly enough of it. Many had fallen due to the heat. Price had even sent couriers to hasten up surgeons and his bodyguard to fetch water for the soldiers, but locating good water was difficult. The Confederates found the wells McKean had destroyed near Battery F, and this only added to their frustration. One Confederate soldier complained of the wells "having been either filled up or destroyed." Still, the Confederates were jubilant at their success that day.[52]

No such feelings existed across the way inside the Federal lines. The Union army had narrowly missed being routed. It had fallen back almost two miles, suffering severe casualties that included several brigade commanders. As night fell, their line remained deformed. Units lay scattered, brigades broken; gaps in the line still existed. The Federals would certainly face another attack the next day, and one observant soldier from Wisconsin wrote home, "The prospect for the morrow was a dismal one."[53]

But the Confederates were similarly disorganized to the point of chaos. Great gaps remained in their lines as well; some brigades were not even in formation, while others were split apart. Numerous officers were down; regimental and brigade commanders had been killed and wounded, including the injured Price. Unlike the Federals, however, the Confederates could claim a partial victory. An optimistic Van Dorn reported that the army went into camp within 600 yards of Corinth itself, "victorious so far." But there was still much to be done.[54]

12

"THINGS LOOK RATHER BLUE TO-NIGHT"

The first day of the Battle of Corinth ended in confusion, with most units on both sides at least partially disjointed and crippled. Casualties had been heavy, and those who remained in the ranks were terribly fatigued. The Confederate army had marched more than ten miles before the fighting even began that day, and the heat was terrible, somewhere in the nineties. The result was a large number of heatstroke victims. And water was almost impossible to find; in fact, Colonel Andrew J. Babcock of the 7th Illinois reported that his men could find only vinegar to drink that night, and they were glad to get it. The lack of basic elements was still vivid in one Confederate's mind when he wrote in his memoirs years later, "This 3rd day of Oct. was a hard one on us Boys, if we eat anything I don't remember it now, the weather was warm and I remember we suffered very much for drinking water." It was no wonder that when darkness finally covered the battlefield, the two armies were entirely unorganized and in a state of total disorder.[1]

Despite everything, many soldiers reported having a sound night's sleep. Many Confederates took advantage of the captured Federal camps and used whatever they could find to aid their slumber. L. H. Graves said that he "laid down to-night on a Federal oil cloth and covered with a Federal blanket that we captured." Others were too excited to sleep. William Kavanaugh and his friend were "chuck full of talk, and after laying down and pulling the Blankets up over us, we began to relate to each other the experiences of the day, he would talk awhile, and then I would talk awhile, here we lay, both tired and worn out but somehow couldn't get off to sleep."[2]

A few unfortunate skirmishers got no rest at all. They had to guard against a night attack and keep straying enemy pickets in their own lines. A few, such as the pickets of Gates's Confederate brigade, encountered some excitement. At a culvert under the Mobile and Ohio Railroad, the skirmishers found an enemy soldier hiding and quickly took him prisoner. But, as one Confederate remembered, "it seemed he was not alone." One behind the other, eleven Federal soldiers emerged from the culvert "on all fours."[3]

All night, with a welcome chill in the air, both armies rearranged and reorganized, and one soldier noted that "there was some skillful moves made on both sides." The most pressing need was to resupply ammunition. The soldiers realized what the next day would bring. One remembered, "We knew that two mighty Armies were going to grapple with each other in deadly conflict." Most also knew that a night spent in reorganization would exhaust the troops almost as much as the earlier battle had. "All the cry was whiskey," one Federal remembered, and the Union army issued it to its troops. One Northerner reported that he and his regiment "lay down in line of battle and had a dose of whiskey, and I tell you we needed it." Another recorded in his diary, "Things look rather blue to-night. They are issuing whiskey to the men pretty freely for the tremendous hot sun of to-day has been telling on the men." A surgeon commented on the depressed state of the soldiers in the Union Brigade: "The boys looked sad before they went into the fight of Saturday. . . . I tried to have them cheerful[,] talked to them but it was of no use." Another Federal later admitted his fear to his wife: "You must not think I was in that fierce engagement from choice."[4]

The night chill soon turned cold and proved hard on the troops. Many soldiers, because of the hot weather during the day, had thrown away their coats, but they soon realized their mistake. One Confederate, J. W. Harmon, wrapped himself in a captured Union tent. The situation was far worse for the countless wounded. Many were terribly thirsty as well as homesick for their loved ones. If they were fortunate enough to have someone carry them to a hospital, they had to endure long hours of waiting; the hospitals were full, and surgeons were few. Those not so fortunate had to pass the night alongside the dead and wish for help to come, suffering terribly. Those who became prisoners suffered in their own way.[5]

The Federal medical facilities set up by Surgeon Campbell were quickly overrun with wounded during the day's fighting. Campbell asked Rosecrans to turn the Tishomingo Hotel into a hospital, which was done under the supervision of Surgeon P. A. Carpenter of the 5th Iowa. When that hotel became too crowded as well, Rosecrans allowed the Corinth House to be converted to a hospital, which was overseen by surgeon Edgar Winchester of the 52nd Illinois. "All the surgeons worked faithfully and diligently," Campbell reported, but unfortunately, when the battle moved nearer the town, Rosecrans ordered Campbell to move the wounded to nearby "Camp Corral," which was done during the night.[6]

Ed Cronon's experience that day and night is illustrative of the wounded's ordeal. A member of the 8th Wisconsin, Cronon had been hit in the arm as Mower's brigade tried to stem the Confederate tide late on Friday afternoon. When told to move to Corinth, he did so, thinking he had the strength to get there. But Cronon soon found that he was too weak, "staggering like one who is drunk," he remembered. "Some of our boys who were less severely wounded" helped Cronon to a shed that contained nearly 100 wounded. Cronon lay there for hours in pain. "I seemed to be burning up inside," he recalled, "for the want of a drink of water." Cronon spied a Wisconsin soldier he knew, who was pacing back and forth "to ease his pain." He tried to call out to him for some water, but he later realized it was probably only a whisper. "My internal organs seemed burning like a furnace," Cronon continued. Eventually, he remembered, "two men came with a stretcher, and examined me and said, 'This is a case for amputation.'" The men carried him to the Corinth House, where a surgeon removed his arm.[7]

Despite the hardships, when nightfall came at last, the Union army was almost totally inside its inner line of defenses. McKean held the left with Crocker's brigade, while Davies, Mower, and McArthur held the center. When he entered the inner line on the left, McArthur marched to the right and took a position at a point north of town to stabilize that part of the line; his front was guarded by skirmishers of the Yates Sharpshooters (64th Illinois). There, his men began to throw up breastworks. "We—our regiment—were very industrious," Daniel Miller of the 21st Missouri wrote to his brother. Stanley's other brigade, Fuller's, also deployed inside the line. Stanley had ordered Fuller's brigade into Corinth to stabilize the position north of town between the Mobile and Ohio Railroad and Battery Powell, but Fuller arrived late. He stopped for water, and by the time he reached the town, the fighting was over. Stanley later reported, "Colonel Du Bois and myself deemed it best to get the water before engaging them, and before this was accomplished the action had ended for the day." Although the troops were relatively safe within the fortifications, they had positioned themselves haphazardly and would have to re-form to withstand the next day's attacks. And Hamilton's division was still outside the fortifications, one Union soldier writing, "By some unaccountable reason the enemy has his line of battle between us and town." Rosecrans had to see to their recall before the Confederates flowed into the gap and cut them off. However, the Confederates had ended the day just as disorganized as their enemies. Their line, too—particularly the gap between Moore and the rest of Maury's division—needed a lot of attention before they could attempt any assault on the Federals.[8]

Thus, commanders both blue and gray saw the necessity of resolving the confusing situation during the long night; all knew that the battle would rage again the next day, and the side that was better prepared would have a distinct advantage.

Earl Van Dorn was disappointed that he had not finished the battle in one day. He had hoped to do so but "saw, with regret, the sun sink behind the horizon," he wrote in his report. He mused that, given just one more hour of daylight, his troops would have stormed the hastily formed Union line and spent the night in Corinth. Many officers of Van Dorn's command agreed, and although they shared a feeling of complete victory and foresaw no trouble the next morning, many still wanted to attack that night. Lovell later wrote, "Two hours more of daylight on Friday would have given us the most brilliant victory." Van Dorn "did not fail to consider the matter," he wrote, but after talking to Price, he was convinced the troops were too tired and disorganized to fight. He had to be content with the day's achievements and even sent a message to Richmond announcing the success of October 3. He notified the authorities that his army was within three-quarters of a mile of Corinth, having driven the enemy from every one of its positions. He also sent written congratulations to his division commanders. Van Dorn, one Confederate remembered, "received the congratulations of every general officer under his command."[9]

At Van Dorn's headquarters, ironically situated within fifty yards of the position it had occupied in the spring, most officers were pleased, but some were not. One officer related to a friend, "Strange it should have been thought that, a comfortless night adding the cravings of hunger to the pangs of thirst would increase their efficiency, and stranger still it should have been supposed that Rosecrantz would remain idle." One Federal of the 16th Wisconsin wrote home, "They thought they had nothing to do but to take up their arms and march in to Corinth." The veterans of Shiloh, especially, must have been skeptical. Only six months earlier, they had experienced the same situation twenty miles to the north. On the night of April 6, the Confederates had driven the Federals back more than two miles and were confident of success the next day. Indeed, Beauregard had even wired Richmond of a great victory, but it was not to be. Here, on October 3, the Confederates had driven the Federals back almost two miles and lay poised to deliver the final blow the next morning. Only time would tell if the results would be different this time around.[10]

As at Shiloh, an evening attack probably would not have achieved victory. It might have broken the thin and hastily formed line, but Hamilton still lurked on the Confederates' left flank. Had the Southern army had that one extra hour of daylight to attack the fifth Federal line, it no doubt would have been attacked in turn by Hamilton. That could have ended the battle permanently, although not in the manner Van Dorn wished.[11]

With the issue of a night attack resolved, Confederate attention turned to the next day. Van Dorn was concerned about leaving the attack unfinished, but he became even more disturbed when he perceived Federal movement in Corinth. Sounds of wagons and marching feet reverberated in the darkness. Some thought it was a withdrawal, which would have given the Confederates a victory, but others thought it hinted at reinforcements coming to the rescue. The threat of reinforcements bothered Van Dorn, but he must have thought back to late May, when his side had played tricks on some of the very men then defending Corinth.[12]

Van Dorn ignored the sounds and produced a plan to achieve victory on the second day and prevent comparisons to Shiloh. This attack, he reasoned, would succeed regardless of whether Rosecrans had withdrawn or strengthened his position. Van Dorn wanted his left to begin the attack on October 4— the exact opposite of his previous day's plan. Hébert would move from his line west of and parallel to the Mobile and Ohio Railroad to the east side, swinging his division perpendicular to the railroad. Cabell's brigade of Maury's division, which was already on the left, would temporarily attach itself to Hébert's troops; Cabell would simply remain in that sector and form behind the left of Hébert's men, adding more weight to the major assault on the left. Hébert would attack with his entire division down the Purdy road ridge but then swing his left around and into the Union defenses and Corinth.[13]

After Hébert was well engaged, Lovell and Maury would attack en echelon on their fronts, with Maury's two brigades moving in a straight line for the heart of Corinth. With the center and left advancing, Lovell would join in when he saw Maury engaged. He would aim his attack at College Hill, with two brigades in line and one in reserve. The cavalry would cover the flanks— Jackson again on the right, and Armstrong on the left. The artillery would cover the movements, and a predetermined signal would sound the time for the attack. Van Dorn ordered three batteries, placed on the ridge at Lovell's position west of Corinth, to fire into the town at 4:00 A.M. This barrage would be the signal for the infantry to pour into the Union fortifications.[14]

During the night, the different units of the Confederate army moved to their assigned positions and then tried to sleep. Hébert's division had already moved up about 200 yards after the fighting ended for the day and made camp west of and parallel to the Mobile and Ohio Railroad. One Missourian remembered, "Our command was pretty well sheltered through the night from the enemies fire by a Rail Road embankment which we taken advantage of."

Cabell's brigade, now attached to this division, also ended the night roughly in its correct position.[15]

Maury's was the only division that had some major realigning to do. The gap that had formed earlier in the day because of the Turner Creek watershed still posed a problem, so Maury used the night to close it. He ordered Moore to move his brigade to the left until it reached Phifer's right. Moore received this order while awaiting word from Lovell concerning future movements. Moore knew that his own division commander's order superseded that of anyone else of equal rank, so he moved his brigade to the left, across Turner Creek. One member of the 42nd Alabama recorded, "We were marched through a swamp." The brigade eventually took a position on top of a hill overlooking Corinth.[16]

Lovell, like Hébert, had ended the day close to his assigned position. The division was somewhat behind the others, but after reconnecting with Moore, it deployed in line, ready to fight the next day. Lovell called his brigade commanders together during the night and showed them "a crude sketch" of the enemy position, which he said was lightly defended with only a few guns. Thus having achieved a continuous line from Hébert's left to Lovell's right, the Confederate army lay down and slept on its arms. The tired men welcomed any rest they were able to get.[17]

While the army re-formed, the three artillery batteries, all from Maury's division, took their positions west of town "upon an advanced ridge about 600 yards from Corinth." The two reserve units, Hoxton's Tennessee and Sengstak's Alabama batteries, made up two-thirds of the formation. Lieutenant Thomas F. Tobin commanded Hoxton's battery, while Captain Henry H. Sengstak commanded the other. McNally's Arkansas battery from Phifer's brigade, commanded by Lieutenant Frank A. Moore, was the third. Lieutenant Tobin, while positioning one of the guns of Hoxton's battery, placed it too far forward and soon found himself confronted by pickets of the 63rd Ohio. Tobin and his bugler were captured, and the Federals later retrieved the gun. Tobin's captors took him to Rosecrans himself, and the general asked him to give Dabney Maury a message (knowing Tobin would be exchanged). Rosecrans wanted Tobin to tell Maury that he never thought his former pupil at West Point would grow up to give him so much trouble. Meanwhile, the remainder of the Confederate guns sat ready to fire the signal at 4:00 A.M.[18]

While the Confederates planned the attack for the next day, October 4, the Federals, only a few hundred yards to the south and east, contemplated their defense. There was no doubt in Rosecrans's mind that Van Dorn would attack;

he never considered retreat, although he did send all unnecessary wagons to the rear, giving that impression. Rosecrans's only real option was to brace the line and wait. He developed plans to form his line roughly out of the positions the retreating divisions had taken at dark. "Early in the evening I called the chiefs of divisions together," Rosecrans reported, "and explained to them . . . the plans." The officers left with detailed orders for their proposed movements and went to work putting them into operation.[19]

McKean rearranged his division on the far left. He placed Crocker's brigade and three batteries in the main line, positioned so that the infantry flanked Battery Phillips and the artillery was deployed in advantageous positions along the line. The other two small and weary brigades, one of which had originally been stationed north of town, where it built breastworks, were now in position on the left again, in reserve and closer to town. McArthur took position at Corona College, with Oliver to the rear. The detached 18th Wisconsin had returned from its bridge-guarding role and rejoined the brigade, adding more numbers to this section of the line. McKean quickly completed these dispositions and then allowed his men to rest.[20]

Stanley also moved his troops into position during the night, with Rosecrans and his staff watching. It was here, one fatigued but excited soldier recalled, that "we saw the Eighth Wisconsin Regiment with their live eagle carried on a standard." Mower's brigade, except for the 11th Missouri and 5th Minnesota, went into line between the right of Crocker's brigade and Battery Williams. Because of the indentation of Battery Williams's position, where Mower's line stopped and Fuller's took up, this line faced northwest instead of west, as did Crocker's. Fuller's brigade ran northward to Battery Robinett and faced almost southwestward, again because of the indentation of the line. One regiment of Fuller's brigade, the 43rd Ohio, held the territory between Williams and Robinett, while the rest prolonged the line eastward from Robinett to the brink of the hollow of Elam Creek. The 11th Missouri of Mower's brigade took position immediately behind the fort. Unfortunately, the troops of Stanley's division were too worn out to build any breastworks; they simply fell to the ground and slept.[21]

The valley of Elam Creek was a problem spot: Stanley's division could not reach all the way to town. Rosecrans had only part of the 64th Illinois, which was providing skirmishers to the front of Davies's division, to plug this gap through which the Mobile and Ohio Railroad and Elam Creek ran. But they did the best they could. N. R. Dunn of the 64th Illinois wrote home, "Our battalion was ordered into the swamp." In addition, the 5th Minnesota of Mower's brigade, called in from its own bridge-guarding duty, took position north of the Memphis and Charleston Railroad and closer to town, its left near

the depot. Two batteries, the 10th Ohio and 3rd Michigan, provided reinforcements for the men in the valley. Rosecrans took a risk in defending this
sector with so few men, but it was in a deep hollow. Thinking that little action
would occur in the swampy valley, much like the Turner Creek watershed the
day before, Rosecrans wasted few men on the area. Instead, he concentrated
his troops on the ridges where the forts sat.[22]

Farther to the right, Davies had perhaps the most difficult situation of all
the division commanders. Immediately after the fighting ceased on October
3, he had gone to the Tishomingo Hotel to check on his commanders. "In one
room I found my three brigade commanders," Davies later wrote. He found
Baldwin suffering from a nonfatal wound. A surgeon derisively described him
as being "disabled by a slight wound on the hand." Baldwin had turned over
command of his brigade to Colonel John V. Du Bois of Rosecrans's staff
before making his way to the hotel to receive care. He would be fine. The
other two were not so fortunate. Oglesby was in much pain, and the doctors
were not optimistic about his recovery. Hackleman died with Davies present.
Davies's visit to the hotel had a hard impact on him. He was determined to
get a reserve position and went to Rosecrans with the request.[23]

Rosecrans originally acquiesced to Davies's request to form the reserve,
but he soon had second thoughts and decided he had no choice but to put
Davies in line; he simply had too few troops and too much territory to defend.
The division, groggy from sleep, thus moved toward its assigned position, one
soldier recording in his diary, "After moving from place to place through the
night we finely took our position north of town." A soldier of the 52nd Illinois recorded in his diary, "I managed to get about 3 hours sleep last night . . .
we changed our line some 3 times in the night." Davies ultimately formed his
division to the right of the Elam Creek watershed and the soldiers who filled
it. The line, looking northwestward, ran from the hollow to Battery Richardson, a new fort constructed of hay and cotton bales by slaves during the night,
and then on to Battery Powell, which was still being completed as well. One
Federal described the work of the slaves that night, writing home, "I attribute
much of our success at Corinth to the laborers of Black men[.] Our army had
been driven back all day on Friday and from the heat and efforts of the day's
fight were completely exhausted and while they lay and rested from the
fatigues of the day, about 1300 Black men were working all night throwing
Breastworks and at 3 o'clock next morning we had cannon mounted sufficient
to repel the attack and save Corinth to our army all by the foresight and wis-
dom of Ab. Lincoln." The expanse now held by Davies had earlier contained
neither entrenchments nor abatis, except those quickly thrown up by
McArthur's men earlier in the night. Those same slaves cut trees to enable the

artillery to have greater range. Others laid logs or simple materials along the line. The 52nd Illinois later found, when it took position, gabions, or "bottomless baskets made of saplings."[24]

Davies placed two brigades in line and one in reserve. Baldwin's brigade, now commanded by Du Bois, took the position to which McArthur had moved earlier, placing his right on the Purdy road. Du Bois was a staff officer and had been wounded the day before, although he kept it quiet, hoping word would not get back to his family. Du Bois's brigade thus relieved McArthur's men, placing the brigade on the right of the skirmishers in the hollow. Sweeny's brigade continued the line from Du Bois's right to Batteries Richardson and Powell, where some of the men formed along the garden fences of a residence immediately in the rear of Battery Powell. Two regiments of Mersy's brigade remained in reserve, while the other two performed separate duty. The 22nd Ohio remained in Corinth as the provost guard, but the 9th Illinois moved to the right of Battery Powell to support two guns of Welker's battery placed on the right of that redoubt. There, they formed amidst a garden and a nearby private residence. In front of the line were the skirmishers of the Yates and also the Western Sharpshooters, the latter known as the "Squirrel Tails."[25]

Hamilton's made the longest march of any of the divisions that night, but not before more confusing altercations with Rosecrans just before the general conference of division commanders. Hamilton later reported that he had received a message between 8:00 and 9:00 P.M. ordering him to press the enemy and make a bayonet charge at midnight. Hamilton could hardly believe that Rosecrans would contemplate such an action and sent word that he would do no such thing until he had a conference with the commanding general. The two exchanged words. Rosecrans demanded, "What do you mean by disobeying my order?" Hamilton replied that he would obey, but only after he had met personally with Rosecrans to explain why the attack should not be made. Hamilton convinced Rosecrans "after a few moments of reflection without reply," Hamilton noted.[26]

Apparently, Rosecrans then decided that Hamilton should stay where he was and attack at daylight, but Hamilton wanted to rejoin the rest of the army inside Corinth's defenses. After further consultation, during which Rosecrans "looked steadily and thoughtfully down upon the pommel of his saddle for a few minutes," according to Colonel Sanborn, Hamilton persuaded Rosecrans again. The troops marched into Corinth. Rosecrans never mentioned either idea, and historians have not placed much stock in their truth. Some evidence does exist, however. Thomas J. McKean received a curious note during the night that told him, "Hamilton is in rear of enemy. Prepare for an advance movement."[27]

With permission to join the rest of the army, Hamilton placed his brigades to the right of Davies's line. According to Joseph Risedorph, the troops "marched by the left flank for several miles through brush and over logs and fallen timber to regain our place inside the works of Corinth." Two of the regiments formed the extension of Davies's line, the 80th Ohio and 10th Missouri taking position on the right of the 9th Illinois in support of the 6th Wisconsin Battery. The remainder of the division formed in line looking toward the northeast, their right resting on the old Confederate entrenchments of the Beauregard line east of Corinth. This line lay at almost a ninety-degree angle to Davies's line, which faced to the northwest, covering the Purdy and Pittsburg Landing roads.[28]

By the early hours of October 4, the Union line was formed, and the men gained what little sleep they could. But Confederate skirmishers on several occasions "advanced to the edge of the woods," brigade commander Fuller noted. Thus, like the Confederates, those who rested well were few and far between.[29]

These preparations finally ended around 3:00 A.M. By the time the men had settled in and skirmishers had moved forward all along the line, one Union officer recalled that "perfect quiet reigned through our entire lines." Content with his deployments, Rosecrans reportedly retired in good humor. He must have seemed very confident, because when he was warned of a report that the Confederates had planted a battery within 200 yards, Rosecrans replied, "Let 'em plant it." Even in his good mood, however, Rosecrans knew he needed to sleep. After reviewing the newly established lines, he retired to his headquarters at 3:00 A.M. to get whatever rest he could. Writing to Grant, he seemed optimistic. "The batteries are rather better posted and will I trust be better supported," he noted. With that, he went to bed. The troops of both armies slept on their arms as best they could, ready to begin the fight at a moment's notice.[30]

Neither Rosecrans nor the troops rested for long. Promptly at 4:00 A.M., the three Confederate batteries west of town broke the deathly silence. Federal artillery from Battery Robinett responded, and an artillery duel commenced, one Union cannoneer reporting, "We answered them with much cannon shots, since they didn't give us our full night's rest." Eventually, other Union batteries opened up. The Federals' big guns were especially loud. According to one soldier from Iowa, "The noise made by the 64-pound howitzers was terrible, and must have made many a poor rebel quake like an aspen." The Confederates seemed to be aiming at the Federal campfires, which, one Iowan reported, "were soon extinguished." Another described the shells passing in the night as "the prettiest thing[s] a busting in the air I ever saw, most especially when they did not come close." In the bivouac of the 39th Ohio, the regiment's lieutenant colonel ordered the men "to lie still and take it." One of the soldiers proudly wrote to his wife that the officer "had his horse shot while telling us to keep cool." Over at the Union horse corral, one man witnessed the humorous sight of the startled donkeys running "with their wagons," which was corroborated by an Illinois soldier who wrote in his diary, "The shell are flying down among the teams pretty lively and the first thing that waked me up was a shell coming down pretty close." Many rounds landed in town; one of them burst through the Tishomingo Hotel, killing a wounded soldier being carried down the stairs. Surgeons were evacuating the hotel at the time, and one of them described the removal of General Oglesby: "As we carried him out of the east end of the building a shell came through the walls of the west end." Additional rounds landed near the other buildings being used as hospitals. The 63rd Ohio's assistant surgeon, A. B. Monahan, was hit in the right temple by a piece of shell and was knocked from his horse. Only slightly wounded, Monahan recovered within an hour and was more concerned about "Bob my much esteemed horse." Monahan related to his wife, "Bob run off," but he was soon recovered.[31]

The disruption, including the Union counterbattery fire, similarly shook the Confederates. A lieutenant in the 42nd Alabama remembered the shells cutting off large limbs in the trees. "It was extremely unpleasant," he said, "and I prayed for forgiveness of my sins, and made up my mind to go through." Others quickly ate breakfast, consisting of whatever they could find. One Confederate described his meal years later: "three hard tack—very hard—and a slice of fat Raw Bacon—the kind that was generally known as Sow Belly—this was the first time I had ever tried to eat fat Bacon in a raw state—and in justice to that Hog must say it was very good." Regardless of the individual fears and the hasty meals, the Confederate assaults were to begin when the guns opened up. All along the line, the Confederate commanders readied their units. Van Dorn anxiously awaited the sound of musketry to heighten on the left, then in the center, and finally on the right. He believed that Corinth would soon be his.[32]

On the right, Lovell quickly formed his brigades and moved toward the position he was supposed to occupy when the battle on the left opened. With two brigades in front and one in the rear, his division moved forward at about daylight. They proceeded down the ridge they had taken the day before, heading toward the Federal inner line around the forts on the College Hill sector. One Confederate remembered that they moved forward until "the skirmishers came in view of the enemy's works near the Female College when we halted and lay down." Minor skirmishing took place on Villepigue's left as the various pickets realized what was taking place. Some counterbattery fire also erupted on Bowen's right, causing one member of the 22nd Mississippi to note that the "ground on which we lay [was covered] with shot and shells of every description." He also related that the enemy fire was so hot that the unit they were protecting, the Watson Louisiana Battery, "only fired two rounds, before it had to retire." He dolefully continued, "The enemy did not cease, however." Another reported that the men laid down "under a blinding shower of shot and shell."[33]

Once he was in immediate range of the Federal lines, Lovell wanted his full complement of men forward. He therefore ordered Rust, in reserve, to move up and take position in the front line. Rust moved between Villepigue on the left and Bowen on the right. In this formation, the entire line continued forward until it reached a point "within a few hundred yards of two strong works," one soldier remembered. Another described moving "within 3 or 400 yards of a very large fort, very near at the precise spot where we camped last spring." The brigades could see the Union line in the distance and noted the forts and the "long lines of infantry behind formidable-looking breastworks with abatis again in front." The division thus stopped and waited for the sound of battle on the left. When Lovell heard the firing there, his men would storm those works and take Corinth.[34]

One of Rust's men, Albert Goodloe of the 35th Alabama, had a premonition of his death. In the spare time before the attack, he wrote a letter to his wife, trying to comfort her because he felt sure he was about to die. Goodloe feared that his widowed wife would have trouble raising their two boys, one newly born after his enlistment. When Goodloe finished, he gave the letter to his chaplain for delivery. Other Confederates had similar thoughts. Will Ray over in Gates's brigade also believed he would fall and wrote so in his diary. He asked friends to send the diary and a lock of his hair to his wife in that event.[35]

To Lovell's left, Maury also formed his brigades for the attack. Around daylight, the three batteries, which found the growing Union counterbattery fire extremely hot, withdrew through the fog, and final preparations for the attack in the center began. Moore's brigade was in position in line on Phifer's right rear. Maury also intended Cabell's brigade to form in this line, but because Cabell was now on the far left flank, that was impossible. Cabell had received orders to remain in reserve behind Hébert's division, but when Maury, his division commander, ordered him to move to the right and rejoin the division, Cabell immediately set out, having to march across the rear of

Hébert's division. Nevertheless, Maury was ready to attack. He had his two brigades in line; the third, which was on the way, could move forward at any opportune time. Maury and his division now waited, like Lovell on the right, for the sounds of Hébert's attack.[36]

As Lovell, Maury, and the other Confederates prepared to take the offensive, they continued to take fire from the Union guns. The Federals, by this time, had awakened and had begun to fully respond. General Buford, all the way on the Union right, remembered that the cannonade "was grand. The different calibers, metals, shapes, and distances of the guns caused the sounds to resemble the chimes of old Rome when all her bells rang out." Batteries Robinett, Williams, and Phillips and several field batteries opened on the Confederate artillery with counterbattery fire. The artillery fire fell heavily on Lovell's division, but the brigades stood their ground "with the most gratifying steadiness," one Confederate wrote. The skirmishers of both armies also became engaged, and a heated firefight broke out all along the lines.[37]

By daylight, Lovell's and Maury's divisions were ready to attack, but they had still heard nothing from Hébert on the far left. One poor Confederate in Gates's brigade remembered the delay: "Here we lay behind this Rail Road embankment breathlessly awaiting orders that we knew were sure to come to move forward and attack them." But Hébert had not positioned his men for the daylight attack and was therefore in no position to advance. One entire brigade had not even deployed in line; Green's brigade had retired at daylight to a position about 100 yards behind the line for "refreshments." Obviously, Hébert had no intention of attacking at daylight as ordered, and Green, uninformed by Hébert, had no idea that the attack was to take place so early. Green later blamed Hébert for the miscommunication. "The Missourians, and indeed all his division," one man claimed, "were exceedingly denunciatory of the conduct of this officer, the many truculent remarks made not needing repetition here." All the blame cannot fall on Hébert, however. The courier sent to deliver Price's orders to the Louisianan had reportedly fallen asleep at a farmhouse during the night. Without orders, Van Dorn could not expect Hébert to carry out his part of the plan. Thus, Hébert was neither ready to attack at daylight nor prepared to lead the rest of the army toward Corinth. Van Dorn later wrote in his report, "I regretted to observe that my whole plan of attack was by this unfortunate delay disarranged."[38]

The reasons for the breakdown in the Confederate command are not difficult to see. Van Dorn's order to make the attack arrived at Price's headquarters, but Hébert apparently never received the order and was obviously not prepared at daylight. Moreover, Hébert did not even command the division at that time. Green, whose brigade remained behind the lines, had been notified that Hébert was ill and could not perform his duties. As senior brigadier in the division, Green was to take command. Hébert reported the same news to Price.[39]

While all this was taking place, unbeknownst to Van Dorn, he anxiously awaited the attack that should have already commenced. When it did not, Van Dorn sent a staff officer to find out why. Then he sent a second and a third. None of these officers found Hébert, but the Louisianan himself arrived at Van Dorn's headquarters shortly thereafter. At this time, Price officially notified Green to command the division and move forward rapidly. But by now it was nearing 8:00 A.M., and there was still no attack. More time passed while Green not only learned his new duties but also had to form the division. The attack was therefore delayed again.[40]

Hébert never gave any reason for reporting sick, nor did he disclose the type of illness. According to one rumor, Hébert was intoxicated. According to another, Hébert, like many other Confederates, had partaken of sour fruit on the march to Corinth and become a victim of the "bowels being disordered." Several newspapers reported that Hébert was taking narcotics. Others reached a more logical conclusion: Hébert had looked at the situation and decided that the attacks would fail. He therefore wanted no part of them and called it quits. The weight of the evidence indicates that Hébert was actually ill. He had been "quite sick" earlier that spring, and this illness could have been a prolonged bout with the same infirmity. Certainly, Hébert had been almost nonexistent the day before, particularly during the White House fighting, when his division had made so many piecemeal attacks. His sickness could have been emerging then. Why Hébert reported sick is open for debate, but there is no doubt that this illness worked to delay the Confederate attack for more than three hours, rendering the artillery bombardment fruitless. Had the attack taken place while the artillery was still firing, the Federal lines would not have had several hours of daylight to prepare to receive the assault.[41]

As the command problems played out in the Confederate rear, the sun rose, and the men on the front lines could see what they would be attacking. Their courses would take them over a slight hill and up a ridge on which the Federal line sat. An almost continuous line of abatis existed between the two forces, particularly farther west, although an area of standing timber gave some relief to the attackers. This cover was more dense in Maury's front than in Green's, where it consisted of only "a few scattering trees." The tree line ran only so far, however, and opened into a clear and unobstructed area that extended for several hundred yards. The Confederates would have to cross this clear expanse to get to the Federal lines.[42]

The Confederates also detected the Federal works atop the ridges. For the first time, the Confederates saw the forts on the ridges separated by the valley. On Lovell's front, there was a ridge and three batteries: Battery Williams and Battery Phillips, with Robinett farther to the left. In front of Maury's command lay Batteries Robinett and Williams. Across the valley was another ridge on which Batteries Richardson and Powell sat. These formidable redoubts could be clearly seen, as could the Federal infantry thick around them. But they were not on Van Dorn's maps, an example of poor reconnaissance by the commanding general. A surprise thus greeted the Confederates at sunrise. Lovell later wrote, "Had we known accurately the nature of the works and their position we should have taken the place on Friday beyond all doubt. . . . But we lost time in 'groping' our way."[43]

Why Van Dorn did not know about these works is uncertain. Brigade commander Rust later reported that Van Dorn had sent a scout into the Union lines during the night, but "the person had not performed his duty satisfactorily and had not given the requisite and correct information." Van Dorn later admitted he had gained no intelligence overnight about the Federal position, despite trying to do so. Rust added that before he beheld the works on the morning of October 4, he had been "furnished with no plan or chart of the defenses the enemy had constructed and was not informed orally of their position and character." But according to Bowen, in the same division, Lovell had gathered all three brigade commanders and showed them a crude drawing of the enemy line. Who was right, we do not know. However, Rust could have meant that no word came down from army headquarters or that Lovell simply drew the supposed Union line without knowing it was behind stout fortifications. Green also testified that he had not seen the works the night before, noticing them only on the morning of October 4. He related, "Going in in the morning there were fortifications immediately before us. Whether they were there in the evening or built in the night I do not know."[44]

Nevertheless, Green hurriedly assumed command of the division and did all he could to press the attacks. When he took control, Green found the division deployed in the same manner it had been the night before when the fighting ended. His own brigade, now under Colonel W. H. Moore of the 43rd Mississippi, was on Phifer's left. To its left was Gates's brigade. Farther to the left lay Martin's brigade, now commanded by McLain, with Colbert still in reserve. Green took his third brigade, which had fought hard the day before, out of line and replaced it with Colbert's brigade, holding Moore in reserve. By the time this repositioning took place, however, severe skirmishing had already occurred. McLain, on the extreme left, notified his new division commander that his flank was wide open and invited attack. (Cabell had already departed to join Maury.) Green acted swiftly by moving Colbert's brigade back out of line and to the left of McLain. W. H. Moore's brigade then moved back to its former position. Confederate dallying was costing precious hours.[45]

It was now nearly 9:00 A.M., and there was still no attack. Skirmishers fought one another with a fury that almost reached battle proportions, however, as Confederate sharpshooters climbed trees in front of the Union line. Federal artillery rapidly fired into the Confederate lines in response. The Confederate guns had fallen silent long before, but the Union cannon continued their fire, with Cabell's brigade receiving a good part of this shelling. It was still moving across the rear of Green's division but had to stop and take cover on the reverse slope of a hill. Nothing, it seemed, was going right for the Confederates this morning.[46]

Matters were certainly better in the Federal lines, although the Confederate artillery had awakened the Northern soldiers and wounded a number of them. One Ohio soldier told of a cannonball hitting Corporal Creighton Orr of the 43rd Ohio, "nearly severing his head from his body." One soldier nearby was wounded by a flying piece of Orr's skull, and many had brain matter splattered all over them. The firing also interrupted Rosecrans's sleep just as he lay down. He immediately went to the lines, not taking any breakfast. The troops likewise took no time to eat. As it turned out, there was no need for the Federals to rush because the Confederate commanders had trouble launching the attack. The delay in the Confederate assault afforded Rosecrans and his Federals the opportunity not only to review their lines in daylight but also to make any needed adjustments. Rosecrans himself found the lines satisfactory. One Federal found the lull medicinal. He stated, "We had a little breathing spell which I improved by going to sleep." Another was not so pleased: "If they're goin' to take us, why don't they come and do it in the cool of the morning? It'll be hot after a while!" He was right. Rosecrans later recalled, "The morning opened clear and soon grew to be hot. It must have been ninety-four degrees in the shade."[47]

Even then, Rosecrans still wondered whether Van Dorn had retreated or had at least retraced his steps in order to attack Bolivar. When the Confederate artillery opened up, he decided it could be an attempt to "cover their retreat." A soldier of the 5th Iowa remembered, "We began to think Price had given us the slip during the night." To make sure, Rosecrans decided to send out a reconnaissance force to determine exactly where the Confederates were. Stanley's division sent out two companies of each regiment for the operation. Davies sent entire regiments — the 7th Iowa and 7th Illinois.[48]

Near Robinett, Stanley himself commanded one unit of skirmishers; he gave the other command to Mower, even though some had reported him drunk the day before. Davies did not accompany his regiments, sending them out under their own officers. The skirmishers pushed forward, engaged the Confederate skirmishers, and quickly drove them back. The Federals pursued their enemy counterparts but soon found themselves in trouble. The Union skirmishers came face-to-face with the Confederate battle lines, which were "already forming . . . for the assault," one of them noted. The same soldier who thought Price had retreated corrected himself, writing in his diary, "Our delusion was soon apparent." The skirmishers promptly withdrew, but their "hot firing proclaimed the presence of their [Confederate] forces preparing for the assault," one grateful onlooker observed. The skirmishers had done their job; Rosecrans now had his answer about Confederate intentions. There was no doubt that the Confederates would assault in a matter of moments.[49]

While the skirmishers obtained good information for the Union commanders, Mower made a major mistake. Rosecrans had ordered him to "feel" the enemy. Perhaps a little overanxious, Mower enthusiastically drove the Confederates back until they reached the main Confederate lines. When a few shots came from his left rear, Mower, believing it was friendly fire, rode over to stop it. He suddenly found himself "in the midst of a small party of the enemy." Mower tried to flee, but when he did, the Confederates opened fire. His horse fell, and the colonel was "prostrated by an ugly wound in the neck." Helpless, he fell into Confederate hands.[50]

Rosecrans had no time to ponder the loss of one of his best brigade commanders. It was now 9:00 A.M., and the Confederates were finally ready to attack.

13

"A Dreadful Charge Up Hill"

William Rosecrans and his men were fortunate that the enemy was late getting organized on the morning of October 4. But their good fortune soon ran out. By 9:00 A.M., the Confederate left wing had finally worked out its command kinks and moved from its position west of the Mobile and Ohio Railroad, crossing it, Elam Creek, and the adjacent swamp. They formed in front of the Union line while Rosecrans and his men watched the movement, spellbound. One Union soldier described "the flags of the enemy and the glint of the sunlight on their bayonets." The Confederates continued their march in full view of the enemy, moving in column until they reached the attack point. Then the entire line fanned out and formed into a line of battle. One eyewitness remembered the column "opened and spread out magnificently, right and left, like great wings."[1]

Before the attack began, however, Van Dorn's plan went awry again. The original order called for Green's division to begin the attack, followed by Maury and Lovell. But by the time Green was ready to move, his skirmishers were already hotly engaged, and to the units on the right, it sounded like the attack had started. Maury's skirmishers were also engaged in serious fighting. Thus, John C. Moore began his assault at approximately the same time as Green's.[2]

Other factors hurt the Confederate effort more than its timing, however. The Southerners had to rely mainly on the infantry because the terrain and the belt of timber running along the front of the Union lines prevented the use of artillery. One of Price's brigade commanders asked for artillery support, to which Price thundered to the lowly aid: "Go back sir, and tell your General he will find a plenty of cannon in his front and to take them." Price thus ordered Green forward without artillery support, and Green deployed all four brigades in line: W. H. Moore, Gates, McLain, and Colbert, from right to left. Green ordered the two left brigades, McLain's and Colbert's, to charge the Federal line, throwing their lefts forward so that they could obtain a flanking position on the east side of Battery Powell. While these two brigades moved forward, Gates and W. H. Moore were to attack the Union line at Battery Powell and the troops to the west. Green knew his work would be bloody; he could "see the enemy had . . . lines of fortifications, bristling with artillery and strongly supported by infantry." But he still moved on.[3]

As Green's Confederates marched toward the enemy, one soldier remembered that a "cheer now rose from the troops up near the town, and ran like electricity along the line." The entire Confederate division marched "slowly and steadily," one soldier noted, while the skirmishers in front fought with their Federal counterparts. One Federal wrote in his diary that the Confederates moved "with a bravery, a desperation that threatened calamity to our army."[4]

Moving out of the thin timber, which one watching Federal declared was only "3/4 of a mile of the depot and village," the Confederates moved up the hill toward the Federal lines. The Southerners could see their targets on top of the ridge, which one Confederate described as "gay with streaming banners, defiant with glittering bayonets and bristling cannon." When they got within 200 yards of the Federal line, Green ordered the brigades to advance at the double-quick, and the gray regiments charged toward Battery Powell and the lines of infantry that defended the work. The Southerners moved onward with "great rapidity," one observer noted, as each individual unit strove to be the first to enter the Union lines. Tom Sweeny, trying to steady his men in the face of the onslaught, called it "a terribly beautiful sight to see." The charging Confederates, already hit by every gun the enemy could train on them, simply closed ranks and pushed forward, their faces "averted like men striving to protect themselves against a driving storm of hail."[5]

The Confederate attack ran into trouble as soon as it went forward. The two right brigades made good progress toward the Federal line, but those on the left found the going difficult. That wing of the division, McLain's and Colbert's brigades, was forced to move on "worse roads," which slowed them down. The longer distance they had to travel to get to the Union lines also hampered their attack. Despite the difficulties, Colbert's and McLain's brigades soon reached the Federal lines, but then they encountered another surprise. The Federal line did not end with the 10th Iowa, positioned northeast of Battery Powell, in prolongation of Davies's line. The main line bent back at Battery Powell.[6]

Indeed, only three Union regiments were deployed north of Powell. The 9th Illinois of Mersy's brigade was to the immediate right, while the 80th Ohio, 6th Wisconsin Battery, and 10th Iowa of Colonel Samuel A. Holmes's brigade deployed in extension. The main line was back at Battery Powell, running off to the east. The remainder of Holmes's brigade was deployed in this line, which sat on higher ground and could thus fire over the extension of the Battery Powell line. The 56th Illinois was on the fort's immediate right rear, while the 10th Missouri and 12th Wisconsin Battery continued the line to the east. Buford, who told his men "that not one foot of ground must be yielded," supported the 11th Ohio Battery and Battery M of the 1st Missouri Light Artillery to the right of the Wisconsin guns. When Colbert's and McLain's brigades assaulted the Union position, throwing their lefts to the front, they were surprised to meet Hamilton's division situated to the east of Battery Powell, facing northeast. The plan to flank the line was now utterly impossible.[7]

McLain's brigade was the first to make contact with the Federal line when it hit the 10th Iowa, the end of the Federal spur. The Mississippians and Alabamians charged "over a succession of small hills," one of them recalled, with courage and determination, only to meet the steadfast Iowans. The 6th Wisconsin Battery also poured heavy fire into the charging Confederates. This fire stopped the Southerners for a time, but they soon re-formed and moved forward again.[8]

Colbert to the left wheeled his brigade around and moved to the east of the Union spur line. One Federal marveled at the sight: "The long lines of gleaming bayonets could be seen emerging from the woods, East of the railroad, and moving up the Bolivar road in column by division. It was a grand sight and a still grander target for our batteries which cut great gaps in that living mass of humanity." But, he added, those gaps were "quickly filled up almost as soon as opened." As the Confederates moved on, they soon caught a better glimpse of Buford's brigade, which was formed in the rear and ready to meet them. Despite this sight, Colbert's men moved forward to the rear of the spur. This movement shook the Federals in that line, and although the Union spur held its own for a time, the regiments soon broke.[9]

While McLain and Colbert attacked the spur itself and Hamilton's division to the left, Gates and W. H. Moore made their way toward the Union line west of Battery Powell. The brigades lurched forward after Gates gave the command "in a voice that could have been easily heard a mile away," according to one of his soldiers. Another member of Gates's command described the assault: "What a sublime sight it was to see that magnificent body of men moving majestically forward in regular battle array." Soon, however, the majesty wore off: "After passing through a wooded skirt of about two hundred yards we emerged into the open. Now we were in plain view of the enemy, who were posted on the crest of the ridge surrounding the town. Now we raised the Rebel Yell all along the line and pressed gallantly forward. It

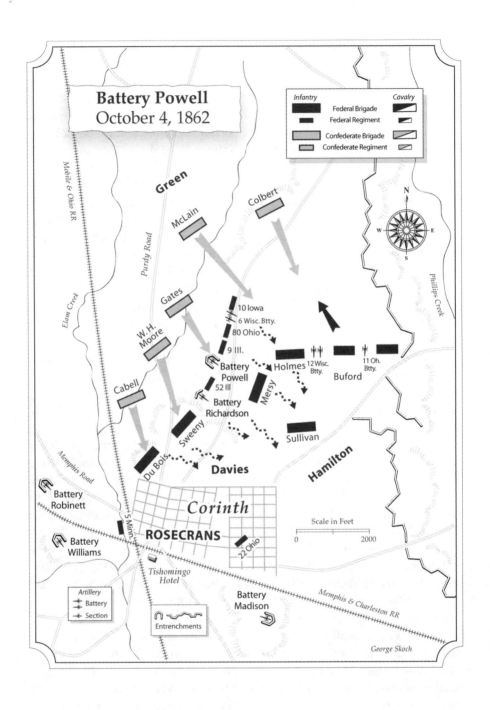

Battery Powell
October 4, 1862

Infantry
Federal Brigade
Federal Regiment
Confederate Brigade
Confederate Regiment

Cavalry

Mobile & Ohio RR

Green

McLain

Colbert

Purdy Road

Gates

W. H. Moore

10 Iowa
6 Wisc. Btty.
80 Ohio
9 Ill.

Battery Powell

52 Ill.

Battery Richardson

Holmes
12 Wisc. Btty.
Buford
11 Oh. Btty.

Cabell

Elam Creek

Mersy

Sweeny

Sullivan

Du Bois

Davies

Hamilton

Memphis Road

5 Minn.

Battery Robinett

Battery Williams

Corinth

ROSECRANS

22 Ohio

Scale in Feet
0   2000

Tishomingo Hotel

Memphis & Charleston RR

Battery Madison

Artillery
Battery
Section

Entrenchments

Phillips Creek

George Skoch

was yet some five or six hundred yards to the works and mostly up grade." Gates's units also found the going rough as they got closer to the Federal line, having to contend with the hastily formed abatis. Green remembered that it was "a hard road to travel, climbing over logs, brush, and fallen timber, while masked batteries of the enemy opened upon us at almost every step with great slaughter." Another soldier remembered, "It was a dreadful charge up hill," and yet another described the awful route: "Passing through a narrow belt of timber, we emerged into open ground in full view of the enemy's breast works, lining the crest of a ridge, some three hundred yards in our front. The enemy's artillery opened a terrific fire on our line as soon as we showed in the open ground, but there was no wavering. Steadily the men went forward to meet death dealing fire from both artillery and infantry, but there was no halt." A Missourian elaborated on the open ground the brigade had to cover: "There was not even a single brush to screen a person from the terrible storm of shot and shell from their heavy siege guns, which were in full view for over a mile, and [it] looked like . . . hell had been let loose. Shells bursting all around you; round shot ploughing the ground everywhere; grape and canister sweeping down the hill almost by the bushel, it is a miracle how anyone escaped."[10]

As Gates came face-to-face with the Federals inside Battery Powell, the Confederates of McLain's brigade continued their advance toward the Union spur, killing and wounding many cannoneers of the 6th Wisconsin Battery. By this time, McLain's men had also reached the battery and penetrated it, while the regiments to the right and left of the Wisconsin guns fell back in retreat. The 10th Iowa retired from its position, seeing that the battery to the left had fallen and that Colbert's troops had gained a portion of its rear. The regiment fled after only fifteen rounds but then regrouped about seventy yards to the rear, where it turned and fired another volley into the following Confederates. This salvo had little effect on the Southerners, who kept coming, and the Union regiment broke again, this time to a point behind the main line. It finally stopped, still together but shaken, behind the 12th Wisconsin Battery.[11]

The 80th Ohio on the left of the 6th Wisconsin Battery likewise fell back, causing one Indianan in the rearward line to disgustedly comment, "as they usually do." When Gates's charge stopped the fire of the Wisconsin battery and McLain's brigade took it, the 80th Ohio began to waver, and its commander, Major Richard Lanning, fell with a mortal wound. Officers in the regiment, as well as Colonel Jesse Alexander of the nearby 59th Indiana, tried to re-form the unit, which they eventually did, but not before the Ohioans fell back. The continuation of Gates's charge next brought the Missourians to the 9th Illinois in the garden. Like the 10th Iowa, it also retired to a position behind Holmes's main line. With the regiments on its flanks gone, little remained of the 6th Wisconsin Battery. The cannoneers had either been killed or retreated in the face of the bayonet. When its commander, Captain Henry Dillon, saw that the battery would fall, he ordered the limbers and caissons to the rear. He knew the men could not remove the guns, but he succeeded in removing everything else except for one disabled limber.[12]

Colbert's and McLain's brigades had succeeded in driving away the Federals east of Battery Powell, but at a fearful cost. Casualties began to mount, including Colonel McLain, whose leg was "cut off by a cannonball," according to one observer. A Federal soldier of the 49th Indiana may have been describing McLain's mortal wounding when he noted, "The commanding officer fell from his horse killed or wounded." But despite the growing Confederate losses, the Union spur was shattered.[13]

The effort west of the fort by the other two brigades of Green's division produced similar favorable results for the Confederates. Immediately to McLain's right, Gates also moved up and attacked. The Federals on the hill met the charge, one Confederate recounting, "The shot shell and shrapnel ploughed through our ranks unmercifully." The Federal barrage caused confusion, and the same Confederate reported, "It is impossible to maintain a solid line, and unavoidably we became more or less scattered." Yet the Southerners did not stop, even though "the very earth shook," one soldier remembered. Colonel Francis M. Cockrell, who later became a U.S. senator, led his 2nd Missouri, pointing his sword and yelling, "Forward, my boys, we must capture that battery." Just then, a Federal bullet cut his beard and a shell fragment hit him, but he was not injured seriously enough to cause him to leave the field.[14]

The Missourians obeyed Cockrell's command and soon swarmed over the parapet of Battery Powell, taking possession of the fort and the guns remaining inside. Colonel Gates himself, still astride his horse, climbed the parapet and, waving the flag of the 1st Missouri Cavalry (dismounted), motioned for his men to continue. Colonel James A. Pritchard of the 3rd Missouri was not as fortunate. He dismounted at the redoubt and was in the process of waving his men forward with his sword when a Federal minié ball slammed into his shoulder.[15]

Lieutenant Henry Gillespie of Gates's brigade was one of the first soldiers to reach the redoubt. He found an enemy artilleryman in the process of firing his gun, and Gillespie ordered him to stop at the point of his sword. The cannoneer did so, and Gillespie took him prisoner. When someone later asked why Gillespie had not used his pistol, he replied that "he forgot entirely that he ever had one." The battle continued to rage while the flag of the 5th Missouri, atop the parapet, announced to all that Battery Powell was in Confederate hands.[16]

While the left of Gates's brigade attacked Battery Powell, the right moved toward Sweeny's line. An "ominous silence took place for a few moments," Sweeny remembered, and then "a sharp rattling of musketry was heard, accompanied by heavy volleys, and the enemy's columns burst from the woods in front." The Confederates moved right behind the retreating Union skirmishers of the Yates and the Western Sharpshooters, whom Davies had ordered out of the way so he could use his artillery. The big guns began firing before all the skirmishers had reached safety, so some Union soldiers fell victim to their own guns; others fell to Confederate bullets. Colonel Patrick E. Burke, commanding the Western Sharpshooters, had his horse shot no fewer than seven times. The Confederates drove the maddened skirmishers back but then proceeded to drive the main line as well. Sweeny's men dropped to the ground by order of Rosecrans himself, who rode along the line, and they held their own for a moment. "A shower of leaden hail was sweeping over our heads," one 2nd Iowa soldier remembered. When the Federal infantry opened up, the Confederate ranks shuddered but did not stop. Gates's Missourians continued to advance amidst the shot, shell, and bullets.[17]

Although Sweeny was hit in the leg by a spent ball, that did not phase the one-armed colonel. He continued to hold his line until Battery Powell fell to the Southerners. Before that, only a few of his men had retreated, one of whom "fired his piece in the air, ducked his head, and ran to the rear," Davies himself reported. "I shall take great pains to find out [his name]," Davies remarked, adding that he would have shot the man if he had been near enough. And Davies certainly meant it, having shot at two men the day before because they had left the line. When Battery Powell fell, however, the stiffening Union line broke. The cannoneers had abandoned Powell, but due to the restlessness of the horses and the small quarters, they had been unable to remove the guns. Another section just to the west also evacuated the hastily formed Battery Richardson. Even worse, the Confederates were pouring through the opening between Battery Powell and the nearby house and garden, and they quickly flanked Sweeny's line from the captured redoubt. The regiment on the left of the fort, the 52nd Illinois, broke and fled to the rear, although Private Charles Murray of Company E refused to leave, yelling, "It was Colonel Sweeny's orders to hold the fort to the last." A Confederate captain confronted Murray, ordered him to surrender, and shot him in the hand with his revolver. Murray responded by shooting the officer and taking his pistol. He also killed a nearby Confederate private and was still fighting hard when other members of his regiment returned to offer assistance.[18]

An Illinois soldier described the attack that flanked Sweeny's line. "The enemy charged on us in solid column," he wrote, "and beautifully done." The commander of the 52nd Illinois, Lieutenant Colonel John S. Wilcox, ordered his prone men to fire: "Up and give it to them," he said. They responded by pouring eight volleys into the Confederates, but the Southerners kept coming. When the redoubt to the right was taken, however, Wilcox ordered his regiment to withdraw. The retreat could have turned into a rout, but the Illinoisans regrouped amid some of the houses on the northern outskirts of Corinth.[19]

The tireless Sweeny could not stop the retreat of the 52nd Illinois, and he found that the remainder of his line had also come apart. The limbers of the various retreating batteries passed behind Sweeny's line at a full gallop, scaring the horses of his own batteries and causing them to bolt. This chaos, Davies remembered, had a "very demoralizing effect upon the stability of the infantry line." The galloping animals also frightened the horses pulling the ammunition wagons in the rear, causing a panic that was brought under control only when Davies himself and his staff ran the animals down.[20]

By this time, W. H. Moore's Confederate brigade also arrived on the scene and attacked Sweeny's position, causing units up and down the line to peel away under the increasing Confederate pressure. The Yates Sharpshooters "were lying flat down and soon the buzz of the balls began to reach us," a member of the regiment remembered. It sounded to him "like the buzz of a large sized whirlygig." He went on to describe how "the balls tore up the dust in great style and the men began to fall." Another observer noted, "In a very short time all the troops on our right had fallen back. It is said on account of a mistake in the order. I don't know but to me it looked as if from fear." Despite the attack, the color-bearer of the 7th Iowa, according to one Federal, "ran out in front two or three rods and fell [so] another one stepped out and picked up the flag." Such heroics notwithstanding, the Confederate charge broke the Union line here as well. With its leader down, the Union Brigade also came apart, and one of its members reported, "They advanced their infantry and they drove us clare into town[;] they fought in the streets about an hour." After a few minutes, only portions of the 2nd and 7th Iowa remained on the main line, but they soon had to retire as well, when parts of the line farther east fell. However, the stand of these two regiments gave Sweeny time to begin regrouping his splintered brigade. Sweeny ordered the 7th and 2nd Iowa to retire and form into his new line, but those units had suffered terribly. One soldier of the 7th Iowa wrote to his sisters that he "got a slite introduction to something less than a pound of secesh lead in the face." He had been "struck in the left cheak just above the mouth—the ball striking the bone and glancing lodged on the back part of the cheak." He described it as "an ugly, though not very paneful wound." The 2nd Iowa's Lieutenant Colonel Noah W. Mills, who had assumed command after Colonel Baker's mortal wounding the day before, was also wounded. Taking command of the regiment now was Major James B. Weaver, who would go on to have a career in national politics, including two presidential runs, most notably as the 1892 Populist Party nominee. He had two spent balls bounce off him, and his horse was wounded. With the wounding of the regiment's other officers, Weaver later boasted to his wife, "I took command on the forenoon on the 2nd day of the fight and took the Regt. triumphantly through."[21]

In the Union Brigade, Captain David B. Henderson took a minié ball in his left foot, leaving it "terribly shattered." He described the wound in vivid detail: "The ball entered my foot on the top and two inches back of the second and third toes, cutting the cords of those toes. It then passed diagonally across the foot and came out three quarters of an inch below the left ankle. Its course was through the large part of the foot." The bullet, he said, was "the worst used up Minnie I ever saw." Surgeons tried to save Henderson's foot, but they had to amputate it, forcing him to wear what he called "my new foot"—a "timber leg." Corinth ended Henderson's career in the 12th Iowa, but not his usefulness. He later served multiple terms in the U.S. House of Representatives, where he played a major role in ensuring the preservation of Civil War battlefields. He retired as Speaker of the House.[22]

Despite the future political power in that Union line, the Confederate attack had rolled over Rosecrans's defenses north of Corinth in a matter of minutes. All four of Green's brigades had taken portions of the Union line. McLain and Colbert had shattered the spur and were moving toward the second Federal position. Gates and W. H. Moore had taken Battery Powell and Battery Richardson and the line to the southwest. Yet the victorious Confederates still faced many obstacles. Colbert and McLain had a well-formed line ahead of them, which was already slowing the Confederate advance. The Southerners would have to attack by frontal assault. Moreover, Gates and W. H. Moore found that although they had taken the Federal line, the enemy was already beginning to counterattack. They had also expended their ammunition, and several officers were down, including McLain and future Confederate general Samuel Gholson, now a captain in the 43rd Mississippi.[23]

But Green's earlier call for reinforcements had not gone unheeded. Cabell's brigade was the only available reserve, and at the time, he was on the right flank of Green's line. Van Dorn ordered Cabell to the rescue. A courier dashed up to him and reported, "Colonel Gates has captured forty guns, but cannot hold them unless you reinforce him at once—follow me." Cabell immediately moved his brigade from the sheltered position he had taken west of the railroad. "The order was received with a shout by the whole brigade," Cabell wrote, and he moved across the tracks and the creek and onto the right rear of W. H. Moore's brigade. There, he prepared to attack.[24]

While Cabell was moving into position, Green's division continued its struggle. The Confederates advanced right on the heels of the retreating Federals, who caused as much havoc among their fellow troops as they did among the enemy as they staggered toward the re-forming line. The 10th Iowa and 80th Ohio of the defunct spur, for example, along with the limbers and caissons of the 6th Wisconsin Battery, threw Holmes's line into confusion. One of its members remembered the Confederates coming at them next: "All at once, the enemy emerged from the woods into the open field in our front. They came, onward, on the double quick—eight lines of infantry at the right shoulder shift." In the rear, the 17th Iowa and 56th Illinois had been put under the immediate command of the injured Sullivan, who "sprang from his sick bed"; fortunately, they held their positions, but it was not easy. Lieutenant Colonel Green B. Raum, commanding the 56th Illinois, reported, the Union "retreat soon became a rout, and they came down pell-mell upon us, running over my men in every direction." And it got worse. Raum noted that as soon as the "debris" had passed, he could see the enemy in possession of Battery Powell and several houses on either side. Despite it all, the Illinoisans stood firm. When the "fugitives" passed, they opened up on the Confederates of McLain's brigade with a terrible fire, re-fusing their left to guard the flank. The 10th Missouri also stood firm in the face of their comrades' retreat, fixing bayonets "and threatening to bayonet those who attempted to force through our lines." The Missourians needed more than bayonets to stop the Confederates, however, and soon took them under fire. But these solid regiments alone could not stop the Southerners, who pressed on. As the Confederates reached the crest of a small hill, they took fire from the 12th Wisconsin Battery, which opened on them and stopped the advance, despite one cannon jamming with a round in the bore. The artillery fire, combined with the small arms of the regiments, caused enormous destruction in the already dazed Confederate ranks. McLain's Confederates could go no farther.[25]

On McLain's left, Colbert also found the Union line more formidable. As McLain's brigade took the spur of the Union line, Colbert's brigade moved to the left, meeting the Union forces under Buford. Severe fighting erupted as the two brigades engaged each other. One Minnesotan marveled, "They drop by the score but still they come." Only days before, these two brigades had met each other on the fields of Iuka, and now they were squaring off again. But this time, Colbert's brigade could not overwhelm the Union line, and Buford's men gained their revenge for the harsh handling they had received at Iuka. This time, Colbert's brigade was stopped, and as a result, the Confederate advance hesitated.[26]

Sam Byers, who had missed the fight at Iuka, stood tall as one of the Union defenders of this line. Anxious about his first chance in battle, he recalled being "too excited to be scared." His regiment, the 5th Iowa, had deployed in a field of high weeds, but that did not stop Byers from getting the best view. Almost hoping to be wounded, which he deemed a "little honor," he began to fire at "nobody in particular." He continued to fire his musket repeatedly, which, a comrade later told him, was senseless. His friend also claimed that Byers had "nearly shot his ear off." Byers only laughed hysterically, pleased to be in the battle.[27]

In the face of such firepower, the two Confederate brigades fell back, but they quickly rushed toward the Union lines a second time. The Federals repulsed the enemy again, only to face a third assault. Buford's brigade, supported by the revamped 11th Ohio Battery, poured heavy fire into the oncoming Confederates. Lieutenant Henry Neil, commanding the Ohioans, rode perhaps forty feet in front of the guns, where he taunted the Confederate column to attack his battery: "Come on! Come on! if you think you can play Iuka over again." He exclaimed to his troops, "Boys, there are the same troops that fought us at Iuka; are you going to let them touch our guns today?" The cannoneers, filled with pride, let loose a "yell of rage" and deadly fire from their guns. The Southerners came to within seventy-five yards of Buford's line, but the Federals stopped them cold. Colbert's brigade would advance no more that day.[28]

Just because Hamilton had checked the Confederate advance on the right did not mean the Union forces' troubles were over. Gates's and W. H. Moore's brigades were still moving forward to the west. Gates, by this time, had moved past Battery Powell toward the town, but he found it difficult to continue. For one thing, he had almost run out of ammunition. In addition, the retreating Federals had begun to reorganize and form a new line, and Union regiments that had previously been in reserve entered the action. There was also resistance from pockets of Federals who had not withdrawn, extending from the first line all the way into town. A member of the Yates Sharpshooters wrote to his father, "Most of the troops fell back two squares but I was too tired to run and stopped in an old log shanty intending to fire till they came [back] up and take my chances." Entering the cabin, he found several wounded soldiers as well as others who were still determined to battle the Confederates. He wrote that there were six of them "poping away at the Rebs."[29]

Gates moved to the rear of Battery Powell and found himself on the flank of Sullivan's line, putting the 56th Illinois in dire straits. Raum saw his unit's predicament and quickly ordered the three left companies to wheel to the left and form at a ninety-degree angle to the rest of the regiment. This deployment gave some protection to the flank until help could arrive.[30]

By taking this action, Holmes's brigade was somewhat stabilized, but not so Davies's line. When Sweeny's brigade fell back, the retreat caused confusion in Mersy's brigade to the rear. This brigade did not hold up as well as Holmes's did when confronted with the same problem. The retreat of the artillery through the lines caused enormous panic and several casualties. That Mersy had only the 12th Illinois and 81st Ohio with which to fight added to his troubles (the 9th Illinois had fought on the spur and retreated separately), and these two regiments also became victims of the retreat. Colonel Morton of the 81st Ohio reported that "a battery in front of us came dashing out full speed through our columns, wounding several men and throwing the column into confusion." Colonel August L. Chetlain of the 12th Illinois reported the same: a battery ran through his regiment, causing the center and right to flee.[31]

As Gates's and W. H. Moore's Confederates pressed on, they found themselves on the outskirts of Corinth. Part of Moore's brigade soon penetrated into the town itself, and a few got as far as the depot. Brigade commander Moore made it to the depot and Tishomingo Hotel area, where he fought with the remnants of his command and others who had made it into town, "hopefully trusting to meet there Lovell's command," one Confederate wrote. They also reached Rosecrans's headquarters, where, one declared, they "posted themselves under cover of the portico." But then things turned sour for the Confederates. The Federals contained the attack and wounded Colonel Moore. Most of the men were out of ammunition, and there were no reinforcements in sight; McLain and Colbert had already been stopped on the left, and Cabell had not yet arrived. Lovell, likewise, had not broken through yet. A withdrawal was the only course of action, and Moore's bloodied remnants began to fall back, finding themselves as riddled with bullets as the headquarters building they had surrounded.[32]

The fight on the Federal right lasted less than an hour. The Confederates charged bravely and took the Federal lines, but the Union regiments eventually slowed the advance. Meanwhile, Cabell's brigade finally began its assault at about the same time Gates and W. H. Moore were nearing the peaks of their advances. Cabell had moved his brigade as quickly as possible, but the timing was confused and the attacks uncoordinated. Had they gone off jointly, the Confederates might have gained more success. As it was, Cabell became engaged just as Gates's and Moore's men began to slow down.[33]

By the time Cabell got moving, there was one factor in his favor: the Union line had taken a hard blow, and the reverberations had spread down the line. Du Bois's brigade did not know whether it would be attacked or have to fall back to conform with a new line. The surgeon of the 57th Illinois described the fright as the Confederates advanced: "They commenced an attack with their whole force, there seemed to be no end to their numbers as they swarmed out of the woods." Despite taking artillery fire, "on they came as if on parade, closing up their ranks as fast as their men fell." When W. H. Moore's and Gates's brigades hit Sweeny's brigade, causing it to withdraw, the 57th Illinois of Du Bois's command did so as well. While in the process of moving from the left to the right flank of the brigade, the regiment became caught in a cross fire between Green's brigades to the rear and the approaching Cabell. By this time, Cabell's presence had become known, and Du Bois realized that he had only two regiments with which to fight. The 7th and 50th Illinois nevertheless maintained their position for a time against what one Federal described as "the drunken Arkansas legions under the command of General Cabell."[34]

At the beginning of the advance, Cabell's left immediately became engaged. Rather than risk a flank action, he ordered the entire brigade to advance, which it did, sweeping the Federal skirmishers back. Du Bois was still fuming later when he wrote an account of the battle in his private journal: "Our skirmishers came in so slowly that we had to retain our fire until they came within 100 yards of us." The mistake was crucial, allowing Cabell's men to reach the line fairly easily. As the men of Cabell's brigade charged over the shabby works, they met the remnants of Du Bois's command but did not falter. One Union colonel, seeing Cabell mount the works and cross over them, tried desperately to save his men, shouting, "Kill that d____d rebel officer." By this time, Cabell was near enough to strike the colonel with his sword, placing "his antagonist at his feet."[35]

The 7th and 50th Illinois held only briefly. Gates and W. H. Moore were in the rear of these two regiments, and Cabell was engaged with the Federals on the front and flank. Du Bois's command thus received fire from the front as well as the right rear. The troops could hardly endure it, and the regiments began to fall back. Battery Richardson had fallen as well, and some of the Illinoisans described the cannoneers in the little fort "swing[ing] their rammers high over their heads as the enemy, yelling like demons, surround[ed] and literally smother[ed] the little squad of men fighting for their guns." The 50th Illinois ran rapidly to the rear, unsuccessfully trying to organize around a clump of buildings. The 7th Illinois, however, turned to give one last fight. Its new location was only thirty yards behind the original line, but the regiment could not hold that position either. More fire from the rear erupted, as well as artillery fire from Battery B of the 2nd Illinois Artillery at Battery Madison. The 7th Illinois, like its comrade units, broke and fled to the rear.[36]

Since Du Bois's line had formed on the outskirts of Corinth, the retreat took the troops directly into the town. The 50th Illinois, which, like the 57th Illinois, had been moved at the last minute, had no chance to redeploy, and it fell back into town. Colonel William Swarthout reported, "On reaching the cross-street [we] became entangled with several other regiments." Lieutenant Colonel Hurlbut reported, "The enemy opened a galling fire on me, which was impossible to pass through." All of Du Bois's orderlies had been shot down by this time, so he alone perceived the disaster unfolding in front of him. The Illinoisans fell back into Corinth ahead of the charging Confederates.[37]

Portions of Cabell's brigade, mostly the 20th Arkansas, continued forward toward the town, but then Cabell found that he was taking fire from the rear. The artillery to the west of Du Bois's position fired into his flank, as did the infantry units that had begun to recover their lost ground from Green's brigades. Cabell faced a severe cross fire from these two positions and lost several of his regimental commanders, including Colonel Henry P. Johnson of the 20th Arkansas, whom the Federals observed "being killed and falling from his horse." John N. Daly of the 18th Arkansas also went down. Shells thrown in from the batteries atop College Hill added to Cabell's problems.[38]

The 20th Arkansas advanced the farthest, making it partway into town and mingling with the men of W. H. Moore's command who had reached the depot. Others made it as well. One member of the 13th Arkansas was especially commended for gallantry. His clothes contained numerous bullet holes, but he received no wound. One eyewitness said that he had been protected by "that unseen shield with which Providence protects its agents."[39]

All was chaos in town. Hospital orderlies, teamsters, and servants, who never dreamed they would witness the battle firsthand, quickly bolted. One Federal described "one of the greatest stampedes of teams, teamsters, non-combatants and negroes that I ever saw." Another remembered, "I was almost persuaded to be a *Christian Coward* and run," but he thought better of it, not wanting to be compared with "contraband."[40]

Fortunately for the Federals, Rosecrans had left his nearby headquarters earlier. During the action, the general had ridden the front lines, steadying his troops and giving directions. He had begun his tour at Battery Robinett, but by the time the final charges took place at Battery Powell, he had moved to that sector. Rosecrans later claimed to have seen a house in the distance, very possibly his headquarters, with its porch full of Confederates. He ordered a section of the 12th Wisconsin Battery to disperse them. Lieutenant Immel did so, firing only one round. After that shot, the porch contained only "dead and dying."[41]

With the Confederate surge obviously petering out, Union troops were ordered to retake their original positions, and all along the line, Federal regiments began the counterattack. As the artillery fired into Battery Powell—sending the Confederates running, but also killing the horses that remained—the Union infantry began its comeback. Although he had not retreated, Buford, on the extreme right, moved his entire brigade northward, still in perfect order, and attacked Colbert's stalled and dazed regiments. The Federal brigade, artillery and all, advanced toward the Confederates "with cheers and volleys, their banners streaming to the winds," Hamilton noted. Another soldier recalled that the entire brigade moved forward "with the accuracy, precision, and steadiness of a review." Despite the earlier fall of its commander, Lieutenant Colonel De Witt C. Rugg, the 48th Indiana was the first to make contact, but all the Federal units entered the fight before it ended. Hamilton thus drove Colbert's men away, and Buford took up an advance position from which he could shell the retreating Confederates. The charge, Hamilton remembered, "was too much even for rebel courage." After "firing two volleys and giving three hearty cheers," one Confederate remembered, they fell back before the weight of Buford's counterattack. The Southerners managed to fire into the flank of the column, hitting the 26th Missouri, but to little effect; the retreat continued with great difficulty. The Federals eventually swept the field of Confederates east of Battery Powell.[42]

While Buford advanced, Sullivan's command counterattacked around the redoubt itself. The 17th Iowa and 56th Illinois charged the bewildered Confederates, and Sullivan himself reported that with "two well-delivered volleys, a charge, [and] a cheer, . . . the enemy fled." The 10th Missouri assaulted near the abandoned guns of the 6th Wisconsin Battery, charging the Confederates of McLain's brigade and driving them back past Battery Powell and the Wisconsin guns. A few Federal soldiers redeployed the pieces and opened a destructive fire on the retreating Southerners, causing further suffering in the Confederate ranks. The 10th Iowa charged right behind the Missourians.[43]

In this charge, the 17th Iowa, which had behaved badly at Iuka, moved up from its reserve position and made its way toward the Confederates. The path of its advance took the regiment to the right of the 10th Missouri, which lay in the direction of Colbert's brigade. While Buford attacked this brigade, Sullivan's 17th Iowa joined in on the left and helped drive the enemy away. In the process, the Iowans captured the 40th Mississippi's flag, which was great validation for the regiment that had once been accused of cowardice. Hamilton officially wrote in his report that the Iowa regiment "nobly redeemed itself from the cloud cast upon it by conduct at Iuka."[44]

Although the counterattack in the sector east of Battery Powell was successful, the Union regiments to the left had problems. The 10th Missouri's attack occurred so quickly that it held the position before Gates's brigade could be driven from Battery Powell. This opened the rear of the 10th Missouri and 10th Iowa to fire from the fort. Heavy casualties resulted before the Federals drove the Confederates out of Battery Powell.[45]

Sweeny, working diligently to re-form his brigade along with Hamilton and other officers, at last seemed ready to charge the Confederates and retake his position. Once he had the Union Brigade and the 52nd Illinois re-formed, he brought the 7th and 2nd Iowa back to the new line. These units then attacked the Confederates, Sweeny's men responding to his order "with a shout that was heard throughout our whole lines." Gates's and W. H. Moore's Confederates, one soldier remembered, "fought stubbornly for a while" but were no match for the regrouped and wild Federals. "A panic seemed to seize all the men," remembered Lieutenant Colonel Finley Hubbell of the 3rd Missouri. Gates fell back from his position, as did W. H. Moore's brigade. One of Gates's soldiers reported, "Hastily and with no regard to order, we retreated to the friendly shelter of the timber, leaving our dead and most of our wounded where they fell." Sweeny, who had a horse shot under him and took a spent ball in the leg, followed the retreating Confederates, who, after turning to fire one last volley, ran away in earnest. With this, Sweeny retook his original position, driving the Confederates back to the abatis, which the Southerners found as difficult to cross going out as coming in.[46]

The 52nd Illinois became the proud captors of Battery Powell itself, and the regiment's lieutenant colonel, John S. Wilcox, became the first man to reach it, with one of Davies's staff officers, Julius Lovell, not far behind. Davies reported that Lovell "sprang from his horse, captured five prisoners in the ditch, and, with the assistance of one of Colonel Sweeny's men and one bugler of the First Missouri Artillery, manned a 20-pounder rifled gun and fired ten or twelve shots at the retreating enemy before the artillerists returned to their posts." The 12th Illinois planted its colors on the parapet near the Confederate 5th Missouri's flag, as did the 52nd Illinois. During the retreat from the battery, Confederate Lieutenant William McCarty noticed that his regiment's colors had been left behind in the confusion. He went back to retrieve them and managed to do so by the slimmest of margins. McCarty took the flag and ran, only ten feet in front of the charging Federals. Somehow, he made it back to his lines safely. Although the flag of the 5th Missouri did not fall captive, other units were less fortunate. In addition to the Iowans who captured the Mississippi banner, the 12th Illinois succeeded in capturing the flag of a Louisiana regiment, most likely the 3rd Louisiana.[47]

With Battery Powell again in Union hands, the destruction became evident. Eighteen Confederates lay in the ditch, thirteen of them dead. The successful Federals then turned a portion of Battery Powell's guns on the retreating Confederates. The Southerners experienced increased confusion due to this artillery fire. Nevertheless, Sweeny soon called off the pursuit to re-form his line and get out of range of artillery fire from Battery Powell and Battery Madison south of town. Davies himself was not immune to the friendly fire, writing that "seven or eight of these passed directly over my head, and one very close, brushing my adjutant general, Captain Lovell, on the right arm and raising a contusion." The Confederates retreated en masse, but many dead soldiers remained behind, including Will Ray. His premonition of death had come true; he had fallen in the attack on Battery Powell.[48]

Farther to the west, the Arkansans of Cabell's brigade also had to retreat. Although he reported that the enemy "presented the appearance of men nearly whipped," in actuality, Cabell was the whipped one. He could do nothing but retreat, taking heavy losses as the men of Du Bois's brigade followed up his withdrawal. Du Bois himself described his men regrouping and fighting in the town: "As we fell back we had to fight our way through the street—crossing muskets over the fences to fire at each other." Lieutenant Colonel Hurlbut, exhausted and overheated, was, in his own words, "much affected by the sun and dropped to the ground" during the advance. The counterattack was just about as destructive as the retreat.[49]

During the counterattack, General Davies himself led the troops west of Battery Powell. Obviously recovered from what Rosecrans termed his "perfect panic," Davies seemed to fear nothing and led his men as they retook their lost ground. Perhaps caught up in the moment, he expected everyone else to join in the work. When he came upon a fellow officer who refused to move forward, Davies immediately shot him and ordered a private to look after him, but the private reported him dead. Such firmness helped turn the tide of the Federal rout and helped decide the Battle of Corinth on the Federal right.[50]

It had been a maddening hour or so, and the Confederate legions had gained early success before being thrown back in retreat. Despite the reverse, the day was not totally lost for Van Dorn, who still had two of his three divisions waiting to attack. Green had terribly shaken the Federal line north of Corinth and still had some pockets of soldiers in Corinth itself. It was quite possible that Green could renew his attack if the rest of the army drove the enemy from their fronts. A watching Van Dorn hoped that Maury and Lovell could indeed build on that success and split the enemy army, drive it away, and retake the critical crossroads at Corinth for good.

14

"THE VERY HEART OF CORINTH"

Although the Confederate attack on the left had failed to provide the rout hoped for, Earl Van Dorn still had two more divisions with which to take Corinth. Cabell had done good work in breaking Du Bois's line, and this breach widened the avenue through which the rest of Maury's brigades, by this time attacking to the west of Cabell, could pass into town. Lovell was still on the right and could also force his way into Corinth. The Federal defenses were cracking; the Confederates only had to apply more pressure.[1]

In fact, Maury's brigades had already begun their attacks, only moments after Green's men had gone forward. Van Dorn had originally planned for Green to attack and Maury to move forward when Green had become well engaged. Maury's men, however, became involved with Union skirmishers, and the attack went off before the scheduled time. John C. Moore and Phifer, only a few minutes behind the attack to the left, suddenly came on the scene as Cabell's forward units reached the town. In fact, Phifer, immediately on Cabell's right, took part of his brigade into the gap Cabell had opened by forcing Du Bois to retreat. Moreover, the Confederates exploited the natural gap between Davies's left and Stanley's right. Nothing but unsupported artillery and skirmishers filled this gap, and Phifer's raging troops soon had the best of them. John C. Moore, on Phifer's right and rear, likewise made his way toward Corinth, one member of his brigade recalling, "Marching 250 yards and rising the crest of a hill the whole of Corinth with its enemy fortifications burst upon our view. The US flag was floating over the forts and in the town." Despite the earlier setbacks, the situation still looked promising for Van Dorn.[2]

Maury's brigades initially deployed one behind the other, and Phifer in front engaged in some fighting with enemy skirmishers as they awaited Hébert's attack on their left. But all morning, Maury only waited. Finally, at the same time the roll of musketry erupted on the left and Green made his advance,

Maury also began his assault. Phifer and John C. Moore ordered their men to move forward through the timber and the undulating hills and hollows. A member of the 6th Texas Cavalry (dismounted) later wrote of the attack: "For over a mile down the line my eye could see every flag and regiment. What a sweep, what a blast of noise and death." The pageantry soon ended. The Union line opened up on the charging Confederates but did little damage because of the timber and the cover of the hills. Soon, however, the Confederates broke through the woods and topped a ridge. This proved disastrous, and the damage began to mount as they moved into the open area in front of the Union line. One Texan remembered, "We charged through fallen timber for 150 or 200 yards which broke our lines all to pieces." Moore reported that the musketry was "the severest fire I ever imagined possible to concentrate on one point in front of a fortification." The Confederates nevertheless moved across the open ground covered with felled trees, only to receive more fire from the Union guns. A member of Stirman's Arkansas Sharpshooters remembered, "We had to charge through where timber was fell to prevent us from charging the breastworks, and while we was through that place the Federals had full play on us with their big guns and short arms." Stirman himself recorded, "It was not long until the abatis had broken our line in to fragments, but we kept up the advance." Federal fire took a fierce toll on the oncoming Confederates, but they continued forward, "maintaining the silence of the grave," according to one soldier.[3]

The watching Federals were taken aback by the slaughter. One Union soldier recorded that the Confederates moved forward "steadily and unflinchingly." Captain Oscar Jackson of the 63rd Ohio, just to the right of Battery Robinett, marveled, "I thought they would never stop coming out of the timber." David Stanley was in awe as he watched the developing situation from what he called "the small hill to the right of Battery Robinett." Peering to the northeast, he watched as the Confederates attacked Davies's division across Elam Creek. "As the smoke cleared up I can safely say I could see every fighting man on the field," he remembered. But then his division came under attack: "We were not long left spectators of the fight," Stanley reported. "Soon a line of battle of a brigade crowned the ridge opposite us," he wrote, adding that "their officers rode well to the front, their flags waved gaily and full of defiant confidence."[4]

In command of the brigade defending Battery Robinett and actually inside the redoubt, John Fuller reported that the Confederates "burst simultaneously from the wood north of Corinth and pushed rapidly for the position of the batteries." He could see four distinct columns—one moving down the Chewalla road, two on the east toward Elam Creek, and one west of the road. The one gun of Battery Robinett that faced that direction immediately opened up on the advancing Confederates, each shot causing great swaths in the Confederate lines. The guns inside Battery Williams as well as Battery F of the 2nd U.S. Artillery and Battery F of the 2nd Illinois Artillery to the south also opened up, one soldier reporting, "When our 60 pound howitzers were let off it seemed as if it killed whole companies." One member of the 47th Illinois of Mower's brigade also declared that his unit was soon "pouring a deadly enfilading fire with telling effect." While this transpired, Fuller saw that his brigade and the little fort defended by Lieutenant Henry Robinett had become the enemy's major target. He also saw that his line, in the position now taken, was open to the Confederates; there was no effective defense as it now stood. To remedy this fault, Fuller made several changes in his deployment. He ordered the 11th Missouri, positioned behind Battery Robinett, to move by the right flank and proceed to a point directly behind Colonel John W. Sprague's 63rd Ohio, which Fuller saw as the concentration point of the Confederate attack. He also ordered them to charge if the front regiment broke. Major Andrew J. Weber, commanding the 11th Missouri, moved to within twenty-five yards of the prone 63rd Ohio and ordered his men to lie down. Fuller also ordered the 43rd Ohio, on the left of Robinett, to wheel to the right and therefore face toward the north. This position allowed them to face the Confederate line as it attacked Battery Robinett.[5]

Fortunately for the Federals, the changes took place quickly as the Confederates neared the Union line, still in dead silence. As the moments passed, the firing in this sector intensified. Fuller ran along the lines of the 63rd and 27th Ohio, steadying the men, who could see the Confederates coming closer. One officer of the 63rd Ohio told his men, "We own the ground behind us. The enemy may go over us but all the rebels yonder can't drive Company H back." He also reminded his men that if all else failed, they could still use their bayonets.[6]

Although badly damaged by the Union artillery, the Confederates still advanced. One of the officers shouted, "Give it to the scoundrels" and then fell wounded by a shell from one of the enemy's guns. The 6th Texas Cavalry, ahead of the other columns, was the first Southern unit to reach the Union line. Many of its officers went down, and one member of the regiment described Captain T. A. Norfleet's death: he was "shot dead—a ball entering his forehead just above one of the eyes." L. H. Graves then took command of the company and led it forward with a pistol in one hand and a sword in the other. But he was soon hit as well, balls entering his chest and thigh.[7]

Right in the middle of the fight, Captain Oscar Jackson's black servant, Old Mose, remained near the officer. Jackson told him to go to the rear to

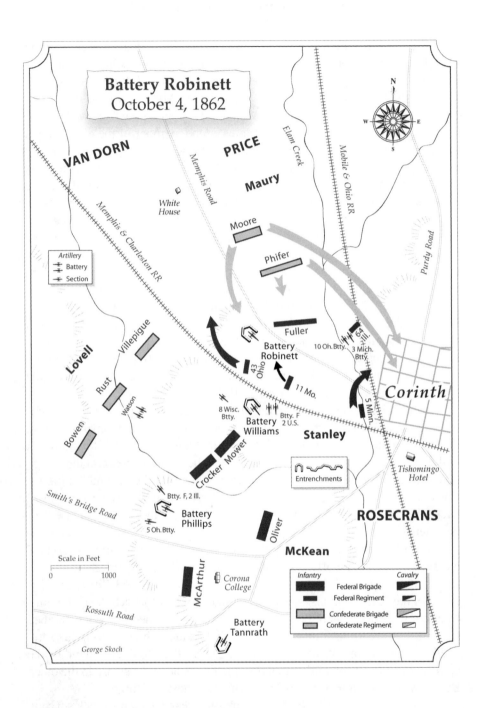

Battery Robinett
October 4, 1862

VAN DORN

PRICE

Maury

Elam Creek

Memphis Road

Mobile & Ohio RR

White House

Moore

Phifer

Purdy Road

Artillery
—⊢⊢— Battery
—⊢— Section

Memphis & Charleston RR

Fuller

Villepigue

64 Ill.

10 Oh. Btty.

3 Mich. Btty.

Lovell

Rust

Battery Robinett

43 Ohio

Corinth

Watson

11 Mo.

Bowen

5 Minn.

8 Wisc. Btty.

Battery Williams

Btty. F 2 U.S.

Stanley

Crocker   Mower

Entrenchments

Tishomingo Hotel

Btty. F, 2 Ill.

ROSECRANS

Battery Phillips

Oliver

5 Oh. Btty.

McKean

Scale in Feet

0   1000

McArthur

Corona College

Kossuth Road

Infantry		Cavalry	
	Federal Brigade		
	Federal Regiment		
	Confederate Brigade		
	Confederate Regiment		

Battery Tannrath

George Skoch

safety and pointed out a log. Jackson had in mind for Old Mose to get behind the log, but the servant seated himself on it instead. "A piece of shell struck the log between his legs and would have cut one of them off if it had hit it," Jackson recalled. Old Mose calmly muttered, "This fellow better git to the other side ob de log," and rolled backward "like a turtle." When fire also came from that direction, Old Mose popped up and shouted, "Hard to tell which side ob dis log better to be at."[8]

When the lead column of the 6th Texas Cavalry, with the 42nd Alabama, 2nd Texas, and 35th Mississippi of Moore's brigade on their right, came up the hill to within 100 yards of the Federal line, the 63rd Ohio and portions of the left of the 27th Ohio rose from their prone positions and fired. The 43rd Ohio west of the fort was also firing rapidly. "The head of the column almost instantly disappeared," Fuller wrote, "and the rear recoiled rapidly to the edge of the woods." Captain Jackson of the 63rd Ohio recalled that "their column appeared to reel like a rope shaken at the end." Many of the Ohioans did not know whether their fire had taken effect, but after the smoke cleared, they saw what one member of the brigade described as "a mass of struggling bodies." A member of the watching 39th Ohio down the line recalled, "The Johnnies seemed very determined and held their line remarkably well for a time but before they got more than half way across the cleared space they wavered and broke for the cover of the wood." Before they did, the Southerners fired at the Union line, but it was erratic and hit mostly the ground in front of the Ohio regiments, "knocking the dirt and chips all over us," one soldier recalled. The 27th Ohio then charged the Confederates, continuing to fire all the while. Those Texans that remained recoiled from the "swarm of Yankees" charging them and fled to the edge of the woods. "Every fellow went as it suited him," Captain Jackson wrote, "and it appeared to suit all to go fast."[9]

One member of Fuller's brigade remembered that, amazingly, "comparative silence reigned for a time." But not everyone had a break. One Confederate participating in the first charge was trapped in no-man's-land and faced musketry from almost every direction. "I was right between our own and the enemies fire," he remembered. "I had to endure it all." The Confederates were soon back, however. The 6th Texas Cavalry re-formed and charged again, this time joined by other units of Phifer's brigade. The Texans, Alabamians, and Mississippians of Moore's brigade also came on again. Once more, the Ohioans drove them back. A 39th Ohio private, watching the action to his left, recalled, "This time the rebs held their formation and course a little longer and got about two thirds of the way." The 63rd Ohio's assistant surgeon was caught up in the excitement, later writing to his wife, "Our regiment repelled two charges of bayonets made by superior numbers and repelled them successfully." But it took a toll. The surgeon reported that the 63rd Ohio lost more men than any other Federal regiment that day. Fuller, behind the lines, reported that he could plainly see the Confederates, as if the thinned 63rd Ohio's line did not exist. Nine of the thirteen line officers were down in that regiment. The stout Ohioans had held, but they could hardly stand another assault. And another one looked likely, since the enemy had re-formed and seemed intent on attacking again. The critical moments of the fight at Battery Robinett had arrived.[10]

While Phifer's men made their attacks on the 63rd and 27th Ohio, John C. Moore's brigade moved forward to their right and left. Three regiments of Moore's brigade—the 42nd Alabama, 35th Mississippi, and 2nd Texas—made their way toward Battery Robinett to the right, rolling over an enemy company sent to hold a pair of guns in advance of the fort. While the 63rd Ohio was battling the Texans of Phifer's brigade, the 43rd Ohio poured an extremely deadly fire into the Confederates west of the fort, which halted them for a while. The battle-hardened Confederates charged again in concert with Phifer's men to the east, but like the last time, they had to fall back. Each time, a period of a few minutes passed as the battered Confederates regrouped and prepared to charge again. Sharpshooters took to the stumps during the lull and pestered the Federal line, and Captain Jackson complained that something needed to be done about them because "the fellow wanted a Colonel or a General and I feared he might take a Captain." Jackson did not have long to worry, however, because another Confederate advance soon began. The Southerners, led by Colonel William P. Rogers, who had served in Jefferson Davis's Mexican War regiment, made one last desperate attempt at the fort, and one Federal marveled that "they rushed like demons at the fort, crossing the ditch and scaling the walls as if by superhuman dexterity." Rogers, with flag in hand and still atop his white charger, led the men toward the ditch and finally reached it. The 42nd Alabama and 2nd Texas jumped the ditch and made it to the parapet but could go no farther. All the while, the 43rd Ohio continued its deadly fire.[11]

The walls of the fort were too high to climb, so the Confederates made their way to the embrasures, trying to enter there. The men of Company C, 1st U.S. Infantry, manning the big guns, saw that the enemy was about to take their fort and resorted to a last-ditch effort. Taking up their rifles, the men fought the Confederates hand to hand. A member of the 1st U.S. Infantry ironically wrote home that his unit had trained as foot soldiers (they were infantry, after all) for one and a half hours every morning. Their training paid off. The

43rd Ohio also fought hand to hand, and Colonel Kirby Smith and his adjutant fell in the melee. Smith was shot in the face, nearly duplicating the wound his father had received in the Mexican War. Only days before, Smith had confided to Stanley, "I want to go into one fight where there is a storm of bullets, just to see how I can behave." Unfortunately, he got his wish. The Federal defense proved successful for a while, but the Confederates found ways to climb the parapet, overpowered the small band of artillerymen, and entered the battery. John C. Moore reported that the color-bearer of the 23rd Arkansas was "last seen . . . going over the breastworks waving a piece over his head and shouting for the Southern Confederacy."[12]

The 43rd Ohio responded by changing its front again, moving slightly to the left and re-fusing its right to direct some of its fire toward Robinett. While doing this, the regiment temporarily fell apart. Because it had lost its colonel, General Stanley himself directed the regiment. Stanley's assistant adjutant general, Captain W. D. Coleman, fell in the effort. After participating in and living through all the bloody battles of Winfield Scott's campaign during the Mexican War, he fell on the fields of Corinth. Despite the loss of his staffer, Stanley succeeded in re-forming the Ohioans, and when regrouped, they faced eastward toward Robinett and let out a terrific fire, cutting down many of the enemy who remained on their side of the fort.[13]

As the fighting continued to intensify, more Confederates began to make their way over the parapet of the redoubt. Still on his horse and holding on to the regiment's flag, Colonel Rogers pushed his men onward. The soldiers responded to Rogers's leadership with a loud cheer and burst forward to renew the attack. But the charge began to peter out due to the thinness of the command and the regrouping Federals. Still, the Confederates had reached the fort.[14]

While the battle for Battery Robinett was taking place, Captain George A. Williams, commanding the 1st U.S. Artillery at Battery Williams, threw two shells into Robinett. One officer indicated that "all our batteries were so arranged as to be brought to bear on one given point," and that forethought aided the Federals. One shell burst directly on top of the fort, and the other exploded on the right side of the work. One Federal watching through field glasses declared, "Fragments of the wretched victims could be seen twenty feet in the air." In the close-order fighting at the fort itself, Lieutenant Robinett fell wounded, and many of his regulars were also cut down, thirteen of twenty-six being killed or wounded. The remaining artillerymen, now reverted to infantrymen, had taken up their muskets and were fighting through the embrasures. Eventually, they gathered "into the angle of the fort," Williams wrote, "as they had been directed to do in such an emergency." Others nearby on the left also

watched as the dramatic fight for the redoubt unfolded. One Federal remembered that the Texans "came clear over into the fort," and the "colonel of the
regiment planted their flag on our fort." Another was amazed to see "men using
their bayonets like pitch forks, and thrusting each other through." Apparently,
soldiers of the idle 39th Ohio had been asked to come to the assistance of Battery Robinett, one soldier recalling, "We were gladly and willing to obey." He
remembered, "There were numbers of men knocked down with fists and butts
of muskets and tramped to death." The writer himself received "one trifling
scratch on the back of his hand made by a bayonet."[15]

While portions of John C. Moore's brigade partially broke through at Robinett on this third assault, Phifer's brigade also broke the Union line to the east.
The 63rd Ohio, sorely hurt by the first two Confederate charges, endured even
more destruction from the flank fire delivered by the Confederates who had
taken hold at Battery Robinett. The left of the 63rd Ohio responded by refusing their wing and firing at the Confederates near the redoubt. This volley
filled the ditch in front of Robinett with Confederates, but it failed to stop the
flank fire. Moreover, while the regiment took fire from the left flank, the third
charge of Phifer's brigade hit the Ohioans' front. The left of the Ohio regiment retreated, passing through the line of the 11th Missouri. Now that they
were the front line, the Missourians stood at their position and promptly
received another staggering volley from the Confederates.[16]

Phifer's brigade, meanwhile, had also driven the left flank of the 27th Ohio
back. That regiment, which had charged earlier, found that its left flank was
wide open to the 9th Texas Cavalry (dismounted). One of its members wrote
a few days later that "the rifle balls war as thick as hale and the shot and shell
jist as thick." Major Zephaniah Spaulding ordered his left to fall back to a line
with the 11th Missouri, but before doing so, they engaged in hand-to-hand
combat with the enemy. In that encounter, Orrin B. Gould shot and killed the
color-bearer of the 9th Texas Cavalry and then sprang forward to take the colors; however, the Texans' commander ordered his Southerners to save the flag.
Gould took the colors anyway, but he was wounded in the process. Later,
when Fuller visited Gould in the hospital, the boy pointed to his wound and
said, "Colonel, I don't care for this, since I got their flag." Unfortunately,
Gould later died, but Fuller sent the flag to the governor, who posthumously
promoted Gould to captain. Despite this act of bravery, part of the 27th Ohio
had to fall back.[17]

With no sign of Lovell at this point, the Confederate surge began to falter.
Phifer's brigade had broken the line to the east of Robinett, and a handful of
John C. Moore's men had moved into the fort itself. Stanley later admitted,
"At this period the fight was close and doubtful." But that was the high-water

mark for the Confederates on the ridge west of Corinth. The 11th Missouri, which was now under control, stood its ground and halted the Confederate advance with the bayonet. The 27th Ohio, just to the right of the 11th Missouri, re-formed its line in conjunction with the Missourians. This new line effectively stopped the Confederate surge there as well, but only after brutal hand-to-hand combat. Over at Robinett itself, the Confederates were facing terrifying slaughter. The fire of the 43rd Ohio and 1st U.S. Infantry proved enough to halt the Confederates on the parapets of the battery. One Federal described the destruction: "The rebels' dead just outside the fort lay three or four deep and the blood ran in streams down the trenches."[18]

With the Confederate advance faltering, a short lull fell over the field. But then, like the divisions to the east, the Union regiments quickly counterattacked to retake the fort and the original line. Fuller ordered the 11th Missouri and the 27th Ohio, along with the regrouped 63rd Ohio and the 39th Ohio to the right, to charge the Confederates that held the line. A dismounted General Stanley himself encouraged the 11th Missouri, literally pushing the men forward with his arms. As they made their way toward the fort, the Federals topped a small rise, where they saw the Confederates near the wall of the fort. Colonel Rogers, seeing his helpless position, told the soldiers gathered nearby, "Men, save yourselves, or sell your lives as dear as possible." He also ordered a soldier to give him a ramrod on which he could place his handkerchief. The soldier quickly obeyed, and Rogers waved the handkerchief to indicate his surrender. Some near the parapet did likewise, but other Confederates around the fort did not see it. They simply saw the enemy and let out a volley. The Federal units responded to this fire, and the party near Robinett quickly fell. Rogers himself, despite body armor, suffered eleven wounds. He became the last of his regiment's many color-bearers to fall that day.[19]

The fire that killed Rogers and the others at Robinett was only part of the Federal countercharge. Despite the loss of Colonel A. W. Gilbert, who was thrown from his horse and dazed, the 39th Ohio attacked the Confederates "with a yell that would have scared the devil," one soldier remembered, and forced them to give ground without firing another shot. The other regiments picked up the attack on their fronts. The charge of the 11th Missouri took part of that regiment into Battery Robinett itself. One Federal related, "Our motto was victory or death, and our brave boys stuck to the motto most determinably." Another dubbed the charge "one of the most brilliant affairs of the war." Stanley himself reported that the hill was "cleared in an instant," while another stated that the Confederate lines "melted like snow." Many of the Southerners threw down their weapons and "called for quarter." The Federal charge succeeded in retaking all the lost territory and sent the confused and disorganized Confederates fumbling to the rear, leaving their dead and wounded. As the Confederates fled for cover, the 11th Missouri fired its first shots, which, as one soldier recalled, "piled the ground with his [the enemy's] killed and wounded."[20]

The attack on Battery Robinett, like that on the Confederate left, was a brief one. By this time, both Green's and Maury's attacks had petered out. Only one assault was still having success, although amazingly, it was not Lovell's. He had not yet launched his attack on the Federal left. The one attack that was still moving forward consisted of the left wing of John C. Moore's brigade and a like portion of Phifer's men, whose advance carried them east of Fuller's line. The 39th Ohio had received orders to move left and look out for a flank attack on the right of the brigade, but the Confederates did not attack Stanley's flank. Rather, they continued toward Corinth, flowing into the gap between Davies's left and Stanley's right. The right wing of the 39th Ohio nevertheless bent back at right angles to the rest of the regiment and fired into the mass of Confederates in the valley of Elam Creek.[21]

Initially, only a small group of skirmishers, part of the 64th Illinois, and two batteries covered the gap. Du Bois's brigade had at one time faced this area with part of the command, but Cabell's attack had forced the Illinois troops to concentrate on their front and then retreat, leaving the defense of the gap to the skirmishers. The infantry and artillery in the valley did good work for a time, however. The 3rd Michigan Battery and 10th Ohio Battery, with the aid of Battery F of the 2nd U.S. Artillery just outside Battery Williams, repelled one attack by the Confederates, but the undaunted Southerners regrouped and came on again. A soldier of the 39th Ohio watching from the high ground near Battery Robinett could hardly believe his eyes. Obviously exaggerating, he described the Confederates moving forward "perhaps sixteen deep." He went on to describe how "the shells from our battery made complete roads through them. You could see the poor fellows throw up their arms and leap into the air, and fall down." But by this time, Cabell had forced Du Bois back, and the 10th Ohio Battery had to retreat. That battery limbered up, still intact. Lieutenant Carl A. Lamberg, commanding the 3rd Michigan Battery, had no such opportunity. By the time he realized that his right flank was entirely open and the Confederates had begun another charge, he could do nothing but order canister fire by the double load. Lamberg ordered his limbers to the rear and retreated at the last possible moment, leaving the guns. The skirmishers then likewise retreated, one member of the 64th Illinois remembering that they "did not leave until the battery was taken and our front was behind us." The Confederates caught up with the infantry, however, and hand-to-hand fighting ensued. But the skirmishers were no match for the Confederates and melted in front of the attack. With the batteries silenced and the infantry on the flank taken care of by Cabell, the men of John C. Moore's and Phifer's brigades moved toward the town.[22]

Rosecrans later stated that he "had the personal mortification of witnessing this untoward and untimely stampede." His hat fell to the ground, but the general remained, shouting for his men to stand firm for the nation. Stanley asserted that he cursed his men, "for which he afterward made some amends." But it helped. Rosecrans picked a good time to stem the tide because the Confederates, with the door wide open, were stampeding across the railroad and Elam Creek toward town. And, as John C. Moore recalled, they "penetrated to the very heart of Corinth." A distraught Federal wrote that "the rebels broke through the center of our line and reached the main street in town." A surgeon was concerned about his patients: "My hospital which was about half a mile on the east side was in great danger from the fire of both armies, the rebels approached within a half mile of it." Once in town, Moore's men met the remnants of Cabell's brigade and Green's division, which had also made it into Corinth minutes earlier.[23]

Maury's attack occurred soon after Green's assault, and together, the units made their way farther into Corinth "with a desperation seldom paralleled," one soldier stated. There they found themselves confronted by small bands of Union troops, disorganized from their retreat on the left. One Federal teamster, in fact, reported that he came to the "public square" in Corinth and met "large numbers of the infantry of Davies's division who had broken and were retreating before the enemy." Another declared that an officer, whom he later claimed to be Rosecrans himself, told him to burn the wagons, as the day was lost. The teamster refused, but he set to building a line of wagons south of town for the withdrawing troops to rally behind. The Confederates drove these small bands through the streets of Corinth, fighting small and isolated battles all the way. Cavalry squads were also on hand, trying to stop the flight of the infantry and halt the Confederate advance. Hand-to-hand fighting erupted in the very yard of Rosecrans's headquarters and in numerous other positions within Corinth. The Federals, unable to muster a line that could stop the Confederates, fell back from house to house. The Southerners drove them back, one soldier remembered, "frequently firing in at the windows and driving them out." The Confederate surge finally reached downtown, and units reported taking horses at the Corinth House. Others made their way to the depot and the crossroads of the railroads and, according to Stirman, rode out horses that had been tied at the Tishomingo Hotel. A brave few even crossed the railroads and planted their colors on the porch of the hotel. All of them fought inside Corinth, one Southerner remembered, "trusting to greet there Lovell's Command equally successful on the opposite side."[24]

The Confederate surge, which Maury later claimed included such high-ranking officers as Maury himself and Phifer, took an undeterminable section of the town. John C. Moore reported that his men "brought off two or three horses which they found hitched in the streets near the Corinth House, their owners being absent." One staff officer later wrote to Beauregard, who was, of course, familiar with the town: "Our division obtained the ground from the Tishomingo Hotel, back of Bragg's old headquarters, and nearly to the house where Major Smith had his quarters. Hébert [Green] was on our left and occupied the works on the ridge northwest from your house." Artilleryman Captain Tobin, who had been captured earlier that morning, related that the Confederate surge "penetrated to the Corinth House and the Tishomingo House and to the square in front of General Bragg's old headquarters and into the yard of General Rosecrans's headquarters." Even some Federals were amazed, John Pray of an Illinois battery writing, "They charged write through the town."[25]

Unfortunately for Van Dorn, by the time the lead troops reached the Tishomingo Hotel, the Confederate drive had lost its power. The attack had spread out over such an extensive area that there were few large groups of Confederates to withstand the counterattack the Federals were already organizing. A captain of the 50th Illinois posted the colors, telling his bearer, "Sergeant hold the colors and I will stand by you while I live." He was immediately shot down. The Confederate surge also weakened as soldiers took in the delicacies they found in town. One Federal, in fact, recorded in his diary that "more than 100 [Confederates] were captured in the bakeries and stores." Thus, when the Federal counterattack began, a Southern officer admitted, "Our lines melted under their fire like snow in thaw."[26]

The 5th Minnesota was one of the many regiments that aided in halting the Confederate surge. That regiment, called some of the "best troops" in the army by its commander, had held a reserve position at the edge of town. The Minnesotans had deployed close to town the night before, and they were the only soldiers west of Corinth who could get to the Confederates. The regiment's commander, Lucius Hubbard, wrote to his aunt, "Our troops became scattered and retreated in confusion, leaving a gap in our lines several hundred yards in length, through which the enemy boldly pushed and in large numbers entered the streets of Corinth." When they saw the enemy charge through the gap, the men of the 5th Minnesota moved to support the two batteries in the valley. Before they could do so, the Confederates took the position, so the 5th Minnesota formed a line facing east. To one of its members, "It seemed at one time as though all was lost." But the regiment lay in such a way that the Confederates had to move directly across the Minnesotans' line of fire to get farther into town. As the Confederates moved southward, the 5th Minnesota on their right flank "poured into them a dozen volleys in rapid succession, which terribly decimated their ranks," Hubbard wrote. The Minnesotans took some fire as well; according to one member, "The bullets were falling as thick as hail." Hubbard continued: "They fought desperately to break through the position I had taken, but my gallant boys would not give an inch." The regiment's division commander was also impressed. Stanley reported, "Few regiments on the field did more effective killing than they." He added, referring to the men's less than stellar performance during the siege the spring before, "If they lost their feathers on May 28, they have recovered them now."[27]

Portions of the 22nd Ohio supported the fire of the 5th Minnesota. That regiment of Mersy's brigade had performed guard duty in Corinth throughout the battle on October 3, having been split up in and about Corinth. Two companies performed duty around the Corinth House, which lay in the direct line of the Confederate advance. When these two companies saw the Confederates coming, they immediately formed a line and poured a destructive fire into the head of the enemy advance. Portions of the 64th Illinois, falling back into town before the Confederate surge, also fired into the charging Southerners. In addition, there were "batteries in mask" to deal death blows to the Confederates, although one of these mistakenly fired into the Yates Sharpshooters. One captain in the regiment reported that artillery fire from the rear created "greater havoc among our skirmishers than the enemy." A section of the 12th Wisconsin Battery and the regrouped 10th Ohio Battery also poured a destructive fire into the Confederates. Finally, idle soldiers around town added to the group making a defense.[28]

Although the Confederate thrust slowly came to a halt, many Southerners had penetrated the town. All they needed was support from others for the victory to remain in their grasp; there was still time for Lovell to press his attack and force his way into Corinth from the west. If so, the two groups of Confederates could unite and hold Corinth, attack the re-formed Union lines in the rear, or support new attacks in sectors where the initial attacks had failed. Lovell was the key, however, and without his help, the Confederates could not hold what they had gained, much less defeat the enemy.

Unfortunately for the Confederates, Lovell did not advance, and the Confederates who had battled their way into Corinth were left unsupported. One soldier in the division reported to his parents, "We laid down while Genl. Price was on our left hotly engaged. I think it was the intention for us to charge but by some means we did not do it." A Missourian went so far as to erroneously record, "Lovell hung back, and failed to burst a cap." That assertion is wrong, but the sentiment is clear. Because of Lovell's neglect, some Confederate units had to go it alone. And the chance for success soon passed. The Federals had already begun to drive the enemy away, and the Confederates saw their hopes dashed. Without Lovell's aid, the Confederates had no chance to turn their small victory into a triumph for the entire army. Moreover, it seemed that those units in Corinth would be sacrificed. The troops had fought their way into the town, but since they received no support, they would have to fight their way back out. One officer noted that the troops in town began to have "the sickening feeling, the prostrating conviction that they were unsupported."[29]

"To advance further was impossible," one Southerner in Corinth remembered. "To stand their ground was but ingloriously to die; to retire was the mournful necessity." The Confederates in Corinth did not have an easy time retiring, however. The 5th Minnesota still tore at their flanks, and the two companies of the 22nd Ohio charged their front, driving them back. The Southerners fought back the best they could, but their ranks were amazingly thin. Many were wounded, others had fallen captive, and most had used up all their ammunition. Those who could get out made their way toward the northern edge of town, one dejected soldier commenting on the hard-won territory: "We had to give [it] back."[30]

Nearing the northern edge of town, the 22nd Ohio, now concentrated into eight companies, and about 700 troops of other scattered regiments pursued the Confederates northward. The 5th Minnesota, coming in from the left, also joined in, Colonel Hubbard reporting that his men "kept close upon their heels for a distance of fifty rods, recapturing the battery the rebels had taken." There, the 5th Minnesota stopped and re-formed the original line. The batteries did not stop firing. They continued to shell the enemy, who "fell back in disorder, but sullenly," until they entered the woods across the way. It was not yet 11:00 A.M.[31]

The Battle of Corinth had ended. In a little more than one hour, certainly less than two, the Confederate attack, which Maury claimed consisted of only 9,000 men, had taken place and ended in defeat. The Confederate armies had performed well in their attempts to capture the inner line of Union fortifications, however. They accomplished this goal in all sectors, but at no place could the tired Southerners hold their gains.[32]

There were many reasons why the Confederates could not take advantage of their successes of October 4. The men had simply become too weary and hungry to withstand the force of the Union counterattacks. By the time the attacks reached their peak, many of the officers had fallen. Most of the troops had also run out of ammunition. But Van Dorn could have overcome several of these serious flaws. Had he established a tactical reserve, the preliminary Confederate victories might have grown into more substantial gains. He also did a poor job of reconnaissance. Totally unaware of the inner line of Federal works, his troops were surprised and no doubt intimidated when they finally saw them at daylight on October 4.[33]

Blame for the defeat cannot be placed on Van Dorn alone, however. During any of the attacks on October 4, an assault by Mansfield Lovell could have changed the situation, but he did not attack as ordered. Lovell had moved his division forward on time and lay poised to attack, but he never did. One Union soldier summed up the fighting on Lovell's front: "As soon as the Rebels opened out with their battery, our artillery opened out along the whole line and they soon quit." "Outside of the skirmishers not a volley had been fired," one of Lovell's men remembered, although Daniel Miller of the 21st Missouri reported that "the rebel sharpshooters were in trees across from our fort and wounded several. A cannoneer fell within our very fort."[34]

Bowen became somewhat engaged, but not enough to consider it a fight. Without orders to do so, he did not attack. "Nearly mad with impatience at what he considered infamous inaction," one Missourian remembered, Bowen tried unsuccessfully to hurry staff officers to obtain orders to assault. He and his command, both "panting for the order to charge," were forced to remain mere spectators. Bowen took some initiative on his own, however. Having been told that the forts contained only a few cannon, he decided to see for himself. He had a small encounter with the enemy's guns when he reconnoitered the Union position. This engagement brought a quick response from the Federals across the way, and Bowen, "under a blinding shower of shot and shell," according to one of his soldiers, realized he faced quite a few Federals. He was "answered by a terrific cannonade from the right, left, and front," Bowen noted, "convincing me that the information given that there were only three guns at this point was erroneous, as I had thus developed at least twenty."[35]

Rust did not become engaged either, although some of his men maneuvered through their old campsites of the past spring. Unlike his comrade in Gates's brigade, Albert Goodloe's premonition of his death had little chance of coming true. Likewise, Villepigue became involved in only a small skirmish that made it necessary to change his front slightly. Beyond these actions, the division did not enter the fight. Corresponding reports from McKean's division corroborate that little fighting took place. They mainly mention the enemy's attempt to use a ravine to move near the Union lines and good work by the extreme left regiment, the 16th Wisconsin, in holding the flank.[36]

Lovell's actions are shrouded in uncertainty, but it is clear that he did not lead his division well. Van Dorn made excuses for him, writing in his report that Lovell was "on the point of assaulting the works" when he was called back. Others were not so kind. One of Price's staff officers correctly opined that "an assault upon College Fort was essential both to security and to hope." He blamed the delay on Lovell's West Point education, focused on methodology and preparation, in comparison to his own boss's swaggering attacks: "An assault upon College Fort was not in accordance with West Point tactics, and Genl. Lovell prudently abstained from making the desperate and bloody effort." Apparently, Lovell was not even on the front line; Bowen reported that he sent "three messages to General Lovell, stating our position and urging his presence." A Missourian stated that Lovell "remained in a safe place at a respectable distance from danger."[37]

By the time Price's retreat began, Lovell finally arrived at the front. He seemed prepared to attack then, but orders to retreat stopped him. By that time, an assault would have been useless and suicidal, and all knew it. One of Lovell's staff officers asked Bowen about the chances of taking the enemy works now that Price had fallen back. Bowen retorted that "the opportunity had been lost." The staffer then pressed the Missourian, asking, "Suppose General Lovell orders you to take it?" Bowen replied, "My brigade will march up and be killed."[38]

Lovell made no excuse for his inactivity, stating only that he had engaged in "reconnoitering these [Federal] positions with a view to the assault." Of course, that assault never came. But the stain of inaction did, both for the men of Price's Corps who had not received the help ordered by Van Dorn and for Lovell's own troops. One of Lovell's Missouri men wrote almost apologetically, "Price's men were making their bloody fight, and the aid of every man was needed. The whole command panting for the order to charge, were left to stand and gaze and listen to the thunder of the conflict raging near them." He added, "The noble attack of the Missourians, elsewhere made, was allowed to fail for want of timely cooperation."[39]

Despite Lovell's later assertions that he had "no reason to be dissatisfied with the part that my troops took in the battle, and think that the official reports will do me full justice," his inaction cost the Confederates at least the chance of victory. It is likely, as has been argued by many historians, that Lovell's attack would have been no more successful than the others on October 4. Whether the attack would have succeeded is less relevant (except in terms of its human cost) than the main issue: the order he was given. Lovell was supposed to attack, just like everyone else. It was not up to him to decide whether to obey; it was his duty to do so. James Longstreet at Gettysburg did not agree with the so-called Pickett's Charge, but he made the attempt. History would look much differently on Longstreet today had he not even tried. Besides, there was a slight chance the attack could have succeeded. There is no way to tell, and although the chances are very good that Lovell's men would have been slaughtered like Price's, the Missionary Ridge effect is always in the back of the mind: No one thought it would succeed. Everyone thought it was suicidal. But it worked.[40]

W ithout an advance by Lovell, and realizing the uselessness of further bloodshed, Van Dorn ordered his beaten army to retreat. He would lead them to safer pastures. But he realized what a terrible fight it had been, calling Corinth "the bloodiest [battle] I ever saw of the fourteen I have been in." The retreat was grueling in itself; Federal artillerymen kept firing at the Confederates as long as they could see them in the expanse between the recovered Union lines and the belt of timber offering safety. "The work of destruction still continues," one Union soldier wrote in his diary. "Our batteries continue their terrible fire, and hundreds of rebels fall before their death hail."[41]

As Van Dorn and Price (whom one soldier described as "lingering with the rearmost files") sat atop their horses watching the beaten army straggle back, they were touched with "sorrow and pity." Van Dorn knew his army was shattered, and he had lost two close staff members during the battle: young Clement Sullivane had been captured, and J. D. Balfour had been killed outright. Price, almost beside himself, looked on with "unmitigated anguish." He could only cry, Maury remembered. "The big tears coursed down the old man's bronzed face" as he watched his boys stream back in defeat. Above the cry of the wounded and the sound of footsteps, he cried in agony, "My boys are running! . . . How could they do otherwise—they had no support—they are nearly all killed!" Van Dorn tried to comfort him, but Price could only point toward Corinth and weep.[42]

Given the catastrophe developing around him, Van Dorn had to think of a way to avoid further disaster. He had to hold Rosecrans's army in place until he could get his troops on the road to Chewalla. To do this, he placed the only semicoherent body of troops he had left, Lovell's almost fresh division, in the path of the expected Union pursuit. Maury reported sarcastically that Lovell was "in fine order; they had done no fighting." When the order to move to the left arrived, Lovell seemed disturbed, stating, "I've got a good position here, and I can whip anything that comes out of Corinth." Nevertheless, Lovell followed the order and quickly fell back from his strong position.[43]

With his center broken and nothing but shattered units standing between him and the Federals, Van Dorn ordered Lovell to send his strongest brigade to Price's center. Lovell did so, sending Villepigue, who marched his brigade to the left. Villepigue made his way over the Memphis and Charleston Railroad and formed across Price's center between Elam and Turner Creeks. The victorious Federals saw this as another formation for attack, but Van Dorn contemplated no such action. The Mississippian had ordered Villepigue to the center solely to protect Price's Corps, but he achieved the complete opposite effect. The Federals, perceiving another threat and preparing to meet it, seemed of no mind to follow the retreating Confederates. Only cavalry tested the line, and one of Villepigue's batteries soon dispersed them. Thus, Villepigue's movement gave Van Dorn the time he needed to extract his army from danger.[44]

With the rear covered, "a second retreat from Corinth was begun," according to one Confederate soldier. Many of these same troops had been with Beauregard when he evacuated in May. Now they were retreating again. Moreover, this was the second retreat of the fall; most of the Confederate army had marched with Price as he left Iuka. The Confederates had lost again.[45]

Van Dorn still had the remainder of Lovell's fresh division at his disposal, however, so he ordered them back two miles to Cane Creek, where they could cover the flanks and act as a second line of defense if the Federals pursued. Obviously, Van Dorn had to retreat the same way he had come into Corinth, having left his wagon train between the rivers. Lovell received the order just as he closed the gap created by Villepigue's removal. Under this new order, his men marched to the rear "without the slightest confusion and in the most excellent order," Lovell boasted. Bowen took a position at Cane Creek, with Rust to the front on the hill the troops had carried the day before. A regiment of Bowen's brigade, the 1st Missouri under Lieutenant Colonel A. C. Riley, moved forward as skirmishers for both brigades. The 2nd Mississippi Cavalry, under Lovell, also covered the exposed western flank. There, the men of Lovell's division waited as the torn remnants of Price's Corps began marching past.[46]

Price's battered corps went to the rear as soon as Lovell's men took their positions. Because they were almost leaderless due to the staggering number of casualties among the officers, Price's men made their way rearward with little organization. They were also nearing exhaustion due to two days of fighting and a lack of food and water. The men expressed mixed feelings as they retreated. One soldier believed they could still whip the Federals. "They can't do anything for us out of their breast works," he mused. Another felt thankful he had survived the battle. Writing to his parents, he warned them not to worry about his safety. "A person who has passed through Shiloh and Corinth surely will die a natural death," he told them. But not all were so fortunate. One Confederate described a lieutenant of the 37th Alabama who had been wounded the day before and had his arm amputated: the man was marching as "calm and undisturbed as if nothing had occurred to ruffle his mind or cause him bodily pain." The officer, with his sleeveless shirt, even whistled "Dixie." At least one officer was impressed with the bloodied but still defiant Missourians falling back: Villepigue exclaimed, "Magnificent! Magnificent! With an hundred thousand such men I could fight my way across Europe."[47]

Obviously, the Missourians were less interested in fighting across Europe than in getting away from Corinth safely. The troops thus moved as ordered and made their way solemnly to the rear, taking the same road that had brought them forward with such high hopes. Green got word to move the division back across the Mobile and Ohio Railroad, but before he could do so, more orders arrived telling him to march up the road until he received further directions. Maury likewise received orders to march his division on the road toward Chewalla.[48]

As the dilapidated units of Price's command marched past, Lovell brought up the rear, keeping a wary eye on the Federals. Seeing no more action in his front, Villepigue formed his brigade and marched toward Chewalla behind Price. When that brigade passed Rust's position, Bowen's brigade and the 1st Missouri likewise formed and marched out, joining Villepigue's men. But the march was slow, "very much annoyed and delayed by the wagons," Bowen reported. Rust's unit, the only one left on the field, waited "exactly forty minutes," he recalled, and then formed and moved toward Chewalla, acting as rear guard for the entire army. He brought out a few wounded that had been left in field hospitals along the way.[49]

The Confederate army's progress on the afternoon of October 4 was slow. It retreated only partway to Chewalla; some bivouacked there, while the rest camped at points along the road. Desperate for sleep and rest, the troops lay down and took advantage of the respite. At least one officer questioned why they did not move a few more miles and put the Tuscumbia or even the Hatchie River between them and the enemy, but Van Dorn himself called the halt at Chewalla. Fortunately for the beaten army, few Federals pursued, so the Confederates were able to enjoy their rest. They would need it.[50]

15

"A Second Retreat"

The Battle of Corinth ended so abruptly that it caught everyone by surprise, and the suddenly victorious Union commanders were at a loss as to what to do next. Some thought the quiet was only a lull and the Confederates would renew their attacks in the afternoon. Others hoped they had wounded the Confederate army severely and wanted to pursue and destroy what was left of it. Rosecrans developed plans for a pursuit, but he was in no hurry. He realized that Van Dorn's army still posed a threat, and word from the front lines verified as much. One Iowan reported that some of his regiment's men "went out in front a short time after they left to get some trophys but they soon came back with the rebels yelling in the rear." Taking no chances, Rosecrans called Mower's brigade from its relative safety west of town to steady Davies's broken and bloodied line north of Corinth. He also dispatched the 57th Illinois into town to corral and guard the numerous Confederate prisoners, who were eventually herded into a large warehouse southeast of town. Most of the rank and file, however, collapsed. Stanley remembered, "When the excitement of battle was over they lay down exhausted on the ground."[1]

Making Rosecrans particularly cautious was the lingering Confederate cavalry in his rear. These horsemen had been in action for hours, guarding the flanks of the Confederate army and making a sweep south of town during the second day's fight. They had even been involved in a small cavalry fight. Confederate cavalry brigade commander Jackson had taken his men east of town during the battle on the morning of October 4, obviously thinking he would intercept the Federal retreat after the infantry and artillery drove them out of Corinth. One of his men remembered that "the roar of the guns and small arms was incessant." Another, a trooper of the 7th Tennessee Cavalry, reported, "The earth seemed to tremble with the thunder of artillery and the roar of small arms." When all went silent, the cavalrymen thought Rosecrans had surrendered, but they soon learned otherwise. Their task was then to get themselves back to the army for their own retreat. Jackson passed south of Corinth, "in full view of the enemy's works," one of the troopers remembered. Rosecrans, in fact, notified Grant that "Rebel cavalry [was] reported in your old camp to the south." Afterward, Jackson's brigade tested the College Hill fortifications on its way back to the main army, but to no avail.[2]

Despite the skirmishing, it soon became clear that the Confederates were leaving for good and that the Union had won a stellar but bloody victory. Whether it would be a total victory depended on whether Van Dorn escaped.

Amazingly, the Federal pursuit did not begin until the next morning, October 5. But Rosecrans thought he had good reasons to delay. His army was dazed, so he decided to stay the night in Corinth, feed his army, rest and regroup, and follow the next morning. The reappearance of more Confederates immediately after the Southerners fell back only reinforced Rosecrans's decision to delay a pursuit. Still thinking defensively, he ordered his divisions to re-form their lines and prepare to resist any attack. Davies recalled his men from their brief pursuit of the retreating Confederates and formed them on the original line they had held that morning. The four regiments from Mower's brigade soon arrived and formed in the rear of Davies's line, creating a strong reserve and strengthening the weak center. Hamilton, to Davies's right, also ordered his troops back to their original line, not only to repel another Confederate attack but also to gather the different units that had already begun to scatter. Stanley and McKean on the far left also realigned their divisions, which were in somewhat better order than the others. In these positions, the Federals waited for a renewed Confederate attack that never came.[3]

Rosecrans soon had evidence that no new attack was imminent. His army could see the Confederates blowing up their ammunition wagons, a sure sign of retreat. Villepigue's brigade soon vanished as well. The Federals moved forward cautiously, finding Confederates hiding behind stumps and logs for safety. An Alabama lieutenant surrendered only when "a rascal threatened to shoot me," he said. The Union soldier took the lieutenant's sword and his watch, but when the Confederate appealed to an officer, the watch was returned. One group of Union soldiers later reported that they had gone forward "two miles and had seen nary enemy." General McArthur and his brigade was the largest unit that moved forward searching for the Southern army, and it verified the enemy's full retreat.[4]

The Federals saw awful sights on the battlefield once they began to explore. Dead and wounded were everywhere. One Federal counted "20 that lay tuching others." Another marveled at a house that "was literally shot away" but still contained several women. Many Union soldiers described the

Confederate dead, almost all mentioning their blackened faces, which they believed came from drinking whiskey and gunpowder. A member of the 11th Iowa wondered whether the darkened bodies had anything to do with the barrels of vinegar the Federals had left in their camps when they retreated. After the battle, he mused, "there was no vinegar to be found." The Federals also came upon an unexpected sight. The retreating Confederates somehow managed to lose the captured Colonel Mower. Federal skirmishers described Mower as "a hatless rider" spurring a mule, racing toward them. The retreating Confederates sent a "shower of lead" after the escaping prisoner of war, but he returned to Union lines safely, despite being wounded in the neck. When he reported to Rosecrans, he had not lost his sense of humor. Having heard unjust reports of a binge the day before, Mower told Rosecrans, "If they had reported me for being 'shot in the neck' today instead of yesterday, it would have been correct." The pursuing Federals also found the abandoned gun of the 1st Minnesota Artillery in Cane Creek.[5]

The men of Fuller's brigade found the Confederates who had stormed Battery Robinett dead in and around the ditch, including Colonel Rogers. He had taken eleven bullets. Under his clothing, the Federals found a bit of paper stating his name, rank, and instructions for reaching his relatives. Sam Byers of the 5th Iowa termed him "the bravest of the brave" but noticed that "some vandal had robbed him of his boots." Rosecrans, moved by Rogers's actions during the battle, ordered his soldiers to lay him to rest near Robinett with full military honors. Near Rogers lay a dead Confederate tightly grasping a hammer in one hand and "rat tail files" in the other, with which he had planned to spike the cannon.[6]

The vast majority of the Federal army remained in line, however, and celebrated the victory that now seemed complete. One soldier remembered, "The Battle being over the victory ours We then got something to Eat." Rosecrans celebrated by riding the lines and announcing the good news to his weary veterans: "Soon afterward Rosecrans rode past and informed us Price was outflanked and in full retreat," one soldier remembered. Another recalled him "riding along the line—He told us they were whipped on both flanks. . . . [and] that we must eat a hearty supper get a good night rest and be ready to follow in the morning." An Iowan recorded in his diary that Rosecrans's ride caused "the wildest enthusiasm," and one Minnesotan stated, "A shout went up as I never heard before. Hats were thrown in the air." As he rode along the line, Rosecrans also dispelled the rumor that he himself had been killed.[7]

There were some tense moments, however, during Rosecrans's victory ride. He stopped to address many of the brigades, telling Fuller's Ohio boys, "I know now that I stand in the presence of brave men and I take off my hat to you. I know this from what I have heard and from what I have seen at a distance, and also from these piles of dead along your front, and I thank you in our country's name for your great valor." Rosecrans had no such cheery sentiments for other troops along the lines. When he reached Davies's position, he let out a string of insults. An incensed Davies later wrote to Rosecrans, reminding him what he had said and condemning it: "You said upon the battle-field, among the piles of dead and groans of the wounded, slain by the Second Division, Army of West Tennessee, that they were a set of cowards; that they never should have any military standing in your army till they had won it on the field of battle; that they had disgraced themselves, and no wonder the rebel army had thrown its whole force upon it during the two days' engagement." It is a wonder that Rosecrans lived through his postbattle ride.[8]

Only McArthur's troops did not join in the respite and celebration. His brigade had seen hard fighting on October 3 but had remained relatively unengaged on the next day and was therefore comparatively fresh. Rosecrans ordered McArthur to follow the Confederate retreat. He took a portion of his brigade—the 16th Wisconsin and 21st Missouri—and eventually made his way toward the old Confederate works northwest of town. He started at Battery C but found no Confederates in the vicinity. He proceeded northward past Battery D to Battery E, where he caught his first glimpse of the retreating Southerners. He failed to overtake them but, in the process, made his way to the railroad. Ultimately, McArthur followed the Confederates at a safe distance until he went into camp at Alexander's, the place where he and Oliver had made a stand only two days previously. McArthur had no major contact with the Confederates, but he did gather an immense number of prisoners and a large amount of equipment. He also found one of Van Dorn's hospitals containing many wounded Confederates. The Federals took some of them prisoner, but many others were beyond capture. "Oh, how many gave up the ghost," remembered one Federal.[9]

Back at Corinth, Rosecrans finished his victory ride and returned to town, where he found the reinforcements Grant had sent. At Jackson, Tennessee, Grant had done all he could to move reinforcements to the area, including sending James B. McPherson with two mini-brigades. Michael K. Lawler's and John D. Stevenson's four regiments traveled as far as possible on the railroad, eventually having to disembark at Ramer's Crossing because the Confederate cavalry had disabled the track. The sounds of artillery could distinctly be heard as they marched. They arrived in Corinth at 4:00 P.M.—a few hours late, but in good shape and ready for the pursuit, despite the heat. The brigades marched into town and set up camp on the public square. Rosecrans ordered McPherson to lead the pursuit the next morning.[10]

Obviously, a battle of the magnitude of Corinth, and one that had been fought on the fringes of town and at times right in the heart of it, had a major effect on the citizens who lived there and nearby. Many of the Southern-leaning civilians had heeded Beauregard's order to leave in mid-April 1862. Even more left with the Confederate army in late May. In October, however, there were still some families left in Corinth, and it fell to them to endure the brunt of the battle. One local citizen later remembered, "If there is a place within the boundaries of the Union that has smelled the breath of war, that place is Corinth."[11]

Although both armies scavenged off the locals on their marches to and from the battle, those civilians in town suffered the most. Sutlers, for example, were stripped of their goods during the battle. One Illinois teamster reported that Davies told him to take "anything I wanted for the Boys . . . no matter who it belonged to." He thus told of being confronted by a sutler whose barrels of water he was taking for his troops near the White House. As he loaded the wagon, the teamster watched the sutler "with a full determination to shoot him if he opened his mouth as I had two pistols loaded and would rather shoot a Northern traitor than a rebel." The sutler yelled "in a cross tone" as the wagon left, and the teamster yelled back, "Friend, no more of your gab."[12]

It was a most difficult time for the women and children caught in Corinth during the fighting. Mrs. J. E. Gift remarked that, during the night between the two days of fighting, "The women and children trembled between hope and fear, saying over and over again, what will to-morrow bring?" That day, of course, brought the heavy fighting right into Corinth. The women and children wondered where they would be safest. "To go away with the streets full of soldiers, the very air full of the noise of battle, with shells and bullets flying, seemed impossible," Mrs. Gift recalled. "The only place that presented itself was a refuge under the house which stood on brick pillows [pillars] several feet from the ground."[13]

Most Corinthians tried to leave town or find a barricade to hide behind. As an Illinois soldier in Hamilton's division neared Corinth on the early morning of October 3, he noted in his diary that he saw a "woman and children leaving their homes." "The sutlers and citizens were making good time of it," another soldier remembered; "they were a running over the other to see how [they] could get to the Creek to hide." At least one woman was hit by a projectile, according to an Illinois soldier. During the morning bombardment of the town, the soldier was "thinking how nice this was on the [hated] sutlers;" then "a shell went a bouncing along the ground and struck a poor woman in the back who was leaving town and turned her over end over end. Moving, it did not damage her—could not keep from laughing at her."[14]

One of the civilians stuck in town during the battle was not even a native of Corinth. Dr. Mitchell, a minister from Florence, Alabama, had been in a Federal prison camp and was on his way home when he got caught in Corinth by the events. On the morning of October 4, Mitchell's host knocked on his door and asked to have a prayer before such a critical day: "before it shall close we may be in eternity." Mitchell continued praying with a group of ladies during the fighting, and one recalled that the house "became a very Bethel."[15]

The civilians actually caught on the battle lines had the roughest time. One family near the White House on the first day was caught in an artillery duel. Two women ran from the small cabin waving a quilt, but the firing did not cease. They thought better of being out in the open and scurried back to the cover of the cabin. On the second day, a poor woman and her daughter who lived near Battery Powell found that their only place of refuge was in their well, which was dry at the time. The two females were "assisted down a ladder and covered with a few loose planks by a Federal lieutenant," one Corinthian remembered. They came through the battle safely. An Illinois soldier told a similar story, or perhaps it was just a different version of the same one. This time, an entire family consisting "of father, mother and five children" took refuge in a dry well.[16]

After the battle, Mrs. Gift recorded that "a chaplain of an Illinois regiment . . . who was kind enough to be thinking of the non-combatants, rode up and announced that the worst had passed, and we might come out of our hiding place." In addition, "a few skirmishers had taken refuge in the kitchen, [and] he also ordered them out and back to the ranks." She went on to describe how "the citizens began to hunt for each other to see if any were missing and compare experiences." Later, she remembered, "we turned away from this sad sight, went back to our homes to take up again the thread of life."[17]

Part of that life was caring for the wounded. As it had after Shiloh, it fell on the locals to help the army surgeons tend to the wounded. Mrs. Gaston, of the female seminary, reported doing just that; in particular, she helped one soldier who had been hiding out for days and had a "brain fever." Other civilians went out on the battlefield immediately after the battle but were forced to return quickly when rumors of a renewed Confederate attack spread. One of them was the wife of a Union major, who, according to one soldier, "came a running in as fast as her horse could bring her." She told the soldier, "I saw the rest a running and I thought I might, for I don't want to be taken prisoner by the Rebels."[18]

Not all the civilians affected by the battle were Southern citizens. There were some Federal family members in town who were caught up in the horrific battle and its aftermath. One Union soldier's wife had been in town for a visit when the battle caught everyone by surprise. As her husband left for the fight, he told her, "Pray for me, my wife, and if I fall, God protect you!" When the battle ended, she went out amid the gruesome scenes on the battlefield to look for him. She happened to see a wounded soldier lying partially under a dead horse whose head had been shot off. It was her husband and the family horse, which, she recalled, they had both loved and petted in more peaceful times. "He was utterly senseless, and there was a dreadful wound in his head," she remembered. She got him to a hospital and wrote to a friend: "Even as I write, my heart throbs achingly to hear the deep groans and sharp cries."[19]

In the heat of the moment, at least one of these nonnatives got more excited than she should have. The wife of a Union officer was hiding with Mrs. Gift and other women underneath a house during the battle. "In her excitement," Gift remembered, "she said: 'O, I wish they would kill all those old rebels!'" An awkward silence followed. "It is needless to say," Gift recalled, that "she received a response from one of the company which silenced her."[20]

Those African Americans caught in town during the fight were mostly appropriated to work on the skimpy fortifications ringing Corinth. One Illinois soldier remembered that, during the night, "Davie's division . . . had all the Negroes a cutting down the timber to give the artillery a chance and throwed up a fort on the right." They were some of the unsung Union heroes of the Battle of Corinth.[21]

The chaos of October had an effect on countywide services as well. Because of the fighting, the elections scheduled for October 1862 were canceled, and the sheriff, board of police, and other officials maintained their jobs for another term (the last county election had taken place in 1860), until elections could be held in more peaceful times.[22]

By the evening of October 4, the action around Corinth had ended, but the bloodshed still taxed all those involved. One Federal wrote to his wife, "I slept alongside a dead rebel whose right hip was shot right off." Even Rosecrans was shaken, admitting that he "sought the shade of a tree." Yet the battle most upset the Confederates. One grizzled Southerner summed up the fighting succinctly when he wrote home, "We lost a good many men and then had to retreat." Indeed, Van Dorn had taken a sound beating, but it did not end there.

Unknown to him, his army was now between two powerful forces, each ready to march at first light to destroy him. Van Dorn knew that Rosecrans at Corinth was in his rear, but he had yet to learn that a force from Bolivar was almost to the Hatchie River in his front. Moreover, if Van Dorn marched across the Tuscumbia River toward the Hatchie crossing—a vital route for the Confederate escape—the Confederate army would find itself between two rivers, with the enemy in control of the crossings of each.[23]

Van Dorn felt sure that he could outrun the Federals with the head start Rosecrans had afforded him. He could get across the Tuscumbia River and burn the bridge, thereby halting the Union advance for several hours. The Mississippian also correctly reasoned that an enemy force would move from Bolivar to intercept his crossing of the Hatchie River. He had no proof as yet, but he made preparations for anything. Van Dorn knew he had not escaped yet, but he felt sure that if he could cross the Hatchie River before the Bolivar troops arrived, he could march to safety. Given Rosecrans's weak pursuit, Van Dorn felt optimistic.

Although he did not know it yet, Van Dorn's concerns were justified. In addition to sending McPherson from Jackson, Grant had ordered Ord and Hurlbut at Bolivar to march to Pocahontas and the rear of Confederate operations. Ord was absent on an inspection trip, but Hurlbut, his second in command, had taken his own division south on the morning of October 4. After sending all the sick and the excess wagons "within the fortifications," Hurlbut had proceeded toward Middleton and Pocahontas with two brigades— Jacob G. Lauman's and James C. Veatch's, both veterans of Shiloh—and two additional regiments. He met Confederate cavalry but pressed them back to the east side of Muddy Creek, three miles west of Davis Bridge on the Hatchie. The skirmishing, one Illinois Federal recorded in his diary, "hurried us up in a double quick."[24]

Fearing the probability of Federal forces moving from Bolivar, Van Dorn temporarily considered another way out of his desperate situation: march to Rienzi, south of Corinth, and possibly even attack Corinth again from that direction. He dispatched Armstrong and Jackson, with the balance of the cavalry, to Rienzi with orders to hold it for him. But Price insisted that it was "madness to make the attempt," and Maury told Van Dorn bluntly: "You are the only man I ever saw who loves danger for its own sake. When any daring enterprise is before you, you cannot adequately estimate the obstacles in your way." Van Dorn decided to return to his original plan.[25]

But even that plan seemed to be in jeopardy by the next morning, when Van Dorn received word that his worst fears had come to pass. Colonel Wirt Adams, guarding the bridge over the Hatchie River, was engaging the force from Bolivar and needed help. Infantry began to move to the front while the news spread through the army that they were trapped. The teamsters wore a "somber and cheerless look," one soldier remembered. Another noted that he "had visions of swimming the stream." Fortunately, Van Dorn had one more option: the Bone Yard road. Named after the nearby hamlet of Bone Yard, the road branched off the main thoroughfare between the rivers and ran southward to the Hatchie, crossing it at Crum's Mill. Armstrong's cavalry had earlier damaged the bridge to reduce the Federals' ability to get to Van Dorn wherever he went. Now, the bridge was suddenly important to Confederate survival. Fortunately, Armstrong's men had only partially destroyed the crossing and were now working feverishly to repair it. All the while, Maury moved toward the Hatchie, while Lovell held the rear. It was a tight spot.[26]

Fortunately for Van Dorn, the pressure on his rear was slight. Rosecrans sent his divisions forward on the morning of October 5, even establishing a complex system of rockets to show the exact whereabouts of each column. But in a comedy of errors, the divisions soon became hopelessly lost and intermingled, negating a vigorous pursuit. To further compound the problem, Rosecrans remained in Corinth to coordinate the movements, thus separating himself from the actual march.[27]

McKean moved at daylight, passing the hill above Cane Creek that his men had defended two days ago. One Wisconsin soldier noted, "The dead nearly all lay close to the road, and we passed directly by them." He reported that most had been "robbed of their clothing" and, after two days of extreme heat, were "in a horrid condition." Officers detailed men from each company to identify the dead and write their names on cards for the burial details. Other divisions stacked up in the confusion, and Hamilton blamed Rosecrans: "Much confusion and delay occurred from want of a commander," he stated. Rosecrans was back in Corinth, writing to his wife to let her know he was safe, while his army languished on the road. Being the most senior of the four division commanders, Hamilton contemplated taking command to straighten out the mess, but he decided against it because the troops were not in contact with the enemy. Had they come in contact, Hamilton noted, "I should not have hesitated to exercise my right of seniority in the absence of the general commanding."[28]

McArthur's and McPherson's small commands were thus the only troops to meet the enemy. As they followed the retreating Confederates, the Federals found their way littered with every possible type of equipment. "All along the road we passed wagons, tents, clothing, [and] arms of all kinds," one Federal remembered. But then McArthur had to halt when a Confederate delegation under a flag of truce appeared. Led by Colonel William S. Barry (recently the president of the Mississippi secession convention) of the 35th Mississippi, the group was going to Corinth to establish terms for burial of the Confederate dead. That left only McPherson to lead the pursuit.[29]

Protection of the Confederate rear at the Tuscumbia River fell on the shoulders of John Bowen, and he met McPherson late in the day on October 5 at a large hill about a mile east of the river. The Union line moved up the hill, steadily pushing the Confederate skirmishers back. When the Northerners moved on Bowen's left flank, he fell back to the west, taking a commanding position on another hill near the bridge. The major Union thrust at this second position came at the Confederate center, where the 15th Mississippi held the line. Bowen himself took command of this regiment, advanced it several yards, and then ordered a sheet of musketry poured into the Federals, driving them back for good. What one soldier described as "quite a severe little action" had ended. Bowen soon destroyed the bridge and marched westward to rejoin his division.[30]

The critical area of operations for Van Dorn was not on the Tuscumbia River, however, but on the Hatchie. Even before Bowen made his stellar defense of the Tuscumbia River crossing, Van Dorn fought a battle for the life of his army on the Hatchie River while his columns continually moved onto the Bone Yard road. Van Dorn still needed to check Hurlbut, because it would take some time to get the trains and men onto the Bone Yard road and across the Hatchie River at Crum's Mill.[31]

And the Federals were indeed coming fast. The entire command had heard the sounds of battle on October 4, but not on the next morning. Hurlbut thus surmised that he would meet the Confederates at some point, whether victorious or defeated. He did not know the Confederates had lost and retained little organization, so he took no chances, ordering his men out early on the morning of October 5.[32]

Although Hurlbut was performing well, he soon found himself replaced. Having heard of the action around Corinth, Ord ended his inspection trip early, caught up with his command, and took charge. Dressed in a white "linen Duster," white socks, and civilian shoes, Ord looked so much like a civilian that his troops had to ask his identity. Ord and his men soon reached the little village of Metamora, which stood on the ridge overlooking the Hatchie River. There, they saw the enemy ready to contest the bridge, and more. The colonel of the 25th Indiana, William H. Morgan, saw "the enemy coming up the road in large force, apparently making for the same point." The commanders deployed the men not already in line, and the batteries also moved up and unlimbered. Ord made ready for an all-out battle for the high ground around the village, opening up on the Confederates below.[33]

The Southerners, realizing they could not take the heights of Metamora, held their position in the valley and responded with "very spirited" fire of their own, one Federal noted. Then reinforcements began to arrive. The first units were from John C. Moore's depleted brigade, and when the enemy artillery opened up, Maury remembered that "in the next second the lane was cleared." The fire splattered Moore, Maury, and their men with sand but did little damage, except that a portion of the 2nd Texas was cut off and therefore did not deploy. Because of this development, Moore had even fewer men with which to fight. Still, most of the remaining troops deployed behind Burr's Branch, a small creek that flowed north into the Hatchie several hundred yards above the bridge.[34]

Then the battle began in earnest. Ord ordered his entire line forward, and the Federals moved eastward off the Metamora ridge. One Illinois soldier described the action: "The fight was now general along the whole line, the enemy behind fences and houses, we advancing over and around these obstacles." Another described the Federal movement through "brush, blackberry bushes, and fences." Moore's depleted brigade soon broke, leaving four guns behind, which the crews could not bring off because of dead horses. The Federals subsequently hauled the captured prizes off with oxen.[35]

The broken Confederate troops began to move across the river at whatever point they could. Many, even hundreds, "had to take to the water to make their escape," one observer noted. Some drowned or were shot by the Federals. Others, such as Albert McCollom, were captured. "I was so hot and tired that I didn't care about trying to swim with my clothes on and risk getting shot in the back, so of course I surrendered," he informed his brother. Others fell captive in similar situations, among them Van Dorn's nephew, who served as the general's aide. One Confederate described the scene well: "Gen. Price's army got to Davises Bridge on the Hatches River just in time to get whipped right good," he wrote home.[36]

Fortunately, more reinforcements arrived to aid Van Dorn's defense of the river line. Phifer's and Cabell's brigades and Green's division were moving to the front and went into line east of the river as they arrived, halting the Union advance. Ord thus found his various regiments bottlenecked at the "miserable bridge." He immediately began to straighten out the chaos, realizing that the Confederates were re-forming on the heights on the other side of the river. He also straightened out Hurlbut, whom he had to call twice from the rear to come forward and command his men.[37]

Ord soon sent his soldiers across the bridge. But what the Union regiments found on the east side of the Hatchie River caused even more confusion. The Federal commanders obviously did not know the terrain, because they issued orders the men could not carry out. The regiments were supposed to move alternately left and right of the road, leaving enough room for the other regiments to form between them. The first regiments across immediately took a cross fire of musketry and artillery from the Confederate position, which one soldier recalled was "well served and exceedingly accurate both at long and short ranges." The regiments intended to go to the left of the road had no trouble, but those on the right found there was no room to deploy, much less to make room for the rest of the men. The river, flowing north, made a sharp westward turn south of the road and followed the thoroughfare for a way before turning sharply to the north again and crossing the road at the bridge. Veatch later reported that the area to the south of the road could hardly support a company, much less an entire regiment. Another soldier described the area as providing "scarcely room to form a Company." All the while, one Illinois soldier recalled, the enemy "kept up a deadly fire of grape and Canister on the Bridge where the troops were massed and crossing."[38]

While pushing his men across the bridge, General Ord himself took a ball in the leg. No doubt, his white coat made him a perfect target for some Confederate. As he remembered it, Ord was "scolding" Hurlbut for not being up front with his men when he was hit. He immediately thought the worst, believeing his foot was shattered. He called out to an aide, "I am hit in the foot," just as his horse, also stung by the bullet, bolted. The skittish animal quickly calmed down, and Ord could see that the ball had hit him just above the ankle. He immediately went to an ambulance in the rear. Fearing that the wound posed a grave danger, Ord gave the command back to Hurlbut. At a field hospital, the doctors found that Ord's leg bone had not shattered; the bullet had passed between the two bones. A surgeon was able to perform a simple operation and remove the bullet from the opposite side of the leg. Ord, writing to his children later, made light of the incident, saying, "Papa only got a little bullet into his leg." But his injury did affect the steadiness of his men.[39]

All the while, the Union regiments were stacking up in the miserable area between the road and the river, and the situation was becoming desperate. But Hurlbut soon had his men advancing toward the Confederate lines deployed atop a range of hills in a large field. The Southern position proved so good that they soon ran out of ammunition. After withdrawing to an even higher range of hills on the other side of the field and replenishing their ammunition, the Confederates held tight with the aid of Green's arriving division, and Hurlbut declined to follow. During this lull, the artillery of both sides took over. The resting infantrymen took the opportunity to send details to the river for water.[40]

While the remainder of the Confederate army moved onto the Bone Yard road, Green's division lay in its position for about three hours, with the enemy in full view the entire time. The Confederates expected either to be assaulted or to attack themselves, but nothing happened. By 3:30 P.M., the Federals seemed content with their progress. The artillery of each side shook the hills and hollows around the Hatchie River, but the battle had ended.[41]

Both sides could claim victory, but neither could back that claim with substantial proof. The Union army had fallen short of its ultimate goal: destruction of the Confederate army. It had also suffered 570 casualties, most of which occurred during the confusion on the right of the road, just east of the bridge. One Federal observed, "I don't know much about hard fighting, but the Artillerymen said they never saw such fighting and they were at Shilo." The Confederates could likewise claim only a marginal victory. Their casualties were also numerous (their officers kept no record of the totals), but probably not as high as the Federals'. Ord reported that his own casualties were of "a greater number than the enemy."[42]

Nightfall brought an end to the operations. Because of the stand made at Davis Bridge, the weary Confederate command reached Crum's Mill safely, where Armstrong's cavalry had repaired the bridge. But the crossing proved slow and tedious. All through the night, wagons rolled across, followed by the infantry. The men were startled to see Price himself there, ensuring that the makeshift bridge stayed together. As dark approached, Price had a bonfire built on the western shore. As each surprised driver crossed the bridge and caught a glimpse of the commander, he stopped and pondered the sight. Price would yell, "Drive up! Drive up! Drive up!" to keep the column moving. Later in the night, Confederate officer Ras Stirman reported seeing Price "asleep in a chair by a small fire worn out from fatigue." The Missourian stayed, one Confederate noted, "until every wheel had rolled across to the west side of the Hatchie." After completing the crossing, the units camped on the west side of the river. Eventually, Van Dorn marched on toward Holly Springs, where he received badly needed reinforcements in the form of exchanged prisoners. When the dilapidated Army of West Tennessee reached Holly Springs, it was the first time in quite a while that its men felt entirely safe.[43]

But Rosecrans was eager to catch the Confederate army, and he had his men up early each morning in pursuit. Around 3:00 A.M. on October 6, for example, Rosecrans suddenly appeared at Davies's headquarters, calling out, "General! General! It is time for reveille. Get the Second in motion as soon as possible." The marches were long and tiresome, especially after two days of hard fighting. One officer remembered, "We were stumbling along, almost dead with fatigue." Rosecrans arrived at Ripley on the night of October 7, but the Confederates were long gone by this time.[44]

Rosecrans wanted to continue chasing the Confederates, but Grant called him back and ordered the fatigued Union army to return to Corinth. This sparked some heated communication between Grant and Rosecrans. At first, Grant had chastised Rosecrans for not following the Confederates promptly; however, when he realized that no good would come from a belated pursuit, he ordered the army back. Rosecrans, in contrast, believed that he was in an ideal position to forever destroy the Confederates. Since Grant held the ultimate command, however, his orders had to be obeyed, and the army returned to Corinth. In all, Rosecrans reported that his cavalry had pursued the enemy fifty-three miles, and his infantry had logged forty-one. A turn in the weather that ushered in a cold snap only added to the strain. One Federal described the weather as "cold and rainy," and another reported a one-inch snowfall. Yet another wondered about the "sunny south."[45]

Back at Corinth, the situation slowly began to return to normal, even as the armies continued to engage each other along the Confederates' line of retreat. But it took a great deal of effort to repair what had been wounded, damaged, or stricken. And there was not much time to do it. One Federal who examined the field in the days immediately after the battle wrote, "The sight was awful to behold. Thousands of wounded men [were] laying in the hot sun and begging for water." One surgeon even noted that smoke hovered over the battlefield for several days—at least until October 11.[46]

The wounded were initially the primary concern, and their care began almost as soon as the shooting stopped. The Federals collected all their wounded, but one soldier reported that the North had suffered far fewer casualties than the South had. He added, "There is fifteen or twenty rebel surgeons waiting on them all the time." Another soldier also noted the vast number of Confederate wounded: "I have seen several hundreds of them myself in one hospital." By and large, the Federals were sympathetic to the Confederate wounded, who were soon shipped to Iuka for care by their own doctors. One Confederate remarked in a letter to his father, "We have been treated with great kindness by the officers and men of the Federal army, who have done all in their power to alleviate our sufferings." Federal surgeons were busy indeed. Assistant surgeon Myron Underwood of the 12th Iowa wrote to his wife, "For three days after the battle I had not time to lay my head down but was constantly upon the move." He added, "The wounded must be attended to before anything else." James Zearing, surgeon of the 57th Illinois, wrote to his wife, "We have had an immense amount of labor to perform during the past week taking care of the wounded." Northern officials wanted to help too. The acting governor of Wisconsin, J. T. Lewis, wrote to Charles Hamilton, "To what extent have Wisconsin troops suffered[?]" He asked, "Had we better send surgeons and nurses and how many[?]"As late as October 18, one soldier wrote to his father, "It is two weeks to day since Corinth witnessed her bloody battle and the wounded are still around us by hundreds."[47]

Both sides also had an immense number of prisoners to deal with. The Confederates took as many as they could with them, putting them on cars at Holly Springs and shipping them to Jackson, where some "were taken to the state house and allowed to sleep in the halls and doorways wherever they could find a place," according to one Wisconsin prisoner. Eventually they went to Vicksburg, Mississippi, and waited until they were paroled. At least one Confederate took advantage of the presence of Union soldiers to obtain some novel food items: "I went among the prisoners and exchanged bread for coffee." The Federals had many more prisoners to deal with, however, having rounded up numerous Confederates both during the battle and on the pursuit afterward. One surgeon marveled at the sight of the captured Southerners: "The Rebel prisoners as usual are of all shades of uniform, the grey and butternut predominating," he said. "We [also] have here a part of Gen. Lovell's guard, a French company of Zouaves from New Orleans. They are very dashing in their dress." Most Confederate prisoners were paroled in a couple of days, although some, mostly the wounded, were sent north; part of the 57th Illinois accompanied some 600 of them.[48]

As for the dead, the initial hot and humid weather made the battlefield simply awful. "Passed over the battle ground," one soldier wrote the next day, "the most sickening sight I ever saw, far worse than at Pittsburg. The dead bodies lay all along the road and smelt awfully. Maggots were making terrible work with them." One soldier gave specific details: "13 dead Rebels . . . were swelled to their utmost tension." Many a sad letter went out from Corinth in the weeks after the battle, telling of the deaths of loved ones and often providing bone-chilling descriptions of how they died. Dabney Maury himself wrote to Colonel Rogers's widow: "It is my painful duty to write to you relative to the death of your brave husband," he began. Even more wrenching, one soldier wrote his own farewell to his wife: "I have been told by my Surgeon that I could not live but a few days longer," William Brown wrote on October 8. He wanted to say his good-byes, assuring his wife, "I was shot at my post doing my duty." "Ere this reaches you," he concluded, "the spirit of your husband will have passed from Earth to Eternity. . . . Cherish the memory that I was engaged in the performance of a Sacred Duty and prepare to meet me in heaven. Farewell, Farewell." He died the next day.[49]

The people on the home front were obviously anxious to hear news from or about their loved ones. "Cousin Pearce was in the late battle at Corinth. I have not yet learned whether he escaped unhurt and unharmed or not," one home-front letter read. When the fateful letters announcing the death of a loved one began to arrive, their kin would never treat life the same way again, even after the war ended. Similarly, many of the mangled and wounded had not recovered by the time they returned home. Some never recovered from the wounds they suffered in Mississippi. The campaign was as tragic in human terms as any that had ever raged.[50]

Eventually, the dead had to be buried, especially considering the heat. It took time, however, and one Federal of the 27th Ohio wrote on October 8, "Their dead were [still] not all buried yesterday—3 days after the battle." A Missourian wrote on October 9, "The rebels are still not all buried, and many are not to be found. Wounded ones are still being found." Another wrote on October 9, "The woods stink yet with unburied dead." Because of the delay, most of the dead were buried near where they fell. An artilleryman noted, "This storming of the redoubt was the most desperate and murderous charge that has been made during the war, this is shown by the rebel graves that cover the space before the fort. Gen. Rogers is buried within 10 steps of the ditch, and his men lie in long trenches close by." A member of the 47th Illinois described how "the long trenches were soon filled with blue and gray shrouded in army blankets." Another noted, "Graves are scattered all around through the woods." Over the days following the battle, the Federal soldiers methodically buried the bodies and gathered the dead's gear, often finding items of interest. An Ohio private found Confederate canteens that "contained a mixture of bad whiskey and gunpowder, which," he said, "seemed to make them utterly reckless and in a manner crazy." One Illinois soldier was almost ashamed to find only parched acorns in some Confederate haversacks; it made him think differently of the Confederates, who were willing to fight for their cause on such meager rations. It led him to conclude, "This war won't be ended until there is a total failure of the acorn crop."[51]

In addition to tending to the dead, wounded, and prisoners, there was an effort to survey the destruction to Corinth itself, which had been heavily damaged during the battle. "The enemy have finished what we began," one Federal wrote home; "they have thrown shot and shell through nearly every house in town." He described some of the residences as "pretty fine buildings" but added, "they are not so fine now." Another described the early-morning bombardment and commented, "It looked as if they would ruin and take the town."

One Federal gave a detailed description of the damage: "Several houses which were full of supplies for the army were hit, and a hotel also was riddled with cannon shot." Another noted that "Corinth now has the appearance of one great cemetery, except the splendid monuments we see in such places. In the place of these we see a small board with the name of the soldier and regiment to which he belonged inscribed upon it."[52]

The campaign was over, and Van Dorn's army was depleted, having lost 4,233 men in the fighting. With his army of "about 22,000 men," Van Dorn had suffered 22 percent casualties, a figure comparable to the losses in the bigger and more famous battles. The battle took a heavy toll on the Union army as well. Its engaged force numbered 21,147, of which 2,520 became casualties—a 12 percent casualty rate. Perhaps one grizzled Confederate summed up the fierceness of the campaign best. There emerged, he said, "many battles where greater numbers were engaged and where very hard battles have taken place, but I do not believe any field of slaughter can show forth more courageous fighting and determination to overcome than was shown on the gore stained field of Corinth." One Union veteran of the campaign concluded in understatement, "We have had hard times during this [past] month."[53]

The nation was watching the events at Corinth. In a congratulatory message to Grant, Abraham Lincoln asked, "How does it all sum up?" Newspapers large and small, such as the *New York Herald* and *New York Tribune*, ran front-page stories on the battle. The other armies of both North and South fighting in other theaters soon heard the news and began to digest its meaning, with one Confederate general in east Tennessee writing of "our disaster at Corinth." George McClellan offered Washington congratulations "from the bottom of my heart."[54]

In fact, the face of the entire war changed dramatically with the engagements of September and October 1862. During the span of a month, the Confederacy saw three separate armies contemplate an invasion of Federal-held territory. The eastern thrust, Lee's Antietam campaign, ended in defeat before Iuka even took place. The best hope for Confederate success disappeared with that campaign. The Emancipation Proclamation, a direct result of Antietam, ruined any hope of European recognition of the South. With Lee's invasion halted, the weight fell on Bragg and Van Dorn. Bragg, after the Confederate defeat at Corinth, quickly headed for a showdown. That invasion attempt ended four days after Corinth, on October 8 at the Battle of Perryville. Though not a tactical defeat for Bragg, it effectively ended the invasion, and Bragg returned home without any startling achievements. Van Dorn's and Price's failure at Corinth simply capped a disastrous Confederate offensive in the fall of 1862.[55]

As far as Corinth is concerned, its importance — or "sum," as Lincoln described it — lay in the fact that the Federals held firm their location in north Mississippi. From that position, the Union forces would later launch the Vicksburg campaign. Although it would take several months and many tries, the Federals ultimately took Vicksburg. Had the Federals not retained their foothold in north Mississippi, they would have had to retake that lost ground, delaying the capture of Vicksburg, perhaps indefinitely. The Federals won no large strategic victory in the campaign itself, but they maintained a position from which they were able to gain a greater victory, one of the greatest of the war. Mansfield Lovell saw this clearly. Writing to his wife, he confessed, "I can't say I feel entirely easy about the future prospect of affairs here."[56]

The social aspects of the Union retention of Corinth were perhaps just as important as the military ones. With the strategic front moving southward down the Mississippi Valley and then eastward, Corinth became a behind-the-lines occupation center, which brought all kinds of contact among partisans, civilians, and the Union army. Most notably, Corinth became an extremely important area in the evolving U.S. policy toward freed slaves. The retention and occupation of Corinth thus allowed the Federal government to experiment with a new factor in the war: the contraband.

16

"We Are Getting Things in Good Order Again"

When the dust settled around Corinth in mid-October, both Union and Confederate officials began to make sense of what had happened and reorganize their armies. Part of that effort invovled writing their reports, which caused the fighting to begin again, within each army. Rosecrans had made derogatory remarks about Davies's division, and they hit the papers. Davies took Rosecrans to task over his insults, and Rosecrans responded, "I shall overlook the cowardly stampeding of those under my immediate observance on the second day." Davies was hardly appeased, and he also criticized David Stanley, Rosecrans's pet. He added another jab at Rosecrans himself: "I regret exceedingly that I had not the advice and suggestions of our commanding general on this day." It is not surprising that Davies left Corinth soon after the battle. Hamilton also hurled a barb at Rosecrans, faulting him for not leading the pursuit himself. Rosecrans fought back. Word had gotten out about several misadventures by the commanding general during the battle, and Rosecrans wanted his subordinates' reports to exonerate him of any charges. For example, word spread that Rosecrans had fled the field in fear. He thus ordered Davies and Hamilton to revise their reports to show that he had given orders during the battle and had toured the lines. It all boiled down to petty egotism. With friends like these, who needed Confederates?[1]

The same turmoil occurred in the Southern high command, however. Numerous Confederates faulted Lovell for his inaction, with Maury writing, "I cannot recount the events of the Corinth Campaign without placing the Cause of failure where it belongs—on Gen. Lovell." In the most notable effort, John S. Bowen preferred charges against Van Dorn himself. Eventually, Van Dorn won in a court of inquiry, and he compared Bowen's charges to "Cowper's fly on the dome of St. Paul's, who, with a vision that extended only a few inches around him, was found discoursing on the architecture of the entire building." Nevertheless, the charges scarred Van Dorn's reputation, and he wrote to his wife, "I have passed through a terrible ordeal . . . the army failed and the people damned me." Van Dorn tried to comfort his wife, saying that he would lead the troops to new victories. But that was not to be. A new Confederate commander had arrived to defend Mississippi: John C. Pemberton.[2]

Most of the units that fought at Corinth later battled at such places as Champion Hill, Vicksburg, Atlanta, Franklin, and Nashville, but the majority of the higher-level officers did not. Only one general who commanded a force in a pitched battle, Ord, went on to command in the Vicksburg campaign. Van Dorn successfully led the cavalry until an irate husband ended his career, and his life, in May 1863. Price finally got to go home and fought the rest of the war in the trans-Mississippi, having little effect on the outcome. Rosecrans moved up to command the Army of the Cumberland through the bloody battles of Stones River and Chickamauga, but after that defeat, he was removed from command. He then went west to Missouri to face his old adversary Price.[3]

As for Corinth itself, it too underwent a thorough military reorganization, most notably Grant's late October order dividing his command into four separate districts: Memphis, Jackson, Corinth, and Columbus, Kentucky. Officers came and went. Richard J. Oglesby survived his wound at Corinth but finally had to resign because of it. He returned to Illinois and eventually became its governor. Numerous other officers changed positions because of promotion or loss of command. Rosecrans eventually had his friend Stanley join him in the Army of the Cumberland, while Rosecrans's departure left Hamilton in command at Corinth. Command of other divisions changed hands as well; for instance, Isaac F. Quinby arrived and took command of Hamilton's division. Lower-level offices, such as post commander, also changed hands frequently.[4]

By November, when Grant began his thrust into central Mississippi in the first stages of the Vicksburg campaign, the district of Corinth was down to a single division, with artillery and cavalry attached. Most divisions had marched westward by early November 1862 to join Grant, leaving Davies's Second Division with the job of garrisoning Corinth and protecting Grant's flank and rear from Confederates in Alabama and Braxton Bragg in Tennessee. One of those left behind wrote in his diary, "The town looks quite desolate, as all but one Division have left." Over the course of the next year, aggregate troop levels in Corinth hovered around 10,000 to 15,000—generally nearer the lower figure. Thomas Sweeny replaced Davies but served for only a short time. It was a major development when the man who would become synonymous with occupied Corinth arrived in late October to take command of the post and the troops: Brigadier General Grenville Dodge.[5]

Although Dodge later became more famous for his part in building the post-war transcontinental railroad, he played a major role during the conflict, commanding the post of Corinth. A native of New England, Dodge had obtained an engineering degree and headed west to build railroads. He became an Iowan, and that is where he was when the war began. He fought at Pea Ridge and other places before obtaining his general's commission and working on the railroads feeding Grant's army. Then Grant called him south on October 30 to command Corinth. When Dodge first took charge of the Second Division of the Army of the Tennessee, Grant assured him that it was not "a Division of cowards," as Rosecrans had called the unit. Dodge soon took over the Corinth district as well, which was being tossed about due to organizational changes in the Department of the Tennessee. Initially he served under Hamilton, then in the 17th Corps under James McPherson, and finally, in Stephen Hurlbut's 16th Corps, where he and Corinth's garrison remained. Dodge generally stayed in Corinth, but sickness and business affairs kept him away from August to October 1863, which he spent in Iowa and New York City. For the vast majority of the time, however, Dodge commanded three brigades under Tom Sweeny, August Mersy, and Moses M. Bane. Mersy commanded at Corinth when Dodge was away.[6]

Dodge was not entirely enthusiastic about his new job. "It is a larger command than a division," he wrote to his brother in November 1862, "and . . . in a very important point, yet I prefer a division on the move." He even asked Grant for a mobile command and was refused. He thus remained in Corinth, headquartered in two fine houses. Fortunately, the situation was returning to normal around the post. The town was once again a major supply depot and garrison in the Memphis-to-Corinth Federal line in northern Mississippi and southwestern Tennessee. "We are getting things in good order again," an Illinois surgeon wrote to his wife; "a fight messes up things in the army like washday at home, though the soldiers are more cheerful than the women on such occasions." With time on their hands, thousands of soldiers began relating their experiences to those at home. Several units sent either captured battle flags or their own terribly scarred colors home as souvenirs. The army's judicial system restarted as well, and Robert Murphy's trial for evacuating Iuka resumed. A similar court-martial took place for brigade commander Silas Baldwin, who had left his troops because of a minor hand wound. He was found guilty, but President Lincoln himself overturned the verdict. Baldwin was not welcomed back to Corinth, however, and Dodge placed him under arrest when he returned to his regiment. Eventually, Baldwin left the army in disgrace. Additional cases involved other high-ranking officers, including Colonel Francis M. Cornyn.

This heated case finally erupted into a shoot-out in which Cornyn's lieutenant colonel killed him in a room adjoining the courtroom.[7]

Even before Dodge's arrival, Rosecrans had put the Federals to work cleaning up the area and preparing for another fight. Some soldiers moved the wounded to Iuka or to northern hospitals; others, such as the 57th Illinois, escorted Confederate prisoners northward to St. Louis. Still others built and then manned and operated a vast assortment of army and government buildings, including storehouses, wagon shops, carpenter shops, harness shops, blacksmith shops, slaughter yards, and corrals. The chief work, however, was securing the fortifications that already existed and building new ones to complete the garrison. In response to rumors of another Southern attack, Rosecrans began strengthening Corinth almost to invulnerability as early as late October, prompting one soldier to write to his family, "We had been preparing *for them*." Other Federals reported that they built forts "twice as large" as those used during the battle, and "Corinth soon became literally a walled city." One colonel reported that Corinth was "fiercely fortified."[8]

The keys to the new defenses were the inner forts guarding the approaches to the town. In the days and weeks after the battle, these were made more impregnable by connecting one to another. Some of the "old Rebel fortifications," according to one soldier, were even used on the east side of town. In the process, the laborers removed some "out-works in front" and replaced them with substantial lines of earthworks. "Dirt is flying," an Illinoisan remembered, "and the line of defense rapidly assumes proper proportions." In particular, the area between Batteries Robinett and Powell, which the Confederates had exploited during their attack, was covered with a line of earthworks. One soldier, in describing the new fortifications, reported, "There is a line of Earthworks here now, then there were none." Another noted that the new line was "nearly on the line with that held by the brigade October 4th." Other formidable lines went up all around the town. At the forts themselves, the soldiers built underground magazines and bunkers to protect ammunition, and several covered passageways were built to allow safe movement within the garrison, even under fire. All the work was done under the tutelage of engineer officers, mostly Captain Frederick Prime.[9]

Numerous soldiers worked on the fortifications. One member of the 52nd Illinois left a detailed description and even a sketch of the fortifications that he and the thousands of other soldiers had built. "The ditch is about 14 feet wide at the top & 6 at the bottom," he wrote, "from 4 to 8 feet deep & the breastwork is about 7 feet high boarded up on the inside & with a sort of a bank, 2½ feet high & 4½ wide, to stand on to shoot, the rest is 4½ feet higher." With such stout earthworks ringing Corinth, the Federals hoped to never again face the tense moments experienced during the October battle. One Federal even boasted, "Should the Rebels make another attempt to take Corinth they will find far different work from that of Oct 3rd & 4th."[10]

The major development in the fortifications came around the female seminary. Batteries Phillips, Tannrath, and Lothrop had guarded the approaches to the high ground around the college, but these were detached works. The Federals' common sense told them that another Southern attack would come from the south, so they connected these three forts and other newly built ones into a large walled bastion, with the three original forts now acting as salients within the larger work. The Federals even fashioned a stockade across a creek and a ravine on the eastern side. Inside the fort was the college, which one soldier described as having "a dilapidated appearance." The Federals named the entire walled fortification Fort College Hill or Fort Randall, and several regiments, including the 2nd and 7th Iowa, garrisoned the inside. Sweeny also kept his headquarters there.[11]

With thousands of men working, the fortifications proceeded quickly. In fact, they were finished by November 7, prompting one Federal to label the town "a very Gibraltar in strength." The Confederates were also convinced as much. Lovell reported on the work taking place at Corinth: "The enemy has strongly fortified Memphis, Bolivar and Corinth, the latter particularly." He went on to say, "Corinth is being made immensely strong and is evidently intended as a permanent position." Even so, Lovell still talked of retaking Corinth, which would "throw the enemy back upon the Mississippi and rid us of an ugly salient point in our right rear."[12]

Convinced that they would spend several months in Corinth, most Federal units erected winter quarters, although at least one soldier had a problem with the camps' location on the battlefield. "In our camp are the graves of several of the 2nd and 7th Iowa," a member of the 50th Illinois wrote, "but lightly covered with earth." Most soldiers, however, were enthused about their more permanent quarters. Some regiments built log or board barracks with windows and doors; the companies alternated the work—some building the barracks while others stood guard. One soldier of the 81st Ohio described these dwellings as "made . . . of boards and clapboards rived from native trees." A member of the 57th Illinois gave more detail about the structures: "very substantial quarters in rear of Fort Robinett, consisting of log houses 20x28 feet, with a cook-house and dining-room attached. They were built uniform, and made a very pretty camp." The 81st Ohio had similar log huts measuring about 16 by 10 feet each. One soldier described them: "The logs were notched and fitted nicely; it was daubed between the logs with Mississippi clay. It was covered with clapboards riven in the old style by some of the boys whose energetic fathers had built log huts and had riven boards in Ohio, and had taught their sons the useful art." Each hut had a window or two and a chimney, along with numerous bunks that made them "cosy war cabin[s]." The 50th Illinois chose to build fewer but larger barracks, measuring 116 by 16 feet. The 52nd Illinois had the fanciest barracks, building exquisite "gothic cottages," as one historian described them. The colonel's residence contained two rooms, and almost all the structures had porches and were fashioned much more carefully than the log or frame barracks of the other regiments. The 52nd Illinois even had a tall flagpole, on which the men placed a birdhouse. The 2nd Iowa and 66th Indiana were not so well off and remained in their Sibley tents, but the men took the time to build a foundation of "logs for three or four feet," as well as a fireplace and chimney. "They look comfortable and are so," wrote one Iowan. "In various ways," an Ohio soldier remembered, "all made themselves comfortable."[13]

The 39th Iowa had log huts, and the unit's Lieutenant Colonel James Redfield provided a detailed explanation of his accommodations to his wife:

The house is 12 ft by 16 ft inside and is divided into two rooms, one for an office and the other for a bedroom. I have a small portico in front covering the door, and two flower beds planted one on each side of the door. I have planted seeds of the Cypress vine — *corrobunlus*. My bed room floor is graced with a good carpet which one of the boys gave me. I have a good bed a cotton & straw tick & sheets & blankets, also a good pillow, all of which except the blankets, have been given me by one and another. I have a blind to my window on the west end of the house. Taking it altogether I am as comfortable as I could expect under the circumstances.[14]

The Federals also occupied outlying areas "to give notice at Corinth of the approach of the enemy in case of an advance," one Union soldier wrote. A reporter noted that "the city itself [was] almost lost in the little villages built about it by the troops." The local paper described "each camp being a town corporate, surrounding the city proper." The soldiers stationed at these outposts made the best of it, often constructing, one member of the 18th Missouri noted, "comfortable log houses." These outlying garrisons guarded major transportation routes, including roads and railroads, and they came up with some novel features to aid them in doing so. Dodge described the growing use of blockhouses at railroad trestles, remarking that "a company in a blockhouse or stockade was equal to a regiment attacking." Another novel garrison was aboard a moving railcar that had been fortified and manned with cannon.

The boys called it the "gunboat" and the "iron-clad" because it looked so much like a boat. A major stationary installation sat on the Mobile and Ohio Railroad south of Corinth and was known as Camp Davies. In November 1862, soldiers of the 66th Illinois began to build the ten-acre camp surrounded by a thirteen-foot-high stockade made of logs, fully equipped with "portholes" to allow the soldiers to shoot out. To further protect the garrison, the men dug a deep ditch around the stockade. Several gates offered access to the garrison, but these were kept shut and were guarded by the various units inside. For even more safety, soldiers later erected an earthen fortification within the walls of the stockade. To make life comfortable, the soldiers built wooden barracks, dug artesian wells, and even erected a Masonic hall. Similarly, other regiments occupied such places as Kossuth, Glendale, Farmington, Chewalla, Bethel, Moscow, and Rienzi, and all made their quarters as comfortable as possible amid the raging war.[15]

For the most part, soldier life at Corinth was enjoyable during the Union occupation. One Federal described his mess mates as "the most commodious, perhaps the most comfortable, in the Company." He described "daily scripture reading, prayer, and sacred songs" in the barracks, along with "almost daily a political argument between Frank Dunlap, warm under the collar Democrat, and myself, just as warm a Republican." The 50th Illinois even went so far as to build a church in its camp. Needing a bell, the men obtained one at the Tishomingo Hotel. One member recalled, "The boys thought that the bell would be in better form calling the Fiftieth to prayer than the hungry to grub, and so toiling and almost blinded by sweat, they bore the prize to the church." Others, however, noted a distinctly secular tone in Corinth. "It is Sabbath Day," one Illinois soldier wrote in his diary, "yet no church bell gives us warning to repair to the House of God." Although chaplains did preach in camp from time to time, he noted, "instead of songs of thanksgiving and hearing from God's word—our ears are pierced with the shrill notes of fife and Kettle drums, and any instruction we may hear—are military orders read to us by the Adjutant after *dress parade*." His unit's chaplain had resigned, and he lamented the irony that "we have *good* Genls to muster us in battle array . . . but *alas now* are we *without* a leader or champion, to martial us against the *arch enemy* of our Souls." Another Federal noted that "the moral tone of the soldiers is very low. Stealing ceases to be a sin and other things in a like proportion." He added in a note to his father, "There is not much of the war to be seen[—]a great collection of tents and long trains of wagons[,] dirty swearing men and fifty cents a meal make the whole thing."[16]

A peaceful Corinth soon offered the soldiers many amenities, however, including dances and balls "attended by the indefatigable dancing descendents of Ham," one soldier remembered. On New Year's in 1863, there was "a grand military ball" at the Tishomingo Hotel, which was "beautifully and tastefully decorated with evergreens and with the battle-stained flags of all the regiments that belonged to the garrison." A band furnished music, and nearby towns furnished the women. There was also a theater, one soldier recalled, "the enterprise of some of the leading inhabitants." The actors were army soldiers detailed in the hospitals, and the music came from the regimental bands. One soldier wrote that, after a show, "the audience dispersed with a rather favorable feeling toward the efforts of the amateur performers." Other entertainments included a billiard hall, a photographic establishment, and a music hall, where the post band played on their brand new "silver instruments." The soldiers also fabricated their own entertainment. On Christmas in 1862, the officers had horse races on the drill grounds south of Corinth, and on August 6, 1863, when a day of thanksgiving was proclaimed, the 50th Illinois celebrated with a picnic.[17]

A member of the 2nd Iowa, C. W. Hildreth, published a newspaper called the *Corinth Chanticleer*. He offered a weekly special in which he presented the news from around Corinth as well as the nation, along with other bits of poetry, stories, and literature. Many businesses advertised in the paper, and several operated at a handsome profit. One soldier mentioned a watchmaker: "He has his tools with him, and has watches and other jewelry to sell. He has a shop in Corinth and makes a lot of money through his watchmaking." Unfortunately, prices were extremely high in Corinth—twice as high as in Memphis.[18]

When spring rolled around in 1863, the soldiers began to spruce up their barracks and campsites. Many were glad to be at Corinth. In February, the Federals marked the anniversary of Fort Donelson, and in April they remembered the anniversary of Shiloh with artillery salutes and cheers. The 81st Ohio had a grand supper after drill on April 7, 1863, and one soldier remarked afterward that "all retired glad they were at Shiloh a year ago, and that they were here now." Others caught a spring-cleaning fever. One regiment went out foraging for small pines trees, which the men planted in their company streets. "What an effect!" one soldier recalled. "The bare white tents were relieved by the grateful green of the pines, and the soldiers were in ecstasies on beholding the wonderful change." He added, "It was found that it paid even for soldiers to give some attention to the amenities of life."[19]

Many of the Federal soldiers were proud of the progress they saw in Corinth. A newspaper extolled the differences in "the northern and southern armies— their habits—and mode of living." The writer reminded the soldiers of the dilapidated state of Corinth when the Federals took over in May 1862 and noted the cleanliness of the place in 1863. He pointed out that "the streets have been curbed and sidewalks laid," in addition to other amenities, such as gardens. He labeled the town "our own beautiful city of Corinth." By late 1862 and 1863, Corinth was indeed a calm place compared with the chaos of October, and the local newspaper remarked on "the good order which characterizes our city."[20]

The Northern soldiers never quite got used to the odd weather in the Deep South, however. The heat was oppressive in the summer. The winter had its oddities as well. One Federal wrote in late October 1862, "This morning awoke and found one inch of snow oerspreading the ground. *Never before* have I seen snow covering all the face of Nature while yet the trees were arrayed in summer attire." Another wrote, "It seems rather queer to lay down at night after the middle of December & sleep comfortably in the open air." One Iowan wrote in January 1863, "Last night I heard the frogs croaking which seemed very strange this season of the year."[21]

In fact, it was a life of ease. "We don't have much too doo but stand picket guard," one Federal wrote. An Indianan even admitted, "I don't have anything at all to do now. It has now been over two months since I have done any duty at all whatever." Likewise, food was normally not an issue for the soldiers in Corinth. One member of the 66th Indiana wrote, "We have bilt a Coock house for each Company and we will have fore men to Coock for us out of each Company. We have plenty of bred and meat to eat." Another soldier described the fare: "Uncle Sam is getting richer every day[;] he furnished us with hams and flour all the time. I haven't eat a hard cracker for a long time." The men of the 50th Illinois cooked a goose, but they roasted it too long (two days) and gave the inedible bird "away to company B for a foot ball."[22]

At times, there were major festivities to break some of the monotony at Corinth. For example, Iowa governor Samuel J. Kirkwood visited his troops in the summer of 1863. Many of the officers went away on leave during the lull time, and others had their wives and children spend time with them in camp. Among these were Dodge's wife and the wives of Colonels Bane and Cummings. Lower-level soldiers likewise had their wives in town. The 50th Illinois even built a separate house for one of its members when his wife arrived. Many were glad to see the army wives in town. One soldier recalled, "The presence of a number of ladies in camp adds a charm beyond expression to the surroundings."[23]

Despite the ease of camp life, numerous unwelcome events reminded the Corinth soldiers that they were still in a war zone. Boredom was a concern, leading to the heavy use of alcohol. "Some of the boys have procured some whiskey," one soldier wrote, "and [are] endeavoring to fire the *inner man* and by so doing are rendering themselves quite odious." An Illinoisan wrote in his diary, a "good meny of the boys drink to much." One soldier described seeing several empty bottles outside an officer's tent one morning. Holidays were especially notorious for drinking, such as George Washington's birthday: "I have never seen so many drunk men and so much fighting in the regt before," said one soldier. Another wrote that at Christmas "there was no evidence in sight that Santa Claus had paid the camp a visit," so the boys obtained a fix from the local sutler. On a more sinister note, several soldiers described fairly frequent executions for crimes such as desertion, frequently caused by boredom and alcohol. One Illinois soldier described an execution in July 1863, during which the offender was seated in his coffin and "launched into eternity." The entire garrison witnessed the horrific event.[24]

There were also freak accidents and unwise behavior. In July, upon hearing the official news of Vicksburg's surrender, soldiers fired off salutes that resulted in the wounding of one man. As the men became more and more bored, they also made some foolish decisions. Lieutenant Elias Davis of Company B, 66th Indiana, was arrested for being caught absent from his picket post with, his indictment read, "a woman who he said was telling his fortune." Not all such arrests were warranted, however. General Dodge ordered Captain George Wyckoff arrested for leaving his post, but Wyckoff produced proof that brigade commander Bane had ordered him to do so. "The genl sent me his written apology," Wyckoff wrote, "and ordered me to be released and Col. Bane arrested in my place."[25]

One of the most irritating occurrences for the soldiers in Corinth was the growth of the Copperhead movement in the North, which seemed to climax (at least at Corinth) in the early winter of 1863. The reaction was swift and decisive from Corinth's garrison. The Illinois officers called a meeting at the music hall on January 29 and then sent home resolutions "to show to Governor Yates and to all our friends at home that we are still in favor of a vigorous prosecution of the war, and that we will uphold our President and Governor in all their efforts to crush the rebellion and restore the Union." One soldier described the antiwar Democrats as "Northern traitors." He went on to say, "Southern rebels who profess to be just what they are and fight for their principles are men that I can respect and regret that it is my duty to fight them but these men up there who profess to be Union men and at the same time [are] doing all in their power to destroy it are not worthy the respect of a dog." One soldier even mentioned that the Copperheads had been given a derogatory name in Corinth: "copper bottoms."[26]

Corinth soldiers were similarly disgusted by the numerous hours of marching and drilling. One Federal described "squad drill" in the morning, followed by regimental and brigade drill in the afternoon. Sometimes there were larger reviews, such as the one in mid-October 1862, held when the wind was high and the roads were dusty. One soldier remarked that due to "the soiling of the Officers uniforms — The Commander hastened through — requiring but few evolutions of the line." Soldiers often witnessed humorous episodes during drill, such as the time the band of the 57th Illinois paraded down the line of soldiers and the bass drummer "stubbed his toe, falling forward and rolling on top of the drum." He did not miss a beat, however; he double-quicked it to the still-marching band and resumed his correct place and step. As the line of soldiers laughed, the regiment's colonel, Frederick J. Hurlbut, tried to hide a grin. One soldier remembered that the colonel "tried hard to look the martinet, as he stroked his long red whiskers to hide the smile on his countenance." Once back in camp, the drummer was often congratulated for his "dexterity."[27]

The garrisoning soldiers frequently complained about the bad water as well. One Federal wrote in his diary that it was "*quite poor* and should be filtered or strained before use." According to an Illinois soldier, the only water near one of the batteries was that "which ran through an abatis between the town and Fort Robinett," and another declared to a friend, "We have to dig a hundred and 78 feet for water." Of course, the many dead bodies littering the watersheds made for horrible conditions, and health was a concern. The result of the bad water continued to be sickness in the garrison. One Ohio soldier remembered, "Day after day could be heard the muffled drum, and a burial-party with reversed arms would march to the place of interment with the remains of a comrade, and then the three volleys would be heard."[28]

Some units tried to remedy the bad water situation. The 57th Illinois bored an eighty-foot well in its camp, but one soldier recalled, "The water coming from this well was of a bluish color and very strongly impregnated with iron." Apparently, a team of "three Negroes, a mule, a few pullies with their ropes and tackle, and the simple auger" made the rounds in Corinth, drilling wells for soldiers. "Almost every regiment had one of these wells bored for its accommodation," one Ohioan wrote, "all done by the same mule and Negroes who had enjoyed the monopoly of well-boring about Corinth for a number of years."[29]

Although boredom was the norm, Corinth and its outlying areas could be dangerous at times. A storm blew down an oak tree onto the barracks of an Ohio regiment. As one soldier described it: "Some of the guns [left inside] were bent and useless, as we would have been, had we tarried a few seconds longer." Accidental friendly fire also claimed some lives. And then there were the Confederates. "Guerillas and small parties of the enemy's cavalry hovered about us," one Ohioan remembered, "making it a matter of interest and of a little danger to venture out of our lines." Dodge himself wrote to his brother, "I fight now daily the enemy."[30]

Despite these problems, many soldiers enjoyed their stay in Corinth. Over time, most were shipped to other scenes of war, however, most notably the Vicksburg campaign. Only Dodge's small division was left to garrison the town. Most soldiers were sad to leave Corinth and their nice barracks. A member of the 27th Ohio, Luther Meily, wrote, "I never did leave any place with as much reluctance." He also quoted a soldier from the 81st Ohio: "[he] says that we have the best site. The best water and the best constructed barracks (at our own expense) within any present Military Department in the United States." The members of the 81st Ohio even went so far as to request the 27th's barracks when it left. That was fine with the 27th Ohio; they were happy to give their barracks to fellow Ohioans. However, Meily continued: "All the men and most all the officers say they will burn them or blow them up before any Illinois Troops shall inhabit them."[31]

All the while, the soldiers stationed in Corinth kept their minds firmly focused on the war. Some even walked over their battlefields and remembered those excruciating days in October. One soldier told a friend, "I did something over there that I never did before in my life," pointing toward the White House, which had seen so much action on October 3. When asked what he had done, the soldier replied that he had prayed during the fight. His friends did not believe him, to which the ruffled confessor replied, "Yes; I'll be d____d if I didn't." His friends had a chuckle over him "*swearing* that he prayed." A touring Indianan reported finding many relics and seeing a grave of 300 Confederates in front of Battery Robinett. An Iowa surgeon similarly described in a letter home, "Large trees are around us, cut off by our cannon balls and shell, branches shot and hanging, tops lying all around, splintered and broken, shells unexploded and fragments of shells are lying on the ground." Another soldier, describing the garrison to a friend, became caught up in remembering the scenes of October; he mentioned the White House and noted, "You can see its roof towards the Northwest." He then recounted parts of the battle and, almost overcome with patriotism, simply ended, "This is historic ground."[32]

17

"Establishing Friendly Relations with the Inhabitants"

Even amid the military work being done at Corinth in the days and months after the battle, there was humanitarian and charitable work going on: that of seeing to the immense number of fugitive slaves known as contrabands. By late 1862, the U.S. government had already changed its policy on slaves several times. After Lincoln issued the preliminary Emancipation Proclamation in September 1862, Dodge wrote to his brother, "You have no idea of the consternation old Abes Proclamation is making." At that point, all bets were off, and the Union forces were required to aid and enlist the services of the former slaves. Corinth, because of its location, became a major part of that process. And it happened more quickly than anyone had envisioned because the slaves took the initiative and began flocking to Union lines. "They will not even wait until 1st January," Dodge wrote in explanation. "I do not know what we shall do with them."[1]

The acceptance of blacks into the army and as wards of the government was not universally welcomed. Numerous soldiers in Corinth offered their protests. "You know . . . [this] army is an Egyptian host that hates darkies and fulminates against the abolitionists," one soldier wrote, and "it is a matter of curiosity to see the intense prejudice against the blacks." Other contemporary examples abound, most notably the frequent derogatory references to blacks. One soldier complained about the army, saying, its "mind is so full of the everlasting nigger." Another described a social event: "Last night there was a nigger wedding and dance here." Dodge himself used the term frequently. Even when derogatory language was not used, prejudice was still apparent. One officer wrote to his son about the child's dog, which had accompanied him to war: "He plays with some negro children a good deal but I guess that wont spoil him."[2]

The white soldiers had other problems with the contrabands, especially when they thought the black soldiers were receiving special treatment. An Illinois artillery battery was seven months behind in its pay, one member complained, but he insisted that "the Negroes are paid up quite regularly and promptly." He added, "There is a storm brewing in the army on this and other accounts. . . . Wo be then to the Abolitionists." An Illinois infantryman commented in disgust, "Sambo is as good food for powder as is his white brother."[3]

The army had ways of ensuring cooperation from its racist soldiers, however. When Dodge appointed several members of the 81st Ohio to recruit blacks, those who were "not in sympathy with arming the negroes, talked it, and even abused Mr. Lincoln" were quickly replaced. When a general officer asked if there were any dissenters from the policy, those who replied affirmatively were put in the guardhouse, according to a chaplain, "there to revise the opinion he had invited them to express."[4]

While there were those who did not support or desire black participation in the war, many others accepted the idea or at least remained ambivalent until more information was forthcoming. One Iowan asked rhetorically, "These poor children if we looked only at the present, would be much better off with their old masters but is there not something in store for them in the great future?"[5]

One of those who wanted something done—perhaps more out of a practical desire than any moral persuasion—was Grenville Dodge. Thousands of contrabands flooded into his command. One Ohioan told of the influx of slaves into Corinth: "They had not heard the news of the Emancipation Proclamation, but they did know that freedom could be obtained at Corinth." One slave said, "Massa tole us dat you all Yankees at Corinth would make we 'uns work on de big forts tell we died, an' den give us some beef on a cracker, an' throw in a hole alive an' bury us!" Asked why he had come anyway, the slave replied, "Oh, we knowed massa *lied!*" What was Dodge to do with these people? He decided on his own accord to encamp them beginning in November 1862, although his predecessors had apparently done the same thing, perhaps as early as September. Soon the idea of encamping and protecting the contrabands caught on, and Grant appointed Chaplain John Eaton to take charge of that work in his department.[6]

The initial effort was haphazard, to say the least. Dodge had few resources to provide the contrabands. One Iowan reported that they were first quartered "in old tents, huts, hovels, and sheds." According to one of the white garrison soldiers, "[we] gave up our school rooms and even our porch & hall until shanties could be provided." The slaves were extremely poor, having come out of captivity with little or nothing. One Federal wrote that "raids were made into the enemy's country and invariably returned with a number of men, women & children who had traveled by foot in wind and rain or sunshine and dust—for many miles. . . . They came not as the Hebrews out of Egypt— ladened with the riches of the land—what few possessions they had accumulated were left behind and they hardly escaped with their lives." One soldier told a pitiful story of the contrabands' extreme poverty: "I shot a hog and when I gutted it the old Negro come and got the guts and carried them to the house."[7]

Dodge was not willing to wait for the army or Congress to make decisions while these people were starving and hurting. He first provided the contrabands with dead soldiers' used uniforms and equipment. The results were mixed. "It is laughable to see a negro boy 3 ft. high dressed in the pants and shirt jacket of a 6 foot soldier," one Federal remarked. He noted, however, "how proud it makes the little chalk eyed fellows to notice them." But anything was better than nothing; other children, one soldier observed, were going "around in their native purity." One boy of about three years old was given a wooden musket; he learned the manual of arms so well while watching the soldiers drill that he became as proficient as any infantrymen.[8]

Strapped as he was to provide for his own command, Dodge began to put the adult contrabands to work. He set many of the former slaves up on an occupied plantation and had them grow all sorts of crops. They also tended smaller gardens in the hope of growing food for themselves. Over time, the contrabands' work turned a profit. Dodge also used the slaves in a vast intelligence operation whereby he sent scouts out all over the western Confederacy. Many of them were former slaves who gained information from their relatives and friends.[9]

Dodge took the ultimate step when he officially organized a contraband camp at Corinth in December 1862 and placed it under the command of 66th Illinois chaplain James M. Alexander. The camp itself sat east of town, just inside the old Confederate earthworks; it eventually contained a number of houses, a moss-covered church, a commissary, and an assortment of other buildings on streets named after Federal military commanders. An internal police force kept the peace. This contraband camp was a city unto itself—ironically, larger than Corinth. In comparison to other contraband camps in the Mississippi Valley, the one at Corinth was described as a model operation. It eventually had up to 6,000 inhabitants at times, although the normal population was apparently closer to 2,500. Unfortunately, the camp was not immune to danger. One Federal soldier recorded in his diary that there was a "big fire last night about 12 o clock, [and] the negro meeting house burnt up."[10]

A number of additional buildings went up near the camp. The American

Missionary Association quickly sent its associates to the contraband camps, Corinth included. Missionaries such as George and Mary Carruthers, the Reverend and Mrs. Edward Pierce, Lois Hinman, and the Reverend and Mrs. Abner D. Olds toiled hard on behalf of the freedmen at Corinth. They soon erected a hospital to care for the ex-slaves and a school that served as many as 150 students, both children and adults.[11]

Federal officers soon found the contraband camp to be a logical place to organize black military units. Dodge began recruiting black men in the fall and winter of 1862, before there was any official sanction to establish black regiments. And it almost got him into trouble. He received word that the Confederates "swear they will hang me if they catch me. They have offered a reward for my head." He added, "I tell them to come and get it." Dodge was evidently more worried about his own side's reaction. He was soon called to Washington for a consultation with President Lincoln. Afraid he was going to be reprimanded, much as John C. Fremont and others had been earlier in the war, Dodge was relieved to find that Lincoln wanted to talk about the transcontinental railroad. Back at Corinth, Dodge had no choice. His white soldiers were balking at guarding the contraband camp, and, according to Dodge, "several conflicts ensued when our sentinels shot one or two of the contrabands." Alexander gave Dodge the perfect solution: if Dodge provided the equipment and arms, he would train the black troops and take over the guard duty. Two black companies, commanded by white officers, resulted. They were outfitted with weapons and uniforms and generally provided guards for the camp.[12]

By the spring, permission to raise black units had arrived. Dodge formed a regiment on May 21, 1863, rewarding worthy and competent white soldiers with commissions. He later began another unit at Corinth, although there were insufficient men. "I think Colonel Cornyn will have to make another raid or two before enough men of color can be found to fill the second regiment," one observer noted. But the first regiment was well on its way to providing good service. Chaplain Alexander went into the regiment as colonel, and John Phillips of the 57th Illinois replaced him as head of the camp. The regiment became known as the 1st Alabama Infantry (African Descent), but it was later renamed the 55th United States Colored Troops (USCT), which were regular army units, not state units. The soldiers built their barracks near the camp, prompting a newspaper reporter to observe, "They are quartered in very neat barracks" that are "quite as neat as those of the white regiments, and are kept in excellent order." He reported that the black regiment on parade needed more work but added, "It was apparent that the officers were more to blame for it than the men." At times, the fervor of recruiting went too far. The

Corinth Chanticleer advised of the need for some "distinguishing mark or badge" for the white soldiers; recruiters sometimes tried to sign them up, thinking they were light-skinned slaves in old soldiers' clothing.[13]

Perhaps the high point of contraband recruitment in Corinth came during "a formal presentation to the negro regiment of the national colors." Many local whites attended the event, and they were serenaded by black schoolchildren. Then an opening prayer was given by the chaplain, who kneeled on the stage; "many of the black soldiers follow[ed] his example by kneeling on the ground beside their muskets," an impressed observer noted. Colonel Moses M. Bane of the 50th Illinois gave the main address; he then presented "with his left hand—his right hand and arm he sacrificed at Shiloh—the starry emblem of freedom into the hands of the black color-bearer of the 1st Alabama regiment, adjuring him to bear it with honor, and to desert it never." Two of the black soldiers also spoke, and one man from Iowa found them to be "rather amusing" and noted that they "made some good hits without knowing it." According to a Northern newspaper correspondent, one black soldier spoke "with more fluency and good sense than one would have expected." The former slave declared, "Why, they's not much blood in a man any how, and if he is not willing to give it for the freedom of his children and friends, he does not deserve to be called a man." The correspondent described another black soldier who spoke as "a bit of a wag." He closed by saying, "We to-day for the first time have had given to us the stars, but many of us have received *stripes* before." Colonel James B. Weaver of the 2nd Iowa gave a short speech to conclude the festivities. A dress parade with General Dodge and other Federal officers in attendance ended the affair. The soldiers were obviously moved: there were, according to one observer, "tears on many a dark cheek."[14]

Many whites were impressed with the black soldiers. "If they fight as well as they look, wo be to the rebels. —I have faith in them, I mean the Negroes," wrote one white soldier. A correspondent in the local paper similarly lauded the blacks as excellent soldiers, arguing that the former slaves were physically adapted to rigorous duties, knew "nothing but perfect obedience," and were "natural imitators," having learned the manual of arms quickly. Finally, they were completely loyal. "There is not a copperhead to be found among them," he concluded.[15]

Perhaps the peak of the army's relationship with the contrabands came when Adjutant General Lorenzo Thomas visited Corinth in May 1863. Lincoln had sent Thomas to the Mississippi Valley to recruit black troops, and he made twelve different stops. The troops at Corinth, both white and black, prepared for his visit by cleaning the camps and making everything ready. Thomas first spoke to the white troops. According to one participant, "The troops were massed in close column by regiments in front of General Dodge's headquarters, when General Thomas stepped forward and, after acknowledging the salute tendered him, delivered an eloquent and soul stirring address upon the progress of the war." When the general was finished, "he was cheered to the echo." Another soldier commented, "He made a good speech. He came here to organize Negro Regiments. We shall have at least one and I think two of these Regiments [in] a very short time at this place. I believe [if we] . . . give them a chance they will fight." Others spoke as well, including Oglesby, Sweeny, and Dodge. Later, Thomas toured the contraband camp and its attendant schools and military barracks and spoke to the former slaves. He said "that the President had sent him out here so far to tell them they were free & to tell all the soldiers they must receive them, treat them kindly, provide work for them and pay them, feed them if hungry, clothe them if naked, and to make soldiers of the strong & healthy men so that they might fight for the liberty of their wives & children and against the rebellion." With Thomas's praise for the camp, Superintendent Alexander told John Eaton, "I am now prepared to die."[16]

Over time, the contrabands at Corinth made a life for themselves in the camp. Soldiers mentioned large-scale weddings among the blacks, one describing "a grand conjugal day." Another described "sixty persons, thirty men and thirty women, coupled off, arranged themselves in a circle around the minister, and were all married at once." He added, "I noticed that several of the couples had three or four pledges of their affection standing immediately behind them." The freed slaves likewise participated in large religious revivals. "Thare is Quite a refirmation breaking out among the darkey's," one soldier wrote; "I should judge thare was nearly three thousand of them, [and] they have Prayer Meeting nearly every night." Obviously, the former slaves were responding well to the newfound freedom made possible by the army's capture, retention, and occupation of Corinth.[17]

In addition to the large number of contrabands flowing into their lines, the Union forces had to deal with the local population. In most cases, the soldiers were saddened by the citizens' plight. "This rebellion has cost the south great sacrifices in men and means," one Union soldier wrote; "their country is made desolate their farms destroyed their crops taken many houses and towns burnt and goods destroyed." Another noted, "Farmers are doing but little near here." One soldier questioned how the population could survive with so little agricultural work. "It is a mystery to me how the citisins of Tenn. & Miss will live this year. Nearly every team is taken from them; foraging parties are ordered to leave families 60 days rations if they can find plenty if not, take it all." One Federal remarked sarcastically, "This war has played havoc on planters cotton crops—as thousands of acres along the road are rapidly going to waste. The Negroes 'who *love* their masters so dearly' have nearly all absconded, leaving their masters to mourn a *double loss*."[18]

When the choice came down to feeling sorry for the inhabitants or going hungry, however, almost all Federals opted to forage for whatever they could find. "The troops were kept continually on forage expeditions," one soldier wrote, "until there was not any corn of any consequence within a space of twenty-five miles in diameter about Corinth." Another spoke of raiding "in the name of Uncle Samuel." Sometimes the Federal soldiers took pleasure in taking from the citizens of Corinth. One soldier on picket duty told of an episode in which he and others took apples, milk, and eggs from a local who wanted to sell them to only one particular officer. When the citizen complained to a higher authority, the soldier remembered, "he told us to go to our quarters and said that we done right but we ought to have made a smoother job of it." At other times, the punishment could be severe. One soldier remembered that his "Regiment [was] made to stand at parade-rest this afternoon for 2 hours because some one had burnt a house contrary to orders. Thus do the innocent suffer for the guilty."[19]

The citizens who remained in Corinth were mostly Unionists, since the majority of the die-hard Confederates had evacuated with the Confederate army earlier in the war. As a result, they were much better treated and even prospered during the occupation. Sutlers, stores, theaters, and all sorts of other establishments operated in Corinth. Most were closed on Sunday, however; one soldier thankfully reported, "All the stores, and even the barber shops, observe the Sabbath quite as much as is done in Cincinnati." Of course, the "celebrated Tishomingo Hotel" was the center of attention, but one soldier found "nothing about it that is prepossessing. What it had in palmist days, while in the hands of the Confederates I cannot say."[20]

Many Northerners, including officers' wives, agents, and missionaries, came to Corinth to live, and many lodged with private citizens. In particular, one young girl provided some insight into civilian life in Corinth. Maud Morrow was the daughter of a sick Union officer, and she and her mother had come from Ohio immediately after the battle to care for him. They stayed with the sick officer in his room, first at the female seminary, which Maud called "the Castle Beautiful," and then at the Tishomingo Hotel, which she described with less reverence as "the historic dilapidated old hotel through which a cannon ball passed during the progress of the battle." Maud saw some sights that a little girl should never have to witness. She once walked in on surgeons amputating both legs of a severely wounded soldier. "Sick at heart," she remembered, "I hurried on and delayed my return until I felt sure the operation was well over with." But most of her memories were better. She later recalled, "Night after night I have sat on the upper porch [of the Tishomingo Hotel] listening entranced to the regimental band," which, she noted, "would play from dark until bedtime, and I could not be induced to leave my post until the last note died away in the silence." She also remembered the contrabands, particularly "Uncle Sandy and Aunt Katy," who admitted having some doubts about the Federals before they arrived. "I thought they was some kind of wild animals with horns on their heads and they would eat me up," Aunt Katy laughed. Though only nine years old, Maud "organized and taught a [contraband] school on the upper veranda of the Tishomingo," she proudly remembered. She taught the children the alphabet and some ciphering using the cards that numbered the rooms in the hotel. Her lessons could not compete with the arrival of trains, however, and "each whistle that pierced the air was a signal to suspend lessons, and teacher and pupils alike would scramble to the front and leaning far over the rotten railing would wave and cheer at the blue-coated soldiers being borne on ward to victory or defeat, life or death, God alone knew."[21]

Naturally, the civilians who most caught the Federal soldiers' eyes were the ladies of the area. There were quite a few women in and around the camps, and some even took up residence at distant outposts such as Camp Davies; the wife of the colonel of the 66th Illinois lived there for a time. Not all were commented on for their beauty, however. One Iowa soldier wrote of a laundress in the camp of the 1st U.S. Infantry: "She is ugly to a degree which is horrible." But most of the females who garnered any attention were far from ugly. "The charms of a Mississippi belle—a sweet secesher—so entrapped a son of Erin, an artillerist, that he to-day became the happy husband of this lady love," one soldier recorded. Most soldiers were not interested in marriage, however; they wanted only the companionship of the rare females in Civil War Corinth. Thus, much effort was made to bring in women for dances and balls. "The district was ransacked for ladies," one soldier wrote, "and they succeeded in scaring up about 25 mostly officers wives and daughters and a few natives." The dances were high-level affairs. One surviving dance card, including the names of the officers who participated, shows that some twenty-five dances—everything from the Virginia reel to waltzes, quadrilles, and polkas—were danced at the New Year's Eve ball at the Tishomingo Hotel.[22]

Soldiers usually found the local women friendly, if not supportive. "We were posted near a house and a few of us spent most of the time in the house chatting with the old lady and her daughter," one soldier remembered. Another woman attacked members of the 7th Illinois with a hoe and told the colonel,

"You the leader of these vandals, clear out of my yard." But according to an observer, "The affable Colonel soon succeeded in quieting her, and we believe he succeeded in persuading the old lady to give him his supper." Some women were helpful. One woman allowed a soldier and his wounded comrade to spend the night in her house, and "the next morning she prepared us some coffee and biscuits for breakfast, that was all she had to offer us, but it tasted mighty good to me for this was the first food I had tasted since the morning before." Despite the locals' friendliness, some Federals did not try to cultivate relationships. One soldier wrote, "We have a high old time down here going out foraging. I shot 3 big hogs the other day and made the rebels' chicken and geese get up and howl. The women and children begging for them like good chaps. That's the way to do them, the ornery cusses."[23]

Relations with the local citizens were not always so cut and dried, however. There were many supporters of the Union cause in general and of Grenville Dodge in particular. Conversely, there were many who opposed him. Telling the difference between the two could be difficult, and keeping them apart was almost impossible. One soldier related Dodge's solution: "Every man in the district is required to take the oath of allegiance, or register themselves as enemies of the United States and be treated as such." Another noted in more detail:

> Of late all able bodied men have been pressed into the Service. And a good idea it is. Our lines are filled with citizens who are living off of the Soldiers and Government, swindling one, and acting as Spies against the other. Some of these citizens are men who left the Northern States to prevent going into the Union Army and many are old citizens who remain among us for no good to Government, but to live off of our Soldiers and do all the injury they can against us, and the rest are a worthless, no account set, who neither benefit themselves or any other person. So you see the best thing we can do with the whole Tribe is make them go into our army and fight with us for their protection, or make them leave our Lines, and go to their Rebel friends.[24]

Dodge made concessions to the civilians he trusted. He allowed trade with Mississippi civilians through Corinth, writing to his brother, "If you could come down here with a few thousand dollars you can double your money in a short time in the purchase of cotton." He would have gotten involved in the trade himself, but such investment was "very risky as well as prohibited to an US officer." He also took in Unionist families who were being pestered by the Confederates because of their loyalty. One soldier described a pitiful group of "some Alabamians Suffering with the cold[;] their Children's crying . . . is awful. . . . I went & got a teem to howl some wood for them, [and] they returned their thanks to me & said God bless you, they had come here for protection." One woman's husband had been "hung, holding up for the union caus, [but] he Succeded in kiling three Rebels' before they took him, [and] her brother is in the union army." Dodge also took in others from the Purdy and Bethel, Tennessee, area. Later, he assessed a tax on the Confederate people of his district to pay for the white refugees, whom he sent into loyal territory for safety. Individual Union soldiers also had weak spots in their hearts for the Unionists, one soldier reporting that the 50th Illinois built a small house for "five orphan children."[25]

But the Corinth garrison did not spend all its time drilling or helping the area's civilians, both white and black; it also participated in raids, skirmishes, and expeditions. Several took place shortly after the battle's completion in October, including an expedition by the 81st Ohio and 9th Illinois on a "tour of observation" southward. While Grant moved toward Vicksburg along the line of the Mississippi Central Railroad to the west, a portion of the expedition made it all the way to Tupelo and "captured several officers who were too drunk to leave when the place was evacuated." Numerous contrabands followed the retiring Federals back toward Corinth. Another expedition responded to Nathan Bedford Forrest's 1862 winter raid on the Mobile and Ohio Railroad in northwestern Tennessee. Dodge sent portions of the Corinth garrison northward to cut off the Confederate cavalry. When the unsuccessful troops returned to Corinth, they found it "isolated, as it were, from the rest of the world." The Memphis and Charleston was not running, and the Mobile and Ohio was broken. And they learned that "all the quartermaster & commissary stores were removed to the fort next to our camp as were also the heavy guns on the east side of town." The garrison had to go on reduced rations for several weeks. It was during this isolation that many false reports emerged. For instance, the garrison learned (erroneously) that Richmond had been captured, as had Vicksburg. One soldier joked, "Here all the *reliable* news reached us, even in advance of the occurrences themselves."[26]

The major raid took place in late April and early May 1863, when Dodge led his three brigades, with artillery and cavalry, eastward by river and along the railroad toward a concentration of Confederates in northern Alabama. Hoping to disrupt Braxton Bragg's lines of supply as well as launch Abel Streight's famous "mule march," Dodge had a small fight at Town Creek, Alabama, before returning to Corinth. One Ohioan wrote that the men enjoyed the trip: "Our soldiers, who have for a year seen only the dull desolation of Corinth, are delighted with the view of civilization and refinement." As always, large numbers of contrabands as well as loyal whites followed the units back to Corinth. Dodge marveled, "They came in every conceivable conveyance from their masters' private carriage to a wheelbarrow."[27]

There were other expeditions and raids throughout the Union occupation of Corinth, along with some scouting and foraging parties that ranged out many miles. The 7th Illinois, in fact, mounted mules to extend their range. One of the new troopers reported his experiences with the obstinate animals: "Of all the stubborn and aggravating beings on earth the mule is the chiefest. It would make a saint swear to lead a mule. Whenever they discover a soldier is vexed, they draw back their ears and look so provokingly mean at him, taking all the delight imaginable in tormenting and teasing their master." In all the skirmishing, Dodge's main antagonist around Corinth, northeastern Mississippi, and northwestern Alabama was the Confederate cavalry commander, Brigadier General Phillip D. Roddey. The two generals fought each other on various battlefields, as well as through letters dealing with everything from the exchange of prisoners to the treatment of civilians. "If you purpose to drive out of your lines all Union men and their families," Dodge wrote to Roddey in January 1863, "I desire to know that fact."[28]

The major reason for Corinth's occupation was to allow the Federals to utilize the railroads that passed through the town and keep them away from the Confederates. One soldier noted, "This railroad was a bone of contention through most of the war after it fell into our hands. . . . General Hurlbut said later, it took more men to defend it than it would to clear the whole State of Mississippi of rebels." Although the railroads repeatedly proved their worth, ironically, they would also be part of the reason why Corinth lost its importance to the Union forces. As operations heated up around Chattanooga, Tennessee, in late 1863, much of the Army of the Tennessee in Mississippi was shuttled via the Memphis and Charleston to that area. Most of the Corinth garrison also departed, thereby putting the lightly defended town of Corinth out of the spotlight.[29]

Many Federal troops, along with Sherman himself, moved through Corinth in the fall of 1863 in their travels from Memphis to Chattanooga. In fact, large numbers moved through the town in the early days of October, on the anniversary of the battle, and many remembered the significance of the occasion. Once again, one of the chief complaints was the bad water. Most of Corinth's garrison also moved eastward; Dodge took his entire division to Pulaski, Tennessee, and then on to the Atlanta campaign. Brigadier General John D. Stevenson took command of the backwater Corinth district, but he was not happy about it. With only the 108th, 113th, and 120th Illinois, along with two black units and a few engineer companies, he complained to Hurlbut in Memphis, "I feel I have imposed upon me a responsibility that can only result in disaster and disgrace." Fortunately, only a few minor skirmishes erupted.[30]

The weakening of Corinth's garrison was just a precursor to the eventual evacuation of the place. By January 1864, with Chattanooga in Union hands, Sherman hit on the idea of making a raid through Mississippi to Meridian, one of the only major rail junctions left in the state. Rather than call his troops back from Chattanooga, where they would eventually begin the Atlanta campaign, he decided to use the resources still in Mississippi—mainly, the 17th Corps around Vicksburg and the 16th Corps at Memphis and along the railroad in northern Mississippi. Thus, Sherman called his troops in to prepare for the offensive. Corinth—or, more precisely, the railroad—was no longer needed for the Union war effort and could be spared. The Federals prepared to leave the crossroads town once and for all.[31]

On January 11, 1864, corps commander Hurlbut in Memphis ordered Stevenson to evacuate Corinth and send all the stores, guns, and sick to Memphis. He was to haul away everything he could, including the lumber used in buildings; then he was to "destroy thoroughly" all that was left. Hurlbut ordered that all this be done "with the greatest promptitude," and Stevenson worked hard over the next several weeks to comply. He sent the heavy guns away, along with quartermaster and ordnance supplies. Stevenson found his task daunting, however. "I have at least 600 wives and children of Federal soldiers that require to be cared for," he wrote to Hurlbut. He also asked what to do with "traders with Treasury permits." One of the biggest issues, of course, was the closing of the contraband camp. Despite the magnitude of the job, Sherman was impatient, writing to Grant, "The Sixteenth Corps has become so domiciled at Memphis and along the railroad that it is like pulling teeth to get them started." Nevertheless, by January 23, Stevenson sent the last of his supplies out of Corinth, as well as "an immense train of refugees," with another large train waiting to be loaded. He had his command entirely out of town by January 25. Everything that was left, including barracks, fortifications, and the stockades at Camp Davies and elsewhere, was torched, as was Corona College. Confederate officials reported that the buildings were burning as late as Monday, January 27, but by then, the Federals were long gone. Hurlbut ordered his commanders not to look back, but to "leave the country to God and the cavalry."[32]

Confederate forces soon returned to Corinth. Southern refugees also slowly reentered the area. One civilian wrote, "Well, we can bring our niggers back now, the d___d Yankees have left Corinth." The Confederate military depart-

ment under Leonidas Polk quickly began to reconstruct the town and its facilities, bringing in cannon and rebuilding the fortifications. West of town, they
built what was called Fort Williams, apparently on the site of the original Fort
Williams on the Memphis and Charleston Railroad. They also repaired the
Mobile and Ohio Railroad northward to Corinth, although several Federal
raids from Memphis that summer continually damaged the track.[33]

Throughout the summer and into the fall of 1864, the post of Corinth under
Colonel J. C. Reid and later Colonel William R. Miles provided logistical support for John Bell Hood's doomed invasion of Tennessee and the subsequent
retreat. Pontoon boats, meal, hard bread, rice, and soap were all gathered and
stockpiled at Corinth, and a hospital was set up to accommodate the wounded
and the sick. The shattered and retreating Confederate army arrived at Corinth
on December 31, where the men were issued supplies and received six
months' pay. But the town and the surrounding area, much like the Confederacy itself, was much different from the Corinth of 1862. J. T. Peterson of
the 12th Louisiana sadly noted, "The country we pass through . . . [has] been
devastated and laid waste." Most units continued southward due to another
Federal incursion that put Corinth out of the war for good. Benjamin Grierson led his second major raid through Mississippi in late December 1864 and
early January 1865, shattering both the Mobile and Ohio and the Mississippi
Central Railroads. By that time, repair was out of the question, and the remaining Confederate units left Corinth in early January, bound for Tupelo and elsewhere.[34]

But the Federals were not totally through with Corinth. In mid-January,
one division moved by boat along the Tennessee River to Eastport, where the
men built winter quarters and kept an eye on Corinth and its vicinity. Colonel
Jonathan Moore's two-brigade division, along with a brigade of cavalry,
marched from Eastport to Corinth and arrived on January 19, 1865. Slight
skirmishing ensued as small elements of Colonel Lawrence S. Ross's Confederate cavalry brigade fled Corinth ahead of the approach of a large number of Federals. Before they left, however, the Confederate troopers set fire
to anything of value, including the Tishomingo Hotel.[35]

Some of the men in the approaching Union division had been at Corinth
earlier in the war. The 14th Wisconsin, for instance, had participated in both
the siege and the battle. One soldier who had been there in 1862 wrote to his
mother, "The old place looked as natural as ever. We found the 'Tishomingo
Hotel' in flames, probably set on fire by the Rebs who left the place on learning of our approach." Conversely, another wrote, "The country as far as we
went is completely destroyed it don't look like the same place that it did 2
years ago." The Federals left Corinth just as quickly as they appeared, how-

ever. One soldier recalled, "The troops halted in Corinth an hour or two for the men to make their coffee, and the object of the reconnaissance having been accomplished, the expedition turned back the same day."[36]

All during the upheaval and the occupation, the county government continued to function in the areas not controlled by the Federals, and despite its Unionism and recent occupation, Tishomingo County still participated in the Mississippi state government. For instance, the county received its share of relief funds from the state legislature, even during the Federal occupation, and the board of police continued to raise and submit taxes to the state as late as 1865. The county participated in state elections, the most notable being the October 1863 gubernatorial election during the occupation. Local county elections took place in October 1864, and a new slate of leaders, including the sheriff, board of police, school commissioners, and other officers, was elected. The primary concern was for the indigent. The board of police made several efforts throughout the war years to transport corn into the county for needy families. Although Corinth's leaders, such as ousted mayor Edward C. Gillenwaters, were active throughout the war in caring for the "poor families now in Corinth who are dependent on the Government," the town government apparently was not officially reorganized until after the war, when Gillenwaters resumed control of Corinth's affairs.[37]

The growth of an already predominant Unionist sentiment in Tishomingo County was unmistakable. Throughout the Union occupation, and even later toward the end of the war, Unionist sentiment in Mississippi had grown, whether by personal choice or because that seemed to be the way the war was going, and the northeast corner of Mississippi led the way. Judge R. A. Hill was a leading proponent of working with the Federals, and his efforts paid off. By January 1865, George H. Thomas, commanding the Department of the Cumberland, ordered all Federals in the area to recognize the newly established Federal government in the county. "Authority is hereby granted to the residents of Tishomingo County, Miss.," the order read, "to hold regular sessions of circuit, probate, and police courts of the county." He also gave permission to operate the railroads "within the limits of the county, strictly for the convenience of the citizens thereof." It was seemingly what the people of the county had wanted all along, but it took four years of hardship, spiked by the violent year of 1862, to get it done.[38]

By early May 1865, the war was practically over. Most action had shifted southward to Mobile or in response to James Harrison Wilson's raid through Alabama. Corinth was again isolated and quiet. The Confederate departmental commander surrendered his forces in early May, so most troops in the region gave up and went home. Some correspondence occurred concerning isolated units of Forrest's and Roddey's commands in northern Mississippi and their desire to surrender at Corinth. By May 22, Federal cavalry troops of the Fifth Division, Cavalry Corps, Military Division of the Mississippi, had scattered and garrisoned several localities in the area, such as Tuscumbia, Alabama; Purdy, Tennessee; and Iuka, Eastport, Okolona, and Aberdeen, Mississippi. Part of that force commanded by Edward Hatch reoccupied Corinth. There, the 19th Tennessee Cavalry officially surrendered and was paroled.[39]

The war was over, and for Corinth, it was a good thing. The fighting had severely afflicted the town and its people. Now the long road to reconstruction began.

EPILOGUE

As the decades passed, Corinth retained a central place in the memories of the veterans who fought there. Over the years, more and more soldiers began to write their reminiscences of the events that took place around the railroad town, and many were printed in publications such as *Confederate Veteran* or the *National Tribune*. Others had unique postwar experiences related to their Corinth activities. J. W. Crawford of the 4th Minnesota had been hit in the head during the fighting and received care from a fellow officer, Major W. T. Kittredge. Years later, while reading a medical journal, Kittredge learned that doctors had removed the bullet from behind Crawford's eye, and he lived to tell the story. A sadder case was the wife of Sam Davis of the 35th Mississippi. His comrades reported seeing him moving toward the enemy before they lost him in the smoke of the battlefield. His wife, holding on to the last ounce of hope, looked for her husband at sundown every evening until the day she died, forty-nine years later. One Confederate veteran still felt the toll of Corinth years later, writing in his journal: "Corrinth the mere mention of the name to this day depresses my soul as no other name on this earth. Why. Because it was here that the first dart of doubt pierced my soul of the ultimate success of the Confederate cause."[1]

After the war was over, the Corinth area was a mess. According to an observer who toured the battlefield, "The forest trees in all directions [were] rent and torn by shot and shell." He also noted the many burial places. "This great battle-ground is dotted—here and there—in some places thick as meadow mole-hills—with the graves of Federal and the exposed remains of Confederate dead," he wrote. He found that the "Federal dead were all neatly interred in the usual way, with head and foot boards in every instance." The Confederates, however, were not so well entombed. He saw "vast numbers of Confederate 'bones'—whole skeletons and parts of skeletons—lying exposed, and bleaching on the field, in the bushes, and on the hill-sides, under logs, and on stumps," in contrast to "the neatly-enclosed and well-marked graves of the Federal soldiers, all buried at the proper depth."[2]

Matters did not get much better over the next decade. During the turmoil of Reconstruction, Corinth's citizens, both black and white, dealt with the massive changes taking place. After an attempt at lenient Reconstruction, during which Southerners resumed control of their own governments, military Reconstruction arrived. The most noticeable aspect of this second phase of Reconstruction in Corinth was military occupation, which the inhabitants were well used to. The 16th and 34th U.S. Infantry Regiments, under such men as Brevet Lieutenant Colonel Lloyd Wheaton, spent time in Corinth, as did others. The military officers took over the government and ran all aspects of life in town, from ensuring voting rights to closing saloons.[3]

Even during the volatile days of Reconstruction, the nation did not forget what had happened at Corinth. National cemeteries had been established during the war, but in the South, most cemeteries were not set up until after the war, when tensions had calmed and workers could safely perform the ghastly duty of removing bodies. The Federal government began building cemeteries at many of the famous battlefields such as Shiloh, Vicksburg, Stones River, and elsewhere. One of those was the Corinth National Cemetery, which came into being in 1866 and was situated in the southeastern quadrant of the railroads, about three-quarters of a mile southeast of downtown. The attempt to beautify the cemetery is evident in the original report of the site: "The main avenues have been ornamented by excellent shade trees and evergreens, and a number of trees have been set out, at uniform distances, around the entire grounds near the fence." A superintendent kept his residence as well as an office there, and the government had to drill a well to provide "a good and permanent supply of water"—not unexpected at Corinth. Workers disinterred Federal soldiers from battlefield graves at Corinth, Iuka, Farmington, Davis Bridge, Brices Cross Roads, Parker's Cross Roads, Holly Springs, and Britton's Lane, as well as "from various camps and hospitals in Tennessee and Mississippi." Appropriately, the local railroads were utilized to bring the remains to Corinth. By 1869, 5,688 dead had been reinterred at Corinth National Cemetery. They came from 273 different regiments and fifteen different states. All but 1,793 were unknown. Only a handful of Confederates were placed in the cemetery; most were left on the battlefields, their whereabouts destined to be lost. Never honored by their government, which by that time was nonexistent, they remained in their hastily dug mass graves. Only the privileged few were cared for, such as Colonel Rogers at Battery Robinett. One visitor noted that Rogers was the only Confederate "buried deep enough to prevent the rains from washing the dirt away and exposing the bones."[4]

Over the years, time removed most evidence that anything horrendous had happened at Corinth, especially at the Confederate burial trenches. However, many of the earthworks were still discernible as late as 1884, when one onlooker noted, "The old redoubts which encompass the town on every hand, tell of the fearful conflict that once raged over them—on the green slopes beyond the earthworks those who hurled themselves against them in vain lie in unmarked graves—dust and ashes these twenty-odd years—the grave of only one is known of all those who perished in that fierce assault." That one grave, of course, belonged to Colonel Rogers, buried by Rosecrans's order at Battery Robinett. The traveler noted, "No stone marks the spot where he fell. A plain, white picket fence encloses his grave."[5]

By the turn of the century, even the fortifications were being removed. One veteran wrote in the early 1900s of Battery Robinett, "The walls of this old fort are leveled down, but the ladies of Corinth have enclosed the ground where the old fort once stood. This place is just outside the town on a hill overlooking the town." For years, this commemoration by the local chapter of the United Daughters of the Confederacy (UDC) was all that told visitors of the carnage at Corinth.[6]

While most of the physical links to the battle melted away over time, the Battle of Corinth was memorialized during the climax of the commemoration carried out by veterans around the turn of the century. Members of the UDC in Texas, as well as family members, erected a granite monument to Colonel Rogers in 1912. One onlooker described it as "twenty feet high and five feet square at base standing over the spot where Rogers fell." Likewise, the remains of General Joseph L. Hogg, who had died of disease during the siege in May 1862, were moved to the Battery Robinett site and reinterred in 1918 with a large tombstone. In addition, the UDC placed a monument to the unknown Confederate dead near Rogers's and Hogg's resting places, and the local United Confederate Veterans also placed a monument in downtown Corinth, which was eventually moved to the court square.[7]

Eventually, the horrors of the Civil War were forgotten as new generations were born and matured and fought new wars to commemorate. Yet Corinth always retained a tinge of remembrance. One veteran who returned in 1915 could not forget what had happened there, but he was more in awe of the changes that had taken place over the years. Old veterans, he declared, "would scarce believe it was the same Corinth of fifty one and fifty two years ago. It will be remembered in the spring of 1862 as a small country town, with the muddiest streets, the worst water and more fatal sickness than any place this army ever camped. Now it has beautiful streets shaded with Magnolia and other trees, with more beautiful flowers than any other little city that this writer has ever had the pleasure to visit, and might well be called the city of roses."[8]

After the early monuments and commemorations at Corinth, there was a long period of inactivity, even during the years surrounding the Civil War centennial. As a result, much of the historic fabric of the remaining war-era fortifications, buildings, and sites was lost. In particular, the major fortifications were steadily eroded or removed; those affected by urbanization were the first to go. None of the inner line of fortifications lasted more than several decades, and only Battery F on the Halleck line remains in the early twenty-first century. The Confederate line east of town, the direction in which Corinth ultimately sprawled, has been almost totally lost, but large sections of the line north of town still remain, including a very well-protected section of a large salient near the Mobile and Ohio Railroad. Farther outside of Corinth, many of the May 1862 Union siege works weathered the years and still stand today. Likewise, although urbanization, modernization, and renovation took a toll on what was left of Corinth after the conflict, a few war-era houses survived the long decades and are still in use today.[9]

Other than the UDC site at Battery Robinett, the first serious proposal to establish a commemorative military park at Corinth originated from local leaders in the 1940s. Little came of the scheme or from later attempts in the 1970s to get National Historic Landmark recognition. The first tangible effort occurred during the national bicentennial in 1976. As part of the celebration, Corinth commemorated its battle with a re-created earthen fort portraying Battery Robinett. Fortunately, the re-created fortification was not built on the exact site of the original; rather, it was located a few hundred feet to the west in the UDC park. Thus, the original imprint and Colonel Rogers's burial site were preserved. Also erected were state historical signs denoting the fighting at Battery Robinett, several of which identified the approximate positions of individual regiments. Because it was a city park, funding was not always a priority, and over the years, the site deteriorated.[10]

Preservation activity began to rebound in the 1990s, as it did nationwide, and the effect on Corinth was monumental. The first major step in preserving and interpreting Corinth's Civil War history came in 1991 when the National Park Service designated numerous localities around Corinth as National Historic Landmarks. This designation opened the gates for all kinds of federal work at Corinth, and the local population responded in 1993 by forming a nonprofit preservation group known as the Siege and Battle of Corinth Commission. By the next decade, the commission had preserved nearly 1,000 acres of historic battlefield and related sites. The commission also lobbied hard for a federal presence at Corinth, and that goal was eventually successful when Mississippi senators Trent Lott and Thad Cochran introduced legislation to make Corinth a national park. The Corinth Battlefield Preservation Act of 2000 authorized the Battery Robinett property and the existing National Historic Landmark sites, as well as others to be determined later, to become a separate unit of Shiloh National Military Park. The Corinth Civil War Interpretive Center opened its doors with a dedication service on a hot and muggy afternoon in July 2004.[11]

Today, with the donation of hundreds of acres of battlefields and earthworks, the Corinth unit is preserving and interpreting the important Civil War sites of north Mississippi and southwest Tennessee. Tourists at Corinth can view the well-preserved earthworks, walk among the original downtown houses that played host to numerous generals, visit the site of Davis Bridge, see the contraband camp where a novel experiment proved successful, and view the original site of the railroads' crossing, which led to all the conflict in the first place. Visitors can also see the original site of Battery Robinett, which, for better or worse, has come to exemplify the fighting at Corinth, much as Pickett's Charge and the Hornet's Nest epitomize Gettysburg and Shiloh. Although there was much more to the Battle of Corinth than the fighting that took place at Battery Robinett, and certainly more to the siege and the occupation, Battery Robinett has become the focal point, thanks to the early monument, the later city park, and eventually the National Park Service center. Thus, if visitors are willing to brave the humidity and heat of a summer afternoon or the cold wind of winter, they can still walk a few hundred feet up the hill to the original site of Battery Robinett (ground-penetrating radar located the original outline of the redoubt). There, the long-silent dead who are still buried on the site seemingly call out Corinth's importance, not just to their own lives and families of 150 years ago but also to our nation today. General Hogg's burial site demonstrates the inglorious nature of disease in warfare. The monument to the unknown dead calls for the silent commemoration of long-forgotten soldiers. And the stately monument and burial site of Colonel Rogers, just in front of the original Battery Robinett, exclaims the carnage that once took place on that now tranquil spot of ground.

And while they are there, visitors can also ponder the larger issues that brought the armies to that bald hill west of Corinth, the first stumbling attempts to deal with the issue of freedom for all Americans. That is where the carnage of war, as illustrated by Corinth's decisive year of 1862, met the loftier ideals of liberty and helped make our nation what it is today.

ORDER OF BATTLE AT THE BATTLE OF CORINTH

Confederate Forces

Army of West Tennessee: Major General Earl Van Dorn

Price's Corps—Army of the West: Major General Sterling Price

First Division: Brigadier General Louis Hébert (sick), Brigadier General
    Martin E. Green
First Brigade: Colonel Elijah Gates
    16th Arkansas
    2nd Missouri
    3rd Missouri
    5th Missouri
    1st Missouri Cavalry (dismounted)
    Wade's (Mo.) Battery
Second Brigade: Colonel W. Bruce Colbert
    14th Arkansas
    17th Arkansas
    3rd Louisiana
    40th Mississippi
    1st Texas Legion
    3rd Texas Cavalry (dismounted)
    Clark's (Mo.) Battery
    St. Louis (Mo.) Battery
Third Brigade: Brigadier General Martin E. Green, Colonel W. H. Moore
    (wounded)
    7th Mississippi Battalion
    43rd Mississippi
    4th Missouri

6th Missouri
3rd Missouri Cavalry (dismounted)
Guibor's (Mo.) Battery
Landis's (Mo.) Battery
Fourth Brigade: Colonel John D. Martin (killed), Colonel Robert McLain
(wounded)
37th Alabama
36th Mississippi
37th Mississippi
38th Mississippi
Lucas's (Mo.) Battery

Second Division: Brigadier General Dabney H. Maury
Moore's Brigade: Brigadier General John C. Moore
42nd Alabama
15th Arkansas
23rd Arkansas
35th Mississippi
2nd Texas
Bledsoe's (Mo.) Battery
Cabell's Brigade: Brigadier General William L. Cabell (wounded)
18th Arkansas
19th Arkansas
20th Arkansas
21st Arkansas
Jones's Arkansas Battalion
Rapley's Arkansas Battalion
Appeal (Ark.) Battery
Phifer's Brigade: Brigadier General C. W. Phifer
3rd Arkansas Cavalry (dismounted)
6th Texas Cavalry (dismounted)
9th Texas Cavalry (dismounted)
Stirman's Sharpshooters
McNally's (Ark.) Battery
Reserve Artillery
Hoxton's (Tenn.) Battery
Sengstak's (Ala.) Battery
Armstrong's Cavalry Brigade: Brigadier General Frank C. Armstrong
2nd Missouri Cavalry

1st Mississippi Partisan Rangers
2nd Mississippi Cavalry

District of the Mississippi

First Division: Major General Mansfield Lovell
First Brigade: Brigadier General Albert Rust
    4th Alabama Battalion
    31st Alabama
    35th Alabama
    9th Arkansas
    3rd Kentucky
    7th Kentucky
    Hudson's (Miss.) Battery
Second Brigade: Brigadier General J. B. Villepigue
    33rd Mississippi
    39th Mississippi
    12th Louisiana
    1st Confederate Infantry Battalion
    Louisiana Zouave Battalion
    McClung's (Tenn.) Battery
Third Brigade: Brigadier General John S. Bowen
    6th Mississippi
    15th Mississippi
    22nd Mississippi
    Caruther's Mississippi Battalion
    1st Missouri
    Watson's (La.) Battery
Jackson's Cavalry Brigade: Colonel W. H. Jackson
    1st Mississippi Cavalry
    7th Tennessee Cavalry

Union Forces

Major General William S. Rosecrans

Army of the Mississippi

Second Division: Brigadier General David S. Stanley
First Brigade: Colonel John W. Fuller
    27th Ohio
    39th Ohio
    43rd Ohio
    63rd Ohio
    Jenk's Co. Illinois Cavalry
    3rd Michigan Battery
    8th Wisconsin Battery
    Battery F, Second U.S. Artillery
Second Brigade: Colonel Joseph A. Mower (wounded, captured)
    26th Illinois
    47th Illinois
    5th Minnesota
    11th Missouri
    8th Wisconsin
    2nd Iowa Battery

Third Division: Brigadier General Charles S. Hamilton
First Brigade: Brigadier General Napoleon B. Buford
    48th Indiana
    59th Indiana
    5th Iowa
    4th Minnesota
    26th Missouri
    Battery M, First Missouri Artillery
    11th Ohio Battery
Second Brigade: Brigadier General Jeremiah C. Sullivan (wounded),
    Colonel Samuel A. Holmes
    56th Illinois
    10th Iowa
    17th Iowa
    10th Missouri
    Company E, 24th Missouri

80th Ohio
6th Wisconsin Battery
12th Wisconsin Battery
Cavalry Division: Colonel John K. Mizner
    7th Illinois Cavalry
    11th Illinois Cavalry
    2nd Iowa
    7th Kansas
    3rd Michigan
    5th Ohio (4 Co.)
Unattached
    64th Illinois
    1st U.S. Artillery

Army of West Tennessee

Second Division: Brigadier General Thomas A. Davies
First Brigade: Brigadier General Pleasant A. Hackleman (killed), Colonel
    Thomas W. Sweeny
    52nd Illinois
    2nd Iowa
    7th Iowa
    Union Brigade:
        58th Illinois
        8th Iowa
        12th Iowa
        14th Iowa
Second Brigade: Brigadier General Richard J. Oglesby (wounded), Colonel
    August Mersy
    9th Illinois
    12th Illinois
    22nd Ohio
    81st Ohio
Third Brigade: Colonel Silas D. Baldwin (wounded), Colonel John V. Du
    Bois
    7th Illinois
    50th Illinois
    57th Illinois
Artillery: Major George H. Stone
    Battery D, 1st Missouri Artillery

Battery H, 1st Missouri Artillery
Battery I, 1st Missouri Artillery
Battery K, 1st Missouri Artillery
Unattached
14th Missouri

Sixth Division: Brigadier General Thomas J. McKean
First Brigade: Colonel Benjamin Allen, Brigadier General John McArthur
21st Missouri
16th Wisconsin
17th Wisconsin
Second Brigade: Colonel John M. Oliver
Independent Co. Illinois Cavalry
15th Michigan
18th Missouri (4 Co.)
14th Wisconsin
18th Wisconsin
Third Brigade: Colonel Marcellus M. Crocker
11th Iowa
13th Iowa
15th Iowa
16th Iowa
Artillery
Battery F, 2nd Illinois Artillery
1st Minnesota Battery
3rd Ohio Battery (section)
5th Ohio Battery
10th Ohio Battery

NOTES

Preface

1. *OR*, 1, 10(1): 667; *OR*, 1, 10(2): 403; *OR*, 1, 7: 888; Timothy B. Smith, "'A Siege from the Start': The Spring 1862 Campaign against Corinth, Mississippi," *Journal of Mississippi History* 66, 4 (2004): 403.

2. Thomas M. Stevenson, *History of the 78th Regiment O.V.V.I., Its "Muster-in" to Its "Muster-out": Comprising Its Organization, Marches, Campaigns, Battles and Skirmishes* (Zanesville, OH: Hugh Dunne, 1865), 151; John Tyler Jr. to William L. Yancey, October 15, 1862, John Tyler Jr. Letter, UMC; *OR*, 1, 10(1): 667; *OR*, 1, 10(2): 403; Smith, "Siege from the Start," 403; *OR*, 1, 7: 888; Steven E. Woodworth, *Jefferson Davis and His Generals: The Failure of Confederate Command in the West* (Lawrence: University Press of Kansas, 1990), 103; James L. McDonough, *Shiloh: In Hell before Night* (Knoxville: University Press of Tennessee, 1977), 9.

3. G. W. Dudley, *The Battle of Iuka* (Iuka, MS: Iuka Vidette, 1896); G. W. Dudley, *The Battle of Corinth and the Court Martial of Gen. Van Dorn* (n.p.: n.p., 1899); Ben Earl Kitchens, *Rosecrans Meets Price: The Battle of Iuka, Mississippi* (Florence, AL: Thornwood Book Publishers, 1987); Monroe F. Cockrell, ed., *The Lost Account of the Battle of Corinth and Court-Martial of Gen. Van Dorn* (Jackson, TN: McCowat-Mercer Press, 1955); Franklin L. Riley, "G. W. Dudley," *Publications of the Mississippi Historical Society* 5 (1902): 290–291; Peter Cozzens, *The Darkest Days of the War: The Battles of Iuka and Corinth* (Chapel Hill: University of North Carolina Press, 1997); Earl J. Hess, *Banners to the Breeze: The Kentucky Campaign, Corinth, and Stones River* (Lincoln: University of Nebraska Press, 2000); Steven Nathaniel Dossman, *Campaign for Mississippi: Blood in Mississippi* (Abilene, TX: McWhiney Foundation Press, 2006). An original draft copy of Dudley's "lost" account of Corinth is in the Bolivar-Hardeman County Public Library.

4. Smith, "Siege from the Start," 403–424; John F. Marszalek, "Halleck Captures Corinth," *Civil War Times* 45, 1 (February 2006): 46–52; Patrick Michael Hotard, "The Campaign (Siege) of Corinth, Mississippi, April–June 1862" (M.A. thesis, Southeastern Louisiana University, 2005). For an example of this new approach, see George C. Rable, *Fredericksburg! Fredericksburg!* (Chapel Hill: University of North Carolina Press, 2002).

Prologue: Crossroads

1. *OR*, 1, 10(1): 667; *OR*, 1, 10(2): 403; *OR*, 1, 7: 888; *OR*, 1, 6: 432; *OR*, 1, 8: 673; Timothy B. Smith, "'A Siege from the Start': The Spring 1862 Campaign against Corinth, Mississippi," *Journal of Mississippi History* 66, 4 (2004): 403.

2. Dunbar Rowland, *Mississippi*, 2 vols. (Spartanburg, SC: Reprint Company, 1976), 1:60; Rosemary Taylor Williams, *Cross City Chronicles* (n.p.: n.p., n.d.), 29–30; Alcorn County Historical Association, *The History of Alcorn County, Mississippi* (Dallas: Nationalshare Graphics, 1983), 6–8. Corinth remained a part of Tishomingo County until April 15, 1870, at which time Alcorn County, named after Governor James Lusk Alcorn, came

into existence. There is some debate as to the spelling of Lasley's name. Some sources say Lesley, but the 1860 census for Tishomingo County clearly lists him as William Lasley.

3. Alcorn County Historical Association, *History of Alcorn County,* 6–7; Williams, *Cross City Chronicles,* 29–30.

4. Kate Cumming, *A Journal of Hospital Life in the Confederate Army of Tennessee from the Battle of Shiloh to the End of the War: With Sketches of Life and Character, and Brief Notices of Current Events during that Period* (Louisville, KY: John P. Morton, 1866), 22; Williams, *Cross City Chronicles,* 29–30; Mrs. F. A. Inge, "Corinth, Miss. in Early War Days," *Confederate Veteran* 17, 9 (September 1909): 443; John H. Aughey, *The Iron Furnace: Or, Slavery and Secession* (Philadelphia: William S. and Alfred Martien, 1863), 232; Mrs. F. A. Inge, "Corinth, Miss. in War Times," *Confederate Veteran* 23, 9 (September 1915): 412–413; Alcorn County Historical Association, *History of Alcorn County,* 7; M. A. Miller Sketchbook of 1860 Corinth, 1, 3, 8, Northeast Mississippi Regional Library, Corinth (copy in M. A. Miller File, CWIC). For a description of Miller's sketchbook, see Joseph Todd Sanders, "M. A. Miller's Sketchbook of 1860 Corinth: The Built Environment of a Mississippi Boomtown" (M.A. thesis, Mississippi State University, 1992).

5. *Lucy's Journal* (Greenwood, MS: Baff Printing Company, 1967), 1, 25; Dawn Alexander, *Corona College as an Example of Antebellum Southern Education* (n.p.: n.p., n.d.), 8–13; Williams, *Cross City Chronicles,* 29–30; Inge, "Corinth, Miss. in Early War Days," 443; Aughey, *Iron Furnace,* 232; Inge, "Corinth, Miss. in War Times," 412–413; Alcorn County Historical Association, *History of Alcorn County,* 7; John A. Duckworth to William Rosser, undated, John A. Duckworth Letter, SHSI (copy in 2nd Iowa File, CWIC); M. A. Miller Sketchbook, 1, 3, 8. For the original diary published as *Lucy's Journal,* see Eliza Lucy Irion Diary, Irion-Neilson Family Papers, MDAH. For a handwritten diploma dated June 20, 1859, see box 1, folder 1, R. E. Price Collection, University of Mississippi.

6. M. A. Miller Sketchbook, 7; Margaret Greene Rogers, *Civil War Corinth: 1861–1865* (Corinth, MS: Rankin Printery, 1989), 2, 15; Alcorn County Historical Association, *History of Alcorn County,* 7–8; Frank Moore, ed., *The Rebellion Record: A Diary of American Events, with Documents, Narratives, Illustrative Incidents, Poetry, etc.,* 11 vols. (New York: D. Vann Nostrand, 1861–1868), 5:156–157.

7. Walter A. Overton Diary, April 16, May 26, June 16 and 29, August 16, and October 22, 1860, MDAH; excerpts of the diary can be found in Beulah M. D'Olive Price, ed., "Excerpts from Diary of Walter A. Overton, 1860–1862," *Journal of Mississippi History* 17, 3 (July 1955): 191–204.

8. Walter A. Overton Diary, October 22–25, 1860; *Manufactures of the United States in 1860: Compiled from the Original Returns of the Eighth Census under the Direction of the Secretary of the Interior* (Washington, DC: Government Printing Office, 1865), 294; Francis A. Walker, *A Compendium of the Ninth Census (June 1, 1870) Compiled Pursuant to a Concurrent Resolution of Congress and under the Direction of the Secretary of the Interior* (Washington, DC: Government Printing Office, 1872), 688–689, 699, 798; James H. McLendon, "The Development of Mississippi Agriculture," *Journal of Mississippi History* 13, 2 (April 1951): 81; Ranae Smith Vaughn and Cynthia Whirley Nelson, eds., *His-*

tory of Old Tishomingo County, Mississippi Territory (Iuka, MS: Tishomingo County Historical and Genealogical Society, 2005), 100; Williams, *Cross City Chronicles*, 29.

9. Walter A. Overton Diary, January 10, 1861; Rogers, *Civil War Corinth*, 29–30; Williams, *Cross City Chronicles*, 29–30.

10. John Tyler Jr. to William L. Yancey, October 15, 1862, John Tyler Jr. Letter, UMC.

11. Joseph C. G. Kennedy, *Population of the United States in 1860: Compiled from the Original Returns of the Eighth Census under the Direction of the Secretary of the Interior* (Washington, DC: Government Printing Office, 1864), 267–269.

12. Percy L. Rainwater, *Mississippi: Storm Center of Secession, 1856–1861* (Baton Rouge: Louisiana State University Press, 1938), 199; Walter A. Overton Diary, December 10–21, 1860; *Journal of the State Convention and Ordinances and Resolutions Adopted in January, 1861, with an Appendix* (Jackson, MS: E. Barksdale, 1861), 8; J. L. Power, *Proceedings of the Mississippi State Convention, Held January 7th to 26th, A.D. 1861* (Jackson, MS: Power and Cadwallader, 1861), 13; Bruce S. Allardice, *More Generals in Gray* (Baton Rouge: Louisiana State University Press, 1995), 196–197.

13. John Tyler Jr. to William L. Yancey, October 15, 1862; Walter A. Overton Diary, March 5, 1861. For more on the region, see Kristy Armstrong White, "Life in Civil War Tishomingo County, Mississippi" (M.A. thesis, Mississippi State University, 1998).

CHAPTER 1. THE GREAT RALLLYING POINT

1. Clement A. Evans, *Confederate Military History: A Library of Confederate States History Written by Distinguished Men of the South, and Edited by General Clement A. Evans*, 12 vols., vol. 7, pt. 2, *Mississippi* (Atlanta: Confederate Publishing Company, 1899), 52; *OR*, 1, 7: 888; J. T. Lance to brother, January 27, 1862, Settle Family Letters, Univeristy of Mississippi; David W. Ogden, "Reminiscences," undated, 30, William S. Ray Papers, University of Arkansas.

2. Frank Moore, ed., *The Rebellion Record: A Diary of American Events, with Documents, Narratives, Illustrative Incidents, Poetry, etc.*, 11 vols. (New York: D. Vann Nostrand, 1861–1868), 5:156; O. Edward Cunningham, *Shiloh and the Western Campaign of 1862*, ed. Gary D. Joiner and Timothy B. Smith (New York: Savas Beatie, 2007), 395.

3. Mrs. F. A. Inge, "Corinth, Miss. in Early War Days," *Confederate Veteran* 17, 9 (September 1909): 443; Walter A. Overton Diary, February 16, April 27, and November 21, 1861, MDAH; Stacy D. Allen, "Crossroads of the Western Confederacy," *Blue and Gray Magazine* 19, 6 (Summer 2002): 7. For more on the Corinth Rifles, see James C. Harris, *Story of the Corinth Rifles and Its Flag Bearer, Co. A 9th Miss. Inf Regt., C.S.A.* (Corinth, MS: n.p., n.d.); Gale Judkins, "James E. Stewart," James E. Stewart Biographical File, Alcorn County Genealogical Society Archives.

4. Inge, "Corinth, Miss. in Early War Days," 442–443.

5. Ibid., 443.

6. W. H. Riddick to Miss Sallie, June 1, 1861, HC; *OR*, 1, 52(2): 84–85; James W. Silver, ed., *A Life for the Confederacy: As Recorded in the Pocket Diaries of Pvt. Robert*

A. *Moore, Co. G 17th Mississippi Regiment Confederate Guards Holly Springs, Missis-sippi* (Jackson, TN: McCowat-Mercer Press, 1959), 21; *OR*, 1, 4: 370, 388; *OR*, 1, 7: 688, 710; Minutes of the Military Board, January 29, 1861–November 23, 1861, RG 9, series 394, box 416, MDAH; M. P. Lowry, "General M. P. Lowry: An Autobiography," September 30, 1867, Lowry Autobiographical Essay, University of Southern Mississippi; Dunbar Rowland and H. Grady Howell Jr., *Military History of Mississippi: 1803–1898, Including a Listing of All Known Mississippi Confederate Military Units* (Madison, MS: Chickasaw Bayou Press, 2003), 368–369; N. B. M. to friend, 1861, Malloy Papers, MSU. For the histories of each individual regiment, see Rowland and Howell, *Military History of Mississippi*.

7. Ogden, "Reminiscences," 29–30; Roland Oliver to wife, February 23, 1862, Roland Oliver Papers, Louisiana Tech University; A. R. Belser to sister, June 5, 1861, HC; Jesse R. Kirkland to wife, June 19 and 22, 1861, Jesse R. Kirkland Papers, MDAH; Robert G. Evans, ed., *The 16th Mississippi Infantry: Civil War Letters and Reminiscences* (Jackson: University Press of Mississippi, 2002), 4–5, 8; W. L. Culberson to sisters, February 28, 1862, 19th Louisiana File, CWIC; Alexander Livaudais Diary, March 30, 1862, 18th Louisiana File, CWIC; Rufus W. Daniel Diary, March 23, 1862, Arkansas History Commission.

8. Silver, *A Life for the Confederacy*, 22, 26; Alexander Livaudais Diary, March 30, 1862.

9. Alice Gray Sears Diary, April 22, May 27, and June 9, 1861, Sears-Featherston Sword Research Collection, MDAH; Roland Oliver to wife, March 20, 1862; Silver, *A Life for the Confederacy*, 24, 28; J. J. Wilson to brother, June 14, 1861, J. J. Wilson Papers, MDAH.

10. *OR*, 1, 7: 694–696; J. J. Wilson to brother, June 14, 1861; Walter A. Overton Diary, April 29, June 10, August 5, and December 14, 1861; Silver, *A Life for the Confederacy*, 22, 28; Evans, *The 16th Mississippi Infantry*, 5–6; N. B. M. to friend, 1861; Susan P. Gaston, "Reminiscences of the War," undated, in "History of Old Tishomingo County," 1, Alcorn County Chancery Clerk Archives.

11. Walter A. Overton Diary, April 29, June 10, August 5, and December 14, 1861; S. M. Nabors, *History of Old Tishomingo County* (Corinth, MS: n.p., 1940), 24; "History of Old Tishomingo County," 31.

12. Inge, "Corinth, Miss. in Early War Days," 443; W. L. Culberson to sisters, February 28, 1862, 19th Louisiana File, CWIC; James S. Slaughter to unknown, December 13, 1861, 5th Mississippi File, CWIC; J. J. Wilson to father, July 10, 1861; Roland Oliver to wife, March 20, 1862; Gaston, "Reminiscences of the War," 1.

13. Jesse R. Kirkland to wife, June 27, 1861; Inge, "Corinth, Miss. in Early War Days," 443; Walter A. Overton Diary, April 29, June 10, August 5, and December 14, 1861; Roland Oliver to wife, March 20, 1862; N. B. M. to friend, 1861; Rufus W. Daniel Diary, March 30 and April 2, 1862; Narcissa L. Black Diary, April 7 and May 26 and 27, 1862, MDAH.

14. Freeman Williams to father, December 6, 1861, HC; *OR*, 1, 4: 404; Reuben Davis, *Recollections of Mississippi and Mississippians* (Boston: Houghton, Mifflin, 1890), 420.

15. See Rowland and Howell, *Military History of Mississippi*, for later organization areas. For more on the second wave of enlistments, see Kenneth W. Noe, *Reluctant Rebels: The Confederates Who Joined the Army after 1861* (Chapel Hill: University of North Carolina Press, 2010).

16. Thomas L. Connelly, *Army of the Heartland: The Army of Tennessee, 1861–1862* (Baton Rouge: Louisiana State University Press, 1967); *OR*, 1, 7: 422, 672; *OR*, 1, 8: 634; John S. West to brother and sister, February 22, 1862, John S. West Letter, MSU.

17. *OR*, 1, 7: 674. The Army of the Tennessee was not officially given that name until December 1862. It was still officially known as the Army of West Tennessee during the spring of 1862, although the name "Army of the Tennessee" was beginning to appear in print.

18. For Halleck, see John F. Marszalek, *Commander of All Lincoln's Armies: A Life of General Henry W. Halleck* (Cambridge, MA: Harvard University Press, 2004).

19. Thomas Richardson to wife, March 26, 1862, Thomas Richardson Letter, LSU; Walter A. Overton Diary, February 8, March 3, 24, and 25, and May 15, 1862; S. S. Calhoon to P. G. T. Beauregard, August 3, 1876, P. G. T. Beauregard Papers, MDAH; "History of Old Tishomingo County," 31–32.

20. John Tyler Jr. to William L. Yancey, October 15, 1862, John Tyler Jr. Letter, UMC; Frank Batchelor to Julia, March 29, 1862, HC; *OR*, 1, 10(1): 775; P. G. T. Beauregard, "The Campaign of Shiloh," in *Battles and Leaders of the Civil War*, 4 vols. (New York: Century Company, 1884–1887), 1:577.

21. Thomas Richardson to wife, March 26, 1862; John H. Gates to Eliza, April 6, 1862, John Hooper Gates Papers, TSLA; Braxton Bragg to wife, March 23, 1862, Braxton Bragg Papers, LC.

22. Thomas Richardson to wife, March 26, 1862; Walter A. Overton Diary, March 18, 1862.

23. Inge, "Corinth, Miss. in Early War Days," 443; Maria Jane Southgate Hawes, *Reminiscences of Mrs. Maria Jane Southgate Hawes: Daughter of James Southgate and Jane Smith, Born Nov. 30, 1836* (n.p.: n.p., 1918); Bruce S. Allardice, *Confederate Colonels: A Biographical Register* (Columbia: University of Missouri Press, 2008), 210.

24. P. G. T. Beauregard to W. P. Johnston, March 9, 1877; A. H. Gladden to Daniel Ruggles, March 15, 1862, A. H. Gladden Papers, University of South Carolina; Daniel to Miss Honnoll, April 4, 1862, Robert W. Honnell Papers, Duke University; James L. McDonough, *Shiloh: In Hell before Night* (Knoxville: University of Tennessee Press, 1977), 69; Thomas Richardson to wife, March 26, 1862.

25. Larry J. Daniel, *Shiloh: The Battle that Changed the Civil War* (New York: Simon and Schuster, 1997), 123; Inge, "Corinth, Miss. in Early War Days," 443.

26. For Shiloh, see Wiley Sword, *Shiloh: Bloody April*, rev. ed. (Dayton, OH: Morningside, 2001); McDonough, *Shiloh*; Daniel, *Shiloh*; and Cunningham, *Shiloh and the Western Campaign of 1862*. An old but still useful source is David W. Reed's *The Battle of Shiloh and the Organizations Engaged* (1902; reprint, Knoxville: University of Tennessee Press, 2008).

27. W. A. Howard to his wife, April 11, 1862, 33rd Tennessee File, SNMP; Braxton Bragg to wife, March 23, 1862.

28. John H. Gates to Eliza, April 6, 1862; Gaston, "Reminiscences of the War," 1; Inge, "Corinth, Miss. in Early War Days," 444.

29. Cunningham, *Shiloh and the Western Campaign of 1862*, 329; Inge, "Corinth, Miss. in Early War Days," 444.

30. F. F. Kiner, *One Year's Soldiering: Embracing the Battles of Fort Donelson and Shiloh and the Capture of Two Hundred Officers and Men of the Fourteenth Iowa Infantry, and Their Confinement Six Months and a Half in Rebel Prisons* (Priot Lake, MN: Morgan Avenue Press, 2000), 31; J. Robins to H. H. Price, April 18, 1862, H. H. Price Papers, Duke University; A. Tomlinson to H. H. Price, April 18, 1862, Price Papers; Andrew Devilbliss to Mary, April 16, 1862, Civil War Miscellaneous Series, Tulane University; Jack D. Welsh, *Medical Histories of Confederate Generals* (Kent, OH: Kent State University Press, 1995), 15; Alcorn County Historical Association, *The History of Alcorn County, Mississippi* (Dallas: Nationalshare Graphics, 1983), 9; Richard B. Harwell, ed., *Kate: The Journal of a Confederate Nurse* (Baton Rouge: Louisiana State University Press, 1959), 12, 14, 19, 22, 26–27; Inge, "Corinth, Miss. in Early War Days," 444; Mary W. Schaller and Martin N. Schaller, *Soldiering for Glory: The Civil War Letters of Colonel Francis Schaller, Twenty-second Mississippi Infantry* (Columbia: University of South Carolina Press, 2007), 84.

31. W. J. Stubblefield Diary, April 8, 1862, Murray State University; Walter A. Overton Diary, April 7, 1862.

32. Kiner, *One Year's Soldiering*, 31; J. Robins to H. H. Price, April 18, 1862; A. Tomlinson to H. H. Price, April 18, 1862; Andrew Devilbliss to Mary, April 16, 1862; Alcorn County Historical Association, *History of Alcorn County*, 9; Harwell, *Kate*, 12, 14, 19, 22, 26–27; Inge, "Corinth, Miss. in Early War Days," 444; Schaller and Schaller, *Soldiering for Glory*, 84; Bell I. Wiley, *The Life of Johnny Reb: The Common Soldier of the Confederacy* (Indianapolis: Bobbs-Merrill, 1943), 263.

33. Harwell, *Kate*, 12, 14, 19, 22, 26–27; Shelby Foote, *The Civil War: A Narrative*, 3 vols. (New York: Random House, 1958), 1:381; Roland Oliver to wife, April 18, 1862.

34. Walter A. Overton Diary, April 9 and April 29–May 5, 1862; Gaston, "Reminiscences of the War," 2; Roland Oliver to wife, April 18, 1862; Inge, "Corinth, Miss. in Early War Days," 444; J. H. Knighton to "Rod," April 10, 1862, Josiah Knighton and Family Papers, LSU; Robert Franklin Bunting to Sir, May 11, 1862, Robert Franklin Bunting Collection, TSLA; William Eames to wife, April 10, 1862, William Mark Eames Papers, TSLA; Rachel Carter Craighead Diary, April 11, 1862, TSLA.

35. Robert H. Cartmell Diary, August 14, 1862, Robert H. Cartmell Papers, TSLA; W. N. Mattison to wife, June 15, 1862, William N. Mattison Papers, Atlanta History Center; E. B. Sellers to father, May 12, 1862, 1st Texas File, CWIC; Theodore Trimmier to Mary, April 14, 1862, Theodore Gillard Trimmier Papers, TSLA; Houston Huling Parker Diary, April 9 and 11, 1862, MDAH; James S. Oliver Memo, July 25, 1862, James S. Oliver Papers, MDAH. See the Confederate sections of cemeteries at Okolona, Oxford, Columbus, Holly Springs, and Winona for examples.

36. *OR*, 1, 6: 433–435; *OR*, 1, 10(2): 405–407, 409, 416; Dabney H. Maury, *Recollections of a Virginian* (New York: Charles Scribner's Sons, 1894), 167.

37. Earl Van Dorn to Samuel Cooper, April 8, 1862, Letters and Telegrams Sent—Van Dorn's Command, NARA; Albert Castel, *General Sterling Price and the Civil War in the West* (Baton Rouge: Louisiana State University Press, 1968), 81–83; L. H. Graves Diary, April 1862, University of Texas at Austin.

38. *OR*, 1, 10(2): 405, 436; W. W. Worthington to parents, April 10, 1862, L. P. Wulff Collection, University of Tennessee.

39. D. A. Rawlins Diary, April 18, 1862, University of North Texas; Patrick Michael Hotard, "The Campaign (Siege) of Corinth, Mississippi, April–June 1862" (M.A. thesis, Southeastern Louisiana University, 2005), 10; W. H. Tunnard, *A Southern Record: The History of the 3rd Regiment Louisiana Infantry*, ed. Edwin C. Bearss (Dayton, OH: Morningside Bookshop, 1970), 164; Castel, *General Sterling Price*, 84; Newton A. Keen, *Living and Fighting with the Texas 6th Cavalry* (Gaithersburg, MD: Butterneutt Press, 1986), 32; Robert C. Black III, *The Railroads of the Confederacy* (Chapel Hill: University of North Carolina Press, 1952), 144; Harwell, *Kate*, 25; Kate Cumming, *A Journal of Hospital Life in the Confederate Army of Tennessee from the Battle of Shiloh to the End of the War: With Sketches of Life and Character, and Brief Notices of Current Events during that Period* (Louisville, KY: John P. Morton, 1866), 21; Francis Marion Cockrell Scrapbooks, 97, UMC; Robert G. Hartje, *Van Dorn: The Life and Times of a Confederate General* (Nashville: Vanderbilt University Press, 1967), 173, 175.

40. H. L. Honnoll to father, May 8, 1862; "Personal Memoirs of I. V. Smith," undated, 20, UMC; Hartje, *Van Dorn*, 173, 175; D. T. Pounds to mother, April 17, 1862, Pounds Family Papers, TSLA.

41. John Tyler Jr. to William L. Yancey, October 15, 1862; *OR*, 1, 10(1): 775; Margaret Greene Rogers, *Civil War Corinth* (Corinth, MS: Rankin Printery, 1989), 9; Alfred Roman, *The Military Operations of General Beauregard in the War between the States, 1861–1865: Including a Brief Personal Sketch of His Services in the War with Mexico, 1846–8*, 2 vols. (New York: Harper and Brothers, 1883), 1:382; Tunnard, *Southern Record*, 165; Allen, "Crossroads of the Western Confederacy," 14; Castel, *General Sterling Price*, 85; Thomas C. Reynolds, "General Sterling Price and the Confederacy," Thomas C. Reynolds Papers, Missouri Historical Society; Cecil A. Duke, "Confederate Intrenchments," Historical Reports, SNMP; Rufus W. Daniel Diary, April 23, 24, and 26, 1862.

42. *OR*, 1, 10(1): 778; John H. Aughey, *The Iron Furnace: Or, Slavery and Secession* (Philadelphia: William S. and Alfred Martien, 1863), 255; Castel, *General Sterling Price*, 85; Reynolds, "General Sterling Price and the Confederacy."

43. T. J. Koger to wife, May 12, 1862, T. J. Koger Collection, MDAH; Thomas A. Williams to his brother, May 2, 1862, Haller Nutt Papers, Huntington Library; Evans, *Confederate Military History*, 7(2): 52; Daniel Stout to his wife, April 26, 1862, Stout Civil War Letters, University of Memphis.

CHAPTER 2. "I LEAVE HERE TO-MORROW MORNING"

1. John B. Rice to wife, May 1, 1862, Robert S. Rice Papers, RBHPC; *OR*, 1, 10(1): 27; Jacob Ammen to A. B. Martin, March 6, 1862, Jacob Ammen Papers, U.S. Military Academy; Samuel D. Lougheed to wife, April 20, 1862, Samuel D. Lougheed Papers, University of Washington.

2. *OR*, 1, 10(1): 672.

3. James Scully to wife, May 2, 1862, James Wall Scully Papers, Duke University; *OR*, 1, 10(1): 672, 705.

4. U. S. Grant, *Personal Memoirs of U. S. Grant* (New York: Charles L. Webster, 1885), 220; Patrick Michael Hotard, "The Campaign (Siege) of Corinth, Mississippi, April–June 1862" (M.A. thesis, Southeastern Louisiana University, 2005), 5.

5. David Harrison Thomas to brother, April 26, 1862, David Harrison Thomas Papers, Ohio Historical Society; *OR*, 1, 10(1): 672; John F. Marszalek, *Commander of All Lincoln's Armies: A Life of General Henry W. Halleck* (Cambridge, MA: Harvard University Press, 2004), 121–122; Stephen E. Ambrose, *Halleck: Lincoln's Chief of Staff* (Baton Rouge: Louisiana State University Press, 1962), 47; Steven E. Woodworth, *Nothing But Victory: The Army of the Tennessee, 1861–1865* (New York: Knopf, 2005), 205.

6. Manning F. Force, *From Fort Henry to Corinth* (New York: Charles Scribner's Sons, 1881), 183.

7. Wallace J. Schutz and Walter N. Trenerry, *Abandoned by Lincoln: A Military Biography of General John Pope* (Chicago: University of Illinois Press, 1990), 85; Charles W. Gallentine to sister, May 17, 1862, Charles W. Gallentine Letters, Newberry Library; Elmore to "Dearest One," April 17, 1862, Elmore (Union Soldier) Letter, Filson Historical Society; Henry Buck to Helen, April 28, 1862, Henry A. Buck Papers, Detroit Public Library; *OR*, 1, 10(2): 235; Robert H. Cartmell Diary, August 14, 1862, Robert H. Cartmell Papers, TSLA. One author puts Halleck's numbers as few as 86,000; see Larry J. Daniel, *Days of Glory: The Army of the Cumberland, 1861–1865* (Baton Rouge: Louisiana State University Press, 2004), 85.

8. Vivian Kirkpatrick McCarty, ed., "Civil War Experiences," *Missouri Historical Review* 43, 3 (April 1949): 244; Henry Buck to Helen, April 28, 1862; Grant, *Personal Memoirs*, 220; John B. Rice to wife, May 1, 1862.

9. *OR*, 1, 10(2): 101, 106, 144; William T. Sherman, *Memoirs of General William T. Sherman: Written by Himself* (New York: D. Appleton, 1875), 232.

10. Richard L. Kiper, *Major General John A. McClernand: Politician in Uniform* (Kent, OH: Kent State University Press, 1999), 118; Woodworth, *Nothing But Victory*, 206; Gail Stephens, *Shadow of Shiloh: Major General Lew Wallace in the Civil War* (Indianapolis: Indiana Historical Society Press, 2010), 112.

11. Shelby Foote, *The Civil War: A Narrative*, 3 vols. (New York: Random House, 1958), 1:373; Stephen D. Engle, *Don Carlos Buell: Most Promising of All* (Chapel Hill: University of North Carolina Press, 1999), 241, 244.

12. Richard O'Connor, *Thomas: Rock of Chickamauga* (New York: Prentice-Hall, 1948), 171–172.

13. *OR*, 1, 52(1): 245; Sherman, *Memoirs,* 250; O'Connor, *Thomas*, 172.

14. William J. Christie to brother, May 16, 1862, William J. Christie Letters, LSU; *OR*, 1, 10(2): 132; John F. Marszalek, "Halleck Captures Corinth," *Civil War Times* 45, 1 (February 2006): 49.

15. Phineas R. Freeman to wife, May 4, 1862, Amori B. Cook Papers, Archives of Michigan; Charles Watson to wife, May 16, 1862, Charles Watson Letters, 52nd Illinois File, CWIC; Frank Jones to his mother, May 20, 1862, Frank J. Jones Civil War Letters, Cincinnati Historical Society; Ambrose, *Halleck*, 49; *OR*, 1, 10(1): 665; *OR*, 1, 8: 603. For an overview of the campaign, see Timothy B. Smith, "'A Siege from the Start': The Spring 1862 Campaign against Corinth, Mississippi," *Journal of Mississippi History* 66, 4 (2004): 403–424.

16. Henry Buck to Helen, April 28, 1862; William Brown to sister, May 3, 1862, William Brown Letters, SHSW; John Hill Ferguson Diary, May 1, 1862, MacMurray College (copy in TSLA); *OR*, 1, 10(1): 664–665; George Lanphear to children, May 22, 1862, Lanphear Family Letters, University of Tennessee.

17. Charles W. Wills, *Army Life of an Illinois Soldier: Including a Day by Day Record of Sherman's March to the Sea* (Washington, DC: Globe Printing Company, 1906), 85; *OR*, 1, 10(1): 672–673; W. A. Neal, *An Illustrated History of the Missouri Engineer and the 25th Infantry Regiments: Together with a Roster of Both Regiments and the Last Known Address of All that Could Be Obtained* (Chicago: Donohue and Henneberry, 1889), 52.

18. *OR*, 1, 10(1): 672–673.

19. Marszalek, *Commander of All Lincoln's Armies*, 123; Ezra J. Warner, *Generals in Blue: Lives of the Union Commanders* (Baton Rouge: Louisiana State University Press, 1964), 195–196; Marszalek, "Halleck Captures Corinth," 49, 52; Ephraim A. Wilson, *Memoirs of the War* (Cleveland, OH: W. M. Bayne, 1893), 114; Greg Barton to sister, May 17, 1862, HC; *The Story of the Fifty-fifth Regiment Illinois Volunteer Infantry in the Civil War, 1861–1865* (n.p.: n.p., n.d.), 143; unknown to wife, May 11, 1862, Gail and Stephen Rudin Collection, Cornell University; Henry Buck to Helen, April 28, 1862.

20. Erasmus Stirman to sister, May 12, 1862, Rebecca Stirman Davidson Family Papers, University of Arkansas; William M. Parkinson to wife and children, May 2 and 6, 1862, William M. Parkinson Letters, Emory University; Frank L. Jones to his mother, May 20, 1862, Michael B. Ballard Collection, MSU; Wright C. Shaumburg Journal, May 12, 1862, Schaumburg-Wright Family Papers, HNOC; John B. Rice to wife, May 1, 6, 8, 11, and 14, 1862; Alpheus S. Bloomfield to father, May 5, 1862, Alpheus S. Bloomfield Papers, LC; Thomas A. Williams to Haller Nutt, May 2, 1862, Haller Nutt Papers, Huntington Library; George Thomas to Minerva, April 27, 1862, Thomas Family Correspondence, University of Notre Dame; George Kryder to his wife, May 19, 1862, George Kryder Papers, BGSU; J. G. Burggraf to wife, May 12, 1862, John G. Burggraf Collection, Willamette University; S. B. Maxey to his wife, May 5 and 6, 1862, Samuel Bell Maxey Papers, Texas State Archives.

21. Cyrus S. Bolton Diary, April 29, 1862, Ohio Historical Society; George W. Lennard to Clara, May 12, 1862, George W. Lennard Collection, Arizona State University; Henry Buck to Helen, April 28, 1862; P. P. Lash to wife, May 2, 1862, 30th Indiana File, CWIC;

Hugh Johnson to wife, June 1, 1862, 2nd Iowa Cavalry File, CWIC; Richard W. Burt to editor, May 10, 1862, 76th Ohio File, CWIC.

22. Hugh Johnson to wife, June 1, 1862; P. P. Lash to wife, May 2, 1862; Richard W. Burt to editor, May 10, 1862; Henry Buck to Helen, April 28, 1862; Cyrus S. Bolton Diary, April 29, 1862; George W. Lennard to Clara, May 12, 1862.

23. August Schilling Diary, April 26, 1862, BCHS; *OR*, 1, 10(1): 713-734; Warner, *Generals in Blue*, 196.

24. *OR*, 1, 10(1): 721, 799-800; Peter Cozzens and Robert I. Girardi, eds., *The Military Memoirs of General John Pope* (Chapel Hill: University of North Carolina Press, 1998), 66; Thomas Jesse Rankin to Sarah, April 28, 1862, 7th Mississippi File, CWIC; George W. Lennard to Clara, May 3, 1862.

25. Lewis Mathewson to parents, May 2, 1862, Lewis Mathewson Papers, Ohio Historical Society; John Hill Ferguson Diary, May 1, 1862; *OR*, 1, 10(1): 713-715, 721, 802-803.

26. John Hill Ferguson Diary, May 3, 1862; Frank L. Jones to his mother, May 20, 1862, Michael B. Ballard Collection, MSU; Lewis Mathewson to parents, May 2, 1862; John Pope, "Report of Major General Pope," in *Supplemental Report of the Joint Committee on the Conduct of the War, in Two Volumes* (Washington, DC: Government Printing Office, 1866), 2:71; Hotard, "Campaign (Siege) of Corinth," 52; *OR*, 1, 10(1): 713-715, 721, 802-803; *OR*, 1, 10(2): 158, 160; John B. Rice to wife, May 4, 1862; W. L. Broaddus to wife, May 5, 1862, William L. Broaddus Papers, Duke University; John Hill Ferguson Diary, May 3, 1862; Frank Moore, ed., *The Rebellion Record: A Diary of American Events, with Documents, Narratives, Illustrative Incidents, Poetry, etc.*, 11 vols. (New York: D. Vann Nostrand, 1861-1868), 5:4-6; Wills, *Army Life of an Illinois Soldier*, 86; C. C. Briant, *History of the Sixth Regiment Indiana Volunteer Infantry: Of Both the Three Months' and the Three Years' Services* (Indianapolis: William B. Burford, 1891), 131.

27. Frederick Kehrwecker to his brother, May 11, 1862, Kehrwecker Family Papers, BGSU; Lewis Mathewson to parents, May 12, 1862; George W. Lennard to Clara, May 5, 1862; J. V. Frederick, ed., "An Illinois Soldier in North Mississippi: Diary of John Wilson February 15–December 30, 1862," *Journal of Mississippi History* 1, 3 (July 1939): 186; John Hill Ferguson Diary, May 3, 1862; W. L. Broaddus to wife, May 5, 1862; *OR*, 1, 10(2): 160; *OR*, 1, 10(1): 665, 721, 728, 730.

28. Fritz Hashell, ed., "Col. William Camm War Diary, 1861-1865," *Journal of the Illinois State Historical Society* 18, 4 (January 1926): 869; Lewis Mathewson to parents, May 12, 1862; Frederick Kehrwecker to his brother, May 11, 1862; George W. Lennard to Clara, May 5, 1862; Joshua T. Bradford Diary, May 5, 1862, LC; John Hill Ferguson Diary, May 3, 1862; *OR*, 1, 10(2): 160; *OR*, 1, 10(1): 665, 721, 728, 730; W. L. Broaddus to wife, May 5, 1862; Frederick, "An Illinois Soldier in North Mississippi," 186.

29. Lewis Mathewson to parents, May 12, 1862; W. L. Broaddus to wife, May 10, 1862; Moore, *The Rebellion Record*, 5:117; Hotard, "The Campaign (Siege) of Corinth," 54; John Hill Ferguson Diary, May 8, 1862; *OR*, 1, 10(1): 715, 719, 721, 724; *OR*, 1, 10(2): 170; Wills, *Army Life of an Illinois Soldier*, 86.

30. *OR*, 1, 10(1): 678; James Scully to wife, May 2, 1862.

31. W. A. Huddard to father, May 1, 1862, William A. Huddard Papers, University of Tennessee; James Birney Shaw, *History of the Tenth Regiment Indiana Volunteer Infantry: Three Months and Three Years Organizations* (Lafayette, IN: Regimental Association, 1912), 167; Briant, *History of the Sixth Regiment Indiana Volunteer Infantry*, 131.

32. David Harrison Thomas to brother, May 28, 1862; John B. Rice to wife, May 11, 1862; *OR*, 1, 10(1): 672–673, 682; Shaw, *History of the Tenth Regiment Indiana Volunteer Infantry*, 167; Clint to Hannah, May 24, 1862, DeWitt Clinton Loudon Papers, Ohio Historical Society; Cyrus S. Bolton Diary, May 3, 1862; Charles Kroff Diary, May 11, 1862, Sherry M. Cress Collection, University of Oklahoma.

33. William Shanks Diary, May 5, 1862, BGSU; *OR*, 1, 10(1): 673–675, 678, 705.

34. *OR*, 1, 10(1): 674, 678; *OR*, 1, 10(2): 171–172.

35. T. W. Sherman to Adam Badaeu, April 3, 1862, Thomas West Sherman Collection, LC; William F. G. Shanks, *Personal Recollections of Distinguished Generals* (New York: Harper and Brothers, 1866), 36; D. Leib Ambrose, *History of the Seventh Regiment Illinois Volunteer Infantry, from Its First Muster into the U.S. Service, April 25, 1861, to Its Final Muster out, July 9, 1865* (Springfield: Illinois Journal Company, 1868), 67; August Schilling Diary, May 2, 1862; John B. Rice to wife, May 1, 1862.

36. John B. Rice to wife, May 1, 1862; *OR*, 1, 10(1): 738–739; *OR*, 1, 10(2): 158, 189, 192–193; Alvin P. Hovey Memoirs, undated, Alvin P. Hovey Papers, University of Indiana.

37. William M. Parkinson to wife and children, May 6, 1862; Benita K. Moore, ed., *A Civil War Diary: Written by Dr. James A. Black, First Assistant Surgeon, 49th Illinois Infantry* (Bloomington, IN: Author House, 2008), 56; Chester Townsend Hart Diary, May 5, 1862, 15th Illinois File, CWIC; *OR*, 1, 10(1): 739; Charles B. Kimbell, *History of Battery "A" First Illinois Light Artillery Volunteers* (Chicago: Cushing Printing Company, 1899), 49; Thomas J. Williams, *An Historical Sketch of the 56th Ohio Volunteer Infantry during the Great Civil War from 1861 to 1865* (Columbus, OH: Lawrence Press, n.d.), 18.

38. John B. Rice to wife, May 6, 1862; Grant, *Memoirs*, 221, 224.

Chapter 3. "The Ball Has Commenced"

1. *OR*, 1, 10(2): 457–458; W. H. Tunnard, *A Southern Record: The History of the 3rd Regiment Louisiana Infantry*, ed. Edwin C. Bearss (Dayton, OH: Morningside, 1970), 165; Frank Moore, ed., *The Rebellion Record: A Diary of American Events, with Documents, Narratives Illustrative Incidents, Poetry, etc.*, 11 vols. (New York: D. Vann Nostrand, 1861–1868), 5:157; Patrick Michael Hotard, "The Campaign (Siege) of Corinth, Mississippi, April–June 1862" (M.A. thesis, Southeastern Louisiana University, 2005), 38–39.

2. *OR*, 1, 10(2): 457–458; *OR*, 1, 52(2): 309–310.

3. *OR*, 1, 10(2): 457–458, 499–500.

4. Ibid., 457–458, 517–518.

5. Thomas A. Williams to Haller Nutt, May 2, 1862, Haller Nutt Papers, Huntington Library; Wright C. Shaumburg Journal, May 14, 1862, Schaumburg-Wright Family Papers,

HNOC; P. Marchant to Susan, May 7, 1862, HC; Robert H. Cartmell Diary, August 14, 1862, Robert H. Cartmell Papers, TSLA; Thomas A. Colman to parents, May 12, 1862, Colman-Hayter Family Papers, UMC; W. J. McMurray, *History of the Twentieth Tennessee Regiment Volunteer Infantry, C.S.A.* (Nashville: Publication Committee, 1904), 213; L. H. Graves Diary, April 1862, University of Texas at Austin; Joseph M. Bailey Memoir, "Story of a Confederate Soldier, 1861–1865," undated, 16, University of Arkansas; W. J. Stubblefield Diary, May 9, 1862, Murray State University; T. J. Walker Reminiscences, undated, 7, University of Tennessee; Erasmus Stirman to sister, May 12, 1862, Rebecca Stirman Davidson Family Papers, University of Arkanksas.

6. S. H. Dent to his wife, April 23, 1862, S. H. Dent Papers, Auburn University; C. H. George to sister, May 27, 1862, George Family Letters, Auburn University.

7. Bell I. Wiley, *The Life of Johnny Reb: The Common Soldier of the Confederacy* (Indianapolis: Bobbs-Merrill, 1943), 247; T. J. Koger to wife, May 13, 1862, T. J. Koger Collection, MDAH; "History of Company D, 15th Mississippi Infantry," undated, 38, Gore Civil War History Collection, University of Southern Mississippi; Special Order 47, May 1, 1862, William Yerger Papers, MDAH; W. J. Stubblefield Diary, May 8, 1862; Thomas L. Snead, "With Price East of the Mississippi," in *Battles and Leaders of the Civil War*, 4 vols. (New York: Century Company, 1884–1887), 2:719; William H. Kavanaugh Memoirs, undated, 32, William H. Kavanaugh Papers, UMC; C. H. George to sister, May 27, 1862; W. H. Wiseman to family, May 24, 1862, 10th Mississippi File, CWIC; John G. Galliard Memoir, 1895, John G. Galliard Papers, University of South Carolina; W. N. Mattison to wife, May 5 and 15, 1862, William N. Mattison Papers, Atlanta History Center.

8. Grady McWhiney, *Braxton Bragg and Confederate Defeat*, 2 vols. (New York: Columbia University Press, 1969), 1:257; Hotard, "The Campaign (Siege) of Corinth," 31; *OR*, 1, 10(2): 496; William C. Davis, *Breckinridge: Statesman, Soldier, Symbol* (Baton Rouge: Louisiana State University Press, 1974), 316; Sam Davis Elliott, *Soldier of Tennessee: General Alexander P. Stewart and the Civil War in the West* (Baton Rouge: Louisiana State University Press, 1999), 46.

9. *OR*, 1, 10(2): 478, 492, 530–531; W. J. Stubblefield Diary, May 8, 1862; Thomas A. Colman to parents, May 12, 1862; Alexander Livaudais Diary, March 30, 1862, 18th Louisiana File, CWIC.

10. Special Order 43, May 17, 1862, William Yerger Papers, MDAH; *OR*, 1, 10(2): 516, 525, 539, 544; Robert G. Hartje, *Van Dorn: The Life and Times of a Confederate General* (Nashville: Vanderbilt University Press, 1967), 180–181; Louis Stagg to wife, July 18, 1862, Louis Stagg Letters, LSU (copy in 16th Louisiana File, CWIC).

11. A. P. Stewart to unknown, May 6, 1862, Alexander Peter Stewart Letters, Duke University; *OR*, 1, 10(2): 520, 525; Sam R. Watkins, *"Co. Aytch," Maury Grays, First Tennessee Regiment; or, a Side Show of the Big Show* (Nashville: Presbyterian Printing House, 1882), 49; Charles W. Wills, *Army Life of an Illinois Soldier: Including a Day by Day Record of Sherman's March to the Sea* (Washington, DC: Globe Printing Company, 1906), 91; E. S. Holloway to wife, May 25, 1862, Ephraim S. Holloway Papers, Ohio Historical Society.

12. *OR*, 1, 10(2): 482, 484, 496.

13. Ibid., 492, 502, 509, 528.

14. Ibid., 457–458, 482, 509.

15. Special Order 49, May 3, 1862, William Yerger Papers, MDAH; *OR*, 1, 10(1): 801; *OR*, 1, 10(2): 483, 493; George Dobson to family, May 4, 1862, 10th Mississippi File, CWIC.

16. W. J. Stubblefield Diary, May 4, 1862; W. N. Mattison to wife, May 5, 1862; *OR*, 1, 10(2): 487, 489, 492, 496–498, 500; W. A. Huddard to father, May 6, 1862, William A. Huddard Papers, University of Tennessee.

17. Kate Cumming, *A Journal of Hospital Life in the Confederate Army of Tennessee from the Battle of Shiloh to the End of the War: With Sketches of Life and Character, and Brief Notices of Current Events during that Period* (Louisville, KY: John P. Morton, 1866), 23; Stacy D. Allen, "Crossroads of the Western Confederacy," *Blue and Gray Magazine* 19, 6 (Summer 2002): 14; *OR*, 1, 10(2): 487, 489, 492, 496–498, 500; William R. Burke Diary, May 9, 1862, 50th Alabama File, CWIC.

18. J. H. Rogers to Sallie, May 18, 1862, Sarah Rogers Shaw Papers, Wesleyan College.

19. *OR*, 1, 10(1): 807–808; *OR*, 1, 10(2): 489–491; Alred Roman, *The Military Operations of General Beauregard in the War between the States, 1861–1865: Including a Brief Personal Sketch of His Services in the War with Mexico, 1846–8*, 2 vols. (New York: Harper and Brothers, 1883), 1:386; John K. Street to sisters, May 10, 1862, John Kennedy Street Papers, University of North Carolina (copy in 3rd Texas Cavalry File, CWIC); P. G. T. Beauregard to Braxton Bragg, May 9, 1862, Pierre Gustave Toutant Beauregard Papers, LC.

20. Matthew H. Jamison, *Recollections of Pioneer and Army Life* (Kansas City, MO: Hudson Press, 1911), 184; *OR*, 1, 10(1): 805–807.

21. Sharon L. D. Kraynek, ed., *Letters to My Wife: A Civil War Diary from the Western Front* (Apollo, PA: Closson Press, 1995), 22; *OR*, 1, 10(1): 706, 809, 812, 820, 831–838; J. H. Rogers to Sallie, May 18, 1862; James Patton Anderson to R. M. Hood, May 15, 1862, James Patton Anderson Papers, University of Florida.

22. *OR*, 1, 10(1): 806; Moore, *The Rebellion Record*, 5:117; William R. Plum, *The Military Telegraph during the Civil War in the United States, with an Exposition of Ancient and Modern Means of Communication, and of the Federal and Confederate Cipher Systems; Also a Running Account of the War between the States*, 2 vols. (Chicago: Jansen, McClurg, 1882), 1:243.

23. *OR*, 1, 10(1): 806; *Supplement to the Official Records of the Union and Confederate Armies*, 100 vols. (Wilmington, NC: Broadfoot, 1994), pt. 1, 1:722.

24. John M. Palmer, *Personal Recollections of John M. Palmer: The Story of an Earnest Life* (Cincinnati, OH: Robert Clarke, 1901), 103–104.

25. J. H. Rogers to Sallie, May 18, 1862; W. L. Broaddus to wife, May 10, 1862; Palmer, *Personal Recollections,* 105; Kraynek, *Letters to My Wife*, 22–23; *OR*, 1, 10(1): 729, 809, 812–813, 820, 825; Clyde C. Walton, ed., *Private Smith's Journal: Recollections of the Late War* (Chicago: R. R. Donnelley and Sons, 1963), 39; Moore, *The Rebellion Record*, 5:119; Daniel Gober Report, May 10, 1862, HC.

26. *OR*, 1, 10(1): 729, 809, 812–813, 820, 825; Walton, *Private Smith's Journal*, 39; Moore, *The Rebellion Record*, 5:119; J. H. Rogers to Sallie, May 18, 1862; W. L. Broaddus to wife, May 10, 1862; Kraynek, *Letters to My Wife*, 22–23; Gober Report, May 10, 1862; Lyman B. Pierce, *History of the Second Iowa Cavalry: Containing a Detailed Account of Its Organization, Marches, and the Battles in Which It Has Participated; Also, a Complete Roster of Each Company* (Burlington, IA: Hawk-eye Steam Book and Job Printing Establishment, 1865), 22.

27. David McKnight Diary, May 9, 1862, Civil War Collection, Missouri Historical Society; *OR*, 1, 10(1): 806–807, 830; John Hill Ferguson Diary, May 91, 1862, MacMurray College; Thomas A. Colman to parents, May 12, 1862; Wills, *Army Life of an Illinois Soldier*, 88–89.

28. *OR*, 1, 10(1): 806–807, 830; Wills, *Army Life of an Illinois Soldier*, 88–89; David McKnight Diary, May 9, 1862; John Hill Ferguson Diary, May 91, 1862; Thomas A. Colman to parents, May 12, 1862.

29. John Hill Ferguson Diary, May 9, 1862; Lewis Mathewson to parents, May 12, 1862, Lewis Mathewson Papers, Ohio Historical Society; Palmer, *Personal Recollections*, 107–108.

30. John Melvin Williams, *"The Eagle Regiment," 8th Wis. Inf'ty Vols.: A Sketch of Its Marches, Battles and Campaigns from 1861–1865 with Complete Regimental and Company Roster, and a Few Portraits and Sketches of Its Officers and Commanders* (Belleville, WI: Recorder Print, 1890), 47; J. W. Greenman Diary, May 9, 1862, MDAH.

31. *OR*, 1, 10(1): 674, 682, 804–805, 810; Peter Cozzens, *General John Pope: A Life for the Nation* (Urbana: University of Illinois Press, 2000), 67; Peter Cozzens and Robert I. Girardi, eds., *The Military Memoirs of General John Pope* (Chapel Hill: University of North Carolina Press, 1998), 67.

32. *OR*, 1, 10(1): 810.

33. Cumming, *Journal of Hospital Life*, 25; Erasmus Stirman to sister, May 12, 1862; Tunnard, *Southern Record*, 167; *OR*, 1, 10(1): 809, 813, 815–816, 819; *OR*, 1, 10(2): 172; Thomas A. Colman to parents, May 12, 1862; Moore, *The Rebellion Record*, 5:119.

34. George Lanphear to children, June 19, 1862, Lanphear Family Letters, University of Tennessee; Albert Theodore Goodloe, *Confederate Echoes: A Voice from the South in the Days of Secession and the Southern Confederacy* (Nashville: Publishing House of the Methodist Episcopal Church, South, 1907), 97–98; J. H. Rogers to Sallie, May 18, 1862. Federal soldiers also took souvenirs. One Minnesotan later in the campaign sent home several cotton leaves.

35. *OR*, 1, 10(1): 809, 824; *OR*, 1, 10(2): 505.

36. Erasmus Stirman to wife, May 12, 1862; L. H. Graves Diary, April 1862; Ephraim McD. Anderson, *Memoirs: Historical and Personal; Including the Campaigns of the First Missouri Confederate Brigade* (St. Louis: Times Printing Company, 1868), 198; Cumming, *Journal of Hospital Life*, 26; Tunnard, *Southern Record*, 166; *OR*, 1, 10(1): 778, 807–808; *OR*, 1, 10(2): 503, 505–506; Thomas A. Colman to parents, May 12, 1862.

37. T. Harry Williams, *P. G. T. Beauregard: Napoleon in Gray* (Baton Rouge: Louisiana State University, 1954), 151; Goodloe, *Confederate Echoes*, 97–98; W. L. Baily to W. K.

Benson, May 12, 1862, William George Hale Papers, LSU; Thomas H. Colman to his parents, May 12, 1862; William F. Hinkle Diary, May 9, 1862, Indiana Historical Society.

38. Jacob Harrison Allspaugh Diary, May 8, 1862, University of Iowa; *OR*, 1, 10(1): 666–667, 803–804; David W. Ogden Reminiscences, undated, 24, University of Arkansas; Alexis Cope, *The Fifteenth Ohio Volunteers and Its Campaigns: War of 1861–5* (Columbus, OH: n.p., 1916), 147.

39. Pierce, *History of the Second Iowa Cavalry*, 23.

40. *OR*, 1, 10(1): 739; *OR*, 1, 10(2): 179; William W. Cluett, *History of the 57th Regiment Illinois Volunteer Infantry, from Muster in, Dec. 26, 1861, to Muster out, July 7, 1865* (Princeton, IL: T. P. Streeter, 1886), 29; John N. Wiedemyer to wife, May 16, 1862, Gail and Stephen Rudin Collection, Cornell University.

41. *OR*, 1, 10(1): 665–667; John F. Marszalek, *Commander of All Lincoln's Armies: A Life of General Henry W. Halleck* (Cambridge, MA: Harvard University Press, 2004), 123.

42. William M. Parkinson to his sister, June 15, 1862, William M. Parkinson Papers, Emory University; Thomas W. Sweeny, "The Siege and Occupation of Corinth," Thomas William Sweeny Papers, Huntington Library; Stephen E. Ambrose, *Halleck: Lincoln's Chief of Staff* (Baton Rouge: Louisiana State University Press, 1962), 49; DeWitt Loudon to Hannah, May 15, 1862, DeWitt Clinton Loudon Papers, Ohio Historical Society.

43. *OR*, 1, 10(1): 674, 682, 839.

44. Ibid., 685; *OR*, 1, 10(2): 177; U. S. Grant, *Personal Memoirs of U. S. Grant* (New York: Charles L. Webster, 1885), 224; Shelby Foote, *The Civil War: A Narrative*, 3 vols. (New York: Random House, 1958), 1:374.

Chapter 4. "A Siege from the Start"

1. John B. Rice to wife, May 2, 1862, Robert S. Rice Papers, RBHPC; H. L. Honnoll to father, May 8, 1862, Robert W. Honnoll Papers, Duke University; William H. Kavanaugh Memoirs, undated, 31, William H. Kavanaugh Papers, UMC; William W. Cluett, *History of the 57th Regiment Illinois Volunteer Infantry, from Muster in, Dec. 26, 1861, to Muster out, July 7, 1865* (Princeton, IL: T. P. Streeter, 1886), 28; Jason Arter to family, May 16, 1862, 31st Ohio File, CWIC; Charles W. Gallentine to sister, May 17, 1862, Charles W. Gallentine Letters, Newberry Library; Abiel M. Barker to friend, June 5, 1862, 32nd Illinois File, CWIC; D. Leib Ambrose, *History of the Seventh Regiment Illinois Volunteer Infantry, from Its First Muster into the U.S. Service, April 25, 1861, to Its Final Muster out, July 9, 1865* (Springfield: Illinois Journal Company, 1868), 69; William Grose, *The Story of the Marches, Battles and Incidents of the 36th Regiment Indiana Volunteer Infantry* (New Castle, IN: Courier Company, 1891), 115; Asbury L. Kerwood, *Annals of the Fifty-seventh Regiment Indiana Volunteers: Marches, Battles, and Incidents of Army Life by a Member of the Regiment* (Dayton, OH: W. J. Shuey, 1868), 66; Frederick Kehrwecker to his brother, May 29, 1862, Kehrwecker Family Papers, BGSU; William Brown to sister, May 3, 1862, William Brown Letters, SHSW; *OR*, 1, 10(1): 666, 730,

755; *OR*, 1, 10(2): 180, 202, 209–210; John F. Marszalek, "Halleck Captures Corinth," *Civil War Times* 45, 1 (February 2006): 50.

2. Henry V. Boynton to *Cincinnati Daily Commercial*, April 15, 1862, Henry Van Ness Boynton Papers, Massachusetts Historical Society; John B. Rice to wife, May 2, 1862; H. L. Honnoll to father, May 8, 1862; William H. Kavanaugh Memoirs, 31; Cluett, *History of the 57th Regiment Illinois Volunteer Infantry*, 28; Kerwood, *Annals of the Fifty-seventh Regiment Indiana Volunteers*, 66; Jason Arter to family, May 16, 1862; Charles W. Gallentine to sister, May 17, 1862; Abiel M. Barker to friend, June 5, 1862; Ambrose, *History of the Seventh Regiment Illinois Volunteer Infantry*, 69; Grose, *Story of the Marches, Battles and Incidents of the 36th Regiment Indiana Volunteer Infantry*, 115; Frederick Kehrwecker to his brother, May 29, 1862; William Brown to sister, May 3, 1862; *OR*, 1, 10(1): 666, 730, 755; *OR*, 1, 10(2): 180, 202, 209–210; Marszalek, "Halleck Captures Corinth," 50. Illinois governor Richard Yates also visited his state's troops during the siege.

3. Charles W. Gallentine to sister, May 17, 1862; August Schilling Diary, May 20, 1862, BCHS; Thomas Sweeny, "The Siege and Occupation of Corinth," undated, Thomas Sweeny Papers, Huntington Library; George Thomas to Minerva, May 17, 1862, Thomas Family Correspondence, University of Notre Dame; William M. Parkinson to wife and children, May 6, 1862, William M. Parkinson Letters, Emory University; John Q. Adams to wife, May 16, 1862, John Q. Adams Letters, University of Southern Mississippi; Charles Johnson to his mother, May 25, 1862, Charles Johnson Papers, Virginia Tech University; *OR*, 1, 10(1): 742, 744, 749, 756, 760, 771, 856; *OR*, 1, 10(2): 164, 215, 508, 511, 516–517; Ezekiel J. Ellis to sister, May 25, 1862, Ezekiel J. Ellis Letter, LSU.

4. George Thomas to Minerva, May 17, 1862; Charles Wilkins to brother, May 23, 1862, Charles Wilkins Letter, Virginia Tech University; John Q. Adams to wife, May 16, 1862; Richard W. Burt to editor, May 10, 1862, 76th Ohio File, CWIC; *OR*, 1, 10(1): 742, 744, 749, 756, 760, 771, 856; *OR*, 1, 10(2): 164, 215, 508, 511, 516–517.

5. Frank L. Jones to his mother, May 20, 1862, Michael B. Ballard Collection, MSU; Alexis Cope, *The Fifteenth Ohio Volunteers and Its Campaigns: War of 1861–5* (Columbus, OH: n.p., 1916), 151; George Thomas to Minerva, May 17, 1862; William H. Kavanaugh Memoirs, 31; John Q. Adams to wife, May 16, 1862; *OR*, 1, 10(1): 742, 744, 749, 756, 760, 771, 856; *OR*, 1, 10(2): 164, 215, 508, 511, 516–517; B. W. Pearce to father, May 28, 1862, HC.

6. George Thomas to Minerva, May 17, 1862; William W. Belknap, "The Obedience and Courage of the Private Soldier, and the Fortitude of Officers and Men in the Field, in Hospital, and in Prison, with Some Incidents of the War," in *Military Order of the Loyal Legion* (Des Moines, IA: P. C. Kenyon, 1893), 55:160–161; John Q. Adams to wife, May 16, 1862; Gardner Abbott to family, June 7, 1862, Civil War Letters of Mack and Nan Ewing, Archives of Michigan; *OR*, 1, 10(1): 742, 744, 749, 756, 760, 771, 856; *OR*, 1, 10(2): 164, 215, 508, 511, 516–517; Abia Zeller to Sir, May 22, 1862, Abia M. Zeller Papers, Ohio Historical Society.

7. David Harrison Thomas to parents, May 31, 1862, David Harrison Thomas Papers, Ohio Historical Society; Clint to Hannah, May 24, 1862, DeWitt Clinton Loudon Papers,

Ohio Historical Society; C. Mitchell to Will, May 18, 1862, William B. Mitchell Papers, Ohio Historical Society; Charles Wilkins to brother, May 23, 1862; Sam Gold to his father, May 27, 1862, Samuel C. Gold Papers, UMC; Ephraim C. Dawes to Katie, May 27, 1862, Ephraim C. Dawes Papers, Newberry Library; Lewis Mathewson to parents, May 12, 1862, Lewis Mathewson Papers, Ohio Historical Society; W. L. Broaddus to wife, May 13, 1862, William L. Broaddus Papers, Duke University; Ezekiel J. Ellis to sister, May 25, 1862; Eben Lewis to Henry Ewing, July 1, 1862, Civil War Letters of Mack and Nan Ewing, Archives of Michigan; Frank L. Jones to his mother, May 20, 1862; Frank Moore, ed., *The Rebellion Record: A Diary of American Events, with Documents, Narratives, Illustrative Incidents, Poetry, etc.*, 11 vols. (New York: D. Vann Nostrand, 1861–1868), 5:153; William R. Hartpence, *History of the Fifty-first Indiana Veteran Volunteer Infantry: A Narrative of Its Organization, Marches, Battles and Other Experiences in Camp and Prison, from 1861 to 1866* (Cincinnati, OH: Robert Clarke, 1894), 47; William Shanks Diary, May 9 and 15, 1862, BGSU; John B. Rice to wife, May 1 and 8, 1862; Joseph M. Bailey Memoir, "Story of a Confederate Soldier, 1861–1865," undated, 16, University of Arkansas; *OR*, 1, 10(1): 742, 744, 749, 756, 760, 771, 856; *OR*, 1, 10(2): 164, 215, 508, 511, 516–517; Henry B. Wright, *A History of the Sixth Iowa Infantry* (Iowa City: State Historical Society of Iowa, 1923), 107; Charles W. Wills, *Army Life of an Illinois Soldier: Including a Day by Day Record of Sherman's March to the Sea* (Washington, DC: Globe Printing Company, 1906), 87; Regimental History, 5th Tennessee Infantry, undated, Civil War Collection, TSLA.

8. Unknown to wife, May 11, 1862, Gail and Stephen Rudin Collection, Cornell University; E. J. Hart, *History of the Fortieth Illinois Inf. (Volunteers)* (Cincinnati, OH: H. S. Bosworth, 1864), 97; Charles Wilkins to brother, May 23, 1862; Sam Gold to his father, May 27, 1862; Ephraim C. Dawes to Katie, May 27, 1862; W. L. Broaddus to wife, May 13, 1862; Benita K. Moore, ed., *A Civil War Diary: Written by Dr. James A. Black, First Assistant Surgeon, 49th Illinois Infantry* (Bloomington, IN: Author House, 2008), 56; Ezekiel J. Ellis to sister, May 25, 1862; Eben Lewis to Henry Ewing, July 1, 1862; William R. Stimson to family, June 1, 1862, William R. Stimson Collection, LC; Special Order 57, May 26, 1862, William Yerger Papers, MDAH; Regimental History, 5th Tennessee Infantry; Frank L. Jones to his mother, May 20, 1862; Wills, *Army Life of an Illinois Soldier*, 87; Moore, *The Rebellion Record*, 5:153; Hartpence, *History of the Fifty-first Indiana Veteran Volunteer Infantry*, 47; *OR*, 1, 10(2): 164, 215, 508, 511, 516–517; William Shanks Diary, May 9 and 15, 1862; John B. Rice to wife, May 1 and 8, 1862; Bailey, "Story of a Confederate Soldier," 16; *OR*, 1, 10(1): 742, 744, 749, 756, 760, 771, 856.

9. *OR*, 1, 10(1): 742, 744, 856; Fritz Hashell, ed., "Col. William Camm War Diary, 1861–1865," *Journal of the Illinois State Historical Society* 18, 4 (January 1926): 874.

10. James O'Halligan to wife, May 24, 1862, James O'Halligan Papers, Ohio Historical Society; W. A. Huddard to father, May 1, 1862, William A. Huddard Papers, University of Tennessee; W. L. Broaddus to wife, May 24, 1862; John Q. Adams to wife, May 11 and 16, 1862; James Shadle to wife, May 20, 1862, HC; Wills, *Army Life of an Illinois Soldier*, 89; *The Story of the Fifty-fifth Regiment Illinois Volunteer Infantry in the Civil War, 1861–1865* (n.p.: n.p., 1887), 142; Erasmus Stirman to sister, May 12 and 16, 1862,

Rebecca Stirman Davidson Family Papers, University of Arkansas; John N. Wiedemyer to wife, May 16, 1862, Gail and Stephen Rudin Collection, Cornell University; Moore, *The Rebellion Record*, 5:119; Rufus W. Daniel Diary, May 16, 1862, Arkansas History Commission; Charles Kroff Diary, May 11, 1862, Sherry M. Cress Collection, University of Oklahoma.

11. E. S. Holloway to wife, May 25, 1862, Ephraim S. Holloway Papers, Ohio Historical Society; George W. Lennard to Clara, May 3, 1862, George W. Lennard Collection, Arizona State University; Moore, *The Rebellion Record*, 5:119; W. N. Mattison to wife, May 5, 1862, William N. Mattison Papers, Atlanta History Center; Rufus W. Daniel Diary, May 16, 1862; Charles Kroff Diary, May 11, 1862; Wills, *Army Life of an Illinois Soldier*, 89; John Q. Adams to wife, May 11 and 16, 1862; James Shadle to wife, May 20, 1862; Erasmus Stirman to sister, May 12 and 16, 1862; John N. Wiedemyer to wife, May 16, 1862.

12. Wilbur F. Hinman, *The Story of the Sherman Brigade: The Camp, the March, the Bivouac, the Battle; and How "the Boys" Lived and Died during Four Years of Active Field Service* (n.p.: n.p., 1897), 196–204; Cope, *The Fifteenth Ohio Volunteers*, 151–152; Henry Eells to family, June 4, 1862, Samuel Henry Eells Papers, LC; G. B. McDonald, *A History of the 30th Illinois Veteran Volunteer Regiment of Infantry* (Sparta, IL: Sparta News, 1916), 25; Hartpence, *History of the Fifty-first Indiana Veteran Volunteer Infantry*, 47; W. L. Broaddus to daughter, May 16, 1862; Lewis Mathewson to parents, May 2, 1862; Wills, *Army Life of an Illinois Soldier*, 95–96.

13. Charles Wilkins to brother, May 23, 1862; Lewis Mathewson to parents, May 2, 1862; Hashell, "Col. William Camm War Diary," 879; Wills, *Army Life of an Illinois Soldier*, 87–88; Charles W. Gallentine to sister, May 17, 1862; J. V. Frederick, ed., "An Illinois Soldier in North Mississippi: Diary of John Wilson February 15–December 30, 1862," *Journal of Mississippi History* 1, 3 (July 1939): 187; Chester Townsend Hart Diary, May 6, 1862, 15th Illinois File, CWIC; *Story of the Fifty-fifth Regiment Illinois Volunteer Infantry,* 146; John B. Rice to wife, May 11 and 26, 1862; James Scully to wife, May 7, 1862, James Wall Scully Papers, Duke University; Thomas J. Williams, *An Historical Sketch of the 56th Ohio Volunteer Infantry during the Great Civil War from 1861 to 1865* (Columbus, OH: Lawrence Press, n.d.), 18; John Patton to Mary, May 16, 1862, HC; Cope, *Fifteenth Ohio Volunteers,* 143.

14. Hartpence, *History of the Fifty-first Indiana Veteran Volunteer Infantry*, 45.

15. Robert L. Kimberly and Ephraim S. Holloway, *The Forty-first Ohio Veteran Volunteer Infantry in the War of the Rebellion, 1861–1865* (Cleveland, OH: W. R. Smellie, 1897), 28.

16. John J. Hight and Gilbert R. Stormont, *History of the Fifty-eighth Regiment Indiana Volunteer Infantry: Its Organization, Campaigns and Battles from 1861 to 1865* (Princeton, IN: Press of the Clarion, 1895), 73; John Thomas Smith, *A History of the Thirty-first Regiment of Indiana Volunteer Infantry in the War of the Rebellion* (Cincinnati, OH: Western Methodist Book Concern, 1900), 29.

17. John Hill Ferguson Diary, May 19 and 21, 1862, MacMurray College; William M. Parkinson to wife and children, May 2, 1862; *OR*, 1, 10(1): 753–757; Hart, *History of the*

Fortieth Illinois Inf., 96; Lew Wallace, *An Autobiography*, 2 vols. (New York: Harper and Brothers, 1906), 2:575; U. S. Grant, *Personal Memoirs of U. S. Grant* (New York: Charles L. Webster, 1885), 224; David W. Reed, *Campaigns and Battles of the Twelfth Regiment Iowa Veteran Volunteer Infantry: From Organization, September, 1861, to Muster-out, January 20, 1866* (n.p.: n.p., 1903), 84. For an in-depth look at the Halleck-Grant relationship, see Brooks D. Simpson, "After Shiloh: Grant, Sherman, and Survival," in *The Shiloh Campaign*, ed. Steven E. Woodworth (Carbondale: Southern Illinois University Press, 2009), 142–156.

18. Richard L. Kiper, *Major General John A. McClernand: Politician in Uniform* (Kent, OH: Kent State University Press, 1999), 121; Marszalek, "Halleck Captures Corinth," 50.

19. Grant, *Memoirs*, 224–225; Simpson, "After Shiloh," 153; Thomas L. Snead, "With Price East of the Mississippi," in *Battles and Leaders of the Civil War*, 4 vols. (New York: Century Company, 1884–1887), 2:719; William T. Sherman, *Memoirs of General William T. Sherman: Written by Himself* (New York: D. Appleton, 1875), 232.

20. *OR*, 1, 10(2): 182–183.

21. Grant, *Memoirs*, 224; Sherman, *Memoirs*, 236. For more on the Grant-Sherman relationship, see John F. Marszalek, "'A Full Share of All the Credit': Sherman and Grant to the Fall of Vicksburg," in *Grant's Lieutenants: From Cairo to Vicksburg*, ed. Steven E. Woodworth (Lawrence: University Press of Kansas, 2001), 5–20, and Charles Bracelen Flood, *Grant and Sherman: The Friendship that Won the Civil War* (New York: Farrar, Straus, and Giroux, 2005).

22. William M. Parkinson to wife and children, June 15, 1862; P. P. Lash to wife, May 2, 1862, 30th Indiana File, CWIC; Hart, *History of the Fortieth Illinois Inf.*, 93. For the Shiloh civilians, see Timothy B. Smith, "The Forgotten Inhabitants of Shiloh: A Case Study in a Civilian-Government Relationship," *Tennessee Historical Quarterly* 67, 1 (Spring 2008): 36–55.

23. W. L. Broaddus to daughter, May 16, 1862; C. C. Briant, *History of the Sixth Regiment Indiana Volunteer Infantry: Of Both the Three Months' and the Three Years' Services* (Indianapolis: William B. Burford, 1891), 135; Gardner Abbott to family, June 7, 1862; Lewis Mathewson to parents, May 12, 1862.

24. Lewis Mathewson to parents, May 2, 1862; David Harrison Thomas to brother, May 28, 1862, and David Harrison Thomas to parents, May 31, 1862.

25. Lewis Mathewson to parents, May 2, 1862; D. W. Pollock to family, June 8, 1862, David W. Pollock Letters, UMC; George Lanphear to children, May 22, 1862, Lanphear Family Letters, University of Tennessee; Jason Arter to family, May 16, 1862; James Scully to wife, May 14, 1862; Thomas A. Colman to parents, May 12, 1862, Colman-Hayter Family Papers, UMC; Wills, *Army Life of an Illinois Soldier*, 90.

26. Charles W. Gallentine to sister, May 17, 1862; Ezekiel J. Ellis to sister, May 25, 1862; *OR*, 1, 10(2): 538; George Little, *Memoirs of George Little* (Tuscaloosa, AL: Weatherford Printing Company, 1924), 43; John Hill Ferguson Diary, May 18, 1862; T. D. Christie to sister, July 16, 1862, Christie Family Letters, Minnesota Historical Society; *OR*, 1, 10(1): 816; Kate Cumming, *A Journal of Hospital Life in the Confederate Army of Tennessee from the Battle of Shiloh to the End of the War: With Sketches of Life and Char-*

acter, and Brief Notices of Current Events during that Period (Louisville, KY: John P. Morton, 1866), 27; W. J. Stubblefield Diary, May 8, 1862, Murray State University.

27. George Lanphear to children, May 22, 1862; *OR*, 1, 10(1): 724, 820, 834; *OR*, 1, 10(2): 217; Abiel M. Barker to friend, May 10, 1862.

28. "Morning Report," May 5, 1862, William Yerger Papers, MDAH; *OR*, 1, 10(1): 813; *OR*, 1, 10(2): 499, 511, 523.

29. C. H. George to sister, May 27, 1862, George Family Letters, Auburn University; *OR*, 1, 10(2): 541–543.

30. W. J. Stubblefield Diary, May 8, 1862; Cumming, *Journal of Hospital Life*, 25.

31. Cumming, *Journal of Hospital Life*, 27.

32. S. H. Dent to his wife, April 23, 1862, S. H. Dent Papers, Auburn University.

33. Ezekiel J. Ellis to sister, May 25, 1862.

34. *OR*, 1, 10(1): 795, 858; *OR*, 1, 10(2): 192; W. H. Tunnard, *A Southern Record: The History of the 3rd Regiment Louisiana Infantry,* ed. Edwin C. Bearss (Dayton, OH: Morningside, 1970), 170; John B. Rice to wife, May 26, 1862.

CHAPTER 5. "A CONSTANT SUCCESSION OF BATTLES ON A SMALL SCALE"

1. Ezekiel J. Ellis to sister, May 25, 1862, Ezekiel J. Ellis Letter, LSU; George D. Cotton to "My Dear Kemp," June 16, 1862, George D. Cotton Letters, LSU; Gardner Abbott to family, June 7, 1862, Civil War Letters of Mack and Nan Ewing, Archives of Michigan.

2. Joseph Skipworth to wife, May 18, 1862, Joseph Skipworth Papers, Southern Illinois University.

3. William J. Christie to brother, May 16, 1862, William J. Christie Letters, LSU; *OR*, 1, 10(1): 739; David B. Henderson to George, June 13, 1862, David B. Henderson Papers, DCHS; August Schilling Diary, May 17, 1862, BCHS; John B. Rice to wife, May 11, 1862, Robert S. Rice Papers, RBHPC.

4. Clint to Hannah, May 24, 1862, DeWitt Clinton Loudon Papers, Ohio Historical Society; Frank Moore, ed., *The Rebellion Record: A Diary of American Events, with Documents, Narratives, Illustrative Incidents, Poetry, etc.,* 11 vols. (New York: D. Vann Nostrand, 1861–1868), 5:153; *OR*, 1, 10(1): 739; Jobe M. Foxworth Diary, May 8, 1862, MDAH.

5. John B. Rice to wife, May 11 and 18, 1862; *OR*, 1, 10(1): 751, 840.

6. Clint to Hannah, May 24, 1862; John B. Rice to wife, May 18, 1862; *OR*, 1, 10(1): 741, 840, 841, 842–843; *OR*, 1, 10(2): 198–199.

7. *OR*, 1, 10(1): 741, 840, 841, 842–843; *OR*, 1, 10(2): 198–199; John B. Rice to wife, May 18, 1862; Clint to Hannah, May 24, 1862.

8. *The Story of the Fifty-fifth Regiment Illinois Volunteer Infantry in the Civil War, 1861–1865* (n.p.: n.p., 1887), 142.

9. *OR*, 1, 10(1): 747, 840–841; *Story of the Fifty-fifth Regiment Illinois Volunteer Infantry,* 140.

10. August Schilling Diary, May 19, 1862; *OR*, 1, 10(1): 739; Clint to Hannah, May 24, 1862.

11. *OR*, 1, 10(1): 674–675, 678, 702, 704, 706–707; G. D. Molineaux Diary, May 30, 1862, Augustana College; William W. Cluett, *History of the 57th Regiment Illinois Volunteer Infantry, from Muster in, Dec. 26, 1861, to Muster out, July 7, 1865* (Princeton, IL: T. P. Streeter, 1886), 30; H. I. Smith, *History of the Seventh Iowa Veteran Volunteer Infantry during the Civil War* (Mason City, IA: R. Hitchcock, 1903), 64; A. F. Lee to mother and sister, May 26, 1862, HC; Robert L. Kimberly and Ephraim S. Holloway, *The Forty-first Ohio Veteran Volunteer Infantry in the War of the Rebellion, 1861–1865* (Cleveland, OH: W. R. Smellie, 1897), 28.

12. W. A. Huddard to father, May 27, 1862, William A. Huddard Papers, University of Tennessee; D. F. McGowan to Ellen, May 19, 1862, HC; *OR*, 1, 10(1): 674–675, 678, 702, 704, 706–707; Frank L. Jones to his mother, May 20, 1862, Michael B. Ballard Collection, MSU; John H. Foster to son, May 29, 1862, Frank B. Foster Letters, U.S. Military Academy.

13. Ezekiel J. Ellis to sister, May 25, 1862; Charles F. Hubert, *History of the Fiftieth Regiment Illinois Volunteer Infantry in the War of the Union* (Kansas City, MO: Western Veteran Publishing Company, 1894), 112; George D. Cotton to "My Dear Kemp," June 16, 1862; John Thompkins to brother, May 4, 1862, HC; O. Edward Cunningham, *Shiloh and the Western Campaign of 1862*, ed. Gary D. Joiner and Timothy B. Smith (New York: Savas Beatie, 2007), 392.

14. *OR*, 1, 10(1): 675, 844–846; John Thomas Smith, *A History of the Thirty-first Regiment of Indiana Volunteer Infantry in the War of the Rebellion* (Cincinnati, OH: Western Methodist Book Concern, 1900), 30.

15. *OR*, 1, 10(1): 845–847; Smith, *History of the Thirty-first Regiment of Indiana Volunteer Infantry,* 30.

16. *OR*, 1, 10(2): 197–200; Almon F. Rockwell Diary, May 17, 1862, Almon Ferdinand Rockwell Papers, LC.

17. *OR*, 1, 10(2): 201–202.

18. Lewis Mathewson to parents, May 12, 1862, Lewis Mathewson Papers, Ohio Historical Society; Charles Wilkins to brother, May 23, 1862, Charles Wilkins Letter, Virginia Tech University; W. N. Mattison to wife, May 5, 1862, William N. Mattison Papers, Atlanta History Center; Joseph Phillips to Margaret, May 12, 1862, Joseph Phillips Letter, Ohio Historical Society; Charles W. Wills, *Army Life of an Illinois Soldier: Including a Day by Day Record of Sherman's March to the Sea* (Washington, DC: Globe Printing Company, 1906), 89–90; Frederick Kehrwecker to his brother, May 11, 1862, Kehrwecker Family Papers, BGSU; Mary Amelia Boomer Stone, *Memoir of George Boardman Boomer* (Boston: George C. Rand and Avery, 1864), 229–230; *OR*, 1, 10(1): 715, 722, 730–731; *OR*, 1, 10(2): 183–184; John Hill Ferguson Diary, May 10, 1862, MacMurray College.

19. Joseph Phillips to Margaret, May 12, 1862; Wills, *Army Life of an Illinois Soldier*, 89–90; Frederick Kehrwecker to his brother, May 11, 1862; *OR*, 1, 10(1): 715, 722, 730–731; *OR*, 1, 10(2): 183–184; John Hill Ferguson Diary, May 10, 1862; Lewis Math-

ewson to parents, May 12, 1862; Charles Wilkins to brother, May 23, 1862; W. N. Mattison to wife, May 5, 1862; Clyde C. Walton, ed., *Private Smith's Journal: Recollections of the Late War* (Chicago: R. R. Donnelley and Sons, 1963), 40.

20. W. L. Broaddus to wife, May 24, 1862, William L. Broaddus Papers, Duke University; John Hill Ferguson Diary, May 17 and 18, 1862; *OR*, 1, 10(1): 724; *OR*, 1, 10(2): 206; "Confederate Intrenchments," Historical Reports, SNMP; John Q. Adams to wife, May 25, 1862, John Q. Adams Letters, University of Southern Mississippi.

21. *OR*, 1, 10(2): 524, 526–528, 532; Alexander P. Stewart to W. H. McCardle, May 26, 1862, Frederick M. Dearborn Collection, Harvard University.

22. Frank L. Jones to his mother, May 20, 1862; *OR*, 1, 10(1): 775–776, 784; E. S. Holloway to wife, May 25, 1862, Ephraim S. Holloway Papers, Ohio Historical Society; Moore, *The Rebellion Record*, 5:156; Robert G. Hartje, *Van Dorn: The Life and Times of a Confederate General* (Nashville: Vanderbilt University Press, 1967), 180; Sam R. Watkins, *"Co. Aytch," Maury Grays, First Tennessee Regiment; or, a Side Show of the Big Show* (Nashville: Presbyterian Printing House, 1882), 49; Samuel Gold to his father, May 27, 1862, Samuel C. Gold Papers, UMC; Wills, *Army Life of an Illinois Soldier*, 88; Special Order 18, May 25, 1862, William Yerger Papers, MDAH.

23. Ezekiel J. Ellis to sister, May 25, 1862; John G. Galliard Memoir, 1895, John G. Galliard Papers, University of South Carolina; George Dobson to family, May 21, 1862, 10th Mississippi File, CWIC; *OR*, 1, 10(2): 531.

24. Special Order 31, May 5, 1862, William Yerger Papers, MDAH; *OR*, 1, 10(2): 532; Stanley F. Horn, *The Army of the Tennessee* (Indianapolis: Bobbs-Merrill, 1941), 147–148; Hartje, *Van Dorn*, 179–180.

25. Cyrus S. Bolton Diary, May 20, 1862, Ohio Historical Society; *OR*, 1, 10(2): 532–533; Nathaniel Cheairs Hughes Jr., *General Williah J. Hardee: Old Reliable* (Baton Rouge: Louisiana State University Press, 1965), 118; George Dobson to family, May 21, 1862.

26. *OR*, 1, 10(2): 533, 535; *OR*, 1, 52(2): 316; A. D. Kirwan, ed., *Johnny Green of the Orphan Brigade: The Journal of a Confederate Soldier* (Lexington: University Press of Kentucky, 1956), 41; John S. Jackman Journal, May 22, 1862, LC.

27. Arthur Fulkerson to sister, May 22, 1862, HC; Kate Cumming, *A Journal of Hospital Life in the Confederate Army of Tennessee from the Battle of Shiloh to the End of the War: With Sketches of Life and Character, and Brief Notices of Current Events during that Period* (Louisville, KY: John P. Morton, 1866), 27; *OR*, 1, 10(2): 532, 534–535.

28. *OR*, 1, 10(2): 537, 539; J. H. Rogers to father, May 25, 1862, Sarah Rogers Shaw Papers, Wesleyan College; George Dobson to family, May 24, 1862.

29. Ezekiel J. Ellis to sister, May 25, 1862; *OR*, 1, 10(2): 538.

30. *OR*, 1, 10(2): 540; Alfred Roman, *The Military Operations of General Beauregard in the War between the States, 1861–1865: Including a Brief Personal Sketch of His Services in the War with Mexico, 1846–8*, 2 vols. (New York: Harper and Brothers, 1883), 1:577.

31. S. M. Meek to wife, May 22, 1862, CWIC; *OR*, 1, 10(2): 540; Roman, *Military Operations of Beauregard*, 1:577.

32. *OR*, 1, 10(1): 739.

33. Ibid., 724.

34. John Hill Ferguson Diary, May 23, 1862; *OR*, 1, 10(1): 708; *OR*, 1, 10(2): 208.

35. Erasmus Stirman to sister, May 26, 1862, Rebecca Stirman Davidson Family Papers, University of Arkansas; Walter A. Overton Diary, May 24, 1862, MDAH; *OR*, 1, 10(1): 722; John Hill Ferguson Diary, May 23, 26, and 27, 1862.

36. *OR*, 1, 10(1): 675, 678–679.

37. Ibid., 724–725.

38. Ibid., 675, 679, 726, 740; *OR*, 1, 10(2): 190–191, 224; Stacy D. Allen, "Crossroads of the Western Confederacy," *Blue and Gray Magazine* 19, 6 (Summer 2002): 21–22; Alonzo L. Brown, *History of the Fourth Regiment of Minnesota Infantry Volunteers during the Great Rebellion 1861–1865* (St. Paul: Pioneer Press Company, 1892), 49; Alexis Cope, *The Fifteenth Ohio Volunteers and Its Campaigns: War of 1861–5* (Columbus, OH: n.p., 1916), 150; W. L. Broaddus to wife, May 25, 1862; G. D. Molineaux Diary, May 28, 1862.

39. George C. Jenkins Diary, May 25, 1862, 2nd Illinois Light Artillery, Battery B File, CWIC; *OR*, 1, 10(1): 725; *OR*, 1, 10(2): 541; William M. Lamers, *The Edge of Glory: A Biography of General William S. Rosecrans, U.S.A.* (New York: Harcourt, Brace, and World, 1961), 85; Ole A. Hanse to brother, June 3, 1862, Ole A. Hanse Letter, Brown University.

40. John Hill Ferguson Diary, May 25 and 28, 1862; W. L. Broaddus to wife, May 30, 1862; James Birney Shaw, *History of the Tenth Regiment Indiana Volunteer Infantry: Three Months and Three Years Organizations* (Lafayette, IN: Regimental Association, 1912), 167; Patrick Michael Hotard, "The Campaign (Siege) of Corinth, Mississippi, April–June 1862" (M.A. thesis, Southeastern Louisiana University, 2005), 87; David McKnight Diary, May 28, 1862, Civil War Collection, Missouri Historical Society; *OR*, 1, 10(1): 716, 722–723; *OR*, 1, 52(1): 35–36; Craig L. Symonds, *Stonewall of the West: Patrick Cleburne and the Civil War* (Lawrence: University Press of Kansas, 1997), 83–84; S. S. Stanton to W. J. Hardee, May 29, 1862, HC; Marion Bennett Ledger, undated, unpaginated, University of Tennessee.

41. *OR*, 1, 10(1): 675, 679, 682, 849–852; Moore, *The Rebellion Record*, 5:154.

42. Fritz Hashell, ed., "Col. William Camm War Diary, 1861–1865," *Journal of the Illinois State Historical Society* 18, 4 (January 1926): 877; John B. Rice to wife, May 28, 1862; E. J. Hart, *History of the Fortieth Illinois Inf. (Volunteers)* (Cincinnati, OH: H. S. Bosworth, 1864), 98; *OR*, 1, 10(1): 739–743, 756–760; *OR*, 1, 52(1): 247; *OR*, 1, 10(2): 193.

43. John B. Rice to wife, May 28, 1862; Hart, *History of the Fortieth Illinois Inf.*, 98; *OR*, 1, 10(1): 739–743, 756–760; *OR*, 1, 52(1): 247; *OR*, 1, 10(2): 193; Granville W. Hough, ed., "Diary of a Soldier in Grant's Rear Guard (1862–1863)," *Journal of Mississippi History* 45, 3 (August 1983): 197.

44. *OR*, 1, 10(1): 686, 716, 723, 725, 740; Asbury L. Kerwood, *Annals of the Fifty-seventh Regiment Indiana Volunteers: Marches, Battles, and Incidents of Army Life by a Member of the Regiment* (Dayton, OH: W. J. Shuey, 1868), 69; John B. Rice to wife, May 26, 1862; John Hill Ferguson Diary, May 29, 1862.

45. Alf Shields to his brother, May 26, 1862, Alfred Shields Letters, Indiana Histori-
cal Society; Liberty P. Warner to family, July 1862, Liberty Warner Papers, BGSU; Charles
Wilkins to brother, May 23, 1862; W. L. Broaddus to wife, May 16 and 18, 1862; Austin
O. Green Diaries, May 29, 1862, UMC; John Sibrel to John Meeks, May 27, 1862, Meeks
Family Papers, Indiana State Library; Samuel Gold to his father, May 27, 1862; Hart, *His-
tory of the Fortieth Illinois Inf.*, 97; George Lanphear to children, May 22, 1862, Lanphear
Family Letters, University of Tennessee; Robert F. Engs and Corey M. Brooks, eds., *Their
Patriotic Duty: The Civil War Letters of the Evans Family of Brown County, Ohio* (New
York: Fordham University Press, 2007), 27; John B. Rice to wife, May 26 and 31, 1862;
Rufus W. Daniel Diary, May 28, 1862, Arkansas History Commission; D. W. Pollock to
family, May 31, 1862, David W. Pollock Letters, UMC; John Hill Ferguson Diary, May
17, 1862; "Confederate Intrenchments," Historical Reports, SNMP; Shaw, *History of the
Tenth Regiment Indiana Volunteer Infantry*, 167.

46. Samuel Gold to his father, May 27, 1862; Hart, *History of the Fortieth Illinois Inf.*,
97; Engs and Brooks, *Their Patriotic Duty*, 27; John B. Rice to wife, May 26 and 31, 1862;
Charles Wilkins to brother, May 23, 1862; W. L. Broaddus to wife, May 16 and 18, 1862;
George Lanphear to children, May 22, 1862; Austin O. Green Diaries, May 29, 1862; John
Sibrel to John Meeks, May 27, 1862; Rufus W. Daniel Diary, May 28, 1862; Alpheus S.
Bloomfield to father, May 5, 1862, Alpheus S. Bloomfield Papers, LC; D. W. Pollock to
family, May 31, 1862; Alf Shields to his brother, May 26, 1862; John Hill Ferguson Diary,
May 17, 1862; "Confederate Intrenchments," Historical Reports, SNMP; Liberty P. Warner
to family, July 1862; Shaw, *History of the Tenth Regiment Indiana Volunteer Infantry*, 167.

CHAPTER 6. "TO THE LAST EXTREMITY"

1. *OR*, 1, 10(1): 731, 862–865; John H. Aughey, *The Iron Furnace: Or, Slavery and
Secession* (Philadelphia: William S. and Alfred Martien, 1863), 252–253; Lyman B. Pierce,
*History of the Second Iowa Cavalry: Containing a Detailed Account of Its Organization,
Marches, and the Battles in Which It Has Participated; Also, a Complete Roster of Each
Company* (Burlington, IA: Hawk-eye Steam Book and Job Printing Establishment, 1865),
23–24; Hugh Johnson to wife, June 1, 1862, 2nd Iowa Cavalry File, CWIC; T. J. Koger
to wife, June 2, 1862, T. J. Koger Collection, MDAH; Philip H. Sheridan, *Personal Memoirs of P. H. Sheridan: General United States Army*, 2 vols. (New York: Charles L. Webster, 1888), 1:145–152.

2. P. G. T. Beauregard to John B. Villepigue, May 28, 1862, P. G. T. Beauregard
Papers, MDAH; John E. Magee Diary, April 10, 1862, Duke University; Alfred Roman,
*The Military Operations of General Beauregard in the War between the States,
1861–1865: Including a Brief Personal Sketch of His Services in the War with Mexico,
1846–8*, 2 vols. (New York: Harper and Brothers, 1883), 1:380–381; T. Harry Williams,
P. G. T. Beauregard: Napoleon in Gray (Baton Rouge: Louisiana State University, 1954),
151; Jason Arter to family, May 16, 1862, 31st Ohio File, CWIC; Lamar Butler to
unknown, May 29, 1862, William Yerger Papers, MDAH; J. H. Phillips to father, May 19,

1862, 22nd Illinois File, CWIC; Thomas L. Connelly, *Army of the Heartland: The Army of Tennessee, 1861–1862* (Baton Rouge: Louisiana State University Press, 1967), 176–177; Ezra J. Warner, *Generals in Gray: Lives of the Confederate Commanders* (Baton Rouge: Louisiana State University Press, 1959), 139–140; *OR*, 1, 10(2): 196, 232, 547; Jack D. Welsh, *Medical Histories of Confederate Generals* (Kent, OH: Kent State University Press, 1995), 103.

3. *OR*, 1, 10(2): 506. For more on the Davis and Beauregard controversy, see Williams, *P. G. T. Beauregard*, 96–112.

4. *OR*, 1, 10(2): 529–530; Williams, *P. G. T. Beauregard*, 153.

5. *OR*, 1, 10(2): 546.

6. Ezekiel J. Ellis to sister, May 25, 1862, Ezekiel J. Ellis Letter, LSU; Thomas L. Snead, "With Price East of the Mississippi," in *Battles and Leaders of the Civil War*, 4 vols. (New York: Century Company, 1884–1887), 2:720; *OR*, 1, 10(2): 544–547, 775; P. G. T. Beauregard Confidential Memorandum, May 23, 1862, HC.

7. *OR*, 1, 10(1): 765; Roman, *Military Operations of Beauregard*, 1:389.

8. *OR*, 1, 10(1): 766–767.

9. Ibid.

10. Ibid.

11. Ibid., 767–768.

12. William H. Kavanaugh Memoirs, undated, 31, William H. Kavanaugh Papers, UMC; Kate Cumming, *A Journal of Hospital Life in the Confederate Army of Tennessee from the Battle of Shiloh to the End of the War: With Sketches of Life and Character, and Brief Notices of Current Events during that Period* (Louisville, KY: John P. Morton, 1866), 29–30; *OR*, 1, 10(2): 555, 871; Eugene F. Falconnet Diary, around May 30, 1862, Eugene Frederic Falconnet Papers, TSLA.

13. *OR*, 1, 10(1): 768.

14. Ibid., 785, 795.

15. *OR*, 1, 10(2): 557–558; *OR*, 1, 10(1): 560, 785; *OR*, 1, 8: 178.

16. Eugene F. Falconnet Diary, around May 30, 1862.

17. *OR*, 1, 10(1): 871–873.

18. Eugene F. Falconnet Diary, around May 30, 1862; *OR*, 1, 10(2): 503, 557.

19. *OR*, 1, 10(1): 768–770; Roman, *Military Operations of Beauregard*, 1:390.

20. *OR*, 1, 10(1): 768–770.

21. Ibid., 769–770; *OR*, 1, 10(2): 206.

22. *OR*, 1, 10(1): 769–770; *OR*, 1, 10(2): 206; Charles F. Hubert, *History of the Fiftieth Regiment Illinois Volunteer Infantry in the War of the Union* (Kansas City, MO: Western Veteran Publishing Company, 1894), 114; W. A. Neal, *An Illustrated History of the Missouri Engineer and the 25th Infantry Regiments: Together with a Roster of Both Regiments and the Last Known Address of All that Could Be Obtained* (Chicago: Donohue and Henneberry, 1889), 54; Fritz Hashell, ed., "Col. William Camm War Diary, 1861–1865," *Journal of the Illinois State Historical Society* 18, 4 (January 1926): 874–875; Alonzo L. Brown, *History of the Fourth Regiment Minnesota Infantry Volunteers during the Great Rebellion 1861–1865* (St. Paul: Pioneer Press Company, 1892), 49;

Cloyd Bryner, *Bugle Echoes: The Story of the Illinois 47th* (Springfield, IL: Phillips Bros. Printers, 1905), 47; Charles H. Smith, *The History of Fuller's Ohio Brigade, 1861–1865: Its Great March, with Roster Portraits, Battle Maps and Biographies* (Cleveland, OH: Press of A. J. Watt, 1909), 73.

23. *OR*, 1, 10(1): 870, 872; John K. Bettersworth, ed., *Mississippi in the Confederacy: As They Saw It* (Baton Rouge: Louisiana State University Press, 1961), 83; Susan P. Gaston, "Reminiscences of the War," undated, in "History of Old Tishomingo County," 2, Alcorn County Chancery Clerk Archives.

24. John E. Magee Diary, May 29, 1862; Sam R. Watkins, *"Co. Aytch," Maury Grays, First Tennessee Regiment; or, a Side Show of the Big Show* (Nashville: Presbyterian Printing House, 1882), 53; James Thomas to his sister, June 3, 1862, James S. Thomas Letters, Indiana Historical Society; Jacob Harrison Allspaugh Diary, May 8, 1862, University of Iowa; Hubert, *History of the Fiftieth Regiment Illinois Volunteer Infantry,* 115; George Lanphear to children, May 22, 1862, Lanphear Family Letters, University of Tennessee; Bettersworth, *Mississippi in the Confederacy,* 83; P. B. McKay to wife, June 2, 1862, McKay Family Letter, Virginia Military Institute; *OR*, 1, 10(1): 771, 773, 854; William R. Hartpence, *History of the Fifty-first Indiana Veteran Volunteer Infantry: A Narrative of Its Organization, Marches, Battles and Other Experiences in Camp and Prison, from 1861 to 1866* (Cincinnati, OH: Robert Clarke, 1894), 46; James Birney Shaw, *History of the Tenth Regiment Indiana Volunteer Infantry: Three Months and Three Years Organizations* (Lafayette, IN: Regimental Association, 1912), 167; "Camouflage," *Confederate Veteran* 21, 3 (March 1913): 102–103; Wright C. Shaumburg Journal, May 12, 1862, Schaumburg-Wright Family Papers, HNOC.

25. Gaston, "Reminiscences of the War," 2; John E. Magee Diary, May 29, 1862; Watkins, *"Co. Aytch,"* 53; William R. Burke Diary, May 9, 1862, 50th Alabama File, CWIC; George Lanphear to children, May 22, 1862; Bettersworth, *Mississippi in the Confederacy,* 83; P. B. McKay to wife, June 2, 1862; *OR*, 1, 10(1): 771, 773, 854; John S. Jackman Journal, May 30, 1862, LC; Wright C. Shaumburg Journal, May 12, 1862; Beauregard to Van Dorn, April 28, 1862, Letters Received—Van Dorn's Command, Army of the West, NARA.

26. *OR*, 1, 10(2): 560; Watkins, *"Co. Aytch,"* 53–54; Marcus J. Wright, *Diary of Brigadier-General Marcus J. Wright, C.S.A. April 23, 1861–February 26 1863* (n.p.: n.p., n.d.), 5.

27. George W. Lennard to Clara, May 8, 1862, George W. Lennard Collection, Arizona State University; John B. Rice to wife, May 11, 1862, Robert S. Rice Papers, RBHPC; *OR*, 1, 10(1): 675–676; *OR*, 1, 10(2): 164, 167, 169, 173, 184, 189, 205–206, 213–217, 222–224.

28. William J. Christie to brother, May 31, 1862, William J. Christie Letters, LSU; *OR*, 1, 10(2): 225, 710; Henry R. Strong Diary, May 30, 1862, Indiana Historical Society.

29. U. S. Grant, *Personal Memoirs of U. S. Grant* (New York: Charles L. Webster, 1885), 226.

30. *OR*, 1, 10(1): 710, 723; C. C. Briant, *History of the Sixth Regiment Indiana Volunteer Infantry: Of Both the Three Months' and the Three Years' Services* (Indianapolis: William B. Burford, 1891), 132–133.

31. *OR*, 1, 10(1): 676.

32. Gardner Abbott to family, June 7, 1862, Civil War Letters of Mack and Nan Ewing, Archives of Michigan; *OR*, 1, 10(1): 676, 680; Almon F. Rockwell Diary, May 30, 1862, Almon Ferdinand Rockwell Papers, LC; Wilbur F. Hinman, *The Story of the Sherman Brigade: The Camp, the March, the Bivouac, the Battle; and How "the Boys" Lived and Died during Four Years of Active Field Service* (n.p.: n.p., 1897), 205.

33. John B. Rice to wife, May 31, 1862; *OR*, 1, 10(1): 740, 743–744, 747, 752; *OR*, 1, 10(2): 228; Asbury L. Kerwood, *Annals of the Fifty-seventh Regiment Indiana Volunteers: Marches, Battles, and Incidents of Army Life by a Member of the Regiment* (Dayton, OH: W. J. Shuey, 1868), 69; Hinman, *Story of the Sherman Brigade*, 207.

34. John Melvin Williams, *"The Eagle Regiment," 8th Wis. Inf'ty Vols.: A Sketch of Its Marches, Battles and Campaigns from 1861–1865 with Complete Regimental and Company Roster, and a Few Portraits and Sketches of Its Officers and Commanders* (Belleville, WI: Recorder Print, 1890), 48; Kerwood, *Annals of the Fifty-seventh Regiment Indiana Volunteers*, 69; John B. Rice to wife, May 31, 1862; *OR*, 1, 10(1): 740, 743–744, 747, 752; *OR*, 1, 10(2): 228; Hinman, *Story of the Sherman Brigade*, 207.

35. August Schilling Diary, May 31, 1862, BCHS; D. W. Pollock to family, June 8, 1862, David W. Pollock Letters, UMC; William R. Stimson to family, June 1, 1862, William R. Stimson Collection, LC; Cyrus S. Bolton Diary, May 30, 1862, Ohio Historical Society; Benita K. Moore, ed., *A Civil War Diary: Written by Dr. James A. Black, First Assistant Surgeon, 49th Illinois Infantry* (Bloomington, IN: Author House, 2008), 57; Peter Cozzens and Robert I. Girardi, eds., *The Military Memoirs of General John Pope* (Chapel Hill: University of North Carolina Press, 1998), 69; Frank Moore, ed., *The Rebellion Record: A Diary of American Events, with Documents, Narratives, Illustrative Incidents, Poetry, etc.*, 11 vols. (New York: D. Vann Nostrand, 1861–1868), 5:156; Hashell, "Col. William Camm War Diary," 879.

36. Moore, *The Rebellion Record*, 5:156; H. I. Smith, *History of the Seventh Iowa Veteran Volunteer Infantry during the Civil War* (Mason City, IA: R. Hitchcock, 1903), 71; John B. Rice to wife, May 31, 1862; Charles S. Cotter to unknown, May 30, 1862, 1st Ohio Battery File, CWIC; Gaston, "Reminiscences of the War," 4.

37. August Schilling Diary, May 30, 1862; Charles S. Cotter to unknown, May 30, 1862; Cyrus S. Bolton Diary, May 30, 1862; Hubert, *History of the Fiftieth Regiment Illinois Volunteer Infantry*, 115; Kerwood, *Annals of the Fifty-seventh Regiment Indiana Volunteers*, 70; John J. Hight and Gilbert R. Stormont, *History of the Fifty-eighth Regiment Indiana Volunteer Infantry: Its Organization, Campaigns and Battles from 1861 to 1865* (Princeton, IN: Press of the Clarion, 1895), 74; *OR*, 1, 10(1): 667, 676, 680, 856–857; Hinman, *Story of the Sherman Brigade*, 209; Joseph Skipworth to wife, June 1, 1862, Joseph Skipworth Papers, Southern Illinois University.

38. *OR*, 1, 10(1): 857; Smith, *History of Fuller's Ohio Brigade*, 73; Moore, *The Rebellion Record*, 5:157; Gaston, "Reminiscences of the War," 5–7, 9; W. L. Broaddus to wife, May 30, 1862, William L. Broaddus Papers, Duke University; Abiel M. Barker to friend, May 10, 1862, 32nd Illinois File, CWIC; William R. Stimson to family, June 1, 1862.

39. John F. Marszalek, *Commander of All Lincoln's Armies: A Life of General Henry*

W. Halleck (Cambridge, MA: Harvard University Press, 2004), 125; Stephen E. Ambrose, *Halleck: Lincoln's Chief of Staff* (Baton Rouge: Louisiana State University Press, 1962), 53; Jack D. Welsh, *Medical Histories of Union Generals* (Kent, OH: Kent State University Press, 1996), 144; Peter Cozzens, *General John Pope: A Life for the Nation* (Urbana: University of Illinois Press, 2000), 70; *The Story of the Fifty-fifth Regiment Illinois Volunteer Infantry in the Civil War, 1861–1865* (n.p.: n.p., 1887), 147; Joseph Mitchell Strickling Diary, May 30, 1862, 39th Ohio File, CWIC.

40. David McKnight Diary, May 29, 1862, Civil War Collection, Missouri Historical Society; *OR*, 1, 10(1): 676, 679, 745, 861; George W. Lennard to Clara, May 30, 1862; Thomas Sweeny, "The Siege and Occupation of Corinth," undated, Thomas Sweeny Papers, Huntington Library.

41. Gaston, "Reminiscences of the War," 8; W. J. Stubblefield Diary, June 20, 1862, Murray State University; *OR*, 1, 10(2): 563; *OR*, 1, 10(1): 763–764, 770, 777; A. D. Kirwan, ed., *Johnny Green of the Orphan Brigade: The Journal of a Confederate Soldier* (Lexington: University Press of Kentucky, 1956), 41.

42. Albert T. Goodloe to Mollie, June 2, 1862, Albert Theodore Goodloe Papers, TSLA; William R. Plum, *The Military Telegraph during the Civil War in the United States, with an Exposition of Ancient and Modern Means of Communication, and of the Federal and Confederate Cipher Systems; Also a Running Account of the War between the States*, 2 vols. (Chicago: Jansen, McClurg, 1882), 1:247–248; *OR*, 1, 10(1): 746, 763, 779, 796, 867, 872; Shelby Foote, *The Civil War: A Narrative*, 3 vols. (New York: Random House, 1958), 1:384.

43. Connelly, *Army of the Heartland*, 177; A. P. Stewart to William H. McCardle, April 30, 1878, William H. McCardle Papers, MDAH; *OR*, 1, 10(1): 710–712; Sweeny, "The Siege and Occupation of Corinth."

44. William M. Parkinson to wife and children, June 15, 1862, William M. Parkinson Letters, Emory University; *OR*, 1, 10(2): 635; *OR*, 1, 10(1): 858, 860, 874; *OR*, 1, 52(1): 31; Sweeny, "The Siege and Occupation of Corinth"; Bryner, *Bugle Echoes*, 48; Marcus Frost to his sisters, June 21, 1862, Marcus O. Frost Letters, *CWTI* Collection, USAMHI; Joseph Skipworth to wife, June 8, 1862.

45. Gaston, "Reminiscences of the War," 2; *OR*, 1, 10(1): 669, 771, 773; Moore, *The Rebellion Record*, 5:157; Ephraim A. Wilson, *Memoirs of the War* (Cleveland, OH: W. M. Bayne, 1893), 120.

46. John Beach to mother, May 31, 1862, HC; Ephraim C. Dawes to Katie, May 30, 1862, Ephraim C. Dawes Papers, Newberry Library; John B. Rice to wife, May 31, 1862; Charles Cotter to unknown, May 30, 1862; *OR*, 1, 10(1): 694, 699, 710.

47. Gaston, "Reminiscences of the War," 8; Matt Kemper to brother and sister, June 9, 1862, HC; *OR*, 1, 10(1): 744, 857–858; Moore, *The Rebellion Record*, 5:157.

48. Gale Judkins, "Edward C. Gillenwaters," Edward C. Gillenwaters Biographical File, Alcorn County Genealogical Society; Charles Johnson to his mother, July 11, 1862, Charles Johnson Papers, Virginia Tech University; "History of Old Tishomingo County," 32–33, 46.

49. For county records, see Records of Police Court, 1857–1862, Old Tishomingo

County; Probate Docket No. 2, 1860–1865, Old Tishomingo County; Appraisements, 1861–1870, Old Tishomingo County; Land Deed Record Book X, 1859–1866, Old Tishomingo County; Administrator Bonds and Letters, 1858–1870, Book 1, Old Tishomingo County; Probate Court Minutes, Book Q, 1861–1865, Old Tishomingo County; Miscellaneous Records, Book 9, 1860–1867, Old Tishomingo County; and "History of Old Tishomingo County," 32–33, 46, all in Alcorn County Chancery Clerk Archives.

50. John B. Rice to wife, May 31, 1862; *OR*, 1, 10(1): 743; Hinman, *Story of the Sherman Brigade*, 209; Moore, *The Rebellion Record*, 5:157.

CHAPTER 7. "MOST ANXIOUS PERIOD OF THE WAR"

1. A. P. Stewart to William H. McCardle, April 30, 1878, William H. McCardle Papers, MDAH; William Preston Johnston, "Albert Sidney Johnston at Shiloh," in *Battles and Leaders of the Civil War*, 4 vols. (New York: Century Company, 1884–1887), 1:568; Stacy D. Allen, "Crossroads of the Western Confederacy," *Blue and Gray Magazine* 19, 6 (Summer 2002): 10; *OR*, 1, 6:877; Timothy B. Smith, "'A Siege from the Start': The Spring 1862 Campaign against Corinth, Mississippi," *Journal of Mississippi History* 66, 4 (2004): 424.

2. O. P. Newberry to mother, May 22, 1862, Oliver Perry Newberry Papers, Newberry Library; Frank Moore, ed., *The Rebellion Record: A Diary of American Events, with Documents, Narratives, Illustrative Incidents, Poetry, etc.*, 11 vols. (New York: D. Vann Nostrand, 1861–1868), 5:157; *OR*, 1, 10(2): 403; *OR*, 1, 16(2): 95; T. J. Koger to his wife, May 13, 1862, T. J. Koger Collection, MDAH; P. B. McKay to wife, June 2, 1862, McKay Family Letter, Virginia Military Institute; Smith, "Siege from the Start," 424.

3. "Retreat of the Rebel Army from Corinth," *New York Times,* May 31, 1862; "The Evacuation of Corinth," *New York Herald,* June 1, 1862; Catherine Broun Diary, May 5 and 6, 1862, Philip H. Broun Family U.S. Civil War Papers, Rice University; *OR*, 1, 11(3): 209; Samuel K. Carrigan to William, May 25, 1862, Samuel K. Carrigan Letters, University of Tennessee; John Brown Jr. to wife, April 30 and May 21 and 30, 1862, John Brown Jr. Collection, Kansas Historical Society; Samuel Ayers to Sir, April 5, 1862, Samuel Ayers Letters, Kansas Historical Society; Mary A. Crowell to cousin, April 28, 1862, Mary Crowell Letter, University of Notre Dame; Moore, *The Rebellion Record*, 5:155; Abraham Lincoln to John C. Fremont, May 30, 1862, Lincoln Collection, Brown University.

4. John W. Morrison to wife, June 1, 1862, John W. Morrison Letters, Brigham Young University; John F. Kimbley to Maggie, June 1, 1862, HC; *OR*, 1, 10(1): 744, 772; Wallace J. Schutz and Walter N. Trenerry, *Abandoned by Lincoln: A Military Biography of General John Pope* (Chicago: University of Illinois Press, 1990), 85; William J. Christie to his brother, May 31, 1862, William J. Christie Letters, LSU; David P. Bunn Diary, May 30, 1862, ISHL; Lew Wallace, *An Autobiography*, 2 vols. (New York: Harper and Brothers, 1906), 2:579–581; Shelby Foote, *The Civil War: A Narrative*, 3 vols. (New York: Random House, 1958), 1:385–386; Steven E. Woodworth, *Nothing But Victory: The Army of*

the Tennessee, 1861–1865 (New York: Knopf, 2005), 207; Henry J. B. Cummings to Hopy, February 7, 1863, Henry Johnson Brodhead Cummings Papers, SHSI (copy in 39th Iowa File, CWIC); John F. Marszalek, *Commander of All Lincoln's Armies: A Life of General Henry W. Halleck* (Cambridge, MA: Harvard University Press, 2004), 124. Pope's biographers, Schutz and Trenerry, figured the exact distance Halleck averaged per day—3,432 feet.

5. *OR*, 1, 10(1): 676, 681, 710, 716, 773; *OR*, 1, 10(2): 226; William T. Sherman, *Memoirs of General William T. Sherman: Written by Himself* (New York: D. Appleton, 1875), 234.

6. *OR*, 1, 10(1): 772–773; William M. Polk, *Leonidas Polk: Bishop and General*, 2 vols. (New York: Longmans, Green, 1915), 2:118; John G. Galliard Memoir, 1895, John G. Galliard Papers, University of South Carolina.

7. James Phelan to Jefferson Davis, June 18, 1862, James Phelan Letter, LSU; George Thomas to Minerva, June 9, 1862, Thomas Family Correspondence, University of Notre Dame; Wright C. Shaumburg Journal, May 12, 1862, Schaumburg-Wright Family Papers, HNOC; John A. Wilson to "Lizzie," June 11, 1862, John A. Wilson Letters, MDAH; George W. Lennard to Clara, May 30, 1862, George W. Lennard Collection, Arizona State University; Isaac Gaillard Foster to his father, June 10, 1862, James Foster Family Correspondence, LSU; P. B. McKay to wife, June 2, 1862.

8. *OR*, 1, 10(1): 762–763, 771–775.

9. Ibid., 779; Steven E. Woodworth, *Jefferson Davis and His Generals: The Failure of Confederate Command in the West* (Lawrence: University Press of Kansas, 1990), 105.

10. William J. Christie to brother, May 31, 1862.

11. Ephraim C. Dawes to Katie, May 30, 1862, Ephraim C. Dawes Papers, Newberry Library; George D. Cotton to "My Dear Kemp," June 16, 1862, George D. Cotton Letters, LSU.

12. John Tyler Jr. to William L. Yancey, October 15, 1862, John Tyler Jr. Letter, UMC; William S. Rosecrans, "The Battle of Corinth," in *Battles and Leaders of the Civil War*, 4 vols. (New York: Century Company, 1884–1887), 2:740; Margaret Greene Rogers, *Civil War Corinth* (Corinth, MS: Rankin Printery, 1989), 16–17; Charles H. Smith, *The History of Fuller's Ohio Brigade, 1861–1865: Its Great March, with Roster Portraits, Battle Maps and Biographies* (Cleveland, OH: Press of A. J. Watt, 1909), 75; Joseph K. Nelson, "Recollections of My Early Life," Miscellaneous Collection, USAMHI (copy in 81st Ohio File, CWIC); William H. Chamberlain, *History of the Eighty-first Regiment Ohio Infantry Volunteers during the War of the Rebellion* (Cincinnati, OH: Gazette Steam Printing House, 1865), 21–22.

13. Henry W. Halleck to Edwin M. Stanton, June 10, 1862, Lincoln Collection, University of Chicago; *OR*, 1, 17(2): 3; Richard O'Connor, *Thomas: Rock of Chickamauga* (New York: Prentice-Hall, 1948), 174; Jack D. Welsh, *Medical Histories of Union Generals* (Kent, OH: Kent State University Press, 1996), 145; Charles Grundy to Henry, May 15, 1862, Charles Grundy Letter, LSU. One soldier also referred to diarrhea as the "Tennessee Quickstep."

14. Marszalek, *Commander of All Lincoln's Armies*, 126; Philip H. Sheridan, *Personal*

Memoirs of P. H. Sheridan: General United States Army, 2 vols. (New York: Charles L. Webster, 1888), 1:171; James M. McPherson, *Battle Cry of Freedom: The Civil War Era* (New York: Oxford University Press, 1988), 512.

15. Earl J. Hess, *Banners to the Breeze: The Kentucky Campaign, Corinth, and Stones River* (Lincoln: University of Nebraska Press, 2000), 3–6; James Lee McDonough, *War in Kentucky: From Shiloh to Perryville* (Knoxville: University of Tennessee Press, 1994), 32–36; Larry J. Daniel, *Days of Glory: The Army of the Cumberland, 1861–1865* (Baton Rouge: Louisiana State University Press, 2004), 85; Kenneth W. Noe, *Perryville: This Grand Havoc of Battle* (Lexington: University Press of Kentucky, 2001), 24; Marszalek, *Commander of All Lincoln's Armies*, 126, 129–130.

16. Stephen E. Ambrose, *Halleck: Lincoln's Chief of Staff* (Baton Rouge: Louisiana State University Press, 1962), 56; *OR*, 1, 10(1): 671.

17. William Shanks Diary, May 5, 1862, BGSU; Frederick Kehrwecker to brother, July 22, 1862, Kehrwecker Family Papers, BGSU; Liberty P. Warner to friends, July 14, 1862, Liberty Warner Papers, BGSU; George D. Cotton to "My Dear Kemp," June 16, 1862; Charles Fox to sister, July 27, 1862, Charles Fox Letter, University of Tennessee.

18. Ezra J. Warner, *Generals in Gray: Lives of the Confederate Commanders* (Baton Rouge: Louisiana State University Press, 1959), 317; Alvin P. Hovey Memoirs, undated, Alvin P. Hovey Papers, University of Indiana; John W. Morrison to wife, June 29 and August 1, 1862; "A Visit to Our Regiments Near Corinth," July 21, 1862, *Wisconsin State Journal* (copy in 8th Wisconsin File, CWIC).

19. Lewis Stafford to Kate Newland, July 5 and 31, 1862, Kate Newland Collection, Kansas Historical Society. For Ord, see Bernarr Cresap, *Appomattox Commander: The Story of General E. O. C. Ord* (San Diego: A. S. Barnes, 1981); T. D. Christie to brother, September 2, 1862, Christie Family Letters, Minnesota Historical Society; Peter Cozzens, *General John Pope: A Life for the Nation* (Urbana: University of Illinois Press, 2000), 71; U. S. Grant to wife, June 1862, Ulysses S. Grant Civil War Letter, University of California–Santa Barbara; *OR*, 1, 17(2): 32; Robert H. Cartmell Diary, August 14, 1862, Robert H. Cartmell Papers, TSLA; *OR*, 1, 17(2): 17, 18.

20. William J. Christie to brother, July 2, 1862; *OR*, 1, 17(2): 29, 42–43, 46–47, 53, 63–64, 68, 90, 97, 101; Ambrose, *Halleck*, 58; E. B. Long, *The Civil War Day by Day: An Almanac 1861–1865* (New York: Da Capo, 1971), 233; Foote, *The Civil War*, 1:544.

21. *OR*, 1, 17(2): 30; Thomas L. Snead, "With Price East of the Mississippi," in *Battles and Leaders of the Civil War*, 4 vols. (New York: Century Company, 1884–1887), 2:722; Mansfield Lovell to G. W., October 26, 1862, Mansfield Lovell Papers, Huntington Library; Nathan to Rachel, May 26, 1862, Union Soldier's Letter, University of Tennessee; Orlando Geer to sister, June 13, 1862, Orlando C. Geer Letter, University of Tennessee; *OR*, 1, 10(2): 243; *Corinth War Eagle*, August 7, 1862; Foote, *The Civil War*, 1:546.

22. Jacob Brunner to his wife, October 13, 1862, Jacob Brunner Letters, Ohio Historical Society; *OR*, 1, 17(2): 144.

23. James Phelan to Jefferson Davis, June 18, 1862; Andrew Nelson Lytle, *Bedford Forrest and His Critter Company* (New York: Minton Balch, 1931), 86; Clem Watson to

Mary, July 15, 1862, Clement Stanford Watson Family Papers, Tulane University; John W. Miller to his uncle, August 19, 1862, Miller Family Letters, University of Mississippi; W. N. Mattison to wife, July 18, 1862, William N. Mattison Papers, Atlanta History Center; P. D. Stephenson Memoirs, undated, 2, LSU (copies of Stephenson's memoirs are in the Nat C. Hughes Collection, University of Memphis); Rufus W. Cater to Fannie, June 22, 1862, Douglas J. and Rufus W. Cater Papers, LC; Special Order 35, May 9, 1862, William Yerger Papers, MDAH; John G. Galliard Memoir, 1895; Eugene F. Falconnet Diary, around May 30, 1862, Eugene Frederic Falconnet Papers, TSLA; George Dobson to family, May 24, 1862, 10th Mississippi File, CWIC.

24. N. L. Watts to wife, September 4, 1862, N. L. Watts Letter, MDAH; F. A. Rawlins Diary, July 12 and 28 and August 18, 1862, University of North Texas; Louis Stagg to wife, July 18, 1862, Louis Stagg Letters, LSU; William H. Kavanaugh Memoirs, undated, 33, William H. Kavanaugh Papers, UMC; J. H. Rogers to father, June 24, 1862, Sarah Rogers Shaw Papers, Wesleyan College; Sam R. Watkins, *"Co. Aytch," Maury Grays, First Tennessee Regiment; or, a Side Show of the Big Show* (Nashville: Presbyterian Printing House, 1882), 55; A. P. Stewart to D. H. Hill, July 21, 1862, Daniel Harvey Hill Papers, University of North Carolina.

25. *OR*, 1, 17(2): 594–595, 599, 601, 606, 614, 619, 623; T. Harry Williams, *P. G. T. Beauregard: Napoleon in Gray* (Baton Rouge: Louisiana State University, 1954), 155.

26. *OR*, 1, 17(2): 636; James Phelan to Jefferson Davis, June 18, 1862.

27. Snead, "With Price East of the Mississippi," 724–725; James Phelan to Jefferson Davis, June 18, 1862.

28. *OR*, 1, 17(2): 613, 654; Snead, "With Price East of the Mississippi," 724–725.

29. McDonough, *War in Kentucky*, 74–75; Sam Davis Elliott, *Isham G. Harris of Tennessee: Confederate Governor and United States Senator* (Baton Rouge: Louisiana State University Press, 2010), 118–119.

30. Watkins, *"Co. Aytch,"* 59; *OR*, 1, 17(2): 656–658; Isham W. Thomas to his wife, July 22, 1862, Isham W. Thomas Letters, MSU; *Chattanooga Daily Rebel*, September 7, 1862; F. A. Rawlins Diary, September 3, 1862; Snead, "With Price East of the Mississippi," 726.

31. J. C. Parrott to wife, September 27, 1862, James C. Parrott Papers, SHSI; Daniel Miller to brother, September 26, 1862, Herman B. Miller Papers, Missouri Historical Society; August Schilling Diary, July 6, 1862, BCHS; William J. Christie to brother, July 11, 1862; J. H. Phillips to father, June 5, 1862, 22nd Illinois File, CWIC; H. I. Smith, *History of the Seventh Iowa Veteran Volunteer Infantry during the Civil War* (Mason City, IA: R. Hitchcock, 1903), 72; George Lanphear to children, June 19, 1862, Lanphear Family Letters, University of Tennessee; Charles Johnson to his mother, July 11, 1862, Charles Johnson Papers, Virginia Tech University; Alcorn County Historical Association, *The History of Alcorn County, Mississippi* (Dallas: National Sharegraphics, 1983), 10; *Corinth War Eagle*, August 7, 1862; James M. Thurston Diary, September 21, 1862, Massachusetts Historical Society; Charles Thurber to mother, August 30, 1862, Charles Thurber Collection, UMC.

32. John Tyler Jr. to William L. Yancey, October 15, 1862; Rosecrans, "Battle of

Corinth," 740; William S. Rosecrans, "Rosecrans's Campaigns," in *Report of the Joint Committee on the Conduct of the War, at the Second Session Thirty-eighth Congress* (Washington, DC: Government Printing Office, 1865), 20.

33. Charles Johnson to his mother, July 11, 1862; T. D. Christie to father, July 4, 1862; William S. Stewart to Parents, July 4, 1862, William S. Stewart Papers, UMC; "From the Eighth Regiment," August 5, 1862, 8th Wisconsin File, CWIC; George Lanphear to children, June 19, 1862; "Civil War Narrative by Captain Joel W. Strong, Company I, 10th Missouri Infantry Volunteers," undated, 7, Joel Strong Papers—Alphabetical Files, Missouri Historical Society.

34. John Melvin Williams, *"The Eagle Regiment," 8th Wis. Inf'ty Vols.: A Sketch of Its Marches, Battles and Campaigns from 1861–1865 with Complete Regimental and Company Roster, and a Few Portraits and Sketches of Its Officers and Commanders* (Belleville, WI: Recorder Print, 1890), 48–50; Charles Thurber to mother, July 30, 1862; John Boatman to parents, June 14, 1862, HC; George Lanphear to children, June 19, 1862; Alonzo L. Brown, *History of the Fourth Regiment of Minnesota Infantry Volunteers during the Great Rebellion 1861–1865* (St. Paul: Pioneer Press Company, 1892), 64; David B. Henderson to George, August 26, 1862, David B. Henderson Papers, DCHS; William S. Stewart to Parents, September 9, 1862; William J. Christie to brother, July 2 and 11, 1862; *Corinth War Eagle*, August 7, 1862.

35. *Corinth War Eagle*, August 7, 1862.

36. Willit Haynes to friends, September 17, 1862, Willit Samuel Haynes Letters, Bradley University; August Schilling Diary, August 26 and 28, 1862; Smith, *History of Fuller's Ohio Brigade, 1861–1865*, 74; Ezra J. Warner, *Generals in Blue: Lives of the Union Commanders* (Baton Rouge: Louisiana State University Press, 1964), 375; Brown, *History of Fourth Regiment Minnesota Infantry Volunteers*, 69.

37. Horace Wardner, "Reminiscences of a Surgeon," in *Military Essays and Recollections: Papers Read before the Commandery of the State of Illinois, Military Order of the Loyal Legion of the United States*, 3 vols. (Chicago: Dial Press, 1899), 3:188; D. W. Pollock to family, August 7 and 25, 1862, David W. Pollock Letters, UMC; S. S. Seward to Thomas Davies, September 15, 1862, Letters Sent, RG 393, E 287, NARA; Charles Thurber to mother, July 30, 1862; Lyman B. Pierce, *History of the Second Iowa Cavalry: Containing a Detailed Account of Its Organization, Marches, and the Battles in Which It Has Participated; Also, a Complete Roster of Each Company* (Burlington, IA: Hawk-eye Steam Book and Job Printing Establishment, 1865), 26, 28; *Corinth War Eagle*, August 7, 1862; William S. Stewart to Parents, September 9, 1862; Martin Miller to sister, August 17, 1862, HC. For the various skirmishes that occurred over the summer, see *OR*, 1, 10(1): 918, 924; *OR*, 1, 17(1): 5–8, 12–13, 17–20, 20–26, 28–29, 35–36, 39–52; E. O. C. Ord to Richard Oglesby, June 28, 1862, Letters Sent, RG 393, E 287, NARA.

38. N. R. Dunn to his father, October 2, 1862, N. R. Dunn Letters, University of Michigan.

39. Albert Spelman to wife, June 6, 1862, HC; T. D. Christie to brother, July 10 and 19, 1862; William J. Christie to brother, July 2 and 11, 1862; Williams, *"The Eagle Regiment,"* 48–49; John W. Morrison to wife, August 28, 1862; Alexander G. Downing,

Downing's Civil War Diary, ed. Olynthus B. Clark (Des Moines: Historical Department of Iowa, 1916), 71–72; T. D. Christie to brother, July 10, 1862; T. D. Christie to sister, September 8, 1862; William S. Stewart to Parents, September 9, 1862.

40. D. W. Pollock to family, August 7, 1862; L. F. Hubbard to his aunt, October 13, 1862, Lucius F. Hubbard and Family Papers, Minnesota Historical Society; Martin Miller to sister, September 16, 1862; T. D. Christie to brother, July 19, 1862; "A Visit to Our Regiments Near Corinth," *Wisconsin State Journal,* July 21, 1862; Arthur Borland to sister, September 10, 1862, HC; N. R. Dunn to his father, October 2, 1862; Steven Werly Diary, August 10, 1862, UMC.

41. James W. Boyd to Edwin M. Stanton, February 14, 1865, Neff-Guttridge Collection, Indiana State University; Willit Haynes to friends, October 2, 1862; Mildred Throne, ed., *The Civil War Diary of Cyrus F. Boyd: Fifteenth Iowa Infantry, 1861–1863* (Des Moines: State Historical Society of Iowa, 1953), 71; Robert W. Banks, "The Civil War Letters of Robert W. Banks," ed. George C. Osborn, *Journal of Mississippi History* 5 (1943): 141–154; C. B. Smith to brother, July 31, 1862, 4th Minnesota File, CWIC; Special Order 8, October 1, 1862, Special Orders Issued, RG 393, E 294, NARA. For more on Unionism in Mississippi, see Timothy B. Smith, *Mississippi in the Civil War: The Home Front* (Jackson: University Press of Mississippi, 2010).

42. Henry McEwing to Hank, July 4, 1862, Civil War Letters of Mack and Nan Ewing, Archives of Michigan; Laurens Wolcott to mother, August 17, 1862, HC; Willit Haynes to friends, October 1, 1862; Daniel Miller to brother, September 27, 1862; John W. Morrison to wife, July 10 and August 28, 1862; Downing, *Downing's Civil War Diary,* 71–72; T. D. Christie to brother, July 10, 1862; T. D. Christie to sister, September 8, 1862; William S. Stewart to Parents, September 9, 1862; Williams, *"The Eagle Regiment,"* 48–49.

43. *OR,* 1, 46(3): 40–41.

44. D. F. McGowan to Ellen, June 13, 1862, HC; Robert McDougall to Henry Ewing, July 26, 1862, Civil War Letters of Mack and Nan Ewing, Archives of Michigan; Jeremiah C. Sullivan to C. S. Hamilton, September 12, 1862, Eldridge Collection, Huntington Library; Downing, *Downing's Civil War Diary,* 68.

CHAPTER 8. "A DEEPER DESIGN"

1. For Antietam, see Stephen W. Sears, *Landscape Turned Red: The Battle of Antietam* (New Haven, CT: Ticknor and Fields, 1983); James M. McPherson, *Crossroads of Freedom: Antietam: The Battle that Changed the Course of the Civil War* (New York: Oxford University Press, 2002).

2. For Perryville, see Kenneth W. Noe, *Perryville: This Grand Havoc of Battle* (Lexington: University Press of Kentucky, 2001).

3. *OR,* 1, 17(2): 688.

4. Albert Castel, *General Sterling Price and the Civil War in the West* (Baton Rouge: Louisiana State University Press, 1968), 3–7; Robert E. Shalhope, *Sterling Price: Portrait of a Southerner* (Columbia: University of Missouri Press, 1971),17; Ezra J. Warner,

Generals in Gray: Lives of the Confederate Commanders (Baton Rouge: Louisiana State University Press, 1959), 246–247.

5. Albert O. McCollom to his family, September 24, 1862, Robert and Sephronica Clark McCollom Papers, University of Arkansas; Castel, *General Sterling Price*, 93; J. C. Ives to Earl Van Dorn, September 9, 1862, Lusk Family Papers, MDAH.

6. W. C. Porter, "War Diary of W. C. Porter," ed. J. V. Frederick, *Arkansas Historical Quarterly* 11, 4 (1952): 302; Homer L. Calkin, "Elkhorn to Vicksburg," *Civil War History* 2, 1 (March 1956): 29; Robert W. Banks, "The Civil War Letters of Robert W. Banks," ed. George C. Osborn, *Journal of Mississippi History* 5 (1943): 143; Henry Little, "The Diary of General Henry Little, C.S.A.," ed. Albert Castel, *Civil War Times Illustrated* 11, 6 (October 1972): 45 (the original diary is filed under Lewis Henry Little Diary, *CWTI* Collection, USAMHI); Samuel B. Barron, *The Lone Star Defenders: A Chronicle of the Third Texas Cavalry Regiment in the Civil War* (Washington, DC: Zenger, 1983), 102, 104; F. A. Rawlins Diary, September 9 and 12, 1862, University of North Texas.

7. Peter Cozzens, *The Darkest Days of the War: The Battles of Iuka and Corinth* (Chapel Hill: University of North Carolina Press, 1997), 54; Ben Earl Kitchens, *Rosecrans Meets Price: The Battle of Iuka, Mississippi* (Florence, AL: Thornwood Book Publishers, 1987), 27, 35, 48–50, 59; David McKinney Diary, September 8 and 9, 1862, USAMHI; Jeremiah C. Sullivan to C. S. Hamilton, September 12, 1862, Eldridge Collection, Huntington Library; Murphy to Rosecrans, September 13, 1862, Court Martial Case File KK 303, Robert C. Murphy, NARA; U. S. Grant to J. C. Kelton, October 25, 1862, U. S. Grant Letters, ISHL; Banks, "Civil War Letters of Robert W. Banks," 143–145; *OR*, 1, 17(2): 702–703; W. H. Tunnard, *A Southern Record: The History of the 3rd Regiment Louisiana Infantry*, ed. Edwin C. Bearss (Dayton, OH: Morningside, 1970), 182; F. A. Rawlins Diary, September 15, 18–19, 1862; Calkin, "Elkhorn to Vicksburg," 30–31; Porter, "War Diary of W. C. Porter," 302; Avington Wayne Simpson Diary, September 17, 1862, UMC; W. P. Rogers to his wife, September 24, 1862, William P. Rogers Papers, University of Texas at Austin; Little, "Diary of General Henry Little," 46; Barron, *Lone Star Defenders*, 106; James A. Walden, *The Journals of James A. Walden Part I—Confederate Soldier*, ed. W. J. Lemke (Fayetteville, AR: Washington County Historical Society, 1954), 39.

8. *OR*, 1, 17(2): 706.

9. Thomas L. Snead, "With Price East of the Mississippi," in *Battles and Leaders of the Civil War*, 4 vols. (New York: Century Company, 1884–1887), 2:732.

10. J. C. Parrott to wife, September 27, 1862, James C. Parrott Papers, SHSI; *OR*, 1, 17(2): 206.

11. *OR*, 1, 17(2): 210, 213; U. S. Grant, *Personal Memoirs of U. S. Grant* (New York: Charles L. Webster, 1885), 241; Alexander G. Downing, *Downing's Civil War Diary*, ed. Olynthus B. Clark (Des Moines: Historical Department of Iowa, 1916), 68.

12. *OR*, 1, 17(2): 214.

13. Ibid., 218, 222, 228; Charles Floyd to "Dear Friend," September 13, 1862, Charles H. Floyd Papers, ISHL.

14. *OR*, 1, 17(1): 68; J. R. Zearing to his wife, September 21, 1862, James Robert Zear-

ing Collection, Chicago Historical Society; General Order 196, September 16, 1862, Thomas J. McKean Papers, MDAH.

15. Charles Hamilton letter, September 17, 1862, Charles Smith Hamilton Papers, University of Illinois; Grant, *Memoirs*, 241; David McKinney Diary, September 19, 1862; *OR*, 1, 17(2): 225; *OR*, 1, 17(1): 94; William M. Lamers, *The Edge of Glory: A Biography of General William S. Rosecrans, U.S.A.* (New York: Harcourt, Brace, and World, 1961), 104; E. A. Webb to his sister, September 16, 1862, Edward A. Webb Papers, WRHS; Richard S. Reeves Diary, September 18, 1862, Richard S. Reeves Miscellaneous Papers, Minnesota Historical Society.

16. E. A. Webb to his sister, September 16, 1862; Richard S. Reeves Diary, September 18, 1862; Mark Mayo Boatner III, *The Civil War Dictionary* (New York: David McKay, 1988), 791; *OR*, 1, 17(1): 81, 82, 85, 118; August Schilling Diary, September 18, 1862, BCHS; James M. Thurston Diary, September 17, 1862, Massachusetts Historical Society; Ezra J. Warner, *Generals in Blue: Lives of the Union Commanders* (Baton Rouge: Louisiana State University Press, 1964), 350, 470; John Wilcox to his wife, September 22, 1862, John S. Wilcox Papers, ISHL. McArthur commanded the Sixth Division of the Army of the Tennessee, Davies had the Second Division, and Ross took over for McClernand when he left.

17. Richard S. Reeves Diary, September 19, 1862; *OR*, 1, 17(1): 69, 79; S. H. M. Byers, "How Men Feel in Battle," *American History Illustrated* 22, 2 (April 1987): 11; David McKinney Diary, September 19, 1862; D. J. Williams to his parents, September 18, 1862, Robert S. Williams Letters, NMMA; Hiram P. Howe to his parents, October 19, 1862, Hiram P. Howe Papers, LC; Edwin C. Bearss, *Decision in Mississippi: Mississippi's Important Role in the War between the States* (Jackson: Mississippi Commission on the War between the States, 1962), 34; Grant, *Memoirs*, 242, 244; *OR*, 1, 17(1): 73; Charles S. Hamilton, "The Battle of Iuka," in *Battles and Leaders of the Civil War*, 4 vols. (New York: Century Company, 1884–1887), 2:734; Francis Vinton Greene, *The Mississippi* (New York: Charles Scribner's Sons, 1882), 39; Terrence J. Winschel, "A Fierce Little Fight in Mississippi," *Civil War Times Illustrated* 33, 3 (July/August 1994): 55; Lamers, *Edge of Glory*, 108–109; William H. Miller, "Battle of Iuka," 10, William H. Miller Papers, Missouri Historical Society. Originally, Hamilton was to march on the Fulton road, Stanley on the Jacinto road.

18. William D. Evans to Caroline, September 26, 1862, William D. Evans Papers, WRHS; Grant, *Memoirs*, 244; Lyle Dickey to "Ann," September 21, 1862, Wallace-Dickey Papers, ISHL; Seth Daily to his father, November 13, 1862, David W. Daily Papers, Indiana Historical Society.

19. *OR*, 1, 17(2): 708; *OR*, 1, 17(1): 122; Bearss, *Decision in Mississippi*, 40; G. W. Dudley, *The Battle of Iuka* (Iuka, MS: Iuka Vidette, 1896), 5.

20. Alonzo L. Brown, *History of the Fourth Regiment of Minnesota Infantry Volunteers during the Great Rebellion 1861–1865* (St. Paul: Pioneer Press Company, 1892), 82; Lamers, *Edge of Glory*, 109; J. Q. A. Campbell Diary, September 19, 1862, WRHS; *OR*, 1, 17(1): 90, 94, 104–105; Bearss, *Decision in Mississippi*, 41–42, 61; D. W. Pollock to

his family, September 24, 1862, David W. Pollock Letters, UMC; "War Times at Iuka, Miss.," *Confederate Veteran* 11, 3 (March 1903): 120; W. C. W., "The Fight at Iuka," *Southern Bivouac* 1, 7 (December 1885): 445–446. For Iuka, see William L. Coker, *Valley of Springs: The Story of Iuka* (Hattiesburg: University of Southern Mississippi, 1968); Jack W. Gunn, "The Battle of Iuka," *Journal of Mississippi History* 14 (1962): 142–157.

21. *OR*, 1, 17(1): 68, 90, 94–95, 97–98, 100–102, 125, 127–131; *OR*, 1, 17(2): 708; Tunnard, *Southern Record*, 182, 184; Dudley, *Battle of Iuka*, 5; Victor M. Rose, *Ross' Texas Brigade* (Louisville, KY: Courier-Journal Company, 1881), 72; Winschel, "A Fierce Little Fight in Mississippi," 56; Kitchens, *Rosecrans Meets Price*, 96, 98; Brown, *History of Fourth Regiment Minnesota Infantry Volunteers*, 86; Bearss, *Decision in Mississippi*, 42; Henry M. Neil, "A Battery at Close Quarters: Being the Story of the Eleventh Ohio Battery at Iuka and Corinth," in *Sketches of War History, 1861–1865: A Compilation of Miscellaneous Papers Compiled for the Ohio Commandery of the Loyal Legion, February, 1885–February, 1909* (Wilmington, NC: Broadfoot, 1993), 347–348, 351; Lamers, *Edge of Glory*, 111; Frank Moore, ed., *The Rebellion Record: A Diary of American Events, with Documents, Narratives, Illustrative Incidents, Poetry, etc.*, 11 vols. (New York: D. Vann Nostrand, 1861–1868), 5:484; Hamilton, "Battle of Iuka," 735; Kitchens, *Rosecrans Meets Price*, 102; Douglas Hale, *The Third Texas Cavalry in the Civil War* (Norman: University of Oklahoma Press, 1993), 126; Bearss, *Decision in Mississippi*, 42–43; W. P. Helm, "Close Fighting at Iuka, Miss.," *Confederate Veteran* 19, 4 (April 1911): 171.

22. George W. Pepper, *Under Three Flags; or the Story of My Life as Preacher, Captain in the Army, Chaplain, Consul, with Speeches and Interviews* (Cincinnati, OH: Curts and Jennings, 1899), 91; *OR*, 1, 17(1): 73, 80, 90–91, 95–99, 100–104, 107–109, 111–112, 128–129; Hiram P. Howe to his parents, October 19, 1862; Brown, *History of Fourth Regiment Minnesota Infantry Volunteers*, 101; Cozzens, *Darkest Days*, 84, 109; Charles Vanamburg to his father, September 20–26, 1862, Vanamburg Family Papers, USAMHI; Bearss, *Decision in Mississippi*, 43, 48; *OR*, 1, 17(1): 97, 128; Miller, "Battle of Iuka," 15, 26, 35; Kitchens, *Rosecrans Meets Price*, 115–116; Byers, "How Men Feel in Battle," 12; Tunnard, *Southern Record*, 183; W. F. Howell to W. A. Pinson, September 24, 1862, Rosemonde and Emile Kuntz Collection, Tulane University; Dudley, *Battle of Iuka*, 9; Joseph M. Bailey Memoir, "The Story of a Confederate Soldier," 17, Joseph M. Bailey Papers, University of Arkansas; Neil, "A Battery at Close Quarters," 348, 350; Helm, "Close Fighting at Iuka, Miss.," 171.

23. *OR*, 1, 17(1): 122, 125, 132, 134–136; Little, "Diary of General Henry Little," 46; Dudley, *Battle of Iuka*, 6; Warner, *Generals in Gray*, 189; Phillip Thomas Tucker, *The Confederacy's Fighting Chaplain: Father John B. Bannon* (Tuscaloosa: University of Alabama Press, 1992), 81; *New Orleans Daily Picayune*, August 11, 1901; Albert Castel, "The Battle without a Victor . . . Iuka," *Civil War Times Illustrated* 11, 6 (October 1972): 16.

24. William D. Evans to "Caroline," September 26, 1862; *OR*, 1, 17(1): 86–87, 89, 91, 106, 109–111, 117, 122, 128; Hamilton, "Battle of Iuka," 735; Bearss, *Decision in Mississippi*, 51–53; Moore, *The Rebellion Record*, 5:488.

25. William S. Stewart to Parents, September 23, 1862, William S. Stewart Papers, UMC; Grant, *Memoirs*, 244; H. P. Andrews to his wife and children, September 19, 1862,

Henry P. Andrews Papers, ISHL; William Wade Diary, September 20, 1862, USAMHI; John Whitten Diary, inside front cover, LC; *OR*, 1, 17(1): 77; N. R. Dunn to father, October 1, 1862, N. R. Dunn Letters, University of Michigan. For acoustic shadows, see Charles D. Ross, *Civil War Acoustic Shadows* (Shippensburg, PA: White Mane Books, 2001).

26. Snead, "With Price East of the Mississippi," 733; Finley L. Hubbell, "Diary of Lieut. Col. Hubbell, of 3d Regiment Missouri Infantry, C.S.A.," *The Land We Love* 6, 2 (December 1868): 99; L. S. Ross to his wife, September 24, 1862, Ross Family Papers, Baylor University; Castel, *General Sterling Price*, 103; *OR*, 1, 17(1): 122; Dabney H. Maury, "Recollections of Campaign against Grant in North Mississippi in 1862–63," *Southern Historical Society Papers* 13 (1885): 290.

27. W. B. Britton to "Messrs. Editors," September 22, 1862, William A. Britton Letters, WRHS; *OR*, 1, 17(1): 67, 70, 83; Dudley, *Battle of Iuka*, 13; Kitchens, *Rosecrans Meets Price*, 159–160; "Personal Memoirs of Brigadier General David Sloan Stanley, Late Major General, U.S. Volunteers," 169, West-Stanley-Wright Family Papers, USAMHI (Stanley later published his memoirs as *Personal Memoirs of Major General D. S. Stanley, U.S.A.* [Cambridge, MA: Harvard University Press, 1917]); Bernarr Cresap, *Appomattox Commander: The Story of General E. O. C. Ord* (San Diego: A. S. Barnes, 1981), 86; John W. Fuller, "Our Kirby Smith," in *Sketches of War History, 1861–1865: Papers Read before the Ohio Commandery of the Military Order of the Loyal Legion of the United States, 1886–1888* (Cincinnati: Robert Clarke, 1888), 171.

28. Joel Strong, "Civil War Narrative by Captain Joel W. Strong, Company I, 10th Missouri Infantry Volunteers," 7–8, Joel Strong Alphabetical File, Missouri Historical Society; W. P. Rogers to his wife, September 24, 1862; Thomas Smith Manuscript, "Sketches of the Confederate War," 4, MDAH; James Vanderbilt to his mother, September 25, 1862, James C. Vanderbilt Civil War Letters, Indiana State Library; Thomas B. Wilson Diary, September 16, 1862, TSLA; Grant, *Memoirs*, 245; *OR*, 1, 17(1): 68, 74, 83; Brown, *History of Fourth Regiment Minnesota Infantry Volunteers*, 110; August Schilling Diary, September 21, 1862; James M. Thurston Diary, September 21, 1862.

29. August Schilling Diary, September 21, 1862; James M. Thurston Diary, September 21, 1862; *OR*, 1, 17(1): 74; Strong, "Civil War Narrative," 7.

30. William Arkins Diary, September 22, 1862, William Arkins and Family Papers, Minnesota Historical Society; Hamilton, "Battle of Iuka," 736; *OR*, 1, 17(1): 74, 119; Cresap, *Appomattox Commander*, 87; Maury, "Recollections of Campaign against Grant," 292.

31. Robert G. Hartje, *Van Dorn: The Life and Times of a Confederate General* (Nashville: Vanderbilt University Press, 1967), 6–77; Earl Van Dorn Biographical File, J. F. H. Claiborne Papers, University of North Carolina; Charles N. Elliott, "Van Dorn's Blitzkrieg Stumbles: Comanches, Command Decisions, and Combat in the Baton Rouge Campaign of 1862," in *Confederate Generals in the Western Theater: Essays on America's Civil War,* vol. 2 (Knoxville: University of Tennessee Press, 2010), 53–72; *OR*, 1, 17(2): 697; *OR*, 1, 17(1): 376; R. R. Hutchinson, "Missourians East of the Mississippi River," 25, Thomas L. Snead Papers, Missouri Historical Society; W. J. Stubblefield Diary, September 12, 1862, Murray State University.

32. *OR*, 1, 17(2): 709–712, 714; H. J. Reid, "Twenty-second Mississippi," 13, J. F. H. Claiborne Papers, University of North Carolina.

33. Phillip Thomas Tucker, *Westerners in Gray: The Men and Missions of the Elite Fifth Missouri Infantry Regiment* (Jefferson, NC: McFarland, 1995), 64; Castel, *General Sterling Price*, 104–106; *Charleston Mercury*, October 8, 1862; newspaper article by Colonel Celcus Price, Earl Van Dorn Papers, Alabama Department of Archives and History; Special Order, October 2, 1862, General and Special Orders—Price's Command, Army of the West, NARA; Price to Snead, October 1, 1862, Letters Sent—Price's Command, NARA.

34. *OR*, 1, 17(1): 374; Castel, *General Sterling Price*, 106.

35. *OR*, 1, 17(1): 374.

36. Ibid., 377–378, 416, 432, 435, 441, 454.

37. Ibid.; Calkin, "Elkhorn to Vicksburg," 33.

38. *OR*, 1, 17(1): 377; Hartje, *Van Dorn*, 214.

39. John Tyler Jr. to William L. Yancey, October 15, 1862, John Tyler Jr. Letter, UMC; *OR*, 1, 17(1): 377; C. M. Griven to Van Dorn, September 18, 1862, Earl Van Dorn Papers, LC; *OR*, 1, 17(1): 434, 453; Castel, *General Sterling Price*, 106; Charles Stevens, "The Corinth Diary of Private Charles Stevens," *Blue and Gray Education Society Papers* 18 (Fall 2006): 12 (original diary in HC).

40. *OR*, 1, 17(2): 714–715.

41. Ibid., 715; *OR*, 1, 17(1): 378; Breckinridge to Van Dorn, September 20, 1862, Civil War Papers, MDAH; Maury to Emily Van Dorn Miller, November 5, 1902, Emily Van Dorn Miller Papers, MDAH; Van Dorn to G. W. Randolph, October 1, 1862, Earl Van Dorn Papers, Alabama Department of Archives and History.

42. Willit Haynes to friends, October 2, 1862, Willit Samuel Haynes Letters, Bradley University; Grant, *Memoirs*, 245; *OR*, 1, 17(2): 233; Neil, "Battery at Close Quarters," 351–352; John B. Sanborn, "An Army Experience," in *Sketches of War History, 1861–1865: A Compilation of Miscellaneous Papers Compiled for the Ohio Commandery of the Loyal Legion, February, 1885–February, 1909* (Wilmington, NC: Broadfoot, 1993), 358; Kenneth P. Williams, *Lincoln Finds a General: A Military Study of the Civil War* (New York: Macmillan, 1956), 81; Warner, *Generals in Blue*, 410. Rosecrans was appointed major general on September 17; after arguing his case, he gained that rank on October 25, retroactive to March 21, 1862. Grant, *Memoirs*, 245; Warner, *Generals in Blue*, 113–114, 301; *OR*, 1, 17(2): 232.

43. *OR*, 1, 17(2): 240; John Fuller to David S. Stanley, August 23, 1887, West-Stanley-Wright Family Papers, USAMHI; Grant, *Memoirs*, 245; William S. Rosecrans, "The Battle of Corinth," in *Battles and Leaders of the Civil War*, 4 vols. (New York: Century Company, 1884–1887), 2:741; Fuller, "Our Kirby Smith," 171; Monroe F. Cockrell, ed., *The Lost Account of the Battle of Corinth and Court-Martial of Gen. Van Dorn* (Wilmington, NC: Broadfoot, 1991), 54; D. S. Stanley, "The Battle of Corinth," in *Personal Recollections of the War of the Rebellion: Addresses Delivered before the Commandery of the State of New York, Military Order of the Loyal Legion of the United States*, 2nd series (New York: G. P. Putnam's Sons, 1897), 271.

44. Daniel Miller to brother, September 27, 1862, Herman B. Miller Papers, Missouri Historical Society; *OR*, 1, 17(1): 143–144; *OR*, 1, 17(2): 240–241, 243.

45. *OR*, 1, 17(2): 243; Grant, *Memoirs*, 245–246; J. R. Zearing to his wife, September 21, 1862; *OR*, 1, 17(2): 240, 245; Rosecrans, "Battle of Corinth," 740–741.

46. *OR*, 1, 17(2): 243; Rosecrans, "Battle of Corinth," 741.

47. Rosecrans, "Battle of Corinth," 741.

CHAPTER 9. "MY POSITION IS PRECARIOUS"

1. For Antietam's importance, see James M. McPherson, *Crossroads of Freedom: Antietam: The Battle that Changed the Course of the Civil War* (New York: Oxford University Press, 2002).

2. For the Kentucky campaign, see Kenneth W. Noe, *Perryville: This Grand Havoc of Battle* (Lexington: University Press of Kentucky, 2001).

3. *OR*, 1, 17(1): 378, 385; Will Snyder to Parents, November 25, 1862, NMMA.

4. *OR*, 1, 17(1): 385; Robert W. Banks, "The Civil War Letters of Robert W. Banks," ed. George C. Osborn, *Journal of Mississippi History* 5 (1943): 146; Robert G. Hartje, *Van Dorn: The Life and Times of a Confederate General* (Nashville: Vanderbilt University Press, 1967), 216; Homer L. Calkin, "Elkhorn to Vicksburg," *Civil War History* 2, 1 (March 1956): 33–34; W. H. Tunnard, *A Southern Record: The History of the 3rd Regiment Louisiana Infantry*, ed. Edwin C. Bearss (Dayton, OH: Morningside, 1970), 191; *Corinth Daily Corinthian*, October 18, 1978.

5. *OR*, 1, 17(1): 385; Hartje, *Van Dorn*, 216.

6. Finley L. Hubbell, "Diary of Lieut. Col. Hubbell, of 3d Regiment Missouri Infantry, C.S.A.," *The Land We Love* 6, 2 (December 1868): 99; *OR*, 1, 17(2): 717; *OR*, 1, 17(1): 378, 385, 404, 421; Robert Ingersoll to his brother, September 26, 1862, R. G. Ingersoll Papers, ISHL.

7. *OR*, 1, 17(1): 421.

8. Ibid., 378, 385, 392, 421; William McCuray to Mrs. Dantzler, October 11, 1862, Absolem F. Dantzler Papers, Duke University.

9. Phillip Thomas Tucker, *The Forgotten Stonewall of the West: Major General John Stevens Bowen* (Macon, GA: Mercer University Press, 1997), 129; Hartje, *Van Dorn*, 219; *OR*, 1, 17(1): 425.

10. George L. Griscom Diary, October 3, 1862, University of Texas at Austin; Hartje, *Van Dorn*, 219–220; *OR*, 1, 17(1): 378, 404, 417, 421–422, 456; Alonzo L. Brown, *History of the Fourth Regiment of Minnesota Infantry Volunteers during the Great Rebellion 1861–1865* (St. Paul: Pioneer Press Company, 1892), 114.

11. *OR*, 1, 17(1): 404; *OR*, 1, 17(2): 252, 352; Charles C. Labuzan Diary, October 2, 1862, 42nd Alabama File, CWIC.

12. *OR*, 1, 17(1): 353, 418.

13. N. R. Dunn to his father, October 2, 1862, N. R. Dunn Letters, University of Michigan; W. Q. Gresham to his wife, September 23, 1862, Walter Q. Gresham Papers, LC; Bela

T. St. John Diary, October 2, 1862; Bela T. St. John Papers, LC; John Fuller to W. N. Vagleson, September 25, 1862, Letters Sent—Fuller's Brigade, NARA; *OR*, 1, 17(1): 157–158, 167, 242; Charles Cowell, "An Infantryman at Corinth: The Diary of Charles Cowell," *Civil War Times Illustrated* 13, 7 (November 1974): 10.

14. *OR*, 1, 17(1): 158, 242; *OR*, 1, 17(2): 250; William S. Rosecrans, "The Battle of Corinth," in *Battles and Leaders of the Civil War*, 4 vols. (New York: Century Company, 1884–1887), 2:743.

15. William S. Rosecrans, "Rosecrans's Campaigns," in *Report of the Joint Committee on the Conduct of the War, at the Second Session Thirty-eighth Congress* (Washington, DC: Government Printing Office, 1865), 21; Rosecrans, "Battle of Corinth," 743; *OR*, 1, 17(1): 166, 179.

16. Myron Underwood to unknown, undated, Myron Underwood Papers, University of Iowa; 166; Henry M. Neil, "A Battery at Close Quarters: Being the Story of the Eleventh Ohio Battery at Iuka and Corinth," in *Sketches of War History, 1861–1865: A Compilation of Miscellaneous Papers Compiled for the Ohio Commandery of the Loyal Legion, February, 1885–February, 1909* (Wilmington, NC: Broadfoot, 1993), 7:352.

17. *OR*, 1, 17(1): 352; John B. Sanborn, "An Army Experience," in *Sketches of War History, 1861–1865: A Compilation of Miscellaneous Papers Compiled for the Ohio Commandery of the Loyal Legion, February, 1885–February, 1909* (Wilmington, NC: Broadfoot, 1993), 7:358.

18. J. R. Zearing to wife, October 11, 1862, James Roberts Zearing Collection, Chicago Historical Society; David B. Henderson to George, November 17, 1862, David B. Henderson Papers, DCHS.

19. Byron Kirby to Thomas J. McKean, October 1, 1862, Thomas J. McKean Papers, MDAH; *OR*, 1, 17(1): 352, 357; *OR*, 1, 17(2): 251–252; W. H. Tucker, *The Fourteenth Wisconsin Vet. Vol. Infantry (General A. J. Smith's Command) in the Expedition and Battle of Tupelo: Also, Wanderings through the Wilds of Missouri and Arkansas in Pursuit of Price* (Indianapolis: n.p., 1892), 4; unknown to Andrew Hickenlooper, October 1, 1862, Thomas J. McKean Papers, MDAH; James K. Newton, *A Wisconsin Boy in Dixie: The Selected Letters of James K. Newton*, ed. Stephen E. Ambrose (Madison: University of Wisconsin Press, 1961), 38. The drums heard at Kossuth no doubt came from part of Stanley's division, not the enemy.

20. *OR*, 1, 17(1): 352–353; Tucker, *Fourteenth Wisconsin Vet. Vol. Infantry*, 6.

21. James Monroe Tyler Diary, October 2, 1862, SHSW; *OR*, 1, 17(1): 336, 353; John Oliver to Thomas J. McKean, undated, Thomas J. McKean Papers, MDAH; John Oliver to unknown, undated, ibid.

22. *OR*, 1, 17(1): 353.

23. Ibid., 336; John J. Safely to Mary Frances McEwen, October 9, 1862, McEwen Family Papers, Missouri Historical Society; Mildred Throne, ed., *The Civil War Diary of Cyrus F. Boyd: Fifteenth Iowa Infantry, 1861–1863* (Des Moines: State Historical Society of Iowa, 1953), 71; Alexander G. Downing, *Downing's Civil War Diary*, ed. Olynthus B. Clark (Des Moines: Historical Department of Iowa, 1916), 72.

24. *OR*, 1, 17(1): 178–179, 286; Charles H. Smith, *The History of Fuller's Ohio*

Brigade, 1861–1865: Its Great March, with Roster Portraits, Battle Maps and Biographies (Cleveland, OH: Press of A. J. Watt, 1909), 82; Cloyd Bryner, *Bugle Echoes: The Story of the Illinois 47th* (Springfield, IL: Phillips Bros. Printers, 1905), 58; Joseph Mitchell Strickling Diary, October 3, 1862, 39th Ohio File, CWIC.

25. *OR*, 1, 17(1): 219, 271; C. J. Sergent Diary, October 2, 1862, NMMA; John J. McKee Diary, October 2, 1862, Civil War Miscellaneous Collection, USAMHI; Union soldier to Adam, October 16, 1862, Adam Durkes Papers, UMC.

26. *OR*, 1, 17(1): 149–150, 158, 336; Victor Hoar, "Colonel William C. Falkner in the Civil War," *Journal of Mississippi History* 27 (1965): 56.

27. A. B. Monahan to wife, October 9 and 11, 1862, 63rd Ohio File, SNMP; *OR*, 1, 17(2): 254.

28. *OR*, 1, 17(1): 167; Rosecrans, "Battle of Corinth," 745.

29. Temple Clark to Thomas J. McKean, October 3, 1862, Thomas J. McKean Papers, MDAH; *OR*, 1, 17(1): 336–337; *OR*, 1, 17(2): 254; Throne, *Civil War Diary of Cyrus F. Boyd*, 71.

30. Joseph Risedorph, "Battle of Corinth," 2, Joseph Risedorph Papers, Minnesota Historical Society; J. Q. A. Campbell Diary, October 3, 1862, WRHS; *OR*, 1, 17(1): 205, 209, 220, 226, 229; J. V. Frederick, ed., "An Illinois Soldier in North Mississippi: Diary of John Wilson February 15–December 30, 1862," *Journal of Mississippi History* 1, 3 (July 1939): 190.

31. *OR*, 1, 17(1): 205, 251–252, 285; D. Leib Ambrose, *History of the Seventh Regiment Illinois Volunteer Infantry, from Its First Muster into the U.S. Service, April 25, 1861, to Its Final Muster out, July 9, 1865* (Springfield: Illinois Journal Company, 1868), 91–92; Charles F. Hubert, *History of the Fiftieth Regiment Illinois Volunteer Infantry in the War of the Union* (Kansas City, MO: Western Veteran Publishing Company, 1894), 131, 135; William H. Chamberlain, *History of the Eighty-first Regiment Ohio Infantry Volunteers during the War of the Rebellion* (Cincinnati, OH: Gazette Steam Printing House, 1865), 25; James M. Thurston Diary, October 3, 1862, Massachusetts Historical Society.

32. *OR*, 1, 17(1): 167–168, 252, 268, 272; *OR*, 1, 52(1): 286.

33. A. B. Monahan to wife, October 9 and 11, 1862, 63rd Ohio File, SNMP; *OR*, 1, 17(1): 179; *OR*, 1, 17(2): 255; George Hovey Cadman to wife, October 13, 1862, George Hovey Cadman Papers, University of North Carolina; Joseph Mitchell Strickling Diary, October 3, 1862, 39th Ohio File, CWIC.

34. *OR*, 1, 17(1): 177.

35. Court Martial Case File KK 303, Robert C. Murphy, NARA; *OR*, 1, 17(1): 160, 167.

36. S. C. Lyford to Thomas J. McKean, October 3, 1862, Thomas J. McKean Papers, MDAH; *OR*, 1, 17(1): 167.

37. William Brown to his wife, September 28, 1862, William Brown Letters, SHSW; *OR*, 1, 17(1): 378, 385, 404; *Natchez Courier*, September 26, 1862; Victor M. Rose, *Ross' Texas Brigade* (Louisville, KY: Courier-Journal Company, 1881), 72; Monroe F. Cockrell, ed., *The Lost Account of the Battle of Corinth and Court-Martial of Gen. Van Dorn* (Jackson, TN: McCowat-Mercer Press, 1955), 21; Albert Castel, *General Sterling Price and the Civil War in the West* (Baton Rouge: Louisiana State University Press, 1968), 110;

Alice Hirsch, "Company G, 22nd Mississippi Infantry," Isaac E. Hirsh Papers, MSU, 18; Hartje, *Van Dorn*, 220; Griffin A. Stanton Civil War Journal, September 28, 1862, University of Memphis; George R. Elliott Diary, October 3, 1862, TSLA; Balzar Grebe, "Autobiography and Civil War Diary," 15, Balzar Grebe Papers, LC. Others corroborated the reports of earthquakes in the area.

38. John Tyler Jr. to William L. Yancey, October 15, 1862, John Tyler Jr. Letter, UMC; *OR*, 1, 17(1): 378, 385, 404; August Schilling Diary, October 3, 1862, BCHS.

39. *OR*, 1, 17(1): 167, 337, 342, 353–354; E. A. Pollard, *Southern History of the War*, 2 vols. (New York: Richardson, 1866), 1:516.

40. *OR*, 1, 17(1): 342, 344, 353–354; Newton, *Wisconsin Boy in Dixie*, 39; T. D. Christie to father, October 27, 1862, Christie Family Letters, Minnesota Historical Society.

41. *OR*, 1, 17(1): 337, 354.

42. Ibid., 253, 337, 354; Ambrose, *History of Seventh Regiment Illinois Volunteer Infantry*, 92.

43. *OR*, 1, 17(1): 378, 404; John Tyler Jr. to William L. Yancey, October 15, 1862.

44. John Tyler Jr. to William L. Yancey, October 15, 1862; Hartje, *Van Dorn*, 221.

45. James Gordon, "The Battle and Retreat from Corinth," *Publications of the Mississippi Historical Society* 4 (1901): 65; *OR*, 1, 17(1): 425.

46. *OR*, 1, 17(1): 378, 404, 407.

47. Ibid., 378, 385, 389, 393, 435.

48. Ibid., 378; Castel, *General Sterling Price*, 110.

49. Newton, *Wisconsin Boy in Dixie*, 38–39.

50. W. C. Holmes, "The Battle of Corinth," *Confederate Veteran* 27, 8 (August 1919): 291; R. S. Bevier, *History of the First and Second Missouri Confederate Brigades, 1861–1865* (St. Louis: Bryan, Brand, 1879), 148.

51. John Tyler Jr. to William L. Yancey, October 15, 1862; *OR*, 1, 17(1): 378; Hartje, *Van Dorn*, 221.

52. Castel, *General Sterling Price*, 110; John Tyler Jr. to William L. Yancey, October 15, 1862.

CHAPTER 10. "WE WERE OBLIGED TO FALL BACK GRADUALLY"

1. Albert Castel, *General Sterling Price and the Civil War in the West* (Baton Rouge: Louisiana State University Press, 1968), 110; *OR*, 1, 17(1): 386.

2. William S. Rosecrans, "Rosecrans's Campaigns," in *Report of the Joint Committee on the Conduct of the War, at the Second Session Thirty-eighth Congress* (Washington, DC: Government Printing Office, 1865), 21.

3. *OR*, 1, 17(1): 289–290, 337, 342, 347, 349, 354, 356; William W. Cluett, *History of the 57th Regiment Illinois Volunteer Infantry from Muster in, Dec. 26, 1861, to Muster out, July 7, 1865* (Princeton, IL: T. P. Streeter, 1886), 39; W. H. Tucker, *The Fourteenth Wisconsin Vet. Vol. Infantry (General A. J. Smith's Command) in the Expedition and Battle of Tupelo: Also, Wanderings through the Wilds of Missouri and Arkansas in Pursuit of*

Price (Indianapolis: n.p., 1892), 7; N. D. Starr and T. W. Holman, *The 21st Missouri Regiment Infantry Veteran Volunteers: Historical Memoranda* (Fort Madison, IA: Roberts and Roberts, 1899), 12. For a well-done study of artillery at Corinth, see Thomas E. Parson, "A Study of the Artillery at the Battles of Corinth, Davis Bridge and Young's Bridge, October 3–5, 1862," CWIC.

4. *OR*, 1, 17(1): 407–408; Frederick S. Prime to Thomas J. McKean, October 3, 1862, Thomas J. McKean Papers, MDAH; John Tyler Jr. to William L. Yancey, October 15, 1862, John Tyler Jr. Letter, UMC. There may have been more Federal earthworks to the south of the Memphis and Charleston Railroad. John Tyler, one of Price's staff officers, mentioned "earthworks recently constructed by the enemy to the south of the Memphis and Charleston Rail-Road." Other sources bear this out as well. See Cluett, *History of the 57th Regiment Illinois Volunteer Infantry*, 39.

5. T. D. Christie to sister, October 28, Christie Family Letters, Minnesota Historical Society.

6. *OR*, 1, 17(1): 289, 297.

7. Ibid., 407–408.

8. J. T. Peterson, "Historical Sketch of Co. E, 12th La. Regt. Vols.," undated, Evander McNair Graham Family Papers, Louisiana Tech University; L. B. Claiborne Memoirs, 16, *CWTI* Collection, USAMHI; James Mellor to his wife, October 15, 1862, Edward Cronon Papers, University of Wisconsin; *Corinth War Eagle*, August 7, 1862; H. J. Reid, "Twenty-second Mississippi," 14, J. F. H. Claiborne Papers, University of North Carolina. Other Federals referred to Villepigue as "Villepinge."

9. J. R. Zearing to wife, October 6, 1862, James Roberts Zearing Collection, Chicago Historical Society; *OR*, 1, 17(1): 252, 347, 356, 358, 397; Leslie Anders, *The Twenty-first Missouri: From Home Guard to Union Regiment* (Westport, CT: Greenwood Press, 1975), 99, 105.

10. *OR*, 1, 17(1): 252, 397; Marion Morrison, *A History of the Ninth Regiment Illinois Volunteer Infantry* (Monmouth, IL: John S. Clark, 1864), 40.

11. *OR*, 1, 17(1): 397–398; Charles C. Labuzan Diary, October 3, 1862, 42nd Alabama File, CWIC.

12. *OR*, 1, 17(1): 292–293, 342, 344; Henry V. Hoagland to his wife, September 24, 1863, Henry V. Hoagland Papers, NSHS; D. Leib Ambrose, *History of the Seventh Regiment Illinois Volunteer Infantry, from Its First Muster into the U.S. Service, April 25, 1861, to Its Final Muster out, July 9, 1865* (Springfield: Illinois Journal Company, 1868), 93–94.

13. *OR*, 1, 17(1): 407–408.

14. Ibid., 404, 407–408, 412.

15. Ibid., 410–412; Dunbar Rowland, *Mississippi*, 2 vols. (Spartanburg, SC: Reprint Company, 1976), 1:910–911.

16. *OR*, 1, 17(1): 412, 419; Tucker, *Fourteenth Wisconsin Vet. Vol. Infantry*, 8; W. C. Holmes, "The Battle of Corinth," *Confederate Veteran* 27, 8 (August 1919): 291; "Col. H. J. Reid," *Confederate Veteran* 14, 3 (March 1906): 132; Reid, "Twenty-second Mississippi," 14.

17. *OR*, 1, 17(1): 342, 344, 347; T. D. Christie to sister, October 28, 1862; Joseph M. Stetson to his parents, October 6, 1862, Joseph M. Stetson Letters, NMMA.

18. *OR*, 1, 17(1): 268, 342, 344, 347; R. S. Bevier, *History of the First and Second Missouri Confederate Brigades, 1861–1865* (St. Louis: Bryan, Brand, 1879), 149.

19. J. R. Zearing to wife, October 6, 1862; *OR*, 1, 17(1): 421; James K. Newton, *A Wisconsin Boy in Dixie: The Selected Letters of James K. Newton,* ed. Stephen E. Ambrose (Madison: University of Wisconsin Press, 1961), 40–41; Holmes, "Battle of Corinth," 291.

20. *OR*, 1, 17(1): 254, 291, 337, 342, 344, 347–348, 354–356; Ambrose, *History of the Seventh Regiment Illinois Volunteer Infantry,* 95; Charles F. Hubert, *History of the Fiftieth Regiment Illinois Volunteer Infantry in the War of the Union* (Kansas City, MO: Western Veteran Publishing Company, 1894), 131–132.

21. *OR*, 1, 17(1): 355, 359; Mildred Throne, ed., *The Civil War Diary of Cyrus F. Boyd: Fifteenth Iowa Infantry, 1861–1863* (Des Moines: State Historical Society of Iowa, 1953), 72; William W. Belknap, *History of the Fifteenth Regiment, Iowa Veteran Volunteer Infantry, from October, 1861, to August, 1865, When Disbanded at the End of the War* (Keokuk, IA: R. B. Ogden and Son, 1887), 209.

22. *OR*, 1, 17(1): 160, 211; S. C. Lyford to Thomas J. McKean, undated, Thomas J. McKean Papers, MDAH; William S. Rosecrans to Thomas J. McKean, October 3, 1862, ibid.

23. *OR*, 1, 17(1): 253, 398, 405, 421; Phillip Thomas Tucker, *The Forgotten Stonewall of the West: Major General John Stevens Bowen* (Macon, GA: Mercer University Press, 1997), 131; W. G. Whitfield, "Battle of Corinth, Miss.," undated, 35th Alabama File, CWIC.

24. *OR*, 1, 17(1): 398, 405.

25. Ambrose, *History of the Seventh Regiment Illinois Volunteer Infantry,* 96; *OR*, 1, 17(1): 254, 290, 344; Hubert, *History of the Fiftieth Regiment Illinois Volunteer Infantry,* 133; J. R. Zearing to wife, October 11, 1862; Verdine E. Carpenter to Charles Carpenter, October 13, 1862, Laura Ingalls Wilder Family Correspondence, Wisconsin Historical Society.

26. *OR*, 1, 17(1): 296, 344, 358; Charles C. Labuzan Diary, October 3, 1862; For more on the 42nd Alabama, see Samuel L. Askew III, "An Analysis of Unit Cohesion in the 42nd Alabama Infantry" (M.A. thesis, U.S. Army Command and General Staff College, 2003).

27. *OR*, 1, 17(1): 291, 293, 337, 342, 344–345, 347–349, 350–351, 354–356; Hubert, *History of the Fiftieth Regiment Illinois Volunteer Infantry,* 134–135; Ambrose, *History of the Seventh Regiment Illinois Volunteer Infantry,* 95.

28. Obituary of Colonel John D. Martin, undated, NMMA; *OR*, 1, 17(1): 252, 268; Robert G. Hartje, *Van Dorn: The Life and Times of a Confederate General* (Nashville: Vanderbilt University Press, 1967), 223; John Tyler Jr. to William L. Yancey, October 15, 1862.

29. *OR*, 1, 17(1): 252, 268.

30. *OR*, 1, 17(1): 272; William H. Chamberlain, *History of the Eighty-first Regiment Ohio Infantry Volunteers during the War of the Rebellion* (Cincinnati, OH: Gazette Steam

Printing House, 1865), 26; Union soldier to Adam, October 16, 1862, Adam Durkes Papers, UMC.

31. *OR*, 1, 17(1): 252, 268; Charles Wright, *A Corporal's Story: Experiences in the Ranks of Company C, 81st Ohio Vol. Infantry, during the War for the Maintenance of the Union, 1861–1864* (Philadelphia: James Beale, 1887), 56, 58.

32. *OR*, 1, 17(1): 272, 386; Chamberlain, *History of the Eighty-first Regiment Ohio Infantry Volunteers*, 26; Wright, *A Corporal's Story*, 57; unknown Union soldier to "Friend Adam," October 16, 1862, Adam Durkes Papers, UMC.

33. *OR*, 1, 17(1): 252–253; Wright, *A Corporal's Story*, 57.

34. *OR*, 1, 17(1): 253; Bevier, *History of the First and Second Missouri Confederate Brigades*, 148; John Tyler Jr. to William L. Yancey, October 15, 1862.

35. *OR*, 1, 17(1): 272, 283–284; obituary of Colonel John D. Martin; G. A. Foote to his father, October 26, 1862, Foote Family Papers, Filson Historical Society; John Tyler Jr. to William L. Yancey, October 15, 1862; Morrison, *History of the Ninth Regiment Illinois Volunteer Infantry*, 39; William Travis Sketchbooks, William D. T. Travis Papers, ISHL.

36. *OR*, 1, 17(1): 168, 253, 272.

37. Union soldier to Adam, October 16, 1862; C. J. Sergent Diary, October 3, 1862, NMMA.

38. C. J. Sergent Diary, October 3, 1862; James M. Thurston Diary, October 3, 1862, Massachusetts Historical Society; Phillip Thomas Tucker, *Westerners in Gray: The Men and Missions of the Elite Fifth Missouri Infantry Regiment* (Jefferson, NC: McFarland, 1995), 68; Ephraim McD. Anderson, *Memoirs: Historical and Personal; Including the Campaigns of the First Missouri Confederate Brigade* (St. Louis: Times Printing Company, 1868), 232; Homer L. Calkin, "Elkhorn to Vicksburg," *Civil War History* 2, 1 (March 1956): 34; Castel, *General Sterling Price*, 111.

39. John Tyler Jr. to William L. Yancey, October 15, 1862; Tucker, *Westerners in Gray*, 68; Castel, *General Sterling Price*, 111.

40. William McCuray to Mrs. Dantzler, October 11, 1862, Absolem F. Dantzler Papers, Duke University; *OR*, 1, 17(1): 386; Bruce S. Allardice, *More Generals in Gray* (Baton Rouge: Louisiana State University Press, 1995), 152; Dabney H. Maury, "Recollections of Campaign against Grant in North Mississippi in 1862–63," *Southern Historical Society Papers* 13 (1885): 294; obituary of Colonel John D. Martin; John Tyler Jr. to William L. Yancey, October 15, 1862; Union soldier to Adam, October 16, 1862.

41. *OR*, 1, 17(1): 168, 253, 272; Charles Cowell, "An Infantryman at Corinth," *Civil War Times Illustrated* 13, 7 (November 1974): 11.

42. L. H. Graves Diary, October 3, 1862, University of Tennessee; *OR*, 1, 17(1): 386; Peter Cozzens, *The Darkest Days of the War: The Battles of Iuka and Corinth* (Chapel Hill: University of North Carolina Press, 1997), 203.

43. Will H. Judkins Diary, October 3, 1862, Indiana State Library.

44. *OR*, 1, 17(1): 253–254, 390; Anderson, *Memoirs*, 232; Stephen Werly Diary, October 3, 1862, UMC.

45. *OR*, 1, 17(1): 253–254, 390.

46. Ibid., 254–255.

CHAPTER 11. "VICTORIOUS SO FAR"

1. H. G. Kennett to Thomas J. McKean, October 3, 1862, Thomas J. McKean Papers, MDAH; *OR*, 1, 17(1): 290, 337–338, 342, 344–345, 359.

2. J. R. Zearing to wife, October 6, 1862, James Roberts Zearing Collection, Chicago Historical Society; *OR*, 1, 17(1): 290, 337–338, 342, 344–345, 359; August Schilling Diary, October 3, 1862, BCHS; D. Leib Ambrose, *History of the Seventh Regiment Illinois Volunteer Infantry, from Its First Muster into the U.S. Service, April 25, 1861, to Its Final Muster out, July 9, 1865* (Springfield: Illinois Journal Company, 1868), 96; Peter Cozzens, *The Darkest Days of the War: The Battles of Iuka and Corinth* (Chapel Hill: University of North Carolina Press, 1997), 186.

3. T. D. Christie to sister, October 28, Christie Family Letters, Minnesota Historical Society.

4. *OR*, 1, 17(1): 290, 342, 344–345, 359; Frederick C. Prime to Thomas J. McKean, October 3, 1862, Thomas J. McKean Papers, MDAH; C. Goddard to Thomas J. McKean, October 3, 1862, ibid.

5. August Schilling Diary, October 3, 1862; *OR*, 1, 17(1): 290, 342, 344–345, 359; H. C. Adams Journal, October 3, 1862, Henry Clay Adams Papers, University of Iowa; Mildred Throne, ed., *The Civil War Diary of Cyrus F. Boyd: Fifteenth Iowa Infantry, 1861–1863* (Des Moines: State Historical Society of Iowa, 1953), 72; Van Reeves to family, October 1862, 11th Iowa File, CWIC.

6. *OR*, 1, 17(1): 405.

7. Ibid., 398, 405.

8. Ibid., 359, 364, 366, 398, 412, 426; Henry Clay Adams Civil War Journals, October 3, 1862, 30, University of Iowa; William W. Belknap, *History of the Fifteenth Regiment, Iowa Veteran Volunteer Infantry, from October, 1861, to August, 1865, When Disbanded at the End of the War* (Keokuk, IA: R. B. Ogden and Son, 1887), 211, 229; A. H. Brown Diary, NMMA; Throne, *Civil War Diary of Cyrus F. Boyd*, 72; Charles Cady to his family, October 16, 1862, Charles Cady Papers, University of Iowa.

9. *OR*, 1, 17(1): 359, 364, 366, 398, 412, 426; Charles Cady to his family, October 16, 1862; A. H. Brown Diary; Throne, *Civil War Diary of Cyrus F. Boyd*, 72; Henry Clay Adams Civil War Journals, October 3, 1862, 30; Belknap, *History of the Fifteenth Regiment, Iowa Veteran Volunteer Infantry*, 211, 229.

10. *OR*, 1, 17(1): 398, 405; Throne, *Civil War Diary of Cyrus F. Boyd*, 73.

11. H. C. Adams Journal, October 3, 1862; *OR*, 1, 17(1): 338, 359; Throne, *Civil War Diary of Cyrus F. Boyd*, 72–73.

12. Joseph M. Bailey Memoirs, "The Story of a Confederate Soldier," 17, Joseph M. Bailey Papers, University of Arkansas; Charles Cowell, "An Infantryman at Corinth," *Civil War Times Illustrated* 13, 7 (November 1974): 11; *OR*, 1, 17(1): 386, 390; John Tyler Jr. to William L. Yancey, October 15, 1862, John Tyler Jr. Letter, UMC.

13. *OR*, 1, 17(1): 168, 205; William S. Rosecrans, "The Battle of Corinth," in *Battles and Leaders of the Civil War*, 4 vols. (New York: Century Company, 1884–1887), 2:746.

14. Joseph Risedorph, "Battle of Corinth," 3, Joseph Risedorph Papers, Minnesota His-

torical Society; Alonzo L. Brown, *History of the Fourth Regiment Minnesota Infantry Volunteers during the Great Rebellion 1861–1865* (St. Paul: Pioneer Press Company, 1892), 129; Charles F. Hubert, *History of the Fiftieth Regiment Illinois Volunteer Infantry in the War of the Union* (Kansas City, MO: Western Veteran Publishing Company, 1894), 136; *OR*, 1, 17(1): 168, 205, 216, 221–222, 227.

15. Charles S. Hamilton, "Hamilton's Division at Corinth," in *Battles and Leaders of the Civil War*, 4 vols. (New York: Century Company, 1884–1887), 2:757–758; *OR*, 1, 52(1): 286; Jack D. Welsh, *Medical Histories of Union Generals* (Kent, OH: Kent State University Press, 1996), 147; William M. Lamers, *The Edge of Glory: A Biography of General William S. Rosecrans, U.S.A.* (New York: Harcourt, Brace, and World, 1961), 141; *Memoir of Gen. A. C. Ducat* (Chicago: Rand, McNally, 1897), 32–33.

16. *OR*, 1, 17(1): 168, 255, 337; Robert G. Hartje, *Van Dorn: The Life and Times of a Confederate General* (Nashville: Vanderbilt University Press, 1967), 226.

17. *OR*, 1, 17(1): 168, 255, 337; William H. Chamberlain, *History of the Eighty-first Regiment Ohio Infantry Volunteers during the War of the Rebellion* (Cincinnati, OH: Gazette Steam Printing House, 1865), 27; Charles Wright, *A Corporal's Story: Experiences in the Ranks of Company C, 81st Ohio Vol. Infantry, during the War for the Maintenance of the Union, 1861–1864* (Philadelphia: James Beale, 1887), 59; Mark A. Plummer, *Lincoln's Rail-Splitter: Governor Richard J. Oglesby* (Urbana: University of Illinois Press, 2001), 76.

18. *OR*, 1, 17(1): 255, 268, 276, 386, 390; Thomas Hogan to his father, October 12, 1862, Thomas Hogan Letters, Civil War Collection, Missouri Historical Society; Ephraim McD. Anderson, *Memoirs: Historical and Personal; Including the Campaigns of the First Missouri Confederate Brigade* (St. Louis: Times Printing Company, 1868), 233; R. S. Bevier, *History of the First and Second Missouri Confederate Brigades, 1861–1865* (St. Louis: Bryan, Brand, 1879), 149.

19. *OR*, 1, 17(1): 255, 268, 272, 276, 386; Wright, *A Corporal's Story*, 60; Cozzens, *Darkest Days*, 204; Franklin B. Reed to brother, October 20, 1862, Franklin B. Reed Papers, SHSI; Bevier, *History of the First and Second Missouri Confederate Brigades*, 150; Chamberlain, *History of the Eighty-first Regiment Ohio Infantry Volunteers*, 27; Union soldier to Adam, October 16, 1862, Adam Durkes Papers, UMC.

20. *OR*, 1, 17(1): 255, 268, 276, 386; Cozzens, *Darkest Days*, 204.

21. *OR*, 1, 17(1): 255–256, 267.

22. Ibid., 255, 272; Henry S. Doty to his brother, August 25, 1862, 52nd Illinois Papers, NMMA; John S. Wilcox to his wife, October 9, 1862, John S. Wilcox Papers, ISHL. For more on the 52nd Illinois, see John Swaddling, *Historical Memoranda of the 52nd Regiment Illinois Infantry Volunteers from Its Organization, Nov. 19th, 1861, to Its Muster out, by Reason of Expiration of Service, on the 6th Day of July, 1865* (Elgin, IL: Gilbert and Post, 1868) (copy in 52nd Illinois File, CWIC).

23. Franklin B. Reed to brother, October 20, 1862; David B. Henderson to George, November 17, 1862, David B. Henderson Papers, DCHS; E. B. Soper, "A Chapter from the History of Company D, Twelfth Iowa Infantry Volunteers," in *War Sketches and Incidents as Related by the Companions of the Iowa Commandery Military Order of the Loyal*

Legion of the United States (Des Moines, IA: n.p., 1898), 2:137; *OR*, 1, 17(1): 251, 255–256, 272; Cozzens, *Darkest Days*, 154.

24. Franklin B. Reed to brother, October 20, 1862; David B. Henderson to George, August 26, 1862; *OR*, 1, 17(1): 255–256, 272, 394, 401; Newton A. Keen, *Living and Fighting with the Texas 6th Cavalry* (Gaithersburg, MD: Butterneutt Press, 1986), 39; Union soldier to Adam, October 16, 1862.

25. Wright, *A Corporal's Story*, 60.

26. Franklin B. Reed to brother, October 20, 1862; David B. Henderson to George, August 26, 1862; Soper, "Chapter from the History of Company D, Twelfth Iowa Infantry Volunteers," 137; David W. Reed, *Campaigns and Battles of the Twelfth Regiment Iowa Veteran Volunteer Infantry from Organization, September, 1861, to Muster out, January 20, 1866* (n.p.: n.p., n.d.), 89.

27. J. C. Parrott to wife, October 6 and 20, 1862, James C. Parrott Papers, SHSI; *OR*, 1, 17(1): 255–256, 272, 284, 394, 401; Union soldier to Adam, October 16, 1862.

28. *OR*, 1, 17(1): 255–256, 272, 284, 394, 401.

29. Ibid., 255–256, 272, 284, 394, 401; J. C. Parrott to wife, October 6, 1862; Union soldier to Adam, October 16, 1862; Audley S. H. Boyd to Thomas E. Wilson, December 27, 1862, 3rd Missouri Cavalry File, CWIC.

30. Anderson, *Memoirs*, 232; William Kavanaugh Memoirs, undated, 44, William H. Kavanaugh Papers, UMC; William A. Ruyle Memoir, 9, *CWTI* Collection, USAMHI.

31. William Kavanaugh Memoirs, 45.

32. *OR*, 1, 17(1): 179, 183, 197, 199, 256; *OR*, 1, 17(2): 256–257; Cloyd Bryner, *Bugle Echoes: The Story of the Illinois 47th* (Springfield, IL: Phillips Bros. Printers, 1905), 58; Sharon L. D. Kraynek, ed., *Letters to My Wife: A Civil War Diary from the Western Front* (Apollo, PA: Closson Press, 1995), 37; Charles Stevens, "The Corinth Diary of Private Charles Stevens," *Blue and Gray Education Society Papers* 18 (Fall 2006): 15.

33. Stevens, "Corinth Diary of Private Charles Stevens," 15; *OR*, 1, 17(1): 197, 201, 203; Kraynek, *Letters to My Wife*, 37.

34. John Melvin Williams, *"The Eagle Regiment," 8th Wis. Inf'ty Vols.: A Sketch of Its Marches, Battles and Campaigns from 1861–1865 with Complete Regimental and Company Roster, and a Few Portraits and Sketches of Its Officers and Commanders* (Belleville, WI: Recorder Print, 1890), 51–52; Bryner, *Bugle Echoes*, 59–60; Kraynek, *Letters to My Wife*, 37; J. O. Barrett, *The Soldier Bird: "Old Abe": The Live War-Eagle of Wisconsin that Served a Three Year's Campaign in the Great Rebellion* (Madison, WI: Atwood and Culver, 1876), 42.

35. Edward Cronon, "Personal Recollections of the Civil War," undated, 3–4, Edward Cronon Papers, University of Wisconsin; *OR*, 1, 17(1): 179, 181.

36. Plummer, *Lincoln's Rail-Splitter*, 77; Welsh, *Medical Histories of Union Generals*, 145; *OR*, 1, 17(1): 256, 271, 272–273, 282, 388, 390; Wright, *A Corporal's Story*, 60; A. C. Riley, "Confederate Col. A. C. Riley, His Reports and Letters," ed. Riley Bock, *Missouri Historical Review* 85, 3 (April 1991): 266; *OR*, 1, 17(2): 270; Chamberlain, *History of the Eighty-first Regiment Ohio Infantry Volunteers*, 27–28; Horace Wardner, "Reminiscences of a Surgeon," in *Military Essays and Recollections: Papers Read before the*

Commandery of the State of Illinois, Military Order of the Loyal Legion of the United States, 3 vols. (Chicago: Dial Press, 1899), 3:189; Cowell, "An Infantryman at Corinth," 11; Augustus L. Chetlain, *Recollections of Seventy Years* (Galena, IL: Gazette Publishing Company, 1899), 95; T. W. Sweeny Report, October 15, 1862, George Sawin Letters, Chicago Historical Society.

37. Myron Underwood to wife, October 19, 1862, Myron Underwood Papers, University of Iowa.

38. *OR*, 1, 17(1): 256–257, 273, 390.

39. Ibid., 256–257, 273, 390; Phillip Thomas Tucker, *The South's Finest: The First Missouri Brigade from Pea Ridge to Vicksburg* (Shippensburg, PA: White Mane, 1993), 68.

40. Franklin B. Reed to brother, October 20, 1862; Cronon, "Personal Recollections of the Civil War," 4; Stevens, "Corinth Diary of Private Charles Stevens," 16–17; *OR*, 1, 17(1): 197, 204, 247, 255–257, 273, 280, 390; Soper, "Chapter from the History of Company D, Twelfth Iowa Infantry Volunteers," 137; Cozzens, *Darkest Days*, 212; Hugh T. Carlisle Reminiscences, 82, Civil War Miscellaneous Collection, USAMHI; "A Condensed History of the 47th Regiment of Illinois Vol. Infantry," 8, John N. Cromwell Papers, ISHL.

41. Wright, *A Corporal's Story*, 62; Cronon, "Personal Recollections of the Civil War," 4; *OR*, 1, 17(1): 204, 247, 255–257, 273, 280, 390; David S. Stanley, "The Battle of Corinth," in *Personal Recollections of the War of the Rebellion: Addresses Delivered before the Commandery of the State of New York, Military Order of the Loyal Legion of the United States*, 2nd series (New York: G. P. Putnam's Sons, 1897), 273; Soper, "Chapter from the History of Company D, Twelfth Iowa Infantry Volunteers," 137; Franklin B. Reed to brother, October 20, 1862; Cozzens, *Darkest Days*, 212; Stevens, "Corinth Diary of Private Charles Stevens," 16–17.

42. *OR*, 1, 17(1): 197, 204, 247, 255–257, 273, 280, 390; Stanley, "Battle of Corinth," 273; Wright, *A Corporal's Story*, 62; Cozzens, *Darkest Days*, 212.

43. *OR*, 1, 17(1): 197, 257, 387; Dabney H. Maury, "Recollections of Campaign against Grant in North Mississippi in 1862–63," *Southern Historical Society Papers* 13 (1885): 295; William Kavanaugh Memoirs, 45.

44. *OR*, 1, 17(1): 401.

45. Ibid., 205, 234–235.

46. Risedorph, "Battle of Corinth," 3–4; Brown, *History of the Fourth Regiment Minnesota Infantry Volunteers*, 112; *OR*, 1, 17(1): 209, 218; Hamilton, "Hamilton's Division at Corinth," 758; Abraham Slough to wife, October 12, 1862, 59th Indiana File, CWIC.

47. *OR*, 1, 17(1): 205–206, 227, 230, 401; Rosecrans, "Battle of Corinth," 747.

48. Rosecrans, "Battle of Corinth," 747; *OR*, 1, 17(1): 205–206, 227, 230, 401.

49. *OR*, 1, 17(1): 338, 343, 355, 359, 405; Anders, *The Twenty-first Missouri*, 101; H. C. Adams Journal, October 3, 1862; *OR*, 1, 17(1): 338, 359; Throne, *Civil War Diary of Cyrus F. Boyd*, 72–73.

50. *OR*, 1, 17(1): 179, 183, 422, 426, 428.

51. Ibid., 338, 355, 359, 405, 427, 433; Leslie Anders, *The Twenty-first Missouri: From Home Guard to Union Regiment* (Westport, CT: Greenwood Press, 1975), 101.

52. *OR*, 1, 17(1): 379, 387; Alice Hirsch, "Company G, 22nd Mississippi Infantry," 19–20, Isaac E. Hirsh Papers, MSU; Rosecrans, "Battle of Corinth," 748; Albert Castel, *General Sterling Price and the Civil War in the West* (Baton Rouge: Louisiana State University Press, 1968), 112–113; John Tyler Jr. to William L. Yancey, October 15, 1862.

53. James M. Thurston Diary, October 3, 1862, Massachusetts Historical Society; "The Battle of Corinth," E. B. Quiner Papers, SHSW; Castel, *General Sterling Price*, 112–113.

54. *OR*, 1, 17(1): 379, 387.

Chapter 12. "Things Look Rather Blue To-night"

1. William Kavanaugh Memoirs, undated, 34, William H. Kavanaugh Papers, UMC; *OR*, 1, 17(1): 293.

2. L. H. Graves Diary, October 4, 1862, University of Texas at Austin; William Kavanaugh Memoirs, 46–47.

3. N. R. Dunn to father, October 14, 1862, N. R. Dunn Letters, University of Michigan; Ephraim McD. Anderson, *Memoirs: Historical and Personal; Including the Campaigns of the First Missouri Confederate Brigade* (St. Louis: Times Printing Company, 1868), 234.

4. James M. Thurston Diary, October 3, 1862, Massachusetts Historical Society; Charles Cowell, "An Infantryman at Corinth," *Civil War Times Illustrated* 13, 7 (November 1974): 11–12; George Hovey Cadman to his wife, October 13, 1862, George Hovey Cadman Papers, University of North Carolina; *OR*, 1, 17(1): 227; Charles H. Smith, *The History of Fuller's Ohio Brigade, 1861–1865: Its Great March, with Roster Portraits, Battle Maps and Biographies* (Cleveland, OH: Press of A. J. Watt, 1909), 82; Alonzo L. Brown, *History of the Fourth Regiment of Minnesota Infantry Volunteers during the Great Rebellion 1861–1865* (St. Paul: Pioneer Press Company, 1892), 130; William Kavanaugh Memoirs, 47; Myron Underwood to wife, October 19, 1862, Myron Underwood Papers, University of Iowa; George Sawin to wife, October 12, 1862, George Sawin Letters, Chicago Historical Society.

5. J. W. Harmon Memoirs, 19, TSLA.

6. *OR*, 1, 17(1): 177.

7. Edward Cronon, "Personal Recollections of the Civil War," undated, 4, Edward Cronon Papers, University of Wisconsin; Joseph Risedorph, "Battle of Corinth," 4, Joseph Risedorph Papers, Minnesota Historical Society.

8. Daniel Miller to brother, October 9, 1862, Herman B. Miller Papers, Missouri Historical Society; *OR*, 1, 17(1): 179, 183, 249, 290, 345; J. W. Harmon Memoirs.

9. Mansfield Lovell to G. W., October 26, 1862, Mansfield Lovell Papers, Huntington Library; *OR*, 1, 17(1): 379, 433, 435, 457; Phillip Thomas Tucker, *Westerners in Gray: The Men and Missions of the Elite Fifth Missouri Infantry Regiment* (Jefferson, NC: McFarland, 1995), 72; Emily Van Dorn Miller, *A Soldier's Honor, with Reminiscences of Major General Earl Van Dorn, by His Comrades* (New York: Abbey Press Publishers, 1903), 152; Albert Castel, *General Sterling Price and the Civil War in the West* (Baton

Rouge: Louisiana State University Press, 1968), 114; John Tyler Jr. to William L. Yancey, October 15, 1862, John Tyler Jr. Letter, UMC.

10. Verdine E. Carpenter to Charles Carpenter, October 13, 1862, Laura Ingalls Wilder Family Correspondence, Wisconsin Historical Society; *OR*, 1, 17(1): 435; Castel, *General Sterling Price*, 114; John Tyler Jr. to William L. Yancey, October 15, 1862.

11. Timothy B. Smith, *The Untold Story of Shiloh: The Battle and the Battlefield* (Knoxville: University of Tennessee Press, 2006), 6–7, 31–32; William S. Rosecrans, "The Battle of Corinth," in *Battles and Leaders of the Civil War*, 4 vols. (New York: Century Company, 1884–1887), 2:748.

12. John Tyler Jr. to William L. Yancey, October 15, 1862; George L. Griscom Diary, October 4, 1862, University of Texas at Austin; *OR*, 1, 17(1): 379, 396, 422, 431; Brown, *History of the Fourth Regiment Minnesota Infantry Volunteers*, 121; Anderson, *Memoirs*, 235.

13. *OR*, 1, 17(1): 379.

14. Ibid.

15. Ibid., 390, 401; William Kavanaugh Memoirs, 46, 49.

16. *OR*, 1, 17(1): 398; Charles C. Labuzan Diary, October 3, 1862, 42nd Alabama File, CWIC.

17. *OR*, 1, 17(1): 405, 422.

18. Ibid., 180, 184, 394; Frank Moore, ed., *The Rebellion Record: A Diary of American Events, with Documents, Narratives, Illustrative Incidents, Poetry, etc.*, 11 vols. (New York: D. Vann Nostrand, 1861–1868), 5:501; William M. Lamers, *The Edge of Glory: A Biography of General William S. Rosecrans, U.S.A.* (New York: Harcourt, Brace, and World, 1961), 154.

19. *OR*, 1, 17(1): 169, 257.

20. Daniel Miller to brother, October 9, 1862; *OR*, 1, 17(1): 338, 343, 345, 355, 359–360.

21. Rosecrans, "Battle of Corinth," 748; *OR*, 1, 17(1): 168–169, 179, 198, 200, 258, 291, 446; Smith, *History of Fuller's Ohio Brigade*, 82–83.

22. N. R. Dunn to his father, October 8, 1862; Moore, *The Rebellion Record*, 5:501.

23. Horace Wardner, "Reminiscences of a Surgeon," in *Military Essays and Recollections: Papers Read before the Commandery of the State of Illinois, Military Order of the Loyal Legion of the United States*, 3 vols. (Chicago: Dial Press, 1899), 3:189; *OR*, 1, 17(1): 179, 183, 257, 290.

24. F. T. Gilmore to David Stanley, January 13, 1897, West-Stanley-Wright Family Papers, USAMHI; C. J. Sergent Diary, October 2, 1862, NMMA; Risedorph, "Battle of Corinth," 4; Daniel Miller to brother, October 9, 1862; Moore, *The Rebellion Record*, 5:501; *OR*, 1, 17(1): 168–169, 269, 289; Rosecrans, "Battle of Corinth," 748; Cowell, "An Infantryman at Corinth," 12; Monroe F. Cockrell, ed., *The Lost Account of the Battle of Corinth and Court-Martial of Gen. Van Dorn* (Jackson, TN: McCowat-Mercer Press, 1955), 66; Lamers, *Edge of Glory*, 142; John Lomax to his son, December 12, 1862, John Lomax Papers, UMC; John S. Wilcox to his wife, October 9, 1862, John S. Wilcox Papers, ISHL; James M. Thurston Diary, October 4, 1862. For evidence of Battery Richardson, see Moore, *The Rebellion Record*, 5:501; Comte de Paris, *History of the Civil War in*

America, 2 vols. (Philadelphia: Porter and Coates, 1876), 2:412; Charles F. Hubert, *History of the Fiftieth Regiment Illinois Volunteer Infantry in the War of the Union* (Kansas City, MO: Western Veteran Publishing Company, 1894), 139; Henry Coppee, *Life and Services of Gen. U. S. Grant* (New York: Richardson and Company, 1868), 128–129; Benson Lossing, *Pictorial History of the Civil War in the United States of America*, 2 vols. (Hartford, CT: T. Belknap, 1868), 2:519; William H. Chamberlain, *History of the Eighty-first Regiment Ohio Infantry Volunteers during the War of the Rebellion* (Cincinnati, OH: Gazette Steam Printing House, 1865), 28–29.

25. *OR*, 1, 17(1): 257–259, 291; Hubert, *History of the Fiftieth Regiment Illinois Volunteer Infantry,* 139; W. B. McCord, "Battle of Corinth," in *Glimpses of the Nation's Struggle. Fourth Series. Papers Read before the Minnesota Commandery of the Military Order of the Loyal Legion of the United States, 1892–1897* (St. Paul: H. L. Collins, 1898), 577; C. J. Sergent Diary, October 2, 1862; Risedorph, "Battle of Corinth," 4; Jared C. Lobdell, ed., "The Civil War Journal and Letters of Colonel John Van Deusen Du Bois, April 12, 1861–October 16, 1862," *Missouri Historical Review* 61, 1 (October 1966): 48.

26. Charles S. Hamilton, "Hamilton's Division at Corinth," in *Battles and Leaders of the Civil War*, 4 vols. (New York: Century Company, 1884–1887), 2:758; Brown, *History of the Fourth Regiment Minnesota Infantry Volunteers*, 128.

27. *OR*, 1, 17(1): 161, 168, 206; Hamilton, "Hamilton's Division at Corinth," 758; Brown, *History of the Fourth Regiment Minnesota Infantry Volunteers*, 128; C. Goddard to Thomas J. McKean, October 3, 1862, Thomas J. McKean Papers, MDAH.

28. *OR*, 1, 17(1): 161, 168, 206; Hamilton, "Hamilton's Division at Corinth," 758.

29. Alphonso Barto to his family, October 17, 1862, Alphonso Barto Papers, ISHL; *OR*, 1, 17(1): 184.

30. *OR*, 1, 17(1): 161, 169, 227; Moore, *The Rebellion Record*, 5:501.

31. George Hovey Cadman to wife, October 13, 1862; August Schilling Diary, October 3, 1862, BCHS; *OR*, 1, 17(1): 169, 274; "What I Saw at the Battle of Corinth," E. B. Quiner Papers, SHSW; Leslie Anders, *The Twenty-first Missouri: From Home Guard to Union Regiment* (Westport, CT: Greenwood Press, 1975), 102–103; Wardner, "Reminiscences of a Surgeon," 189; David McKnight Diary, October 4, 1862, Civil War Collection, Missouri Historical Society; Moore, *The Rebellion Record*, 5:502; Cowell, "An Infantryman at Corinth," 12; A. B. Monahan to wife, October 9 and 11, 1862, 63rd Ohio File, SNMP; Chamberlain, *History of the Eighty-first Regiment Ohio Infantry Volunteers,* 30; Mary Swords to "Dear friends," October 21, 1862, Elizabeth (McClain) Sword Papers, 1822–1885, Duke University; J. Q. A. Campbell Diary, October 3, 1862, WRHS; H. C. Adams Journal, October 4, 1862, Henry Clay Adams Papers, University of Iowa; James M. Thurston Diary, October 4, 1862; Daniel Miller to brother, October 9, 1862; Marion Morrison, *A History of the Ninth Regiment Illinois Volunteer Infantry* (Monmouth, IL: John S. Clark, 1864), 40–41.

32. Morrison, *History of the Ninth Regiment Illinois Volunteer Infantry*, 40–41; William Kavanaugh Memoirs, 49; Will Snyder to parents, November 25, 1862, NMMA; H. J. Reid, "Twenty-second Mississippi," 14–15, J. F. H. Claiborne Papers, University of North Carolina; *OR*, 1, 17(1): 405, 408.

33. William Kavanaugh Memoirs, 49; Reid, "Twenty-second Mississippi," 14–15; *OR*, 1, 17(1): 405, 408; Will Snyder to parents, November 25, 1862.

34. Will Snyder to parents, November 25, 1862; *OR*, 1, 17(1): 405, 408.

35. Albert Theodore Goodloe, *Some Rebel Relics: From the Seat of War* (Nashville: Publishing House of the Methodist Episcopal Church, South, 1893), 44–45; Anderson, *Memoirs*, 236.

36. *OR*, 1, 17(1): 394, 398, 401; Joseph Mitchell Strickling Diary, October 4, 1862, 39th Ohio File, CWIC.

37. *OR*, 1, 17(1): 217, 247, 408, 411–412.

38. William Kavanaugh Memoirs, 49; *OR*, 1, 17(1): 390; Tucker, *Westerners in Gray*, 7; *OR*, 1, 17(1): 379; R. S. Bevier, *History of the First and Second Missouri Confederate Brigades, 1861–1865* (St. Louis: Bryan, Brand, 1879), 150.

39. *OR*, 1, 17(1): 387, 390, 401.

40. Ibid., 379, 387.

41. R. Walpole to friends, November 4, 1862, Bomar Family Papers, Emory University; Charles Cady to his family, October 16, 1862, Charles Cady Papers, University of Iowa; M. D. Hardiman to Van Dorn, May 1, 1862, Telegrams Received—Van Dorn's Command, Army of the West, NARA; Albert Castel, "Victory at Corinth," *Civil War Times Illustrated* 17, 6 (October 1978): 22; Bell I. Wiley, *The Life of Johnny Reb: The Common Soldier of the Confederacy* (Indianapolis: Bobbs-Merrill, 1943), 251; Robert G. Hartje, *Van Dorn: The Life and Times of a Confederate General* (Nashville: Vanderbilt University Press, 1967), 229; John Johnston Reminiscences, Confederate Collection, TSLA; Louis Hébert, "An Autobiography of Louis Hébert," University of North Carolina. It is possible that Hébert had something to hide. In an autobiographical sketch written years later, he completely left out the events surrounding the Battle of Corinth. After going into some detail about Iuka, he skipped directly to his Vicksburg exploits. The words "after some days" were his only reference to Corinth.

42. Anderson, *Memoirs*, 234.

43. *OR*, 1, 17(1): 379, 387; Anderson, *Memoirs*, 234; Lamers, *Edge of Glory*, 145; Mansfield Lovell to G. W., October 26, 1862.

44. *OR*, 1, 17(1): 416–417, 431–432, 457.

45. Ibid., 390–391.

46. Ibid., 190, 401–402; Smith, *History of Fuller's Ohio Brigade*, 84–85.

47. *OR*, 1, 17(1): 169; Rosecrans, "Battle of Corinth," 748–749; Smith, *History of Fuller's Ohio Brigade*, 84; Charles Wright, *A Corporal's Story: Experiences in the Ranks of Company C, 81st Ohio Vol. Infantry, during the War for the Maintenance of the Union, 1861–1864* (Philadelphia: James Beale, 1887), 63; George Hovey Cadman to his wife, October 13, 1862.

48. J. Q. A. Campbell Diary, October 3, 1862; *OR*, 1, 17(1): 161, 184–185, 259; Rosecrans, "Battle of Corinth," 752.

49. *OR*, 1, 17(1): 161, 169, 184–185, 259; Hubert, *History of the Fiftieth Regiment Illinois Volunteer Infantry*, 140; J. Q. A. Campbell Diary, October 3, 1862.

50. *OR*, 1, 17(1): 180, 198; Rosecrans, "Battle of Corinth," 752.

CHAPTER 13. "A DREADFUL CHARGE UP HILL"

1. *OR*, 1, 17(1): 273, 276, 384; William S. Rosecrans, "The Battle of Corinth," in *Battles and Leaders of the Civil War*, 4 vols. (New York: Century Company, 1884–1887), 2:749; Frank A. Montgomery, *Reminiscences of a Mississippian in Peace and War* (Cincinnati, OH: Robert Clarke, 1901), 92; Frank Moore, ed., *The Rebellion Record: A Diary of American Events, with Documents, Narratives, Illustrative Incidents, Poetry, etc.*, 11 vols. (New York: D. Vann Nostrand, 1861–1868), 5:502; "Reminiscences by a Confederate Soldier of the Battles of Iuka and Corinth," NMMA.

2. *OR*, 1, 17(1): 384, 398.

3. Ibid., 387, 391; John Tyler Jr. to William L. Yancey, October 15, 1862, John Tyler Jr. Letter, UMC.

4. *OR*, 1, 17(1): 274, 391; Ephraim McD. Anderson, *Memoirs: Historical and Personal; Including the Campaigns of the First Missouri Confederate Brigade* (St. Louis: Times Printing Company, 1868), 236–237; J. Q. A. Campbell Diary, October 3, 1862, WRHS.

5. N. R. Dunn to father, October 14, 1862, N. R. Dunn Letters, University of Michigan; *OR*, 1, 17(1): 274, 391.

6. *OR*, 1, 17(1): 391.

7. Ibid., 207, 217; Abraham Slough to wife, October 12, 1862, 59th Indiana File, CWIC.

8. W. H. Tunnard, *A Southern Record: The History of the 3rd Regiment Louisiana Infantry*, ed. Edwin C. Bearss (Dayton, OH: Morningside, 1970), 192.

9. Joseph Risedorph, "Battle of Corinth," 5–6, Joseph Risedorph Papers, Minnesota Historical Society; Tunnard, *Southern Record*, 192.

10. William Kavanaugh Memoirs, undated, 50, William H. Kavanaugh Papers, UMC; Joseph M. Bailey Memoirs, "The Story of a Confederate Soldier," 17, Joseph M. Bailey Papers, University of Arkansas; *OR*, 1, 17(1): 391; Homer L. Calkin, "Elkhorn to Vicksburg," *Civil War History* 2, 1 (March 1956): 35; Thomas Hogan to father, October 12, 1862, Thomas Hogan Letters, Missouri Historical Society.

11. *OR*, 1, 17(1): 235, 240; Anderson, *Memoirs*, 236.

12. *OR*, 1, 17(1): 207, 219, 239–240; Abraham Slough to wife, October 12, 1862.

13. W. McCurdy to Mrs. A. F. Dantzler, October 11, 1862, Absolem F. Danztler Papers, Duke University; *OR*, 1, 17(1): 218; Allardice, *Confederate Colonels*, 268.

14. William Kavanaugh Memoirs, 51; *OR*, 1, 17(1): 259–260, 274, 391; Leslie Anders, *The Twenty-first Missouri: From Home Guard to Union Regiment* (Westport, CT: Greenwood Press, 1975), 103; Phillip Thomas Tucker, *Westerners in Gray: The Men and Missions of the Elite Fifth Missouri Infantry Regiment* (Jefferson, NC: McFarland, 1995), 80; Phillip Thomas Tucker, *The South's Finest: The First Missouri Brigade from Pea Ridge to Vicksburg* (Shippensburg, PA: White Mane, 1993), 73–75; Jack D. Welsh, *Medical Histories of Confederate Generals* (Kent, OH: Kent State University Press, 1995), 44; Anderson, *Memoirs*, 236; R. S. Bevier, *History of the First and Second Missouri Confederate Brigades, 1861–1865* (St. Louis: Bryan, Brand, 1879), 153.

15. Tucker, *The South's Finest*, 73–75; Tucker, *Westerners in Gray*, 80; Finley L. Hubbell, "Diary of Lieut. Col. Hubbell, of 3d Regiment Missouri Infantry, C.S.A." *The Land We Love* 6, 2 (December 1868): 101; Bevier, *History of the First and Second Missouri Confederate Brigades*, 156.

16. Anderson, *Memoirs*, 240.

17. George Bargus Diary, October 4, 1862, *CWTI* Collection, USAMHI; *OR*, 1, 17(1): 262, 273–274; Union soldier to Adam, October 16, 1862, Adam Durkes Papers, UMC.

18. *OR*, 1, 17(1): 259–260, 269, 274, 276–277; Tucker, *Westerners in Gray*, 72; Jack D. Welsh, *Medical Histories of Union Generals* (Kent, OH: Kent State University Press, 1996), 330.

19. James M. Thurston Diary, October 4, 1862, Massachusetts Historical Society; *OR*, 1, 17(1): 277; John S. Wilcox to his wife, October 9, 1862, John S. Wilcox Papers, ISHL.

20. *OR*, 1, 17(1): 259.

21. Ibid., 258, 274, 278; Franklin B. Reed to brother, October 20, 1862, Franklin B. Reed Papers, SHSI; M. E. Sykes to his wife, October 22, 1862, M. E. Sykes Letters, MSU; Robert Kepner to sisters, October 7, 1862, Mead Family Papers, University of Iowa; N. R. Dunn to father, October 14, 1862; J. B. Weaver to Sir, March 10, 1893, Weaver and Vinson Family Correspondence, University of Iowa; J. B. Weaver to wife, October 6 and 12, 1862, James B. Weaver Letters, University of Iowa.

22. "A Few Incidents in the Life of Speaker Henderson's Successor," undated, David B. Henderson Papers, University of Iowa; "From the 12th Regiment," undated newspaper clipping, W. W. Warner Collection, SHSI; D. B. Henderson to William Larrabee, May 26, 1863, William Larrabee Collection, Montauk Historic Site; David B. Henderson to George, November 17, 1862, David B. Henderson Papers, DCHS. For more information on Henderson, see Timothy B. Smith, "The Politics of Battlefield Preservation: David B. Henderson and the National Military Parks," *Annals of Iowa* 66 (Summer–Fall 2007): 293–320; *Burial of General Rosecrans, Arlington National Cemetery, May 17, 1902* (Cincinnati, OH: Robert Clarke, 1903), 32–33.

23. Welsh, *Medical Histories of Confederate Generals*, 79.

24. *OR*, 1, 17(1): 402; Bevier, *History of the First and Second Missouri Confederate Brigades*, 154. The statement about forty pieces of captured artillery is misleading. Gates indeed had control of these guns, but only because he had entered the Federal artillery parking lot. Gates had not wrested these guns from the Federals, and he lost them when he moved back toward his own lines. In actuality, he captured only eleven guns.

25. Joel Strong, "Civil War Narrative by Captain Joel W. Strong, Company I, 10th Missouri Infantry Volunteers," 8–9, Joel Strong Alphabetical File, Missouri Historical Society; *OR*, 1, 17(1): 207, 218–219, 233, 238, 241; Tucker, *The South's Finest*, 78.

26. *OR*, 1, 17(1): 217; Richard S. Reeves Diary, October 4, 1862, Richard S. Reeves Papers, Minnesota Historical Society.

27. S. H. M. Byers, "How Men Feel in Battle," *American History Illustrated* 22, 2 (April 1987): 12.

28. *OR*, 1, 17(1): 207, 218–219; Henry M. Neil, "A Battery at Close Quarters: Being the Story of the Eleventh Ohio Battery at Iuka and Corinth," in *Sketches of War History,*

1861–1865: A Compilation of Miscellaneous Papers Compiled for the Ohio Commandery of the Loyal Legion, February, 1885–February, 1909 (Wilmington, NC: Broadfoot, 1993), 7:353; John B. Sanborn, "An Army Experience," ibid., 358.

29. N. R. Dunn to father, October 14, 1862.

30. *OR*, 1, 17(1): 233.

31. Ibid., 285, 289.

32. Ibid., 391; "What I Saw at the Battle of Corinth," E. B. Quiner Papers, SHSW; Tucker, *Westerners in Gray*, 82; Moore, *The Rebellion Record*, 5:502; Dunbar Rowland and H. Grady Howell Jr., *Military History of Mississippi: 1803–1898, Including a Listing of All Known Mississippi Confederate Military Units* (Madison, MS: Chickasaw Bayou Press, 2003), 738; Clement A. Evans, *Confederate Military History: A Library of Confederate States History Written by Distinguished Men of the South, and Edited by General Clement A. Evans*, 12 vols. (Atlanta: Confederate Publishing Company, 1899), 7(2): 255; Wimer Bedford Memoir, undated, 26, LC.

33. *OR*, 1, 17(1): 402.

34. J. R. Zearing to wife, October 6, 1862, James Roberts Zearing Collection, Chicago Historical Society; *OR*, 1, 17(1): 291, 298; Charles F. Hubert, *History of the Fiftieth Regiment Illinois Volunteer Infantry in the War of the Union* (Kansas City, MO: Western Veteran Publishing Company, 1894), 139, 142; D. Leib Ambrose, *History of the Seventh Regiment Illinois Volunteer Infantry, from Its First Muster into the U.S. Service, April 25, 1861, to Its Final Muster out, July 9, 1865* (Springfield: Illinois Journal Company, 1868), 99.

35. Jared C. Lobdell, ed., "The Civil War Journal and Letters of Colonel John Van Deusen Du Bois, April 12, 1861–October 16, 1862," *Missouri Historical Review* 61, 1 (October 1966): 48; E. A. Pollard, *Southern History of the War*, 2 vols. (New York: Richardson, 1866), 1:520; *OR*, 1, 17(1): 291.

36. *OR*, 1, 17(1): 248, 291, 293, 295; Hubert, *History of the Fiftieth Regiment Illinois Volunteer Infantry*, 142–143; Lobdell, "Civil War Journal and Letters of Du Bois," 48.

37. *OR*, 1, 17(1): 248, 291, 293, 295, 297–298; Lobdell, "Civil War Journal and Letters of Du Bois," 48.

38. Lobdell, "Civil War Journal and Letters of Du Bois," 48; Pollard, *Southern History of the War*, 1:520; *OR*, 1, 17(1): 260, 402.

39. Pollard, *Southern History of the War*, 1:520; *OR*, 1, 17(1): 298, 402; Lobdell, "Civil War Journal and Letters of Du Bois," 48.

40. Edwin Dean Memoirs, 12, Civil War Miscellaneous Collection, USAMHI; Nehemiah Davis Starr to "Miss Henrietta," October 9, 1862, Nehemiah Davis Starr Letters, Leslie Anders Collection, USAMHI; Garret W. Schreurs Diary, October 4, 1862, SHSI (copy in 7th Iowa File, CWIC).

41. Rosecrans, "Battle of Corinth," 749–750.

42. *OR*, 1, 17(1): 206–207, 209, 220, 224.

43. Ibid., 228, 231, 233, 235.

44. Ibid., 209, 237–238.

45. Ibid., 231.

46. Ibid., 210, 248, 260–261, 274, 276, 285, 391; Hubbell, "Diary of Lieut. Col. Hubbell," 101; Bailey, "Story of a Confederate Soldier," 18; Tucker, *Westerners in Gray*, 87; Anderson, *Memoirs*, 236; Tucker, *The South's Finest*, 79.

47. Tucker, *Westerners in Gray*, 87; *OR*, 1, 17(1): 260, 270, 277, 285; Anderson, *Memoirs*, 236; Tucker, *The South's Finest*, 79. The 3rd Louisiana was the only Louisiana regiment on this part of the field.

48. *OR*, 1, 17(1): 260, 285.

49. Pollard, *Southern History of the War*, 1:520; *OR*, 1, 17(1): 298, 402; Lobdell, "Civil War Journal and Letters of Du Bois," 48.

50. Charles Cowell, "An Infantryman at Corinth," *Civil War Times Illustrated* 13, 7 (November 1974): 13–14; William S. Rosecrans to U. S. Grant, October 4, 1862, William S. Rosecrans Papers, University of California at Los Angeles.

Chapter 14. "The Very Heart of Corinth"

1. Robert G. Hartje, *Van Dorn: The Life and Times of a Confederate General* (Nashville: Vanderbilt University Press, 1967), 233.

2. *OR*, 1, 17(1): 379; Frank Moore, ed., *The Rebellion Record: A Diary of American Events, with Documents, Narratives, Illustrative Incidents, Poetry, etc.*, 11 vols. (New York: D. Vann Nostrand, 1861–1868), 5:503; Charles C. Labuzan Diary, October 4, 1862, 42nd Alabama File, CWIC.

3. *OR*, 1, 17(1): 185, 398–399; A. O. McCollom to his friends, October 16, 1862, Robert and Sephronica Clark McCollom Papers, University of Arkansas; E. A. Pollard, *Southern History of the War*, 2 vols. (New York: Richardson, 1866), 1:519; George S. Milan to unknown, undated, 6th Texas Cavalry File, CWIC; Newton A. Keen, *Living and Fighting with the Texas 6th Cavalry* (Gaithersburg, MD: Butterneutt Press, 1986), 40; Marion Morrison, *A History of the Ninth Regiment Illinois Volunteer Infantry* (Monmouth, IL: John S. Clark, 1864), 41; Henry Steele Commager, ed., *The Blue and the Gray: The Story of the Civil War as Told by Participants*, 2 vols. (Indianapolis: Bobbs-Merrill, 1950), 1:366; Pat M. Carr, ed., *In Fine Sprits: The Civil War Letters of Ras Stirman* (Fayetteville, AR: Washington County Historical Society, 1986), 52 (copy in Stirman's Arkansas Sharpshooters File, CWIC).

4. Oscar L. Jackson, *The Colonel's Diary: Journals Kept before and during the Civil War by the Late Colonel Oscar L. Jackson of Newcastle, Pennsylvania, Sometime Commander of the 63rd Regiment O.V.I.* (n.p.: n.p., 1922), 71; David S. Stanley, "The Battle of Corinth," in *Personal Recollections of the War of the Rebellion: Addresses Delivered before the Commandery of the State of New York, Military Order of the Loyal Legion of the United States*, 2nd series (New York: G. P. Putnam's Sons, 1897), 274–275; Augustus Chetlain, "The Battle of Corinth," in *Military Essays and Recollections: Papers Read before the Commandery of the State of Illinois, Military Order of the Loyal Legion of the United States* (Chicago: A. C. McClurg, 1894), 2:378; *OR*, 1, 17(1): 180.

5. H. C. Adams Journal, October 4, 1862, Henry Clay Adams Papers, University of

Iowa; Cloyd Bryner, *Bugle Echoes: The Story of the Illinois 47th* (Springfield, IL: Phillips Bros. Printers, 1905), 63; *OR*, 1, 17(1): 185, 192, 202, 343; Mildred Throne, ed., *The Civil War Diary of Cyrus F. Boyd: Fifteenth Iowa Infantry, 1861–1863* (Des Moines: State Historical Society of Iowa, 1953), 74; John W. Sprague Papers, 63rd Ohio File, CWIC.

6. *OR*, 1, 17(1): 185, 188; Pollard, *Southern History of the War*, 1:519; Commager, *The Blue and the Gray*, 1:367; Jackson, *The Colonel's Diary*, 71.

7. L. H. Graves Diary, October 4, 1862, University of Texas at Austin; Pollard, *Southern History of the War*, 1:519; Commager, *The Blue and the Gray*, 1:367.

8. Jackson, *The Colonel's Diary*, 81.

9. William D. Evans to "Caroline," October 8, 1862, William D. Evans Papers, WRHS; *OR*, 1, 17(1): 185, 188, 192; Jackson, *The Colonel's Diary*, 72–73; Commager, *The Blue and the Gray*, 1:367; H. S. Halbert to "Sir," June 20, 1881, 6th Texas Cavalry Papers, NMMA; Joseph Mitchell Strickling Diary, October 4, 1862, 39th Ohio File, CWIC.

10. A. B. Monahan to wife, October 9 and 11, 1862, 63rd Ohio File, SNMP; *OR*, 1, 17(1): 185, 192; Morrison, *History of the Ninth Regiment Illinois Volunteer Infantry*, 42; Commager, *The Blue and the Gray*, 1:368; Joseph Mitchell Strickling Diary, October 4, 1862.

11. Marion Bennett Ledger, University of Tennessee; *OR*, 1, 17(1): 191, 399; Sharon L. D. Kraynek, ed., *Letters to My Wife: A Civil War Diary from the Western Front* (Apollo, PA: Closson Press, 1995), 38; Jackson, *The Colonel's Diary*, 73, 79; Francis Vinton Greene, *The Mississippi* (New York: Charles Scribner's Sons, 1882), 50; Joseph E. Chance, *The Second Texas Infantry: From Shiloh to Vicksburg* (Austin, TX: Eakin Press, 1984), 74–75; Commager, *The Blue and the Gray*, 1:368; John W. Fuller, "Our Kirby Smith," in *Sketches of War History, 1861–1865: Papers Read before the Ohio Commandery of the Military Order of the Loyal Legion of the United States* (Cincinnati, OH: Robert Clarke, 1888), 2:175; Monroe F. Cockrell, *The Lost Account of the Battle of Corinth and Court-Martial of Gen. Van Dorn* (Jackson, TN: McCowat-Mercer Press, 1955), 51.

12. *OR*, 1, 17(1): 180, 185–186, 191, 400; Fuller, "Our Kirby Smith," 176; Stanley, "Battle of Corinth," 276; Charles Wilkins to his friend, August 8, 1862, 1st U.S. Infantry Papers, NMMA.

13. *OR*, 1, 17(1): 181, 191.

14. J. W. Harmon Memoirs, 20, TSLA; Chance, *Second Texas Infantry*, 75; T. B. Arnold, "The Battles around Corinth, Miss.," *Confederate Veteran* 5, 5 (May 1897): 199.

15. *OR*, 1, 17(1): 248; Alexander G. Downing, *Downing's Civil War Diary*, ed. Olynthus B. Clark (Des Moines: Historical Department of Iowa, 1916), 73; Throne, *Civil War Diary of Cyrus F. Boyd*, 75; Lyman B. Pierce, *History of the Second Iowa Cavalry: Containing a Detailed Account of Its Organization, Marches, and the Battles in Which It Has Participated; Also, a Complete Roster of Each Company* (Burlington, IA: Hawk-eye Steam Book and Job Printing Establishment, 1865), 36; W. B. Britton to editors, October 9, 1862, William P. Britton Papers, WRHS; Joseph Mitchell Strickling Diary, October 4, 1862.

16. *OR*, 1, 17(1): 185, 192.

17. Ibid., 186, 188, 202; Charles H. Smith, *The History of Fuller's Ohio Brigade, 1861–1865: Its Great March, with Roster Portraits, Battle Maps and Biographies* (Cleveland, OH: Press of A. J. Watt, 1909), 101; B. F. Stephens to Mrs. E. D. Bowen, October 14, 1862, 9th Texas Cavalry File, CWIC.

18. *OR*, 1, 17(1): 186, 188, 202; Downing, *Downing's Civil War Diary*, 73; Stanley, "Battle of Corinth," 276.

19. John Fuller to David Stanley, August 23, 1887, West-Stanley-Wright Family Papers, USAMHI; F. T. Gilmore to David Stanley, January 13, 1897, ibid.; Harvey L. Carter and Norma L. Peterson, eds., "William S. Stewart Letters, January 13, 1861, to December 4, 1862, Part III," *Missouri Historical Review* 61, 4 (July 1967): 476; Stanley, "Battle of Corinth," 276; David W. Ogden, "Reminiscences," 26, William S. Ray Papers, University of Arkansas; *OR*, 1, 17(1): 188; Chance, *Second Texas Infantry*, 74–76; R. T. Martin, "Remembrances of an Arkansan," *Confederate Veteran* 12, 2 (February 1909): 69; David S. Stanley, "An Order to Charge at Corinth," in *Battles and Leaders of the Civil War*, 4 vols. (New York: Century Company, 1884–1887), 2:759; Fuller, "Our Kirby Smith," 175; George Hovey Cadman to his wife, October 13, 1862, George Hovey Cadman Papers, University of North Carolina; Arnold, "Battles around Corinth, Miss.," 199; William S. Stewart to mother, October 12, 1862, William S. Stewart Papers, UMC. The events surrounding Rogers's death are shrouded in uncertainty.

20. *OR*, 1, 17(1): 181, 186, 196, 202; George Hovey Cadman to his wife, October 13, 1862; John K. Bettersworth, ed., *Mississippi in the Confederacy: As They Saw It* (Baton Rouge: Louisiana State University Press, 1961), 96; William Stewart to his mother, October 12 and 17, 1862.

21. George Hovey Cadman to his wife, October 13, 1862; *OR*, 1, 17(1): 189; Greene, *The Mississippi*, 50; Arnold, "Battles around Corinth, Miss.," 199.

22. N. R. Dunn to his father, October 8 and 14, 1862, N. R. Dunn Letters, University of Michigan; *OR*, 1, 17(1): 194, 196, 247, 249, 399; George Hovey Cadman to his wife, October 13, 1862.

23. *OR*, 1, 17(1): 169, 217, 379, 399; Stanley, "Battle of Corinth," 275; William M. Lamers, *The Edge of Glory: A Biography of General William S. Rosecrans, U.S.A.* (New York: Harcourt, Brace, and World, 1961), 149; William D. Evans to Caroline, October 8, 1862, William D. Evans Papers, WRHS; J. R. Zearing to wife, October 6, 1862, James Roberts Zearing Collection, Chicago Historical Society.

24. Silas T. Trowbridge, "Saving a General," *Civil War Times Illustrated* 11, 4 (July 1972): 22; *OR*, 1, 17(1): 169, 217, 379, 399; Charles F. Hubert, *History of the Fiftieth Regiment Illinois Volunteer Infantry in the War of the Union* (Kansas City. MO: Western Veteran Publishing Company, 1894), 147; Carr, *In Fine Sprits*, 52; Alonzo L. Brown, *History of the Fourth Regiment of Minnesota Infantry Volunteers during the Great Rebellion 1861–1865* (St. Paul: Pioneer Press Company, 1892), 130; John Tyler Jr. to William L. Yancey, October 15, 1862, John Tyler Jr. Letter, UMC.

25. Dabney H. Maury, "Recollections of Campaign against Grant in North Mississippi in 1862–63," *Southern Historical Society Papers* 13 (1885): 298; *OR*, 1, 17(1): 396, 399, 446; Throne, *Civil War Diary of Cyrus F. Boyd*, 76; Hubert, *History of the Fiftieth Regi-*

ment Illinois Volunteer Infantry, 146; John Tyler Jr. to William L. Yancey, October 15, 1862; John Pray to John Bishop, October 10, 1862, John Pray Letters, 2nd Illinois Light Artillery, Battery B File, CWIC.

26. Hubert, *History of the Fiftieth Regiment Illinois Volunteer Infantry,* 146; *OR*, 1, 17(1): 396, 399, 446; John Pray to John Bishop, October 10, 1862; John Tyler Jr. to William L. Yancey, October 15, 1862.

27. L. F. Hubbard to his aunt, October 13, 1862, Lucius F. Hubbard and Family Papers, Minnesota Historical Society; W. B. McGrorty to unknown, undated, William B. McGrorty and Family Papers, Minnesota Historical Society; *OR*, 1, 17(1): 180, 200–201; Aden Cravens to his wife, October 17, 1862, Aden G. Cravens Letters, Indiana Historical Society.

28. *OR*, 1, 17(1): 169, 249–250, 286–287, 387; W. W. Booten, "A Federal Boy Soldier at Corinth," *Confederate Veteran* 5, 1 (January 1897): 6.

29. Will Snyder to Parents, November 25, 1862, NMMA; John Tyler Jr. to William L. Yancey, October 15, 1862; R. S. Bevier, *History of the First and Second Missouri Confederate Brigades, 1861–1865* (St. Louis: Bryan, Brand, 1879), 154.

30. John Tyler Jr. to William L. Yancey, October 15, 1862; *OR*, 1, 17(1): 201, 287, 387; J. K. Ferguson Civil War Diary, 72, University of Memphis.

31. L. F. Hubbard to his aunt, October 13, 1862; *OR*, 1, 17(1): 201, 287, 387; N. R. Dunn to his father, October 8, 1862; Maury, "Recollections of Campaign against Grant," 297.

32. Maury, "Recollections of Campaign against Grant," 301.

33. *OR*, 1, 17(1): 380.

34. Ibid., 405, 411–412; Daniel Miller to brother, October 9, 1862, Herman B. Miller Papers, Missouri Historical Society; Henry Clay Adams Civil War Journals, October 4, 1862, 31, University of Iowa; Albert Theodore Goodloe, *Some Rebel Relics: From the Seat of War* (Nashville: Publishing House of the Methodist Episcopal Church, South, 1893), 45–46; W. C. Holmes, "The Battle of Corinth," *Confederate Veteran* 27, 8 (August 1919): 292; Will Snyder to Parents, November 25, 1862.

35. Henry Clay Adams Civil War Journals, October 4, 1862, 31; *OR*, 1, 17(1): 405, 411–412; Daniel Miller to brother, October 9, 1862; Goodloe, *Some Rebel Relics*, 45–46; Holmes, "Battle of Corinth," 292; Will Snyder to Parents, November 25, 1862; R. R. Hutchinson, "Missourians East of the Miss. River," 25–26, Thomas L. Snead Papers, Missouri Historical Society.

36. *OR*, 1, 17(1): 345, 405, 411–412; W. G. Whitfield, "Battle of Corinth, Miss.," undated, 35th Alabama File, CWIC.

37. Hutchinson, "Missourians East of the Miss. River," 25–26; *OR*, 1, 17(1): 380, 405, 422; John Tyler Jr. to William L. Yancey, October 15, 1862; Audley S. H. Boyd to Thomas E. Wilson, December 27, 1862, 3rd Missouri Cavalry File, CWIC.

38. *OR*, 1, 17(1): 422.

39. Hutchinson, "Missourians East of the Miss. River," 25–26; *OR*, 1, 17(1): 380, 405, 422; John Tyler Jr. to William L. Yancey, October 15, 1862.

40. M. V. Lovell to his son, October 22, 1862, Lionel Baxter Collection, University of

Mississippi; M. V. Lovell to his son, October 22, 1862, Lionel Baxter Collection, *CWTI* Collection, USAMHI.

41. Van Dorn to wife, October 14, 1862, Earl Van Dorn Papers, Alabama Department of Archives and History; W. B. McGrorty letter, October 1862, William B. McGrorty and Family Papers, Minnesota Historical Society; John N. Ferguson Diary, October 4, 1862, LC; George Sawin to his wife, October 12, 1862, George Sawin Letters, Chicago Historical Society; J. Q. A. Campbell Diary, October 3, 1862, WRHS.

42. John Tyler Jr. to William L. Yancey, October 15, 1862; Maury, "Recollections of Campaign against Grant," 299; *OR*, 1, 17(1): 396; Bevier, *History of the First and Second Missouri Confederate Brigades*, 155; Albert Castel, *General Sterling Price and the Civil War in the West* (Baton Rouge: Louisiana State University Press, 1968), 118.

43. *OR*, 1, 17(1): 380, 405, 411; James Gordon, "The Battle and Retreat from Corinth," *Publications of the Mississippi Historical Society* 4 (1901): 69; Maury, "Recollections of Campaign against Grant," 297.

44. *OR*, 1, 17(1): 380, 405, 411; Maury, "Recollections of Campaign against Grant," 297; Gordon, "Battle and Retreat from Corinth," 69.

45. Goodloe, *Some Rebel Relics*, 56.

46. *OR*, 1, 17(1): 380, 405, 413; Gordon, "Battle and Retreat from Corinth," 70; Joseph J. Hunter, "A Sketch of the History of Noxubee Troopers, 1st Mississippi Cavalry, Company 'F,'" Joseph J. Hunter Manuscript, MDAH.

47. W. C. Porter, "War Diary of W. C. Porter," ed. J. V. Frederick, *Arkansas Historical Quarterly* 11, 4 (1952): 304; W. H. Tunnard, *A Southern Record: History of the 3rd Regiment Louisiana Infantry*, ed. Edwin C. Bearss (Dayton, OH: Morningside, 1970), 192; A. C. Riley, "Confederate Col. A. C. Riley, His Reports and Letters—Part II," ed. Riley Bock, *Missouri Historical Review* 85, 3 (April 1991): 266; James E. Payne, *History of the Fifth Missouri Volunteer Infantry* (n.p.: Press of James Payne, 1899), 36.

48. *OR*, 1, 17(1): 380, 391, 394.

49. Ibid., 380, 405, 408–409, 413.

50. Ibid., 380; John Tyler Jr. to William L. Yancey, October 15, 1862.

CHAPTER 15. "A SECOND RETREAT"

1. H. C. Adams Journal, October 3, 1862, Henry Clay Adams Papers, University of Iowa; *OR*, 1, 17(1): 181, 199, 261; William W. Cluett, *History of the 57th Regiment Illinois Volunteer Infantry, from Muster in, Dec. 26, 1861, to Muster out, July 7, 1865* (Princeton, IL: T. P. Streeter, 1886), 45.

2. *OR*, 1, 17(1): 162; Frank A. Montgomery, *Reminiscences of a Mississippian in Peace and War* (Cincinnati, OH: Robert Clarke, 1901), 92–93; John Milton Hubbard, *Notes of a Private* (Bolivar, MS: R. P. Shackelford, 1973), 43.

3. *OR*, 1, 17(1): 181, 199, 210, 261.

4. Ibid., 170, 338; Marion Morrison, *A History of the Ninth Regiment Illinois Volunteer Infantry* (Monmouth, IL: John S. Clark, 1864), 42; George Hovey Cadman to

his wife, October 13, 1862, George Hovey Cadman Papers, University of North Carolina.

5. William S. Rosecrans, "The Battle of Corinth," in *Battles and Leaders of the Civil War*, 4 vols. (New York: Century Company, 1884–1887), 2:752; Lewis F. Phillips Memoirs, 27, *CWTI* Collection, USAMHI; E. A. Pollard, *Southern History of the War*, 2 vols. (New York: Richardson, 1866), 1:520; Sharon L. D. Kraynek, ed., *Letters to My Wife: A Civil War Diary from the Western Front* (Apollo, PA: Closson Press, 1995), 38; Thomas Pollock to his wife and children, October 9, 1862, Thomas Pollock Letters, UMC; Alexander G. Downing, *Downing's Civil War Diary*, ed. Olynthus B. Clark (Des Moines: Historical Department of Iowa, 1916), 74; "A Condensed History of the 47th Regiment of Illinois Vol. Infantry," 9, John N. Cromwell Papers, ISHL.

6. Rosecrans, "Battle of Corinth," 752; Pollard, *Southern History of the War*, 1:520; James Gordon, "The Battle and Retreat from Corinth," *Publications of the Mississippi Historical Society* 4 (1901): 69; S. H. M. Byers, "How Men Feel in Battle," *American History Illustrated* 22, 2 (April 1987): 13–14; John K. Bettersworth, ed., *Mississippi in the Confederacy: As They Saw It* (Baton Rouge: Louisiana State University Press, 1961), 97.

7. Henry Clay Adams Civil War Journals, October 4, 1862, 32–33, University of Iowa; George Hovey Cadman to wife, October 13, 1862; Joseph Risedorph, "Battle of Corinth," 7, Joseph Risedorph Papers, Minnesota Historical Society; *OR*, 1, 17(1): 170; Mildred Throne, ed., *The Civil War Diary of Cyrus F. Boyd: Fifteenth Iowa Infantry, 1861–1863* (Des Moines: State Historical Society of Iowa, 1953), 76; C. J. Sergent Diary, October 4, 1862, NMMA.

8. Charles H. Smith, *The History of Fuller's Ohio Brigade, 1861–1865: Its Great March, with Roster Portraits, Battle Maps and Biographies* (Cleveland, OH: Press of A. J. Watt, 1909), 89; *OR*, 1, 17(1): 267.

9. Phinehas Orlando Avery Diary, October 9, 1862, Phinehas Orlando Avery Papers, NSHS; *OR*, 1, 17(1): 338, 345; Leslie Anders, *The Twenty-first Missouri: From Home Guard to Union Regiment* (Westport, CT: Greenwood Press, 1975), 104; John McArthur to Thomas J. McKean, undated, Thomas J. McKean Papers, MDAH.

10. *OR*, 1, 17(1): 367, 370, 372–373; W. A. Neal, *An Illustrated History of the Missouri Engineer and the 25th Infantry Regiments: Together with a Roster of Both Regiments and the Last Known Address of All that Could Be Obtained* (Chicago: Donohue and Henneberry, 1889), 67; Wimer Bedford Memoir, undated, 24, LC; James B. McPherson Report, October 13, 1862, James Birdseye McPherson Collection, Chicago Historical Society.

11. Josie Frazee Cappleman, "Local Incidents of the War between the States," in *Publications of the Mississippi Historical Society* 4(1901): 81.

12. Charles Cowell, "An Infantryman at Corinth," *Civil War Times Illustrated* 13, 7 (November 1974): 11.

13. "Personal Reminiscences of the Battle of Corinth," *Jackson Clarion Ledger,* April 16, 1908 (copy in the Civil War Corinth Subject File, MDAH); Charles F. Hubert, *History of the Fiftieth Regiment Illinois Volunteer Infantry in the War of the Union* (Kansas City,

MO: Western Veteran Publishing Company, 1894), 148; Cowell, "An Infantryman at Corinth," 12, 14.

14. J. V. Frederick, ed., "An Illinois Soldier in North Mississippi: Diary of John Wilson February 15–December 30, 1862," *Journal of Mississippi History* 1, 3 (July 1939): 190; Cowell, "An Infantryman at Corinth," 12, 14.

15. "Personal Reminiscences of the Battle of Corinth."

16. Peter Cozzens, *The Darkest Days of the War: The Battles of Iuka and Corinth* (Chapel Hill: University of North Carolina Press, 1997), 204; "Personal Reminiscences of the Battle of Corinth"; Hubert, *History of the Fiftieth Regiment Illinois Volunteer Infantry,* 148.

17. "Personal Reminiscences of the Battle of Corinth."

18. "Aftermath of Corinth Battle Left Citizens Horrified," *Jackson Clarion Ledger,* July 25, 1982; Cowell, "An Infantryman at Corinth," 14.

19. H. I. Smith, *History of the Seventh Iowa Veteran Volunteer Infantry during the Civil War* (Mason City, IA: R. Hitchcock, 1903), 84–85; Charles Stevens, "The Corinth Diary of Private Charles Stevens," *Blue and Gray Education Society Papers* 18 (Fall 2006): 29; Horace Wardner, "Reminiscences of a Surgeon," in *Military Essays and Recollections: Papers Read before the Commandery of the State of Illinois, Military Order of the Loyal Legion of the United States,* 3 vols. (Chicago: Dial Press, 1899), 3:189.

20. "Personal Reminiscences of the Battle of Corinth."

21. Cowell, "An Infantryman at Corinth," 12.

22. "History of Old Tishomingo County," 30, Alcorn County Chancery Clerk Archives.

23. Andrew J. Patrick to his father, October 15, 1862, Andrew J. Patrick Letter, University of Southern Mississippi; *OR,* 1, 17(1): 176, 378; Rosecrans, "Battle of Corinth," 752; George Hovey Cadman to wife, October 13, 1862.

24. Garrett Smith Ainsworth Diary, October 4, 1862, Univeristy of Southern Mississippi; *OR,* 1, 17(2): 255–258; *OR,* 1, 17(1): 158, 305; Bernarr Cresap, *Appomattox Commander: The Story of General E. O. C. Ord* (San Diego: A. S. Barnes, 1981), 88; Henry C. Ewing Diary, October 4, 1862, University of the Pacific; Willit Haynes to friends, October 2, 1862, Willit Samuel Haynes Letters, Bradley University.

25. *OR,* 1, 17(1): 162, 261, 380, 384; Dabney H. Maury, "Recollections of General Earl Van Dorn," *Southern Historical Society Papers* 19 (1891): 196; Robert G. Hartje, *Van Dorn: The Life and Times of a Confederate General* (Nashville: Vanderbilt University Press, 1967), 234–235; John Tyler Jr. to William L. Yancey, October 15, 1862, John Tyler Jr. Letter, UMC.

26. Ephraim McD. Anderson, *Memoirs: Historical and Personal; Including the Campaigns of the First Missouri Confederate Brigade* (St. Louis: Times Printing Company, 1868), 241; Morrison, *History of the Ninth Regiment Illinois Volunteer Infantry,* 47; G. A. Foote to his father, October 26, 1862, Foote Family Papers, Filson Historical Society; James C. Parrott to his wife, October 20, 1862, James C. Parrott Papers, SHSI; *OR,* 1, 17(1): 380, 388; Dabney H. Maury, "Recollections of Campaign against Grant in North Mississippi in 1862–63," *Southern Historical Society Papers* 13 (1885): 303–304; Anderson, *Memoirs,* 243; Samuel B. Barron, *The Lone Star Defenders: A Chronicle of the Third*

Texas Cavalry Regiment in the Civil War (Washington, DC: Zenger, 1983), 122; Davis M. Sullivan, "John Albert Pearson, Jr.: Arkansas Soldier and Confederate Marine," *Arkansas Historical Quarterly* 45, 3 (1986): 255; Hartje, *Van Dorn*, 236; Frank Moore, ed., *The Rebellion Record: A Diary of American Events, with Documents, Narratives, Illustrative Incidents, Poetry, etc.*, 11 vols. (New York: D. Vann Nostrand, 1861–1868), 5:506; H. Grady Howell, *Going to Meet the Yankees: A History of the "Bloody Sixth" Mississippi Infantry, C.S.A.* (Jackson, MS: Chickasaw Bayou Press, 1981), 132.

27. H. G. Kennett to C. S. Hamilton, October 9, 1862, Charles S. Hamilton Papers, University of Illinois; C. Goddard to C. S. Hamilton, October 7, 1862, ibid.; *OR*, 1, 17(1): 182, 210, 261, 338; *OR*, 1, 17(2): 266; William M. Lamers, *The Edge of Glory: A Biography of General William S. Rosecrans, U.S.A.* (New York: Harcourt, Brace, and World, 1961), 159.

28. H. C. Adams Journal, October 4 and 5, 1862; Charles Wright, *A Corporal's Story: Experiences in the Ranks of Company C, 81st Ohio Vol. Infantry, during the War for the Maintenance of the Union, 1861–1864* (Philadelphia: James Beale, 1887), 67; *OR*, 1, 17(1): 182–183, 210, 211, 261, 338; *OR*, 1, 17(2): 263–264; William S. Rosecrans to his wife, October 5, 1862, William Starke Rosecrans Papers, UCLA; W. H. Tucker, *The Fourteenth Wisconsin Vet. Vol. Infantry (General A. J. Smith's Command) in the Expedition and Battle of Tupelo: Also, Wanderings through the Wilds of Missouri and Arkansas in Pursuit of Price* (Indianapolis: n.p., 1892), 14.

29. W. B. Britton to editors, October 9, 1862, William P. Britton Papers, WRHS; George Hovey Cadman to wife, October 13, 1862; *OR*, 1, 17(1): 161, 170, 345; *OR*, 1, 17(2): 265; J. A. Bigger Diary, October 16, 1862, MDAH; Maury, "Recollections of Campaign against Grant," 300; Lamers, *Edge of Glory*, 154, 162; *Fayette (MS) Gazette*, October 24, 1862; 36th Mississippi Muster and Pay Roll, June 30 to August 31, 1862, 36th Mississippi Muster and Pay Rolls, NARA; Richard S. Reeves Diary, October 4, 1862, Richard S. Reeves Papers, Minnesota Historical Society; Octavia Sulivane to her sister, February 5, 1863, Octavia Sulivane Letter, Murray J. Smith Collection, USAMHI.

30. James R. Binford, "Recollections of the Fifteenth Regiment of Mississippi Infantry, C.S.A.," 34, Patrick Henry Papers, MDAH; R. R. Hutchinson, "Missourians East of the Miss. River," 26, Thomas L. Snead Papers, Missouri Historical Society; Thomas E. Parson, "Hell on the Hatchie: The Fight at Davis Bridge, Tennessee," *Blue and Gray Magazine* 24, 4 (Holiday 2007): 49; *OR*, 1, 17(1): 368, 413; John S. Bowen Papers, n.d., Missouri Historical Society; Phillip Thomas Tucker, *The Forgotten Stonewall of the West: Major General John Stevens Bowen* (Macon, GA: Mercer University Press, 1997), 142–150; T. G. Prichett to his sister, October 22, 1862, T. G. Prichett Letter, NMMA.

31. For Hurlbut, see Juliet Gilman Sager, "Stephen A. Hurlbut, 1815–1882," *Journal of the Illinois State Historical Society* 28, 2 (July 1935): 53–80, and Jeffrey N. Lash, *A Politician Turned General: The Civil War Career of Stephen Augustus Hurlbut* (Kent, OH: Kent State University Press, 2003). For more on the Battle of Davis Bridge, see Parson, "Hell on the Hatchie," 6–24, 43–51; Timothy B. Smith, "The Forgotten Battle of Davis' Bridge," *North and South* 2, 5 (June 1999): 68–79; and Robert W. McDaniel, "Forgotten Heritage: The Battle of Hatchie Bridge, Tennessee," *West Tennessee Historical Society Papers* 31 (October 1977): 111.

32. *OR*, 1, 17(1): 305, 308; *OR*, 1, 17(2): 259.

33. Henry C. Ewing Diary, October 5, 1862; Cresap, *Appomattox Commander*, 89–90; *OR*, 1, 17(1): 322, 329; Bela T. St. John Diary, October 5, 1862, Bela T. St. John Papers, LC; William F. Wilder Reminiscences, 30–31, LC; Willit Haynes to his sisters, October 8, 1862.

34. *OR*, 1, 17(1): 322, 328, 333, 392–393, 399; Maury, "Recollections of Campaign against Grant," 303; Monroe F. Cockrell, ed., *The Lost Account of the Battle of Corinth and Court-Martial of Gen. Van Dorn* (Jackson, TN: McCowat-Mercer Press, 1955), 37; McDaniel, "Forgotten Heritage," 111; J. L. Harris to his uncle, October 14, 1862, J. L. Harris Papers, ISHL; H. E. Ranstead, *A True Story and History of the Fifty-third Regiment Illinois Veteran Volunteer Infantry: Its Campaigns and Marches: Incidents that Occurred on Marches and in Camp. What Happened to Some of Its Members and What Became of Others. Short Stories of Marches and How the Army Lived* (n.p.: n.p., 1910), 6.

35. *OR*, 1, 17(1): 322, 325, 327, 381, 399–400; Henry C. Ewing Diary, October 5, 1862; William F. Wilder Reminiscences, 30–31.

36. *OR*, 1, 17(1): 302, 322, 396, 400; Albert O. McCollom to his brother, October 19, 1862, Robert and Sephronica Clark McCollom Papers, University of Arkansas; James C. Veatch Report, October 9, 1862, Helen Coleman Collection, Indiana Historical Society; Jacob Brunner to his wife, October 13, 1862, Jacob Brunner Letters, Ohio Historical Society; George L. Griscom Diary, October 5, 1862, University of Texas at Austin; Barron, *Lone Star Defenders*, 121; Hartje, *Van Dorn*, 237.

37. *OR*, 1, 17(1): 302, 305, 307, 312, 323, 395; E. O. C. Ord to brother, October 1862, Edward Otho Cresap Ord Papers, University of California–Berkeley (copy in E. O. C. Ord File, CWIC).

38. Willit Haynes to his friend, October 8, 1862; *OR*, 1, 17(1): 306, 323, 326, 331; Henry C. Ewing Diary, October 5, 1862.

39. *OR*, 1, 17(1): 306, 312, 323; Cresap, *Appomattox Commander*, 91; E. O. C. Ord to brother, October 1862, Ord Papers, University of California–Berkeley; E. O. C. Ord to children, November 1862, Edward Otho Cresap Ord Papers, Stanford University (copy in E. O. C. Ord File, CWIC).

40. *OR*, 1, 17(1): 307, 312, 323; Bela T. St. John Diary, October 5, 1862; William F. Wilder Reminiscences, 30–31.

41. *OR*, 1, 17(1): 306, 391–392; Anderson, *Memoirs*, 212; Joseph M. Bailey Memoirs, "The Story of a Confederate Soldier," 18, Joseph M. Bailey Papers, University of Arkansas.

42. Willit Haynes to his sisters, October 8, 1862; Frank J. Crawford to Father Richardson, October 8, 1862, 53rd Illinois File, CWIC; General Order 112, October 8, 1862, Garrett Smith Ainsworth Papers, University of Southern Mississippi; Charles Cady to his family, October 16, 1862, Charles Cady Papers, University of Iowa; *OR*, 1, 17(1): 302, 304, 306–307; *Chicago Tribune*, October 11, 1862.

43. R. T. Martin, "Remembrances of an Arkansan," *Confederate Veteran* 12, 2 (February 1909): 69; Anderson, *Memoirs*, 243–244; Barron, *Lone Star Defenders*, 122–123, 125; W. H. Tunnard, *A Southern Record: The History of the 3rd Regiment Louisiana*

Infantry, ed. Edwin C. Bearss (Dayton: Morningside, 1970), 193; Pat M. Carr, ed., *In Fine Sprits: The Civil War Letters of Ras Stirman* (Fayetteville, AR: Washington County Historical Society, 1986), 53; *OR*, 1, 17(1): 381, 392, 396, 406, 424; J. A. Bigger Diary, October 16, 1862, University of Mississippi; Phillip Thomas Tucker, *The Confederacy's Fighting Chaplain: Father John B. Bannon* (Tuscaloosa: University of Alabama Press, 1992), 96; James K. Newton, *A Wisconsin Boy in Dixie: The Selected Letters of James K. Newton*, ed. Stephen E. Ambrose (Madison: University of Wisconsin Press, 1961), 43; Daniel Ruggles to Van Dorn, October 8, 1862, Earl Van Dorn Papers, LC; Isaiah Steedman to his son, June 1, 1891, Isaiah G. W. Steedman Letters, *CWTI* Collection, USAMHI; Martin Green to Captain Hutchinson, October 23, 1862, Thomas L. Snead Papers, NARA; Barron, *Lone Star Defenders*, 122–123, 125; Tunnard, *Southern Record,* 193; John Bennett to his brother, October 7, 1862, Bennett Family Papers, LSU; Binford, "Recollections of the Fifteenth Regiment of Mississippi Infantry," 34; Diary of George R. Elliot, Confederate Collection, TSLA; S. M. Thornton to his wife, November 18, 1862, Thornton Collection, MSU.

44. D. Leib Ambrose, *History of the Seventh Regiment Illinois Volunteer Infantry, from Its First Muster into the U.S. Service, April 25, 1861, to Its Final Muster out, July 9, 1865* (Springfield: Illinois Journal Company, 1868), 110; William D. Evans to "Caroline," William D. Evans Papers, WRHS; C. Goddard to C. S. October 7, 1862; *OR*, 1, 17(1): 338; *OR*, 1, 17(2): 158, 265; T. A. Montgomery to brother, October 17, 1862, T. A. Montgomery Letters, Cornell University; Henry M. Neil, "A Battery at Close Quarters: Being the Story of the Eleventh Ohio Battery at Iuka and Corinth," in *Sketches of War History, 1861–1865: A Compilation of Miscellaneous Papers Compiled for the Ohio Commandery of the Loyal Legion, February, 1885–February, 1909* (Wilmington, NC: Broadfoot, 1993), 7:354; Alonzo L. Brown, *History of the Fourth Regiment of Minnesota Infantry Volunteers during the Great Rebellion 1861–1865* (St. Paul: Pioneer Press Company, 1892), 137–138; John Edwards to his brother, October 19, 1862, NMMA; August Schilling Diary, October 8 and 9, 1862, BCHS.

45. John Edwards to his brother, October 19, 1862; W. B. Britton to editors, October 9, 1862; *OR*, 1, 17(2): 158–159; William S. Rosecrans to his wife, October 15, 1862; Theodore Edgar Saint John to "Janie," October 26, 1862, Theodore Edgar Saint John Papers, LC; Garrett Smith Ainsworth Diary, October 10, 1862; Edward Stanfield to his father, October 12, 1862, Edward P. Stanfield Letters, Indiana Historical Society; Henry C. Ewing Diary, October 12, 1862; T. Kilby Smith to his wife, October 11, 1862, T. K. Smith Collection, Huntington Library; John Anderson to W. E. Lodge, November 14, 1862, William E. Lodge Papers, University of Illinois; David Dewolf to "Dear Na," July 9, 1862, David Dewolf Papers, ISHL.

46. Myron Underwood to his wife, October 19, 1862, Myron Underwood Papers, University of Iowa; Risedorph, "Battle of Corinth," 8.

47. George M. Reeder to "Officer in Charge of the Train," November 4, 1862, Letter of Command, U.S. Army, Corinth District, Oct. 1862–Nov. 1863, Adjutant General's Office and 110th U.S. Colored Infantry, MDAH; Special Order 3, October 8, 1863, Special Orders Issued, RG 393, E 293, NARA; J. A. Bigger Diary, October 16, 1862, MDAH;

Robert Kepner to sisters, October 7, 1862, Mead Family Papers, University of Iowa; Thomas Hogan to father, October 12, 1862, Thomas Hogan Letters, Missouri Historical Society; J. R. Zearing to wife, October 6 and 11, 1862, James Roberts Zearing Collection, Chicago Historical Society; Myron Underwood to wife, October 19, 1862; William D. Evans to Caroline, October 8, 1862; J. T. Lewis to C. S. Hamilton, October 7, 1862, Charles S. Hamilton Papers, University of Illinois; James Mellor to wife, October 15, 1862, Edward Cronon Papers, University of Wisconsin; N. R. Dunn to father, October 14, 1862, N. R. Dunn Letters, University of Michigan; David Spurgin to wife, October 9, 1862, 16th Iowa File, CWIC.

48. M. V. Miller to unknown, October 30, 1862, HC; Newton, *Wisconsin Boy in Dixie*, 43; *OR*, 2, 4: 608; I. V. Smith Memoirs, undated, 25, UMC; J. R. Zearing to wife, October 11, 1862; Special Order 4, October 8, 1862, Special Orders Issued, RG 393, E 293, NARA.

49. James M. Thurston Diary, October 5, 1862, Massachusetts Historical Society; C. J. Sergent Diary, October 2, 1862, NMMA; N. R. Dunn to father, October 5, 1862; J. C. Parrott to wife, October 20, 1862; William P. Rogers, "The Diary and Letters of William P. Rogers, 1846–1862," ed. Florence Damon Pace, *Southwestern Historical Quarterly* 32, 4 (April 1929): 298; William McCuray to Mrs. Dantzler, October 11, 1862, Absolem F. Dantzler Papers, Duke University; O. W. Fox to Mrs. William Brown, October 17, 1862, William Brown Letters, SHSW; William Brown Jr. to wife, October 8, 1862, HC; Frederick, "Illinois Soldier in North Mississippi," 190; J. B. Corts et al. to Major Charley Sterne, November 1, 1862, J. B. Courts Letter, UMC; Franklin Reid to Archible and Nohala Culver, October 22, 1862, John W. Morrison Letters, Brigham Young University.

50. Elva Wright to Jane McPherson, undated, Wilson Family Papers, Virginia Historical Society; Lieutenant [?] to Mrs. William Brown, October 17, 1862, William Brown Papers, SHSW; J. B. Courts et al. to Major Charley Stern, November 1, 1862; John Eaton, *Grant, Lincoln and the Freedmen: Reminiscences of the Civil War, with Special Reference to the Work for the Contrabands and Freedmen of the Mississippi Valley* (New York: Longmans, Green, 1907), 7.

51. William D. Evans to Caroline, October 8, 1862; *OR*, 2, 4: 608; W. B. Britton to editors, October 9, 1862; N. R. Dunn to father, October 5, 1862; Wright, *A Corporal's Story*, 65; Mildred Throne, ed., "An Iowa Doctor in Blue: The Letters of Seneca B. Thrall, 1862–1864," *Iowa Journal of History* 58, 2 (April 1960): 99; Cloyd Bryner, *Bugle Echoes: The Story of the Illinois 47th* (Springfield, IL: Phillips Bros. Printers, 1905), 65; T. A. Montgomery to brother, November 10, 1862; Daniel Miller to brother, October 9, 1862, Herman B. Miller Papers, Missouri Historical Society; T. D. Christie to sister, October 28, Christie Family Letters, Minnesota Historical Society; Joseph Mitchell Strickling Diary, October 5, 1862, 39th Ohio File, CWIC; Robert J. Burdette Memoir, undated, 47th Illinois File, CWIC; Jared C. Lobdell, ed., "The Civil War Journal and Letters of Colonel John Van Deusen Du Bois, April 12, 1861–October 16, 1862," *Missouri Historical Review* 61, 1 (October 1966): 48.

52. D. F. McGowan to Fannie, October 5, 1862, HC; Steven Werly Diary, October 4,

1862, UMC; Daniel Miller to brother, October 9, 1862; W. B. Britton to editors, October 9, 1862.

53. *OR*, 1, 17(1): 378; Confederate States Army Casualties, Lists and Narrative Reports 1861–1865, Roll 2: Mississippi, NARA; Thomas L. Livermore, *Numbers and Losses in the Civil War in America* (Boston: Houghton Mifflin, 1900), 94; A. B. Monahan to his wife, October 12, 1862, 63rd Ohio File, SNMP; Homer L. Calkin, "Elkhorn to Vicksburg," *Civil War History* 2, 1 (March 1956): 35; Wright Schaumburg Journal, Schaumburg-Wright Family Papers, HNOC; A. F. Brown, "Van Dorn's Operations in Northern Mississippi—Recollections of a Cavalryman," *Southern Historical Society Papers* 6, 4 (1878): 152; Moore, *The Rebellion Record*, 5:500; J. W. Harmon Memoirs, Confederate Collection, TSLA.

54. "Another Great Battle at Corinth," *New York Herald,* October 6, 1862; "The Seat of War in the South-West," *New York Tribune,* October 7, 1862; Mansfield Lovell to his wife, October 26, 1862, Mansfield Lovell Papers, Huntington Library; *OR*, 1, 17(1): 160; *OR*, 1, 16(2): 929; *OR*, 1, 19(2): 388.

55. William S. Rosecrans to his wife, October 15, 1862; James L. McDonough, *War in Kentucky: From Shiloh to Perryville* (Knoxville: University of Tennessee Press, 1994), 309, 360.

56. Mansfield Lovell to his wife, October 26, 1862.

CHAPTER 16. "WE ARE GETTING THINGS IN
GOOD ORDER AGAIN"

1. *OR*, 1, 17(1): 214–215, 255–256, 267; D. Leib Ambrose, *History of the Seventh Regiment Illinois Volunteer Infantry, from Its First Muster into the U.S. Service, April 25, 1861, to Its Final Muster out, July 9, 1865* (Springfield: Illinois Journal Company, 1868), 118–119.

2. Maury to Emily Van Dorn Miller, May 10, 1872, Civil War Papers, MDAH; *OR*, 1, 17(1): 414–416, 452, 457, 459; Arthur W. Bergeron, "Mansfield Lovell," in Roman J. Heleniak and Lawrence L. Hewitt, *Leadership during the Civil War: The 1989 Deep Delta Civil War Symposium: Themes in Honor of T. Harry Williams* (Shippensburg, PA: White Mane, 1992), 102; Phillip Thomas Tucker, "Forgotten Confederate General: John Stevens Bowen," *Journal of Mississippi History* 50, 3 (August 1988): 141; R. R. Hutchinson, "Missourians East of the Mississippi," 26, Thomas L. Snead Papers, Missouri Historical Society; Price to Van Dorn, October 13, 1862, Earl Van Dorn Papers, Alabama Department of Archives and History; William N. Nugent, *My Dear Nellie: The Civil War Letters of William N. Nugent to Eleanor Smith Nugent,* ed. William M. Cash and Lucy Somerville Howorth (Jackson: University Press of Mississippi, 1977), 101; William Candace Thompson, "From Shiloh to Port Gibson," *Civil War Times Illustrated* 3, 6 (October 1964): 22; Van Dorn to wife, October 14, 1862, Van Dorn Papers; R. Walpole to "Esteemed Friends," November 4, 1862, Bomar Family Papers, Emory University; Diary of Sarah Jane Johnston, Confederate Collection, TSLA.

3. Thomas C. Reynolds, "General Sterling Price and the Confederacy," Thomas C. Reynolds Papers, Missouri Historical Society; *Jackson Daily Mississippian*, September 29, 1862; "The Battle of Corinth," November 15, 1862, Theodore J. Robinette Civil War Scrapbook, Robinette Family Papers, University of the Pacific.

4. *OR*, 1, 17(2): 297; General Order 21, July 6, 1863, HC; H. J. B. Cummings to Commanding Officer, July 10, 1863, and George B. Hoge to Commanding Officer, November 8, 1863, Letters Sent, RG 393, E 287, NARA.

5. *OR*, 1, 17(2): 310, 313; I. F. Quinby to wife, October 27, 1862, Isaac F. Quinby Letter, Vicksburg National Military Park (copy in Isaac F. Quinby File, CWIC); Stanley P. Hirshson, *Grenville M. Dodge: Soldier, Politician, Railroad Pioneer* (Bloomington: Indiana University Press, 1967), 66; Charles Stevens, "The Corinth Diary of Private Charles Stevens," *Blue and Gray Education Society Papers* 18 (Fall 2006): 35–36; Ambrose, *History of the Seventh Regiment Illinois Volunteer Infantry*, 120. For troop levels, see *OR*, 1, 17(2): 337, 513; *OR*, 1, 24(3): 20, 75, 163, 249, 371, 453, 568; OR, 1, 31(3): 293, 564.

6. Charles F. Hubert, *History of the Fiftieth Regiment Illinois Volunteer Infantry in the War of the Union* (Kansas City, MO: Western Veteran Publishing Company, 1894), 169; Grenville Dodge to Nate, May 27, 1863, Dodge Family Papers, Denver Public Library; Jeffrey N. Lash, *A Politician Turned General: The Civil War Career of Stephen Augustus Hurlbut* (Kent, OH: Kent State University Press, 2003), 116; *OR*, 1, 17(2): 364, 461, 516–517, 565; *OR*, 1, 24(3): 35, 38, 44, 59, 75, 181; "General Dodge," *Corinth Chanticleer,* September 18, 1863; Hirshson, *Grenville M. Dodge*, 64, 79; Jack D. Welsh, *Medical Histories of Union Generals* (Kent, OH: Kent State University Press, 1996), 100.

7. Grenville Dodge to Nate, November 16, 1862; J. R. Zearing to his wife, October 11, 1862, James Roberts Zearing Collection, Chicago Historical Society; Hirshson, *Grenville M. Dodge*, 70; Myron Underwood to his wife, October 19, 1862, Myron Underwood Papers, University of Iowa; Court-Martial Case File KK303, Robert C. Murphy, NARA; Robert Armstrong Diary, August 10, 1863, Indiana Historical Society; Joseph Risedorph, "Iuka Campaign," 1, Joseph Risedorph Papers, Minnesota Historical Society; Charles Wright, *A Corporal's Story: Experiences in the Ranks of Company C, 81st Ohio Vol. Infantry, during the War for the Maintenance of the Union, 1861–1864* (Philadelphia: James Beale, 1887), 84–85; Ben Earl Kitchens, *Rosecrans Meets Price: The Battle of Iuka, Mississippi* (Florence, AL: Thornwood Book Publishers, 1987), 181–183; William W. Cluett, *History of the 57th Regiment Illinois Volunteer Infantry, from Muster in, Dec. 26, 1861, to Muster out, July 7, 1865* (Princeton, IL: T. P. Streeter, 1886), 54–56; "Letter of Lieut. Col. Wm. E. Small," *Annals of the State Historical Society of Iowa* 1, 2 (April 1863): 87; "Correspondence," *Annals of the State Historical Society of Iowa* 1, 3 (July 1863): 140; Horatio N. Marsden to Charles Woodruff, May 20, 1863, William F. Jones Papers, UMC; James Redfield to wife, May 24, 1863, Redfield-Thornburg Family Papers, SHSI (copy in 39th Iowa File, CWIC); "Local Department," *Corinth Chanticleer*, June 12, 1863; "Ordnance Receipt," October 15, 1863, and "List of Quartermaster Stores Received," April 1, 1863, HC.

8. Theodore Saint John to "Janie," October 26, 1862, Theodore Edgar Saint John Papers, LC; *OR*, 1, 17(2): 155; Granville W. Hough, ed., "Diary of a Soldier in Grant's

Rear Guard (1862–1863)," *Journal of Mississippi History* 45, 3 (August 1983): 206; U. S. Grant, *Personal Memoirs of U. S. Grant* (New York: Charles L. Webster, 1885), 247; *Memphis Daily Appeal*, October 24, 1862; John A. Duckworth to William Rosser, undated, John A. Duckworth Letter, SHSI (copy in 2nd Iowa File, SNMP); Joseph Lester to his father, November 1, 1862, Joseph Lester Papers, LC; Edward Stanfield to his father, October 31, 1862, Edward P. Stanfield Letters, Indiana Historical Society; William G. Christie to brother, November 1, 1862, Christie Family Letters, Minnesota Historical Society; William H. Chamberlain, *History of the Eighty-first Regiment Ohio Infantry Volunteers during the War of the Rebellion* (Cincinnati, OH: Gazette Steam Printing House, 1865), 39; "Captain John C. Appler," *Confederate Veteran* 31, 1 (January 1923): 28; Henry J. B. Cummings to wife, January 9, 1863, Henry Johnson Brodhead Cummings Papers, SHSI; Richard D. Andrews to aunt and uncle, November 26, 1862, Richard D. Andrews Letter, 21st Missouri File, CWIC; Uriah M. Glover to parents, February 10, 1863, Uriah M. Glover Letters, 66th Indiana File, CWIC.

9. George M. Reeder to "Captain Smith," November 5, 1862, Letter of Command, U.S. Army, Corinth District, Oct. 1862–Nov. 1863, Adjutant General's Office and 110th U.S. Colored Infantry, MDAH; John A. Duckworth to William Rosser, undated; Chamberlain, *History of the Eighty-first Regiment Ohio Infantry Volunteers,* 39; Hubert, *History of the Fiftieth Regiment Illinois Volunteer Infantry,* 169–170.

10. Laurens W. Wolcott to sister, November 8, 1862, HC; Emory S. Huston to uncle, May 1, 1863, HC; Stevens, "Corinth Diary of Private Charles Stevens," 31, 33–35; Abraham Slough to wife, October 24, 1862, 59th Indiana File, CWIC.

11. Fort Randall Map, undated, HC; John A. Duckworth to William Rosser, undated.

12. Hubert, *History of the Fiftieth Regiment Illinois Volunteer Infantry,* 170; Mansfield Lovell to G. W., October 26, 1862, Mansfield Lovell Papers, Huntington Library; N. R. Dunn to father, October 14, 1862, N. R. Dunn Letters, University of Michigan.

13. Laurens W. Wolcott to sister, May 12, 1863; Theodore Saint John to "Janie," October 26, 1862; Walter Lindley to mother, April 12, 1863, HC; Hubert, *History of the Fiftieth Regiment Illinois Volunteer Infantry,* 170, 182; James Redfield to wife, April 4, 1863; Joseph E. Brent, *Occupied Corinth: The Contraband Camp and the First Alabama Infantry of African Descent, 1862–1864* (Corinth, MS: City of Corinth, 1995), 31, 33; Ebenezer Pearce to parents, February 1, 1863, HC; Chamberlain, *History of the Eighty-first Regiment Ohio Infantry Volunteers,* 39; Simeon Royse to parents, February 5, 1863, John W. Royse Papers, Duke University; Frederick Sherwood Diary, May 13, 1863, Earl Hess Collection, USAMHI; George Bargus Diary, October 8, 1863, *CWTI* Collection, USAMHI; Cluett, *History of the 57th Regiment Illinois Volunteer Infantry,* 49, 52–53, 59; Wright, *A Corporal's Story,* 70–71; John A. Duckworth to William Rosser, undated; Joseph K. Nelson, "Recollections," 31, Civil War Miscellaneous Collection, USAMHI.

14. James Redfield to wife, April 4 and May 16, 1863.

15. N. R. Dunn to father, October 14, 1862; John K. Mahon, ed., "The Civil War Letters of Samuel Mahon, Seventh Iowa Infantry," *Iowa Journal of History* 51, 3 (July 1953): 242; Grenville M. Dodge, "Use of Block-Houses during the Civil War," *Annals of Iowa* 6, 4 (January 1904): 298; George Wyckoff to wife, March 6 and April 24, 1863, and May

19, no year, Wyckoff Family Papers, Missouri Historical Society; Lorenzo A. Barker Diary, December 17, 1862, and May 6 and 22 and June 25 and 29, 1863, Archives of Michigan; Brent, *Occupied Corinth*, 27, 29; "Local Department," *Corinth Chanticleer*, June 12, 1863; Hubert, *History of the Fiftieth Regiment Illinois Volunteer Infantry,* 212; John N. Doak to Emma, February 10 and May 4, 1863, John N. Doak Letters, 66th Illinois File, CWIC; J. C. Parrott to wife, October 20, 1862, James C. Parrott Papers, SHSI; Charles H. Smith, *The History of Fuller's Ohio Brigade, 1861–1865: Its Great March, with Roster Portraits, Battle Maps and Biographies* (Cleveland, OH: Press of A. J. Watt, 1909), 133; "Letter from Corinth," *Cincinnati Daily Gazette,* June 20, 1863. For Camp Davies, see Camp Davies File, CWIC; Mark Boatman to brother, January 7, 1863, HC; George Bargus Diary, September 28, 1863, *CWTI* Collection, USAMHI.

16. Nelson, "Recollections," 31; Stevens, "Corinth Diary of Private Charles Stevens," 29, 31, 35, 38; N. R. Dunn to father, October 14, 1862.

17. "Programme of the Grand Military Ball Given by the Commissioned Officers of the Garrison of Corinth on New Year's Eve (December 31, 1862)," HC; Lorenzo A. Barker Diary, October 19, 1863; Thomas W. Sweeny to Henry J. B. Cummings, July 2, 1863, Henry Johnson Brodhead Cummings Papers, SHSI; Hubert, *History of the Fiftieth Regiment Illinois Volunteer Infantry,* 211; Emory S. Huston to uncle, May 1, 1863, HC; Chamberlain, *History of the Eighty-first Regiment Ohio Infantry Volunteers,* 41, 46; "Local Department," *Corinth Chanticleer*, June 12, 1863; "Headquarters Pass," April 5, 1863, HC.

18. *Corinth Chanticleer*, June 12, 1863; Daniel Miller to brother, October 9, 1862, Herman B. Miller Papers, Missouri Historical Society; Ed H. Rees to Cal, September 9, 1863, Ed H. Rees Letter, Virginia Tech University.

19. Chamberlain, *History of the Eighty-first Regiment Ohio Infantry Volunteers,* 49–50; Ambrose, *History of the Seventh Regiment Illinois Volunteer Infantry*, 144–145; Hubert, *History of the Fiftieth Regiment Illinois Volunteer Infantry,* 185; Henry J. B. Cummings to wife, February 23, 1863.

20. "The Deformed Transformed," *Corinth Chanticleer*, June 12, 1863; "Local Department," *Corinth Chanticleer*, June 12, 1863.

21. Stevens, "Corinth Diary of Private Charles Stevens," 32–33; Laurens W. Wolcott to sister, December 24, 1862; James Redfield to wife, January 26, 1863.

22. Simeon Royse to parents, February 5 and 11 and March 13, 1863; Uriah Glover to father, June 4, 1863, Uriah M. Glover Letters, 66th Indiana File, CWIC; John M. Ruby to sister, December 6, 1863, HC; John A. Duckworth to William Rosser, undated; John Pray to John Bishop, January 22, 1863, John Pray Letters, 2nd Illinois Light Artillery, Battery B File, CWIC; Ambrose, *History of the Seventh Regiment Illinois Volunteer Infantry*, 133; Hubert, *History of the Fiftieth Regiment Illinois Volunteer Infantry,* 177; Hiram Matthew to wife, July 27, 1863, HC; John N. Doak to Emma, April 15, 1863, John N. Doak Letters, 66th Illinois File, CWIC; Robert Armstrong Diary, May 31, 1863; Hiram Matthew to wife, February 1 and March 9, 1863, Hiram Matthew Papers, Virginia Tech University.

23. "Items of Interest," *Corinth Chanticleer*, June 12, 1863; Henry J. B. Cummings to wife, January 9 and March 15, 1863; Hubert, *History of the Fiftieth Regiment Illinois Volunteer Infantry,* 182, 184; "Local," *Corinth Chanticleer,* September 18, 1863.

24. Lorenzo A. Barker Diary, July 23, 1863; Robert Armstrong Diary, July 23, 1863; John A. Duckworth to William Rosser, undated; Hubert, *History of the Fiftieth Regiment Illinois Volunteer Infantry*, 177–178; Stevens, "Corinth Diary of Private Charles Stevens," 37; John N. Doak to Emma, March 6, 1863; Cluett, *History of the 57th Regiment Illinois Volunteer Infantry*, 64; Ambrose, *History of the Seventh Regiment Illinois Volunteer Infantry*, 166; Wright, *A Corporal's Story*, 90–91; Nelson, "Recollections"; Charles Watson to wife, July 25, 1863, Charles Watson Letters, 52nd Illinois File, CWIC; Frederick Sherwood Diary, May 13, 1863.

25. Lorenzo A. Barker Diary, July 7, 1863; T. W. Sweeny to Commander 66th Indiana, May 20, 1863, HC; George Wyckoff to wife, March 15, 1863.

26. I. M. Browne to friend, February 16, 1863, Ivan Lange Collection, SHSI (copy in 39th Iowa File, CWIC); Ambrose, *History of the Seventh Regiment Illinois Volunteer Infantry*, 135–138; Hubert, *History of the Fiftieth Regiment Illinois Volunteer Infantry*, 198; Laurens W. Wolcott to sister, March 11, 1863; John N. Doak to Emma, February 10, 1863; Hiram Matthew to brother, February 24, 1863, HC; Grenville Dodge to Cale, February 5, 1863, and Grenville Dodge to Nate, February 19, 1863, Dodge Family Papers, Denver Public Library.

27. Stevens, "Corinth Diary of Private Charles Stevens," 31; Wright, *A Corporal's Story*, 71; Cluett, *History of the 57th Regiment Illinois Volunteer Infantry*, 50; Smith, *History of Fuller's Ohio Brigade*, 132.

28. Hershel Hunniston to friend, undated, HC; Chamberlain, *History of the Eighty-first Regiment Ohio Infantry Volunteers*, 40; Stevens, "Corinth Diary of Private Charles Stevens," 31; Wright, *A Corporal's Story*, 76; Cluett, *History of the 57th Regiment Illinois Volunteer Infantry*, 59; Henry J. B. Cummings to wife, January 9, 1863.

29. Henry J. B. Cummings to wife, January 9, 1863; Wright, *A Corporal's Story*, 76; Stevens, "Corinth Diary of Private Charles Stevens," 31; Hershel Hunniston to friend, undated; Chamberlain, *History of the Eighty-first Regiment Ohio Infantry Volunteers*, 40; Cluett, *History of the 57th Regiment Illinois Volunteer Infantry*, 59.

30. Laurens W. Wolcott to sister, June 6, 1863; Nelson, "Recollections"; Grenville Dodge to Nate, May 27, 1863; "Local Department," *Corinth Chanticleer*, June 12, 1863; Horatio N. Marsden to Charles Woodruff, May 20, 1863, William F. Jones Papers, UMC; U. S. Grant to C. A. Reynolds, January 22, 1863, Butler-Gunsaulus Collection, University of Chicago; Chamberlain, *History of the Eighty-first Regiment Ohio Infantry Volunteers*, 37; "Letter from Corinth," *Cincinnati Daily Gazette*, June 20, 1863; George M. Reeder to P. E. Burke, December 25, 1862, Letter of Command, U.S. Army, Corinth District, Oct. 1862–Nov. 1863, Adjutant General's Office and 110th U.S. Colored Infantry, MDAH; John N. Doak to Emma, January 18 and October 4, 1863; Frederick Sherwood Diary, June 17, 1863.

31. Luther M. Meily to sister, May 9, 1863, Luther Melancthon Meily Letters, Civil War Collection, TSLA.

32. Walter Lindley to mother, April 12, 1863; Wright, *A Corporal's Story*, 77; Mildred Throne, ed., "An Iowa Doctor in Blue: The Letters of Seneca B. Thrall, 1862–1864," *Iowa Journal of History* 58, 2 (April 1960): 99; John A. Duckworth to William Rosser, undated.

CHAPTER 17. "ESTABLISHING FRIENDLY RELATIONS
WITH THE INHABITANTS"

1. Grenville Dodge to Nate, November 16, 1862, Dodge Family Papers, Denver Public Library; Stanley P. Hirshson, *Grenville M. Dodge: Soldier, Politician, Railroad Pioneer* (Bloomington: Indiana University Press, 1967), 62; Martha M. Bigelow, "Freedmen of the Mississippi Valley, 1862–1865," *Civil War History* 8 (March 1962): 38–47.

2. N. R. Dunn to father, October 18, 1862, N. R. Dunn Letters, University of Michigan; D. Leib Ambrose, *History of the Seventh Regiment Illinois Volunteer Infantry, from Its First Muster into the U.S. Service, April 25, 1861, to Its Final Muster out, July 9, 1865* (Springfield: Illinois Journal Company, 1868), 127; John Pray to John Bishop, January 22, 1863, John Pray Letters, 2nd Illinois Light Artillery, Battery B File, CWIC; Grenville Dodge to Cale, February 5, 1863, Dodge Family Papers; John N. Doak to Emma, January 18, 1863, John N. Doak Letters, 66th Illinois File, CWIC; James Redfield to wife, August 9, 1863, Redfield-Thornburg Family Papers, SHSI.

3. John Pray to John Bishop, January 22, 1863; Charles F. Hubert, *History of the Fiftieth Regiment Illinois Volunteer Infantry in the War of the Union* (Kansas City, MO: Western Veteran Publishing Company, 1894), 199.

4. John Eaton, *Grant, Lincoln and the Freedmen: Reminiscences of the Civil War, with Special Reference to the Work for the Contrabands and Freedmen of the Mississippi Valley* (New York: Longmans, Green, 1907), 55; Joseph K. Nelson, "Recollections of My Early Life," Miscellaneous Collection, USAMHI.

5. John A. Duckworth to William Rosser, undated, John A. Duckworth Letter, SHSI.

6. William H. Chamberlain, *History of the Eighty-first Regiment Ohio Infantry Volunteers during the War of the Rebellion* (Cincinnati, OH: Gazette Steam Printing House, 1865), 37; Cam Walker, "Corinth: The Story of a Contraband Camp," *Civil War History* 20, 1 (March 1974): 6–7; Warren B. Armstrong, "Union Chaplains and the Education of the Freedmen," *Journal of Negro History* 52, 2 (April 1967), 104–115. For accounts of other camps, see the Mary Tyler Peabody Mann Papers, LC.

7. George N. Carruthers, "Incidents and Deductions from Army Life in the Southwest," 1864, George North Carruthers Papers, LC; Joseph E. Brent, *Occupied Corinth: The Contraband Camp and the First Alabama Infantry of African Descent, 1862–1864* (Corinth, MS: City of Corinth, 1995), 9–10, 14; Walker, "Corinth: Story of a Contraband Camp," 10; D. W. Harrston to J. W. Barnes, August 21, 1863, Grenville M. Dodge Papers, SHSI (copy in 7th Kansas Cavalry File, CWIC); Levi Coffin, *Reminiscences of Levi Coffin, the Reputed President of the Underground Railroad; Being a Brief History of the Labors of a Lifetime in Behalf of the Slave, with the Stories of Numerous Fugitives, Who Gained Their Freedom through His Instrumentality, and Many Other Incidents* (Cincinnati, OH: Robert Clarke, 1880), 636; R. J. Oglesby to Nathan Kimball, April 22, 1863, 16th Army Corps, RG 393, NARA; John A. Duckworth to William Rosser, undated; Charles Wright, *A Corporal's Story: Experiences in the Ranks of Company C, 81st Ohio Vol. Infantry, during the War for the Maintenance of the Union, 1861–1864* (Philadelphia: James Beale, 1887), 82; Mark Boatman to brother, January 7, 1863, HC.

8. Bailey O. Bowden Diary, May 25, 1863, *CWTI* Collection, USAMHI (copy in 122nd Illinois File, CWIC); John A. Duckworth to William Rosser, undated; Charles Watson to wife, February 4, 1863, Charles Watson Letters, 52nd Illinois File, CWIC; Hubert, *History of the Fiftieth Regiment Illinois Volunteer Infantry,* 217.

9. Samuel A. Agnew Diary, December 9, 1863, University of North Carolina; Walker, "Corinth: Story of a Contraband Camp," 17–18; Hirshson, *Grenville M. Dodge,* 68, 73.

10. Carruthers, "Incidents and Deductions from Army Life in the Southwest"; Brent, *Occupied Corinth,* 9–10, 14; Walker, "Corinth: Story of a Contraband Camp," 10; D. W. Harrston to J. W. Barnes, August 21, 1863; Coffin, *Reminiscences of Levi Coffin,* 636; R. J. Oglesby to Nathan Kimball, April 22, 1863; Mary E. Carruthers to S. S. Jocelyn, September 15, 1863, and Mary E. Carruthers Certificate of Commission, September 22, 1863, American Missionary Association Archives, Amistad Research Center, Tulane University; Walker, "Corinth: Story of a Contraband Camp," 8, 13–14; Brent, *Occupied Corinth,* 3, 10–11, 13–14; "Letter from Corinth," *Cincinnati Daily Gazette,* June 20, 1863; Frederick Sherwood Diary, September 1, 1863, Earl Hess Collection, USAMHI.

11. Walker, "Corinth: Story of a Contraband Camp," 12; Brent, *Occupied Corinth,* 9–11; "Letter from Corinth."

12. "An Iowa Emancipator," *Annals of Iowa* 30, 4 (April 1950): 302–304; Walker, "Corinth: Story of a Contraband Camp," 9, 15; Brent, *Occupied Corinth,* 2, 18; Nelson, "Recollections of My Early Life"; "Letter from Corinth"; "A Card," *Corinth Chanticleer,* June 12, 1863; "Local Department," *Corinth Chanticleer,* June 12, 1863; Grenville Dodge to Nate, May 24, 1863.

13. "A Card"; "Local Department"; "An Iowa Emancipator," 302–304; Nelson, "Recollections of My Early Life"; Walker, "Corinth: Story of a Contraband Camp," 9, 15; "Letter from Corinth"; Brent, *Occupied Corinth,* 2, 18.

14. "Letter from Corinth"; Hubert, *History of the Fiftieth Regiment Illinois Volunteer Infantry,* 178; John K. Mahon, ed., "The Civil War Letters of Samuel Mahon, Seventh Iowa Infantry," *Iowa Journal of History* 51, 3 (July 1953): 245.

15. James Redfield to wife, May 31, 1863; "First Alabama Infantry," *Corinth Chanticleer,* June 12, 1863.

16. Eaton, *Grant, Lincoln and the Freedmen,* 55; Bailey O. Bowden Diary, May 15, 1863; Hubert, *History of the Fiftieth Regiment Illinois Volunteer Infantry,* 198–199; James Redfield to wife, May 16, 1863; Walker, "Corinth: Story of a Contraband Camp," 14; Brent, *Occupied Corinth,* 14.

17. Chamberlain, *History of the Eighty-first Regiment Ohio Infantry Volunteers,* 42; Wright, *A Corporal's Story,* 82; Frederick Sherwood Diary, January 18, 1863.

18. John Lomax to William Lomax, December 12, 1862, John Lomax Papers, UMC; John N. Doak to Emma, April 12, 1863; Emory S. Huston to uncle, May 1, 1863, HC; Charles Stevens, "The Corinth Diary of Private Charles Stevens," *Blue and Gray Education Society Papers* 18 (Fall 2006): 41; John Tyler Jr. to William L. Yancey, October 15, 1862, John Tyler Jr. Letter, UMC.

19. Chamberlain, *History of the Eighty-first Regiment Ohio Infantry Volunteers,* 37; Horatio N. Marsden to Charles Woodruff, May 20, 1863, William F. Jones Papers, UMC;

William Maple to Mathers, June 23, 1863, HC; James M. Thurston Diary, October 9, 1862, Massachusetts Historical Society; J. W. Barnes to Colonel Alexander, September 8, 1863, Letter of Command, U.S. Army, Corinth District, Oct. 1862–Nov. 1863, Adjutant General's Office and 110th U.S. Colored Infantry, MDAH.

20. "Letter from Corinth"; John A. Duckworth to William Rosser, undated; Hubert, *History of the Fiftieth Regiment Illinois Volunteer Infantry*, 199.

21. Stevens, "Corinth Diary of Private Charles Stevens," 29, 39; "Aftermath of Corinth Battle Left Citizens Horrified," *Jackson Clarion Ledger*, July 25, 1982; "Recollections of a 'Yankee' Girl Who Visted Occupied Corinth," May 16, 1954, unidentified newspaper clipping in Corinth Subject File, MDAH.

22. John A. Duckworth to William Rosser, undated; Chamberlain, *History of the Eighty-first Regiment Ohio Infantry Volunteers*, 42; Mahon, "Civil War Letters of Samuel Mahon," 242; Wimer Bedford Memoir, undated, 16, LC; "Programme of the Grand Military Ball Given by the Commissioned Officers of the Garrison of Corinth on New Year's Eve (December 31, 1862)," HC; Hubert, *History of the Fiftieth Regiment Illinois Volunteer Infantry*, 178; Lorenzo A. Barker Diary, March 14 and April 4, 1863, Archives of Michigan; B. F. Stadler to parents, March 13, 1863, HC; George E. Spencer to Colonel Miller, July 30, 1863, Letter of Command, U.S. Army, Corinth District, Oct. 1862–Nov. 1863, Adjutant General's Office and 110th U.S. Colored Infantry, MDAH; J. W. Barnes to Colonel Miller, September 8, 1863, ibid.

23. Charles Watson to wife, July 6, 1863, Charles Watson Letters, 52nd Illinois File, CWIC; Stevens, "Corinth Diary of Private Charles Stevens," 30; Horatio N. Marsden to Charles Woodruff, May 20, 1863; Ambrose, *History of the Seventh Regiment Illinois Volunteer Infantry*, 175; William Kavanaugh Memoirs, undated, 55, William H. Kavanaugh Papers, UMC; Mark Boatman to brother, January 7, 1863, HC.

24. "Local Department"; John M. Ruby to sister, December 6, 1863, HC.

25. Grenville Dodge to Nate, November 16 and December 28, 1862; Hirshson, *Grenville M. Dodge*, 62; Samuel A. Agnew Diary, October 21, 1863; Lorenzo A. Barker Diary, December 31, 1862; Ambrose, *History of the Seventh Regiment Illinois Volunteer Infantry*, 141; Frederick Sherwood Diary, January 17, 1863; Hubert, *History of the Fiftieth Regiment Illinois Volunteer Infantry*, 184, 202; "An Iowa Emancipator," 305.

26. Wright, *A Corporal's Story*, 72; Chamberlain, *History of the Eighty-first Regiment Ohio Infantry Volunteers*, 43–46; Laurens W. Wolcott to sister, December 24, 1862, HC; George M. Reeder to Captain Carmichael, December 25 and 29, 1862, Letter of Command, U.S. Army, Corinth District, Oct. 1862–Nov. 1863, Adjutant General's Office and 110th U.S. Colored Infantry, MDAH; *OR*, 1, 17(1): 300–301, 549–551; Henry J. B. Cummings to John R. Simpson, December 31, 1862, Henry Johnson Brodhead Cummings Papers, SHSI; I. M. Browne to friend, February 16, 1863, Ivan Lange Collection, SHSI; William W. Cluett, *History of the 57th Regiment Illinois Volunteer Infantry, from Muster in, Dec. 26, 1861, to Muster out, July 7, 1865* (Princeton, IL: T. P. Streeter, 1886), 50–52; Mahon, "Civil War Letters of Samuel Mahon," 241; Charles H. Smith, *The History of Fuller's Ohio Brigade, 1861–1865: Its Great March, with Roster Portraits, Battle Maps and Biographies* (Cleveland, OH: Press of A. J. Watt, 1909), 122–128; Ambrose, *History*

of the Seventh Regiment Illinois Volunteer Infantry, 122–125, 128; Laurens W. Wolcott to sister, January 6, 1863.

27. *OR*, 1, 23(1): 246–250; R. J. Oglesby to Nathan Kimball, April 22, 1863; John Hunt to mother, May 3, 1863, John R. Hunt Letters, *CWTI* Collection, USAMHI (copy in 81st Ohio File, CWIC); Robert Armstrong Diary, May 2, 1863, Indiana Historical Society (copy in 66th Indiana File, CWIC); Hiram Matthew to wife, May 3, 1863, Hiram Matthew Papers, Virginia Tech University; Hirshson, *Grenville M. Dodge*, 71; Horatio N. Marsden to Charles Woodruff, June 8, 1863; Ambrose, *History of the Seventh Regiment Illinois Volunteer Infantry*, 146–159; Henry J. B. Cummings to wife, May 3, 1863; Sereno Bridge to wife, May 10, 1863, HC; "Letter from Corinth"; Chamberlain, *History of the Eighty-first Regiment Ohio Infantry Volunteers*, 46–48, 54; Cluett, *History of the 57th Regiment Illinois Volunteer Infantry*, 60–63; Smith, *History of Fuller's Ohio Brigade*, 132–133; Grenville M. Dodge, *The Battle of Atlanta and Other Campaigns, Addresses, etc.* (Council Bluffs, IA: Monarch Printing Company, 1911), 115–116.

28. Martin V. Miller to sister, August 19 and September 19, 1863, HC; Lorenzo A. Barker Diary, December 19, 1862, and April 14, 1863; Robert Armstrong Diary, July 30, 1863; Samuel A. Agnew Diary, October 8, 1863; James Redfield to wife, August 3, 1863; James Redfield to sir, July 20, 1863, Redfield-Thornburg Family Papers, SHSI; Hubert, *History of the Fiftieth Regiment Illinois Volunteer Infantry*, 202; Ambrose, *History of the Seventh Regiment Illinois Volunteer Infantry*, 173, 177–178; Cluett, *History of the 57th Regiment Illinois Volunteer Infantry*, 65; Stevens, "Corinth Diary of Private Charles Stevens," 36; D. W. Harrston to J. W. Barnes, August 21, 1863; *OR*, 2, 5: 185; *OR*, 2, 6: 123.

29. H. T. Noble et al., *Military History and Reminiscences of the Thirteenth Regiment of Illinois Volunteer Infantry in the Civil War in the United States, 1861–1865* (Chicago: Woman's Temperance Publishing Association, 1892), 347–348.

30. Samuel A. Agnew Diary, October 12, 1863; H. T. Card to family, October 7, 1863, H. T. Card Letter, LSU; Noble et al., *Military History and Reminiscences of the Thirteenth Regiment of Illinois Volunteer Infantry*, 347–349; James Shadle to wife, October 7, 1863, HC; *OR*, 1, 31(3): 197; George Wyckoff to wife, November 8, 1863, Wyckoff Family Papers, Missouri Historical Society; *OR*, 1, 32(2): 70; *OR*, 1, 31(1): 2, 623; Cluett, *History of the 57th Regiment Illinois Volunteer Infantry*, 66; John N. Doak to Emma, November 15, 1863; Samuel A. Agnew Diary, October 17, 1863.

31. For the Meridian campaign, see Buck T. Foster, *Sherman's Mississippi Campaign* (Tuscaloosa: University of Alabama Press, 2006).

32. *OR*, 1, 32(2): 70, 76, 84, 124–125, 134–135, 157–158, 167–168, 180–181, 190–191, 200–201, 213, 630; Walker, "Corinth: Story of a Contraband Camp," 10, 19; Frederick H. Dyer, *A Compendium of the War of the Rebellion*, 3 vols. (Cedar Rapids, IA: Torch Press, 1908), 3:1732; Brent, *Occupied Corinth*, 14, 29; George Bargus Diary, November 21, 1863, *CWTI* Collection, USAMHI; *OR*, 1, 45(2): 655; Special Order 146, January 24, 1864, Special Post Fund Orders Issued, RG 393, E 296, NARA.

33. *OR*, 1, 32(2): 636; Eliza Suggs, *Shadow and Sunshine* (Omaha, NE: n.p., 1906), 45; Richard Taylor to P. G. T. Beauregard, November 18, 1864, P. G. T. Beauregard Papers, MDAH; *OR*, 1, 45(2): 655; Samuel A. Agnew Diary, January 30 and May 2, 1864; *OR*, 1,

39(3): 855. For the Federals' Mississippi raids in 1864, see Edwin C. Bearss, *Forrest at Brice's Cross Roads and in North Mississippi in 1864* (Dayton, OH: Morningside, 1979).

34. R. E. Corry to wife, June 17, 1864, Robert Emmet Corry Letters, Auburn University; *OR*, 1, 52(2): 778; *OR*, 1, 45(1): 866, 1249; *OR*, 1, 45(2): 655, 681–682, 717, 723, 737–738, 749–750, 753–755, 759, 773; Jack D. Welsh, *Two Confederate Hospitals and Their Patients: Atlanta to Opelika* (Macon, GA: Mercer University Press, 2005), 94–95; W. J. McMurray, *History of the Twentieth Tennessee Regiment Volunteer Infantry, C.S.A.* (Nashville: Publication Committee, 1904), 148; Edwin C. Bearss, "Grierson's Winter Raid on the Mobile and Ohio Railroad," *Military Affairs* 24, 1 (Spring 1960): 20–37; J. T. Peterson, "Historical Sketch of Co. E, 12th La. Regt. Vols.," undated, Evander McNair Graham Family Papers, Louisiana Tech University.

35. *OR*, 1, 45(1): 83, 94; Wales W. Wood, *A History of the Ninety-fifth Regiment Illinois Infantry Volunteers, from Its Organization in the Fall of 1862, until Its Final Discharge from the United States Service, in 1865* (Chicago: Tribune Company's Book and Job Printing Office, 1865), 151–152.

36. James K. Newton, *A Wisconsin Boy in Dixie: The Selected Letters of James K. Newton*, ed. Stephen E. Ambrose (Madison: University of Wisconsin Press, 1961), 138; Byron R. Abernethy, ed., *Private Elisha Stockwell, Jr. Sees the Civil War* (Norman: University of Oklahoma Press, 1958), 147, 200; Wood, *History of the Ninety-fifth Regiment Illinois Infantry Volunteers*, 152.

37. Records of Police Court, 1857–1862, Old Tishomingo County; Probate Docket No. 2, 1860–1865, Old Tishomingo County; Appraisements, 1861–1870, Old Tishomingo County; Land Deed Record Book X, 1859–1866, Old Tishomingo County; Administrator Bonds and Letters, 1858–1870, Book 1, Old Tishomingo County; Probate Court Minutes, Book Q, 1861–1865, Old Tishomingo County; Miscellaneous Records, Book 9, 1860–1867, Old Tishomingo County; and "History of Old Tishomingo County," 32–33, all in Alcorn County Chancery Clerk Archives; S. M. Nabors, *History of Old Tishomingo County* (Corinth, MS: n.p., 1940), 24–25; Dunbar Rowland, *Mississippi*, 2 vols. (Spartanburg, SC: Reprint Company, 1976), 2:419; Gale Judkins, "Edward C. Gillenwaters," Edward C. Gillenwaters Biographical File, Alcorn County Genealogical Society; Board Minutes, August 25 and September 9, 1865, 1, 7, Mayor and Selectmen Board Minutes, 1865–1887, Corinth City Hall Archives; Special Order 2, September 29, 1862, Special Orders Issued, RG 393, E 293, NARA.

38. *OR*, 1, 49(1): 612–613. For more on Unionism in Mississippi, see Timothy B. Smith, *Mississippi in the Civil War: The Home Front* (Jackson: University Press of Mississippi, 2010), 125–142.

39. *OR*, 1, 49(2): 752, 791, 830, 906; *OR*, 1, 49(1): 392.

Epilogue

1. Cornelius C. Platter Diary, November 24, 1864, University of Georgia; George Bargus Diary, October 4, 1863, *CWTI* Collection, USAMHI; Alonzo L. Brown, *History of the*

Fourth Regiment of Minnesota Infantry Volunteers during the Great Rebellion 1861–1865 (St. Paul: Pioneer Press Company, 1892), 127; Samuel H. Davis, "Chronicle of a Mississippi Soldier: The Civil War Letters of Samuel H. Davis of Kemper County," ed. Henry E. Mattox, *Journal of Mississippi History* 52, 3 (1990): 214; T. J. Walker Reminiscences, 7, University of Tennessee; John Clinton Memo, undated, William Hicks Jackson Papers, TSLA.

2. W. H. Tunnard, *A Southern Record: The History of the 3rd Regiment Louisiana Infantry,* ed. Edwin C. Bearss (Dayton, OH: Morningside, 1970), 208.

3. Special Order 105, October 30, 1869; Special Order 5, January 26, 1869; Lloyd Wheaton to John Tyler, February 7, 1868; and Lloyd Wheaton to N. Mask, August 22 and November 8, 1867, all in Proceedings of Councils, RG 393, E 297, NARA. See also E 288, Letters Sent, April 1867–July 1870, and E 290, Register of Letters Received and Endorsements Sent, April 1867–July 1870, RG 393, NARA.

4. U.S. Quartermaster Department, *Roll of Honor: Names of Soldiers Who Died in Defense of the American Union Interred in the National Cemeteries,* 27 vols. (Washington, DC: Government Printing Office, 1869), 20:1; Ben Earl Kitchens, *Rosecrans Meets Price: The Battle of Iuka, Mississippi* (Florence, AL: Thornwood Book Publishers, 1987), 177. For more on national cemeteries, see Dean W. Holt, *American Military Cemeteries: A Comprehensive Illustrated Guide to the Hallowed Grounds of the United States, Including Cemeteries Overseas* (Jefferson, NC: McFarland, 1992); Tunnard, *Southern Record,* 208.

5. "A Writer," *Southern Bivouac* 3, 2 (October 1884): 87.

6. David W. Ogden Reminiscences, undated, 28, William S. Ray Papers, University of Arkansas.

7. "Monument at Corinth," *Confederate Veteran* 2, 8 (August 1894): 249; "Monument to Colonel Rogers," *Confederate Veteran* 21, 3 (March 1913): 102–103; David W. Ogden Reminiscences, 26–29; Ezra J. Warner, *Generals in Gray: Lives of the Confederate Commanders* (Baton Rouge: Louisiana State University Press, 1959), 140.

8. David W. Ogden Reminiscences, 29–30.

9. Margaret Greene Rogers, *Civil War Corinth* (Corinth, MS: Rankin Printery, 1989), 43.

10. Ibid.; *Corinth Civil War Boundary Adjustment Study: Corinth Unit of the Shiloh National Military Park: Environmental Assessment* (Washington, DC: National Park Service, 2004), 1–3; Corinth National Historic Register Nomination, 1976, Corinth Battlefield 0-1999 Subject File, MDAH; Corinth National Historic Landmark Nomination, 1971, Corinth Civil War 1 Subject File, MDAH; Chester L. Sumners to Theodore G. Bilbo, March 30, 1940, Corinth Civil War 2 Subject File, MDAH. For the earliest ideas about the preservation of Corinth, see the voluminous newspaper clippings in the various Corinth Subject Files, MDAH.

11. *Special Resource Study: Corinth, Mississippi* (Washington, DC: National Park Service, 2003), 1, 90–95; *Corinth Civil War Boundary Adjustment Study,* 1–3; Robert K. Sutton, ed., *Rally on the High Ground: The National Park Service Symposium on the Civil War* (Fort Washington, PA: Eastern National, 2001).

BIBLIOGRAPHY

Manuscript Collections

Alabama Department of Archives and History, Montgomery, Alabama
  Earl Van Dorn Papers
Alcorn County Chancery Clerk Archives, Corinth, Mississippi
  Administrator Bonds and Letters, 1858–1870, Book 1, Old Tishomingo County
  Appraisements, 1861–1870, Old Tishomingo County
  History of Old Tishomingo County
  Land Deed Record Book X, 1859–1866, Old Tishomingo County
  Miscellaneous Records, Book 9, 1860–1867, Old Tishomingo County
  Probate Court Minutes, Book Q, 1861–1865, Old Tishomingo County
  Probate Docket No. 2, 1860–1865, Old Tishomingo County
  Records of Police Court, 1857–1862, Old Tishomingo County
Alcorn County Genealogical Society Archives, Corinth, Mississippi
  Edward C. Gillenwaters Biographical File
  James E. Stewart Biographical File
Amistad Research Center, Tulane University, New Orleans, Louisiana
  American Missionary Association Archives
Archives of Michigan, Lansing, Michigan
  Civil War Diary of Lorenzo A. Barker
  Civil War Letters of Mack and Nan Ewing
  Amori B. Cook Papers
Arizona State University, Tempe, Arizona
  George W. Lennard Collection
Arkansas History Commission, Little Rock, Arkansas
  Rufus W. Daniel Diary
Atlanta History Center, Atlanta, Georgia
  William N. Mattison Papers
Auburn University, Auburn, Alabama
  Robert Emmet Corry Letters
  S. H. Dent Papers
  George Family Letters

Augustana College, Rock Island, Illinois
    G. D. Molineaux Diary
Baylor University, Waco, Texas
    Ross Family Papers
Bolivar-Hardeman County Public Library, Bolivar, Tennessee
    Battle of Corinth
Bowling Green State University, Bowling Green, Ohio
    Kehrwecker Family Papers
    George Kryder Papers
    William Shanks Diary
    Liberty Warner Papers
Bradley University, Peoria, Illinois
    Willit Samuel Haynes Letters
Brigham Young University, Provo, Utah
    John W. Morrison Letters
Brown County Historical Society, New Ulm, Minnesota
    August Schilling Diary
Brown University, Providence, Rhode Island
    Ole A. Hanse Letter
    Lincoln Collection
Chicago Historical Society, Chicago, Illinois
    James Birdseye McPherson Collection
    George Sawin Letters
    James Roberts Zearing Collection
Cincinnati Historical Society, Cincinnati, Ohio
    Frank J. Jones Civil War Letters
Corinth City Hall Archives, Corinth, Mississippi
    Mayor and Selectmen Board Minutes, 1865–1887
Corinth Civil War Interpretive Center, Corinth, Mississippi
    Camp Davies File
    Hedges Collection of Civil War Corinth
    M. A. Miller Sketchbook
    E. O. C. Ord Letters
    Thomas E. Parson, "A Study of the Artillery at the Battles of Corinth, Davis Bridge
        and Young's Bridge, October 3–5, 1862"
    Isaac F. Quinby Letter
    Regimental Files
        Richard D. Andrews Letter—21st Missouri File
        Robert Armstrong Diary—66th Indiana File
        Jason Arter Letter—31st Ohio File
        Abiel M. Barker Letters—32nd Illinois File
        Bailey O. Bowden Diary—122nd Illinois File

Audley S. H. Boyd Letter—3rd Missouri Cavalry File
I. M. Browne Letter—39th Iowa File
Robert J. Burdette Memoir—47th Illinois File
William R. Burke Diary—50th Alabama File
Richard W. Burt Letter—76th Ohio File
Charles S. Cotter Letter—1st Ohio Battery File
Frank J. Crawford Letter—53rd Illinois File
W. L. Culberson Letter—19th Louisiana File
Henry J. B. Cummings Letters—39th Iowa File
John N. Doak Letters—66th Illinois File
George Dobson Letters—10th Mississippi File
John A. Duckworth Letter—2nd Iowa File
Uriah M. Glover Letters—66th Indiana File
D. W. Harrston Letter—7th Kansas Cavalry File
Chester Townsend Hart Diary—15th Illinois File
Historical Memoranda of the 52nd Regiment—52nd Illinois File
John R. Hunt Letter—81st Ohio File
George C. Jenkins Diary—2nd Illinois Light Artillery, Battery B File
Hugh Johnson Letters—2nd Iowa Cavalry File
Charles C. Labuzan Diary—42nd Alabama File
P. P. Lash Letter—30th Indiana File
Alexander Livaudais Diary—18th Louisiana File
George S. Milan Letter—6th Texas Cavalry File
Joseph K. Nelson Recollections—81st Ohio File
J. H. Phillips Letters—22nd Illinois File
John Pray Letters—2nd Illinois Light Artillery, Battery B File
Thomas Jesse Rankin Letter—7th Mississippi File
James Redfield Letters—39th Iowa File
Van Reeves Letter—11th Iowa File
Garret W. Schreurs Diary—7th Iowa File
E. B. Sellers Letter—1st Texas File
James S. Slaughter Letter—5th Mississippi File
Abraham Slough Letters—59th Indiana File
C. B. Smith Letter—4th Minnesota File
John W. Sprague Papers—63rd Ohio File
David Spurgin Letters—16th Iowa File
Louiss Stagg Letters—16th Louisiana File
B. F. Stephens Letter—9th Texas Cavalry File
Ras Stirman Letters—Stirman's Arkansas Sharpshooters File
John Kennedy Street Letters—3rd Texas Cavalry File
Joseph Mitchell Strickling Diary—39th Ohio File
Various Newspapers—8th Wisconsin File

    Charles Watson Letters—52nd Illinois File
    W. G. Whitfield, "Battle of Corinth, Miss."—35th Alabama File
    W. H. Wiseman Letter—10th Mississippi File
Cornell University, Ithaca, New York
    T. A. Montgomery Letters
    Gail and Stephen Rudin Collection
Denver Public Library, Denver, Colorado
    Dodge Family Papers
Detroit Public Library, Detroit, Michigan
    Henry A. Buck Papers
Dubuque County Historical Society, Dubuque, Iowa
    David B. Henderson Papers
Duke University, Special Collections Library, Durham, North Carolina
    William L. Broaddus Papers
    Absolem F. Dantzler Papers
    Robert W. Honnoll Papers
    John E. Magee Diary
    H. H. Price Papers
    John W. Royse Papers
    James Wall Scully Papers
    Alexander Peter Stewart Letters
    Mary Elizabeth (McClain) Sword Papers, 1822–1885
Emory University, Atlanta, Georgia
    Bomar Family Papers
    Honnell Family Papers
    William Parkinson Papers
Filson Historical Society, Louisville, Kentucky
    Elmore (Union Soldier) Letter
    Foote Family Papers
Harvard University, Cambridge, Massachusetts
    Frederick M. Dearborn Collection
Rutherford B. Hayes Presidential Center, Fremont, Ohio
    Robert S. Rice Papers
Hedges Collection of Civil War Corinth, Corinth, Mississippi
    George Barton Letter
    Frank Batchelor Letter
    John Beach Letter
    P. G. T. Beauregard Memorandum
    R. Belser Letter
    John Boatman Letter
    Mark Boatman Letters
    Arthur I. Borland Letter

Sereno Bridge Letter
William Brown Letter
Charles Cotter Letter
Fort Randall Map
Arthur Fulkerson Letter
"General Orders 21"
Daniel Gober Report
"Headquarters Pass"
Hershel Hunniston Letter
Emory S. Huston Letter
Matt Kemper Letter
John F. Kimbley Letter
A. F. Lee Letter
Walter Lindley Letters
"List of Quartermaster Stores Received"
William Maple Letter
P. Marchant Letter
Hiram Matthew Letters
D. F. McGowan Letters
S. M. Meek Letter
Martin V. Miller Letters
"Ordnance Receipt"
John Patton Letter
Ebenezer Pearce Letter
"Programme of the Grand Military Ball Given by the Commissioned Officers of the
    Garrison of Corinth on New Year's Eve (December 31, 1862)"
W. H. Riddick Letter
John M. Ruby Letter
James Shadle Letters
Albert Spelman Letter
B. F. Stadler Letter
S. S. Stanton Letter
Charles Stevens Diary
Thomas W. Sweeny Letter
John Thompkins Letter
Freeman Williams Letter
Laurens W. Wolcott Letters
Historic New Orleans Collection, New Orleans, Louisiana
    Schaumburg-Wright Family Papers
Huntington Library, San Marino, California
    Eldridge Collection
    Mansfield Lovell Papers

Haller Nutt Papers
T. K. Smith Collection
Thomas William Sweeny Papers
Illinois State Historical Library, Springfield, Illinois
Henry P. Andrews Papers
James W. Anthony and Charles E. Smith Papers
Alphonso Barto Papers
David P. Bunn Diary
George Lemon Childress Diary
John N. Cromwell Papers
Crum Family Papers
David Dewolf Papers
Charles H. Floyd Papers
U. S. Grant Letters
John A. Griffin Papers
Frank E. Hanaford Civil War Reminiscences
J. L. Harris Papers
R. G. Ingersoll Papers
William D. T. Travis Papers
Wallace-Dickey Papers
John S. Wilcox Papers
Indiana Historical Society, Indianapolis, Indiana
Robert Armstrong Diary
Aden G. Cavins Letters
Helen Coleman Collection
David W. Daily Papers
William F. Hinkle Diary
John D. Martin Journal
Alfred Shields Letters
Edward P. Stanfield Letters
Henry R. Strong Diary
James S. Thomas Letters
James C. Veatch Papers
Indiana State Library, Indianapolis, Indiana
Will H. Judkins Diary
Meeks Family Papers
James C. Vanderbilt Civil War Letters
Indiana State University, Terre Haute, Indiana
Neff-Guttridge Collection
Kansas Historical Society, Topeka, Kansas
Samuel Ayers Letters
John Brown Jr. Collection
Kate Newland Collection

Library of Congress, Washington, D.C.
    Pierre Gustave Toutant Beauregard Papers
    Wimer Bedford Papers
    Alpheus S. Bloomfield Papers
    Joshua T. Bradford Diary
    Braxton Bragg Papers
    George North Carruthers Papers
    Douglas J. and Rufus W. Cater Papers
    Samuel Henry Eells Papers
    John N. Ferguson Papers
    Balzar Grebe Papers
    Walter Q. Gresham Papers
    Hiram P. Howe Papers
    John S. Jackman Journal
    Joseph Lester Papers
    Mary Tyler Peabody Mann Papers
    Almon Ferdinand Rockwell Papers
    Theodore Edgar Saint John Papers
    Thomas West Sherman Collection
    Bela T. St. John Papers
    William R. Stimson Collection
    Earl Van Dorn Papers
    John Whitten Diary
    William Frank Wilder Papers
Louisiana State University, Baton Rouge, Louisiana
    Bennett Family Papers
    H. T. Card Letter
    William J. Christie Letters
    George D. Cotton Letters
    Ezekiel John Ellis Letter
    James Foster Family Correspondence
    Charles Grundy Letter
    William George Hale Papers
    Josiah Knighton and Family Papers
    James Phelan Letter
    Thomas Richardson Letter
    Louis Stagg Letters
    P. D. Stephenson Memoirs
Louisiana Tech University, Ruston, Louisiana
    Evander McNair Graham Family Papers
    Roland Oliver Papers
MacMurray College, Jacksonville, Illinois
    John Hill Ferguson Diary

Massachusetts Historical Society, Boston, Massachusetts
    Henry Van Ness Boynton Papers
    James M. Thurston Diary
Minnesota Historical Society, St. Paul, Minnesota
    William Arkins and Family Papers
    Christie Family Letters
    Lucius F. Hubbard and Family Papers
    William B. McGrorty and Family Papers
    Richard S. Reeves Papers
    Joseph Risedorph Papers
Mississippi Department of Archives and History, Jackson, Mississippi
    P. G. T. Beauregard Papers
    J. A. Bigger Diary
    Narcissa L. Black Diary
    Civil War Letters
    Jobe M. Foxworth Diary
    J. W. Greenman Diary
    Patrick Henry Papers
    Joseph J. Hunter Manuscript
    Irion-Neilson Family Papers
    Jesse R. Kirkland Papers
    T. J. Koger Collection
    Letter of Command, U.S. Army, Corinth District, Oct. 1862–Nov. 1863, Adjutant General's Office and 110th U.S. Colored Infantry
    Lusk Family Papers
    William H. McCardle Papers
    Thomas J. McKean Papers
    Samuel M. Meek and Family Papers
    Emily Van Dorn Miller Papers
    Minutes of the Military Board
    James S. Oliver Papers
    Walter A. Overton Diary
    Houston Huling Parker Diary
    Sears-Featherston Sword Research Collection
    Thomas Smith Manuscript
    Subject Files
        Civil War Corinth 1
        Civil War Corinth 2
        Corinth Battlefield 0-1999
    N. L. Watts Letter
    J. J. Wilson Papers
    John A. Wilson Letters
    William Yerger Papers

Mississippi State University, Starkville, Mississippi
    Michael B. Ballard Collection
    Isaac E. Hirsh Papers
    Malloy Papers
    M. E. Sykes Letters
    Isham W. Thomas Letters
    Thornton Collection
    John S. West Letter
Missouri Historical Society, St. Louis, Missouri
    John S. Bowen Papers
    Civil War Collection
        Thomas Hogan Letters
        David McKnight Diary
    McEwen Family Papers
    Herman B. Miller Papers
    William H. Miller Papers
    Thomas C. Reynolds Papers
    Thomas L. Snead Papers
    Joel Strong Alphabetical File
    Wyckoff Family Papers
Montauk Historical Site, Clermont, Iowa
    William Larrabee Collection
Murray State University, Murray, Kentucky
    W. J. Stubblefield Diary
National Archives and Records Administration, Washington, D.C.
    Record Group 109
        Confederate Regimental Muster and Pay Rolls
            36th Mississippi Infantry
        Confederate States Army Casualties, Lists and Narrative Reports 1861–1865
        General and Special Orders—Price's Command, Army of the West
        Letters Sent—Price's Command, Army of the West
        Letters and Telegrams Sent—Van Dorn's Command, Army of the West
        Thomas L. Snead Papers
        Telegrams Received—Van Dorn's Command, Army of the West
    Record Group 153
        Court Martial Case File KK 303—Robert C. Murphy
    Record Group 393
        Letters Sent—Fuller's Brigade, Army of the Mississippi
        Letters Sent, June–September 1862—Post of Corinth
        Letters Sent, April 1867–July 1870—Post of Corinth
        Proceedings of Councils—Post of Corinth
        Register of Letters Received and Endorsements Sent, April 1867–July 1870—Post
            of Corinth

Special Orders Issued, September 1862–September 1863—Post of Corinth
Special Orders Issued, October 1863–January 1864—Post of Corinth
Nebraska State Historical Society, Lincoln, Nebraska
    Phinehas Orlando Avery Papers
    Henry V. Hoagland Papers
Newberry Library, Chicago, Illinois
    Ephraim C. Dawes Papers
    Charles W. Gallentine Letters
    Oliver Perry Newberry Papers
Northeast Mississippi Museum Association, Corinth, Mississippi
    A. H. Brown Diary
    Michael J. Dodge Letter—10th Iowa Papers
    Henry S. Doty Letter—52nd Illinois Papers
    John Edwards Letters
    H. S. Halbert Letter—6th Texas Cavalry Papers
    Colonel John D. Martin Obituary
    T. G. Prichett Letters
    "Reminiscences by a Confederate Soldier of the Battles of Iuka and Corinth"
    C. J. Sergent Diary
    Will Snyder Letter
    Joseph M. Stetson Letters
    M. Ebenezer Wescott Letters
    Charles Wilkins Letter—1st United States Infantry Papers
    Robert S. Williams Letters
Northeast Regional Library, Corinth, Mississippi
    M. A. Miller Sketchbook of 1860 Corinth
Ohio Historical Society, Columbus, Ohio
    Cyrus S. Bolton Diary
    Jacob Brunner Letters
    Ephraim S. Holloway Papers
    DeWitt Clinton Loudon Papers
    Lewis Mathewson Papers
    William B. Mitchell Papers
    James O'Halligan Papers
    Joseph Phillips Letter
    David Harrison Thomas Papers
    Abia M. Zeller Papers
Rice University, Houston, Texas
    Philip H. Broun Family U.S. Civil War Papers
Shiloh National Military Park, Shiloh, Tennessee
    Historical Reports
        Cecil A. Duke, "Confederate Intrenchments"

Regimental Files
    John A. Duckworth Letter—2nd Iowa File
    W. A. Howard Letter—33rd Tennessee Infantry File
    A. B. Monahan Letters—63rd Ohio File
    Armand Pallissard Letter—53rd Illinois File
Southern Illinois University, Carbondale, Illinois
    Joseph Skipworth Papers
Stanford University, Stanford, California
    Edward Otho Cresap Ord Papers
State Historical Society of Iowa, Des Moines, Iowa
    Henry Johnson Brodhead Cummings Papers
    Grenville M. Dodge Papers
    John A. Duckworth Letter
    Ivan Lange Collection
    Redfield-Thornburg Family Papers
    Garret W. Schreurs Diary
    W. W. Warner Collection
State Historical Society of Iowa, Iowa City, Iowa
    James C. Parrott Papers
    Franklin B. Reed Civil War Letters
State Historical Society of Wisconsin, Madison, Wisconsin
    William Brown Letters
    E. B. Quiner Papers
    James Monroe Tyler Diary
Tennessee State Library and Archives, Nashville, Tennessee
    Robert Franklin Bunting Collection
    Robert H. Cartmell Papers
    Civil War Collection
        George R. Elliot Diary
        5th Tennessee Infantry
        J. W. Harmon Memoirs
        John Johnston Reminiscences
        Sarah Jane Johnston Diary
        Luther Melancthon Meily Letters
        Thomas B. Wilson Diary
    Rachel Carter Craighead Diary
    William Mark Eames Papers
    Eugene Frederic Falconnet Papers
    John Hill Ferguson Diary
    John Hooper Gates Papers
    Albert Theodore Goodloe Papers
    William Hicks Jackson Papers

Pounds Family Papers
Theodore Gillard Trimmier Papers
Texas State Archives, Austin, Texas
Samuel Bell Maxey Papers
Tulane University, New Orleans, Louisiana
Civil War Miscellaneous Series
Rosemonde and Emile Kuntz Collection
Clement Stanford Watson Family Papers
United States Army Military History Institute, Carlisle, Pennsylvania
Leslie Anders Collection
Nehemiah David Starr Letters
Civil War Miscellaneous Collection
Hugh T. Carlisle Reminiscences
Edwin Dean Memoirs
John J. McKee Diary
Joseph K. Nelson Recollections
William Wade Diary
Civil War Times Illustrated Collection
George Bargus Diary
Lionel Baxter Collection
Mansfield Lovell Letter
Bailey O. Bowden Diary
L. B. Claiborne Memoirs
Marcus O. Frost Letters
John R. Hunt Letters
Lewis Henry Little Diary
David McKinney Diary
Lewis P. Phillips Memoirs
Isaiah G. W. Steedman Letters
Harrisburg Civil War Roundtable Collection
William A. Ruyle Memoir
Earl Hess Collection
Frederick Sherwood Diary
Murray J. Smith Collection
Octavia Sulivane Letter
Vanamburg Family Papers
West-Stanley-Wright Family Papers
United States Military Academy, West Point, New York
Jacob Ammen Papers
Frank B. Foster Letters
University of Arkansas, Fayetteville, Arkansas
Joseph M. Bailey Papers
Rebecca Stirman Davidson Family Papers

Robert and Sephronica Clark McCollom Papers
David W. Ogden Reminiscences
William S. Ray Papers
University of California at Berkeley, Berkeley, California
   Edward Otho Cresap Ord Papers
University of California at Los Angeles, Los Angeles, California
   William Starke Rosecrans Papers
University of California at Santa Barbara, Santa Barbara, California
   Ulysses S. Grant Civil War Letter
University of Chicago, Chicago, Illinois
   Butler-Gunsaulus Collection
   Lincoln Collection
University of Florida, Gainesville, Florida
   James Patton Anderson Papers
University of Georgia, Athens, Georgia
   Cornelius C. Platter Diary
University of Illinois, Urbana, Illinois
   Charles Smith Hamilton Papers
   William E. Lodge Papers
University of Indiana, Bloomington, Indiana
   Alvin P. Hovey Papers
University of Iowa, Iowa City, Iowa
   Henry Clay Adams Civil War Journals
   Jacob Harrison Allspaugh Diary
   Charles Cady Papers
   David B. Henderson Papers
   Mead Family Papers
   Myron Underwood Papers
   Weaver and Vinson Family Correspondence
   James B. Weaver Letters
University of Memphis, Memphis, Tennessee
   J. K. Ferguson Civil War Diary
   Royal French Letter
   Nat C. Hughes Collection
   Griffin A. Stanton Civil War Journal
   Stout Civil War Letters
University of Michigan, Ann Arbor, Michigan
   N. R. Dunn Letters
University of Mississippi, Oxford, Mississippi
   Baxter Collection
      Mansfield Lovell Letter
   J. A. Bigger Diary
   J. M. Love Diary

Miller Family Letters
R. E. Price Collection
Settle Family Letters
University of Missouri, Columbia, Missouri
Francis Marion Cockrell Scrapbooks
Colman-Hayter Family Papers
J. B. Courts Letter
Adam Durkes Papers
Samuel C. Gold Papers
Austin O. Green Diaries
William F. Jones Papers
William H. Kavanaugh Papers
John Lomax Papers
David W. Pollock Letters
Thomas Pollock Letters
Avington Wayne Simpson Diary
I. V. Smith Memoirs
William S. Stewart Papers
Charles H. Thurber Collection
John Tyler Jr. Letter
Stephen Werly Diary
University of Missouri, St. Louis, Missouri
Dyson-Bell–Sans Souci Papers
University of North Carolina, Chapel Hill, North Carolina
Samuel A. Agnew Diary
George Hovey Cadman Papers
J. F. H. Claiborne Papers
H. J. Reid, "The 22nd Mississippi Regiment"
Earl Van Dorn Biographical File
Jeremy F. Gilmer Papers
Louis Hébert, "An Autobiography of Louis Hébert"
Daniel Harvey Hill Papers
John Kennedy Street Papers
University of North Texas, Denton, Texas
F. A. Rawlins Diary
University of Notre Dame, South Bend, Indiana
Mary Crowell Letter
Thomas Family Correspondence
University of Oklahoma, Norman, Oklahoma
Sherry M. Cress Collection
University of the Pacific, Stockton, California
Henry C. Ewing Diary
Robinett Family Papers

University of South Carolina, Columbia, South Carolina
    John G. Galliard Papers
    Adley H. Gladden Papers
University of Southern Mississippi, Hattiesburg, Mississippi
    John Q. Adams Letters
    Garrett Smith Ainsworth Papers
    Gore Civil War History Collection
    Lowry Autobiographical Essay
    Andrew J. Patrick Letter
University of Tennessee, Knoxville, Tennessee
    Marion Bennett Ledger
    Samuel K. Carrigan Letter
    Charles Fox Letter
    Orlando C. Geer Letter
    William A. Huddard Papers
    Lanphear Family Letters
    Union Soldier's Letter
    T. J. Walker Reminiscences
    L. P. Wulff Collection
University of Texas, Austin, Texas
    L. H. Graves Diary
    George L. Griscom Diary
    William P. Rogers Papers
University of Washington, Seattle, Washington
    Samuel D. Lougheed Papers
University of Wisconsin, La Crosse, Wisconsin
    Edward Cronon Papers
Vicksburg National Military Park, Vicksburg, Mississippi
    Isaac F. Quinby Letter
Virginia Historical Society, Richmond, Virginia
    Wilson Family Papers
Virginia Military Institute, Lexington, Virginia
    McKay Family Letter
Virginia Tech University, Blacksburg, Virginia
    Charles Johnson Papers
    Hiram Matthew Correspondence
    Ed H. Rees Letter
    Charles Wilkins Letter
Wesleyan College, Macon, Georgia
    Sarah Rogers Shaw Papers
Western Reserve Historical Society, Cleveland, Ohio
    William P. Britton Letters
    J. Q. A. Campbell Diary

William D. Evans Papers
Edward A. Webb Papers
Willamette University, Salem, Oregon
     John G. Burggraf Collection
Wisconsin Historical Society, Madison, Wisconsin
     Laura Ingalls Wilder Family Correspondence

NEWSPAPERS

Charleston Mercury
Chattanooga Daily Rebel
Chicago Tribune
Cincinnati Daily Gazette
Corinth Chanticleer
Corinth Daily Corinthian
Corinth War Eagle
Fayette Gazette
Harper's Weekly
Jackson Clarion Ledger
Jackson Daily Mississippian
Memphis Daily Appeal
Mobile Daily Tribune
Natchez Courier
New Orleans Daily Picayune
New York Herald
New York Times
New York Tribune
Northeast Mississippi Daily Journal
Wisconsin State Journal

PRIMARY AND SECONDARY SOURCES

Abernethy, Byron R., ed. *Private Elisha Stockwell, Jr. Sees the Civil War*. Norman: University of Oklahoma Press, 1958.
Alcorn County Historical Association. *The History of Alcorn County, Mississippi*. Dallas: National Sharegraphics, 1983.
Alexander, Dawn. *Corona College as an Example of Antebellum Southern Education*. N.p.: n.p., n.d.
Allardice, Bruce S. *Confederate Colonels: A Biographical Register*. Columbia: University of Missouri Press, 2008.
———. *More Generals in Gray*. Baton Rouge: Louisiana State University Press, 1995.

Allen, Stacy D. "Crossroads of the Western Confederacy." *Blue and Gray Magazine* 19, 6 (Summer 2002): 6–64.

Ambrose, D. Leib. *History of the Seventh Regiment Illinois Volunteer Infantry, from Its First Muster into the U.S. Service, April 25, 1861, to Its Final Muster out, July 9, 1865.* Springfield: Illinois Journal Company, 1868.

Ambrose, Stephen E. *Halleck: Lincoln's Chief of Staff.* Baton Rouge: Louisiana State University Press, 1962.

Anders, Leslie. *The Twenty-first Missouri: From Home Guard to Union Regiment.* Westport, CT: Greenwood Press, 1975.

Anderson, Ephraim McD. *Memoirs: Historical and Personal; Including the Campaigns of the First Missouri Confederate Brigade.* St. Louis: Times Printing Company, 1868.

Armstrong, Warren B. "Union Chaplains and the Education of the Freedmen." *Journal of Negro History* 52, 2 (April 1967), 104–115.

Arnold, T. B. "The Battles around Corinth, Miss." *Confederate Veteran* 5, 5 (May 1897): 199–200.

Askew, Samuel L., III. "An Analysis of Unit Cohesion in the 42nd Alabama Infantry." Master's thesis, U.S. Army Command and General Staff College, 2003.

Aughey, John H. *The Iron Furnace: Or, Slavery and Secession.* Philadelphia: William S. and Alfred Martien, 1863.

Banks, Robert W. "The Civil War Letters of Robert W. Banks," ed. George C. Osborn. *Journal of Mississippi History* 5 (1943): 141–154.

Barrett, J. O. *The Soldier Bird: "Old Abe:" The Live War-Eagle of Wisconsin that Served a Three Year's Campaign in the Great Rebellion.* Madison, WI: Atwood and Culver, 1876.

Barron, Samuel B. *The Lone Star Defenders: A Chronicle of the Third Texas Cavalry Regiment in the Civil War.* Washington, DC: Zenger, 1983.

Bearss, Edwin C. *Decision in Mississippi: Mississippi's Important Role in the War between the States.* Jackson: Mississippi Commission on the War between the States, 1962.

———. *Forrest at Brice's Cross Roads and in North Mississippi in 1864.* Dayton, OH: Morningside, 1979.

———. "Grierson's Winter Raid on the Mobile and Ohio Railroad." *Military Affairs* 24, 1 (Spring 1960): 20–37.

Beauregard, P. G. T. "The Campaign of Shiloh." In *Battles and Leaders of the Civil War*, 4 vols., 1:569–593. New York: Century Company, 1884–1887.

Belknap, William W. *History of the Fifteenth Regiment, Iowa Veteran Volunteer Infantry, from October, 1861, to August, 1865, When Disbanded at the End of the War.* Keokuk, IA: R. B. Ogden and Son, 1887.

———. "The Obedience and Courage of the Private Soldier, and the Fortitude of Officers and Men in the Field, in Hospital, and in Prison, with Some Incidents of the War." In *Military Order of the Loyal Legion,* 157–171. Des Moines, IA: P. C. Kenyon, 1893.

Bergeron, Arthur W., Jr. "Mansfield Lovell." In Roman J. Heleniak and Lawrence L. Hewitt, *Leadership during the Civil War: The 1989 Deep Delta Civil War Symposium: Themes in Honor of T. Harry Williams.* Shippensburg, PA: White Mane, 1992.

Bettersworth, John K., ed. *Mississippi in the Confederacy: As They Saw It*. Baton Rouge: Louisiana State University Press, 1961.

Bevier, R. S. *History of the First and Second Missouri Confederate Brigades, 1861–1865*. St. Louis: Bryan, Brand, 1879.

Bigelow, Martha M. "Freedmen of the Mississippi Valley, 1862–1865." *Civil War History* 8 (March 1962): 38–47.

Black, Robert C., III. *The Railroads of the Confederacy*. Chapel Hill: University of North Carolina Press, 1952.

Boatner, Mark Mayo, III. *The Civil War Dictionary*. New York: David McKay, 1988.

Booten, W. W. "A Federal Boy Soldier at Corinth." *Confederate Veteran* 5, 1 (January 1897): 6.

Brent, Joseph E. *Occupied Corinth: The Contraband Camp and the First Alabama Infantry of African Descent, 1862–1864*. Corinth, MS: City of Corinth, 1995.

Briant, C. C. *History of the Sixth Regiment Indiana Volunteer Infantry: Of Both the Three Months' and the Three Years' Services*. Indianapolis: William B. Burford, 1891.

Brown, A. F. "Van Dorn's Operations in Northern Mississippi—Recollections of a Cavalryman." *Southern Historical Society Papers* 6 (1878): 151–161.

Brown, Alonzo L. *History of the Fourth Regiment of Minnesota Infantry Volunteers during the Great Rebellion 1861–1865*. St. Paul: Pioneer Press Company, 1892.

Bryner, Cloyd. *Bugle Echoes: The Story of the Illinois 47th*. Springfield, IL: Phillips Bros. Printers, 1905.

Burial of General Rosecrans, Arlington National Cemetery, May 17, 1902. Cincinnati, OH: Robert Clarke, 1903.

Byers, S. H. M. "How Men Feel in Battle." *American History Illustrated* 22, 2 (April 1987): 11–17.

Calkin, Homer L. "Elkhorn to Vicksburg." *Civil War History* 2, 1 (March 1956): 7–43.

"Camouflage." *Confederate Veteran* 21, 3 (March 1913): 102–103.

Cappleman, Josie Frazee. "Local Incidents of the War between the States." In *Publications of the Mississippi Historical Society*, 4(1901): 79–87.

"Captain John C. Appler." *Confederate Veteran* 31, 1 (January 1923): 28.

Carr, Pat M., ed. *In Fine Sprits: The Civil War Letters of Ras Stirman*. Fayetteville, AR: Washington County Historical Society, 1986.

Carter, Harvey L., and Norma L. Peterson, eds. "William S. Stewart Letters, January 13, 1861, to December 4, 1862, Part III." *Missouri Historical Review* 61, 4 (July 1967): 463–488.

Castel, Albert. "The Battle without a Victor . . . Iuka." *Civil War Times Illustrated* 11, 6 (October 1972): 12–18.

———. *General Sterling Price and the Civil War in the West*. Baton Rouge: Louisiana State University Press, 1968.

———. "Victory at Corinth." *Civil War Times Illustrated* 17, 6 (October 1978): 12–22.

Chamberlain, William H. *History of the Eighty-first Regiment Ohio Infantry Volunteers during the War of the Rebellion*. Cincinnati, OH: Gazette Steam Printing House, 1865.

Chance, Joseph E. *The Second Texas Infantry: From Shiloh to Vicksburg*. Austin, TX: Eakin Press, 1984.

Chetlain, Augustus. "The Battle of Corinth." In *Military Essays and Recollections: Papers Read before the Commandery of the State of Illinois, Military Order of the Loyal Legion of the United States*, 2:373–382. Chicago: A. C. McClurg, 1894.

———. *Recollections of Seventy Years*. Galena, IL: Gazette Publishing Company, 1899.

Cluett, William W. *History of the 57th Regiment Illinois Volunteer Infantry, from Muster in, Dec. 26, 1861, to Muster out, July 7, 1865*. Princeton, IL: T. P. Streeter, 1886.

Cockrell, Monroe F., ed. *The Lost Account of the Battle of Corinth and Court-Martial of Gen. Van Dorn*. Jackson, TN: McCowat-Mercer Press, 1955.

Coffin, Levi. *Reminiscences of Levi Coffin, the Reputed President of the Underground Railroad; Being a Brief History of the Labors of a Lifetime in Behalf of the Slave, with the Stories of Numerous Fugitives, Who Gained Their Freedom through His Instrumentality, and Many Other Incidents*. Cincinnati, OH: Robert Clarke, 1880.

Coker, William L. *Valley of Springs: The Story of Iuka*. Hattiesburg: University of Southern Mississippi, 1968.

"Col. H. J. Reid." *Confederate Veteran* 14, 3 (March 1906): 132–133.

Commager, Henry Steele, ed. *The Blue and the Gray: The Story of the Civil War as Told by Participants*, 2 vols. Indianapolis: Bobbs-Merrill, 1950.

Comte de Paris. *History of the Civil War in America*, 2 vols. Philadelphia: Porter and Coates, 1876.

Connelly, Thomas L. *Army of the Heartland: The Army of Tennessee, 1861–1862*. Baton Rouge: Louisiana State University Press, 1967.

Cope, Alexis. *The Fifteenth Ohio Volunteers and Its Campaigns: War of 1861–5*. Columbus, OH: n.p., 1916.

Coppee, Henry. *Life and Services of Gen. U. S. Grant*. New York: Richardson, 1868.

Corinth Civil War Boundary Adjustment Study: Corinth Unit of the Shiloh National Military Park: Environmental Assessment. Washington, DC: National Park Service, 2004.

"Correspondence." *Annals of the State Historical Society of Iowa* 1, 3 (July 1863): 140.

Cowell, Charles. "An Infantryman at Corinth." *Civil War Times Illustrated* 13, 7 (November 1974): 10–14.

Cozzens, Peter. *The Darkest Days of the War: The Battles of Iuka and Corinth*. Chapel Hill: University of North Carolina Press, 1997.

———. *General John Pope: A Life for the Nation*. Urbana: University of Illinois Press, 2000.

Cozzens, Peter, and Robert I. Girardi, eds. *The Military Memoirs of General John Pope*. Chapel Hill: University of North Carolina Press, 1998.

Cresap, Bernarr. *Appomattox Commander: The Story of General E. O. C. Ord*. San Diego: A. S. Barnes, 1981.

Cumming, Kate. *A Journal of Hospital Life in the Confederate Army of Tennessee from the Battle of Shiloh to the End of the War: With Sketches of Life and Character, and Brief Notices of Current Events during that Period*. Louisville, KY: John P. Morton, 1866.

————. *Kate, the Journal of a Confederate Nurse*. Edited by Richard B. Harwell. Baton Rouge: Louisiana State University Press, 1959.

Cunningham, O. Edward. *Shiloh and the Western Campaign of 1862,* ed. Gary D. Joiner and Timothy B. Smith. New York: Savas Beatie, 2007.

Daniel, Larry J. *Days of Glory: The Army of the Cumberland, 1861–1865*. Baton Rouge: Louisiana State University Press, 2004.

————. *Shiloh: The Battle that Changed the Civil War*. New York: Simon and Schuster, 1997.

Davis, Reuben. *Recollections of Mississippi and Mississippians*. Boston: Houghton, Mifflin, 1890.

Davis, Samuel H. "Chronicle of a Mississippi Soldier: The Civil War Letters of Samuel H. Davis of Kemper County," ed. Henry E. Mattox. *Journal of Mississippi History* 52, 3 (August 1990): 199–214.

Davis, William C. *Breckinridge: Statesman, Soldier, Symbol*. Baton Rouge: Louisiana State University Press, 1974.

Dodge, Grenville M. *The Battle of Atlanta and Other Campaigns, Addresses, Etc*. Council Bluffs, IA: Monarch Printing Company, 1911.

————. "Use of Block-Houses during the Civil War." *Annals of Iowa* 6, 4 (January 1904): 297–301.

Dossman, Steven Nathaniel. *Campaign for Mississippi: Blood in Mississippi*. Abilene, TX: McWhiney Foundation Press, 2006.

Downing, Alexander G. *Downing's Civil War Diary*, ed. Olynthus B. Clark. Des Moines: Historical Department of Iowa, 1916.

Dudley, G. W. *The Battle of Corinth and the Court Martial of Gen. Van Dorn*. N.p.: n.p., 1899.

————. *The Battle of Iuka*. Iuka, MS: Iuka Vidette, 1896.

Dyer, Frederick H. *A Compendium of the War of the Rebellion*, 3 vols. Cedar Rapids, IA: Torch Press, 1908.

Eaton, John. *Grant, Lincoln and the Freedmen: Reminiscences of the Civil War, with Special Reference to the Work for the Contrabands and Freedmen of the Mississippi Valley*. New York: Longmans, Green, 1907.

Elliott, Charles N. "Van Dorn's Blitzkrieg Stumbles: Comanches, Command Decisions, and Combat in the Baton Rouge Campaign of 1862." In *Confederate Generals in the Western Theater: Essays on America's Civil War*, 2:53–72. Knoxville: University of Tennessee Press, 2010.

Elliott, Sam Davis. *Isham G. Harris of Tennessee: Confederate Governor and United States Senator*. Baton Rouge: Louisiana State University Press, 2010.

————. *Soldier of Tennessee: General Alexander P. Stewart and the Civil War in the West*. Baton Rouge: Louisiana State University Press, 1999.

Engle, Stephen D. *Don Carlos Buell: Most Promising of All*. Chapel Hill: University of North Carolina Press, 1999.

Engs, Robert F., and Corey M. Brooks, eds. *Their Patriotic Duty: The Civil War Letters of the Evans Family of Brown County, Ohio*. New York: Fordham University Press, 2007.

Evans, Clement A. *Confederate Military History: A Library of Confederate States History Written by Distinguished Men of the South, and Edited by General Clement A. Evans*, 12 vols. Atlanta: Confederate Publishing Company, 1899.

Evans, Robert G., ed. *The 16th Mississippi Infantry: Civil War Letters and Reminiscences*. Jackson: University Press of Mississippi, 2002.

Flood, Charles Bracelen. *Grant and Sherman: The Friendship that Won the Civil War*. New York: Farrar, Straus, and Giroux, 2005.

Foote, Shelby. *The Civil War: A Narrative*, 3 vols. New York: Random House, 1958.

Force, Manning F. *From Fort Henry to Corinth*. New York: Charles Scribner's Sons, 1881.

Foster, Buck T. *Sherman's Mississippi Campaign*. Tuscaloosa: University of Alabama Press, 2006.

Frederick, J. V., ed. "An Illinois Soldier in North Mississippi: Diary of John Wilson February 15–December 30, 1862." *Journal of Mississippi History* 1, 3 (July 1939): 182–194.

Fuller, John W. "Our Kirby Smith." In *Sketches of War History, 1861–1865: Papers Read before the Ohio Commandery of the Military Order of the Loyal Legion of the United States*, 2:161–179. Cincinnati, OH: Robert Clarke, 1888.

Goodloe, Albert Theodore. *Confederate Echoes: A Voice from the South in the Days of Secession and the Southern Confederacy*. Nashville: Publishing House of the Methodist Episcopal Church, South, 1907.

———. *Some Rebel Relics: From the Seat of War*. Nashville: Publishing House of the Methodist Episcopal Church, South, 1893.

Gordon, James. "The Battle and Retreat from Corinth." *Publications of the Mississippi Historical Society* 4 (1901): 63–72.

Grant, U. S. *Personal Memoirs of U. S. Grant*. New York: Charles L. Webster, 1885.

Greene, Francis Vinton. *The Mississippi*. New York: Charles Scribner's Sons, 1882.

Grose, William. *The Story of the Marches, Battles and Incidents of the 36th Regiment Indiana Volunteer Infantry*. New Castle, IN: Courier Company, 1891.

Gunn, Jack W. "The Battle of Iuka." *Journal of Mississippi History* 14 (1962): 142–157.

Hale, Douglas. *The Third Texas Cavalry in the Civil War*. Norman: University of Oklahoma Press, 1993.

Hamilton, Charles S. "The Battle of Iuka." In *Battles and Leaders of the Civil War*, 4 vols., 2:734–736. New York: Century Company, 1884–1887.

———. "Hamilton's Division at Corinth." In *Battles and Leaders of the Civil War*, 4 vols., 2:757–758. New York: Century Company, 1884–1887.

Harris, James C. *Story of the Corinth Rifles and Its Flag Bearer, Co. A 9th Miss. Inf. Regt., C.S.A.* Corinth, MS: n.p., n.d.

Hart, E. J. *History of the Fortieth Illinois Inf. (Volunteers)*. Cincinnati, OH: H. S. Bosworth, 1864.

Hartje, Robert G. *Van Dorn: The Life and Times of a Confederate General*. Nashville: Vanderbilt University Press, 1967.

Hartpence, William R. *History of the Fifty-first Indiana Veteran Volunteer Infantry: A Narrative of Its Organization, Marches, Battles and Other Experiences in Camp and Prison, from 1861 to 1866*. Cincinnati, OH: Robert Clarke, 1894.

Hashell, Fritz, ed. "Col. William Camm War Diary, 1861–1865." *Journal of the Illinois State Historical Society* 18, 4 (January 1926): 793–969.

Hawes, Maria Jane Southgate. *Reminiscences of Mrs. Maria Jane Southgate Hawes: Daughter of James Southgate and Jane Smith, Born Nov. 30, 1836.* N.p.: n.p., 1918.

Helm, W. P. "Close Fighting at Iuka, Miss." *Confederate Veteran* 19, 4 (April 1911): 171.

Hess, Earl J. *Banners to the Breeze: The Kentucky Campaign, Corinth, and Stones River.* Lincoln: University of Nebraska Press, 2000.

Hight, John J., and Gilbert R. Stormont. *History of the Fifty-eighth Regiment Indiana Volunteer Infantry: Its Organization, Campaigns and Battles from 1861 to 1865.* Princeton, IN: Press of the Clarion, 1895.

Hinman, Wilbur F. *The Story of the Sherman Brigade: The Camp, the March, the Bivouac, the Battle; and How "the Boys" Lived and Died during Four Years of Active Field Service.* N.p.: n.p., 1897.

Hirshson, Stanley P. *Grenville M. Dodge: Soldier, Politician, Railroad Pioneer.* Bloomington: Indiana University Press, 1967.

Hoar, Victor. "Colonel William C. Falkner in the Civil War." *Journal of Mississippi History* 27 (1965): 42–62.

Holmes, W. C. "The Battle of Corinth." *Confederate Veteran* 27, 8 (August 1919): 290–292.

Holt, Dean W. *American Military Cemeteries: A Comprehensive Illustrated Guide to the Hallowed Grounds of the United States, Including Cemeteries Overseas.* Jefferson, NC: McFarland, 1992.

Horn, Stanley F. *The Army of Tennessee.* Indianapolis: Bobbs-Merrill, 1941.

Hotard, Patrick Michael. "The Campaign (Siege) of Corinth, Mississippi, April–June 1862." M.A. thesis, Southeastern Louisiana University, 2005.

Hough, Granville W., ed. "Diary of a Soldier in Grant's Rear Guard (1862–1863)." *Journal of Mississippi History* 45, 3 (August 1983): 194–214.

Howell, H. Grady. *Going to Meet the Yankees: A History of the "Bloody Sixth" Mississippi Infantry, C.S.A.* Jackson, MS: Chickasaw Bayou Press, 1981.

Hubbard, John Milton. *Notes of a Private.* Bolivar, MS: R. P. Shackelford, 1973.

Hubbell, Finley L. "Diary of Lieut. Col. Hubbell, of 3d Regiment Missouri Infantry, C.S.A." *The Land We Love* 6, 2 (December 1868): 97–105.

Hubert, Charles F. *History of the Fiftieth Regiment Illinois Volunteer Infantry in the War of the Union.* Kansas City, MO: Western Veteran Publishing Company, 1894.

Hughes, Nathaniel Cheairs, Jr. *General William J. Hardee: Old Reliable.* Baton Rouge: Louisiana State University Press, 1965.

Inge, Mrs. F. A. "Corinth, Miss. in Early War Days." *Confederate Veteran* 17, 9 (September 1909): 442–444.

———. "Corinth, Miss. in War Times." *Confederate Veteran* 23, 9 (September 1915): 412–413.

"An Iowa Emancipator." *Annals of Iowa* 30, 4 (April 1950): 302–305.

Isbell, Timothy T. *Shiloh and Corinth: Sentinels of Stone.* Jackson: University Press of Mississippi, 2007.

Jackson, Oscar L. *The Colonel's Diary: Journals Kept before and during the Civil War by the Late Colonel Oscar L. Jackson of Newcastle, Pennsylvania, Sometime Commander of the 63rd Regiment O.V.I.* N.p.: n.p., 1922.

Jamison, Matthew H. *Recollections of Pioneer and Army Life.* Kansas City, MO: Hudson Press, 1911.

Johnston, William Preston. "Albert Sidney Johnston at Shiloh." In *Battles and Leaders of the Civil War*, 4 vols., 1:540–568. New York: Century Company, 1884–1887.

Journal of the State Convention and Ordinances and Resolutions Adopted in January, 1861, with an Appendix. Jackson, MS: E. Barksdale, 1861.

Keen, Newton A. *Living and Fighting with the Texas 6th Cavalry.* Gaithersburg, MD: Butterneutt Press, 1986.

Kennedy, Joseph C. G. *Population of the United States in 1860: Compiled from the Original Returns of the Eighth Census under the Direction of the Secretary of the Interior.* Washington, DC: Government Printing Office, 1864.

Kerwood, Asbury L. *Annals of the Fifty-seventh Regiment Indiana Volunteers: Marches, Battles, and Incidents of Army Life by a Member of the Regiment.* Dayton, OH: W. J. Shuey, 1868.

Kimbell, Charles B. *History of Battery "A" First Illinois Light Artillery Volunteers.* Chicago: Cushing Printing Company, 1899.

Kimberly, Robert L., and Ephraim S. Holloway, *The Forty-first Ohio Veteran Volunteer Infantry in the War of the Rebellion, 1861–1865.* Cleveland, OH: W. R. Smellie, 1897.

Kiner, F. F. *One Year's Soldiering: Embracing the Battles of Fort Donelson and Shiloh and the Capture of Two Hundred Officers and Men of the Fourteenth Iowa Infantry, and Their Confinement Six Months and a Half in Rebel Prisons.* Priot Lake, MN: Morgan Avenue Press, 2000.

Kiper, Richard L. *Major General John A. McClernand: Politician in Uniform.* Kent, OH: Kent State University Press, 1999.

Kirwan, A. D., ed. *Johnny Green of the Orphan Brigade: The Journal of a Confederate Soldier.* Lexington: University Press of Kentucky, 1956.

Kitchens, Ben Earl. *Rosecrans Meets Price: The Battle of Iuka, Mississippi.* Florence, AL: Thornwood Book Publishers, 1987.

Kraynek, Sharon L. D., ed. *Letters to My Wife: A Civil War Diary from the Western Front.* Apollo, PA: Closson Press, 1995.

Lamers, William M. *The Edge of Glory: A Biography of General William S. Rosecrans, U.S.A.* New York: Harcourt, Brace, and World, 1961.

Lash, Jeffrey N. *A Politician Turned General: The Civil War Career of Stephen Augustus Hurlbut.* Kent, OH: Kent State University Press, 2003.

"Letter of Lieut. Col. Wm. E. Small." *Annals of the State Historical Society of Iowa* 1, 2 (April 1863): 87.

Little, George. *Memoirs of George Little.* Tuscaloosa, AL: Weatherford Printing Company, 1924.

Little, Henry. "The Diary of General Henry Little, C.S.A," ed. Albert Castel. *Civil War Times Illustrated* 11, 6 (October 1972): 4–6, 8–11, 41–47.

Livermore, Thomas L. *Numbers and Losses in the Civil War in America.* Boston: Houghton Mifflin, 1900.

Lobdell, Jared C., ed. "The Civil War Journal and Letters of Colonel John Van Deusen Du Bois, April 12, 1861–October 16, 1862." *Missouri Historical Review* 61, 1 (October 1966): 21–50.

Long, E. B. *The Civil War Day by Day: An Almanac 1861–1865.* New York: Da Capo, 1971.

Lossing, Benson. *Pictorial History of the Civil War in the United States of America,* 2 vols. Hartford, CT: T. Belknap, 1868.

Lucy's Journal. Greenwood, MS: Baff Printing Company, 1967.

Lytle, Andrew Nelson. *Bedford Forrest and His Critter Company.* New York: Minton Balch, 1931.

Mahon, John K., ed. "The Civil War Letters of Samuel Mahon, Seventh Iowa Infantry." *Iowa Journal of History* 51, 3 (July 1953): 233–266.

Manufactures of the United States in 1860: Compiled from the Original Returns of the Eighth Census under the Direction of the Secretary of the Interior. Washington, DC: Government Printing Office, 1865.

Marszalek, John F. *Commander of All Lincoln's Armies: A Life of General Henry W. Halleck.* Cambridge, MA: Harvard University Press, 2004.

———. "'A Full Share of All the Credit': Sherman and Grant to the Fall of Vicksburg." In *Grant's Lieutenants: From Cairo to Vicksburg,* ed. Steven E. Woodworth, 5–20. Lawrence: University Press of Kansas, 2001.

———. "Halleck Captures Corinth." *Civil War Times* 45, 1 (February 2006): 46–52.

Martin, R. T. "Remembrances of an Arkansan." *Confederate Veteran* 12, 2 (February 1909): 69.

Maury, Dabney H. "Recollections of Campaign against Grant in North Mississippi in 1862–63." *Southern Historical Society Papers* 13 (1885): 285–311.

———. "Recollections of General Earl Van Dorn." *Southern Historical Society Papers* 19 (1891): 191–201.

———. *Recollections of a Virginian.* New York: Charles Scribner's Sons, 1894.

McCarty, Vivian Kirkpatrick, ed. "Civil War Experiences." *Missouri Historical Review,* 43, 3 (April 1949), 237–250.

McCord, W. B. "Battle of Corinth." In *Glimpses of the Nation's Struggle. Fourth Series. Papers Read before the Minnesota Commandery of the Military Order of the Loyal Legion of the United States, 1892–1897,* 567–584. St. Paul: H. L. Collins, 1898.

McDaniel, Robert W. "Forgotten Heritage: The Battle of Hatchie Bridge, Tennessee." *West Tennessee Historical Society Papers* 31 (October 1977): 109–116.

McDonald, G. B. *A History of the 30th Illinois Veteran Volunteer Regiment of Infantry.* Sparta, IL: Sparta News, 1916.

McDonough, James L. *Shiloh: In Hell before Night.* Knoxville: University of Tennessee Press, 1977.

———. *War in Kentucky: From Shiloh to Perryville.* Knoxville: University of Tennessee Press, 1994.

McLendon, James H. "The Development of Mississippi Agriculture." *Journal of Mississippi History* 13, 2 (April 1951): 81.

McMurray, W. J. *History of the Twentieth Tennessee Regiment Volunteer Infantry, C.S.A.* Nashville: Publication Committee, 1904.

McPherson, James M. *Battle Cry of Freedom: The Civil War Era.* New York: Oxford University Press, 1988.

———. *Crossroads of Freedom: Antietam: The Battle that Changed the Course of the Civil War.* New York: Oxford University Press, 2002.

McWhiney, Grady. *Braxton Bragg and Confederate Defeat,* 2 vols. New York: Columbia University Press, 1969.

Memoir of Gen. A. C. Ducat. Chicago: Rand, McNally, 1897.

Miller, Emily Van Dorn. *A Soldier's Honor, with Reminiscences of Major General Earl Van Dorn, by His Comrades.* New York: Abbey Press Publishers, 1903.

Montgomery, Frank A. *Reminiscences of a Mississippian in Peace and War.* Cincinnati, OH: Robert Clarke, 1901.

"Monument at Corinth." *Confederate Veteran* 2, 8 (August 1894): 249.

"Monument to Colonel Rogers." *Confederate Veteran* 21, 3 (March 1913): 102–103.

Moore, Benita K., ed. *A Civil War Diary: Written by Dr. James A. Black, First Assistant Surgeon, 49th Illinois Infantry.* Bloomington, IN: Author House, 2008.

Moore, Frank, ed. *The Rebellion Record: A Diary of American Events, with Documents, Narratives, Illustrative Incidents, Poetry, etc.,* 11 vols. New York: D. Vann Nostrand, 1861–1868.

Morrison, Marion. *A History of the Ninth Regiment Illinois Volunteer Infantry.* Monmouth, IL: John S. Clark, 1864.

Nabors, S. M. *History of Old Tishomingo County.* Corinth, MS: n.p., 1940.

Neal, W. A. *An Illustrated History of the Missouri Engineer and the 25th Infantry Regiments: Together with a Roster of Both Regiments and the Last Known Address of All that Could Be Obtained.* Chicago: Donohue and Henneberry, 1889.

Neil, Henry M. "A Battery at Close Quarters: Being the Story of the Eleventh Ohio Battery at Iuka and Corinth." In *Sketches of War History, 1861–1865: A Compilation of Miscellaneous Papers Compiled for the Ohio Commandery of the Loyal Legion, February, 1885–February, 1909,* 7:343–354. Wilmington, NC: Broadfoot, 1993.

Newton, James K. *A Wisconsin Boy in Dixie: The Selected Letters of James K. Newton,* ed. Stephen E. Ambrose. Madison: University of Wisconsin Press, 1961.

Noble, H. T., et al. *Military History and Reminiscences of the Thirteenth Regiment of Illinois Volunteer Infantry in the Civil War in the United States, 1861–1865.* Chicago: Woman's Temperance Publishing Association, 1892.

Noe, Kenneth W. *Perryville: This Grand Havoc of Battle.* Lexington: University Press of Kentucky, 2001.

———. *Reluctant Rebels: The Confederates Who Joined the Army after 1861.* Chapel Hill: University of North Carolina Press, 2010.

Nugent, William N. *My Dear Nellie: The Civil War Letters of William N. Nugent to*

Eleanor Smith Nugent, ed. William M. Cash and Lucy Somerville Howorth. Jackson: University Press of Mississippi, 1977.

O'Connor, Richard. *Thomas: Rock of Chickamauga*. New York: Prentice-Hall, 1948.

Palmer, John M. *Personal Recollections of John M. Palmer: The Story of an Earnest Life*. Cincinnati, OH: Robert Clarke, 1901.

Parson, Thomas E. "Hell on the Hatchie: The Fight at Davis Bridge, Tennessee." *Blue and Gray Magazine* 24, 4 (Holiday 2007): 6–24, 43–51.

Payne, James E. *History of the Fifth Missouri Volunteer Infantry*. N.p.: Press of James Payne, 1899.

Pepper, George W. *Under Three Flags; Or the Story of My Life as Preacher, Captain in the Army, Chaplain, Consul, with Speeches and Interviews*. Cincinnati, OH: Curts and Jennings, 1899.

Pierce, Lyman B. *History of the Second Iowa Cavalry: Containing a Detailed Account of Its Organization, Marches, and the Battles in Which It Has Participated; Also, a Complete Roster of Each Company*. Burlington, IA: Hawk-eye Steam Book and Job Printing Establishment, 1865.

Plum, William R. *The Military Telegraph during the Civil War in the United States, with an Exposition of Ancient and Modern Means of Communication, and of the Federal and Confederate Cipher Systems; Also a Running Account of the War between the States*, 2 vols. Chicago: Jansen, McClurg, 1882.

Plummer, Mark A. *Lincoln's Rail-Splitter: Governor Richard J. Oglesby*. Urbana: University of Illinois Press, 2001.

Polk, William M. *Leonidas Polk: Bishop and General*, 2 vols. New York: Longmans, Green, 1915.

Pollard, E. A. *Southern History of the War*, 2 vols. New York: Richardson, 1866.

Pope, John. "Report of Major General Pope." In *Supplemental Report of the Joint Committee on the Conduct of the War, in Two Volumes*. Washington, DC: Government Printing Office, 1866.

Porter, W. C. "War Diary of W. C. Porter," ed. J. V. Frederick. *Arkansas Historical Quarterly* 11, 4 (1952): 286–314.

Power, J. L. *Proceedings of the Mississippi State Convention, Held January 7th to 26th, A.D. 1861. Including the Ordinances, as Finally Adopted, Important Speeches, and a List of Members, Showing the Postoffice, Profession, Nativity, Politics, Age, Religious Preference, and Social Relations of Each*. Jackson, MS: Power and Cadwallader, 1861.

Price, Beulah M. D'Olive, ed. "Excerpts from Diary of Walter A. Overton, 1860–1862." *Journal of Mississippi History* 17, 3 (July 1955): 191–204.

Rable, George C. *Fredericksburg! Fredericksburg!* Chapel Hill: University of North Carolina Press, 2002.

Rainwater, Percy L. *Mississippi: Storm Center of Secession, 1856–1861*. Baton Rouge: Louisiana State University Press, 1938.

Ranstead, H. E. *A True Story and History of the Fifty-third Regiment Illinois Veteran Volunteer Infantry: Its Campaigns and Marches: Incidents that Occurred on Marches and in Camp. What Happened to Some of Its Members and What Became of Others. Short Stories of Marches and How the Army Lived.* N.p.: n.p., 1910.

Reed, David W. *The Battle of Shiloh and the Organizations Engaged,* rev. ed. Washington, DC: Government Printing Office, 1909.

———. *Campaigns and Battles of the Twelfth Regiment Iowa Veteran Volunteer Infantry from Organization, September, 1861, to Muster out, January 20, 1866.* N.p.: n.p., n.d.

Riley, A. C. "Confederate Colonel A. C. Riley, His Reports and Letters—Part II," ed. Riley Bock. *Missouri Historical Review* 85, 3 (April 1991): 264–287.

Riley, Franklin L. "G. W. Dudley." *Publications of the Mississippi Historical Society* 5 (1902): 290–291.

Rogers, Margaret Greene. *Civil War Corinth.* Corinth, MS: Rankin Printery, 1989.

Rogers, William P. "The Diary and Letters of William P. Rogers, 1846–1862," ed. Florence Damon Pace. *Southwestern Historical Quarterly* 32, 4 (April 1929): 259–299.

Roman, Alfred. *The Military Operations of General Beauregard in the War between the States, 1861–1865: Including a Brief Personal Sketch of His Services in the War with Mexico, 1846–8,* 2 vols. New York: Harper and Brothers, 1883.

Rose, Victor M. *Ross' Texas Brigade.* Louisville, KY: Courier-Journal Company, 1881.

Rosecrans, William S. "The Battle of Corinth." In *Battles and Leaders of the Civil War,* 4 vols., 2:737–757. New York: Century Company, 1884–1887.

———. "Rosecrans's Campaigns." In *Report of the Joint Committee on the Conduct of the War, at the Second Session Thirty-eighth Congress.* Washington, DC: Government Printing Office, 1865.

Ross, Charles D. *Civil War Acoustic Shadows.* Shippensburg, PA: White Mane Books, 2001.

Rowland, Dunbar. *Mississippi,* 2 vols. Spartanburg, SC: Reprint Company, 1976.

Rowland, Dunbar, and H. Grady Howell Jr. *Military History of Mississippi: 1803–1898, Including a Listing of All Known Mississippi Confederate Military Units.* Madison, MS: Chickasaw Bayou Press, 2003.

Sager, Juliet Gilman. "Stephen A. Hurlbut, 1815–1882." *Journal of the Illinois State Historical Society* 28, 2 (July 1935): 53–80.

Sanborn, John B. "An Army Experience." In *Sketches of War History, 1861–1865: A Compilation of Miscellaneous Papers Compiled for the Ohio Commandery of the Loyal Legion, February, 1885–February, 1909,* 7:357–359. Wilmington, NC: Broadfoot, 1993.

Sanders, Joseph Todd. "M. A. Miller's Sketchbook of 1860 Corinth: The Built Environment of a Mississippi Boomtown." M.A. thesis, Mississippi State University, 1992.

Schaller, Mary W., and Martin N. Schaller. *Soldiering for Glory: The Civil War Letters of Colonel Francis Schaller, Twenty-second Mississippi Infantry.* Columbia: University of South Carolina Press, 2007.

Schenker, Carl R., Jr. "Ulysses in His Tent: Halleck, Grant, Sherman, and 'The Turning Point of the War.'" *Civil War History* 56, 2 (June 2010): 175–221.

Schutz, Wallace J., and Walter N. Trenerry. *Abandoned by Lincoln: A Military Biography of General John Pope.* Chicago: University of Illinois Press, 1990.

Sears, Stephen W. *Landscape Turned Red: The Battle of Antietam.* New Haven, CT: Ticknor and Fields, 1983.

Shalhope, Robert E. *Sterling Price: Portrait of a Southerner.* Columbia: University of Missouri Press, 1971.

Shanks, William F. G. *Personal Recollections of Distinguished Generals.* New York: Harper and Brothers, 1866.

Shaw, James Birney. *History of the Tenth Regiment Indiana Volunteer Infantry: Three Months and Three Years Organizations.* Lafayette, IN: Regimental Association, 1912.

Sheridan, Philip H. *Personal Memoirs of P. H. Sheridan: General United States Army*, 2 vols. New York: Charles L. Webster, 1888.

Sherman, William T. *Memoirs of General William T. Sherman: Written by Himself.* New York: D. Appleton, 1875.

Silver, James W., ed. *A Life for the Confederacy: As Recorded in the Pocket Diaries of Pvt. Robert A. Moore, Co. G 17th Mississippi Regiment Confederate Guards Holly Springs, Mississippi.* Jackson, TN: McCowat-Mercer Press, 1959.

Simpson, Brooks D. "After Shiloh: Grant, Sherman, and Survival." In *The Shiloh Campaign*, ed. Steven E. Woodworth, 142–156. Carbondale: Southern Illinois University Press, 2009.

Smith, Charles H. *The History of Fuller's Ohio Brigade, 1861–1865: Its Great March, with Roster Portraits, Battle Maps and Biographies.* Cleveland, OH: Press of A. J. Watt, 1909.

Smith, H. I. *History of the Seventh Iowa Veteran Volunteer Infantry during the Civil War.* Mason City, IA: R. Hitchcock Printer, 1903.

Smith, John Thomas. *A History of the Thirty-first Regiment of Indiana Volunteer Infantry in the War of the Rebellion.* Cincinnati, OH: Western Methodist Book Concern, 1900.

Smith, Timothy B. "The Forgotten Battle of Davis' Bridge." *North and South* 2, 5 (June 1999): 68–79.

———. "The Forgotten Inhabitants of Shiloh: A Case Study in a Civilian-Government Relationship." *Tennessee Historical Quarterly* 67, 1 (Spring 2008): 36–55.

———. *Mississippi in the Civil War: The Home Front.* Jackson: University Press of Mississippi, 2010.

———. "The Politics of Battlefield Preservation: David B. Henderson and the National Military Parks." *Annals of Iowa*, 66 (Summer–Fall 2007): 293–320.

———. "'A Siege from the Start': The Spring 1862 Campaign against Corinth, Mississippi." *Journal of Mississippi History* 66, 4 (2004): 403–424.

———. *The Untold Story of Shiloh: The Battle and the Battlefield.* Knoxville: University of Tennessee Press, 2006.

Snead, Thomas L. "With Price East of the Mississippi." In *Battles and Leaders of the Civil War*, 4 vols., 2:717–734. New York: Century Company, 1884–1887.

Soper, E. B. "A Chapter from the History of Company D, Twelfth Iowa Infantry Volunteers." In *War Sketches and Incidents as Related by the Companions of the Iowa Commandery Military Order of the Loyal Legion of the United States*, 2:129–142. Des Moines, IA: n.p., 1898.

Special Resource Study: Corinth, Mississippi. Washington, DC: National Park Service, 2003.

Stanley, David S. "The Battle of Corinth." In *Personal Recollections of the War of the Rebellion: Addresses Delivered before the Commandery of the State of New York, Military Order of the Loyal Legion of the United States*, 2nd series, 267–279. New York: G. P. Putnam's Sons, 1897.

———. "An Order to Charge at Corinth." In *Battles and Leaders of the Civil War*, 4 vols., 2:759. New York: Century Company, 1884–1887.

———. *Personal Memoirs of Major General D. S. Stanley, U.S.A.* Cambridge, MA: Harvard University Press, 1917.

Starr, N. D., and T. W. Holman. *The 21st Missouri Regiment Infantry Veteran Volunteers: Historical Memoranda*. Fort Madison, IA: Roberts and Roberts, 1899.

Stephens, Gail. *Shadow of Shiloh: Major General Lew Wallace in the Civil War*. Indianapolis: Indiana Historical Society Press, 2010.

Stevens, Charles. "The Corinth Diary of Private Charles Stevens." *Blue and Gray Education Society Papers* 18 (Fall 2006): 1–60.

Stevenson, Thomas M. *History of the 78th Regiment O.V.V.I., Its "Muster-in" to Its "Muster-out": Comprising Its Organization, Marches, Campaigns, Battles and Skirmishes*. Zanesville, OH: Hugh Dunne, 1865.

Stone, Mary Amelia Boomer. *Memoir of George Boardman Boomer*. Boston: George C. Rand and Avery, 1864.

The Story of the Fifty-fifth Regiment Illinois Volunteer Infantry in the Civil War, 1861–1865. N.p.: n.p., 1887.

Suggs, Eliza. *Shadow and Sunshine*. Omaha, NE: n.p., 1906.

Sullivan, Davis M. "John Albert Pearson, Jr.: Arkansas Soldier and Confederate Marine." *Arkansas Historical Quarterly* 45, 3 (1986): 250–260.

Supplement to the Official Records of the Union and Confederate Armies, 100 vols. Wilmington, NC: Broadfoot, 1994.

Supplemental Report of the Joint Committee on the Conduct of the War, in Two Volumes. Washington, DC: Government Printing Office, 1866.

Sutton, Robert K., ed. *Rally on the High Ground: The National Park Service Symposium on the Civil War*. Fort Washington, PA: Eastern National, 2001.

Swaddling, John. *Historical Memoranda of the 52nd Regiment Illinois Infantry Volunteers from Its Organization, Nov. 19th, 1861, to Its Muster out, by Reason of Expiration of Service, on the 6th Day of July, 1865*. Elgin, IL: Gilbert and Post, 1868.

Sword, Wiley. *Shiloh: Bloody April*. New York: William Marrow, 1974; rev. ed., Dayton, OH: Morningside, 2001.

Symonds, Craig L. *Stonewall of the West: Patrick Cleburne and the Civil War*. Lawrence: University Press of Kansas, 1997.

Thompson, William Candace. "From Shiloh to Port Gibson." *Civil War Times Illustrated* 3, 6 (October 1964): 20–25.

Throne, Mildred, ed. *The Civil War Diary of Cyrus F. Boyd: Fifteenth Iowa Infantry, 1861–1863*. Des Moines: State Historical Society of Iowa, 1953.

———. "An Iowa Doctor in Blue: The Letters of Seneca B. Thrall, 1862–1864." *Iowa Journal of History* 58, 2 (April 1960): 97–188.

Trowbridge, Silas T. "Saving a General." *Civil War Times Illustrated* 11, 4 (July 1972): 20–25.

Tucker, Phillip Thomas. *The Confederacy's Fighting Chaplain: Father John B. Bannon.* Tuscaloosa: University of Alabama Press, 1992.

———. "Forgotten Confederate General: John Stevens Bowen." *Journal of Mississippi History* 50, 3 (August 1988): 135–152.

———. *The Forgotten Stonewall of the West: Major General John Stevens Bowen.* Macon, GA: Mercer University Press, 1997.

———. *The South's Finest: The First Missouri Brigade from Pea Ridge to Vicksburg.* Shippensburg, PA: White Mane, 1993.

———. *Westerners in Gray: The Men and Missions of the Elite Fifth Missouri Infantry Regiment.* Jefferson, NC: McFarland, 1995.

Tucker, W. H. *The Fourteenth Wisconsin Vet. Vol. Infantry (General A. J. Smith's Command) in the Expedition and Battle of Tupelo: Also, Wanderings through the Wilds of Missouri and Arkansas in Pursuit of Price.* Indianapolis: n.p., 1892.

Tunnard, W. H. *A Southern Record: The History of the 3rd Regiment Louisiana Infantry,* ed. Edwin C. Bearss. Dayton, OH: Morningside, 1970.

U.S. Quartermaster Department. *Roll of Honor: Names of Soldiers Who Died in Defense of the American Union Interred in the National Cemeteries,* 27 vols. Washington, DC: Government Printing Office, 1869.

Vaughn, Ranae Smith, and Cynthia Whirley Nelson, eds. *History of Old Tishomingo County, Mississippi Territory.* Iuka, MS: Tishomingo County Historical and Genealogical Society, 2005.

W. C. W. "The Fight at Iuka." *Southern Bivouac* 1, 7 (December 1885): 445–446.

Walden, James A. *The Journals of James A. Walden Part I—Confederate Soldier,* ed. W. J. Lemke. Fayettville, AR: Washington County Historical Society, 1954.

Walker, Cam. "Corinth: The Story of a Contraband Camp." *Civil War History* 20, 1 (March 1974): 5–22.

Walker, Francis A. *A Compendium of the Ninth Census (June 1, 1870) Compiled Pursuant to a Concurrent Resolution of Congress and under the Direction of the Secretary of the Interior.* Washington, DC: Government Printing Office, 1872.

Wallace, Lew. *An Autobiography,* 2 vols. New York: Harper and Brothers, 1906.

Walton, Clyde C., ed. *Private Smith's Journal: Recollections of the Late War.* Chicago: R. R. Donnelley and Sons, 1963.

War of the Rebellion: A Compilation of the Official Records of the Union and Confederate Armies, 128 vols. Washington, DC: Government Printing Office, 1880–1901.

"War Times at Iuka, Miss." *Confederate Veteran* 11, 3 (March 1903): 120.

Wardner, Horace. "Reminiscences of a Surgeon." In *Military Essays and Recollections: Papers Read before the Commandery of the State of Illinois, Military Order of the Loyal Legion of the United States,* 3 vols., 3:173–191. Chicago: Dial Press, 1899.

Warner, Ezra J. *Generals in Blue: Lives of the Union Commanders*. Baton Rouge: Louisiana State University Press, 1964.

———. *Generals in Gray: Lives of the Confederate Commanders*. Baton Rouge: Louisiana State University Press, 1959.

Watkins, Sam R. *"Co. Aytch," Maury Grays, First Tennessee Regiment; or, a Side Show of the Big Show*. Nashville: Presbyterian Printing House, 1882.

Welsh, Jack D. *Medical Histories of Confederate Generals*. Kent, OH: Kent State University Press, 1995.

———. *Medical Histories of Union Generals*. Kent, OH: Kent State University Press, 1996.

———. *Two Confederate Hospitals and Their Patients: Atlanta to Opelika*. Macon, GA: Mercer University Press, 2005.

White, Kristy Armstrong. "Life in Civil War Tishomingo County, Mississippi." Master's thesis, Mississippi State University, 1998.

Wiley, Bell I. *The Life of Johnny Reb: The Common Soldier of the Confederacy*. Indianapolis: Bobbs-Merrill, 1943.

Williams, John Melvin *"The Eagle Regiment," 8th Wis. Inf'ty Vols.: A Sketch of Its Marches, Battles and Campaigns from 1861–1865 with Complete Regimental and Company Roster, and a Few Portraits and Sketches of Its Officers and Commanders*. Belleville, WI: Recorder Print, 1890.

Williams, Kenneth P. *Lincoln Finds a General: A Military Study of the Civil War*, 5 vols. New York: Macmillan, 1948–1958.

Williams, Rosemary Taylor. *Cross City Chronicles*. N.p.: n.p., n.d.

Williams, T. Harry. *P. G. T. Beauregard: Napoleon in Gray*. Baton Rouge: Louisiana State University, 1954.

Williams, Thomas J. *An Historical Sketch of the 56th Ohio Volunteer Infantry during the Great Civil War from 1861 to 1865*. Columbus, OH: Lawrence Press, n.d.

Wills, Charles W. *Army Life of an Illinois Soldier: Including a Day by Day Record of Sherman's March to the Sea*. Washington, DC: Globe Printing Company, 1906.

Wilson, Ephraim A. *Memoirs of the War*. Cleveland, OH: W. M. Bayne Printing Co., 1893.

Winschel, Terrence J. "A Fierce Little Fight In Mississippi." *Civil War Times Illustrated* 33, 3 (July/August 1994): 50–59.

Wood, Wales W. *A History of the Ninety-fifth Regiment Illinois Infantry Volunteers, from Its Organization in the Fall of 1862, until Its Final Discharge from the United States Service, in 1865*. Chicago: Tribune Company's Book and Job Printing Office, 1865.

Woodworth, Steven E. *Jefferson Davis and His Generals: The Failure of Confederate Command in the West*. Lawrence: University Press of Kansas, 1990.

———. *Nothing But Victory: The Army of the Tennessee, 1861–1865*. New York: Knopf, 2005.

———, ed. *Grant's Lieutenants: From Cairo to Vicksburg*. Lawrence: University Press of Kansas, 2001.

———. *The Shiloh Campaign*. Carbondale: Southern Illinois University Press, 2009.

Wright, Charles. *A Corporal's Story: Experiences in the Ranks of Company C, 81st Ohio Vol. Infantry, during the War for the Maintenance of the Union, 1861–1864*. Philadelphia: James Beale, 1887.

Wright, Henry B. *A History of the Sixth Iowa Infantry*. Iowa City: State Historical Society of Iowa, 1923.

Wright, Marcus J. *Diary of Brigadier-General Marcus J. Wright, C.S.A. April 23, 1861–February 26 1863*. N.p.: n.p., n.d.

INDEX